D0863024

The World
Table of Contents

Map locator 4
Legend 6

Physical and political maps 8
The World – Physical map 10
The World – Political map 12

Europe
Europe – Physical map 14
Europe – Political map 16
Northern Europe 18
Southern Europe 20
Northern Scandinavia, Svalbard 22
Central Scandinavia 24
Southern Scandinavia, Denmark 26
Southern Finland, Karelia 28
Baltic States 30
Iceland, Faroe Islands, Ireland 32
Great Britain 34
Benelux, Northern France 36
Southern France, Switzerland 38
Western Spain, Portugal 40
Eastern Spain, Balearic Islands 42

Germany, Switzerland 44
Northern Italy, Slovenia, Croatia 46
Southern Italy, Malta 48
Poland 50
Austria, Czech Republic, Hungary 52
Serbia, Romania, Moldova 54
Albania, Macedonia, Greece 56
Western Russia, Moscow region 58
Western Russia, Central Volga region 60
Moldova, Ukraine 62
Western Turkey 64
Eastern Turkey, Caucasus 66

Asia
Asia – Physical map 68
Asia – Political map 70
Western Russia 72
Eastern Russia 74
Near and Middle East 76
Central Asia 78
Southern Asia 80
Northern East Asia 82
Southern East Asia 84
Southeast Asia 86

Australia/Oceania

Australia/Oceania –
  Physical map 88
Australia/Oceania –
  Political map 90
Micronesia, New Guinea 92
Western Australia 94
Eastern Australia 96
New Zealand, South Pacific 98

Africa

Africa – Physical map 100
Africa – Political map 102
Northwestern Africa 104
Northeastern Africa 106
Central Africa 108
Southern Africa, Madagascar 110

North and Central America

North and Central America –
  Physical map 112
North and Central America –
  Political map 114
Alaska, Western Canada,
  Hawaiian Islands 116
Northern Canada, Greenland 118
Southeastern Canada 120
United States 122
Mexico 124
Caribbean Islands 126

South America

South America – Physical map 128
South America – Political map 130
Venezuela, Colombia, Ecuador,
  Peru 132
Suriname, Brazil 134
Chile, Argentina, Paraguay,
  Uruguay 136

Polar zones

Arctic Region 138
Antarctica 140

Thematic maps 142
Climate 144
Vegetation 146
Population density 148
Energy 150

Nations of the World 152
Index of local country names 154

Europe 160
Asia 167
Australia/Oceania 174
Africa 176
North and Central America 185
South America 189

Index of names 192

The World
Map locator

Europe

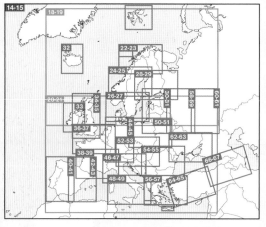

Asia

Africa

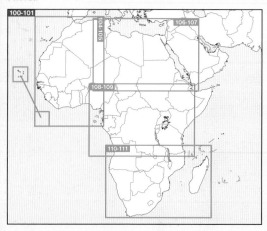

North America

Australia/Oceania

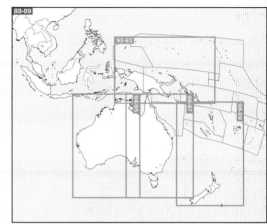

South America

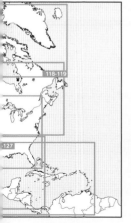

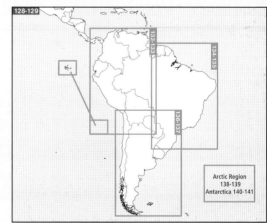

Arctic Region
138-139
Antarctica 140-141

The World
Legend

Bodies of water

River
Intermittent river
Waterfall, rapids
Freshwater lake
Reservoir
Salt lake
Salt pan
Swamp
Coral reef

Topography

Mountains
Region/area
Glacier
Mountain height
Depression

Political and other boundaries

International boundary
National capital
Disputed international boundary
Administrative boundary
Administrative capital
National park

Special symbols

International Airport
National Airport
Elevation above/below sea level
Wall
Motorway
Primary highway
Railway
Ferry
Archeological site
Tourist attraction

Type faces

INDIAN OCEAN	Ocean
Gulf of Mexico	Gulf, bay
Java Trench	Undersea landscapes, trenches
Lake Superior *Nile*	Lake, river
Great Plains	Region/area
ANDES	Mountains
Acongagua	Mountain
North Cape	Cape
Greter Antilles *Mauritius*	Islands, Island
BRAZIL	Sovereign state
North Dakota	State/province

Classification of cities and towns

▢ DALIAN	Town over 1 million inhabitants
○ Colorado Springs	Town 100,000 - 1 million inhabitants
○ Dodge City	Town 10,000 - 100,000 inhabitants
○ Brady	Town under 10,000 inhabitants
• Georg von Neumayer (D)	Research station

Place locator

Search for the name of the sought after area/city in the alphabetically arranged map index. The place names are followed by the page numbers of relevant maps as well as a number-letter combination indicating the area's location in the map. Letters indicate the east-west position and numbers the north-south position of an area.

Example:
Follonica 39 Lf 24
Page 39
Map section Lf 24

The Earth, the so-called blue planet, is the third planet from the sun and the fifth largest planet in the solar system. Formed from a cloud of dust and gas around 4.5 billion years ago, the Earth travels in an elliptical orbit at distances between 147 to 152 million kilometers away from the sun.

The Earth is not a perfect sphere; the area around the poles being relatively flat. The polar diameter of the Earth measures 12,714 kilometers, about 42 kilometers less than the equatorial diameter of the planet. The maximum circumference of the Earth measures 40,075 kilometers. Our planet has a total area of 510 million square kilometers; 71% of the Earth's surface is covered by bodies of water and 29% by land.

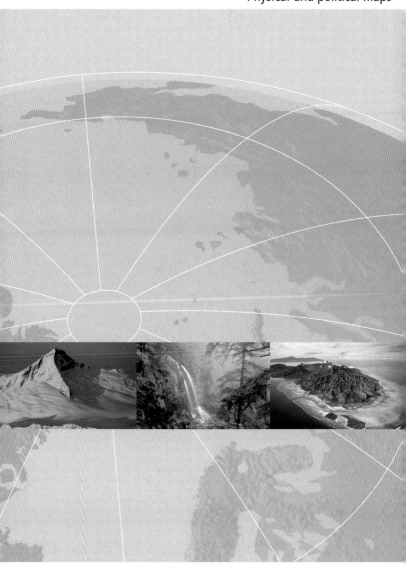

The world
Physical map

Scale 1:170,000,000

| 0 | 1700 | 3400 | 5100 | Kilometers |

| 0 | 1700 | 3400 | Miles |

ARCTIC OCEAN

Beaufort Sea
Queen Elizabeth Islands
Ellesmere Island
Baffin Bay
Greenland
Jan

Wrangel Island
Point Barrow
Parry Islands
Victoria Island
Baffin Island
Davis Strait
3700 Gunnbjørns Field
Denmark Strait

Alaska Peninsula
Bering Strait
Arctic Circle 66°33'
Great Bear Lake
Kap Farvel
Iceland

Bering Sea
Mt. McKinley 6194
Great Slave Lake
Southampton Island
Hudson Bay
Labrador Peninsula
Labrador Sea

Aleutian Islands
Gulf of Alaska
NORTH
AMERICA
Newfoundland

Vancouver Island
L.Winnipeg
L.Superior
L.Huron Saint Lawrence R.
Cape Race

Great Basin
L.Michigan
Appalachian Mountains
ATLANTIC

Cape Mendocino
Mt. Mitchell 2037
Azores
Cape St.Vincent
Strait of Gibraltar

Mt.Whitney 4418
Mt.Elbert 4399
Rio Grande
Bermuda Islands
Madeira
4167
Canary Islands

Death Valley
Lower California
Tropic of Cancer 23°27'
Sargasso Sea

Hawaiian Islands
Gulf of Mexico
Cuba
Bahamas
Hispaniola 9220
Puerto Rico Trench

Hawaii Mauna Kea 4205
Islas Revillagigedo
Orizaba 5700
Caribbean Sea
Lesser Antilles
Cape Verde Islands
Cape Verde

Johnston Atoll
île Clipperton
Popocatepetl 4220
Isthmus of Panama
Guiana Highlands
6663

Palmyra Atoll
Jarvis Island
Galápagos Islands
Chimborazo 6310
Pico da Neblina 3014
Ilha Fernando de Noronha
Ascension

Equator 0°
Pta. Pariñas
Amazon
Pta. São Roque

Phoenix Islands
Marquesas Islands
SOUTH AMERICA
São Francisco
Saint Hel

Samoa Islands
Tuamotu Archipelago
Lake Titicaca 6882
Planalto Central

Fiji Islands
Society Islands
Tahiti
Brazilian Highlands
Pico da Bandeira 2890
Ilhas Martim-Vaz

Tonga Islands
Tubuai Islands
8055
Paraguay

Tropic of Capricorn 23°27'
Pitcairn
Sala-y-Gómez
Islas de los Desventurados
Aconcagua 6963
Río de la Plata
Tristan da Cunha

Kermadec Islands
Easter Island
Gran Chaco
Pampas

North Island
Islas Juan-Fernández
Peninsula Valdés
Gough Island

Chatham Islands
South Island
4058 Cerro San Valentín
Patagonia
Strait of Magellan
Falkland Islands
South Georgia
8264
South Sandwich Islands

Tierra del Fuego
Cape Horn

Antarctic Circle 66°33'
Drake Passage
South Orkney Islands

Antarctic Peninsula
Weddell Sea

Ross Sea
Marie Byrd Land
Vinsonmassiv 5140

West 20°

PACIFIC OCEAN

Line Islands
Polynesia
Cook Islands

AFRICA
1 BURKINA FASO Ouagadougou
2 EQUATORIAL GUINEA Malabo
3 SÃO TOMÉ AND PRINCIPE São Tomé
4 RWANDA Kigali
5 BURUNDI Bujumbura

ASIA
1 AZERBAIJAN Baku
2 ARMENIA Yerevan
3 LEBANON Beirut
4 ISRAEL Jerusalem
5 KUWAIT Kuwait
6 BAHRAIN Manama
7 QATAR Doha

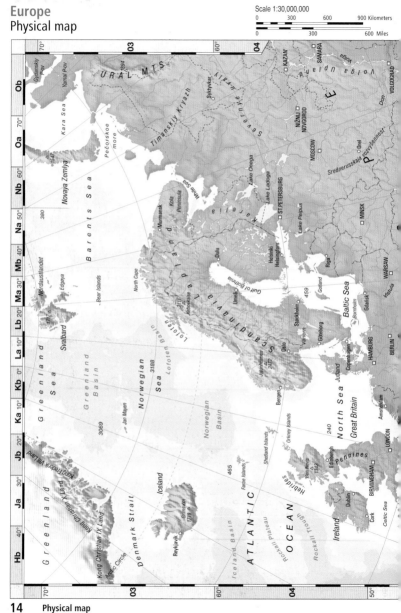

Europe
Physical map

Scale 1:30,000,000

Europe

15

Scale 1:20,000,000

0 200 400 600 Kilometers
0 200 400 Miles

| Ka 20° | Kb 15° | Kc 5° | Kd 0° | La 5° | Lb 10° | Lc |

Rockall Trough

07

33 1343 ▲ Grampian Mts. Aberdeen
Islay Perth Dundee Skagerrak Skagen Göteborg Borås
Londonderry Glasgow Dunfermline Edinburgh 240 81 Frederikshavn
155 IRELAND ÉIRE Sligo Belfast Stranraer Carlisle Newcastle u.Tyne North Kattegat Ålborg Göt Vexi
Galway Galway Bay Dundalk Newry Man Douglas Middlesbrough Jylland Århus Helsingborg
5023 Ireland Dublin Baile Átha Cliath Irish Sea Blackpool Leeds Great Britain Esbjerg DENMARK Malm
Limerick Liverpool Kingston u.Hull 36 Odense Køge Rønn
Tralee 1041 Waterford Rosslare Manchester Sheffield 91 Flensburg German Kiel Stralsund Rostock
Cork Corcaigh Fishguard BIRMINGHAM Nottingham Leicester Groningen Cuxhaven Bight Lübeck Schwerin Szczeci
55° 115 Swansea Cambridge NETHERLANDS HAMBURG Bremen BERLIN

08
4861 Land's End Isles of Scilly Cardiff Bristol Oxford Ipswich Amsterdam Emmen Osnabrück Hannover
73 Barnstaple Southampton LONDON The Hague Utrecht Bielefeld Magdeburg Cottt
185 Devon Plymouth Poole Brighton Calais Rotterdam Düsseldorf Dortmund Leipzig
Channel Islands (UK) Cherbourg Dover Brugge Antwerpen BELGIUM Bonn GERMANY Dresde
50° Le Havre Amiens BRUSSELS COLOGNE Fulda Erfurt Chemi
Brest Lannion Caen Rouen Luxembourg Frankfurt a.M. PRAGUE
Pointe du Raz Dinan Normandie LUX. Mainz Mannheim Würzburg Plze
Quimper Rennes Versailles PARIS Reims Metz Saarbrücken Karlsruhe Nürnberg Regensburg
Belle-Île St.Nazaire Le Mans Troyes Nancy Strasbourg Stuttgart Ulm burg Passau
5294 Nantes Angers Loire Orléans Dijon Mulhouse Freiburg Kempten MUNICH Salzb
163 Niort Tours Bourges Besançon Basle Zürich Innsbruck AUST
la Rochelle Poitiers Autun Vichy Lausanne Berne SWITZERLAND Gross
Royan Limoges Clermont-Ferrand Geneva Mt.Blanc 4800 Bolzano SLOVE
2499 OCEAN

09
560 Pta.da Estaca de Bares MASSIF Lyon Bellinzona Bozen Udine Ljubljana
La Coruña Avilés Gijón CENTRAL Grenoble Novara Trento Padova
Cabo Finisterre Santiago Lugo Oviedo Santander Bilbao Bordeaux Agen Valence Turin MILAN Verona Venice Rijek
Vigo Cantabria Mountains Biarritz Nîmes Avignon Parma Bologna Ferrara Ravenna
Ourense León Burgos S.Sebastián Pau Toulouse Montauban Aix-en-Prov. Provence Genoa La Spezia Livorno SAN MARINO
45° Porto Braga Bragança Zamora Logroño Pamplona Narbonne Montpellier Marseille Nice MC Florence Siena Gran Sasso d'Italia
Vila Nova de Gaia Valladolid PYRÉNÉES ANDORRA Perpignan Golfe du Lion Toulon Ligurian Sea Perugia Terni Tivoli
PORTUGAL Salamanca Zaragoza Andorra la Vella Lleida Manresa Corsica (F) Bastia 2622 Grosseto
Caldas da Rainha Coimbra SPAIN Sabadell BARCELONA Calvi ROME
Penche Abrantes Cáceres MADRID Guadalajara Tarragona Ajaccio 902 ITALY
LISBON Barreiro Trujillo Toledo Teruel Castelló de la Plana Bonifacio Cassino
10° Évora Badajoz Mérida Ciudad Real Cuenca Getafe Submeseta Sur 2132 Sagunt Sassari Olbia NAPLES
Zafra Albacete València Mallorca Nuoro Vesuvius Sale
Sines Beja Huelva Sevilla Córdoba Alcoi Eivissa (Ibiza) Palma de Mallorca Menorca Oristano 1834 Arbatax 3623
Lagos Cabo de Faro São Vicente Jerez d.l.Fr. Granada Linares Jaén Murcia Elx Alacant Formentera 581 Sardinia Tyrrhenian Sea
Cádiz Algeciras Sierra Nevada 3481 Lorca Cartagena Balearic Islands 2784 Cagliari
40° Strait of Gibraltar Gibraltar(UK) Almería Cabo de Gata Capo Teulada Palermo Mes
Tangier Ceuta (E) 2814 Trapani Sicily
El-Araïch Tétouan Al-Hoceima Melilla (E) 2407 Ténès ALGIERS Cap Bougaroun La Galite Bizerte Agrigento Gela
RABAT Kénitra Oran Mostaganem Chlef Blida 2305 Bejaïa Annaba TUNIS Isola di Pantelleria
CASA BLANCA Meknès Fès Taza Oujda Tlemcen Tiaret Sétif Constantine Souk Ahras Jendouba El Kef Hammamet MALT
Khouribga Azrou RIF Bou Saâda Chott el Hodna Biskra Batna Tebessa Kairouan Sousse Valletta
11 MOROCCO Mecheria El Bayadh Djelfa Laghouat Gafsa Gabès Îles de Kerkenah
Tendrara Aïn Sefra Sahara TUNISIA Sfax
Ouarzazate Ar-Rachidia Béchar Figuig ALGERIA Ghardaïa Touggourt El Oued Chott El Jerid Medenine 178 Île de Jerba

| Kc 5° | Kd 0° | La 5° | Lb 10° | Lc |

Scale 1:5,000,000

0   50   100   150 Kilometers
0   50   100 Miles

Le 14° Lf 18° Lg 22° Lh 26° Lj 30° Lk   16° Lj 18° Lk 20° M

A R C T I C   O C E A N

1248   Svalbana

05   Nordvest-
Spitsbergen
nasjonalpark
Lågøya   Storøya   Kvitøya   40
86
Nordaust-Svalbard
naturreservat

Nordaustlandet
naturreservat

130   Oksemidae
1368
Ny-Ålesund   Newtontoppen

06   Spitsbergen   Olgastretet   Svenskøya   Kong Karls Land

Erik Eriksenstretet   Kongsøya

Nordøst-
Svalbard
naturreservat

Peter I Karls
Forland
Forlandet
nasjonalpark
Longyearbyen   Haabergfjellet   Barentsøya   Sørøst-
Svalbard

Gustavfjellet   665   Svalbard (Norway)

07   Barentsburg   1205   Storfjorden   Edgeøya
naturreservat
Kvalpynten   375

Bellsund   Sør-Spitsbergen
nasjonalpark   155   B a r e n t s   S e a

Hornsundtind   Hopen   103
1430
Øyrlandsodden

Scale 1:10,000,000

Le   Lf   Lg   Lh

L o f o t e n   B a s i n

Nord-Kvaløy   Vanna
Vannareid
Arnøy
Skjer
Ringvassøy   Skulgam
Kvaløya   Tromsø   Sverivby
Vikran   Lyngseidet
Skibotn
Lyngen

11   3070

V e s t e r å l e n

Grytøyfjord   Senja   Finnsnes   Nordkjosbotn
Andenes   Øvergård
Andøya   Setermoen
Anderdalen n.p.   Sjøvegan   Andselv   Øvre-Dividal
And-   nasjonalpark
Myre   Stong-   fjorden   landet
Langøya   Harstad   Hamvik
Sortland   Grov   Innset   Tornetrask
Steine   Hinnøya   Bjerkvik   Abisko   Abisko n.p.   Tornetr
Hadseløya   Stokmarknes   Bogen
Austvågøya   Ladingen   Narvik
Vestvågøy   Svolvær   Ballangen   Skarberget   Kebnekaise   Jukkasj
Leknes   Kabelvåg   Ulvsvåg   2111
Henningsvær   Nikkaluokta   Kiruna
Ballstad   Stamsund   Astad   Silas-   Ritsem
Moskenesøya   jaure   Stora Sjøfallets   Sjaunja
Sørvågen   Nordfold   Mørsvik   Akka   nasjonalpark   naturrese
68°   Folda   jaure   Vietas
Værøy   Bago n.p.   Padjelanta   Sarekkåka   L   a   p   o   n   i   a
Røst   Røsvik   nasjonalpark   Sareks
Rosvik   Virihaure   nasjonalpark
 Luring   Stalloluokta   Kvikkjokk   Porjus
Bodø   Fauske
Innbyg   Vesterli   Sulitjelma
Norwegian   Fåuske   Sulitjelma   Jokkmokk
1914
125   Sulitelma   S   W   E   D
Sjonfjorda   Storjord

12   N O R W A Y

Arctic Circle   Vågaholmen   Saltfjellet-   Stødi   Jokkmokk
Storjorda   Svartisen
S e a   nasjonalpark   Jäkkvik   Kåbdalis
Meløjorden   Pieljekaise   Hornavan
Stokkvågen   Mo i Rana   nasjonalpark   Ammarnäs   Arjeplog
Tomma   Hammerberget   Hemavan   Storavan
Nesna   1915   Uddjaure
Dønna   Korgen   Tärnaby   Arvidsjaur
66°   Sandnessjøen   Bleikvassli   Västansjö   Sorsele
Tjøtta   Mosjøen   Slussfors   Glommerstr
Forvika/Vevelstad   Hemavan
Gladstad   Rossvatnet
Vega   Trofors   Hattfjelldal

13   Brønnøysund   Tosbotn   1703

Le   10°   Lf   12°   Lg   14°   Lh   16°   Lj   18°   Lk   2

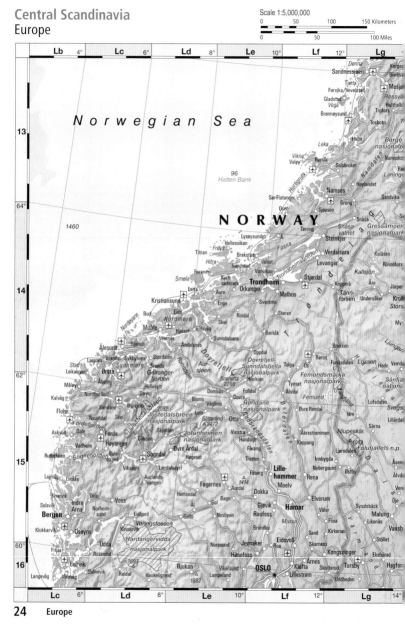

Scale 1:5,000,000

0   50   100   150 Kilometers

0   50   100 Miles

N o r w e g i a n   S e a

96
Halten Bank

1460

N O R W A Y

Trondheim

Kristiansund

Molde

Ålesund

Ørsta

Bergen

OSLO

Hamar

Lille-
hammer

-5000 4000 3000 2000 1000 500 250 100   0 Depression 0   200 2000 4000 6000 +8000

Arjeplog

Ammarnäs
Uddjaure
Hemavan
Storavan
Tärnaby
stansjö
Slussfors
Sorsele
Arvidsjaur
Kittelfjäll
Storuman
Malå
Långsjöby
Björkele
Saxnäs
Risbäck
Vilhelmina
Vägsele
Lycksele
Norråker
Meselefors
Hällnäs
Dorotea
Tallsjö
Grano
Vindeln
Hoting
Åsele
Bjurholm
Strömsund
Solberg
Junsele
Hemling
Hammerdal
Björna
Ramsele
Sidensjö
Forsmo
Nordmaling
Östersund
Stugun
Österforse
Sollefteå
Bjästa
Örnsköldsvik
Brunflo
Kälarne
Bispgården
Decksta
Pilgrimstad
Kramfors
Stavre
Liden
Alandsbro
Bräcke
Ånge
Timrå
Härnösand
Östavall
Stöde
Sundsvall
Ramsjö
Skottsund
Hassela
Gnarp
Ytterhogdal
Hennan
Dellen-
Färila
sjöarna
Ljusdal
Delsbo
Los
Järvsö
Hudiksvall
Edsbyn
Vallsta
Enånger
Bollnäs
Söderhamn
Skattungbyn
Furudal
Holmsveden
Orsa
Bingsjö
Ockelbo
Rättvik
Envken
Gävle
Djurås
Bjursås
Skutskär
Falun
Sandviken
Björbo
Borlänge
Hofors
Smedje-
Hedemora
Tierp
backen
Avesta
Fagersta
Sala
Heby
Bälinge
Uppsala

SWEDEN

Umeälven
Storuman

Ångermanland
Skuleskogens
nationalpark
Höga Kusten
294

Hälsingland

Medel
5

Upland

Ljungan

Arjeplog
Luleälven
Boden
Töre
Haparanda
Tornio
Vidsel
Storforsen
Kalix
Kemi
Simo
Kuivaniemi
Älvsbyn
Antnäs
Luleå
Gammelstaden
Haparanda
skärgårds n.p.
Perämeren
k.puisto
Perämeri
Långträsk
Piteå
Hailuoto
Oulu
Glommersträsk
Bottenviken
Hailuoto
Skellefteälven
Jörn
Byske
Kempele
Norsjö
Boliden
Skellefteå
Brahestad
Raahe
Åsträsk
Skelleftehamn
Burträsk
Lövånger
Kalajoki
Oulainen
Vihanti
124
Robertsfors
Ylivieska
Nivala
Umeå
Holmön
Ängeson
Karleby
Kokkola
Holmsund
Jakobstad
Pietarsaari
Toholampi
Vännäs
Norra Kvarken
Merenkurkku
Fäboda
Evijärvi
Husum
Arnäsvall
Sardön
Lappajärvi
Kauhava
Kyyjärvi
Vaasa
Våsa
Korsnäs
Lapua
Seinäjoki
Soini
Keuruu
FINLAND
Kurikka
Alavus
Teuva
Virrat
Mänttä
Kaskinen
Kauhajoki
Parkano
Vippula
Kristinestad
Kristiinankaupunki
Karvia
Korsnäs
Merikarvia
Kankaanpää
Hämeenkyrö
Ylöjärvi
Orivesi
Noormarkku
Lavia
Nokia
Tampere
Pori
Vammala
Valkeakoski
Rauma
Huittinen
Viiala
Hämeenlinna
Eura
Loimaa
Humppila
Nystad
Uusikaupunki
Forssa
Mynämäki
Somero
Raisio
Turku
Åbo
Salo
Åland/
Ahvenanmaa
Nådendal
Naantali
Lohja
Östhammar
Geta
Pargas
Parainen
Karis
Karjaa
Eckerö
Kumlinge
Dalsbruk
Hangö
Erkenäs
Tammisaari
Mariehamn
Maarianhamina
Föglö
Saaristomeren
kansallispuisto
Kökar

Gulf of Bothnia

Gulf of Finland

Ålands hav
Ahvenanmeri

Central Scandinavia   25

Southern Scandinavia, Denmark
Europe

Scale 1:5,000,000

0 50 100 150 Kilometers

0 50 100 Miles

NORWAY

Leirvik · Skåhevik · Raldal · Rjukan · Vikersund · Klofta · Arnes · Skotterud · Torsby

Langevåg · Valevåg · Haukeligrend · Lampeland · **OSLO** · Lillestrøm · Uddheden

Haugesund · Ølen · Nedstrand · Sand · Åmot · Sauland · Mjøndalen · **Drammen** · Siggerud · Skjanhaug · Antofforss · Sunne · V.Amtervik

Åkrahamn · Kopervik · Hjelmeland · Dalen · Notodden · Kongsberg · Svelvik · Ørebak · Arvika · Fagerås

Skudeneshavn · Pål · Kvitseid · Hvittingfoss · Holmestrand · Askim · Rakkestad · Årjäng · Vålberg · Grums

Stavanger · Jørpeland · Valle · Fyresdal · Nissedal · Silan · Horten · Oslo · Moss · Sarpsborg · Fredrikstad · Säffle

Sandnes · Riska · Ålgård · Bygland · Drangedal · Skien · Tønsberg · Fjorden · Halden · Bengtsfors · Åmål

Bryne · Helle-land · Åseral · Neslandsvatn · Porsgrunn · **Larvik** · Sandefjord · Ed · **S Väne**

Sirevåg · Tonstad · Evje · Svenes · Kragerø · Langesund · Strömstad · Bäckefors · Mellerud

Egersund · Moi · Eiken · Sendeled · Risør · Tanumshede · Munkedal · Färgelanda · Go

Hauge · Liknes · Hageland · Blakstad · **Arendal** · Kungshamn · Uddevalla · **Vänersborg** · **Lidköp**

Flekkefjord · Lyngdal · Vennesla · Grimstad · Lyseki · Trollhättan · Vara

Borhaug · Måløy · **Lillesand** · Orust · Fjord · Stenungsund · Alingsås · Falk

Lindesnes · Mandal · **Kristiansand** · Kuonäv · **Göteborg** · Landvetter · Ulrichram

463 · 81 · 62

Skagerrak

Skagen · **Borås** · Kinna · Svenljun

Hirtshals · Sindal · Albæk · Kungsbacka · Gislave

Hjørring · Frillesås · Ullared · Smålg

Brønderslev · Åabybro · Frederikshavn · Sæby · *Læsø* · Varberg · Tvåaker · ste

Hanstholm · Fjerritslev · Nibe · **Aalborg** · Hals · *Kattegat* · Falkenberg · Oskarsham · Halms

Thisted · Løgstør · Anholt · Gullbrandstorp · Laholm

Hurup · Aars · Støvring · 19 · Laholmsbukten · Torekov · Marka

Thyborøn · Nykøbing M · Hadsund · Båstad · Örkelljung

Lemvig · Skive · Hobro · Ängelholm · Klipp

Holstebro · Viborg · Langå · Trustrup · Grenaa · **Helsingør** · Helsingbo

Vemb · **Jutland** · Randers · Ho

Ringkøbing · Herning · Silkeborg · **Århus** · Odden Ebeltoft · Frederiksværk · Nykøbing S · Landskro

Ringkøbing Fjord · Ikast · Brande · 171 · Skanderborg · Faergehavn · **Helsingør** · Lund

Nørre Nebel · Skjern · **DENMARK** · Frederikssund · **(COPENHAGEN)** **KØBENHAVN** · Mal

Varde · Grindsted · **Vejle** · Juelsminde · Kalundborg · Roskilde

Blåvands Huk · Fredericia · Middelfart · Odense · Slagelse · **Sjælland** · Køge · Svedala

Esbjerg · Kolding · *Fünen* · Ringsted · Fakse · Radvig · Trelleb

Ribe · Vejen · Haderslev · Little Bælt · Faaborg · Nyborg · Næstved · Vordingborg

Skærbæk · Toftlund · Aabenraa · Bejden · Svendborg · Ruckøbing · Stege · Møns Klint

List · Westerland · Tønder · Sønderborg · Sakskøbing · *Lolland* · *Falster*

Amrum · Sylt · Leck · **Flensburg** · Nakskov · Nykøbing F · N.P. Vorpommersche

Wyk · Föhr · Kappeln · *Femern Bælt* · Rødbyhavn · Gedser · Boddenlandschaft · Rüge

North Frisian Islands · Husum · Schleswig · Puttgarden · Fehmarn · Zingst · Barth · Ber

St. Peter-Ording · N.P. Schleswig-Holsteinisches Wattenmeer · Rendsburg · Fehmarn · Warne-münde · Bitz · Stralst

German Bight · Tönning · Büsum · **Kiel** · Plön · 168 · **Rostock** · Darmgarten · Greitsv

Helgoland · **Holstein** · Oldenburg · Bad Segeberg · Travemünde · Nol

East Frisian Islands · Meldorf · **Neumünster** · Eutin · **GERMANY** · **Rostock**

N.P. Niedersächsisches Wattenmeer · Brunsbüttel · Itzehoe

Nordeney Wattenmeer · **Cuxhaven**

NORTH SEA

German Bight

Southern Finland, Karelia
Europe

Scale 1:5,000,000

| 0 | 50 | 100 | 150 Kilometers |

| 0 | 50 | 100 Miles |

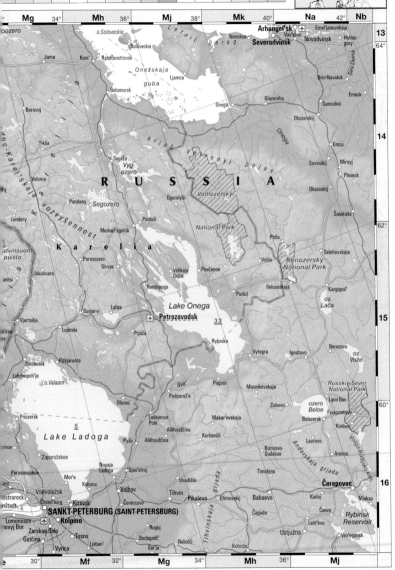

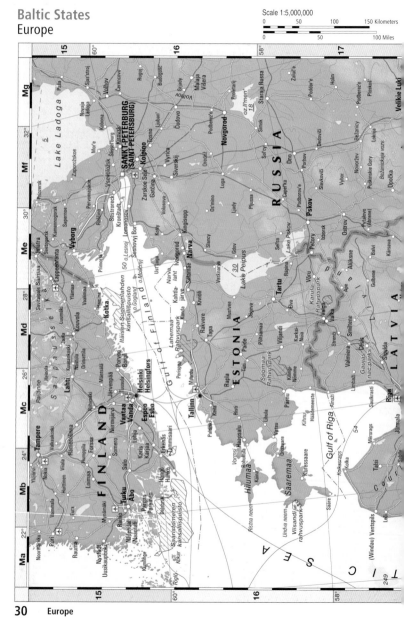

Scale 1:5,000,000

| 0 | 50 | 100 | 150 Kilometers |

| 0 | 50 | 100 Miles |

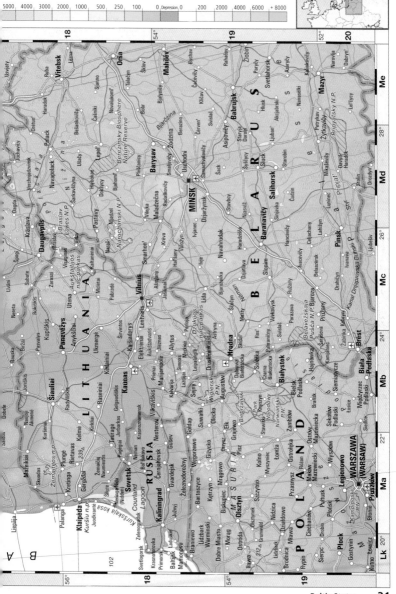

Baltic States **31**

Scale 1:5,000,000

0   50   100   150 Kilometers

0   50   100 Miles

Jg 26°   **Jh** 24°   **Jj** 22°   **Jk** 20°   **Ka** 18°   **Kb**

12   11

66°   68°

Straumnes   *Horn*

Bolungarvík   *N o r w e g i a n   S e a*
Ísafjörður

Pingeyri   Unaðsdalur
Drangajökull
Bíldudalur   Rauðamýri

Bjargtangar   *Arctic Circle*
Patreksfjörður   Brjánslækur
Látrabjarg   **I C E L A N D**   ⊞*Grímsey*

Breiðafjörður   Hólmavík
Þjóðgarðurinn   *Flatey*
Snæfellsjökull   Reykhólar   Drangsnes   *Húnaflói*   Siglufjörður   90
Hellissandur   Stykkishólmur   Hvammstangi   Blönduós   Hofsós   Ólafsfjörður   *Rifstangi*
Arnarstapi   Búðardalur   Laugarbakki   Sauðárkrókur   *Öxar-*   Raufarhöfn
Vegamót   Borðeyri   Varmahlíð   Dalvík   Húsavík   *fjörður*   Kópasker
Kolbeinsstaðir   Dalsmynni   Svalbarðseyri   Skinnastaður   *Þistilfjörður* *Langane*
Faxaflói   Borgarnes   Akureyri   Þórshöfn
Reykholt   Mývatn   *Þjóðgarðurinn í* *Bakkaflói*
Iceland   Krafla   *Jökulsárgljúfrum*
Akranes   Reykjahlíð △818   Grímsstaðir   *Bakkaflói*
Langjökull   *Óðáðahraun*   Vopnafjörður   *Vopna-*
64°   Kevlavík   **Reykjavík** Mosfellsbær   *Þjóðgarðurinn*   1765 △   Herðubreið   *Jökulsá*   *fjörður*   66°
⊞   Hafnarfjörður   Þingvellir   *Pingvellir*   *Hofsjökull*   △1682
Grindavík   Þingvallavatn   *Blafell*   *Sprengisandur*   Askja △   Fossvellir
Hveragerði   △1204   *Þjórsá*   1510 △ Öskjuvatn   Egilsstaðir   Borgarfjörður
Þorlákshöfn   Selfoss   *Kvíslavatn*   △ Kverkfjöll   Seyðisfjörður
Hella   *Þórisvatn*   1929 △   *Snæfell*   Neskaupstaður
Hvolsvöllur   Hekla   *V a t n a j ö k u l l*   △1833   Reyðarfjörður   Eskifjörður
△1491   Grímsvötn   *Þjóðgarðurinn*
14   Vestmannaeyjar   *Mýrdals-*   1719 △   *í Skaftafelli*   Djúpivogur   13
Surtsey   Heimaey   *jökull*   Kirkjubæjar-   Skaftafell   Hvannadals-   *Breiðdalsvík*
Skógar   klaustur   hnúkur △2119   *Papey*
Vík   *Skeiðarársandur*   Höfn
130

14°   **Kd**

6°

Faroe Islands

62°   *ATLANTIC OCEAN*   *Streymoy* Eiði   *Eysturoy*
2135   Sørvágur
Tórshavn
14   **Faroe Islands**   14
(Denmark)

Suðuroy
15   *Vágur*   62°

2110

Ka 18°   **Kb** 16°   **Kc** 14°   **Kg** 4°   **Kh**

Great Britain
Europe

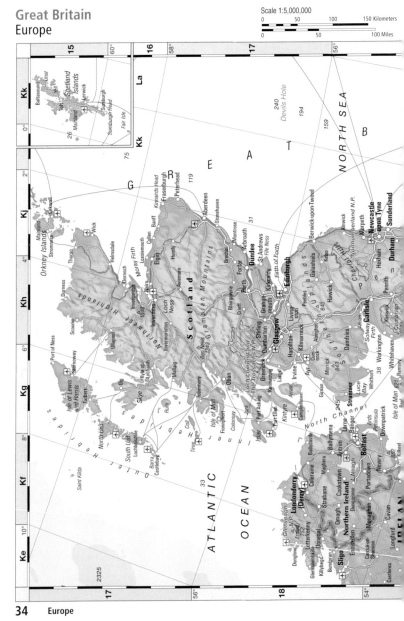

0   50   100   150 Kilometers

0   50   100 Miles

Shetland Islands

Baltasound
Unst
Yell
Lerwick
Mainland
Sumburgh
Sumburgh Head
Fair Isle

NORTH SEA

Devils Hole
240
194
159

Orkney Islands
Kirkwall
Stromness
Mainland
Wick
Helmsdale
Thurso
Durness

Kinnairds Head
Fraserburgh
Peterhead
Aberdeen
Stonehaven

GREAT

Berwick-upon-Tweed
Alnwick
Morpeth
Newcastle upon Tyne
Sunderland
Durham

NORTH SEA

Cullen
Banff
Lossiemouth
Elgin
Huntly
Montrose
Arbroath
Brechin
Forfar
Dundee

St.Andrews
Fife Ness
Firth of Forth
Edinburgh

Cheviot
Northumberland N.P.
Hexham
Kelso
Galashiels
Hawick
Penrith
Carlisle

Scotland
Grampian Mountains
Cairn Gorm
Aviemore
Perth
Blairgowrie
Crieff
Grangemouth
Stirling
Kirkcaldy
Peebles

Dornoch
Inverness
Loch Ness
Invermoriston
Nairn
Fort Augustus
Fort William
Ben Nevis
1344

Glasgow
Hamilton
Livingston
Lanark
840
Solway Firth
Dumfries
Workington
Whitehaven

Ullapool
Scourie
Lochinver

Port of Ness
Stornoway
Isle of Lewis and Harris
Tarbert
Uig
Kyle of Lochalsh
Skye
Mallaig

Outer Hebrides

Tobermory
Isle of Mull
Oban
Loch Lomond and The Trossachs N.P.
Dumbarton
Greenock
Kilmarnock
Ayr
Irvine
Largs
Arran
Campbeltown
Kintyre

Lake District N.P.
Keswick

Merrick
843
Girvan
Stranraer
Luce Bay
38
Whithorn

Isle of Man
Ramsey
621
Douglas

North Channel
245

South Uist
Lochboisdale
Barra
Castlebay

North Uist

Saint Kilda

Inner Hebrides
Coll
Tiree
Staffa
Iona
Colonsay
Islay
Jura
Port Askaig
Port Ellen
Gigha

Rum
Eigg

Inverurie

ATLANTIC

OCEAN

33

2325

Ballycastle
Ballymena
Antrim
Belfast
Larne
Bangor
Ards Peninsula
Downpatrick

Glenveagh
N.P.
752
Errigal
Londonderry
(Derry)
Coleraine
Strabane
Maghera
Cookstown
Magherafelt
L.Neagh
Portadown
Northern Ireland
Dungannon
Omagh
Newry

Dungloe
Letterkenny
Glenties
Donegal
Glencolumbkille
Killybegs
Ballybofey
Bundoran
Sligo
Enniskillen
Carrick on Shannon
Longford

Castlerea
Cavan
Carrick macross
Kells
Dundalk
Kingscourt

IRELAND

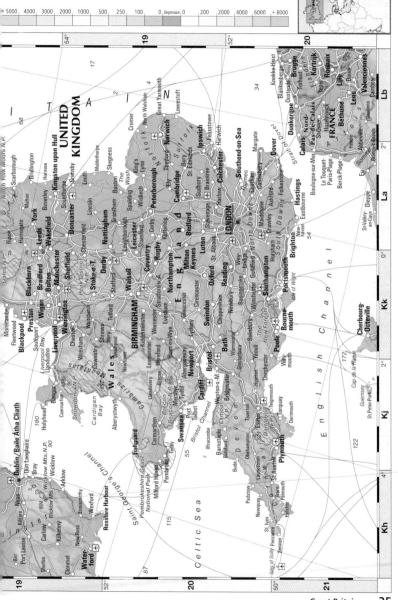

Scale 1:5,000,000

0   50   100   150 Kilometers

0   50   100 Miles

| Kg | 6° | Kh | 4° | Kj | 2° | Kk | 0° |

Aberystwyth · Welshpool · Shrewsbury · Telford · Stafford · **Derby** · **Nottingham** · Grantham · Skegness · Boston

Fishguard · Newtown · **BIRMINGHAM** · **Walsall** · Loughborough · Spalding · The

Pembrokeshire Coast National Park · Llandovery · Kidderminster · Coventry · **Leicester** · Stamford · Wisbech

Milford Haven · Carmarthen · Brecon · Hereford · Worcester · Rugby · Corby · **Peterboro**

Wales · Brecon Beacons-N.P. 886 · Ross-on-Wye · Evesham · **Northampton** · Kettering · Ely

Tenby · Pembroke · 115 · Abergavenny · Gloucester · Stratford-u.-A. · **Milton Keynes** · **Bedford** · St. Ed · Sudbu

Swansea · 55 · Merthyr Tydfil · Lydney · Cirencester · **Oxford** · Luton · Stevenage · Brain

Port Talbot · **Newport** · **Bristol** · **Swindon** · St. Albans · Harlow · **Colche**

Ilfracombe · Weston-s.-M. · **Bath** · Chippenham · **Reading** · **LONDON** · South-on-S

Barnstaple · Bridgwater · Warminster · Newbury · Basingstoke · Weybridge · Maidstone · Chat

Bideford · Exmoor N.P. · Glastonbury · Salisbury · Winchester · **Southampton** · Crawley · Ashford

Bude · Okehampton · Tiverton · Honiton · Yeovil · Dorchester · **Poole** · **Bournemouth** · **Portsmouth** · **Brighton** · **Hastings** · Eastbourne

Padstow · Newquay · St. Ives · **Exeter** · Teignmouth · Weymouth · Isle of Wight · Newhaven · St

Isles of Scilly · Penzance · Truro · St. Austell · Dartmouth · Torquay · The New Forest · Guildford · North Downs · Canter

Sennen · Helston · Falmouth · **Plymouth** · South Downs · Horsham

UNITED KINGDOM

E n g l i s h   C h a n n e l

C e l t i c   S e a

| 20 |

| 50° |

87

Saint George's Channel

Cambrian Mts.

England

Bristol Channel

Devon

Cornwall

Dartmoor N.P.

172 · Cap de la Hague · **Cherbourg-Octeville** · Dieppe · St-Valéry-en-Caux

122 · Guernsey · St Peter-Port · Barneville-Carteret · Valognes · Fécamp · Neufchât en-Bra

Kanalinseln (UK) · Jersey · Ste-Mère-Église · Le Tou · Paris- · Berck-

St Helier · Carentan · **Le Havre** · Trouville-sur-Mer · Yvetot · **Rouen** · Go

Roscoff · Perros-Guirec · Golfe de Saint Malo · Coutances · Bayeux · Ouistreham · Pont-Audemer · Haute

Ploudalmézeau · Lesneven · Lannion · Paimpol · Granville · Saint-Lô · **Caen** · Lisieux · Bernay · Louviers · Vernon

Le Conquet · St-Renan · Morlaix · Guingamp · St-Brieuc · Avranches · Vire · Falaise · Gacé · Évreux · Mant

Brest · Landerneau · Carhaix-Plouguer · Lamballe · Dinan · St-Hilaire-du-Harcourt · Domfront · Argentan · L'Aigle · Verneuil-sur-Avre · Dreux

Douarnenez · Audierne · **Quimper** · Loudéac · **Rennes** · Flers · *Normandie* · Bellême · Rambou

Brittany · Pontivy · St-Méen-le-Grand · Fougères · Mayenne · Alençon · La Ferté-Bernard · Nogent-le-Rotrou · **Chartres**

Penmarch · Concarneau · Quimperlé · Hennebont · Ploërmel · Vitré · Laval · Mamers · Le Mans · Châteaudun · Bonneval

Lorient · Larmor-Plage · Auray · Vannes · Guer · Redon · Château-briant · Château-Gontier · Sablé-sur-Sarthe · **Le Mans** · Château-du-Loir · Vendôme · **Orlé**

Quiberon · La-Roche-Bernard · Pontchâteau · Segré · La Flèche · Château-Renault · Beaugency

Guérande · Trignac · Ancenis · **Angers** · **Tours** · Amboise · Selles-s.-Cher

St-Nazaire · Pornic · Noirmoutier-en-l'Île · Chemillé · Saumur · Chinon · Vierzon

Nantes · Beauvoir-s.-Mer · Challans · Cholet · Doué-la-Fontaine · Loudun

St-Jean-de-Monts · Aizenay · Mauléon · Thouars · Bressuire · Châtellerault

St-Gilles-Croix-de-Vie · La Roche-sur-Yon · La Châtaigneraie

Les Sables-d'Olonne

A T L A N T I C   O C E A N

163

Basse Normandie

Maine

Normandie

Pays de la Loire

Touraine

Vendée

F R A N C E

Centre

Orléan

54

| 21 |

| 48° |

| 22 |

| 46° |

| Kh | 4° | Kj | 2° | Kk | 0° | La | 2° |

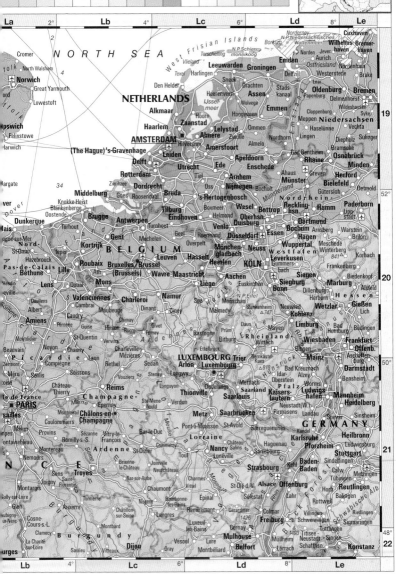

+ 5000 4000 3000 2000 1000 500 250 100 0 Depression 0 200 2000 4000 6000 + 8000

N O R T H   S E A

West Frisian Islands

Norderney
N.P.Niedersächsisches
Borkum Wattenmeer
Terschelling N.P.Schier-
monnikoog
Cromer Vlieland Norden Jever Wilhelms- Bremer-
Cuxhaven
North Walsham Texel Harlingen Leeuwarden Groningen Emden Ostfriesland haven haven
Norwich Den Helder Sneek Delfzijl Aurich Westerstede Brake
Great Yarmouth Heerenveen Drachten Stads Oldenburg Papenburg Delmenhorst Bremen
Lowestoft Alkmaar Hoorn Wolvega Assen Kanaal Cloppenburg Wildeshausen
NETHERLANDS Emmen Meppen Niedersachsen Syke
Ipswich Haarlem Zaanstad IJssel- Ommen Haselünne Diepholz Sulinger
Felixstowe meer Lelystad Nordhorn Lingen Bramsche 19
AMSTERDAM Almere Zwolle Osnabrück Minden
Harwich (The Hague) 's-Gravenhage Hilversum Amersfoort Nijmegen Bad Bentheim Rheine Herford
Margate Delft Leiden Apeldoorn Ahaus Greven Bielefeld Detmold
Rotterdam Utrecht Ede Enschede Münster Gütersloh 52°
Zierikzee Tiel Arnhem Bocholt Münsterland Nordrhein-
Middelburg Dordrecht Oss 's-Hertogenbosch Wesel Paderborn
Dover Goes Roosendaal Breda Boxmeer Rhein Recklingh. Hamm Lippstadt
Knokke-Heist Oosterhout Tilburg Helmond Oberhsn. Bottrop hsn. Brilon
Blankenberge Zundert Eindhoven Duisburg Essen Dortmund Arnsberg Warstein
Oostende Brugge Antwerpen Turnhout Geel Venlo Mönchen- Düsseldorf Bochum Hagen Winterberg 841 Korbach
Dunkerque Torhout Roermond gladbach Neuss Wuppertal Westfalen Frankenberg
Calais Gent Mechelen Overpelt Heerlen Leverkusen Gummers-
Nord- Kortrijk Leuven Hasselt KÖLN bach Siegen Biedenkopf
St-Omer Roubaix BELGIUM Wavre Maastricht Aachen Siegburg Marburg
Ieper Bruxelles/Brussel Euskirchen Bonn Herborn Hessen
Hazebrouck Lille Ath (Brussels) Liège N.P.Eifel Dillenburg Alsfeld
Pas-de-Calais Douai Mons Namur Spa Monschau Blankenheim Neuwied Wetzlar Gießen
Béthune Valenciennes Charleroi Malmedy Daun 747 Koblenz Bad Homburg
Hesdin Lens Maubeuge Ciney Mayen Limburg Büdingen
Arras Cambrai Chimay Givet Prüm Rheinland Wiesbaden Frankfurt
Amiens Caudry Hirson Rocroi Bastogne Bitburg Wittlich Bingen Mainz Aschaffen-
Albert Péronne Rethel Charleville- Ardenne Ettelbruck Trier LUXEMBOURG Bad Münster- Offenb. burg 20
Montdidier St-Quentin Vervins Mézières Luxembourg Kues Mainz Darmstadt
Beauvais Noyon Chauny Laon Sedan LUXEMBOURG Arlon Idar- Bad Kreuznach Worms
Méru Compiègne Soissons Vouziers Stenay Longwy Hunsrück Oberstein Alzey Ludwigs- Mannheim 50°
Senlis Château- Longuyon Pfalz hafen Heidelberg
Thierry Reims Ste-Mene- Thionville Dudelange Saarland Kaisers- Neustadt Sinsheim
PARIS Marne hould Verdun Saarlouis lautern Speyer
Versailles Épernay Metz Saarbrücken Pirmasens Landau GERMANY
Champagne- Bar-le-Duc Pont-à-Mousson St-Avold Sarreguemines Kandel
Coulommiers Châlons-en- Commercy Metz Landau Karlsruhe Heilbronn
Provins Champagne Loraine St-Dizier Nancy Château- Haguenau Pforzheim Ludwigsburg
Sézanne Vitry-le- Toul Salins Sarrebourg Stuttgart 21
Nemours Montereau Romilly-s.-S. François Bar-sur-Aube Lunéville Sarralbe Baden- Sindelfingen
Sens Brienne- Joinville Neufchâteau Charmes Baden Calw
Troyes le-Château Strasbourg Kehl Offenburg Tübingen Metzingen
Montargis Joigny Saint- Chaumont Vittel Alsace Kork Horb Reutlingen
Gien Florentin Nogent- Épinal St-Dié-d.-V. Sélestat Lahr Rottweil Balingen
Auxerre sur-Seine Remiremont Gérardmer Colmar Villingen Schwäbische Alb
Tonnerre Langres Luxeuil- Cernay Freiburg Schwenningen Sigmaringen 48°
Montbard les-Bains Mülheim Riedlingen
Burgundy Vesoul Lure Müllheim Donaueschingen Tuttlingen Singen
Clamecy Châtillon- Gray Belfort Neustadt Schaffhsn. Konstanz
Dijon Montbéliard Lörrach
Mulhouse 22

Scale 1:5,000,000

0   50   100   150 Kilometers
0   50   100 Miles

Kj 2° **Kk** 0° **La** 2° L

Guérande
St-Nazaire
Trignac
Ancenis
Angers
Château-du-Loir
Vendôme
Château-Renault
Orléans
Monta
Pornic
Nantes
Chemillé
Saumur
Amboise
Blois
Beaugency
Sully-sur-Loire
Gien
Noirmoutier-en-l'Île
22
Beauvoir-s.-Mer
Pays de la Loire
Cholet
Doué-la-Fontaine
Tours
Selles-s.-Cher
Aubigny-sur-Nère
Cosne-Cours/L.
St-Jean-de-Monts
Challans
Chinon
Loudun
Vierzon
St-Gilles-Croix-de-Vie
Mauléon
Thouars
Aizenay
Touraine
F R A N C E
Les Sables-d'Olonne
La Roche-sur-Yon
Bressuire
La Châtaigneraie
Châtellerault
Buzançais
Issoudun
Bourges
La Charité-sur-Loire
46° 135
L'Aiguillon-sur-Mer
Luçon
Fontenay-le-Comte
Parthenay
Poitiers
Le Blanc
Argenton-sur-Creuse
Châteauroux
St-Amand-Montrond
Château-Meillant
Nevers
St-Martin-de-Ré
Niort
St-Maixent-l'École
Poitou
Chauvigny
Montmorillon
La Châtre
Moulins
La Rochelle
Surgères
Melle
La Souterraine
Guéret
Commentry
Varennes-sur-Allie
Châtelaillon-Plage
Rochefort
St-Jean-d'Angély
Matha
Ruffec
Confolens
St-Junien
Aubusson
Montluçon
Le Château-d'Oléron
La Tremblade
Marennes
Saintes
Charente
Cognac
Jonzac
Rochechouart
Limoges
St-Léonard-de-Noblat
Eymoutiers
Clermont-Ferrand
A T L A N T I C
23
Royan
Angoulême
Limousin
St-Yrieix-la-Perche
Uzerche
Ussel
Riom
Issoire
d'Auvre
O C E A N
Lesparre-Médoc
Barbezieux
Brantôme
Puy de Sancy
1886
Massif
Pauillac
Chalais
Montpon-Ménesterol
Périgueux
Brive-la-Gaillarde
Tulle
Mauriac
Murat
Auvergne
Bric
Coutras
Central
Lacanau-Océan
St-Médard-en-Jalles
Libourne
Saint-Émilion
Périgord
Cantal
1855
St-Flour
en-V
Andernos-les-Bains
Arcachon
Bordeaux
Bergerac
Sarlat-la-Canéda
St-Céré
Aurillac
Chaud
d'Apcher
Dune du Pilat
Aquitaine
Langon
La Réole
Gourdon
Entraygues-s.-T.
Marvejols
Biscarrosse
Bay of
Mimizan
Villandraut
Castillonnès
Marmande
Fumel
Cahors
Figeac
Decazeville
Espalion
Mende
Mt. Lozè
44°
Castets
Tonneins
Biscay
Roquefort
Nérac
Agen
Moissac
Villeneuve-s.-L.
Lot
Villefranche-de-Rouergue
Rodez
Donostia/
S.Sebastián
Mont-de-Marsan
Condom
Castel-sarrasin
Caussade
Pyrénées
Millau
P.N.des Cévenne
Eibar
Bayonne
Dax
Aire-sur-l'Adour
Mirande
Auch
L'Isle-Jourdain
Montauban
Midi
Gaillac
Albi
St-Affrique
Le Vigan
Ganges
Irun
Biarritz
Orthez
Pau
Tarbes
Lannemezan
Muret
Toulouse
Castres
Lacaune
Lodève
Langued
Tolosa
St-Jean-Pied-de-Port
Sauveterre-de-Béarn
Auterive
Revel
Mazamet
Bédarieux
Montpellier
24
Irurzun
Lourdes
Bagnères-de-Luchon
St-Gaudens
Pamiers
Castelnaudary
Pézenas
Sète
Beaxm
Pamplona (Iruña)
2504
P.N.des Pyrénées
St-Girons
Foix
Limoux
Carcassonne
Roussillon
Béziers
Agde
Golfe
Estella
Navarra
2884
Jaca
Vielha
Quillan
Narbonne
du Lio
Tafalla
Sangüesa
P.N. de Ordesa
y Monte Perdido
3406
P.N. de Aiguestortes
3143
Prades
Rivesaltes
Sistema
Arguedas
ANDORRA
Andorra la Vella
2910
Perpignan
Port-Vendres
Cerbère
42°
Ejea de los Caballeros
Huesca
Benabarre
Tremp
Puigcerdà
Berga
Thuir
Arneda
Calahorra
Almudévar
Barbastro
Ripoll
Olot
Figueres
Iberico
Tudela
Ágreda
Zaragoza
Monzón
S P A I N
Ponts
Vic
1706
Manlleu
Banyoles
Girona
Costa Brava
Tarazona
Sariñena
Balaguer
Aragón
Túrrega
Manresa
Sant Celoni
Palafrugell
Palamós
Illueca
Lleida
Fraga
Catalonia
Granollers
Lloret de Mar
Blanes
25
Calatayud
Cariñena
Belchite
Quinto
Mequinenza
Terrassa
Daroca
Caspe

Kk 0° **La** 2° **Lb** 4°

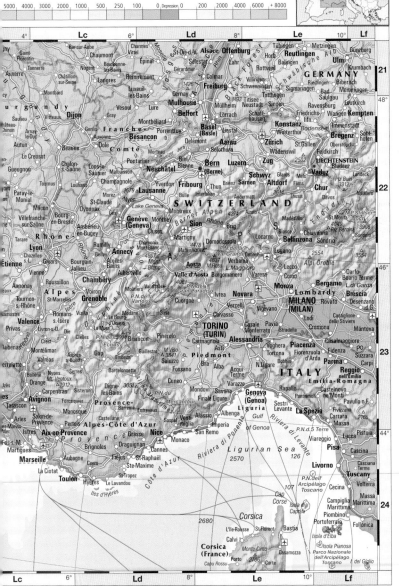

Southern France, Switzerland 39

Scale 1:5,000,000

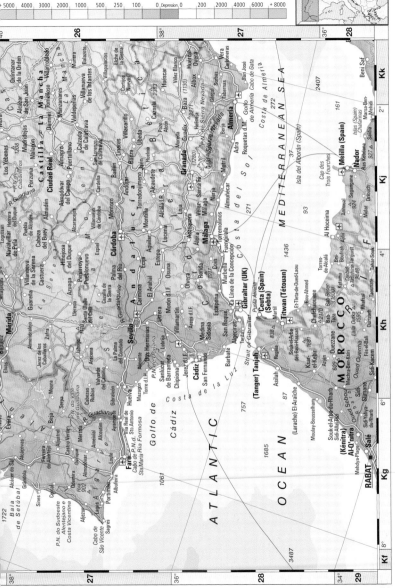

Western Spain, Portugal   41

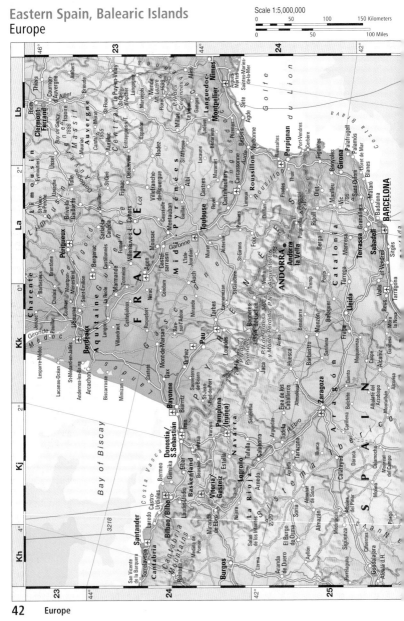

Eastern Spain, Balearic Islands
Europe

Scale 1:5,000,000

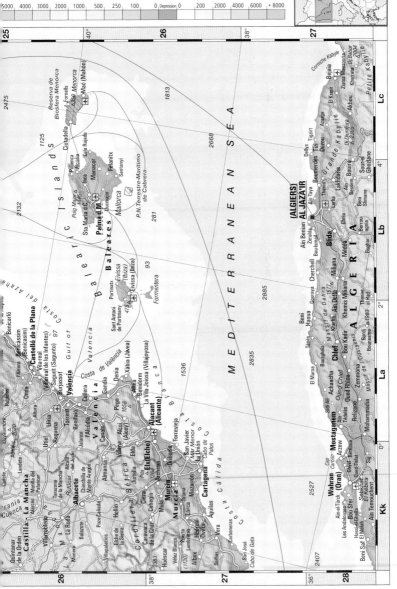

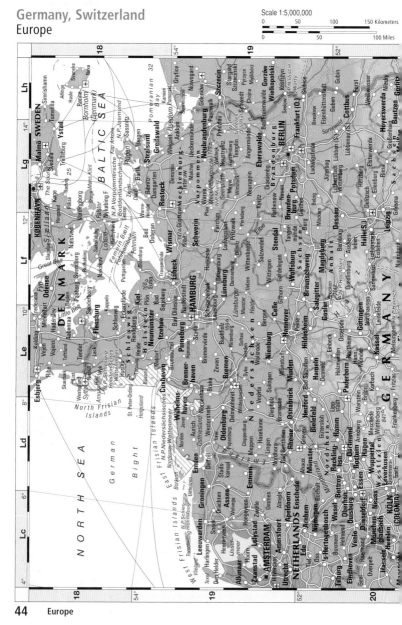

Scale 1:5,000,000

| 0 | 50 | 100 | 150 Kilometers |

| 0 | | 50 | 100 Miles |

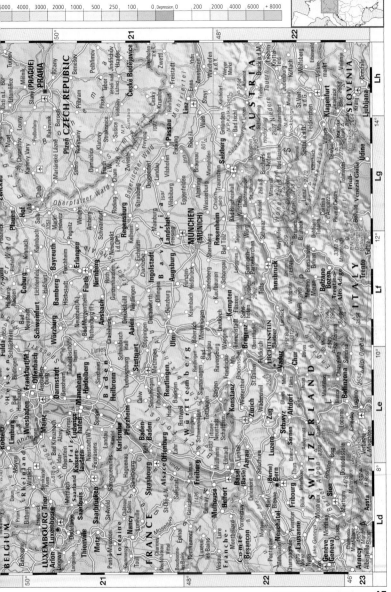

Scale 1:5,000,000

0   50   100   150 Kilometers

0   50   100 Miles

Lc   6°   Ld   8°   Le   10°   Lf   12°

Besancon   Delémont   Aarau   Zürich   Winterthur   Bregenz   Son   Füssen   Garmisch-   Worgl   Kufs
Franche-   Morteau   Jura   Solothurn   Wädenswil   St.Gallen   Oberstdorf   2962   Partenkirchen
Comté   Pontarlier   Biel/   Zug   Schwyz   Feldkirch   LIECHTENSTEIN   Tells   Schwaz   Kitzbühel
Champagnole   Neuchâtel   Bienne   Luzern   Schwyz   2502   Vaduz   Landeck   Mayrhofen   3509   Hoh
Malbuisson   Bern   Sarnen   Altdorf   Mels   Piz Buin   Wildspitze (3774)   Brenner   Bruneco   Ta
Morez   Yverdon   Fribourg   Thun   Brienz   Andermatt   3614   Chur   Davos   Nauders   3768   Bressanone   Bruneck
St-Claude   Nyon   Lausanne   Bulle   Interlaken   S W I T Z E R L A N D   Fims   Ofen   Brixen   Dobbiaco   Cortin
Geneve   Montreux   Sion   Brig   Alpen   Madésimo   P.N.Stilfser   Jocho   Merano   Meran   Brixen   Toblach   d'Ampe
(Geneva)   Monthey   Martigny   4478   Domodóssola   Locarno   Biasca   3905   Bernina   Sondalo   Trentino-   Piève di
Annecy   Cluses   Matterhorn   P.N.della   Bellinzona   Sóndrio   Alto Adige   Marmolada
Bonneville   Mont-Blanc   4807   Val Grande   Lugano   2554   Darfo   Bolzano   Marmolada   Belluno
Aix-les-   Albertville   Mont   A   Verbania   L.Maggiore   Alpi Orobie   Boario Terme   Riva del   Trento   P.N.delle   Belluno
Bains   Moûtiers   4810   Blanc   Aosta   Borgomanero   Lecco   Como   Bergamo   Brescia   Garda   Rovereto   Dolomiti   Vittorio   Conegliano   Trevis
Chambéry   P.N.della   Gran Paradiso   Ivrea   Varese   Schio   Bassano d.G.   Veneto   V
Vanoise   Novara   Monza   Lombardy   Desenzano   Vicenza   Mestre   Ve
Le Bourg   Cuorgnè   Vercelli   MILANO   Rovato   d.G.   Verona   Pádova   (Ve
d'Oisans)   3514   Briançon   Chivasso   Vigevano   (MILAN)   Lodi   Villafranca   Padova
P.N.des   M.Viso   TORINO   Casale   Pavia   Cremona   di Verona   Mántova   Monsélice   Rovigo   Adria
Écrins   3841   (TURIN)   Monferrato   Stradella   Piacenza   Casal-   Legnago
Gap   Guillestre   Pinerolo   Asti   I T A L Y   maggiore   Po   Mirándola   Ferrara
Barcelonnette   Catmagnola   Alessándria   Tortona   Fiorenzuola   Fidenza   Carpi   Pode
Digne-   305.3   Saluzzo   Bra   Alba   d'Arda   Parma   Módena
les-Bains   P.N.du   Cuneo   Acqui   N.Santi   Bóbbio   Reggio   Emilia-Romagna   Bologna   Comacch
Barreme   Mercantour   Fossano   Terme   Varazze   nell'Emilia   Vignola   Lugo   Ravenn
Entrevaux   Mondovi   Savona   Castelnuovo   Pavullo   Imola   Forli   Cervia
Provence   Finale Ligure   Genova   Rapallo   Pontremoli   ne'Monti   Fivizzano   Brisighella   Cesena   Cese
Alpes-Côte d'Azur   Castellane   (Genoa)   Sestri   La Spézia   2765   N.Casentinesi   N.Falterona   SAN MA
Grasse   Ventimiglia   Albenga   Liguria   Levante   Carrara   M.Falterona   San Ma
Draguignan   Nice   Alássio   Gulf of   Massa   Lucca   Pistóia   1654   Urbino   Fossom
Fréjus   Monaco   San Remo   Genoa   Viaréggio   Pisa   Prato   Firenze   Rádio di   Romagna
St-Raphaël   Cannes   Riviera di Ponente   Riviera di Levante   P.N.d.5 Terre   126   Cascina   (Florence)   Arezzo   Sansepolcro   Città di
Ste-Maxime   Côte d'Azur   L i g u r i a n   Livorno   Empoli   Castello   Guald
St-Tropez   2570   Cásciana   Poggibonsi   Arezzo   Cortona   Tadin
Le Lavandou   S e a   Terme   Siena   Città di   Perug
Îles d'Hyères   107   Volterra   Tuscany   Castello
Cecina   Campiglia   Massa   Umbria
Cap   Maríttima   Marittima   Pienza   Monte-
Corse   Piombino   pulciano   L.Tras-   Todi
2680   Portoferraio   Follónica   1738   meno
L'Ile-Rousse   St-Florent   Bastia   Isola d'Elba   Monte-   Orvieto   Narni
Calvi   Corsica   Isola Pianosa   pulciano
(France)   Monte Cinto   Casamozza   Grosseto   L.di   Todi
Capu Rossu   2706   Corte   Acquapendente   Bolsena   Narni
Porto   2622   Parco Nazionale   Orbetello   I.del Giglio   Viterbo   Civita Castellana
Corse   dell'Arcipélago   Lazio
Cateraggio   Toscano   Tarquínia   Civita Castellana
Ajáccio   Civitavécchia
MEDITERRANEAN   Zicavo   VATICAN CITY   ROMA
Capu di Muru   Propriano   (ROME)   Va
SEA   Sartene   Anzio
Bonifácio   P.N.dell' Arcipélago   645   P.N.del C
Santa Teresa   de la Maddalena   Porto Vecchio
Gallura   La Maddalena

Ld   8°   Le   10°   Lf   12°

Northern Italy, Slovenia, Croatia **47**

Scale 1:5,000,000

Southern Italy, Malta **49**

Scale 1:5,000,000

| 0 | 50 | 100 | 150 Kilometers |
| 0 | | 50 | 100 Miles |

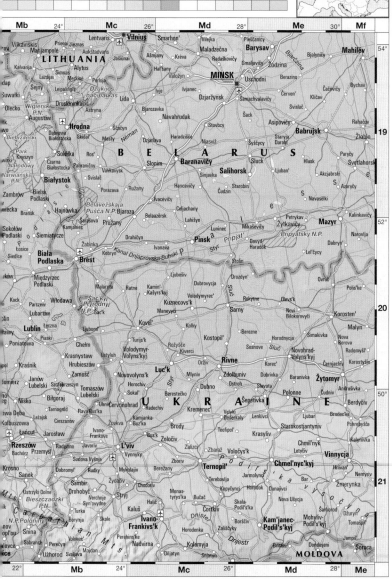

Scale bar: 5000 4000 3000 2000 1000 500 250 100 0 Depression 0 200 2000 4000 6000 +8000

Mb 24° Mc 26° Md 28° Me 30° Mf

54°

Vilkaviškis Prienai Jieznas Lentvaris Vilnius Smarhon' Vilejka Plešcanicy
Marijampole Aukštadvaris Ašmjany Kreva Maladzečna Barysav Bjalyniči Mahilëv
LITHUANIA Alytus Jašiunai Halšany Radaškoviči Smaljaviči Žodzina Bjarčzina Bychav
Kalvarija Lazdijai Simnas Merkine Parloja Valožyn MINSK Uschodni Berazino Čačevičy Kličav Rahacov
Suwałki Sejny Leipalingis Dzūkijos Ivje Ivjanec Berazino Červen' Svislač
dap Druskininkai Lida Dzjaržynsk Samachvalaviči Asipoviči
Olecko Wigierski Astryna Bjarozavka Navahrudak Stovbcy Šack Babrujsk Žlobin
P.N. Augustów Hrodna Ščyn Neman Dzjatlava Haradzišča Njasviž Staryja Darohi Žlobin
Biebrzański Dabrova Skidal Masty Slonim BARANAVIČY Sluck Ljuban' Paryčy
Park Białostocka Sokółka Ros' B E L A R U S Salihorsk Akcjabrski Svetlahorsk
wiski Narodowy Czarna Porozava Ružany Hancaviči Starobin S Navasëlki Azaryčy
Narwiański Białystok Białostocka Pałaniczy Vavkavysk Ivacevičy Čudzin Kalinkavičy Mazyr
P.N. Bielsk Svislač Slonim Sinjavka Luninec Petrykav Žytkaviči Pripyatsky N.P. Narovlja
Zambrów Podlaski Hajnówka Belavežskaja Celjachany Lahišyn Mikaševičy Pripjat Dabra Lel'čycy
wiecka Brańsk Pušča N.P. Bjaroza Belaazërsk Pinsk Davyd Haradok Leľčycy
Sokołów Siemiatycze Kamjaniec Pružany Drahičyn Ivanava Stolin Ovruč Poliss'
Podlaski Łosice Žabinka Kanał Dniaprovska-Buhski Stolin Drozdyn' Novi Korosten'
Siedlce BREST Kóbryn Ratne Kamin'-Kašyrs'kyj Dubrovycja Rokytne Olevs'k Bilokorovyči
Międzyrzec Podlaski Małaryta Ljubešiv Volodymyrec Sarny Berezne Simakivka Malyn Radomyšl'
Kock Parczew Włodawa Šack Sac'kyj Pryrodnyj N.P. Kuznecovs'k Horodnycja Černjaxiv
Lubartów Łęczna Ljubomi Manevyči Kolky Kostopil' Sosnove Novohrad-Volyns'kyj Radomyšl'
Lublin Piaski Chełm Ustyluh Turijs'k Kovel' Rožyšče Kiverci Orživ Rivne Korec' Baranivka Sluč Polonne Cudniv Andrušivka Berdyčiv
Kraśnik Krasnystaw Hrubieszów Volodymyr-Volyns'kyj Novovolyns'k Horoxiv Sokal' Luc'k Mlyniv Dubno Zdolbuniv Ostroh Slavuta Šepetivka Starokostjantyniv Ljubar Brodec'ke Pohrebyšče
Janów Lubelski Szczebrzeszyn Zamość Tomaszów Lubelski Uhniv Červonohrad Radexiv Berestečko Kremenec Dederkaly Lenkivci Krasyliv Chmiľnyk Kalynivka
Nisko Biłgoraj Tarnogród Rava-Rus'ka Žovkva Kamjanka-Buz'ka Brody Teofipol Letyčiv Vinnycja
wa Dęba Leżajsk Bus'k Zoločiv Zalizci Zbaraž Voločys'k Ternopil' Jarmolynci Chmel'nyc'kyj Hnivan' Nemyriv Žmerynka
Kolbuszowa Łańcut Jarosław Ivano-Frankove Javoriv Zoločiv Berežany Zborov U K R A I N E Podiľs'ka Bar Zmerynka Džuryn Tomašpil'
Rzeszów Radymno Przemyśl Sudova Vyšnja Vynnyky L'viv Monastyrys'ka Kopyčynci Horodok Dunajivci Nova Ušycja Šarhorod Jampil'
Bachórz Dobromyl' Rudky Mykolajiv Chodoriv Halič Buča Čortkiv Skala-Podiľs'ka Mohyliv-Podiľs'kyj
Krosno Sanok Sambir Drohobyč Żydačiv Stryj Kaluš Ivano-Frankivs'k Tovste Borščiv Kam'janec-Podil's'kyj Zališčyky Dnistr Dnjestr Bričani Dondušeni Soroca
Ustrzyki Dolne Bieszczadzki N.P. Verchnje Syn'jovydne Turka Skole Horodenka Nadvirna Kolomyja Snjatyn Diljatyn
nov opl'ou Polonina Bieszczadzki Volovec Majdan MOLDOVA
ovce Uzhorod Sobranci Svaljava Perečyn

Mb 24° Mc 26° Md 28° Me

Poland 51

Scale 1:5,000,000

0   50   100   150 Kilometers

0   50   100 Miles

GERMANY

Göttingen · Nordhausen · Halle (S.) · Leipzig · Kassel · Eisenach · Gotha · Weimar · Jena · Gera · Dresden · Meißen · Bautzen · Görlitz · Liberec · Erfurt · Suhl · Plauen · Hof · Chemnitz · Zwickau · Freiberg · Pirna · Hoyerswerda · Weißwasser

Fulda · Coburg · Bamberg · Bayreuth · Karlovy Vary (Karlsbad) · (PRAGUE) PRAHA · Hradec Králové

Würzburg · Erlangen · Fürth · Nürnberg · Plzeň · **CZECH REPU**

Ansbach · Aalen · Nördlingen · Regensburg · Passau · České Budějovice

Ulm · Augsburg · Landshut · **Bavaria** · Ingolstadt · Linz · St. Pölten · WIEN

MÜNCHEN (MUNICH) · Rosenheim · Salzburg · **AUSTRIA**

Bregenz · Kempten · Innsbruck · Graz

LIECHTENSTEIN · Vaduz · Chur · Bozen/Bolzano · Trentino Alto Adige · Klagenfurt · Maribor

ITALY · Trento · Belluno · Udine · **SLOVENIA** · Ljubljana · Zagreb

Bergamo · Brescia · Verona · Vicenza · Padova · Mestre · Venezia (Venice) · Treviso · Trieste · Koper · Karlovac

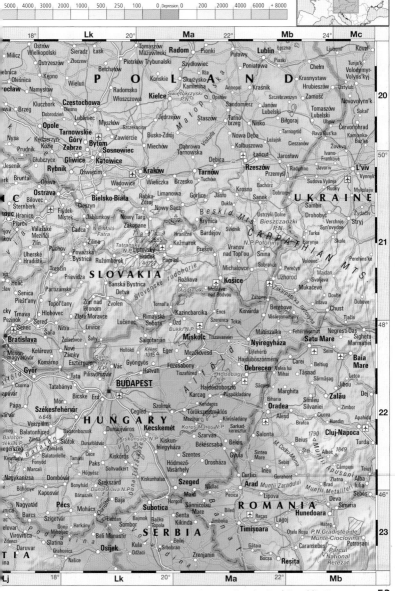

Scale 1:5,000,000

| 0 | 50 | 100 | 150 Kilometers |

| 0 | 50 | 100 Miles |

SLOVAKIA

HUNGARY

BUDAPEST

CROATIA

BOSNIA AND HERZEGOVINA

Sarajevo

MONTENEGRO

Mostar

SERBIA

BEOGRAD (BELGRADE)

Novi Sad

Vojvodina

Subotica

KOSOVO

Priština

Transylvania

Cluj-Napoca

Oradea

Timișoara (Temeschburg)

Arad

Satu Mare

Baia Mare

Bistrița

Zalău

Târgu Mureș

Alba Iulia

Deva

Hunedoara

Reșița

Caransebeș

Drobeta-Turnu Severin

Târgu Jiu

Craiova

Bălești

Calafat

Vidin

Niš

SOFIJA (SOFIA)

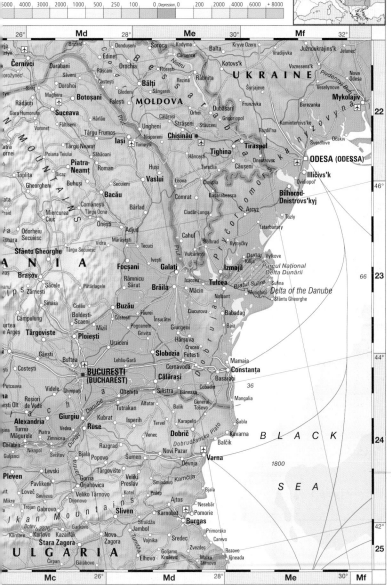

Scale 1:5,000,000

| 0 | 50 | 100 | 150 Kilometers |
| 0 | | 50 | 100 Miles |

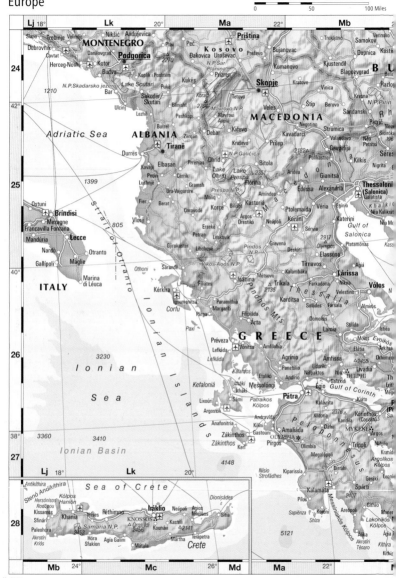

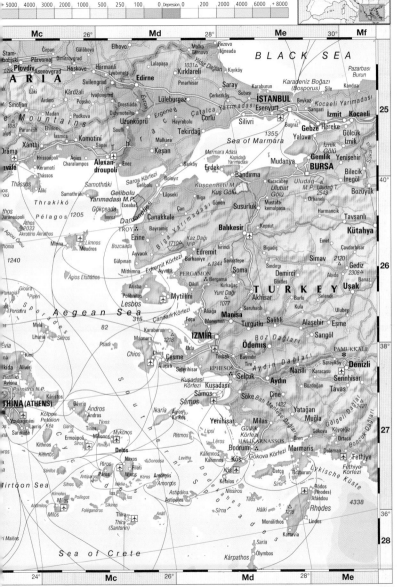

Western Russia, Moscow region
Europe

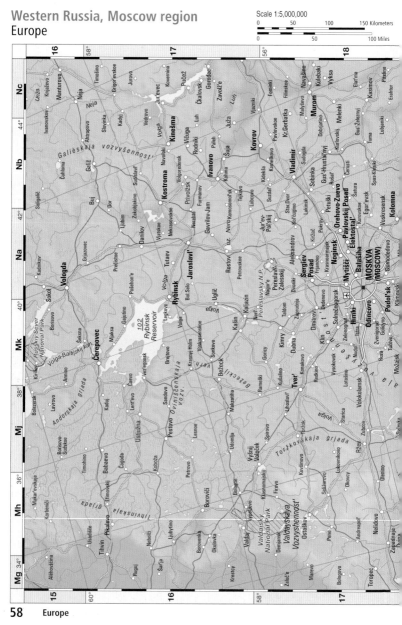

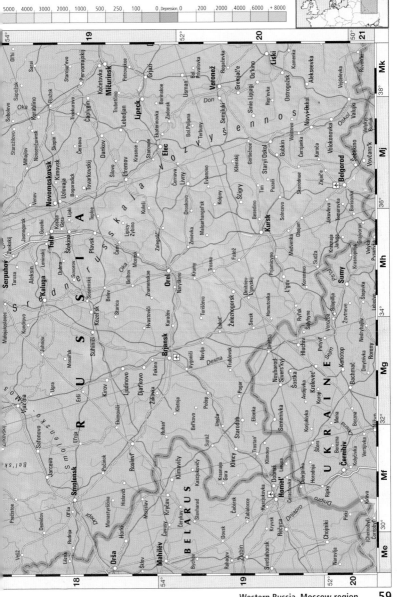

Scale 1:5,000,000

0   50   100   150 Kilometers

0   50   100 Miles

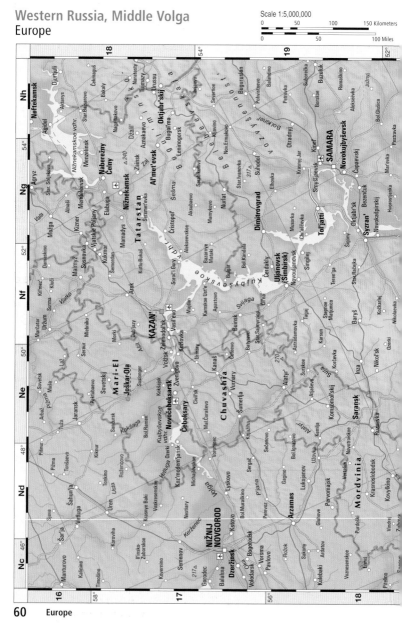

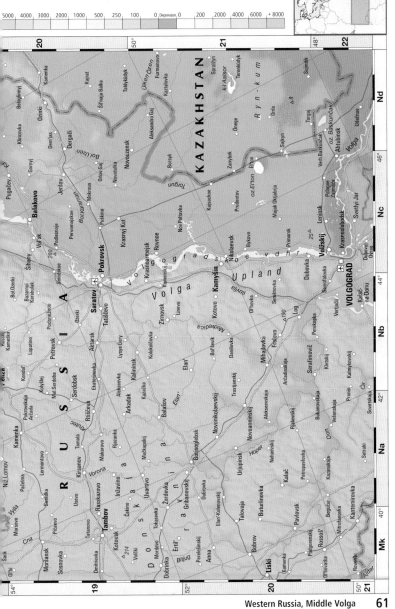

Scale 1:5,000,000

0   50   100   150 Kilometers

0   50   100 Miles

28° Me 30° Mf 32° Mg 34°

Ovruč Polis'ke Kipti Nosivka Ičnja Trostjanec' Ochtyrka
Olevs'k Termachivka Kyjivs'ke vodoschovyšče Bobrovycja Pryluky Sribne Lypova Dolyna Zin'kiv
Nevi Bilokorovyči Korosten' Ivankiv Dymer Brovary Petrivka Varva Lochvycja Hadjač Kotel'va
Simakivka Malyn Borodjanka Buča Vyšhorod Pyrjatyn Čornuchy Romodan Opišnja Dykan'ka
Novohrad- Nova Borova Radomyšl' Kocjubyns'ke Bor- KYJIV Jahotyn Hrebinka Lubny Podil Myrhorod Poltava
Volyns'kyj Černjachiv Hlevacha (KIEV) Perejaslav- Drabiv Oržycja Chorol Rešetylivka
Žytomyr Korostyšiv Fastiv Vasyl'kiv Chmel'nyc'kyj Kaniv Zolotonoša Obolon' Hlobyne
Dubrivka Andrušivka Bila Cerkva Skvyra Uzyn Myronivka Kaniv Irkliiv Čerkasy Hradyz'k
Baranivka Čudniv Berdyčiv Bohuslav Horodyšče Smila Kremenčuc'ke vodoschovyšče Kremenčuk
Polonne Ljubar Pohrebyšče Volodarka Tarašča Korsun'- Čyhyryn Svitlovods'k Dniprodzeržyns'
Starokostjantyniv Brodec'ke Kozjatyn Tetijiv Ševčenkivs'kyj Kam'janka Pavlyš Verchn'odniprov
Chmil'nyk Kalynivka Žaškiv Zvenyhorodka Špola Oleksandrivka Oleksandrija
Letyčiv Vinnycja Monastyryšče Buky Vatutine Novomyrhorod Znam'janka P'jatychatky
Hnivan' Nemyriv Chrystynivka Tal'ne Mala Vyska Kirovohrad Žovti Vody
Nova Ušycja Žmerynka Hajsyn Uman' Novo- Oleksandrivka Šolychivk
Šarhorod Tul'čyn archanhel's'k Tyškivka Rivne Dolyns'k Kryvyj Rih
Mohyliv- Džuryn Ladyžyn Novoukrajinka Bobrynec' Šyroke Ordžo
Podil's'kyj Tomašpil' Bršad' Ul'janovka Pervomajs'k Novyj Buh Kazanka Zelenod
Brieni Dondušeni Soroca Kryžopil' Čečel'nyk Kryve Ozero Balta Vradijivka Južnoukrajins'k Jelanec' Baštanka Bereznehuvate Kacho
Edinet Drochia Florešti Kodyma Kotovs'k Voznesens'k Nova Odesa Snihurivka
Săveni Răscani Rezina Rîbnița Syrjajeve Berezanka Mykolajiv Cherson
Casteşti Bălți Sîngerei Orhei Dubăsari Frunzivka Berezanka Oleksandrivka Čurnpyns'k
Gloden Fălești Călăraşi Strășeni Grigoriopol Razdil'na Kominternivs'ke Očakiv Hola Prystan' Skadovs'k
Botoşani Hărlău Ungheni Nisporeni Stăuceni Kodıma Sverdlove Novomykolajivka
Târgu Frumos Iaşi Tomeşti Chişinău Tighina Tiraspol ODESA (ODESSA) Novofedorivka
Săbăoani Huşi Hănceşti Tarutino Căuşeni Dnestrovsc Illičivs'k
Roman Vaslui Secuieni Leova Cniselia Basarabeasca Ovidiopol' Bilhorod- Čornomors'ke
Buhuşi Bacău Comrat Ciadâr-Lunga Arcyz Dnistrovs'kyj Olenivka
Comăneşti Bârlad Tuzly
Târgu Ocna Oneşti Adjud Cahul Kyrnycky Tatarbunary
Vidra Mărăşeşti Tecuci Bolhrad Dunaj Vylkove
Focşani Iveşti Vulcăneşti Kilija Sulina Parcul National Delta Dunării
ROMANIA Galaţi Izmajil Bratul Sulina Delta of the Danube
Râmnicu Sărat Isaccea Tulcea Bratul Sfântu Gheorghe
Pătârlagele Brăila Măcin Nalbant

Md 28° Me 30° Mf 32°

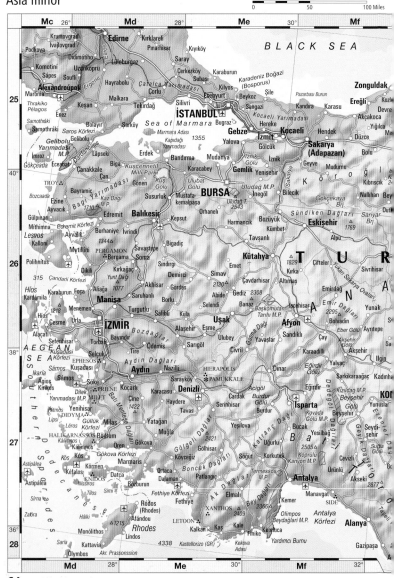

Scale 1:5,000,000

0   50   100   150 Kilometers

0   50   100 Miles

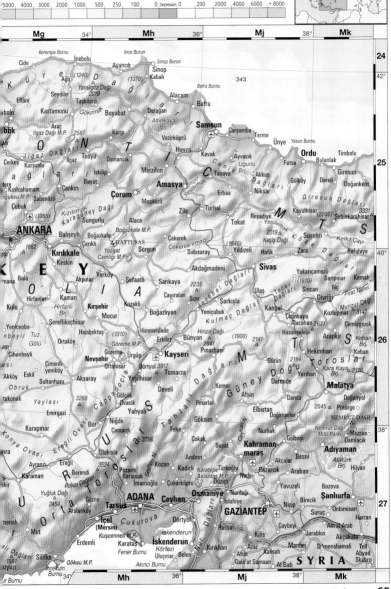

5000 4000 3000 2000 1000 500 250 100 0 Depression 0 200 2000 4000 6000 + 8000

24
42°
25
40°
26
38°
27

Kerempe Burnu   İnce Burun
Cide   İnebolu   Ayancık   Sinop Burun
Ağlı   (1240)   Sinop
Eflâni   Seydiler   Yaralıgöz Dağı   Kabalı   Bafra Burnu   343
Kastamonu   Taşköprü   2019   D   Alaçam
bolu   Boyabat   Gökırmak   Bafra
bük   Araç   Ilgaz Dağı M.P.   Kargı   Vezirköprü   Samsun   Çarşamba   Terme
Çerkes   Kurşunlu   Ilgaz Dağları   Osmancık   Havza   Kavak   Ayvacık   Ünye   Yasun Burnu
ığu.M.P.   Ilgaz   Tosya   İskilip   Merzifon   Taşova   Uğurlu Brj.   Akkuş   Fatsa   Ordu   Tirebolu
Çubuk   Kızılcahamam   Şabanözü   Bayat   Amasya   Erbaa   Niksar   Gölköy   Dereli   Giresun
(1365)   Çankırı   Çorum   Mecitözü   Yeşilırmak   Reşadiye   Köyulhisar (2200)   Şebinkarahisar   3331
ANKARA   Kızılırmak   Karagüney Dağı   Sungurlu   Alaca   Zile   Turhal   Tokat   2019   Keşiş Dağı   Suşehri   Kelkit Çayı
Balışeyh   Boğazkale M.P.   Yozgat   Çamlığı M.P.   Çekerek   Hafik   Zara   Refahiye
Kırıkkale   Boğazkale   HATTUŞAS   Sorgun   Çekerek Irmağı   (1646)   Yıldızeli   Sivas
Keskin   Çerikli   Sulusaray   Akdağmadeni   Yukarıçamozu   Kemah
KE   Y   Akpınar   Yerköy   Şefaatli   Sarıkaya   İncebel Dağları   Ulaş   (1810)   Sarıpınar   İliç   Fırat Nehri
Balâ   Hirfanlı   Kaman   Kırşehir   Çayıralan   2235   Kangal   Sincan   Divriği   Munzur Dağı   3147
Kulu   Brj.   Mucur   Kozaklı   Boğazlıyan   Sızır   Şarkışla   Yeçel Dağları   Çatınkaya   Kozlupınar   Cemişgezek
Yeniceoba   Şereflikoçhisar   Hacıbektaş   Himmetdede   Yeniçubuk   Kulmaç Dağları   Alacahan 2631   Hasançelebi   Arapkir   Keban Brj.
nbeyli   Tuz   (1310)   Erkilet   Hınzır Dağı   (1900)   2141   Hekimhan   Kara Kaya   2116   Keban
Gölü   Ortaköy   Göreme M.P.   Bünyan   2641   Gürün   2164   Yazıhan   Malatya
Cihanbeyli   Çimenli   Göreme   Ürgüp   Kayseri   Pınarbaşı   Darende   Toroslar
Akköy   Eskil   yeniköy   Ortahisar   Dörtyol 3917   Tomarza   Kemer   Afşin   Doğanyol
Sultanhanı   Aksaray   Yeşilhisar   Develi   Pınarlar   Elbistan   Pötürge   NEMRUT DAĞI
Obruk   Yaylası   3268   Gölcük   Ovacık   Göksun   Doğanşehir   2545   Mezraa   Nemrut Dağı
takonak   Emirgazi   Bor   Niğde   Yahyalı   Feke   Nurhak   Gölbaşı   Milli Parkı   Damlacık
Karapınar   Ereğli Ovası   Camardı   Çokak   Kahraman-   Adıyaman
Konya Ovası   Ayrancı   Ereğli   3756   Ulukışla   Andırın   Suşat   maraş   Akçalar   Besni   Atatürk   Hilvan
nra   Karaman   Berendi   Pozantı   Kozan   Kadirli   Türkoğlu   Narlı   Pazarcık   Araban   Bozova   Brj.   Şanlıurfa
kir   Ayrancı   3524   Karaisalı   İmamoğlu   Karatepe   Aslantaş M.P.   Nurdağı   Yavuzeli   Birecik
Yuğluk Dağı   Bolkar Dağları   Çukurköprü   Düziçi   Onbimisan
2454   Gözne   Arslanköy   ADANA   Ceyhan   Osmaniye   İslahiye   Nizip   Suruç   Harran
1591   Tarsus   Dörtyol   GAZİANTEP   Çaybeyi   Akçakale
Mut   İçel   Çukurova   Hassa   Kilis   Jarablos   Sı'reenshamali   Tell Abyad
Dağları   (Mersin)   Kuşçennet M.P.   İskenderun   Kırıkhan   Afrin   Kalsah   Manbej   Skabro
Silifke   Göksu M.P.   Karataş   Körfezi   Belen   Azaz   Qala'at Samaan   Al Bab   SYRIA
Burnu   İncekum   Fener Burnu   Uluçınar   Akıncı Burnu   Al Arab
Burnu   Burnu

Scale 1:5,000,000

0   50   100   150 Kilometers

0   50   100 Miles

Mk   **Na**   **Nb**

Apseronsk   Mineral'nye Vody   Zelenokumsk

Novomihajlovskij   Mostovskoj   Otradnaja   Čerkessk   Suvorovskaja   R U S

Adygea   Pjatigorsk   Georgievsk

Tuapse   Sočinskij nacionál'nyj park   Psebaj   Kurdžinovo   Ust'-Džeguta   Essentuki   Svobody   Novopavlovsk

Hamyški

Lazarevskoe   Zelenčukskaja   Ordžonikidzevskoj   Kislovodsk   Prohladnyj

g.Čuguš 3238   Karačaevsk   Baksan   Majskij

Dagomys   Krasnaja Poljana   Kavkazskij zapovednik   Karachay-Cherkessia   Nacionál'nyj park Priel'brus'e   Nartkala   Malgobek

Soči   Avadkhara   Nal'čik   Terek

Adler   Teberdinskij zapovednik   Teberda   g.El'brus 5642   Tyrnyauz   Kabardino-Balkaria   Sovetskoe

Gagra   b.Dombaj   Dombaj   4046   El'brus   Digora

Bitčvinta   Gudauta   Abkhazia   Zemo Ažara   Kabardino-Balkarski zapovednik   North Ossetia   Alagi

Sokhumi   Mestia   Dyhtau per. 5204 (2829jl)   Mizur

Tqvarčeli   Džvari   4008   Čazaši   Mamisonskij   Severo-Osetinskij zapovednik   Kazbek 5033

Očamčire   S v a n e t i   Tsageri   Oni   Kazbi

Gali   Zugdidi   Ambrolauri   Rioni   South Ossetia   Tkhinval

B L A C K   S E A   Senaki   Tsqaltubo   Tqibuli

1936   Poti   Samtredia   Zestaponi   **Kutaisi**   G E O R G I

Ozurgeti   Bagdati   Surami   Khašuri   Gori

Kobuleti   Mta Mepista karo 2850   Abastumani   Bordžomi   TB

Batumi   Adzharia   Akhaltsikhe   Bakuriani   (TIB

Kemalpaşa   Suakhevi   Akhalkalaki

Fener Burnu   Hopa   Borčka   Posof   Ninotsminda

Ardeşen   Arhavi   Meydancik   Hanak   (2640)   g.Ačkasar 3042

Ordu   Tirebolu   Vakfikebir   Pazar   Artvin   Ortaköy   Čildir   Tashir

Bulanlak   **Trabzon**   Rize   Çayeli   3348   Čildir Gölü   Step'anavan

Giresun   Akçaabat   Araklı   İyidere   Ardanuç   Yusufeli   **Gyumri**   Van

Dereli   Doğankent   Tonya   Altındere Vadisi M.P.   Kaçkar Dağı 3937   Olur   Göle   Aksar   Spitak   A R   Art'ik   4090 g.A

D o ğ u   K a r a d e n i z   D a ğ l a r ı   (2600)   Oltu   Senkaya   **Kars**   Digor   Ch'arent

Torul   3331   Gümüşhane   (1900)   İspir   Sarıkamış   Kağızman   Ashtarak   Echmiadzin

Sebinkarahisar   Siran   Köse   Kaledibi   Narman   Karaurgon   Karakurt   Akçay   Ma

Sușehri   Kelkit   Bayburt   Maden   Ovacik   G ü l l ü   D a ğ l a r ı   Karakurt   Tuzluca   Iğdır   Art

Refahiye   Otlukbeli Dağları   Aşkale   **Erzurum**   Pasinler   Horasan   Ağrı Dağ

Köse Dağları   **T U R K E Y**   Tercan   Eleşkirt   Ağrı   (2010)   (Mt. Ararat) 5165

Erzincan   Üzümlü   Çat   Karayazı   Çakmak Dağı   (2040)

Sarıpınar   Kemah   Kökpınar   Tekman   Hacıömer   Tutak   Diyadin   A r a   D a ğ l a r ı

Sincan   İliç   Pülümür   Yedisu   Göksu   3533

Divriği   Kozlupınar   Munzur Dağları   Munzur Vadisi Milli Parkı   Kiği   Karlıova   B i n g ö l   D a ğ l a r ı   Hınıs   Aktuzla   Patnos   Çaldıran   Sn

2631   Kemaliye   Δ 3147   Çaylar   3193   Yolüstü   Malazgirt   Doğansu   Erciş   Samsu

Arapkir   Çemişgezek   **Tunceli**   Gökçek   Sancak   Şerafettin Dağları   Varto   Muradiye

Hekimhan   Keban   Karakoçan   **Bingöl**   Solhan   Erentepe   Bulanık   Süphan Dağı 4058   Adilcevaz   Erçek Gölü

Kara Kaya   Doğu   Kovancılar   Soğutlu   Yenibaşak   Ahlat   Ercek   Özalp

Yazılkm   2116   **Elazığ**   Palu   Güroymak   Ovakışla   Van Gölü

G ü n e y   D o ğ u   T o r o s l a r   Balta sı   Servi   Kulp   **Muş**   Aşağı Üçdam   Tatvan   **Van**

5000 4000 3000 2000 1000 500 250 100 0 Depression 0 200 2000 4000 6000 + 8000

46° Nd 48° Ne 50° Nf 52° 44°

Terekli-Mekteb
Komsomol'skij
ostrov Čečen

A

KAZAKHSTAN

Syghyndy müysi

Manghystau
Aktau
Zhetibai
Omirzak
Munaishy
-132

Kizljar
Krajnovka

Chechenia
Kargalinskaja
Sulevkent

Agrahanskij
poluostrov

Pesschanyj müysi

Kuryk

Gudermes
Hasavjurt

Rakushechnyi müysi

oragorskij
Groznyi
Argun
Najbere
Kiziljurt
Mahačkala
24

shetia
Šali
Leninkent
Kaspijsk

ikavkaz
°Šatoj
DEF.
Harami
(2177)
Tloh
Bujnaksk

Manasкent

C A S P I A N   S E A

Oboda
Izberbaš

Botlih
g.Addala
Šuhgel'meer
4151
Golotl'
Levasi

Kajakent

Kundy
Mamedkala
Derbent

aneti
meta
Telavi
Kvareli
Kuli
42°

Belidzi
Yalama

Saga-
redzo
Gurdžaani
Balaken
Kurah
Xudat

stavi
Zaqatala
Rutul
Kasumkent
Qusar
Xaçmaz

Gardabani
Qax
Ahty
Quba
Deveç

Šeki
g.Bazardjuzi
4466
Siyezen

Qazax
Tovuz
Mingečevir
qöbät
Qebele
Babadag
3629
Apşeronskij poluostrov

ljevan
Šamkir
Gänžä
Agdas
Ismayilli
Haçi
Sumqayit
Buzovna
25

ARMENIA
Artzvashen
Yevlax
Laki
Göyçay
Šamaxi
Zeynalabdin
Xirdalan
Artyom

Chambarak
zdan
Toganaly
Barda
Ucar
Ahsu
Hövsan
Lökbetan
BAKI
(BAKU)
Qarabattaq adası

Lake Sevan
g.Gamyš Çayli
3725
A Z E R B A I J A N
Kürdämir
Suiti
burnu

EVAN
Vardenis
Agdam
Agdžabedi
Sabirabad
Qazimmemmed
Dobustan
Alat
40°

Martuni
Istisu
Nagornyy-
Karabakh
Xocavand
Bahramtapa
Saatli
Ali Bayramli

Yeghegnadzor
Xankändi
(Stepanakert)
Šuša
Imishli
Salyan
Banka

rki
Goris
Füzuli
Pars Abad
Bilesuvar
Xilli

Bicanak asr.
(2346)
Qubadli
Horadiz
Moradlu
Celilabad

AZERBAIJAN
Sisian
Kapan
Aslanduz
Masalli
26

Naxçivan
Naxçivan
Kadhzaran
Havali
Khoda Afarin
Ghermi
Lekeran

Culfa
Mincivan
Meghri
Kalalaq
Yardimli
Lerik
Qosmeliyon

Qare
ya' Eddin
Jolfa
Almandar
Kharvanaq
Salavat
Astara

Ev Oghli
Kiyamaki Dagh
-3347
Vardin
Razi
Shahrivar
Astara

Khoy
Marand
Alanjeq
Ahar
Meshgin Shahr

I R A N

1025

Bakinskij arhipelag

Nc 46° Nd 48° Ne 50° Nf

Asia
Physical map

Scale 1:65,500,000

0 500 1000 1500 Kilometers

0 500 1000 Miles

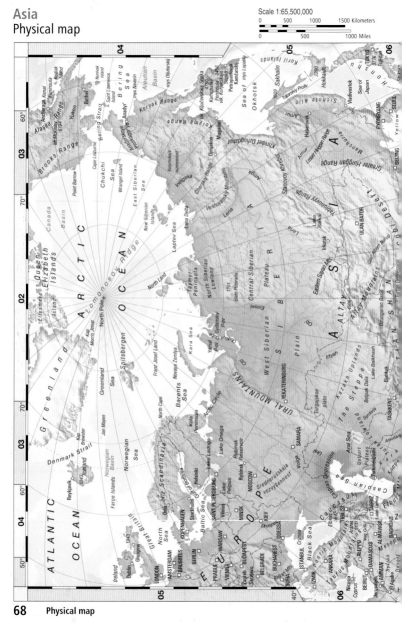

Asia **69**

Asia
Political map

Scale 1:65,500,000

| 0 | 500 | 1000 | 1500 Kilometers |

| 0 | 500 | 1000 Miles |

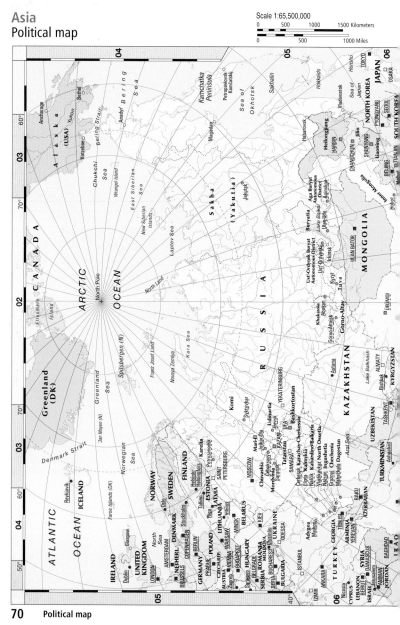

Scale 1:20,000,000

0   200   400   600 Kilometers

0   200   400 Miles

Mo I Rana
Narvik
Hammerfest
2111 △
Kebnekaise
Kiruna
Alta
North Cape
NORWAY
Storuman
Gällivare
S W E D E N
Muonio
Inari
Kirkenes
Inarijärvi
Varangerfjorden
Barents Sea
Umeå
Luleå
Rovaniemi
Sodankylä
Murmansk
Severomorsk
Murmanskoye Rise
Novaya Zemlja
Vaasa
Kemi
Kuusamo
Monečgorsk
Kandalakša
06
Apatity
pik Sedova △
1115
Gulf of Bothnia
Halluoto
Karlo
Kokkola
Oulu
Kola Peninsula
Gremiha
33
m.Kanin Nos
Pečorskoye
more
Kara S
FINLAND
Jyväskylä
Kuopio
Pielinen
Kostomukša
Kandalakšskaja guba
o.Kolgujev
proliv Karskie Vorota
Savonlinna
Joensuu
Karelia
Kem'
White Sea
Ponoj
p-ov Kanin
o.Vajgač
Lappeenranta
Belomorsk
Onežskaja guba
Čёsskaja guba
Amderma
Bajdar...
Vyborg
Segozero
Medvež'egorsk
Severodvinsk
Arhangel'sk
Mezen'
Nar'jan-Mar
15
Lake Ladoga
Petrozavodsk
Onega
Nenets
Autonomous District
Jugorskij p-ov
60°
SAINT PETERSBURG
Lake Onega
Timanskiy krjazh
Boroviči
Kargopol'
Ust'-Varga
Pinega
Pečora
Ust'-Cil'ma
Bolšezemelskaja tundra
Vorkuta
07
Toržok
Čerepovec
Konoša
Vel'sk
K o m i
Pečora
Inta
gora Pajer
gora Narodnaja
1499
Yamal Nene
Tver'
Rybinsk Reservoir
Vologda
Kotlas
Uhta
Sosnogorsk
1617
gora Telposiz
1894
Dubna
Rybinsk
Sergiev-Posad
Vel'sk
Sysola
Syktyvkar
Autonomous Dis
MOSCOW
Kostroma
Vyčegda
Vjatka
(Kirov)
Belojarskij
Orehovo-Zuevo
Kinešma
Šar'ja
Ob'
Sib
Vladimir
Kotel'nič
55°
Rjazan'
NIŽNIJ NOVGOROD
Kirovo-Čepeck
Solikamsk
Khanty-Mansi
Autonomous District
Murom
Berezniki
Serov
W e s t
Šack
Mari-El
Joškar-Ola
1569 △
Kamskoe vdhr.
gora Konžakovskij Kamen'
Hanty-Mansijsk
Neftejugansk
Mordvinia
Čeboksary
Udmurtia
Iževsk
Nižnij Tagil
S i b e r i
Saransk
Chuvashia
KAZAN'
Malmyž
PERM'
Penza
Simbirsk
Kujbyševskoe vdhr.
Naberežnye Čelny
Sarapul
Irbit
08
Kuzneck
Syzran'
Tol'jatti
Dimitrovgrad
Tatarstan
Ufa
Pervoural'sk
Tjumen'
Tobol'sk
Saratov
SAMARA
Oktjabr'skij
YEKATERINBURG
Kamensk-Ural'skij
Irtyš
(Irtyš)
P l a i
Engel's
Balakovo
Novo-kujbyševsk
Buguruslan
UFA
Zlatoust
Miass
Šadrinsk
Zavodoukovsk
Kamyšin
Bashkortostan
Sterlitamak
ČELJABINSK
Kopejsk
Kurgan
Išim
Tara...
Volgogradskoe vodohranilišče
Eršov
Salavat
Magnitogorsk
Troick
Barabinska
Petropavl
OMSK
Oral'
Kumertau
Irklinskoe vdhr.
Kostanaj
Zapadno...
Isil'kul'
nizmennost
Čapaev
Žambejti
Orenburg
Ural
Novotroick
Orsk
Zetikara
Rudnyj

Scale 1:20,000,000

| 0 | 200 | 400 | 600 Kilometer |

| 0 | 200 | | 400 Miles |

PACIFIC

Komandorskie o-va

Pribilof Islands

B e r i n g

Aleutian Basin

Sirsova Ridge

3795

Nunivak Island

Alaska (USA)

St. Matthew Island (USA)

Saint Lawrence Island (USA)

B e r i n g   S e a

m. Olutorskij

m. Ozernoj

Ust'-Kamčatsk

m. Kamčatsk

Northeast Cape

Bambell

m. Navarin

Apuka

1651

m. Ugolnaja

2562

Koryak

Ossora

zaliv o Karaginskij

Olutorskij zaliv

Autonomous District

Karaginskij

S r e d i n n

Alakanuk

Nome

Seward Peninsula

Providenija

Koryak Range

Kamenskoe

Penžinskaja guba

m. Taigonos

Šeljhova

zaliv

Wales

Lavrentija

Chukotskij Poluostrov

Anadyr'

Uėlen

Ėgvekinot

1503

1483

Chukchi Autonomous District

1814

2982

Arctic Circle

Uel'kal'

Kanchalanskaja guba

Čukotskoe Poluostrov'e

Mys Šmidta

Kolymskaja nizmennost'

Alazejskoe ploskogor'e

Ust'-Kuiga

Jana

Omolon

1797

Olojskij hrebet

Anjujskij hrebet

1673

Oloj

1411

Omolon

Sejmčan

Jukagirskoe ploskogor'e

Zyrjanka

Kolyma

Honuu

Moma hrebet

2533

Cherskiy

2043

Nero

Kotzebue Sound

Wevik

Cape Lisburne

ARCTIC OCEAN

CHUKCHI SEA

Wrangel Island

Ušakovo

Čaunskaja guba

ostrov Ajon

Pevek

Proliv Longa

1775

Billino

Čarskij

East Siberian Sea

New Siberian Islands

o Novaja Sibir'

o Ljahovskij

pr. Dmitrija Lapteva

Indigirka

Čerkurtah

Indigirskaja nizmennost'

Deputatskij

Janskij zaliv

m. Svjatoj nos

pr. Dmitrija Lapteva

Buor-Haja guba

Hajyr

Laptev Lakeyevaya

o Katel'nyj

Uc

Ub

Ua

Td

Tc

Tb

Ta

Pd

Pc

Pb

Pa

Ra

Rb

Rc

Rd

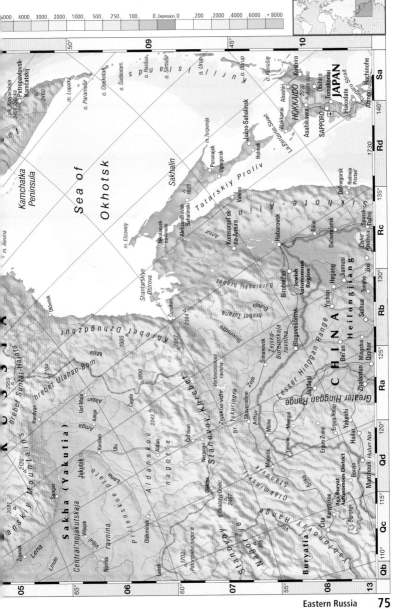

Scale 1:20,000,000

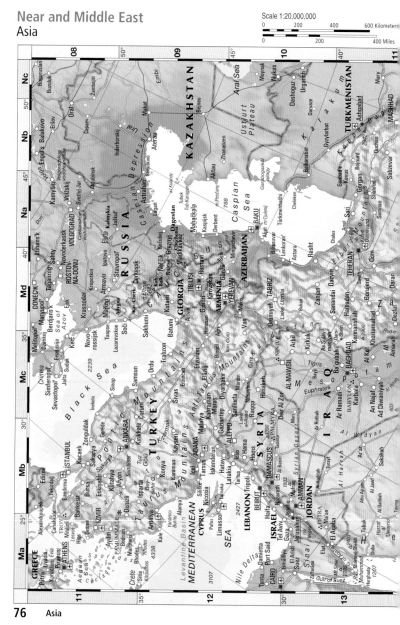

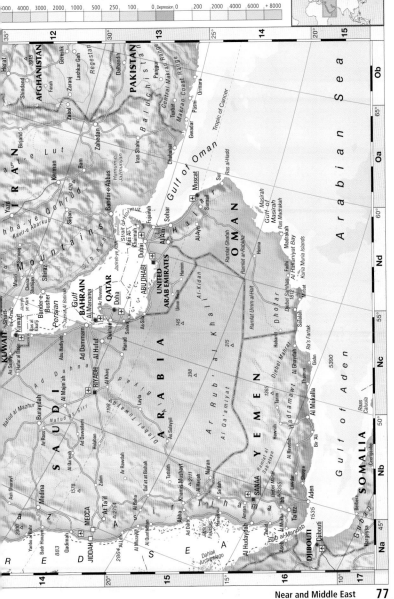

Scale 1:20,000,000

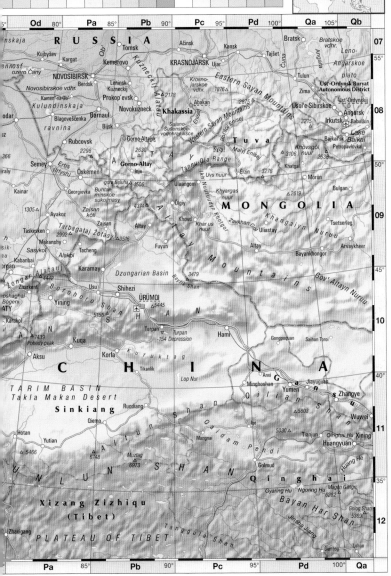

R U S S I A

Tomsk

Kujbyšev
Kargat

Kemerovo

Ačinsk
Kansk

Bratsk
Bratskoe
vdhr.

Leno-
Angarskoe
plato

NOVOSIBIRSK
Berdsk
Leninsk
Kuzneckij

KRASNOJARSK
Ujar

Tulun
Angara
Zima

Ust-Ordynsk Buryat
Autonomous District

ennost *o'b*
ozero Cany
Kulundinskaja

Novosibirskoe vdhr.
Kamen-na-Ob'
Prokop'evsk
Novokuzneck

Krasno-
jarskoe
vdhr.
1876△

Abakan
2875.6

Usol'e-Sibirskoe

Ust'-Ordynskij
3215

Angarsk Babuškin
Irkutsk
Baikal'sk
Petropavlovka

ravnina

Blagoveščenka
Bárnaul
Bijsk

Gorno-Altajsk
2178

Khakassia
Suano-
Sušenskoe
vodohranilisce

Bolšoj Enisej

Tuva

Lake
Baikal

Rubcovsk
2298

2630△

A L T A Y

Kyzyl
Malyj Enisej

Khövsgöl
nuur
2636

Khatgal

Semey
Ertis
(Irtyš)

Öskemen
Inia

Gorno-Altay

qora Beluha 4506

Tannu Ola Range
Erzin
3276

Khatgal
Mörön

Kainar

Georgievka
4374△

Ulaangom

Uvs nuur
Khyargas
nuur

2619△

M O N G O L I A

1305△
Ayakoz
Taskesken

Zajsan
köli
Zajsan

Ölgiy

Khovd
Khar us
nuur

Zavkhan Gol
Khongor
Uliastay

Khangayn Nuruu

Tsetserleg

Tarbagataj Žotasy
2992△
△3516

Altay
Fuyun

3479

Altay

Bayankhongor
Arvaykheer

Makanshy
Sasykol
Alakol
Tacheng

Dzungarian Basin
Bejin Shan

Khangayn Nuruu

Kabanbai
Alataū
Karamay

4442

Gov' Altayn Nuruu

Botohoro Shan
Usu

Shihezi

A Y

Mountains

Yining
ÜRÜMQI
5445

Kuqa
5155
Pobedy peak
7439

Turpan
Turpan
-154 Depression

Hami
Gongpoquan
Saihan Toroi

Aksu

Korla

Kuruktag
Lop Nur

Anxi
Minghoshan
Jiayuguan
Zhangye

C H I N A

Tikanlik

Yumen
5803△

Wuwei

TARIM BASIN
Takla Makan Desert

Sinkiang

Ruoqiang

Q i l i a n
5030△

S h a n

Qinghai Hu
Huangyuan
Xining

Hotan
Yutian

Qiemo

5466△

A l t u n

6748
Muztag
6973

Mangnai

Qaidam Pendi

Golmud

Qinghai
Tianjun

Huang He

K U N L U N   S H A N

Gyaring Hu
Ngoring Hu
Maqên Gangri
6282△

Bayan Har Shan

Golog Shan
5369△

Xizang Zizhiqu
(Tibet)

Zhaxigang

Jin Sha Jiang

Luhuo
Ganzi

P L A T E A U   O F   T I B E T

Tanggula Shan

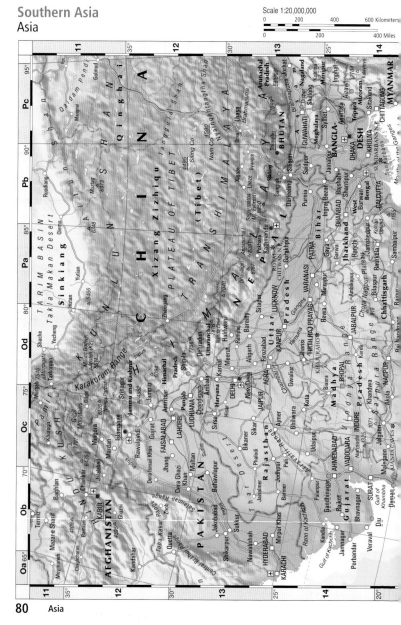

Scale 1:20,000,000

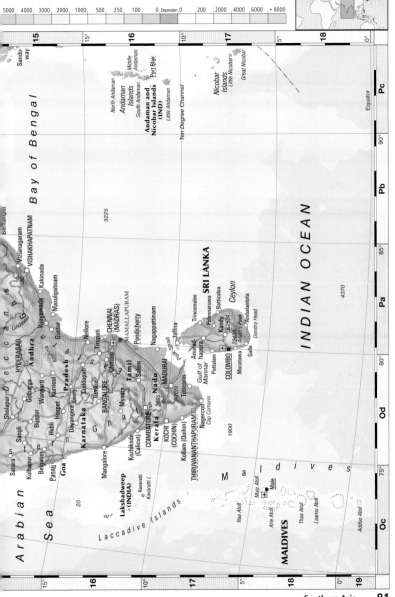

5000 4000 3000 2000 1000 500 250 100 0 Depression 0 200 2000 4000 6000 + 8000

Pc

Equator

Sando
way

North Andaman
Middle
Andaman
Andaman
Islands
South Andaman
Andaman and
Nicobar Islands (IND)
Little Andaman

Port Blair

Nicobar
Islands
(IND)

Little Nicobar

Great Nicobar

Bay of Bengal

Pb

Vizianagaram
VISHAKHAPATNAM
Kakinada

Berhampur

90°

Masulipatnam

Vijayawada

Godavari
1680

3225

INDIAN OCEAN

Pa

Sholapur
Gulbarga

Guntur

Nellore

CHENNAI
(MADRAS)

MAMALLAPURAM

Jaffna

Trincomalee

SRI LANKA

Ceylon

85°

Wangarti
Hospet

Tirupati

Pondicherry

Peh-
ruppattinam

Batticaloa

4370

Bijapur
Kurnool

Krishna

Salem

Peh-
Strait

Anurad-
hapura

Polonnaruwa

Kandy

Adam's Peak

Dayangere Gooty

Cuddapah

Tamil

Gulf of

Puttalam

2243
2524

Ambalantota

80°

Sangli
Hubli

Deccan Plateau

BANGALORE

Mysuru

Nadu

Mannar

COLOMBO

Moratuwa

Dondra Head

Od

Satara
Kolhapur

Belgaum
Panaji

Karnataka

Ghats

2695

Turicorin

Galle

Kochi

Goa

Mangalore

COIMBATORE

Kozhikode
(Calicut)

KOCHI
(COCHIN)

Kollam (Quilon)

Kerala

Cap Comorin

1900

75°

THIRUVANANTHAPURAM

Maldives

Arabian
Sea

Lakshadweep
(INDIA)

Kavaratti I.

20

Laccadive Islands

Male Atoll

Male

Riaa Atoll

Arie Atoll

Thaa Atoll

Laamu Atoll

Addoo Atoll

MALDIVES

Oc

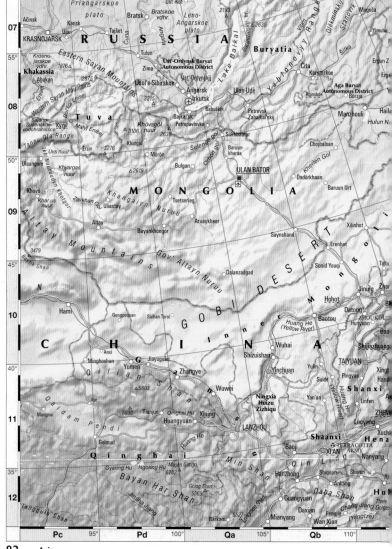

Scale 1:20,000,000

0 — 200 — 400 — 600 Kilometers

0 — 200 — 400 Miles

Scale 1:20,000,000

0   200   400   600 Kilometers

0   200   400 Miles

Pb 90°   Pc   95°   Pd   100°   Qa   105°   Qb   110°

11   35°

Qinghai   Gansu   Baoji   Shaanxi   TERRA
XIAN   ARM
Qin Ling
Bayan Har Shan   Min Shan   Hanzhong   Shiquan   Ankang
Gyaring Hu   Ngoring Hu   Magên Gangri   6282   Longmen Shan   Guangyuan   Daba Shan
Golog Shan   5369   Barkam   Mianyang   Daxian   Fengjie   Chang
Jinsha Jiang   5537   Gantog   Luhuo   Dujiangyan   CHENGDU   Wan Xian
12   C   H   I   N
Xizang Zizhiqu   Ninging Shan   Za Qu   Mekong   Sichuan   Red   Changshou   CHONGQING   Chongqing   Jishou
4495   Sling Co   Bamda   Gongga Shan   Leshan   Zigong   Wu Jiang   Wuling
(Tibet)   4590   7556   Miannang   Luzhou   Xuyong   Huaih
Nam Co   Kyaichentangtha Shan   5966   Xichang   Zunyi   Guizhou   South Chi
30°   PLATEAU OF TIBET   Gartog   Zhongdian   Zhaotong   Liupanshui   GUIYANG   Kaili
Xigaze   Qamxu   Lhasa   Brahmaputra   Panzhihua   Xuanwei   Anshun   Duyun   Hechi
Gyangze   Arunachal   Dibrugarh   4022   Putao   Yunnan   Qujing   Liupanshui   Guangxi Z
Sikkim   Pradesh   7069   Itanagar   3411   Xiaguan   Kaiyuan   Yanshan   Bose
13   Thimphu   BHUTAN   Jorhat   (Dali)   KUNMING   Nanning
Gangtok   Assam   Brahmaputra   3950   KUNMING   Yuxi   Yuanjiang   Mengzi   Zizi
Shiguri   GUWAHATI   Disbur   Nagaland   3822   Myitkyina   Luxi   Cao Bang   Qinzhou
Saidpor   Meghalaya   Shillong   Kohima   Tegcheng   Salween   Pu'er   Thai Nguyen
25°   Sylhet   Manipur   Bhamo   Liuku   Mengzi   Viet Tri
Jamalpur   BANGLA-   Imphal   Chindwin   Jinghong   Red River   Cam Pha   Halor
Rajshahi   Agartala   Aizawl   Indaw   2279   Dien   Black River   HANOI   Haiphong
Shantipur   DHAKA   Tripura   Mizoram   2704   Lashio   Bien Phu   Xam Neua   Gulf of To
KHULNA   Kalaymyo   Jinghong   Muang Xai   7996   Thanh Hóa
14   CALCUTTA   DESH   Sitakund   Irrawaddy   2326   Mengla   Luang   Xam Neua   Vinh
Sundarbans   CHITTAGONG   Mandalay   Shan Plateau   Prabang   2452   Ha Tinh
Cox's Bazar   2704   Meiktila   Taunggyi   Muang Kham   Dong Hoi
Mouths of the Ganges   Pegu Yoma   Inle Lake   L   A   O   S   Plateau
MYANMAR   BAGAN   Makwe   Chiang Rai   Paksan   Savannakhét
20°   Sittwe   Prome   Pyinmana   Nan   Viangchan   Nakhon   Paks
(Akyab)   Toungoo   Chiang Mai   (Vientiane)   Phanom   S
Sando-   Lampang   Mekong   Udon Thani   Savannakhét
way   Henzada   Pegu   Sukhothai   Phitsanulok   Khon Kaen   Ubon
Puthein   Daweiya Range   Nakhon   Khorat Plateau   Ratchathani   Paks
Bay of   (Bassein)   RANGOON   Maula-   Sawan
15   myaing   THAILAND   Nakhon   Muang Khong
Bengal   Kyaikkami   Ayutthaya   Ratchasima   ANGKOR   Stung Treng   Buon
Ye   Kanchanaburi   BANGKOK   Siem Reap   Kompong Thom
15°   Gulf of   Tavoy   Ratchaburi   Chon Buri   Tonlé Sap   Phnom Penh
Martaban   Petchaburi   Pattaya   CAMBODIA
Hua Hin   Trat   Cardamom Mts.   T.P. HO CH
16   Andaman   North Andaman   Andaman   Mergui   Prachuap   Koh Kong
Islands   Middle Andaman   Khirikhan   Gulf of Thailand   Long Xuyen   My T
Andaman and   South Andaman   Sea   Tanintharyi   Sihanoukville   Mekong
Nicobar Islands   (Tehasserim)   (Kompong Som)
(IND)   Port Blair   Chumphon   Mergui   Little Andaman   Isthmus of Kra   Archipelago

Pb 90°   Pc   95°   Pd   100°   Qa   105°

Southern East Asia **85**

Scale 1:20,000,000

0   200   400   600 Kilometers

0   200   400 Miles

MYANMAR

THAILAND

LAOS

VIETNAM

CAMBODIA

MALAYSI

SUMATRA

GREATER SUNDA IS

INDIAN OCEAN

Andaman Sea

Gulf of Martaban

Gulf of Thailand

Mergui Archipelago

Malay Peninsula

Natuna Sea

Java Sea

Java Trench

Henzada
Puthein (Bassein)
Pegu
RANGOON
Maula- myaing
Kyaikkami
Ye
Tavoy
Tanintharyi (Tenasserim)
Mergui
Tavoy
Sukhothai
Phitsanulok
Udon Thani
Nakhon Phanom
Khon Kaen
Savannakhet
Khorat Plateau
Ubon Ratchathani
Nakhon Sawan
Ayutthaya
BANGKOK
Kanchanaburi
Ratchaburi
Petchaburi
Hua Hin
Chon Buri
Pattaya
Trat
Siem Reap
ANGKOR
Muang Khong
Stung Treng
Pakse
Kompong Thom
PHNOM PENH
Cardamom Mts.
Koh Kong
Sihanoukville (Kompong Som)
Long Xuyen
My Tho
T.P. HO CHI MINH (SAIGON)
Phan Thiet
Nha Trang
Da Lat
Buon Ma Thuot
Qui Nhon
Tuy Hoa
Pleiku
Quang Ngai
Hoi An
Da Nang
Hue
Dong Ha
Annam Plateau
Prachuap Khirikhan
Chumphon
Isthmus of Kra
Lang Suan
Khuraburi
Takua Pa
Phang Nga
Phuket
Krabi
Trang
Surat Thani
Koh Samui
Nakhon Si Thammarat
Songkhla
Pattani
Hat Yai
Narathiwat
Betong
Kota Bharu
Kuala Terengganu
Kuala Dungun
Langkawi
Penang
Georgetown
Taiping
Ipoh
Gua Musang
Kuala Lipis
Kampar
Temerloh
Kuantan
Tioman
Padang Endau
KUALA LUMPUR
Kluang
Melaka
Johor Baharu
SINGAPORE
Bintan
Banda Aceh
Sigli
Lhokseumawe
Peureulak
Langsa
Meulaboh
MEDAN
Tebingtinggi
Pematang Siantar
Labuhanhaji
Sinabang
Simeulue
Tuangku
Nias
Gunungsitoli
Padangsidempuan
Natal
Pini
Sibolga
Rantauprapat
Dumai
Pekanbaru
Kep. Lingga
Lingga
Rengat
Sungaidareh
Muarabungo
Bukittinggi
Padang
Padangpanjang
Tanahmasa
Tanahbala
Siberut
Muarasiberut
Sipura
Pagai Utara
Pagai Selatan
Mentawai Archipelago
Bangko
Jambi
Muntok
Bangka
Pangkalpinang
Palembang
Belitung
Toboali
Curup
Bengkulu
Kayuagung
Martapura
Menggala
Bandar Lampung
Enggano
Krakatau
Serang
Bogor
JAKARTA
Purwakarta
Bandung
Ciamis
Cilacap
Cirebon
Pekalongan
SEMARANG
Yogyakarta
BOROBUDUR
Tonlé Sap
Lake Toba
Natuna Besar
Subi Besar
Kep. Anambas
Natuna Sea
Kep. Natuna
Kuching
Sambas
Singkawang
Mempawah
Pontianak
Karimata Strait
Ketapang
Little Nicobar
Great Nicobar
Great Channel

5000 4000 3000 2000 1000 500 250 100   0 Depression, 0   200 2000 4000 6000 + 8000

South China Basin

PHILIPPINES

hina Sea

Mamburao
Marinduque
Matnog
Allen
Calbayog
Samar

Mindoro

Dongangu
Sibuyan
Masbate
Tacloban
Leyte

Calamian Group

San Jose
Coron
Tablas
Roxas
Pandan

Visayas

Dinagat

El Nido

Cadiz
Iloilo
Panay
Bacolod
Cebu

Surigao

6595

PALAU

Taytay

Roxas

Negros
Basay
Santander
Bohol

Butuan

10830

Bislig

3660

Palawan

Puerto Princesa

Siaton
Dipolog
Iligan

Cagayan de Oro

Tagum

Sonsorol I.
Puto Anna

ratly

Quezon

Aborlan

Pagadian

MINDANAO

2954 △ Davao
Mt. Apo

ands

Brooke's Point

Tubbataha Reef

Zamboanga Peninsula

Cotabato

Isulan

General Santos

Helen Reef
Tobi

Balabac

Sulu Sea

Zamboanga

Basilan

Karakelong

Kep.Talaud

18

Kudat

Balabac

Banggi

Jolo

6220

Sangihe

Kep. Sangihe

Morotai

2569

G. Kinabalu 4095
Ranau

Sandakan

Tawi-Tawi

Siau

Galela
1335 △

Kota Kinabalu

Lahad Datu

Sulu Archipelago

Celebes Sea

Kao

Halmahera

Beaufort
Tenom

Sapulut

Tawau

Manado

Bitung

Ternate

Nosliku
Gebe

Sorong

BRUNEI

ala Belait

Miri

Longbawan

Tarakan

Minahasa

Kwandang

Kotamobagu

Halmahera Sea

Gani

Batanta
Salawati

liah

Mulu

Tanjungredeb

Tolitoli

2207 △

Gorontalo

Kasiruta
Bacan

Misool

Adua

elaga

2130

Soloi
3000

Tomini

Kep.Togian

Molucca Sea

Obi

Ceram Sea

Waigeo

Waru

ALIMANTAN

Longnawang

Sangkulirang

Tomini
Pagimana

Gulf of Tomini

Taliabu
Dofa

Mangole

Kep. Sula

Sanana

Amahai

Wahar
3049 △

G.Bihau

(BORNEO)

Sengata

Donggala

Luwuk

Poso

Ampana
Tobol

Beturube

3505 △

Gulf of Tolo

Kep. Banggai

Buru

Seram (Ceram)

Ambon

Ambon

Kep.Banda

Samarinda

2275

SULAWESI (CELEBES)

Palu

ISLANDS

NDS

Balikpapan

Kakah

Watu

Bayu

G.Mekongga

5215

Banda Sea

Kuaro

Mamuju 3074 △
Masamba

Muaratewen

Amuntai

Majene

G.Rantemario △ 3440

Kendari

Kolaka

ange

Palangkaraya

Kandangan
Pagatan

Parepare

Gulf of Bone

Kabaena

Butung

Muna

Misa

Banjarmasin

pembuang

Tg. South

Kep. Laut-Kecil
Laut

UJUNG PANDANG (MAKASSAR)

Watampone
Baubau

Flores Sea

Kep. Daya Barat

Damar

Babar

Kep.Babar

Bulukumba
Selayar

Wetar

Moa

Sermata

Bawan

N E S I A

LESSER SUNDA ISLANDS

Alor

EAST TIMOR

Dili

3310 △
Aliambata

ABAYA

Madura

Kangean

Sumbawa

Komodo

Flores

Lombien

Antar

Timor

Tutuala

Bathurst I.

Beagle Gulf

olingoo

G. Merapi
2829 3332 △

Jangkar
Banyuwangi

Bali

Lombok

Mataram

Sumbawa Besar

Raba

Lubaanbajo

Maumere
Ende

Mikimini

Kupang

Timor Sea

ng

G.Bromo

Denpasar

Bondokodi

△ 1825

Sumba

Waingapu

Savu Sea

Roti

Sawu

AUSTRALIA

A

4865

Hibernia Reef

Ashmore Islands

Cartier I.

Joseph Bonaparte Gulf

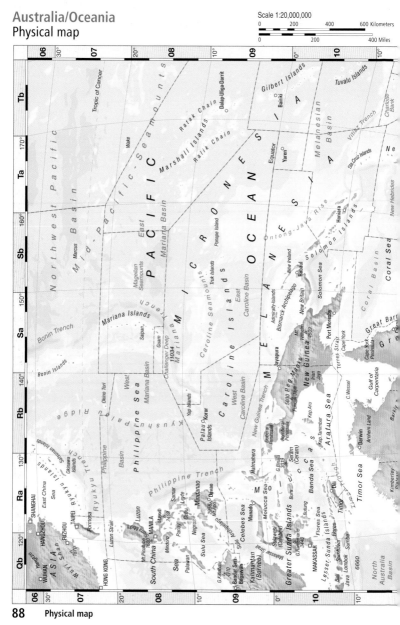

Australia/Oceania
Physical map

Scale 1:20,000,000

0   200   400   600 Kilometers

0   200   400 Miles

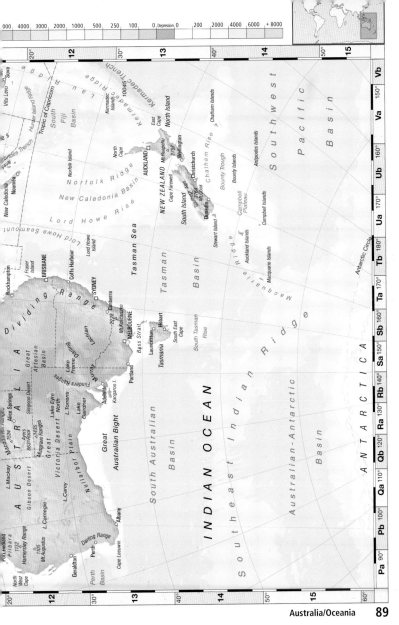

Suva
Vitu Levu
Fiji
Tropic of Capricorn
Hunter Island
Kermadec Ridge
Kermadec Islands
Kermadec Trench
10045
New Caledonia
Nouméa
Norfolk Island
North Cape
East Cape
North Island
Chatham Islands
AUCKLAND
Mt.Ruapehu 2797
Wellington
Norfolk Ridge
New Caledonia Basin
Chatham Rise
Lord Howe Rise
NEW ZEALAND
Christchurch
Cape Farewell
Mt Cook
Bounty Trough
Chatham Islands
Antipodes Islands
Bounty Islands

South West
Pacific Basin

Lord Howe Seamount
Lord Howe Island
Tasman Sea
Tasman Basin
South Island
Dunedin
Stewart Island
Campbell Plateau
Campbell Islands

Fraser Island
Rockhampton
BRISBANE
Coffs Harbour
SYDNEY
Canberra

A U S T R A L I A
Great Dividing Range
Great Artesian Basin
Alice Springs
Simpson Desert
L.Mackay
Ayers Rock 863
MacDonnell Ranges
Musgrave Ranges
Gibson Desert
Great Victoria Desert
L.Carnegie
Lake Eyre North
L.Torrens
Lake Gairdner
Lake Eyre
Flinders Ranges
Murray
Darling
Lachlan
Mt.Kosciuszko 2228
MELBOURNE
Hobart
Launceston
Tasmania
South East Cape
South Tasman Rise
Bass Strait
Portland
Kangaroo I.
Adelaide
Lake Frome

Macquarie Ridge
Macquarie Islands
Auckland Islands

Antarctic Circle

INDIAN OCEAN

Great Australian Bight
South Australian Basin

South East Indian Ridge

Australian-Antarctic Basin

A N T A R C T I C A

Nullarbor Plain
Albany
Pilbara
Port Hedland
1132
North West Cape
Hamersley Range
Mt.Augustus 1105
Darling Range
Perth
Geraldton
Perth Basin
Cape Leeuwin

S o u t h e a s t   I n d i a n   R i d g e

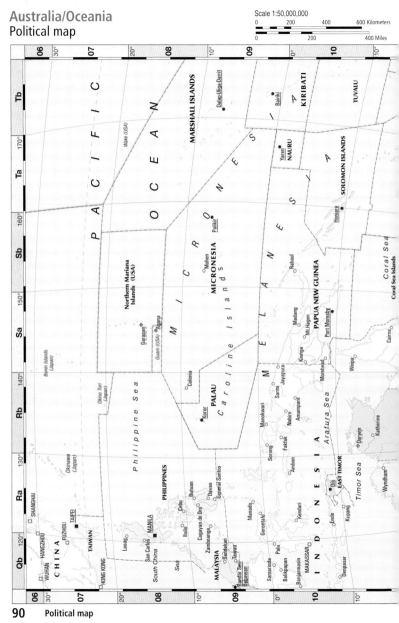

Scale 1:50,000,000

0   200   400   600 Kilometers
0   200   400 Miles

PACIFIC OCEAN

MARSHALL ISLANDS

Dalap-Uliga-Darrit

Wake (USA)

Bairiki
KIRIBATI

TUVALU

MICRONESIA

Yaren
NAURU

Palikir

Mohen

SOLOMON ISLANDS

Honiara

Northern Mariana Islands (USA)

Bonin Islands (Japan)

Rabaul

Coral Sea

Coral Sea Islands

Caroline Islands

MICRONESIA

Garapan
Agana
Guam (USA)

Madang

Mt.Hagen
PAPUA NEW GUINEA

Port Moresby

Kunga

Cairns

Okino Tori (Japan)

Colonia

MELANESIA

Jayapura

Weipa

Morehead

PALAU

Koror

Sarmi

Manokwari

Nabire

Amanpare

Katherine

Philippine Sea

Sorong

Faktak

Arafura Sea

Darwin

Okinawa (Japan)

Ambon

INDONESIA

TIMOR Sea

EAST TIMOR
Dili

Wyndham

PHILIPPINES

Butuan

Davao

General Santos

Manado

Kendari

Gorontalo

Ende

Kupang

SHANGHAI

HANGZHOU

WUHAN

FUZHOU

TAIPEI

TAIWAN

CHINA

HONG KONG

MANILA

Cebu

Iloilo

Cagayan de Oro

Zamboanga

Tawtaw

San Carlos

Sandakan

MALAYSIA

Bandar Seri Begawan

South China Sea

Samarinda

Balikpapan

Banjarmasin

Palu

MAKASSAR

Denpasar

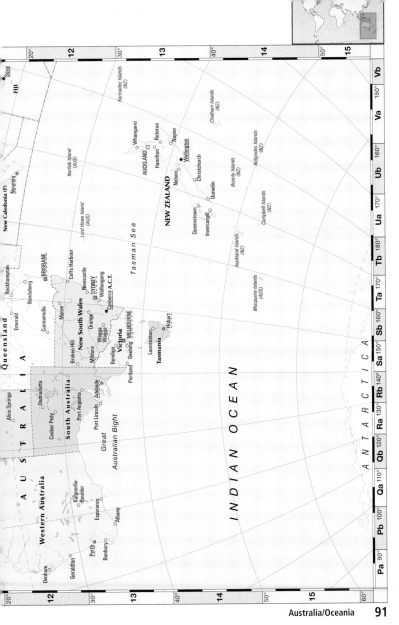

Micronesia, New Guinea
Oceania

Scale 1:50,000,000

0   200   400   600 Kilometers

0   200   400 Miles

130°   135°   140°   145°

Kyushu-Palau-Ridge

5190   *Parece Vela*

15°   4300   Rota I.

Basin   **Guam (USA)** Agana   9650

16°   45   *Challenger Deep* 11034   *M a r i a n a*   *Trench*

6100   Ulithi Atoll   4650

6595   1280   Yap Islands 7875   Fais I.   1700   Gaferut I.

Colonia   Faraulep Atoll   West Fayu

8850   2420   Sorol Atoll   Woleai Atoll   Olimarao Atoll   Lamotrek At

Ngulu Atoll   *C*   *a*   Ifalik Atoll

Kayangel Is.   Eauripik Atoll   *r*   *o*   *l*   *i*

6850   Palau Babelthuap   Koror   1805   2215   4300

Islands   Angaur

17°   3660   *PALAU*   5580

Sonsorol I.   *West Caroline*

Pulo Anna   Merir   *Basin*   4900

Tobi   3715   *Eauripik Rise*

Helen Reef   *E*

18°   1970   1955   3910   2745   3545

Kep. Mapia

Kep. Asia   *New Guinea Trench*   5310

Kep. Ayu   4625   4645   Ninigo Group   Hermit Is.   Ad

Equator Waigeo   Manokwari   Biak   *M*   Wuvulu I.   Manus I.   Is

0°   Gebe   Batanta   Mega   Numfor   Sarmi   Demta   4025   1610   *Bism*

Kofiau   Salawati   Sorong   Ransiki   Yapen   Waren   *Mamberamo*   Vanimo   Wewak   2155

Adua   10   *Doberai*   Teluk   Jayapura   Lumi   *Bism*

Misool   *Peninsula*   Cenderawasih   Taritatu   Sepik   Bopia   Karkar I.

19°   Seram (Ceram)   Wahai   Inanwatan   Nabire   *P*   Telefomin   Madang

Faktak   *Bomberai*   *e*   Mt. Hagen   Mt. Wilhelm

3019   Amahai   Waru   1445   *Peninsula*   Kaimana   Puncak Jaya   *g*   *Central Range*   4509 Goroka   Waitara

Kep. Gorong   Adi   5030   *M*   *u*   *Papua*   Kiunga   Bucari

Kep. Banda   Amamapare   *a*   *n*   *o*   *k*   *e*   *New Guinea*   Mendi   Goroka

INDONESIA   Kepulauan   Kikori

Weber   Kep. Watubela   *Aru*   Kiunga   **PAPUA NEW GUINEA**

Kep. Banda   7440   Kai Besar   Lake Murray

Kep. Kai   Maikoor   Kobroor   40   Bado Digul

Banda Sea   *Basin*   Trangan   15   Kikori   Kerema

Kep. Daya Barat   Wokam   Dolak   Kolhoran   Merauke   Morehead   *Gulf of Papua*

Babar   Yamdena   1345   Tanjung Vals   Port Mor

Leti   Kep. Babar   420   10   35   Dani

455   *Arafura Sea*   *Torres Strait*   Eastern Field

25   70   Prince of Wales I.   Cape York   1445

10°   **AUSTRALIA**

MARSHALL ISLANDS

MICRONESIA

M I C R O N E S I A

PACIFIC OCEAN

Caroline Basin

Senyavin Islands

Mortlock Islands

Hall Islands

Truk Islands

Islands

NAURU
Yaren

Ontong Java Rise

New Ireland
Rabul

Archipelago

New Britain
Solomon Sea

New Britain Trench

SOLOMON ISLANDS

Solomon Islands

Guadalcanal
Honiara

Malaita

San Cristobal

Rennell Rise

d'Entrecasteaux Islands

Louisiade Archipelago

6045
6035
970
935
1390
440
1025
Eniwetok Atoll
Bikini Atoll
Rongelap Atoll
Alinginae Atoll
Rongerik Atoll
Ujelang Atoll
Wotho Atoll
Ujae Atoll
Kwajalein Atoll
1135
Lae Atoll
3710
Fayu I.
Murilo Atoll
Nomwin Atoll
Minto Reef
Oroluk Atoll
640
Kuop Atoll
Mohen
Losap Atoll
Pakin Atoll
Palikir
Ponape I.
Mokil Atoll
5020
Pulusuk I.
60
Pingelap Atoll
Namoluk I.
Ngatik Atoll
Lelu
Satawan Atoll
Kosrae (Kusaie)
4665
245
5750
Nukuoro Atoll
1385
4310
2705
Kapingamarangi Atoll
5920
6680
6310
3945
2790
Nauru
Saint Matthias Group
3710
1685
Mussau I.
Tabar Is.
Lyra Reef
1670
4320
Lihir Group
Nuguria Is.
2250
3145
Namatanai
Tanga Is.
Feni Is.
Green Is.
Kilinailau Is.
Tauu Is.
Ontong Java Atoll
Witu Islands
C.St.George
Buka I.
Kimbe
Bay
Pomio
Tinputz
Bougainville I.
Sag Sag
Hoskins
Nakanai Mts.
8320
2775
Arawa
2470
Kandrian
9140
Mt.Balbi
Buin
Vuranggo
3600
hhafen
Choiseul
Gulf
4900
Vella Lavella
New Georgia Group
Santa Isabel
Gizo
Buala
Trobriand Is.
Auki
4515
Popondetta
Kiriwina I.
New Georgia
Vangunu
Russell Is.
Stewart Is.
5705
Tufi
Goodenough I.
Woodlark I.
Mara
masike
2560
3676
Fergusson I.
Salamo
Normanby I.
3745
Reef Islands
Alotau
Misima I.
San Cristobal
Haurahu
Duff Is.
The Calvados
Chain
Pocklington Reef
Bellona I.
8310
Nendo
Tagula I.
Yela I.

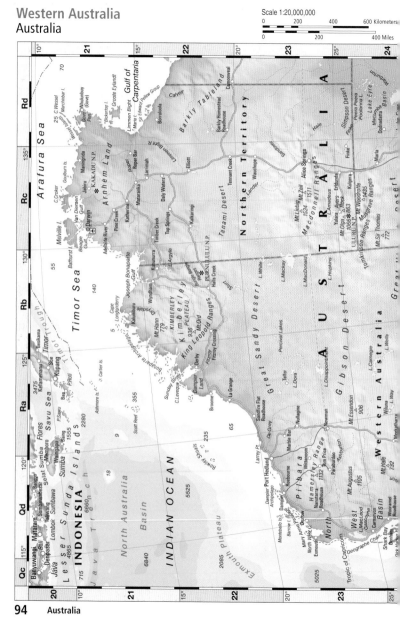

Western Australia
Australia

Scale 1:20,000,000

0   200   400   600 Kilometers

0   200   400 Miles

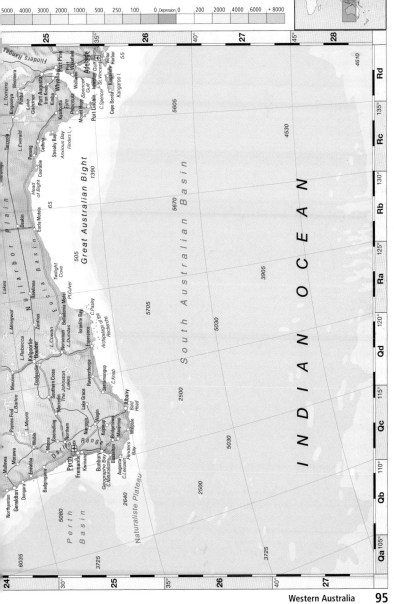

5000 4000 3000 2000 1000 500 250 100 0 Depression 0 200 2000 4000 6000 + 8000

Flinders Ranges

25

35°

26

40°

27

45°

28

Rd

4610

L. Torrens
Woomera
Kimponga
Pimba
Port Augusta
Iron Knob
Kimba
Whyalla
Port Pirie
Crystal Brook
Wallaroo
Port Wakefield
55
Adelaide

Tarcoola
Port Augusta
Mount Hope
Port Lincoln
C. Spencer
Cape Borda
St. Vincent Gulf
Kingscote
Victor Harbor
Kangaroo I.

5005

Kyancutta
Iron Knob
Eyre
Peninsula
Spencer
Gulf
Investigator Str.

135° Rc

Coober
L. Everard
Penong
Ceduna
Anxious Bay
Streaky Bay
Finders I.s

4530

130° Rb

Great Australian Bight

Head of Bight
Eucla
Deakin

65

1390

125° Ra

South Australian Basin

Nullarbor Plain

Eucla Basin

505

Twilight Cove
P.Culver

5670

3905

120° Qd

Lakes

L. Minigwal

Rawlinna

5705

5030

115° Qc

Menzies
L. Barlee
L. Rebecca
L. Cowan
Norseman
Balladonia Motel
L. Dundas
Zanthus
Israelite Bay
C. Pasley
Archipelago of the Recherche

Kalgoorlie-Boulder

Coolgardie
Southern Cross
Merredin
Southern Cross
Lake Grace
Ravensthorpe
C. Knob
Esperance

2500

5030

110° Qb

I N D I A N   O C E A N

Darling Range

Mullewa
Morawa
Prayers Find
L. Moore
Wubin
Moora
Goomalling
Northam
Wongan
Narrogin
Kojonup
Bridgetown
Manjimup
Albany
Bald Head
Walpole

2500

3725

105° Qa

Northampton
Geraldton
Dongara

Perth
Fremantle
Kwinana
Bunbury
Busselton
Blackwood
Geographe Bay
C. Naturaliste
Augusta
C. Leeuwin
Flinders Bay

Naturaliste Plateau

2640

5080

Badgingarra
Eneabba

Perth Basin

6035

3725

24

30°

25

35°

26

40°

27

Eastern Australia
Australia

Scale 1:20,000,000

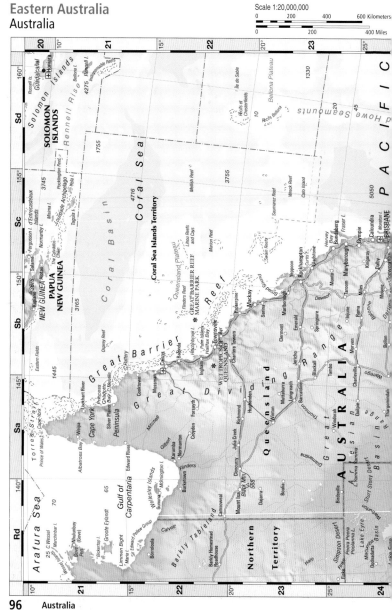

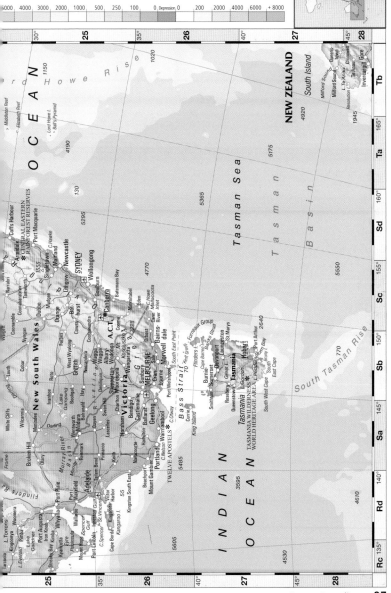

Eastern Australia

97

Scale 1:20,000,000

| 0 | 200 | 400 | 600 Kilometers |

| 0 | 200 | 400 Miles |

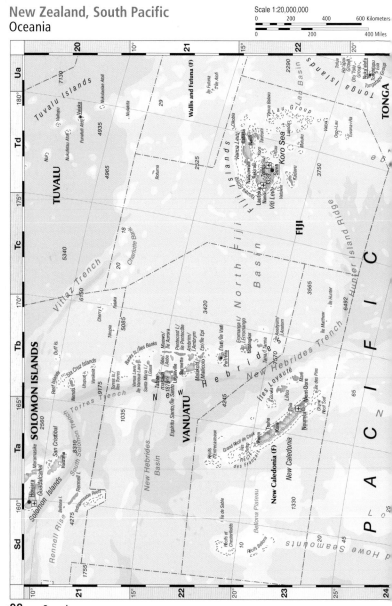

Ua

Td

Tc

Tb

Ta

Sd

TUVALU

Tuvalu Islands

Nanumea Atoll 7130

Vaitupu

Nukufetau Atoll 4935

Funafuti Atoll

Nukulaelae Atoll

Niulakita

Nui I. 4965

Rotuma 2525

Charlotte Bank 18

Vitiaz Trench

5340

6150

5085

9175

Cherry I.

Fataka

Tikopia

20

3420

Reef Islands

Duff Is.

Mendi

Vanikolo

Utupua

Santa Cruz Islands

Banks Is./Îles Banks

Torres Is./Îles Torres

Vanua Lava/Îles Torres

Santa Maria/Gaua

N Tabwe

W maskala

Malo

Oba/Aoba

Espiritu Santo/Île Santo

Maewo/Aurora

Pentecost I./Île Pentecôte

Ambrym/Ambrym

Malakula/Malekula

Epi/Île Epi

Etaté/Île Vaté

Port-Vila

VANUATU

1035

4245

3565

3750

SOLOMON ISLANDS

2560

Honiara

Maramasike

San Cristobal

Guadalcanal

Bellona I.

8310

Rennell I.

4275 Indispensable Reefs

Solomon Islands

Rennell Rise

South Solomon Trench

New Hebrides Basin

Torres Trench

New Hebrides

1755

Wallis and Futuna (F)

29

Île Futuna

Île Alofi

Niuafo'ou

TONGA

2290

Tongatapu Group

'Eua

Tofua

Ha'apai Group

Nuku'alofa

Lau Group

Koro Sea

3750

Vanua Levu

Taveuni

Nabouwalu

Labasa

Ovalau

Nandi

Nausori

Suva

3328

Viti Levu

Vatulele

Kandavu

FIJI

Fiji Islands

North Fiji Basin

Hunter Island Ridge

Île Hunter 6492

Île Matthew

'Anatom

Aneityum/Anatom

Erromango/Erromango

Tana/Tanna

Eromanga I./Lenakango

New Hebrides Trench

Îles Loyauté

Lifou

Maré

Île des Pins

Ouvéa

Nouméa

Mont-Dore

Touho

Koné

Grand Récif de Cook

Récif Ténia

Îles Bélep

Récifs d'Entrecasteaux

Grand Récif Sud

New Caledonia (F)

New Caledonia

1330

65

Bellona Plateau

Île de Sable

Récifs de Chesterfields

Récifs Bellona

10

20

45

of Howe Seamounts

P A C I F I C

25

P L A T

Oceania

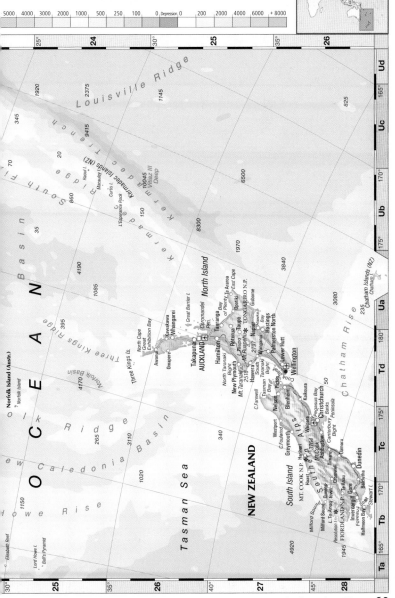

Depth/elevation scale:
5000 4000 3000 2000 1000 500 250 100 0 | Depression 0 | 200 2000 4000 6000 + 8000

O C E A N

Louisville Ridge

2375
1920
1145
825

South Fiji Ridge
Kermadec Trench
9415
10045
Vitiaz III Deep
6500

Kermadec Islands (ZN)
Raoul I.
Macauley I.
Curtis I.
L'Esperance Rock

8300

1970

3840

Chatham Rise
3080
235
Chatham Islands (NZ)
Chatham

North Island

Three Kings Is.
North Cape
Great Exhibition Bay
Kowhawai
Awanui
Whangarei
Kaikohe
Takapuna
AUCKLAND
Kawakawa
Great Barrier I.
Coromandel Pen.
Hamilton
Tauranga
Bay of Plenty
Te Araroa
East Cape
Rotorua
Taupo
Tokanu
Gisborne
Napier
Hastings
Mt Ruapehu 2797
TONGARIRO N.P.
Mt Taranaki 2518
North Taranaki Bight
New Plymouth
South Taranaki Bight
Hawera
Wanganui
Palmerston North
Lower Hutt
Wellington

Three Kings Ridge
4190
395
1085
Norfolk Basin
4170

Norfolk Island (Austr.)
Norfolk Island

C. Farewell
C. Foulwind
Westport
Nelson
Blenheim
Picton
Kaikoura
Pegasus Bay
Christchurch
Banks Peninsula
Canterbury Bight
Greymouth
Hokitika
Haast
Mt Cook 3764
MT. COOK N.P.
Ashburton
Timaru
Oamaru
Southern Alps
Wanaka
Cromwell
Te Anau
Milford Sound
L. Te Anau
FIORDLAND
Milford Sound
Resolution I.
Dunedin
Balclutha
Gore
Invercargill
Foveaux Strait
Halfmoon Bay
Stewart I.
1945

NEW ZEALAND

South Island

Tasman Sea

New Caledonia Basin
265
3110
1020

Lord Howe Rise
1150
1150
Lord Howe I.
Ball's Pyramid
Elizabeth Reef

340
50
4920

Africa
Physical map

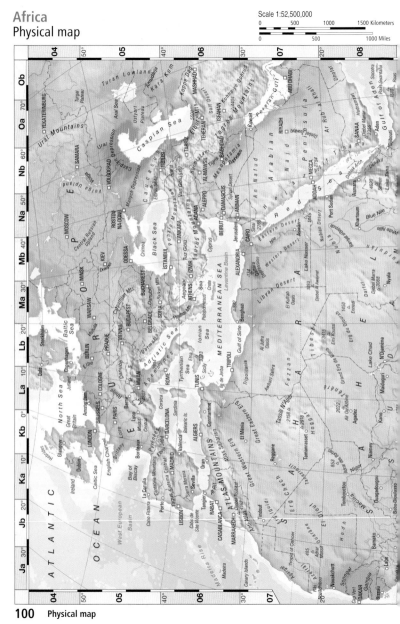

Scale 1:52,500,000

0   500   1000   1500 Kilometers

0   500   1000 Miles

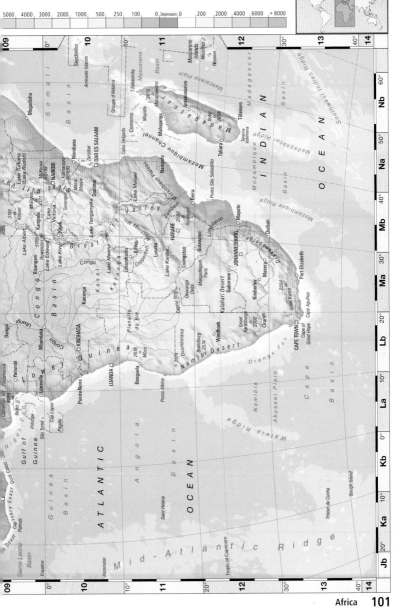

Africa
Political map

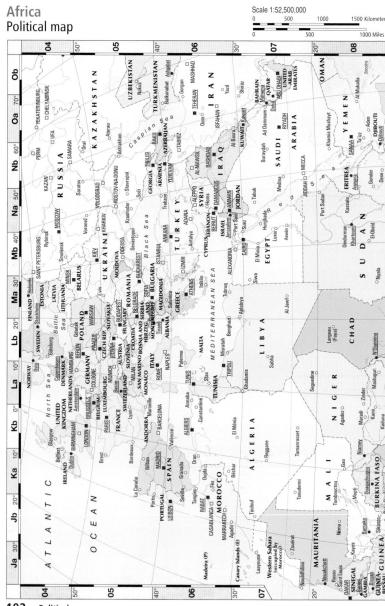

Scale 1:52,500,000

0   500   1000   1500 Kilometers

0   500   1000 Miles

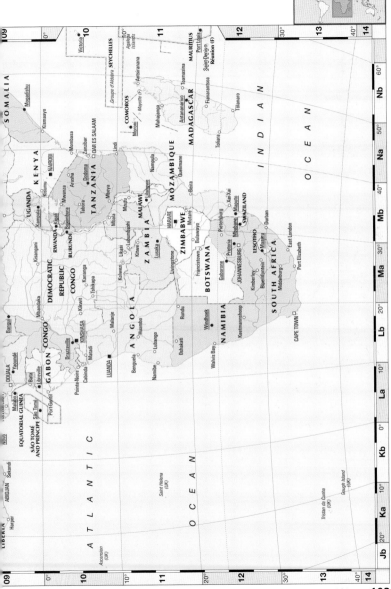

Northwestern Africa
Africa

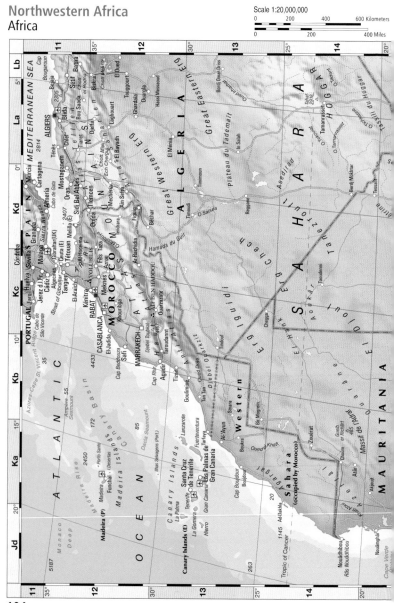

Scale 1:20,000,000

| 0 | 200 | 400 | 600 Kilometers |

| 0 | 200 | 400 Miles |

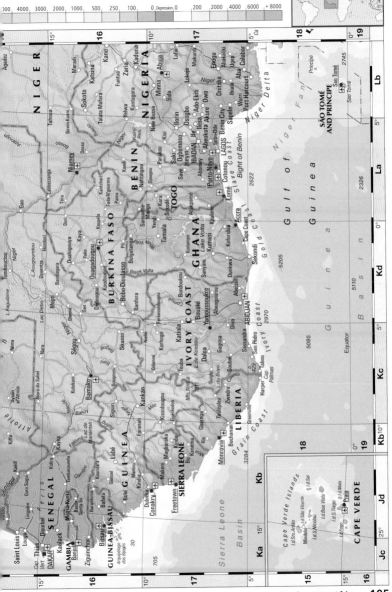

Scale 1:20,000,000

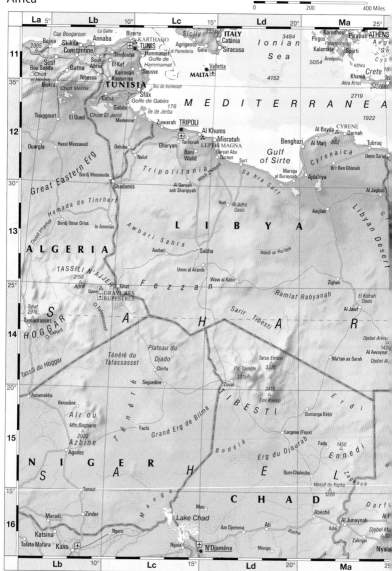

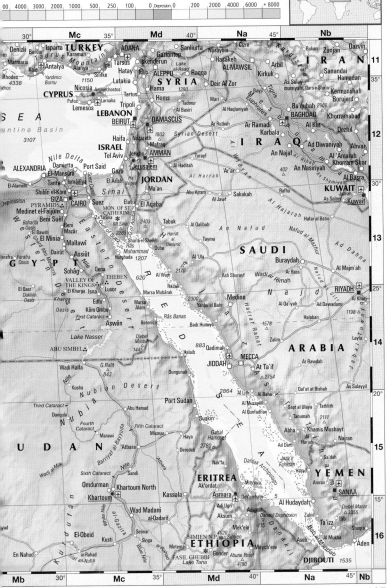

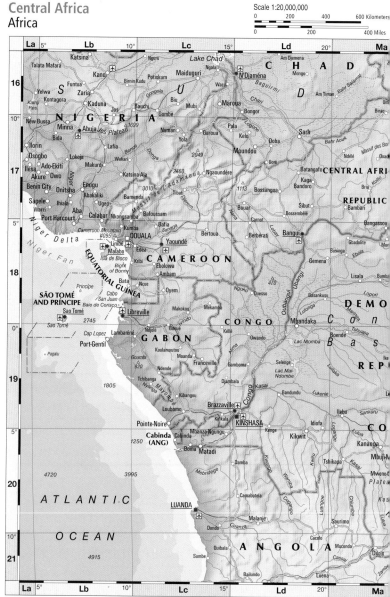

Scale 1:20,000,000

0   200   400   600 Kilometers
0   200   400 Miles

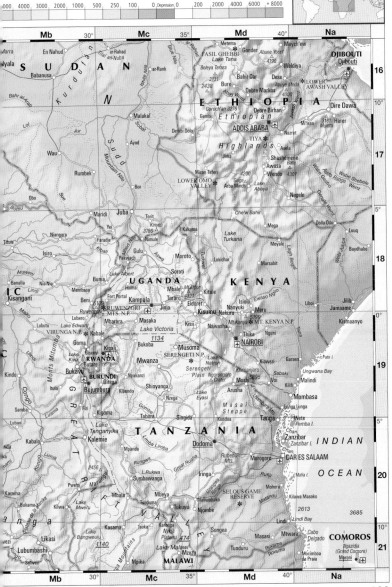

Southern Africa, Madagascar
Africa

Scale 1:20,000,000

0   200   400   600 Kilometres

0   200   400 Miles

Dondo
Cuanza
Saurimo
Cacolo
Muconda
Kasaji **DEM. REP. CONGO**
Ouibala
Cassa
Dilolo
Kolwezi
Likasi
Lubumbashi
Sumbe
Bailundo
Luena
Zambezi
Lumbala
Solwezi
Chililabombwe
Mufulira
Lobito
Moço 2619
Kuito
Huambo
A N G O L A
Lunguè-Bungo
Lumbala
Chingola
Kitwe
Ndola
2420
Benguela
Serra do Neve 2489
Planalto do Bié
Luanginga
Zambezi
Kabompo
Kapiri
Kabwe
Luanshya
Copperbelt
Lubango
Menongue
Cuando
Luena
Kafue
Z A M B I
Namibe
Serra da Chela 2102
Ponta Albina
Humbe
Mongu
Chunga
Namwala
Mazabuka
Lusaka
MANA
Kafue
Barotseland
Senanga
Choma
Zambezi Escarp
Kuvango
Kunene
Ondjiva
Oshakati
Okavango
Rundu
Caprivi Strip
Katima Mulilo
Chobe
Livingstone
Victoria Falls
Kasane
Lake Kariba
Chegu
Kadoma
Z I M B A B W
Etosha Pan
Tsumeb
Grootfontein
Otavi
Okavango Delta
Okavango Swamp
Maun
Nata
Hwange
Kwekwe
Gweru
Otjiwarongo 1857
Waterberg
Eiseb
Hereroland
Rakops
Makgadikgadi Pans
Lake Xau
Francistown
KHAMI RUINS
Bulawayo
ZIM
Brandberg 2574
Spitzkoppe
Karibib 1759
Okahandja
Gobabis
Mamuno
Ghanzi
Serowe
Selebi-Phikwe
Messina
Swakopmund
Walvis Bay
Windhoek
Rehoboth
B O T S W A N A
Mahalapye
Limpopo
MAKAPAN VALLEY
3689
N A M I B I A
Naukluft 1974
Mariental
Kalahari Desert
Molepolole
Gaborone
Potgietersrus
Pie
Lüderitz Bay
Keetmanshoop
Namaland
KGALAGADI TRANSFRONTIER PARK
Lobatse
Mmabatho
Rustenburg
Pretoria
JOHANNESBURG
SOWETO
Mamelodi
Springs
Nossob
Grünau
Karasberge 2202
Groot Karasberge
Kuruman
Vryburg
Hotazel
Klerksdorp
Vereeniging
Volksrust
Lady-smith
Oranjemund
Upington
Warrenton
Welkom
Kroonstad
Winburg
Bethlehem
Orange
Springbok
Orangerivier
Kimberley
Bloemfontein
Maseru
LESOTHO
Aliwal North
Alival-Noord
Kokstad
S O U T H   A F R I C A
Upper Karoo
De Aar
Colesberg
Port St
150
219
Calvinia
Victoria West
Middelburg
Queenstown
Umtata
DRAKENSB
Lamberts Bay
Lambertsbaai
Vanrhynsdorp
Beaufort West
Beaufort-Wes
Graaff-Reinet
Mdantsane
East London
Oos-Londen
Saint Helenabaai
Great Karoo
Somerset-East
Somerset-Oos
CAPE TOWN
TABLE MTN.
Worcester
Stellenbosch
Oudtshoorn 2152
George
Humansdorp
Port Elizabeth
Cape of Good Hope
Riversdale
Little Karoo
Mossel Bay
Mosselbaai
4627
Bredasdorp
Cape Agulhas
90

000 4000 3000 2000 1000 500 250 100 0 Depression 0 200 2000 4000 6000 + 8000

Karonga
Isoka Nyika
Plateau
474
Mzuzu

Songea

Masasi Mtwara

Lindi Lindi Bay 3685

Cabo Delgado

COMOROS

Grande Terre
Assumption Cosmoledo Atoll
Astove I.
Groupe d'Aldabra 4030

10°

Tunduru Ruvuma
Rovuma
Mocímboa
da Praia

Ngazidja
(Grand Comore)
Meroni 2361
Mwali
(Mohéli) 5

Iles Glorieuses (F)

T.Babaomby

Antsiranana

21°

Lake Malawi

Lake Nyassa

Lugenda

Metoro Pemba

Ndzuani
(Anjouan) Mayotte
Dzaoudzi
Mayotte (F) 3200

Ambohitra
1475
Nosy Mitsio
Nosy Be Ambilobe

Ambanja 2876
Maromokotro

Kasungu Nkhotakota

Lichinga

Messalo

Antsohihy Sambava

Chipata

MALAWI
Lilongwe

Dedza Mandimba

Cuamba Nacaroa

Nampula

Antsiranana

15°

Zomba Monte Namuli
Chilwa 2420
Mulanje
3001

Alto Molócuè

380

Mahajanga

Marpantsetra

Tete Zambezi
Changara

Blantyre

Caia

Mocuba

Besalampy T.Vilanandro

Ambondromany

F.Alaotra

T.Masoala
Nosy Ste-Marie

22°

MOZAMBIQUE

Quelimane

2623

Luan de
Nova (F) 10

Ambatondrazaka

Toamasina

gwiza Nyangani Gorongosa
2592 1863
Chimoio
Mutare

51

Tsiroano-
mandidy Antananarivo

Moramanga

Binga
2436

Beira

993

Antsalova

Miandrivazo

Tsiafajavona
2643 Antsirabe

20°

Save

3412

Morondava

MADAGASCAR

Manja

Manakara

Ihas do Bazaruto

Bassas da India

Réunion (F)

Morombe Mangoky

Fianarantsoa

Boby
2658

Manjary

Mananjary

Mapinhane Ponta São Sebastião I.Europa

Ihosy Farafangana

23°

IGER N.P.

2126

3390 Toliara

Vangaindrano

Xai-Xai Inhambane

Mascarene Plain

3670

25°

Baía do Maputo
Maputo

70 Ambovombe Tôlanaro

ZILAND

Saint
uciameer
's Bay

4721

Tanjona
Vohimena

5393

Madagascar

24°

Mozambique

3260

Basin

I N D I A N

30°

Mozambique Ridge

1217

Basin

20

O C E A N

25°

Madagascar Ridge

Scale 1:50,000,000

0   500   1000   1500 Kilometers

0   500   1000 Miles

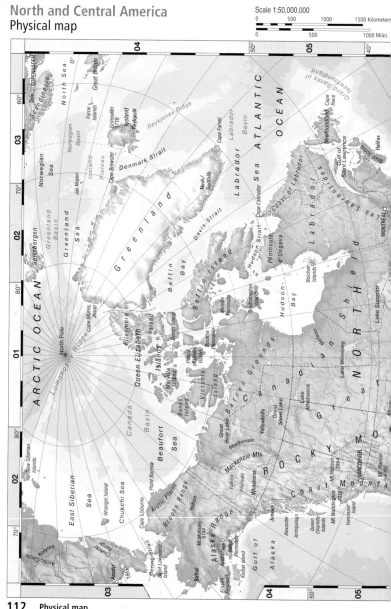

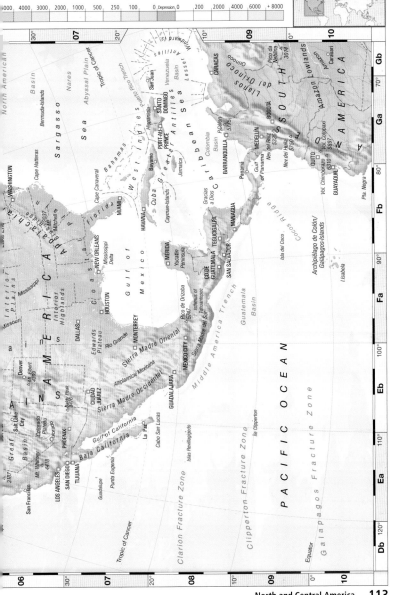

North and Central America
Political map

Scale 1:50,000,000

0   500   1000   1500 Kilometers

0   500   1000 Miles

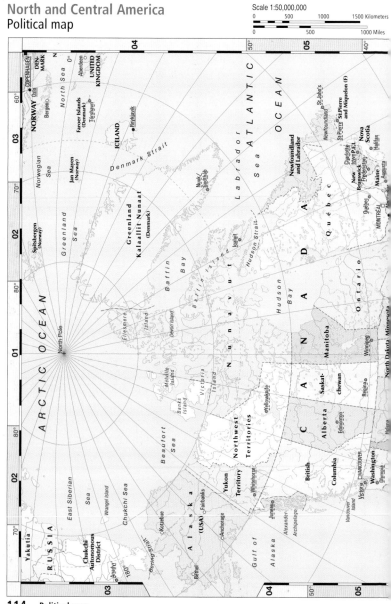

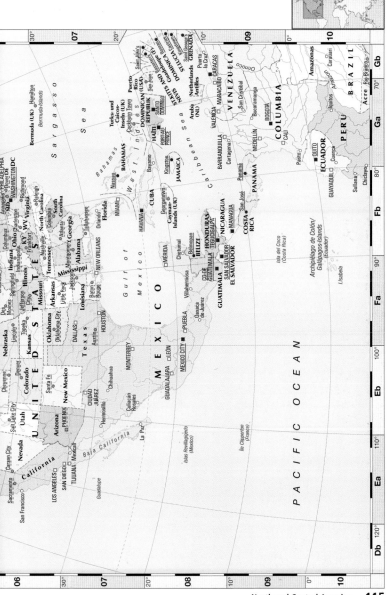

North and Central America **115**

Scale 1:20,000,000

ARCTIC OCEAN

Canada Basin

Chukchi Plateau

Beaufort Sea

Dc
Db
Da
Cd
Cc
Cb
Ca
Bc
Bd
Bb
Ba

Banks Island

Cape Kellet
Sachs Harbour

Franklin
Bay
Amundsen Gulf
Cape Parry

Cape Bathurst

Paulatuk

Tuktoyaktuk

Great Bear Lake

Fort Good Hope

Fort McPherson

Inuvik

Mackenzie Bay

Old Crow

Aklavik

Mackenzie

Fort Radium

36

914

3822

328

155

East Siberian Sea

proliv Longa

Wrangel Island

57

38

Mys Smidta

Ust Belaja

Chukchi Range

Iultin

Egvekinot

Arctic Circle

Chukchi Autonomous District

Chukchi

RUSSIA

Koryak Range

Kanchalan

Anadyr'

Nagornyj

Markovo

Hatyrka

g. Ledjanaja 2562

Apuka

Kara

Point Barrow

Barrow

Ice Cape

Cape Lisburne

Point Hope

Wevok

Kivalina

Kotzebue

Selawik

Noatak

Ambler

Kobuk

BROOKS RANGE

Arctic Plains

Anaktuvuk Peaks
Mt. Doonerak (2633)

Prudhoe Bay

Arctic Village

Mt. Chamberlin
2749

Wiseman

Fort Yukon

Yukon Flats

Circle

Dawson

Stewart

Yukon

Yukon

Whitehorse

1994

Fairbanks

Tanana

Galena

Ruby

Alaska (USA)

Delta Junction

WRANGELL MTS.
Mt. St. Elias 5489

Glennallen

Valdez

Palmer

Anchorage

Cook Inlet

Seward

Kenai

Homer

Kachemak Bay

Prince William Sound

ALASKA RANGE

Mt. McKinley 6194

Kuskokwim Mountains

Stony River

Aniak

Kuskokwim

Bethel

1632

Dillingham

Kvichak Bay

King Salmon

Naknek

Port Heiden

Chignik

Bristol Bay

Alaska Peninsula

Kuskokwim Bay

Cape Newenham

Cape Pierce

Cape Romanzof

Mekoryuk

Nunivak Island

St. Matthew Island

Pribilof Islands

Bering Sea

Bering Strait

Wales

Teller

Nome

Unalakleet

Norton Sound

Seward Peninsula

St. Lawrence Island

Gambell

Savoonga

Northeast Cape

Cape Mohican

Providenija

Lavrentija

Uelen

Gulf of Anadyr

Mys Navarin

Koljucinskaja Guba

Chukchi Peninsula

Chukchi Sea

Ugol'nye Kopi

Kresti

Ottogonskij

Anadyr

Anadyr

65

38

65

257

Aleu...

Cold Bay

Unimak Island

1402

1040

3849

6101

1994

Atognak

Shelikof Strait

Kodiak

Kiliuda Bay

ARCTIC OCEAN

Arctic Circle

60°

65°

70°

75°

80°

85°

55°

70°

75°

80°

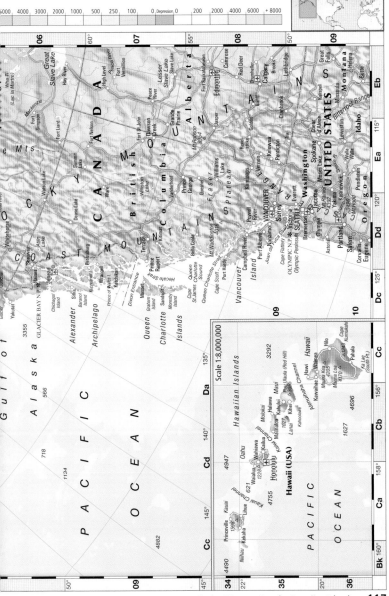

Scale 1:8,000,000

Alaska, Western Canada, Hawaiian Islands **117**

Scale 1:20,000,000

0   200   400   600 Kilometers

0   200   400 Miles

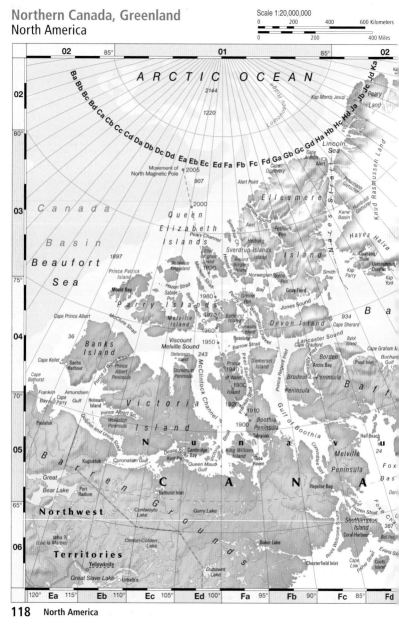

02   85°   01   85°   02

A R C T I C   O C E A N

Ba Bb Bc Bd Ca Cb Cc Cd Da Db Dc Dd Ea Eb Ec Ed Fa Fb Fc Fd Ga Gb Gc Gd Ha Hb Hc Hd Ja Jb Jc Jd Ka

2144

1220

Kap Morris Jesup   Peary Land

02

80°

C a n a d a   B a s i n

Movement of North Magnetic Pole

2005

907

2000

1897

1990

1980

1970

1960

1950

1940

1930

1920

1910

1900

36

243

934

24

387

Queen Elizabeth Islands

Peary Channel   Nansen Sound

Svedrup Ch.

Axel Heiberg Island

Sverdrup Islands

Amund Ringnes Island

Ellef Ringnes Island

Hassel Sound

Foshein Pen.

Lincoln Sea

Cape Aldrich   Alert

Cape Discovery

Alert Point

E l l e s m e r e   I s l a n d

Kane Basin

Peterman Gletscher

Hayes Halvø

Qaanaaq Thule

Ummannaq Dundas

Kap York

Humboldt Gletscher

Smith Sound

Kap Parry

Knud Rasmussen Land

Nares Strait

B e a u f o r t   S e a

Prince Patrick Island

Mackenzie King Island

Hazen Strait

Sabine Pen.

Mould Bay

P a r r y   I s l a n d s

Mercy Bay

Melville Island

Byam Martin Channel

MacKenzie Strait

Grinnell Pen.

Bathurst Island

Cornwallis Island

Wellington Channel

Devon Island

Cape Sherard

Grise Fiord

Jones Sound

B a ...

Norwegian Bay

Bjorne Pen.

Cape Prince Albert

McClure Strait

Lancaster Sound

Cape Crauford

Prince Regent Inlet

Barrow Strait

Resolute

Cornwallis Island

Peel Sound

Borden Peninsula

Arctic Bay

Pond Inlet

Bylot Island

Cape Graham M...

Buchan...

B a f f ...

Brodeur Peninsula

B a n k s   I s l a n d

Sachs Harbour

Cape Kellet

Cape Bathurst

Stefansson Island

Prince of Wales Island

Storkerson Peninsula

Viscount Melville Sound

McClintock Channel

Amundsen Gulf

Franklin Bay

Cape Parry

Holman Island

Prince of Wales Str.

Prince Albert Peninsula

Dolphin and Union Strait

Wollaston Peninsula

V i c t o r i a   I s l a n d

Boothia Peninsula

Gulf of Boothia

Franklin Str.

Talnyoak

Hall Beach

Melville Peninsula

F o x   B a s ...

Paulatuk

B a r r e n   G r o u n d s

Kugluktuk

Coronation Gulf

Dease St.

Kent Pen.

Cambridge Bay

Victoria Strait

Queen Maud Gulf

King William Island

Gjoa Haven

Committee Bay

C A N A ... v u

Repulse Bay

A

Great Bear Lake

Port Radium

Bathurst Inlet

Contwoyto Lake

Garry Lake

Roes Welcome Sound

Southampton Island

Coral Harbour

Frozen Strait

Foxe Ch...

Coats Island

Cape Fisher Strait

Dor...

Evans Str...

N o r t h w e s t

Wha Ti (Lac la Martre)

Clinton-Colden Lake

Baker Lake

Chesterfield Inlet

Cape Low

T e r r i t o r i e s

Yellowknife

Great Slave Lake

Lutselk'e

Dubawnt Lake

120° Ea 115°   Eb 110°   Ec 105°   Ed 100°   Fa 95°   Fb 90°   Fc 85°   Fd

Northern Canada, Greenland **119**

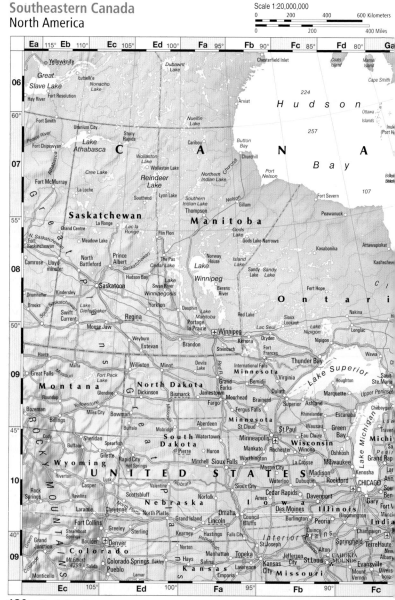

Scale 1:20,000,000

0   200   400   600 Kilometers

0   200   400 Miles

Ea 115° **Eb** 110° **Ec** 105° **Ed** 100° **Fa** 95° **Fb** 90° **Fc** 85° **Fd** 80° **Ga**

06

Yellowknife
Great Slave Lake
Hay River
Lutselk'e
Nonacho Lake
Fort Resolution
Dubawnt Lake
Chesterfield Inlet
Coats Island
Mansel Island
Cape Smith

60°

Fort Smith
Peace River
Fort Chipewyan
Uranium City
Stony Rapids
Nueltin Lake
Arviat

Hudson
224
257
Ottawa Islands
Inuk (Port H)

07

Fort McMurray
Lake Athabasca
C
Wollaston Lake
Cree Lake
Reindeer Lake
La Loche
Southend
Lynn Lake
Caribou
Northern Indian Lake
Churchill River
A
Button Bay
Port Nelson
Churchill
N
Bay
A
Fort Severn
107
Bdei Bston

55°

Saskatchewan
Grand Centre
La Ronge
Lac la Ronge
Flin Flon
Southern Indian Lake
Nelson
Thompson
Gillam
Manitoba
Gods Lake
Gods Lake Narrows
Peawanuck
Kasabonika
Attawapiskat
Kashechew

08

N. Saskatchewan
Fort Saskatchewan
Camrose
Lloydminster
Meadow Lake
North Battleford
Prince Albert
Saskatchewan
The Pas
Cedar Lake
Hudson Bay
Swan River
Norway House
Island Lake
Sandy Lake
Sandy Lake
Fort Hope
C
Drumheller
Kindersley
Saskatoon
Lake Diefenbaker
Winnipegosis
Yorkton
Dauphin
Lake Winnipeg
Berens River
Red Lake
Sioux Lookout
Ontari

50°

Brooks
Swift Current
Regina
Moose Jaw
Weyburn
Estevan
Portage la Prairie
Winnipeg
Kenora
Dryden
Lac Seul
Lake Nipigon
Nipigon
Longlac
Nakina
Cl

Havre
Malta
Williston
Minot
Devils Lake
Brandon
Steinbach
Fort Frances
International Falls
Thunder Bay
Lake Superior
Wawa
Sault Ste. Marie

09

Great Falls
Montana
Roundup
Glendive
Fort Peck Lake
North Dakota
Dickinson
Bismarck
Jamestown
Grand Forks
Fargo
Moorhead
Bemidji
Virginia
Duluth
Minnesota
Houghton
Marquette
Upper Peninsu

45°

Bozeman
Billings
Miles City
Bowman
Mobridge
Aberdeen
Fergus Falls
Brainerd
Superior
Ashland
Rhinelander
Wausau
Escanaba
Chebogan
Traver

Cody
Sheridan
Spearfish
South Dakota
Watertown
St. Cloud
Minnesota
St. Paul
Eau Claire
Green Bay
Oshkosh
Grand Rap
Michi

Wyoming
Buffalo
Gillette
Rapid City
Hot Springs
Pierre
Huron
Mitchell
Sioux Falls
Minneapolis
Mankato
Rochester
Worthington
Winona
La Crosse
Wisconsin
Milwaukee
Kenosha
CHICAGO

10

Riverton
Casper
Lusk
Valentine
Niobrara
Norfolk
Sioux City
Waterloo
Dubuque
Madison
Rockford
Gary
Fort
Sou

Rock Springs
Rawlins
Scottsbluff
Nebraska
Ia
Cedar Rapids
Davenport
Illinois
India

Laramie
Cheyenne
North Platte
Grand Island
Omaha
Council Bluffs
Des Moines
Burlington
Peoria
Bloomington
Champaign

40°

Fort Collins
Steamboat Springs
Boulder
Greeley
Sterling
Kearney
Lincoln
Hastings
Falls City
St. Joseph
Quincy
Springfield
Alton
TerreHaute

09

Grand Junction
Denver
Colorado
Salida
Mt. Elbert 4399
Norton
Hays
Manhattan
Topeka
Lawrence
Jefferson City
St. Louis
CAHOKIA MOUNDS
Evansville
Mount Vernon
Owens

Monticello
Colorado Springs
Pueblo
Oakley
Salina
Emporia
Kansas City
Kansas
Missouri

Ec 105° **Ed** 100° **Fa** 95° **Fb** 90° **Fc**

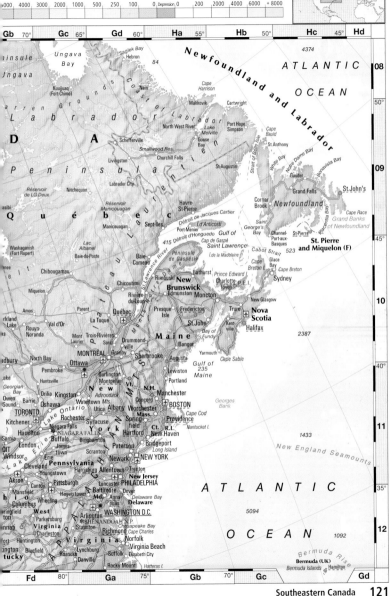

United States
North America

United States **123**

Scale 1:20,000,000

0   200   400   600 Kilometers

0   200   400 Miles

Ea 120°   115°   **Eb**   110°   **Ec**   105°   **Ed**   100°

Oxnard · Pasadena · Needles · Kingman · Lake Havasu City · Flagstaff · Winslow · Gallup · Santa Fe · Las Vegas · Dalhart · Canadian · Oklahoma **O k**

LOS ANGELES · San Bernardino · Prescott · Albuquerque · Amarillo · Altus · Chicka

Long Beach · Santa Ana · Palm Springs · **A r i z o n a** · 3476 · Baldy Peak · **N e w   M e x i c o** · Clovis · Plainview · Lubbock · Wichita Falls

Oceanside · El Cajon · Salton Sea · El Centro · Glendale · **PHOENIX** · Mesa · Roswell · Llano Estacado

SAN DIEGO · Yuma · Casa Grande · Alamo gorda · Hobbs · Lamesa · Big Spring · Fort · Abilene

TIJUANA · Tecate · Mexicali · San Luis Rio Colorado · Tucson · Deming · Las Cruces · El Paso · Pecos · Odessa · **T e x**

Ensenada · Sonoyta · Nogales · Douglas · Agua Prieta · CIUDAD JUAREZ · Van Horn · Fort Stockton · San Angelo

Punta Santo Tomás · **Baja** · San Felipe · Caborca · Sta.Ana · Janos · Nuevo · Brady · **E d w a r d s**

San Quintin · **California** · Puerto Peñasco · CASAS GRANDES · Moctezuma · Casas Grandes · El Sueco · **P l a t e a u** · New Braunfels

Isla de Guadalupe · Punta Peñasco · **Norte** · Bahia Kino · **S o n o r a** · Hermosillo · Madera · Chihuahua · Ojinaga · Rio Bravo del Norte · Del Rio · **SAN AN**

Isla Cedros · Sebastián Vizcaino · Bahía de · Guaymas · **C h i h u a h u a** · Chihuahua · Presidio · Piedras Negras · Eagle Pass

Punta Eugenia · R.BIOSFERA EL VIZCAINO · Sta.Rosalia · Ciudad Obregon · Cuauhtemoc · Delicias · Nueva Rosita · Corpus

Punta Abreojos · **Baja** · Mulege · Navojoa · Hidalgo del Parral · Ciudad Camargo · Jiménez · **C o a h u i l a** · Laredo

California · Loreto · Los Mochis · San Blas · **M e x i c a n** · Monclova · Nuevo Laredo

Rocas Alijos · 691 · Ciudad Constitucion · Isla Magdalena · Guasave · Guamuchil · Ocampo · Gómez Palacio · Ojinaga · Saltillo · MONTERREY · Guadelupe

Tropic of Cancer · **Sur** · Culiacán · Rosales · **D u r a n g o** · Torreón · **P l a t e a u** · **S I E R R A   M A D R E   O R I E N T A L**

La Paz · **M** · 2547 · El Dorado · Concepción del Oro · Nuevo León · **Tam**

3887 · San José del Cabo · **M** · **É** · **X** · Victoria de Durango · Zacatecas · Matehuala · Ciudad · **C**

San Lucas · Cabo San Lucas · Mazatlán · Rosarin · Fresnillo · San Luis Potosí · Acuña

Santiago Ixcuintla · Zacatecas · Aguascalientes · AGS · San Luis Potosí

1415 · **Nayarit** · Islas Marías · San Blas · Tepic · Lagos de Moreno · LEÓN · Guanajuato · QRT.

Puerto Vallarta · **Jalisco** · GUADALAJARA · Guanajuato · Celaya · Pachuca · Hidal

Cabo Corrientes · Tlaquepaque · Ocotlan · Irapuato · Querétaro · Pachuca

I s l a s   R e v i l l a g i g e d o (MEX.) · Nevado de Colima · Ciudad Guzman · Morelia · (MEXICO CITY) · Hidal

Colima · 4265 · **Colima** · Uruapan · Toluca · **MOR**

Manzanillo · Tecoman · J.J.Constitucion · Apatzingan · **Michoacán** · Cuernavaca · XOCHI · **MOR**

Lázaro Cardenas · Guerrero · Iguala · Chilpa

P A C I F I C · Zihuatanejo · 5285 · Acapulco · Chilpancingo · de los E

O C E A N 4840 · 1322 · **M i d d l e** · **A m**

Clipperton Fracture Zone · 5486 · Île Clipperton (F) · Tehua

Ea 115°   **Eb**   110°   **Ec**   105°   **Ed**   100°

5000 4000 3000 2000 1000 500 250 100 0 Depression 0 200 2000 4000 6000 + 8000

ATLANTIC

OCEAN

Fort Smith · McAlester · Conway · Memphis · Florence · Huntsville · Columbia · Florence · Myrtle Beach · Georgetown
Arkansas · Little Rock · Decatur · Gadsden · Marietta · Athens · **South Carolina** · Charleston
Hot Springs · Pine Bluff · Clarksdale · Birmingham · Anniston · Atlanta · Augusta
UNITED STATES · Tupelo · Tuscaloosa · **Alabama** · Macon · Savannah · 3674
LAS · Monroe · Jackson · Meridian · Montgomery · Columbus · **Georgia** · Waycross · 759
Long Prairie · Shreveport · **Mississippi** · Selma · Albany · Valdosta · Brunswick
Tyler · Toledo · Natchez · Hattiesburg · Mobile · Dothan · **Tallahassee** · Jacksonville
Bend Res. · **Louisiana** · Baton Rouge · Gulfport · Pascagoula · Pensacola · Panama City · Gainesville · Ocala · Daytona Beach · 5223
Beaumont · Lake Charles · Lafayette · New Orleans · Chandeleur Islands · Cape St.George · 32 · Tampa · Titusville · Cape Canaveral
Port Arthur · Houma · · St.Petersburg · **Florida** · Orlando · Melbourne · Fort Pierce · Bahama Islands
Pasadena · Galveston Bay · Galveston · Mississippi Delta · Bradenton · Lake Okeechobee · West Palm Beach · Grand Bahama · Freeport · Marsh Harbour · Abaco I.
Lavaca · Matagorda Bay · Matagorda Island · Sarasota · Fort Myers · Boca Raton · Fort Lauderdale · Hollywood · Eleuthera I. · Governor's Harbour
934 · **EVERGLADES N.P.** · Naples · Miami Beach · **MIAMI** · Coral Gables · Nassau
2567 · Cape Sable · Key West · **BAHAMAS** · Andros Town · New Providence Sd.
sville · Andros I.
noros · **Gulf of** · Dry Tortugas · Florida Keys · Straits of Florida · Santaren Channel
Santa María · **Mexico** · 4012 · **HAVANA** · Matanzas · Sagua la Grande · Little Bahama Bank
Madero · Sigsbee · 3265 · Deep · Artemisa · Sta.Clara · Morón · Nuevitas
de Tamiahua · Pinar del Río · Güines · Cienfuegos · Sancti Spíritus · Las Tunas · Camagüey · Bayamo
Isabel Rubio · Golfo de Batabanó · Trinidad · **CUBA** · Manzanillo
Rica · Cabo de San Antonio · Nueva Gerona · Isla de la Juventud · 4887
klapa · **MÉRIDA** · Tizimín · Cancún · **Yucatán** · **Cayman Islands (UK)** · Montego Bay
Veracruz · **CHICHÉN ITZÁ** · Cozumel · Grand Cayman · Georgetown · Savanna-la-Mar · May Pen
eracruz · Bay of · Isla de Cozumel · Yucatán · **JAMAICA**
aba · **Campeche** · Valladolid · Yucatán · **TULUM** · Basin · 15
cán · Tuxtepec · **EDZNA** · Peninsula · Quintana Roo · Bahía de la Ascens.
Oaxaca · Cd.d.Carmen · Champotón · Chetumal · **Caribbean Sea**
ONTE ALBÁN · San Andrés Tuxtla · **Tabasco** · **Campeche** · Bahía de Chetumal · Islas del · Banco de Serranilla (CO.)
i c a · Coatzacoalcos · **Villahermosa** · **CALAKMUL** · Belize City · **BELIZE BARRIER** · Cisne (HN)
erto · Minatitlán · **PALENQUE** · **XULTÚN** · Belmopan · **REEF SYSTEM** · 304
ondida · Isthmus of · San Cristóbal · **TIKAL** · Flores · **BELIZE** · Islas de · Banco de Serrana (CO.)
Puerto Ángel · Tehuantepec · de las Casas · **Chiapas** · Daogrin · Golfo de Honduras · la Bahía · Laguna de · Cabo de · Banco de Serrana (CO.)
Tuxtla Gutiérrez · **AGUATECA** · La Ceiba · Caratasca · Gracias a Dios · Providencia (CO.)
i c a · Salina Cruz · Comitán de Domínguez · Puerto Barrios · **COPÁN** · San Pedro Sula · Trujillo · I.de San Andrés (CO.)
Tapachula · **COPÁN** · **HONDURAS** · Juticalpa · Puerto Cabezas
Mazatenango · **Coban** · Pto. Cortés · **TEGUCIGALPA** · Costa Miskitos
GUATEMALA · **CD. DE GUATEMALA** · Sta.Ana · San Miguel · Ocotal
6663 · Escuintla · San Salvador · **NICARAGUA** · Matagalpa · Rama
SAN SALVADOR · **EL SALVADOR** · Chinandega · León · **LEÓN VIEJO** · Bluefields · Bahía de San Juan del Norte · 4032
u a t e m a l a · Golfo de Fonseca · **MANAGUA** · Lago de Nicaragua · Isthmus of Panamá
Basin · 25 · Golfo de Papagayo · Liberia · Alajuela · Puerto Limón · Colón · Panama Canal
315 · Nicoya · **COSTA RICA** · Puntarenas · **San José** · Golfo de los Mosquitos · La Chorrera · **Panama**
Cabo Blanco · **PANAMA**

Campeche Bank · Yucatán Channel · Cabo Catoche · Yucatán Basin · Cayman Ridge · Cayman Trench

Scale 1:20,000,000

0 200 400 600 Kilometers

0 200 400 Miles

Fb Fc Fd Ga

95° 90° 85° 80° 75°

El Dorado Greenville Columbus Savannah 759
Texarkana Mississippi Alabama Georgia
Long-view Monroe Jackson Meridian Montgomery Albany Waycross Brunswick
Shreveport Natchez Hattiesburg Gulfport Dothan Valdosta Jacksonville 5223
Lufkin Louisiana Baton Rouge Biloxi Mobile Pensa-cola Panama City Tallahassee Gainesville Daytona Beach
Toledo Bend Res. Lake Charles Lafayette Pasca-goula Cape St.George 32 Ocala Titusville Cape Canaveral
HOUS-TON Beaumont Houma New Orleans Chandeleur Islands Tampa Orlando Melbourne
Pasadena Galveston Bay Mississippi Delta St.Petersburg Florida Fort Pierce
Galveston 934 2567 Bradenton Lake Okeechobee West Palm Beach Grand Bahama Marsh Harbour
UNITED STATES Sarasota Boca Raton Freeport Abaco I. Eleuthera I.
Fort Myers Fort Lauderdale Governor's Harbour
G u l f o f EVERGLADES N.P. Hollywood Androd Nassau Exuma Sd.
Naples MIAMI Coral Gables Town BAHAMAS
M e x i c o Cape Sable Great Bahama Bank
Key West Florida Keys Exuma So.
Dry Tortugas Straits of Florida Santaren Channel W e s
Sigsbee 4012 HAVANA Matanzas Sagua la Grande
Deep Artemisa Sta Clara Molon Nuevitas
Pinar del Río Güines Cienfuegos Sancti Spíritus Camagüey Las Tunas Guan
3265 Isabel Rubio Golfo de Batabanó Trinidad C U B A Bayamo
Cabo de San Antonio Nueva Gerona 4887 Manzanillo 7240
Campeche Bank Cabo Catoche Isla de la Juventud Great Santiago de
Cabo Catoche Cancún Cayman Ridge Montego Bay Spanish
MERIDA Tizimín Cayman Islands (UK) Savanna-la-Mar May Pen Ki
Yucatán CHICHEN ITZA Grand Cayman JAMAICA
Campeche Valladolid Isla de Cozumel Georgetown Cayman Trench
Yucatán TULUM Bahía de la Ascens Cayman Basin 15
Bay of Cd.del Carmen EDZNA Peninsula Chetumal Islas del
Campeche Tabasco Villahermosa CALAKMUL Bahía de Chetumal Cisne (HN) Banco de
San Andrés Tuxtla XULTUN Belize City Serranilla (CO.) C a
Coatzacoalcos PALENQUE TIKAL BELIZE BELIZE BARRIER
Minatitlán Chiapas San Cristóbal de las Casas Flores Beltonum REEF SYSTEM 304
Isthmus of Tehuantepec AGUATECA Dangriga Islas de la Bahía Banco de Serrana (CO.)
Salina Cruz Tuxtla Gutiérrez Comitán de Domínguez Golfo de Honduras Pto. Cortés Trujillo Cabo de I.de Providencia (CO.)
Gulf of Tehuantepec Coban COPAN San Pedro Sula Gracias a Dios I. de San Andrés (CO.)
Tapachula CD. DE GUATEMALA Puerto Barrios La Ceiba Juticalpa Puerto
Quezaltenango Mazatenango TEGUCIGALPA HONDURAS Cabezas
GUATEMALA JOYA DE CEREN Laguna de Caratasca
Escuintla Sta.Ana 6663 San HONDURAS Costa de Mosquitos
SAN SALVADOR San NICARAGUA Matagalpa Rama Bahía de San 4032
EL SALVADOR Miguel Choluteca LEON VIEJO Juan del Norte
Golfo de Fonseca Leon MANAGUA Granada Bluefields Isthmus of
25 Lago de Panamá
Nicaragua Colón Panama Canal
Liberia Golfo de Papagayo Alajuela Puerto Limón Golfo de los La Chorrera Panama
COSTA RICA Puntarenas Nueva San José Mosquitos PANAMÁ Panamá
10 Cabo Blanco PARQUE David Gulf of Punta Mala
Bahía de Coronado Palmar Sur LA AMISTAD Chitre Panamá
Santiago Bahía d
3655 PACIFIC OCEAN Punta Burica Puerto Armuelles Punta Naranjas

Fa Fb Fc Fd
95° 90° 85° 80°

South America
Physical map

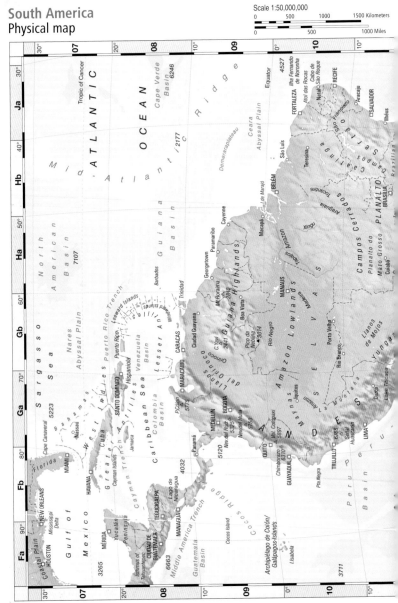

Scale 1:50,000,000

0 500 1000 1500 Kilometers

0 500 1000 Miles

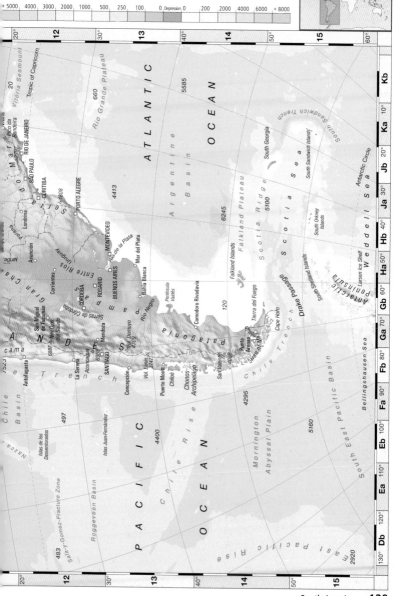

South America
Political map

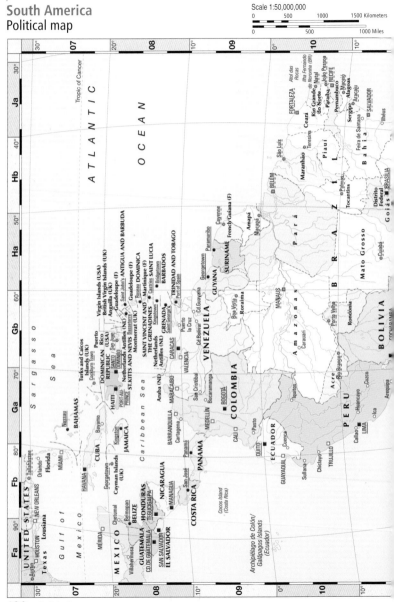

Scale 1:50,000,000

| 0 | 500 | 1000 | 1500 Kilometers |

| 0 | 500 | 1000 Miles |

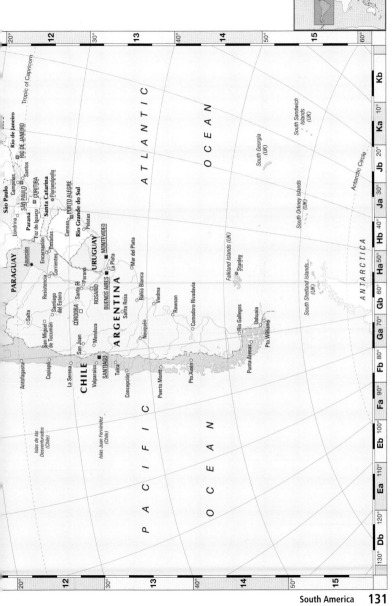

Scale 1:20,000,000

0   200   400   600 Kilometers

0   200   400 Miles

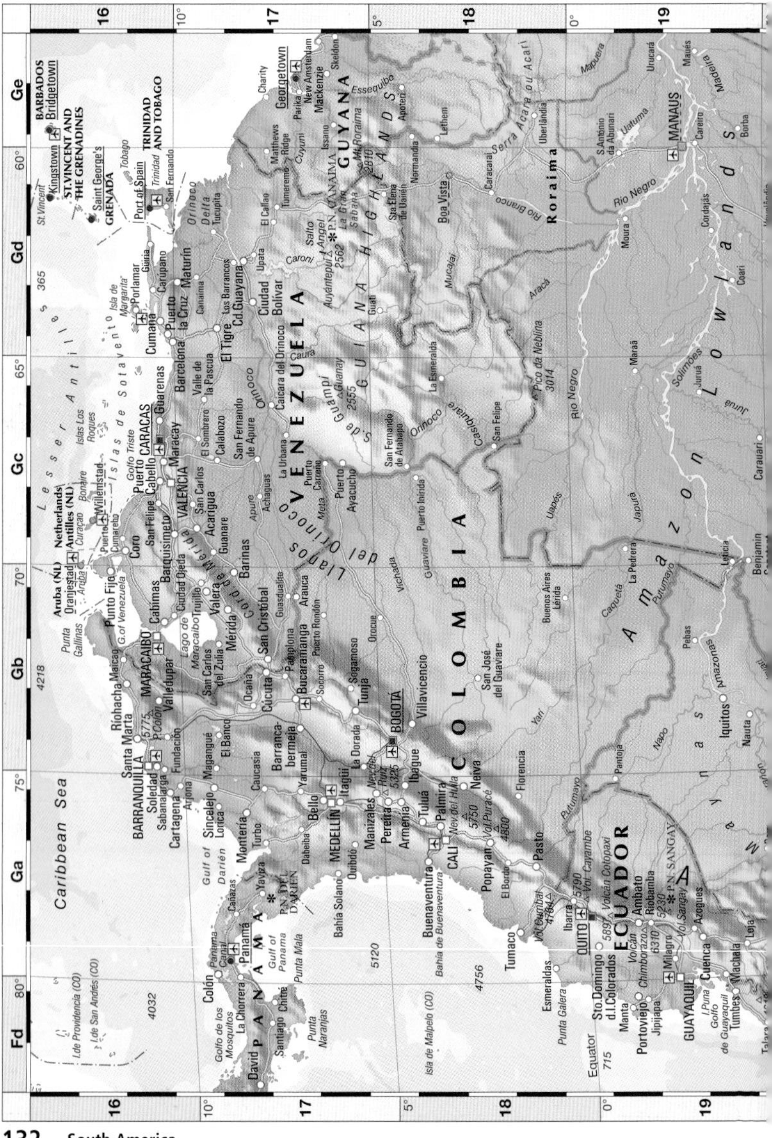

BARBADOS Bridgetown
ST.VINCENT AND THE GRENADINES
Kingstown
Saint George's GRENADA
St Vincent
TRINIDAD AND TOBAGO
Port of Spain

Georgetown
New Amsterdam
Mackenzie
GUYANA
Serra Acarai
MANAUS
Roraima
R o r a i m a

Caracas
VENEZUELA
MARACAIBO
VALENCIA
Barquisimeto
Maracay
Ciudad Bolívar
Ciudad Guayana
Cumaná
Barcelona
Maturín

G U I A N A   H I G H L A N D S

Netherlands Antilles (NL)
Aruba (AU)
Willemstad
Oranjestad
Curaçao
Bonaire

Caribbean Sea

L e s s e r   A n t i l l e s

Islas Los Roques

Lago de Maracaibo

COLOMBIA
BOGOTÁ
MEDELLÍN
CALI
Barranquilla
Cartagena
Santa Marta
Cúcuta
Bucaramanga
Pasto
Popayán

L l a n o s   d e l   O r i n o c o

Río Negro

A m a z o n a s

L o w l a n d s

PANAMA
Panama
Colón
Gulf of Panamá
Gulf of Darién

ECUADOR
QUITO
GUAYAQUIL
Cuenca
Machala
Esmeraldas
Manta
Ambato
Riobamba

Equator
Equator 715

Iquitos
Nauta

P E R U

132   South America

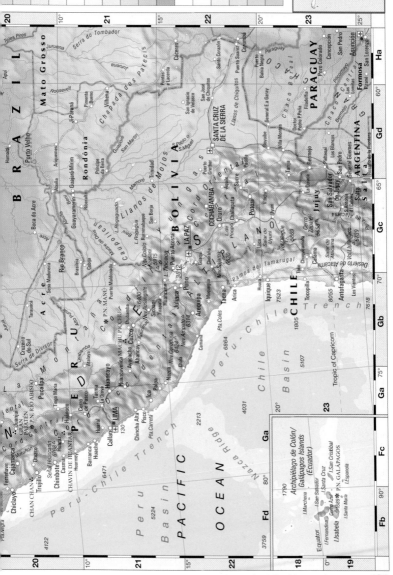

Scale 1:20,000,000

0   200   400   600 Kilometers

0   200   400 Miles

GRID REFERENCES (top): 17 · 18 · 19 · 20

5° · 0° · 5°

GRID ROWS (left): Jb · Ja · Hd · Hc · Hb · Ha

35° · 40° · 45° · 50° · 55°

Mid-Atlantic Ridge
2295
3918
Equator
60
Atol das Rocas

ATLANTIC OCEAN

5148
4925
20
70

Demerara plateau
675
4308
4245
3655
1415
35
110
5

Amazon Cone
Amazon Shelf
Amazon Fan

Mouths of the Amazon
Canal do Norte
Canal da Fora

Guiana Plateau
40
45

Places (Guyana/Suriname/French Guiana):
Charity, Georgetown, New Amsterdam, Mackenzie, Praia, Paia, GUYANA, Essequibo, Apoteri, Nieuw Nickerie, Nieuw Amsterdam, Skeldon, Groningen, Brokopondo, Paramaribo, SURINAME, NR. CENTRAAL SURINAME, Albina, Maroni, Iracoubo, Kourou, French Guiana (F), Mana, Cayenne, Maripasoula, Saint-Georges

Brazil:
Oiapoque, C. Orange, Calçoene, Amapá, Macapá, Santana, Ferreira Gomes, I. Grande de Gurupá, Gurupá, Ponta de Pedras, I. de Marajó, BELÉM, Baía de Marajó, Salinópolis, Capanema, Bragança, Castanhal, Vigia, Santa Isabel, Pinheiro, Turiaçu, Cururupu, Alcântara, São Luís, Santa Rita, Bacabal, Caxias, Teresina, Parnaíba, Luís Correia, Acaraú, Sobral, Camocim, FORTALEZA, Maranguape, Messejana, Aracati, Mossoró, Rio Grande do Norte, Natal, João Pessoa, Santa Rita, RECIFE, Olinda, V. Sta. Antão, Vitória, Caruaru, Pernambuco, Garanhuns, Paulo Afonso, Juazeiro, Petrolina, Pesqueira, Campina Grande, Patos, Sousa, Currais Novos, Santo Antão do Norte, Paraíba, Serra da Fronteira, Piauí, P.N. SERRA CAPIVARA, Monte Alegre, Floriano, Canto do Buriti, Oeiras, Picos, Paulistana, Caracol, Corrente, Gilbués, Balsas, Barra do Corda, Grajaú, Imperatriz, Estreito, Carolina, Palmas, Pedro Afonso, Araguaína, Guaraí, Conceição do Araguaia, Redenção, Santa Terezinha, São Félix do Xingu, Altamira, Senador Pompeu, Iguatu, Crateús, Tauá, Campos Sales, Juazeiro do Norte, Cedro, Crato, Icó

Rivers/features:
Maroni, Coppename, Saramacca, Gran Rio, Serra do Tumucumaque, Serra do Norte, Serra do Cachimbo, Jari, Paru, Xingu, Tapajós, Madeira, Teles Pires, Juruena, Iriri, Tocantins, Araguaia, Parnaíba, Itapecuru, Mearim, Gurupi, Amazon, Maranhão, Pará, Piauí, Ceará, Santarém, Óbidos, Alenquer, Monte Alegre, Almeirim, Gurupá, Prainha, Portel, Baião, Cametá, Tucuruí, Represa de Tucuruí, Marabá, Itupiranga, Tucumã, Ourilândia, Vila Rica, Marajó, Breves, Chaves, Soure, Cabo do Norte, I. de Maracá, Cabo Orange

7°

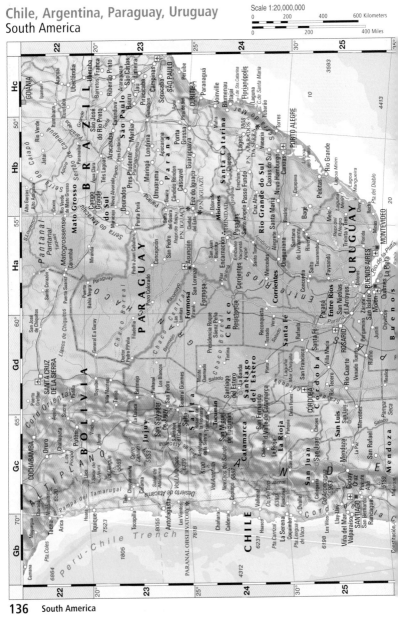

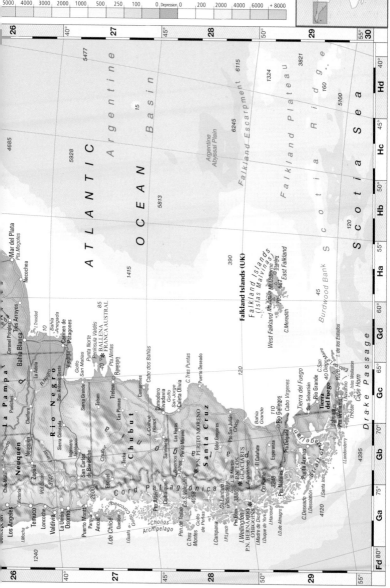

5477

Argentine Basin

6115

1324

3821

Hd

160

4685

5928

6245

Argentine Abyssal Plain

Falkland Escarpment

Falkland Plateau

5100

Hc

ATLANTIC

5813

Hb

OCEAN

Scotia Sea

120

Ha

Mar del Plata
Pta. Mogotes
Necochea

1415

390

Falkland Islands (UK)
Falkland Islands
(Islas Malvinas)
Stanley
West Falkland Mt. Usborne East Falkland
C. Meredith

45

Burdwood Bank

S c o t i a   R i d g e

Gd

Coronel Pringles
Tres Arroyos
L. Trinidad
Anegada
Carmen de Patagones

85
★ BALLENA
FRANCA AUSTRAL
Península Valdés
Punta Norte
Pta. Ninfas
Rawson

Bahía Blanca
La Adela
La Pampa
Puelches
Chadileo
Río Negro
San Antonio Oeste
Viedma
Golfo
San Matías

Bahía
Golfo

Gc

Cabo dos Bahías

120

Tierra del Fuego
Río Grande C. San
40 Diego
San Sebastián

Is. de los Estados

Drake Passage

Neuquén
Zapala
Las Lajas
Picún Leufú
Ingeniero Jacobacci
Sierra Grande
Trelew

Sarmiento
Comodoro Rivadavia
Caleta Olivia
Golfo
San Jorge

Puerto Deseado

110

Cabo Vírgenes

Gb

Chile Chico
Esquel
San Carlos de Bariloche
Chubut
Las Heras
P.N. PERITO MORENO
Santa Cruz
Pto. San Julián
Bahía
Grande
Río Gallegos

C. Vírgenes

Bahía
San Sebastián
Ushuaia
Pto. Williams

Cabo Horn

4395

Gc

Los Angeles
Temuco
Loncoche
Valdivia
La Unión
Osorno
Puerto Montt
Ancud
I. de Chiloé
Chonos
Archipelago

Cord. Patagónica
P.N. Bernardo O'HIGGINS
P.N. Los GLACIARES
Perito Moreno
El Calafate
Esperanza
Pto. Natales
Punta Arenas
Porvenir

Tierra del Fuego
Navarino
Is. Wollaston

Drake Passage

Ga

1240

4120

4395

Fd

Scale 1:30,000,000

0 200 400 600 Kilometers
0 200 400 Miles

125° Dc 130° Db 135° Da 140° Cd 145° Cc 150° Cb 155° Ca 160° Bd 165° Bc 170° Bb 175°

Dd British Columbia — R O C K Y — Watson Lake — Stewart Crossing — Fort Yukon — Alaska (USA) — BROOKS RANGE — Arctic Plains — Chukchi S — Summit Lake — Yukon Territory — Barrow Point Barrow

Ea Dawson Creek — Fort Nelson — Fort Liard — M O U N T A I N S — Mackenzie Mts — Fort McPherson — Prudhoe Bay — 4683 — Chukchi Plateau — 328 — Mackenzie Bay

Alberta — Fort Simpson — Mackenzie — Norman Wells — Inuvik — B e a u f o r t

Eb Peace River — Fort Chipewyan — Hay River — Great Slave Lake — Yellowknife — Great Bear Lake — N o r t h w e s t — T e r r i t o r i e s — Cape Bathurst — Cape Parry — Cape Kellet — S e a — 914

Lake Athabasca — Stony Rapids

Ec Dubawnt Lake — B a r r e n — Coppermine — Bathurst Inlet — G r o u n d s — Amundsen Gulf — Banks Island — Cape Prince Albert — McClure Strait — C a n a d a

Ed C A N A D A — Coronation Gulf — Victoria Island — Prince of Wales — Storkerson Peninsula — Melville Island — Prince Patrick Island — B a s i n — A R C T I

Garry Lake — King William Island — Queen Elizabeth Islands

Fa B a c k G r o u n d s — Baker Lake — McClintock Channel — 1930 1940 1950 — 1970 1960 1990 — 2000 2005 — Movement of North Magnetic Pole — Mackenzie King I. — Sverdrup Islands — Ellef Ringnes I. — Alpha Cordille

Fb N u n a v u t — Chesterfield Inlet — Boothia Peninsula — Prince of Wales Island 1920 1900 — Somerset Island — Axel Heiberg Island — Nansen Sound

06 05 70° 04 75° 03 85° 02 01

Fc Hudson — Rees Welcome Sound — Repulse Bay — Gulf of Boothia — Brodeur Peninsula — Devon Island — Jones Sound — Alert Point — Lancaster Sound — Ellesmere Island — Cape Discovery

Bay — Southampton Island — Melville Peninsula — Arctic Bay — Borden Peninsula — Cape Sherard — N a r e s S t r a i t — Lincoln Sea

Fd Coats Island — 352 — Byloit Island — Qaanaaq Thule — Humboldt Gletscher — Petermann Gletscher — Kap Morris Jesup — Peary Land

Ga Mansel Island — F o x e B a s i n — Prince Charles Island — B a f f i n B a y — Hayes Halvø — Knud Rasmussen Land

Gb P é n i n s u l e d ' U n g a v a — Foxe Peninsula — B a f f i n Basin — Melville Bugt — Kronprins Christian Land

Cape Christian — Cape Raper

Gc Ungava Bay — Hudson Strait — Hall Peninsula — Cumberland Sound — Cumberland Peninsula — Home Bay — 2907 — Upernavik — G r e e n l a n d — Kalaallit Nunaat — (DK) — Kong Frederik VIII Land — G r e e n l

Igaluit — Frobisher Bay — Cape Mercy — Disko — Qeqertarsuaq/ Godhavn — Droning Louise Land — Dove Bugt

Gd Hebron — Newfoundland and Labrador — 2595 — Cape Labrador — Sisimiut/Holsteinsborg — 64 — Disko Bugt — Ilulissat/Jakobshavn — Kangerlussuaq/Søndrestrømfjord — Maniitsoq/Sukkertoppen — Kong Christian IX Land — Scoresby Land — Ittoqqortoormiit/Scoresbysund — 3069

L a b r a d o r — Droning Ingrid Land — Arctic Circle — Scoresby Sound — Gree

Ha S e a — 3115 — Nuuk/Godthåb — Paamiut/Frederikshåb — Kong Christian IX Land

Ha 55° Hb 50° Hc 45° Hd 40° Ja 35° Jb 30° Jc 25° Jd 20° Ka 15° Kb 10° Kc 5°

4000 3000 2000 1000 500 250 100 0 Depression 0 200 2000 4000 6000 +8000

East Siberian Sea

Kolymskaja nizmennost'

Indigirka

Jano-Indigirskaja nizmennost'

Čerskij Range

2243

Janskoe ploskogor'e 2120

Verhojansk

Jakutsk

Amga

Aldanskoe nagor'e

Aldan

Cul'man

Olekma

Ra

120°

Qd

Asyma

Lena

pr.Dmitrija Laptev

o.Novaja Sibir'

o.Bol.Ljahovskij

pr.Sannikova

Janskij zaliv

Chrebet Kular

Jana

Halyt

Čočskij massiv 2081

Verhojanskij

Central'nojakutskaja ravnina

Njurba

Sakha

Olekminskoe

Lena

Qc

115°

New Siberian Islands

o.Kotel'nyj

Zigansk

Lena

Lensk

Qb

44

57

guba Buor-Haja

Lena Delta

Siktjah

Mirnyj

Vilujskoe vdhr.

110°

Olenëk

Olenëk

Nakanno

Central'no-Tunguskoe plato

Qa

Laptev Sea

Olenëkskij zaliv 35

Saskylah

Olenëk

Nižnaja Tunguska

105°

OCEAN

Hatangskij zaliv

m.Dika

Anabarskoe plato

Essej

Pd

100°

Taymyr Peninsula

oz. Tajmyr

Konji

RUSSIA

Central Siberian Plateau

Taymyr

Hatanga

Pc

95°

North Siberian Lowland

1701 plato Putorana

Putorancy

Nižnaja Tunguska

o.Bol.Vrangelja

ostrova Severnaja Zemlja

Byrranga

90°

01 85° 02 80° 03 75° 04 70° 05 65° 06

o.Oktjabr'skoj Revoljucii

o.Komsomolec

North Land

Noril'sk

Enisej Igarka

Turuhansk

Pb

Pjasinskij zaliv

Dikson

Enisejskij zaliv

Pa

85°

Gydanskij p-ov

Tazovskij p-ov

West Siberian Plain

80°

o.Rudol'fa

o.Greem-Bell

m.Želanija

o.Bely

Obskaja Guba

p-ov Jamal

Nižnevartovsk

Ob'

Od

Zemlja Georga

Zemlja Aleksandry

Franz Josef Land (RUST)

360

68

o.Belaja 1052 170

Kara Sea

Surgut

Oc

75°

5449

Kvitøya (N)

Karl's Land

Novaja Zemlja

pik Sedova 1515

1547 pik Sedova

proliv Karskie Vorota

Jugarskij p-ov

Hanty-Mansijsk

Ob'

Ob'

70°

Nordaustlandet

Olgastretet

Barentsøya

Kong Karls Land

Edgeøya

Mean Pack Ice Limit in Summer 63

Vorkuta

gora Pajer 1499

Inta

gora Narodnaja 1894

Tobol'sk

Ob

Spitsbergen

Prins Karls Forland

Hopen

Mean Pack Ice Limit in Winter

Pečorskoe more

Nar'jan-Mar

Pečora

gora Tel'pozis 1617

65°

Svalbard (N)

Bjørnøya (N)

o.Kolguev

p-ov Kanin

Bol'šezemel'skaja tundra

Pečora

Komi

Serov

gora Konžakovskij Kamen' 1569

YEKATERINBURG

URAL MOUNTAINS

910

225

m.Kanin Nos

Timanskij kriaž

Uhta

Solikamsk

Nd

60°

an Sea

North Cape

Hammerfest

Vadsø Vardø

Vaangsfjorden

Kirkenes

Murmansk

Kola Peninsula

Arctic Circle

Mezen'

Syktyvkar

PERM'

NORWAY

Alta

Scale 1:30,000,000

600 Kilometers
0 200 400

0 200 400 Miles

Ha 55°	Hb 50°	Hc 45°	Hd 40°	Ja 35°	Jb 30°	Jc 25°	Jd 20°	Ka

Ha

Scotia Sea
5100
5840

ATLANTIC OCEAN

Georg von Neumayer (D)
Druzhnaya III (RUS)
Kapp Norvegia
SANAE IV
Sarie Ma

60° / Gd

Drake Passage

Elephant Island

3846

Drescher (D)
Aboa (FIN)
Wasa (S)
Svea (S)

Riiser-Larsen Ice Shelf
Borgm

Hainel rionfhield

Aguirre Cerda (RCH)
1 Aguirre Cerda (RCH)
2 Arctowski (PL)
3 Artigas (ROU)
4 Bellingshausen (RUS)
5 C.A.Prat (RCH)
6 Com.Ferraz (BR)
7 Escudero (RCH)
8 Esperanza (RA)
9 Gral.B.O'Higgins (RCH)
10 Great Wall (CHN)
11 King Sejong (ROK)
12 Jubany (RA)
13 Marambio (RA)
14 Presidente Eduardo Frei (RCH)

King George I.
South Shetland Islands
Livingston I.
1-14
I.Joinville

Bransfield Strait

Hero Fracture Zone

65° / Gc

Matienzo (RA)
G.Gonzalez Videla (RCH)
Palmer Station (USA)
Faraday (UK)

Larsen Ice Shelf

Weddell Sea

Halley (UK)

Brunt Ice Shelf
Maudheim (D)

Coats Land

70° / Gb

Biscoe Islands

Antarctic Peninsula

Belgrano II (RA)

Shackleton Range
Filchner Ice Shelf

Rothers (UK)
San Martin (RA)
Mt.Jackson 4190
Fossil Bluff (UK)
Palmer Land

Filchner (D)

Druzhnaya II (RUS)

Recovery Glacier
Argentina Range

75° / Ga

Teniente Luis Carvajal (RCH)
Marguerite Bay
Alexander I.
Soyuz (RUS)

Mt.Edward 1637

Ronne Ice Shelf

Support Force Glacier
Pensacola Mountains

Carcot I.

Sky Blu (UK)

80° / Fd

5245

Bellingshausen Abyssal Plain

Latady I.
Ronne Bay

Behrendt Mts.

Evans Ice Stream
Korff Ice Rise
Fowler Ice Rise

Skytrain Ice Rise

Institute Ice Stream

A N

85° / Fc

Bellingshausen
Sea

Venable Ice Shelf

Bryant Coast

Ellsworth Land

Carlson Inlet

Haag Nunataks

4897
Ellsworth Mountains

Thiel Mts.

2812

31 65° | **32 70°** | **33 75°** | **34 80°** | **35 85°** | **36 So**

90° / Fb

De Gerlache Seamounts

Abbot Ice Shelf

Jones Mountains

1115

Horlick Mts. Queen Ma
Wisconsin Range
Ice Stream A

95° / Fa

South East Pacific Basin

Walker Mts.
Cape Palmer 1036

Hudson Mts.

Hollick-Kenyon Plateau 3022
Mt.Seelig

Mariearie Byrd Land

Ice Stream B

4830

Pine Island Glacier
Cape Flying Fish

Pine Island Bay

West - Antarctica

1920

Ice Stream C

Ice Stream A 406

100° / Ed

5226

Crosson Ice Shelf

Amundsen Sea

Mt.Takahe 3398
Mt.Frakes 3677
Cape Felt

Byrd (USA)

Rockefeller Plateau

Ice Stream D

Ice Stream E

Siple Coast

Ross

105° / Ec

PACIFIC

OCEAN

Mt.Sidley 4181
Mt.Petras 2675
Mt.Siple 3100

Getz Ice Shelf

Mt.Berlin 3498

Ford Ranges

Ice Stream E

Shirase Coast

Roosevelt Island
550

110° / Eb

Amundsen Ridge

Cape Dart
Wrigley Gulf
2000

Sulzberger Ice Shelf
Russkaya (RUS)

Nickerson Ice Shelf

Ford Ranges

Sulzberger Bay

Cape Colbeck

Bay of Whales

115° / Ea

Heezen Fracture Zone

Amundsen Abyssal Plain

4460

4260

3365

Ross Se

120° / Dd

3810
Antarctic Circle

4059

Dd 125°	Dc 130°	Db 135°	Da 140°	Cd 145°	Cc 150°	Cb 155°	Ca 160°	Bd 165°	Bc 170°	Bb 175°

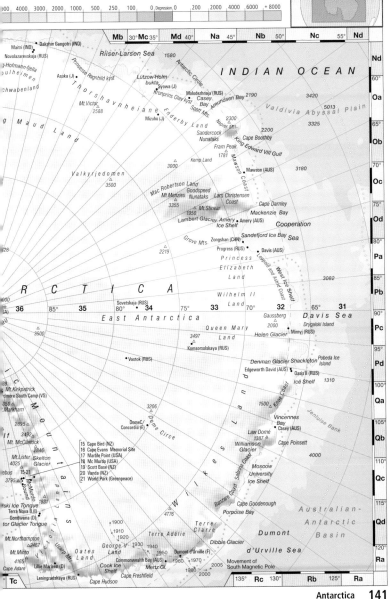

Our planet has experienced countless changes and transformations during its 4.5 billion year history. Natural climate shifts and the powerful forces of plate tectonics have repeatedly altered and continue to shape the topography, vegetation zones, and geology of the Earth.

The first human societies emerged around 10,000 years ago. Humanity has significantly altered the face of our planet in a relatively short period of time through agriculture and industrialization. Recent advances in technology have brought the many cultures of our planet closer together than ever before. Our world is now a global community with an incredible diversity of nations, cultures, religions, and ethnicities.

Scale 1:170,000,000

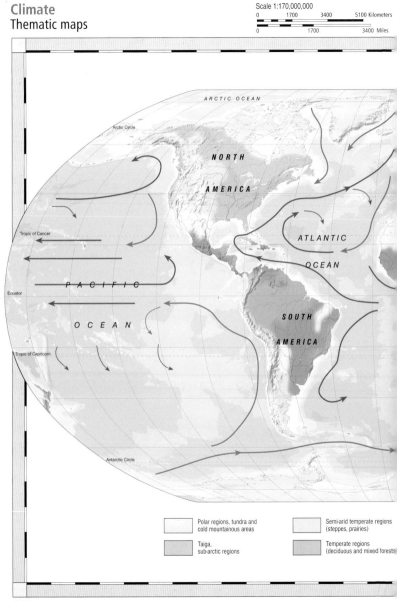

Polar regions, tundra and
cold mountainous areas

Taiga,
sub-arctic regions

Semi-arid temperate regions
(steppes, prairies)

Temperate regions
(deciduous and mixed forests)

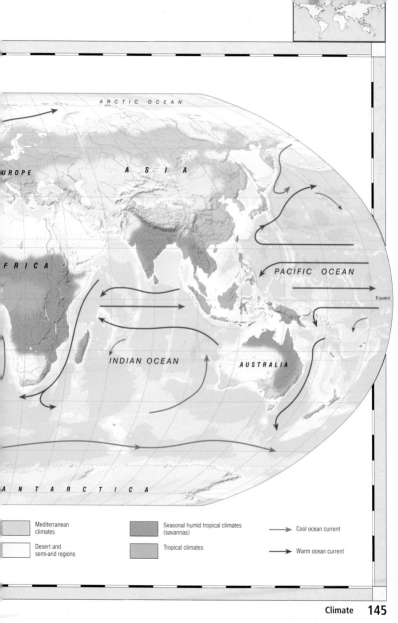

| | Mediterranean climates | | Seasonal humid tropical climates (savannas) | | → | Cool ocean current |
| | Desert and semi-arid regions | | Tropical climates | | → | Warm ocean current |

Vegetation
Thematic maps

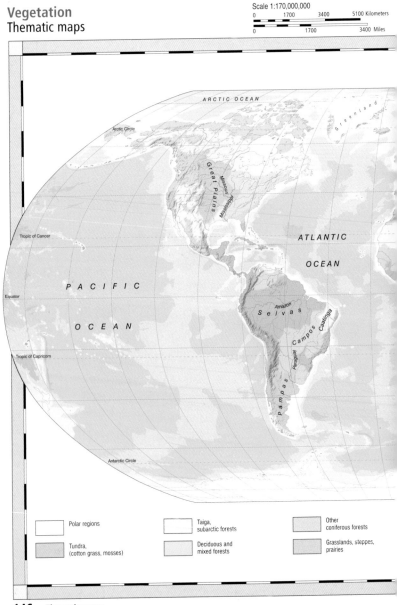

ARCTIC OCEAN

Greenland

Arctic Circle

Great Plains

Missouri

Mississippi

Tropic of Cancer

ATLANTIC

OCEAN

PACIFIC

Equator

Amazon
Selvas

OCEAN

Campos

Caatinga

Paraguai

Tropic of Capricorn

Pampas

Antarctic Circle

Polar regions	Taiga, subarctic forests	Other coniferous forests
Tundra, (cotton grass, mosses)	Deciduous and mixed forests	Grasslands, steppes, prairies

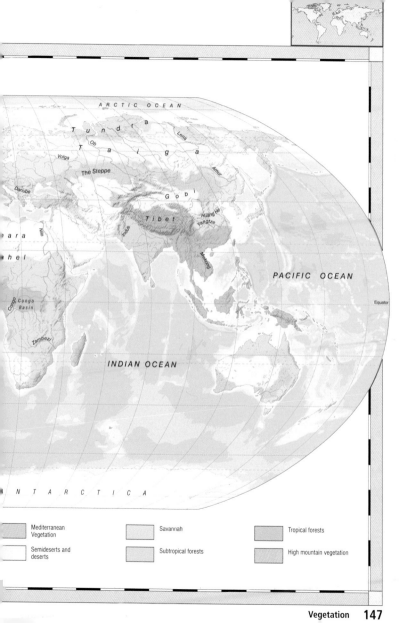

Mediterranean Vegetation

Semideserts and deserts

Savannah

Subtropical forests

Tropical forests

High mountain vegetation

Population density
Thematic maps

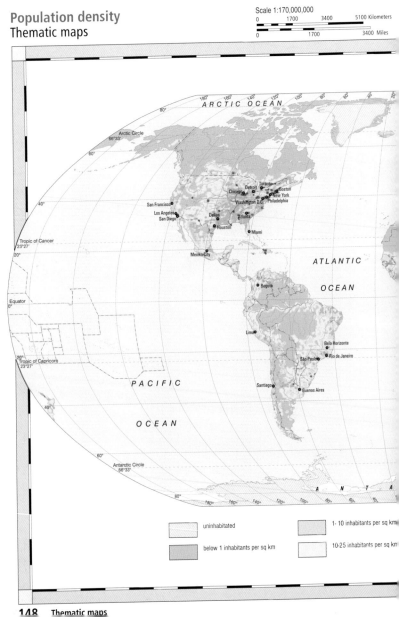

Scale 1:170,000,000

0	1700	3400	5100 Kilometers

0	1700	3400 Miles

ARCTIC OCEAN

Arctic Circle
66°33'

Tropic of Cancer
23°27'

Equator
0°

Tropic of Capricorn
23°27'

Antarctic Circle
66°33'

ATLANTIC OCEAN

PACIFIC OCEAN

San Francisco
Los Angeles
San Diego
Dallas
Houston
Chicago
Detroit
Toronto
Washington D.C.
Atlanta
Boston
New York
Philadelphia
Miami
Mexiko-City
Bogota
Lima
Belo Horizonte
São Paulo
Rio de Janeiro
Santiago
Buenos Aires

A N T A

	uninhabited		1- 10 inhabitants per sq km
	below 1 inhabitants per sq km		10-25 inhabitants per sq km

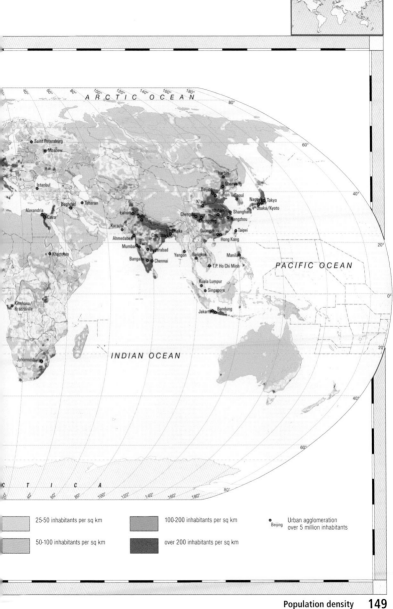

| | 25-50 inhabitants per sq km | | 100-200 inhabitants per sq km | | Urban agglomeration over 5 million inhabitants |
| | 50-100 inhabitants per sq km | | over 200 inhabitants per sq km | | |

Scale 1:170,000,000

| 0 | 1700 | 3400 | 5100 Kilometers |
| 0 | 1700 | | 3400 Miles |

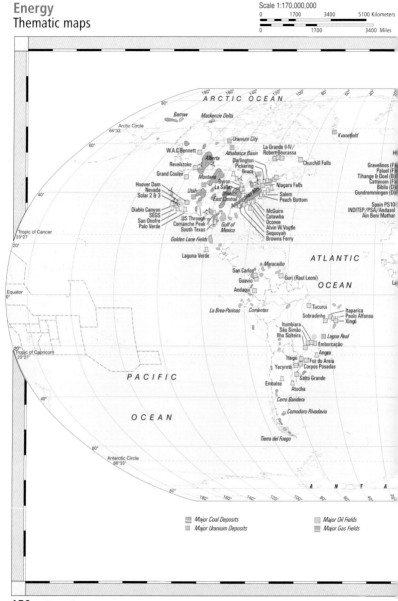

ARCTIC OCEAN

80°

Barrow

Mackenzie Delta

Arctic Circle
66°33'

60°

Uranium City

Kvanefield

W.A.C Bennett

Athabasca Basin

La Grande II-IV/
Robert-Bourassa

Churchill Falls

Gravelines (F)
Paluel (F)
Tihange & Doel (B)
Cattenom (F)
Biblis (D)
Gundremmingen (D)

Revelstoke

Grand Coulee

Alberta

Darlington
Pickering
Bruce

40°

Hoover Dam
Nevada
Solar 2 & 3

Montana

Byron
La Salle
Illinois
East Central

Niagara Falls

Salem
Peach Bottom

Spain PS10
INDITEP/PSA/Andasol
Ain Beni Mathar

Utah

Diablo Canyon
SEGS
San Onofre
Palo Verde

US Through
Comanche Peak
South Texas

Appalachian Mts.

Gulf of
Mexico

McGuire
Catawba
Oconee
Alvin W.Vogtle
Sequoyah
Browns Ferry

Tropic of Cancer
23°27'

20°

Golden Lane Fields

Laguna Verde

Maracaibo

ATLANTIC

San Carlos

Guri (Raul Leoni)

OCEAN

Le

Equator
0°

Guavio
Andaquí

La Brea-Parinas

Corrientes

Tucuruí

Itaparica
Paulo Affonso
Xingó

Sobradinho

Itumbiara
São Simão
Ilha Solteira

Lagoa Real

Emborcação

Tropic of Capricorn
23°27'

20°

PACIFIC

Itaipu
Yacyretá

Angra

Foz do Areia
Corpus Posadas

Salto Grande

Embalse

Atucha

40°

OCEAN

Cerro Bandera

Comodoro Rivadavia

60°

Tierra del Fuego

Antarctic Circle
66°33'

80°

A   N   T   A

180° 160° 140° 120° 100° 80° 60° 40°

| ▨ | Major Coal Deposits | | ▨ | Major Oil Fields |
| ▨ | Major Uranium Deposits | | ▨ | Major Gas Fields |

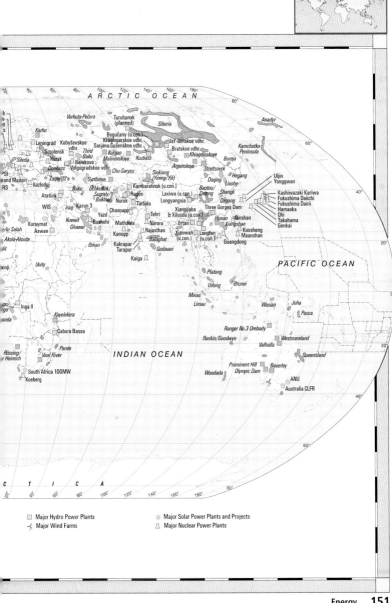

ARCTIC OCEAN

Karhu
Leningrad Kubyševskoe
         vdhr.
Smolensk Kursk Belekovo
Silesia Donbass
Kozlodu Zaporižž'a Volgogradskoe vdhr.
RS

Atatürk Aswan
WIS Iraq Karun 3
In Salah Kuraymat Kuwait Yazd Bushehr
Akola-Akouta

Vorkuta-Pečora Turuhansk
                (planned)
Krasnojarskoe vdhr.
Kungan Sarjano-Sušenskoe vdhr.
Baku Kurgan Kuzbass
Malinovskoye
Chu-Sarysu
Uchkuduk/ Kambaratinsk (u.con.)
Sugraly/ Syrdariya
Bukinei Ragun Laxiwa (u.con.)
Nurek Tarbela Longyangxia
Chasnupp Xiangjiaba
Mathania Tehri & Xiluodu (u.con.)
Narora Ertan
Kanupp Rajasthan Xiaowan (u.con.)
Kakrapar Balaghat Godavari
Tarapur
Kaiga

Siberia
Ust'-Ilimskoe vdhr.
Bratskoe vdhr. Khiagdinskoye
Arginskoye Streltsovsk
Sinkiang Daqing Liaohe
(Yining/Yili) Baotou/ Shengli
              Datong
Three Gorges Dam Daqang
Hunan Qinshan
Xiangshan
Langtan Kuosheng
(u.con.) Maanshan
Guangdong

Anadyr
Kamchatka
Peninsula
Bureja
Hegang
Uljin
Yonggwan
Kashiwazaki Kariwa
Fukushima Daiichi
Fukushima Daini
Hamaoka
Ohi
Takahama
Genkai

PACIFIC OCEAN

Oman Platong
Udang Brunei
Unity Minas Wasian Juha
       Limau Pasca
Inga II
go Ranger No.3 Orebody Westmoreland
go Rankin/Goodwyn Valhalla Queensland
anda Cabora Bassa
Rössing/ Pande
r Heinrich Vaal River Prominent Hill Beverley
South Africa 100MW Olympic Dam
Koeberg Woodada ANU
                    Australia CLFR

INDIAN OCEAN

☐ Major Hydro Power Plants   ● Major Solar Power Plants and Projects
⌐ Major Wind Farms   △ Major Nuclear Power Plants

There were 195 sovereign nations on six continents at the start of the 21st century. During the 20th century, the political makeup of our planet changed frequently and the borders of many nations were redrawn. Two world wars, the end of European colonialism, and the decline of communism lead to the creation and collapse of numerous nations and political entities.

Although most of Africa was under the control of European powers at the start of the 20th century, it is now the continent with the most states; 54. Asia is only slightly behind Africa with 47 states and is followed by Europe (44), North America (23), Australia/Oceania (14), and South America (12). Inhospitable Antarctica is the only "stateless" continent.

Nations of the World
Index of local country names

The local or indigenous name of a country often varies from its English name or designation. The following index lists the English-language names of all the world's nations, followd by their official local names in the second column.

English	International	Continent	Page
Afghanistan	Afghānistān	Asia	16
Albania	Shqipëria	Europe	16!
Algeria	Al-Ğazā´ir / Algérie	Africa	17●
Andorra	Andorra	Europe	16●
Angola	Angola	Africa	17●
Antigua and Barbuda	Antigua and Barbuda	Central America	18!
Argentina	Argentina	South America	18●
Armenia	Armenija (Hayastan)	Asia	16●
Australia	Australia	Australia	17●
Austria	Österreich	Europe	16●
Azerbaijan	Azerbajdzan	Asia	16●
Bahamas	Bahamas	Central America	18●
Bahrain	Al-Bahrain	Asia	16
Bangladesh	Bangladesh	Asia	16●
Barbados	Barbados	Central America	18●
Belarus	Belarus	Europe	16●
Belgium	België / Belgique	Europe	16●
Belize	Belize	Central America	18●
Benin	Benin	Africa	17
Bhutan	Bhutan	Asia	16
Bolivia	Bolivia	South America	18
Bosnia and Herzegowina	Bosna i Hercegovina	Europe	16●
Botswana	Botswana	Africa	17
Brazil	Brasil	South America	18
Brunei	Brunei	Asia	16●
Bulgaria	Bŭlgarija	Europe	16●
Burkina Faso	Burkina Faso	Africa	17
Burundi	Burundi	Africa	17
Cambodia	Kâmpŭchéa	Asia	16

ameroon	Cameroun / Cameroon	Africa	178
anada	Canada	North America	186
ape Verde	Cabo Verde	Africa	177
entral African Republic	République Centrafricaine	Africa	182
had	Tchad	Africa	184
hile	Chile	South America	190
hina	Zhongguo	Asia	174
olombia	Colombia	South America	190
omoros	Comores	Africa	178
ongo, Republic of the	Congo	Africa	178
ongo, Dem. Republic of the	Congo, République démocr.	Africa	178
osta Rica	Costa Rica	Central America	186
ôte d'Ivoire	Côte d'Ivoire	Africa	178
roatia	Hrvatska	Europe	162
uba	Cuba	Central America	186
yprus	Kypros / Kibris	Europe	162
zech Republic	Česká Republika	Europe	160
enmark	Danmark	Europe	161
jibouti	Djibouti	Africa	178
ominica	Dominica	Central America	186
ominican Republic	República Dominicana	Central America	188
ast Timor	Timor Leste	Asia	173
cuador	Ecuador	South America	190
cuatorial Guinea	Guinea Ecuatorial	Africa	179
gypt	Al-Miṣr / Egypt	Africa	176
l Salvador	El Salvador	Central America	186
ritrea	Eritrea	Africa	179
stonia	Eesti	Europe	161
thiopia	Îtyopya	Africa	180
iji	Fiji	Australia/Oceania	174
inland	Suomi / Finland	Europe	166
rance	France	Europe	162
abon	Gabon	Africa	179
ambia	Gambia	Africa	179
eorgia	Gruzija (Sakartvelo)	Asia	169

Nations of the World
Index of local country names

Germany	Deutschland	Europe	16
Ghana	Ghana	Africa	17
Greece	Elláda (Hellás)	Europe	16
Grenada	Grenada	Central America	18
Guatemala	Guatemala	Central America	18
Guinea	Guinée	Africa	17
Guinea-Bissau	Guinea-Bissau	Africa	17
Guyana	Guyana	South America	19
Haiti	Haïti	Central America	18
Honduras	Honduras	Central America	18
Hungary	Magyarország	Europe	16
Iceland	Ísland	Europe	16
India	India (Bhărat)	Asia	16
Indonesia	Indonesia	Asia	16
Iraq	'Īrāq	Asia	16
Iran	Îrân	Asia	16
Ireland	Éire/Ireland	Europe	16
Israel	Yisra'el	Asia	17
Italy	Italia	Europe	16
Jamaica	Jamaica	Central America	18
Japan	Nippon / Nihon	Asia	17
Jordan	Urdunn	Asia	17
Kazakhstan	Kazahstan	Asia	17
Kenya	Kenya	Africa	18
Kiribati	Kiribati	Australia/Oceania	17
Korea, North, Dem. Republic	Choson	Asia	16
Korea, South	Taehan-Min'guk	Asia	17
Kuwait	Al-Kuwait	Asia	16
Kyrgyzstan	Kyrgyzstan	Asia	17
Laos	Lao	Asia	17
Latvia	Latvija	Europe	16
Lebanon	Al-Lubnān	Asia	16
Lesotho	Lesotho	Africa	18
Liberia	Liberia	Africa	18
Libya	Lîbîyâ	Africa	18

Liechtenstein	Liechtenstein	Europe	163
Lithuania	Lietuva	Europe	163
Luxembourg	Luxembourg/Lëtzebuerg	Europe	163
Macedonia	Makedonija	Europe	163
Madagascar	Madagasíkara	Africa	181
Malawi	Malawi	Africa	181
Malaysia	Malaysia	Asia	170
Maledives	Maldives (Divehi Rajje)	Asia	170
Mali	Mali	Africa	181
Malta	Malta	Europe	163
Marshall Islands	Marshall Islands	Australia/Oceania	174
Mauritania	Mawrītāniyah	Africa	181
Mauritius	Mauritius	Africa	181
Mexico	México	Central America	187
Micronesia	Micronesia	Australia/Oceania	174
Moldova	Moldova	Europe	164
Monaco	Monaco	Europe	164
Mongolia	Mongol Ard Uls	Asia	170
Montenegro	Crna Gora	Europe	161
Morocco	Al-Maġrib/Maroc	Africa	176
Mozambique	Moçambique	Africa	181
Myanmar (Burma)	Myanmar	Asia	171
Namibia	Namibia	Africa	182
Nauru	Nauru (Naoero)	Australia/Oceania	174
Nepal	Nepal	Asia	171
Netherlands	Nederland	Europe	164
New Zealand	New Zealand	Australia/Oceania	175
Nicaragua	Nicaragua	Central America	188
Niger	Niger	Africa	182
Nigeria	Nigeria	Africa	182
Norway	Norge	Europe	164
Oman	Saltanat 'Umān	Asia	172
Pakistan	Pākistān	Asia	171
Palau	Palau	Australia/Oceania	175
Panama	Panamá	Central America	188

Nations of the World
Index of local country names

Papua New Guinea	Papua New Guinea	Australia/Oceania	175
Paraguay	Paraguay	South America	190
Peru	Perú	South America	191
Philippines	Pilipinas	Asia	171
Poland	Polska	Europe	164
Portugal	Portugal	Europe	164
Qatar	Qaṭar	Asia	171
Romania	România	Europe	165
Russia	Rossija	Europe	165
Rwanda	Rwanda	Africa	182
Saint Kitts and Nevis	Saint Kitts and Nevis	Central America	188
Saint Lucia	Saint Lucia	Central America	188
St. Vincent and the Grenadines	St. Vincent and the Grenadines	Central America	188
Samoa	Samoa	Australia/Oceania	175
San Marino	San Marino	Europe	165
Sao Tome and Principe	São Tomé e Príncipe	Africa	182
Saudi Arabia	Al-Mamlaka al-'Arabiya as-Sa'ūdiya	Asia	167
Senegal	Sénégal	Africa	183
Serbia	Srbija	Europe	165
Seychelles	Seychelles	Africa	183
Sierra Leone	Sierra Leone	Africa	183
Singapore	Singapore	Asia	172
Slovakia	Slovenská Republika	Europe	165
Slovenia	Slovenija	Europe	165
Solomon Islands	Solomon Islands	Australia/Oceania	175
Somalia	Soomaaliya	Africa	183
South Africa	South Africa/Suid-Afrika	Africa	183
Spain	España	Europe	161
Sri Lanka	Śrī Laṅkā	Asia	172
Sudan	As-Sūdān	Africa	177
Suriname	Suriname	South America	191
Swaziland	Swaziland (kaNgwane)	Africa	183
Sweden	Sverige	Europe	166
Switzerland	Suisse/Schweiz/Svizzera	Europe	166

ria	Suriya	Asia	172
iwan	Taiwan	Asia	173
jikistan	Tadžikistan	Asia	172
nzania	Tanzania	Africa	184
ailand	Muang Thai	Asia	170
go	Togo	Africa	184
nga	Tonga	Australia/Oceania	175
nidad and Tobago	Trinidad and Tobago	Central America	189
nisia	Tūnisiyah / Tunisie	Africa	184
rkey	Türkiye	Europe	166
rkmenistan	Turkmenistan	Asia	173
valu	Tuvalu	Australia/Oceania	176
ganda	Uganda	Africa	184
kraine	Ukrajina	Europe	166
ruguay	Uruguay	South America	191
zbekistan	Uzbekistan	Asia	173
anuatu	Vanuatu	Australia/Oceania	176
atican City	Città del Vaticano	Europe	160
enezuela	Venezuela	South America	191
etnam	Viêt-Nam	Asia	173
nited Arab Emirates	Daulat al-Imārāt al-'Arabiya Al-Muttahida	Asia	168
nited Kingdom of Great Britain and Northern Ireland	United Kingdom of Great Britain and Northern Ireland	Europe	166
nited States of America	United States of America	North America	189
Vestern Sahara	Al-Saharaw	Africa	176
emen	Al-Yaman	Asia	167
ambia	Zambia	Africa	184
imbabwe	Zimbabwe	Africa	185

Nations of the World
Europe

Andorra
Andorra

Location: Southwestern Europe
Area: 467.7 sq km
Highest Point:
Coma Pedrosa (2,946 m)
Capital: Andorra la Vella
Government:
Parliamentary principality
Administrative Divisions:
7 parishes
Population: 69,900
Ethnic Groups: Spaniards (50%),
Catalonians (29%), French (8%),
Portuguese (7%) Britons (2%)
Language:
Catalan (official), Spanish, French
Religion: Catholics (94%)
GDP per capita: 24,000 US$
Currency: 1 euro = 100 cents

Belarus
Belarus

Location: Eastern Europe
Area: 207,600 sq km
Important Rivers:
Dnjepr, Pripyat
Capital: Minsk
Government: Republic
Administrative Divisions:
6 regions and 1 special
municipality (Minsk)
Population: 10.3 million
Ethnic Groups:
Belarusians (78%), Russians (13%),
Poles (4%), Ukrainians (3%)
Language:
Belarusian (official), Russian
Religion:
Russian-Orthodox (60%),
Catholics (8%)
GDP per capita: 6,900 US$
Currency:
1 Belarusian ruble = 100 kopecks

België/Belgique
Belgium

Location: Western Europe
Area: 30,528 sq km
Important Rivers:
Schelde, Maas
Capital: Brussels
Government:
Parliamentary monarchy
Administrative Divisions:
3 regions and 10 provinces
Population: 10.3 million
Ethnic Groups:
Flemish (58%), Wallonian (32%)
Language:
French, Dutch, German
Religion: Catholic (88%)
GDP per capita: 31,400 US$
Currency: 1 euro = 100 cents

Bosna i Hercegovina
Bosnia and
Herzegovina

Location: Southeastern Europe
Area: 52,129 sq km
Capital: Sarajevo
Government: Republic
Population: 4 million
Language:
Bosnian, Serbian, Croatian
Religion:
Muslims (44%), Serbian-Orthodox
(31%), Catholics (17%)
GDP per capita: 6,100 US$
Currency: 1 mark = 100 fenings

Bălgarija
Bulgaria

Location: Southeastern Europe
Area: 110,910 sq km
Highest Point: Musala (2,925 m)
Important Rivers:
Danube, Iskar, Marica

Capital: Sofia
Government: Republic
Administrative Divisions:
8 regions, 1 district
Population: 7.5 million
Ethnic Groups:
Bulgarians (85%), Turks (9%),
Roma (3%), Macedonians (3%)
Language: Bulgarian
Religion:
Orthodox (87%), Muslims (13%)
GDP per capita: 7,600 US$
Currency: 1 lev = 100 stotinki

Česká Republika
Czech Republic

Location: Central Europe
Area: 78,866 sq km
Capital: Prague
Government: Republic
Administrative Divisions:
72 districts
Population: 10.2 million
Ethnic Groups:
Czechs (94%), Slovaks (4%)
Language: Czech, Slovak
Religion:
Catholics (28%), Protestants (3%),
atheist/non-religious (55%)
GDP per capita: 19,500 US$
Currency:
1 Czech koruna = 100 haleru

Città del Vaticano
Vatican City (Holy See)

Location:
Rome, Italy (Southern Europe)
Area: 0.44 sq km
Capital: Vatican City
Government: Elected monarchy
Population: 920
Language: Latin, Italian
Religion: Catholic (100%)
Currency: 1 euro = 100 cents

rna Gora
Montenegro

Location: Southeastern Europe
Area: 13,812 sq km
Capital: Podgorica
Government: Republic
Population: 620,000
Ethnic Groups:
Serbs and Montenegrins (75%),
Bosniaks (8%), Albanians (5%)
Language: Serbian, Albanian
Religion: Orthodox Christians (74%),
Muslims (18%)
GDP per capita: 3,800 US$
Currency: 1 euro = 100 cents

Danmark
Denmark

Location: Northern Europe
Area: 43,094 sq km;
Greenland 2.1 million sq km
Capital: Copenhagen
Government:
Parliamentary monarchy
Administrative Divisions:
14 districts
External Territories:
Faeroes, Greenland
Population: 5.4 million
Language: Danish
Religion: Lutherans (83%)
GDP per capita: 31,200 US$
Currency: 1 krone = 100 Øre

Deutschland
Germany

Location:
Western/Central Europe
Area: 357,021 sq km
Highest Point:
Zugspitze (2,962 m)
Important Rivers: Müritz, Elbe,
Oder, Rhine, Danube

Capital: Berlin
Government: Federal republic
Administrative Divisions:
16 federal states
Population: 82.4 million
Ethnic Groups: Germans (91%),
Turks (2%), Yugoslavs (1%)
Language: German
Religion:
Catholics (34%), Protestants (34%),
Muslims (3.5%)
GDP per capita: 30,500 US$
Currency: 1 euro = 100 cents

Eesti
Estonia

Location: Northeastern Europe
Area: 45,226 sq km
Capital: Tallinn
Government:
Parliamentary republic
Administrative Divisions:
15 regions, 6 districts
Population: 1.3 million
Ethnic Groups:
Estonians (65%), Russians (28%),
Ukrainians (2%), Belarusians (1%),
Finns (1%)
Language:
Estonian (official), Russian
Religion: Lutherans (15%),
Orthodox Christians (14%)
GDP per capita: 16,700 US$
Currency:
1 Estonian krona = 100 senti

Éire/Ireland
Ireland

Location: Western Europe
Area: 70,280 sq km
Important River: Shannon
Capital: Dublin
Government:
Parliamentary republic

Administrative Divisions:
26 counties
Population: 4 million
Language: English, Irish (Gaelic)
Religion:
Catholics (88%), Anglicans (3%)
GDP per capita: 41,000 US$
Currency: 1 euro = 100 cents

Ellás (Hellás)
Greece

Location: Southeastern Europe
Area: 131,940 sq km
Highest Point:
Mt. Olympus (2,917 m)
Capital: Athens
Government:
Parliamentary republic
Administrative Divisions:
10 regions
Population: 10.6 million
Ethnic Groups:
Greeks (96%), Macedonians (4%)
Language: Greek
Religion: Greek-Orthodox (97%),
Muslims (1%)
GDP per capita: 22,200 US$
Currency: 1 euro = 100 cents

España
Spain

Location:
Southwestern Europe
Area: 504,782 sq km
Highest Point:
Pico del Teide (3,718 m)
Important Rivers:
Guadiana, Ebro, Guadalquivir
Capital: Madrid
Government:
Parliamentary monarchy
Administrative Divisions:
17 regions, 52 provinces
Population: 44.3 million

Nations of the World
Europe

Ethnic Groups: Spanish (73%),
Catalonian (18%), Galician (6%),
Basques (2%)
Language: Spanish (Castilian),
Catalan, Basque, Galician
Religion: Catholics (96%)
GDP per capita: 25,500 US$
Currency: 1 euro = 100 cents

France
France

Location: Western Europe
Area: 547,030 sq km
Highest Point:
Mont Blanc (4,808 m)
Important Rivers:
Loire, Rhône, Seine, Garonne
Capital: Paris
Government:
Parliamentary republic
Administrative Divisions:
22 regions, 96 departments,
9 territories
External Territories:
French Guiana, Guadeloupe,
Martinique, Réunion, Mayotte,
Saint Pierre and Miquelon, French
Polynesia, New Caledonia, Wallis
and Futuna
Population: 60.4 million
Ethnic Groups: French (94%),
North Africans (2%)
Language: French
Religion: Catholics (80%),
Protestants (2%), Muslims (5%)
GDP per capita: 29,900 US$
Currency: 1 euro = 100 cents

Hrvatska
Croatia

Location: Southeastern Europe
Area: 56,542 sq km
Capital: Zagreb
Government: Republic

Administrative Divisions:
20 regions, 2 districts
Population: 4.5 million
Language: Croatian
Religion:
Catholics (77%), Orthodox (11%),
Protestants (1%), Muslims (1%)
GDP per capita: 10,700 US$
Currency: 1 kuna = 100 lipa

Ísland
Iceland

Location:
Northern Europe
Area: 103,000 sq km
Highest Point:
Oraefajökull (2,119 m)
Important Body of Water:
Lake Myvatn
Capital: Reykjavik
Government: Republic
Administrative Divisions:
8 regions
Population: 294,000
Ethnic Groups:
Icelandic (94%), Danish (1%)
Language: Icelandic
Religion: Protestants (94%),
Catholics (1%)
GDP per capita: 30,900 US$
Currency:
1 Icelandic krone = 100 aurar

Italia
Italy

Location: Southern Europe
Area: 301,230 sq km
Highest Point:
Monte Bianco (4,808 m)
Important Rivers/Bodies of Water:
Po, Arno, Tiber, Lago di Garda,
Lago di Como
Capital: Rome
Government: Republic

Administrative Divisions:
20 regions, 95 provinces
Population: 58 million
Ethnic Groups: Italians, including
regional minorities (96%)
Language: Italian
Religion: Catholics (85%)
GDP per capita: 29,200 US$
Currency: 1 euro = 100 cents

Kypros/Kibris
Cyprus

Location: Southeastern Europe
Area: 9,250 sq km
Highest Point: Troodos (1,953 m)
Capital: Nicosia
Government: Republic
Administrative Divisions:
6 districts
Population: 776,000
Ethnic Groups:
Greeks (85%), Turks (13%)
Language:
Greek, Turkish, English
Religion:
Orthodox (80%), Muslims (19%)
GDP per capita: 21,000 US$
(figure for the south only)
Currency:
1 Cypriot pound = 100 cents

Latvija
Latvia

Location: Northeastern Europe
Area: 64,589 sq km
Capital: Riga
Government: Republic
Administrative Divisions:
33 districts
Population: 2.3 million
Ethnic Groups:
Latvians (58%), Russians (30%),
Belarussians (4%), Poles (2.5%)
Language: Latvian, Russian

ligion: Lutherans (55%), Catholics
4%), Russian Orthodox (10%)
P per capita: 13,200 US$
rrency: 1 lats = 100 santims

echtenstein
echtenstein

cation: Central Europe
ea: 160 sq km
ghest Point:
auspitze (2,599 m)
pital: Vaduz
overnment:
rliamentary monarchy
dministrative Divisions:
municipalities
pulation: 33,400
hnic Groups:
echtensteiners (63%), Swiss (16%),
ustrians (8%), Germans (4%)
anguage: German
eligion: Catholics (83%),
otestants (7%)
DP per capita: 25,000 US$
urrency:
Swiss franc = 100 rappen

etuva
thuania

ocation: Northeastern Europe
rea: 65,200 sq km
apital: Vilnius
overnment:
rliamentary republic
dministrative Divisions:
) districts
opulation: 3.6 million
thnic Groups: Lithuanians (80%),
ussians (9%), Poles (7%), Bela-
ssians (2%), Ukrainians (1%)
anguage: Lithuanian, Russian
eligion: Catholics (80%)
DP per capita: 13,700 US$
urrency: 1 litas = 100 centas

Luxembourg/
Lëtzebuerg
Luxembourg

Location: Central Europe
Area: 2,586 sq km
Highest Point:
Eisling (562 m)
Important Rivers:
Sauer, Moselle
Capital: Luxembourg
Government:
Constitutional monarchy
Administrative Divisions:
12 cantons
Population: 462,700
Ethnic Groups:
Luxembourgers (73%),
Portuguese (9%), Italians (5%)
Language:
Letzebuergisch, French, German
Religion:
Catholics (95%), Protestants (1%)
GDP per capita: 55,100 US$
Currency: 1 euro = 100 cents

Magyarország
Hungary

Location: Central Europe
Area: 93,030 sq km
Important River/Body of Water:
Danube, Lake Balaton
Capital: Budapest
Government:
Parliamentary republic
Administrative Divisions:
20 districts
Population: 10 million
Ethnic Groups:
Hungarians (97%), Germans (2%),
Slovaks (1%)
Language: Hungarian
Religion:
Catholics (64%), Protestants (24%),
Orthodox (3%)

GDP per capita: 13,900 US$
Currency: 1 forint = 100 filler

Makedonija
Macedonia

Location:
Southeastern Europe
Area: 25,333 sq km
Capital: Skopje
Government: Republic
Administrative Divisions:
38 districts
Population: 2 million
Ethnic Groups:
Macedonian-Style (67%),
Albanian (20%), Turks (5%),
Serbians (3%), Roma (2%)
Language: Macedonian, Albanian,
Turkish, Serbian
Religion:
Macedonian-Orthodox (>50%),
Muslim (<20%)
GDP per capita: 6,700 US$
Currency:
1 Macedonian denar = 100 deni

Malta
Malta

Location:
Southeastern Europe
Area: 316 sq km
Capital: Valletta
Government: Republic
Administrative Divisions:
6 districts
Population: 397,000
Ethnic Groups:
Maltese (96%), British (2%)
Language: Maltese (Semetic
language), English, Italian
Religion: Catholics (95%),
Anglicans (11%)
GDP per capita: 17,700 US$
Currency: 1 lira = 100 cents

Nations of the World
Europe

Moldova
Moldova

Location: Southeastern Europe
Area: 33,700 sq km
Capital: Chisinau
Government: Republic
Administrative Divisions:
40 districts, 10 urban districts
Population: 4.4 million
Ethnic Groups:
Moldavans (65%), Ukrainians (14%),
Russians (13%)
Language:
Moldavan-Romanian, Russian
Religion: Orthodox (60%),
Jewish (1.5%)
GDP per capita: 1,800 US$
Currency: 1 leu = 100 bani

Monaco
Monaco

Location: Western Europe
Area: 1.95 sq km
Capital: Monaco-Ville
Government: Principality
Population: 32,300
Ethnic Groups: Monegasque (19%),
French (47%), Italian (17%), Britons
(4%), Germans (2%)
Language:
French, Monegasque, Italian
Religion: Catholics (90%),
Protestants (6%), Jewish (1%)
GDP per capita: 27,000 US$
Currency: 1 euro = 100 cents

Nederland
The Netherlands
(Holland)

Location: Western Europe
Area: 41,526 sq km
Important River/Body of Water:
Rhine, Ijssellmeer
Capital: Amsterdam (official),
The Hague (de facto)
Government:
Parliamentary monarchy
Administrative Divisions:
12 provinces, 2 external territories
Population: 16.3 million
Ethnic Groups:
Dutch (96%), Turks (2%)
Language: Dutch, Frisian
Religion: Catholics (34%),
Protestants (25%), Muslims (3%)
GDP per capita: 30,500 US$
Currency: 1 euro = 100 cents

Norge
Norway

Location: Northern Europe
Area: 324,220 sq km
Highest Point:
Galdhoppigen (2,470 m)
Capital: Oslo
Government:
Parliamentary monarchy
Administrative Divisions:
19 provinces
External Territories:
Svalbard, Jan Mayen, Bouvet Island,
Peter L. Island
Population: 4.6 million
Ethnic Groups: Norwegians (97%),
Sami/Lapps (1%)
Language: Norwegian, Sami
Religion: Lutheran (88%)
GDP per capita: 42,300 US$
Currency:
1 Norwegian krona = 100 Øre

Österreich
Austria

Location: Central Europe
Area: 83,870 sq km
Highest Point:
Großglockner (3,797 m)
Important River/Body of Water:
Danube, Lake Neusiedler
Capital: Vienna
Government: Federal republic
Administrative Divisions:
9 federal states
Population: 8,2 million
Language: German
Religion: Catholics (85%),
Protestants (6%)
GDP per capita: 32,700 US$
Currency: 1 euro = 100 cents

Polska
Poland

Location: Northeastern Europe
Area: 312,685 sq km
Important River: Oder
Capital: Warsaw
Government: Republic
Administrative Divisions:
49 provinces
Population: 38.6 million
Language: Polish
Religion:
Catholics (94%), Orthodox (2%)
GDP per capita: 13,300 US$
Currency: 1 zloty = 100 groszy

Portugal
Portugal

Location:
Southwestern Europe
Area: 92,391 sq km
Highest Point:
Serra da Estrela (1,991 m)
Important Rivers/Body of Water:
Tejo, Douro, Guadiana
Capital: Lisbon
Government: Republic
Administrative Divisions:
18 districts, 2 autonomous regions
Population: 10.5 million
Language: Portuguese

Religion: Catholics (95%),
Protestants (1%)
GDP per capita: 19,300 US$
Currency:
1 euro = 100 cents

România
Romania

Location:
Southeastern Europe
Area: 237,500 sq km
Highest Point:
Moldoveanu (2,543 m)
Important River: Danube
Capital: Bucharest
Government: Republic
Administrative Divisions:
41 districts
Population: 22.4 million
Ethnic Groups:
Romanians (78%), Hungarians (11%),
Roma (10%)
Language:
Romanian, Hungarian, German
Religion: Romanian Orthodox
(70%), Greek Orthodox (10 %)
GDP per capita: 6,900 US$
Currency: 1 leu = 100 bani

Rossija
Russia

Location:
Eastern Europe/Northern Asia
Area: 17,075,200 sq km
Highest Point: Elbrus (5,642 m)
Important Rivers/Bodies of Water:
Volga, Lena, Yenisey, Caspian Sea,
Baikal
Capital: Moscow
Government:
Presidential federation
Administrative Divisions:
47 districts, 89 territories
Population: 143.7 million

Ethnic Groups: Russians (82%),
Tatars (4%), Ukrainians (3%)
Language:
Russian, minority languages
Religion: Russian Orthodox,
Catholics, Protestants, Armenian
Orthodox, Muslims
GDP per capita: 11,100 US$
Currency:
1 rouble = 100 kopecks

San Marino
San Marino

Location: Southern Europe
Area: 61.2 sq km
Highest Point:
Monte Titano (743 m)
Capital: San Marino Città
Government: Republic
Administrative Divisions:
6 castelli
Population: 28,500
Ethnic Groups:
Sanmarinese (80%), Italian (18%)
Language: Italian
Religion: Catholic (95%)
GDP per capita: 34,600 US$
Currency: 1 euro = 100 cents

Shqipëria
Albania

Location: Southeastern Europe
Area: 28,748 sq km
Highest Point: Korab (2,753 m)
Capital: Tirana
Government: Republic
Administrative Divisions:
27 districts
Population: 3.5 milllion
Ethnic Groups:
Albanians (98%), Greeks (2%)
Language: Albanian
Religion: Muslims (65%),
Orthodox (22%), Catholic (13%)

GDP per capita: 8,200 US$
Currency: 1 lek = 100 quindarka

Slovenija
Slovenia

Location: Central Europe
Area: 20,273 sq km
Capital: Ljubljana
Government: Republic
Population: 2 million
Ethnic Groups: Slovenians (90%),
Croats (3%), Serbs (2%)
Language: Slovene
Religion:
Catholics (90%), Muslims (1%)
GDP per capita: 21,600 US$
Currency: 1 tolar = 100 stotin

Slovenská Republika
Slovakia

Location: Central Europe
Area: 48,845 sq km
Highest Point: Gerlach (2,655 m)
Capital: Bratislava
Government: Republic
Population: 5.4 million
Ethnic Groups: Slovaks (87%),
Hungarians (11%), Czechs (1%)
Language: Slovak (official),
Hungarian, Czech
Religion: Catholics (64%),
Protestants (8%)
GDP per capita: 16,100 US$
Currency:
1 Slovak koruna = 100 hellers

Srbija
Serbia

Location: Southeastern Europe
Area: 88,361 sq km
Capital: Belgrade
Government: Federal republic
Population: 10.2 million

Nations of the World
Europe

Ethnic Groups: Serbs (66%), Albanians (17%), others (17%)
Language: Serbian (official)
Religion: Orthodox (65%), Muslims (22%), Catholic (4%)
GDP per capita: 4,400 US$
Currency: 1 new dinar = 100 para

Schweiz/Suisse Svizzera/Svizra
Switzerland

Location: Central Europe
Area: 41,290 sq km
Highest Point: Monte Rosa (4,637 m)
Important Rivers: Rhine, Rhone
Capital: Bern
Government: Parliementary confederation
Administrative Divisions: 26 cantons
Population: 7.3 million
Ethnic Groups: Swiss (84%), Italians (6%), Spaniards (2%) Germans (2%)
Language: German, French, Italian, Romansh
Religion: Catholics (47%), Protestants (43%), Muslims (1%)
GDP per capita: 32,800 US$
Currency: 1 Swiss franc = 100 centimes

Suomi/Finland
Finland

Location: Northern Europe
Area: 337,031 sq km
Capital: Helsinki
Government: Republic
Administrative Divisions: 5 provinces, 1 autonomous region
Population: 5.2 million
Ethnic Groups: Finns (93%), Swedes (6%), Sami

Language: Finnish, Swedish, Russian, Sami
Religion: Lutheran (98%), Orthodox (1%)
GDP per capita: 30,900 US$
Currency: 1 euro = 100 cents

Sverige
Sweden

Location: Northern Europe
Area: 449,964 sq km
Highest Point: Kebnekaise (2,111 m)
Important Lakes: Vänern, Vättern
Capital: Stockholm
Government: Constitutional monarchy
Administrative Divisions: 24 districts
Population: 9 million
Ethnic Groups: Swedes (91%), Finns (3%), Sami/Lapps (2%)
Language: Swedish, Finnish, Sami
Religion: Lutheran (78%),
GDP per capita: 29,800 US$
Currency: 1 Swedish krona = 100 Ore

Türkiye
Turkey

Location: Southeastern Europe
Area: 780,580 sq km
Highest Point: Ararat (5,156 m)
Capital: Ankara
Government: Republic
Administrative Divisions: 74 provinces
Population: 68.9 million
Ethnic Groups: Turks (70%), Kurdish (20%), Arabs (2%)
Language: Turkish, Kurdish

Religion: Muslim (99%), Christians and Jews (0.2%)
GDP per capita: 8,200 US$
Currency: 1 Turkish lira =100 kurus

Ukrajina
Ukraine

Location: Eastern Europe
Area: 603,700 sq km
Important River: Dnepr
Capital: Kiev
Government: Republic
Administrative Divisions: 25 regions, autonomous region Crimea
Population: 47.7 million
Ethnic Groups: Ukrainians (72%), Russians (22%)
Language: Ukrainian, Russian
Religion: Orthodox, Catholics (10%)
GDP per capita: 5,300 US$
Currency: 1 hryvnia = 100 kopiyok

United Kingdom of Great Britain and Northern Ireland
United Kingdom of Great Britain and Northern Ireland

Location: Western Europe
Area: 244,820 sq km
Highest Point: Ben Nevis (1,344 m)
Important Rivers: Thames, Severn
Capital: London
Government: Constitutional monarchy
Administrative Divisions: 76 boroughs, 36 counties, 66 cities, numerous royal boroughs and districts

External Territories: Channel Islands, Isle of Man, Anguilla, Bermuda, British Virgin Islands, Falkland Islands, Gibraltar, Cayman Islands, Montserrat, Pitcairn, St. Helena, Turks and Caicos, South Georgia and Sandwich Islands
Population: 60.2 million
Ethnic Groups: English (80%), Scots (10%), Irish (3%), Welsh (2%), South Asians (2%), African/Afro-Caribbean (1.5%)
Language:
English, Welsh, Scottish Gaelic, Scots
Religion:
Anglican (57%), Catholic (13%), Presbyterians (7%)
GDP per capita: 30,300 US$
Currency:
1 Pound Sterling = 100 Pence

Asia

Afghānistān
Afghanistan

Location:
Western Asia
Area: 647,500 sq km
Highest Point:
Tirich Mir (7,699 m)
Capital: Kabul
Government: Islamic republic
Administrative Divisions:
31 provinces
Population: 31 million
Ethnic Groups:
Pashtun (40%), Tajiks (25%), Hazara (15%), Uzbeks (5%)
Language: Pashtu, Dari
Religion:
Sunnis (84%), Shiites (15%)
GDP per capita: 800 US$
Currency: 1 afghani = 100 puls

Al-Bahrain
Bahrain

Location: Middle East
Area: 665 sq km
Capital: Al-Manama
Government: Emirate
Population: 699,000
Ethnic Groups: Bahraini (64%), other Arabs (27%), Indians (6%), Pakistani (2%), Westerners (1%)
Language: Arabic
Religion:
Sunnis (59%), Shiites (31%)
GDP per capita: 23,000 US$
Currency: 1 dinar = 100 fils

Al-Kuwait
Kuwait

Location: Middle East
Area: 17,820 sq km
Capital: Kuwait City
Government: Emirate
Administrative Divisions:
5 provinces
Population: 2.4 million
Ethnic Groups:
Kuwaiti (38%), foreigners including Indians and Egyptians (62%)
Language: Arabic
Religion:
Sunnis (66%), Shiites (29%)
GDP per capita: 19,200 US$
Currency:
1 dinar = 100 dirham = 1,000 fils

Al-Lubnān
Lebanon

Location:
Middle East
Area: 10,452 sq km
Highest Point: Lebanon
Capital: Beirut
Government: Republic

Administrative Divisions:
5 provinces
Population: 3.8 million
Ethnic Groups: Lebanese (90%), Palestinians (10%)
Language: Arabic, French
Religion:
Muslims (60%), Christians (40%)
GDP per capita: 6,200 US$
Currency:
1 Lebanese pound = 100 piaster

**Al-Mamlaka
al-'Arabiya
as-Sa'ūdiya**
Saudi Arabia

Location: Middle East
Area: 1,960,582 sq km
Highest Point: Asir (3,133 m)
Capital: Riyadh
Government: Islamic monarchy
Administrative Divisions:
13 regions
Population: 27 million
Ethnic Groups: Saudis, Foreigners; mostly guest workers (27%)
Language: Arabic
Religion: Muslims (98%)
GDP per capita: 12,800 US$
Currency:
1 Saudi riyal = 20 quirshes

Al-Yaman
Yemen

Location: Middle East
Area: 527,970 sq km
Highest Point:
Nabi Shuai (3,760 m)
Capital: Sana'a
Government: Republic
Administrative Divisions:
17 provinces
Population: 21,5 million
Language: Arabic, English

Nations of the World
Asia

Religion: Muslims (99%)
GDP per capita: 900 US$
Currency:
1 Yemeni-real = 100 fils

Armenija (Hayastan)
Armenia

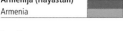

Location:
Western Asia
Area: 29,800 sq km
Capital: Yerevan
Government: Republic
Administrative Divisions:
37 districts
Population: 3 million
Ethnic Groups:
Armenians (93%), Azerbaijanis (3%),
Russians (2%)
Language: Armenian, Russian
Religion:
Armenian Apostolic (95%)
GDP per capita: 4,500 US$
Currency: 1 dram = 100 luma

Azerbajdzan
Azerbaijan

Location:
Middle East
Area: 86,600 sq km
Capital: Baku
Government: Republic
Administrative Divisions:
54 districts, 9 cities,
2 autonomous regions
Population: 7.9 million
Ethnic Groups:
Azerbaijanis (85%), Russians (4%),
Armenians (2%)
Language:
Azeri, Turkish, Russian
Religion:
Sunnis (59%), Shiites (31%)
GDP per capita: 4,800 US$
Currency: 1 manat = 100 gepik

Bangladesh
Bangladesh

Location:
Southeast Asia
Area: 144,000 sq km
Important Rivers:
Ganges, Brahmaputra
Capital: Dhaka
Government: Republic
Administrative Divisions:
4 provinces
Population: 147 million
Ethnic Groups:
Bengalis (95%), Bihari (1%)
Language: Bengali, Urdu, Hindi
Religion:
Muslims (87%), Hindus (12%)
GDP per capita: 2,100 US$
Currency:
1 taka = 100 poisha

Bhutan
Bhutan

Location:
South Asia
Area: 47,000 sq km
Highest Point:
Jomo Lhari (7,314 m)
Capital: Thimphu
Government:
Constitutional monarchy
Administrative Divisions:
18 districts
Population: 2.2 million
Ethnic Groups:
Bhutanese (72%), Nepalese and
other South Asians
Language:
Dzongkha, Tibetan dialects
Religion:
Buddhist (72%), Hindus, Muslims
GDP per capita: 1,400 US$
Currency:
1 ngultrum = 100 chetrum

Brunei
Brunei

Location: Southeast Asia
Area: 5,765 sq km
Capital: Bandar Seri Begawan
Government: Sultanate
Administrative Divisions:
4 districts
Population: 379,000
Ethnic Groups:
Malays (67%), Chinese (16%)
Language: Malay, English
Religion: Muslims (67%),
Buddhist (12%), Christian (10%)
GDP per capita: 23,600 US$
Currency:
1 Brunei dollar = 100 cents

Choson
Democratic Republic
of Korea (North Korea)

Location: East Asia
Area: 120,538 sq km
Capital: Pyongyang
Government:
Authoritarian socialism
Administrative Divisions:
9 provinces, 4 special cities
Population: 23.1 million
Language: Korean
Religion:
Atheists (68%), Buddhist and
Confucianist minoritites
GDP per capita: 1,700 US$
Currency: 1 won = 100 chon

Daulat al-Imārāt
al-'Arabiya
Al-Muttahida
United Arab Emirates

Location: Middle East
Area: 82,880 sq km
Highest Point: Jabal-Sham (3,017 m)

apital: Abu Dhabi
overnment:
onfederation of emirates
dministrative Divisions:
emirates
opulation: 2.6 million
thnic Groups:
abs (70%), foreign guest workers
rimarily South Asians)
anguage: Arabic
eligion:
nnis (81%), Shiites (15%)
DP per capita: 43,400 US$
urrency: 1 dirham = 100 fils

ruzija (Sakartvelo)
eorgia

ocation: Western Asia
rea: 69,700 sq km
ighest Point:
t'a Shkhara (5,201 sq km)
apital: Tbilisi
overnment: Republic
dministrative Divisions:
9 districts and cities,
 autonomous regions
opulation: 4.7 million
thnic Groups:
eorgians (71%), Armenians (8%),
zerbaijanis (5%), Russians (5%)
anguage:
eorgian, Russian, Armenian
eligion:
rthodox (65%), Muslims (11%)
DP per capita: 3,300 US$
urrency: 1 lari = 100 tetri

ndia (Bhārat)
ndia

ocation: South Asia
rea: 3,287,263 sq km
ighest Point:
anda Devi (7,817 m)
mportant Rivers: Indus, Ganges

Capital: New Delhi
Government: Republic
Administrative Divisions:
25 states, 7 territories
Population: 1.095 billion
Language: Hindi, English and
21 other official languages
Religion:
Hindus (80%), Muslims (11%)
GDP per capita: 3,300 US$
Currency: 1 rupee = 100 paisa

Indonesia
Indonesia

Location:
Southeast Asia
Area: 1,919,440 sq km
Capital: Jakarta
Government: Republic
Administrative Divisions:
27 provinces, 3 special regions
Population: 245.4 million
Ethnic Groups:
Javanese (40%), Sundanese (15%),
Madurese (7%), Others (>25%)
Language:
Indonesian, Javanese
Religion:
Muslims (87%), Christians (10%),
Hindus (2%), Buddhists (1%)
GDP per capita: 3,600 US$
Currency: 1 rupiah = 100 dinar

Îrân
Iran

Location: Middle East
Area: 1,648,000 sq km
Highest Point:
Damavand (5,671 m)
Capital: Tehran
Government: Islamic republic
Administrative Divisions:
25 provinces
Population: 68 million

Ethnic Groups:
Persians (50%), Azerbaijanis (20%),
Kurds (8%), Lur (10%), Arabs (2%),
Turkmen (2%)
Language: Persian, Lur, Kurdish
Religion:
Shiites (90%), Sunnis (8%)
GDP per capita: 8,300 US$
Currency: 1 rial = 100 dinar

'Îrāq
Iraq

Location: Middle East
Area: 437,072 sq km
Important Rivers:
Euphrates, Tigris
Capital: Baghdad
Government:
Transitional government
Administrative Divisions:
18 provinces
Population: 26.7 million
Ethnic Groups:
Arabs (80%), Kurds (15%), Turkmen,
Armenians
Language: Arabic
Religion:
Shiites (65%), Sunnis (32%)
GDP per capita: 3,400 US$
Currency: 1 Iraqi dinar = 1,000 fils

Kâmpǔchéa
Cambodia

Location: Southeast Asia
Area: 181,035 sq km
Capital: Phnom Penh
Government:
Constitutional monarchy
Administrative Divisions:
21 provinces
Population: 13.8 million
Ethnic Groups:
Khmer (92%), Vietnamese (5%),
Chinese (2%),Thai (1%)

Language: Khmer, Vietnamese
Religion:
Buddhist (89%), Muslim (2%)
GDP per capita: 2,200 US$
Currency: 1 riel = 10 kak

Kazahstan
Kazakhstan

Location: Central Asia
Area: 2,717,300 sq km
Important Body of Water:
Aral Sea
Capital: Astana
Government: Republic
Administrative Divisions:
19 regions, 2 cities
Population: 15.2 million
Ethnic Groups:
Kazakhs (44%), Russians (36%),
Ukrainians (4%), Germans (4%)
Language: Kazakh, Russian
Religion:
Muslim (50%), Christian (50%)
GDP per capita: 8,200 US$
Currency: 1 tenge = 100 tiin

Kyrgyzstan
Kyrghyzstan

Location: Central Asia
Area: 198,500 sq km
Highest Point: Jengish Chokusu/Pik
Pobedy (7,439 m)
Capital: Bishkek
Government:
Presidential republic
Administrative Divisions:
6 regions, 1 district
Population: 5.2 million
Ethnic Groups:
Kyrgyz (57%), Russians (19%),
Uzbeks (13%), Ukrainians (2%)
Language: Kyrgyz, Russian
Religion:
Primarily Muslim, Christians

GDP per capita: 2,100 US$
Currency: 1 som = 100 tyin

Lao
Laos

Location:
Southeast Asia
Area: 236,800 sq km
Capital: Vientiane
Government: Socialist republic
Administrative Divisions:
16 provinces, 1 prefecture
Population: 6.3 million
Ethnic Groups: circa 70 ethnic
groups incl. Lao-Lum,
Lao-Theung, Lao Soung
Language: Lao
Religion: Buddhists (58%),
Indigenous Religions (34%)
GDP per capita: 1,900 US$
Currency: 1 kip

Malaysia
Malaysia

Location:
Southeast Asia
Area: 329,758 sq km
Capital: Kuala Lumpur
Government:
Constitutional monarchy
Administrative Divisions:
13 states, 2 territories
Population: 24.3 million
Ethnic Groups:
Malays (53%), Chinese (27%),
Indians and Pakistanis (8%)
Language: Bahasa Melayu,
Chinese dialects, Tamil, English
Religion:
Muslim (53%), Buddhist (17%),
Native religions (12%), Hindus (7%)
GDP per capita: 12,100 US$
Currency:
1 Malaysian ringgit = 100 sen

Maldives (Divehi Rajje)
Maldives

Location: South Asia
Area: 298 sq km
Capital: Male
Government: Republic
Administrative Divisions:
20 districts
Population: 359,000
Ethnic Groups: Maldivian
Language: Divehi, English
Religion: Sunni Muslims (99%)
GDP per capita: 3,900 US$
Currency: 1 rufiyaa = 100 laari

Mongol Ard Uls
Mongolia

Location: Central Asia
Area: 1,565,000 sq km
Highest Point:
Huyten Orgil (4,374 m)
Capital: Ulan Bator
Government: Republic
Administrative Divisions:
21 provinces, 1 district
Population: 2.8 million
Ethnic Groups: Mongolians (88%),
Turkic (7%), others
Language:
Mongolian, Kazakh, Russian
Religion: Buddhist Lamaism (90%)
Native Religions
GDP per capita: 1,800 US$
Currency: 1 tugrik = 100 mongo

Muang Thai
Thailand

Location:
Southeast Asia
Area: 513,115 sq km
Capital: Bangkok
Government:
Constitutional monarchy

Administrative Divisions:
3 provinces
Population: 64.8 million
Ethnic Groups:
Thais (80%), Chinese (12%),
Malays (4%), Khmer (3%)
Language:
Thai, English, Chinese
Religion:
Buddhist (95%), Muslim (4%)
GDP per capita: 8,300 US$
Currency: 1 baht = 100 stangs

Myanmar
Myanmar (Burma)

Location: Southeast Asia
Area: 678,500 sq km
Capital: Rangoon
Government: Military regime
Administrative Divisions:
7 states, 7 districts
Population: 47.3 million
Ethnic Groups:
Burmese (69%), Shan (9%),
Karen (6%), Rakhine (4%)
Language: Burmese, other
indigenous languages
Religion: Buddhists (89%),
Christians (5%), Muslims (4%),
indigenous religions (3%)
GDP per capita: 1,900 US$
Currency: 1 kyat = 100 pyas

Nepal
Nepal

Location: South Asia
Area: 140,800 sq km
Highest Point:
Mt. Everest (8,861 m)
Capital: Kathmandu
Government:
Constitutional monarchy
Administrative Divisions:
14 regions

Population: 28.2 million
Ethnic Groups:
Nepalese majority including Bhaman,
Chetri, etc.
Language:
Nepalese, Minority Languages
Religion: Hindus (86%),
Buddhists (6%), Muslims (3%)
GDP per capita: 1,400 US$
Currency:
1 Nepalese rupee = 100 paisa

Nippon/Nihon
Japan

Location:
Pacific Island Chain/East Asia
Area: 377,801 sq km
Highest Point: Mt Fuji (3,776 m)
Important Rivers:
Shinano, Tone, Kitakami
Capital: Tokyo
Government:
Constitutional monarchy
Administrative Divisions:
47 prefectures
Population: 127.4 million
Ethnic Groups:
Japanese (99%), Ainu, Koreans
Language: Japanese
Religion: Shinto (88%),
Buddhism (78%), Christian (4%)
GDP per capita: 31,500 US$
Currency: 1 yen = 100 sen

Pākistān
Pakistan

Location: South Asia
Area: 803,940 sq km
Important Rivers:
Indus and tributaries
Capital: Islamabad
Government: Islamic republic
Administrative Divisions:
4 provinces, 1 district, 2 regions

Population: 165.8 million
Ethnic Groups: Punjabi (50%),
Sindhi (15%), Pashtun (15%)
Language:
Urdu, English, Punjabi, Sindhi
Religion: Muslim (97%)
GDP per capita: 2,500 US$
Currency:
1 Pakistani rupee = 100 paisa

Pilipinas
Philippines

Location: Southeast Asia
Area: 300,000 sq km
Highest Point: Mt. Apo (2,954 m)
Capital: Manila
Government: Republic
Administrative Divisions:
13 regions, 73 provinces
Population: 89.4 million
Ethnic Groups:
Austronesian groups (95%),
Chinese (1.5%)
Language:
Tagalog, English, Spanish
Religion:
Catholic (84%), other Christians
(10%), Muslims (5%)
GDP per capita: 5,100 US$
Currency: 1 Philippine peso =
100 centavos

Qatar
Qatar

Location: Middle East
Area: 11,437 sq km
Capital: Doha
Government: Emirate
Administrative Divisions:
9 districts
Population: 886,000
Ethnic Groups:
Arab (45%), South Asians (34%),
Iranian (16%)

Language: Arabic
Religion: Muslim (93%),
Christians (6%), Hindus (1%)
GDP per capita: 27,500 US$
Currency:
1 Quatar-riyal = 100 dirham

Saltanat 'Umān
Oman

Location:
Middle East
Area: 212,457 sq km
Highest Point:
Jabal-Sham (3,017 m)
Capital: Muscat
Government: Sultanate
Administrative Divisions:
59 Provinces
Population: 3.1 million
Ethnic Groups:
Arabs (88%), Persians (3%), South
Asians (3%), Africans (2%)
Language:
Arabic, Persian, Urdu
Religion:
Muslims (85%), Hindus (14%)
GDP per capita: 13,400 US$
Currency:
1 Omani rial = 100 baizas

Singapore
Singapore

Location:
Southeast Asia
Area: 692.7 sq km
Capital: Singapore
Government: Republic
Administrative Divisions:
5 districts
Population: 4.5 million
Ethnic Groups: Chinese (78%),
Malays (14%), South Asians (7%)
Language:
Malay, English, Chinese, Tamil

Religion:
Buddhist and Taoist (54%),
Muslims (15%), Hindus (4%)
GDP per capita: 28,000 US$
Currency:
1 Singapore dollar = 100 cents

Srī Lankā
Sri Lanka

Location: South Asia
Area: 65,610 sq km
Highest Point:
Pidurutalagala (2,524 m)
Capital: Colombo
Government: Socialist republic
Administrative Divisions:
9 provinces, 25 districts
Population: 20.2 million
Ethnic Groups:
Sinhalese (74%), Tamil (18%)
Language: Sinhala, Tamil
Religion:
Buddhism (70%), Hindus (16%),
Muslims (8%), Catholics (7%)
GDP per capita: 4,300 US$
Currency:
1 Sri Lankan rupee = 100 cents

Suriya
Syria

Location:
Middle East
Area: 185,180 sq km
Important Rivers: Euphrates
Capital: Damascus
Government:
Military governed republic
Administrative Divisions:
13 provinces, 1 district
Population: 18.8 million
Ethnic Groups: Arabs (89%), Kurds
(6%), Armenian (2%)
Language:
Arabic, Kurdish, Armenian

Religion: Sunni Muslims (80%),
Alawite (7%), Christians (9%), Other
Muslims (3%)
GDP per capita: 3,900 US$
Currency:
1 Syrian pound = 100 piasta

Tadžikistan
Tajikistan

Location: Central Asia
Area: 143,100 sq km
Highest Point: Somoni (7,495 m)
Capital: Dushanbe
Government: Republic
Administrative Divisions:
2 regions, 1 district,
1 Autonomous region
Population: 7.3 million
Ethnic Groups:
Tajikistanis (63%), Uzbeks (24%),
Russians (7%)
Language: Tajik, Russian
Religion: Primarily Islam and
Russian Orthodoxy
GDP per capita: 1,200 US$
Currency:
1 Tajik rouble = 100 kopeks

Taehan-Min'guk
Republic of Korea
(South Korea)

Location: East Asia
Area: 98,480 sq km
Capital: Seoul
Government: Republic
Administrative Divisions:
15 provinces
Population: 48.8 million
Language: Korean
Religion:
Christians (32%), Buddhists (23 %),
Confucians (22%)
GDP per capita: 20,400 US$
Currency: 1 won = 100 chon

Taiwan
Taiwan

Location: East Asia
Area: 35,980 sq km
Capital: Taipei
Government: Republic
Administrative Divisions:
16 counties, 5 municipalities,
2 special municipalities
Population: 23 million
Ethnic Groups:
Taiwanese (84%), Mainland
Chinese (14%), Indigenous 2%
Language: Chinese
Religion:
Taoists (34%), Buddhists (43%),
Christians (14%), Confucianism
GDP per capita: 27,600 US$
Currency:
1 New Taiwan dollar = 100 cents

Timor-Leste
East Timor

Location: Southeast Asia
Area: 15,007 sq km
Capital: Dili
Government: Republic
Administrative Divisions:
13 districts
Population: 1 million
Language:
Portuguese, Tetum, Indonesian
Religion:
Catholics (91.4%), Protestant (2.6%),
Muslim (1.7%), Hindu (0.3%)
GDP per capita:
Estimated at 500 US$
Currency: 1 US dollar = 100 cents

Turkmenistan
Turkmenistan

Location: Central Asia
Area: 488,100 sq km

Capital: Ashgabat
Government: Republic
Administrative Divisions:
5 regions
Population: 5 million
Ethnic Groups: Turkmen (73%),
Russians (10%), Uzbeks (9%)
Kazaks (2%), Tartars (1%)
Language: Turkmen, Russian
Religion: Sunni Muslims
GDP per capita: 8,000 US$
Currency: 1 manat = 100 tenge

Urdunn
Jordan

Location: Middle East
Area: 92,300 sq km
Important River: Jordan
Capital: Amman
Government:
Constitutional monarchy
Administrative Divisions:
8 provinces
Population: 5.9 million
Ethnic Groups: Arabs (98%)
Language: Arabic
Religion: Sunni Islam (80%)
GDP per capita: 4,700 US$
Currency:
1 Jordanian dinar = 1,000 fils

Uzbekistan
Uzbekistan

Location: Central Asia
Area: 447,400 sq km
Capital: Tashkent
Government: Republic
Administrative Divisions:
12 regions, 1 autonomous republic
Population: 27 million
Ethnic Groups:
Uzbeks (74%), Russians (6%),
Tajikistanis (5%), Kazaks (4%)
Language: Uzbek, Russians

Religion: Sunni Islam
GDP per capita: 1,800 US$
Currency: 1 Uzbek sum = 100 tijin

Viêt-Nam
Vietnam

Location: Southeast Asia
Area: 329,560 sq km
Important River: Mekong
Capital: Hanoi
Government: Socialist republic
Administrative Divisions:
7 regions, 50 provinces, 3 cities
Population: 84.4 million
Ethnic Groups: Vietnamese (87%),
60 minority groups
Language: Vietnamese
Religion:
Buddhists (55%), Catholic (7%)
GDP per capita: 2,800 US$
Currency: 1 dong = 1 hao = 10 xu

Yisra'el
Israel

Location:
Middle East
Area: 21,946 sq km
Important Bodies of Water/Rivers:
Dead Sea, Jordan
Capital: Jerusalem
Government: Republic
Administrative Divisions:
6 districts
Population: 6.3 million, includes
settlers outside of Isreal proper.
Ethnic Groups: Jewish Israelis
(81%), Israeli Arabs (18%)
Language:
Modern Hebrew, Arabic, English
Religion:
Jewish (81%), Muslims (14%)
GDP per capita: 24,600 US$
Currency:
1 new shekel = 100 agorot

Nations of the World
Asia, Australia/Oceania

Zhongguo
China

Location: East Asia
Area: 9,596,960 sq km
Highest Point:
Muztagh (7,723 m)
Important Rivers:
Yellow, Pearl, Yangtze
Capital: Beijing
Government: Socialist republic
Administrative Divisions:
23 provinces, 5 autonomous regions,
3 cities, 147 special municipalities
Population: 1.3 billion
Ethnic Groups:
Han Chinese (92%), Tibetans, Miao,
Mongol, Manchus
Language:
Chinese, Minority Languages
Religion: Buddhists (9%),
Muslims (2%), Christians (1%)
GDP per capita: 6,800 US$
Currency: 1 yuan = 1,000 fen

Australia/Oceania

Australia
Australia

Location:
Indian/Pacific Ocean
Area: 7,686,850 sq km
Highest Point:
Kosciuszko (2,230 m)
Capital: Canberra
Government:
Parliamentary democracy
Administrative Divisions:
6 states, 2 territories
External Territories: Christmas
Island, Cocos Island, Lord Howe
Island, Norfolk Island
Population: 20.2 million

Ethnic Groups: European
descent (92%), Aborigines (around
1%), Asians (7%)
Language: English
Religion: Catholics (26%), Anglicans
(24%), other Protestants (6%),
Orthodox (3%)
GDP per capita: 31,900 US$
Currency:
1 Australian dollar = 100 cents

Fiji
Fiji

Location: South Pacific
Area: 18,270 sq km
Capital: Suva
Government: Republic
Administrative Divisions:
4 districts, 14 provinces
Population: 906,000
Ethnic Groups:
Fijians (51%), Indians (44%)
Language: English, Fijian, Hindi
Religion: Christians (53%),
Hindus (38%), Muslims (8%)
GDP per capita: 6,000 US$
Currency:
1 Fijian dollar = 100 cents

Kiribati
Kiribati

Location: South Pacific
Area: 810.5 sq km
Capital: Bairiki
Government: Republic
Administrative Divisions:
6 districts
Population: 105,000
Ethnic Groups: Micronesians (99%),
Polynesians, Chinese, Caucasians
Language: Kiribati, English
Religion:
Christians (93%), Baha'i (3%)
GDP per capita: 800 US$

Currency:
1 Australian dollar = 100 cents

Marshall Islands
Marshall Islands

Location: Pacific Ocean
Area: 181 sq km
Capital: Majuro
Government: Republic
Administrative Divisions:
24 districts
Population: 60,000
Ethnic Groups:
Micronesians (97%), Americans
Language: English, Marshallese
Religion: Christians (98%)
GDP per capita: 2,300 US$
Currency:
1 US dollar = 100 cents

Micronesia
Micronesia

Location: Western Pacific
Area: 702 sq km
Capital: Palikir
Government: Federal republic
Administrative Divisions:
4 states
Population: 108,200
Ethnic Groups: Mostly Micronesians
and Polynesians, expats
Language: English, 9 indigenous
languages
Religion: Christian
GDP per capita: 3,900 US$
Currency:
1 US dollar = 100 cents

Nauru (Naoero)
Nauru

Location: South Pacific
Area: 21.3 sq km
Capital: Yaren District

Government: Republic
Administrative Divisions:
  districts
Population: 13,287
Ethnic Groups:
Nauruan (62%), other Pacific
Islanders (25%), East Asians
Language: English, Nauruan
Religion: Christians (90%)
GDP per capita: 5,000 US$
Currency:
 Australian dollar = 100 cents

New Zealand
New Zealand

Location: South Pacific
Area: 268,680 sq km
Highest Point:
Mt. Cook (3,764 m)
Capital: Wellington
Government:
Parliamentary monarchy
Administrative Divisions:
 counties, 3 townships
External Territories:
Cook Islands, Niue, Tokelau
Population: 4 million
Ethnic Groups:
European descent (74%), Maori
(10%), Pacific Islanders (4%)
Language: English, Maori
Religion:
Anglican (22%), Presbyterian (16%),
Catholics (15%)
GDP per capita: 25,500 US$
Currency:
 New Zealand dollar = 100 cents

Palau
Palau

Location: Pacific
Area: 458 sq km
Capital: Koror
Government: Republic

Administrative Divisions:
16 states
Population: 20,000
Ethnic Groups: Palau (83%),
Filipinos (10%), other Micro-
nesians (2%), Chinese (2%)
Language: English, Palauan
Religion:
Christians (65%), Animists (25%)
GDP per capita: 9,000 US$
Currency:
1 US dollar = 100 cents

Papua New Guinea
Papua New Guinea

Location:
Western Pacific
Area: 462,840 sq km
Highest Point:
Mt. Wilhelm (4,508 m)
Important River: Sepik
Capital: Port Moresby
Government:
Constitutional monarchy
Administrative Divisions:
19 provinces, 1 district
Population: 5.6 million
Ethnic Groups:
Mostly New Guineans and
other Melanesians
Language:
English, New Guinean Pidgin, Motu
Religion:
Christians (92%), Animists
GDP per capita: 2,200 US$
Currency: 1 kina = 100 toea

Samoa
Samoa (Western)

Location: Pacific
Area: 2,944 sq km
Capital: Apia
Government:
Constitutional monarchy

Administrative Divisions:
11 districts
Population: 178,000
Ethnic Groups:
Polynesians (90%), Mixed European-
Polynesian (9%)
Language: Samoan, English
Religion: Protestants (71%),
Catholics (22%)
GDP per capita: 5,600 US$
Currency: 1 tala = 100 sene

Solomon Islands
Solomon Islands

Location: Pacific
Area: 28,450 sq km
Capital: Honiara
Government:
Parliamentary monarchy
Administrative Divisions:
8 provinces, 1 district
Population: 553,000
Ethnic Groups: Melanesians (94%),
Polynesians (4%), Micronesians (1%)
Language: English, Pijin
Religion:
Christians (97%), Animists (2%)
GDP per capita: 1,700 US$
Currency:
1 Solomon Island dollar = 100 cents

Tonga
Tonga

Location: Pacific
Area: 748 sq km
Capital: Nuku´alofa
Government:
Constitutional monarchy
Administrative Divisions:
3 island groups
Population: 115,000
Ethnic Groups:
Polynesians (99%)
Language: Tongan, English

Religion:
Christians (90%), Baha'i (4%)
GDP per capita: 2,300 US$
Currency: 1 pa'anga = 100 seniti

Tuvalu
Tuvalu

Location:
Pacific
Area: 26 sq km
Capital: Vaiaku (Funafuti)
Government:
Constitutional monarchy
Administrative Divisions:
9 atolls
Population: 11,800
Ethnic Groups:
Polynesians (96%), Melanesians
Language: Tuvalu, English
Religion:
Protestants (97%), Adventists, Baha'i
GDP per capita: 1,100 US$
Currency:
1 Australian dollar = 100 cents

Vanuatu
Vanuatu

Location:
Pacific
Area: 12,190 sq km
Capital: Port Vila
Government: Republic
Administrative Divisions:
6 provinces
Population: 209,000
Ethnic Groups: Ni-Vanuatu (91%),
Pacific Islanders (3%)
Language:
English, French, Bislama
Religion:
Christians (80%), Animists
GDP per capita: 2,900 US$
Currency:
1 vatu = 100 centimes

Africa

Al-Ǧazā'ir/Algérie
Algeria

Location: North Africa
Area: 2,381,741 sq km
Capital: Algiers
Government: Republic
Administrative Divisions:
48 districts
Population: 32.9 million
Ethnic Groups:
Arabs (70%), Berbers (30%)
Language: Arabic
Religion: Sunni Islam (99%)
GDP per capita: 7,200 US$
Currency: 1 Algerian dinar =
100 centimes

Al-Magrib/Maroc
Morocco

Location: North Africa
Area: 446,550 sq km
Highest Point: Tourkal (4,167 m)
Capital: Rabat
Government:
Constitutional monarchy
Administrative Divisions:
16 regions
Population: 33.2 million
Ethnic Groups: Arab Moroccans
(50%), Berbers (40%)
Language: Arabic, French,
Berber dialects
Religion: Islam (99%)
GDP per capita: 4,200 US$
Currency:
1 dirham = 100 centimes

Al-Misr/Egypt
Egypt

Location: North Africa
Area: 1,001,450 sq km

Highest Point:
Mt. Sinai (2,637 m)
Important River: Nile
Capital: Cairo
Government: Republic
Administrative Divisions:
26 provinces
Population: 78.8 million
Ethnic Groups: Egyptians: of mixed
Arab, Black African and Berber des-
cent (80%), Arabs, Sudanese,
Nubians, Palestinians
Language: Egyptian Arabic
Religion: Sunnis (90%),
Coptic Christians (10%)
GDP per capita: 3,900 US$
Currency:
1 Egyptian pound = 100 piaster

Al-Saharaw
Western Sahara

Location: Northwestern Africa
Area: 266,000 sq km
Government: Territory of Morocco,
annexed in 1979
Administrative Divisions:
4 provinces
Population: 273,000
Ethnic Groups:
Arabs, Berbers, Moroccans
Language: Arabic, Spanish,
Hassaniya Arabic
Religion: Sunni Muslims (100%)
Currency: 1 Moroccan dirham =
100 centimes

Angola
Angola

Location: Southwestern Africa
Area: 1,246,700 sq km
Highest Point:
Morro de Moco (2,629 m)
Important Rivers:
Cuanza, Longa

apital: Luanda
overnment: Republic
dministrative Divisions:
 provinces
opulation: 12.1 million
thnic Groups: Bantu speaking
hnicities (90%)
anguage:
ortuguese, Bantu Languages
eligion: Christians (89%),
nimists (9%)
DP per capita: 3,200 US$
urrency: 1 kwanza = 100 lwei

s-Sūdān
udan

ocation: North Africa
rea: 2,505,813 sq km
mportant River: White Nile
apital: Khartoum
overnment: Republic
dministrative Divisions:
 provinces
opulation: 41 million
thnic Groups: Mixed Black
frican-Arab decent (50%), Black
fricans (30%)
anguage: Arabic, English,
amitic Languages
eligion: Muslim (74%),
nimists (19%), Christians (9%)
DP per capita: 2,100 US$
urrency: 1 Sudanese pound =
00 piaster

enin
enin

ocation: West Africa
rea: 112,622 sq km
ighest Point:
ont Sokbaro (658 m)
mportant Rivers: Niger
apital: Porto Novo
overnment: Republic

Administrative Divisions:
6 Provinces, 78 districts
Population: 7.8 million
Language: French, Fon, Yoruba,
other indigenous Languages
Religion: Animists (62%), Christians
(19%), Muslims (15%)
GDP per capita: 1,300 US$
Currency: 1 CFA franc = 10 centimes

Botswana
Botswana

Location: Southern Africa
Area: 600,370 sq km
Capital: Gaborone
Government: Republic
Administrative Divisions:
11 districts
Population: 1.6 million
Ethnic Groups: Bantu
ethnicities (95%), San (5%)
Language: Setswana, English
Religion: Animists (60%),
Christians (30%)
GDP per capita: 10,500 US$
Currency: 1 pula = 100 thebe

Burkina Faso
Burkina Faso

Location: West Africa
Area: 274,200 sq km
Highest Point:
Tena Kourou (749 m)
Important River: Black Volta
Capital: Ouagadougou
Government: Republic
Administrative Divisions:
45 provinces
Population: 13.9 million
Ethnic Groups:
Volta ethnicities (60%), Mande
(17%), Fulbe (10%)
Language: French, Fulbe,
other indigenous Languages

Religion: Animists (60%), Muslim
(30%), Christians (10%)
GDP per capita: 1,100 US$
Currency:
1 CFA franc = 100 centimes

Burundi
Burundi

Location: East Africa
Area: 27,834 sq km
Important Lake:
Lake Tanganyika
Capital: Bujumbura
Government:
Presidential republic
Administrative Divisions:
15 provinces
Population: 8 million
Ethnic Groups: Hutu (85%),
Tutsi (14 %), Twa (1 %)
Language:
Kirundi, French, Kiswahili
Religion: Christians (70%),
Animists (30%), Muslims (1%)
GDP per capita: 700 US$
Currency: 1 Burundi franc =
100 centimes

Cabo Verde
Cape Verde

Location: Islands off the West
African coast
Area: 4,033 sq km
Capital: Praia
Government: Republic
Administrative Divisions:
15 districts
Population: 421,000
Ethnic Groups: Mixed Afro-
European descent (71%), Blacks
(28%), Whites (1%)
Language: Portuguese, Creole
Religion: Christian (98%)
GDP per capita: 6,200 US$

Currency: 1 Cape Verde escudo = 100 centavos

Cameroun/Cameroon
Cameroon

Location: Central Africa
Area: 475,442 sq km
Capital: Yaoundé
Government: Presidential republic
Administrative Divisions: 10 provinces
Population: 17.3 million
Ethnic Groups: Highlanders (31%), Other Bantu ethnicities (30%), Fulani (10%)
Language: French, English, Indigenous Languages
Religion: Christians (52%), Animists (26%), Muslims (22%)
GDP per capita: 2,400 US$
Currency: 1 CFA franc = 100 centimes

Comores
Comoros

Location: Islands off the East African coast
Area: 2,170 sq km
Capital: Moroni
Government: Islamic republic
Administrative Divisions: 3 island districts
Population: 691,000
Ethnic Groups: Comoros are primarily of mixed Arab, Madagascan and Black African descent
Language: Comoro, French
Religion: Muslims (99%), Christians (1%)
GDP per capita: 700 US$
Currency: 1 Comorian franc = 100 centimes

Congo
Republic of the Congo

Location: Central Africa
Area: 342,000 sq km
Important River: Congo
Capital: Brazzaville
Government: Republic
Administrative Divisions: 9 regions and 4 urban districts
Population: 3.7 million
Ethnic Groups: Bantu ethnicities (88%)
Language: French, Bantu languages
Religion: Catholic (54%), Animists (19%)
GDP per capita: 1,300 US$
Currency: 1 CFA franc = 100 centimes

Congo, République démocratique
Democratic Republic of the Congo

Location: Central Africa
Area: 2,345,410 sq km
Highest Point: Mt. Stanley (5,109 m)
Capital: Kinshasa
Government: Presidential republic
Administrative Divisions: 10 regions, 1 district
Population: 62 million
Ethnic Groups: Bantu ethnicities (80%), Sudanese ethnicities (17%)
Language: French, indigenous languages
Religion: Catholic (48%), Protestants (29%), other Christians
GDP per capita: 700 US$

Currency: 1 Congo franc = 100 makutta

Côte d'Ivoire
Côte d'Ivoire/Ivory Coast

Location: West Africa
Area: 322,462 sq km
Highest Point: Nimba (1,752 m)
Important Rivers: Sassandra, Komoe
Capital: Yamoussoukro
Government: Presidential republic
Administrative Divisions: 49 departments
Population: 17.6 million
Ethnic Groups: Akan (41%), Mandes (27%), Gur (17%)
Language: French, Dioula, and indigenous languages
Religion: Animists (50%), Muslims (30%), Christians (20%)
GDP per capita: 1,400 US$
Currency: 1 CFA franc = 100 centimes

Djibouti
Djibouti

Location: Northeastern Africa
Area: 23,200 sq km
Capital: Djibouti
Government: Republic
Administrative Divisions: 4 districts
Population: 486,500
Ethnic Groups: Somalis (50%), Afar (40%), Arabs, Ethiopians, Europeans
Language: French, Arabic, Cushitic languages
Religion: Muslim (96%), Christians (3%)
GDP per capita: 1,300 US$

Currency: 1 Djibouti franc =
100 centimes

Eritrea
Eritrea

Location:
Northeastern Africa
Area: 121,320 sq km
Capital: Asmara
Government: Republic
Administrative Divisions:
6 provinces
Population: 4.7 million
Ethnic Groups: Tigrinya (50%),
Tigre (30%), Afar (8%)
Language: Arabic, Tigrinya
Religion:
Muslim (50%), Christians (50%)
GDP per capita: 1,000 US$
Currency: 1 birr = 100 cents

Gabon
Gabon

Location:
Central Africa
Area: 267,667 sq km
Highest Point: Bengoué (1,070 m)
Important River: Ogooué
Capital: Libreville
Government:
Presidential republic
Administrative Divisions:
9 provinces
Population: 1.4 million
Ethnic Groups:
Fang (32%), Nzebi (8%), other
African ethnicites
Language:
French, Bantu languages
Religion: Catholic (50%),
Protestants (20%), Animists
GDP per capita: 6,800 US$
Currency:
1 CFA franc = 100 centimes

Gambia
Gambia

Location:
West Africa
Area: 11,295 sq km
Important River: Gambia
Capital: Banjul
Government:
Presidential republic
Administrative Divisions:
6 regions, 35 districts
Population: 1.6 million
Ethnic Groups: Mandingo (44%),
Fulbe (18%), Wolof (12%)
Language:
English, Mandingo, Wolof, other
indigenous languages
Religion: Muslims (90%),
Christians, Animists
GDP per capita: 1,900 US$
Currency: 1 dalasi = 100 butut

Ghana
Ghana

Location:
West Africa
Area: 239,460 sq km
Important River: White Volta
Capital: Accra
Government:
Presidential republic
Administrative Divisions:
10 regions, 110 districts
Population: 22.4 million
Ethnic Groups:
Ashanti (52%), Moshi (16%),
Ewe (13%), Ga (8%), other
indigenous ethnic groups
Language: English, more than
70 other languages
Religion: Christians (60%),
Muslims (16%), Animists
GDP per capita: 2,500 US$
Currency: 1 cedi = 100 pesewa

Guinea-Bissau
Guinea-Bissau

Location: West Africa
Area: 36,125 sq km
Capital: Bissau
Government: Presidential republic
Administrative Divisions:
3 provinces, 8 regions, 1 municipality
Population: 1.4 million
Ethnic Groups: Balantu (25%),
Fulbe (20%), Mandingo (12%)
Language: Portuguese, Creole
Religion: Animists (54%),
Muslim (38%), Christians (8%)
GDP per capita: 900 US$
Currency: 1 Guinea-peso =
100 centavos

Guinea Ecuatorial
Equatorial Guinea

Location: Central Africa
Area: 28,051 sq km
Capital: Malabo
Government:
Presidential republic
Administrative Divisions:
7 provinces
Population: 540,000
Ethnic Groups: Fang
ethnicities (80%), Bubi (10%)
Language: Spanish, English,
indigenous languages
Religion:
Christians (90%), Animists
GDP per capita: Estinates between
30,000 and 51,000 US$
Currency:
1 CFA franc = 100 centimes

Guinée
Guinea

Location: West Africa
Area: 245,857 sq km

Nations of the World
Africa

Highest Point:
Tamgué (1,538 m)
Important River: Niger
Capital: Conakry
Government: Republic
Administrative Divisions:
4 main regions, 30 lesser regions, 1 district
Population: 9.6 million
Ethnic Groups:
Mandingo (45%), Fulbe (30%), Kissi (7%), Kpelle (5%)
Language:
French, indigenous languages
Religion:
Muslim (90%), Christians (2%), Animists
GDP per capita: 2,170 US$
Currency:
1 Guinean franc = 100 cauris

Îtyopya
Ethiopia

Location:
Northeastern Africa
Area: 1,127,127 sq km
Highest Point:
Ras Dejen (4,620 m)
Important Lake/River:
Lake Tsana, Blue Nile
Capital: Addis Ababa
Government: Federal republic
Administrative Divisions:
9 regions, 1 district (Addis Ababa)
Population: 74.7 million
Ethnic Groups: Oromo (40%), Amhara (28%), Tigre (9%), 70 other ethnicities
Language: Amharic, 70 other indigenous languages
Religion: Christians (45%), Muslim (45%), Animists
GDP per capita: 900 US$
Currency:
1 birr = 100 cents

Kenya
Kenya

Location: East Africa
Area: 582,646 sq km
Highest Point:
Mt. Kenya (5,200 m)
Important Body of Water:
Lake Victoria
Capital: Nairobi
Government:
Presidential republic
Administrative Divisions:
7 provinces, 1 district (Nairobi)
Population: 34.7 million
Ethnic Groups: Bantu ethnicities (60%), Nilotes (24%) Massai (2%)
Language: Swahili, English, indigenous languages
Religion: Christian and Animist majority, Muslims (6%)
GDP per capita: 1,100 US$
Currency:
1 Kenyan shilling = 100 cents

Lesotho
Lesotho

Location:
Southern Africa
Area: 30,355 sq km
Highest Point:
Ntlenyana (3,482 m)
Capital: Maseru
Government:
Constitutional monarchy
Administrative Divisions:
10 districts
Population: 2 million
Ethnic Groups: Sotho (99%)
Language: Sesotho, English
Religion: Catholics (44%), Protestants (30%), Animists
GDP per capita: 3,000 US$
Currency: 1 loti = 100 lisente

Liberia
Liberia

Location: West Africa
Area: 111,369 sq km
Highest Point: Wuteve (1,380 m)
Capital: Monrovia
Government: Presidential republic
Administrative Divisions:
11 districts, 4 territories
Population: 3.4 million
Ethnic Groups:
African ethnicities including Kru, Grebo and Kpelle (95%), Americo-Liberians; of African American descent (2.5%)
Language:
English, indigenous languages
Religion: Christians, Animists, Muslim (10%)
GDP per capita: 1,000 US$
Currency:
1 Liberian dollar = 100 cents

Lîbîyâ
Libya

Location: North Africa
Area: 1,759,540 sq km
Highest Point:
Pic Bette (2,285 m)
Capital: Tripoli
Government: Authoritarian Islamic republic
Administrative Divisions:
13 regions
Population: 5.9 million
Ethnic Groups:
Libyans of Arab descent, Berbers, Black Africans
Language:
Arabic, Berber languages
Religion: Muslims (97%)
GDP per capita: 11,400 US$
Currency:
1 Libyan dollar = 1,000 dirham

Madagasíkara
Madagascar

Location: One main island and smaller islands off the southeastern coast of Africa
Area: 587,041 sq km
Highest Point:
Maromokotro (2,876 m)
Important River: Mangoky
Capital: Antananarivo
Administrative Divisions:
6 regions
Population: 18.5 million
Ethnic Groups: Madagascans, of mixed Malayan and Black African descent (99%)
Language:
Malagasy, French, Howa
Religion: Animists (50%), Christians (45%), Muslims (5%)
GDP per capita: 900 US$
Currency: 1 Madagascan franc = 100 centimes

Malawi
Malawi

Location: Southern Africa
Area: 118,484 sq km
Highest Point:
Mulanje (3,000 m)
Important Bodies of Water: Lake Nyasa, Lake Malombe, Lake Chilwa
Capital: Lilongwe
Government:
Presidential republic
Administrative Divisions:
3 regions divided into 27 districts
Population: 13 million
Ethnic Groups: Bantu ethnicities, including the Chewa, Nyanja, Yao, etc. (95%)
Religion: Christians (75%), Animists (15%), Muslims
GDP per capita: 600 US$

Currency:
1 Malawian kwacha = 100 tambala

Mali
Mali

Location: West Africa
Area: 1,240,192 sq km
Important River: Niger
Capital: Bamako
Administrative Divisions:
8 regions, 1 district
Population: 12 million
Ethnic Groups:
Bambara (32%), Fulbe (14%)
Soninke (9%), Taureg (7%),
other indigenous groups
Language: French, Bambara, other Mandé Languages
Religion: Muslim (80%), Christians (1%), Animists
GDP per capita: 1,200 US$
Currency:
1 CFA franc = 100 centimes

Mauritius
Mauritius

Location:
Indian Ocean off eastern Africa
Area: 2,040 sq km
Capital: Port Louis
Government: Republic
Administrative Divisions:
9 districts, 3 dependencies
Population: 1.2 million
Ethnic Groups:
Indians (69%), Creoles of black African descent (27%), Chinese (3%), Whites (3%)
Language: English, Creole, Hindi
Religion: Hindus (52%), Christians (30%), Muslims (13%)
GDP per capita: 13,100 US$
Currency:
1 Mauritian rupee = 100 cents

Mawrītăniyah
Mauritania

Location: West Africa
Area: 1,030,700 sq km
Important River: Senegal
Capital: Nouakchott
Government:
Islamic republic
Administrative Divisions:
13 regions
Population: 3.1 million
Ethnic Groups:
Arab-Berber descent (81%), Wolof (7%), other major ethnicities (9%)
Language:
Arabic, Niger-Congo languages
Religion: Muslim (99%)
GDP per capita: 2,200 US$
Currency: 1 ouguiya = 5 khoums

Moçambique
Mozambique

Location:
Southern Africa
Area: 801,590 sq km
Highest Point:
Binga (2,436 m)
Important Rivers:
Zambezi, Limpopo
Capital: Maputo
Government: Republic
Administrative Divisions:
10 provinces, 1 district
Population: 19.6 million
Ethnic Groups:
Makau (47%), Tsonga (23%), Malawi (12%), Shona (11%)
Language:
Portuguese, Bantu languages
Religion: Animists (50%), Christians, Muslims
GDP per capita: 1,300 US$
Currency:
1 metical = 100 centavos

Nations of the World
Africa

Namibia
Namibia

Location: Southwestern Africa
Area: 825,418 sq km
Highest Point:
Konigstein (2,606 m)
Important Rivers:
Orange, Cunene, Okavango
Capital: Windhoek
Government: Republic
Administrative Divisions:
13 regions
Population: 2 million
Ethnic Groups:
Ovambo (47%), Kavango (9%),
Herero (7%), Damara (7%), Whites,
primarily of German and Afrikaner
descent (6%)
Language:
English, Afrikaans, German
Religion:
Lutherans (52%), Catholics (20%),
Dutch Reformed Church (6%),
Anglicans (5%)
GDP per capita: 7,100 US$
Currency:
1 Namibia dollar = 100 cents

Niger
Niger

Location: West Africa
Area: 1,267,000 sq km
Highest Point:
Gebroun (1,944 m)
Important River: Niger
Capital: Niamey
Government: Presidential republic
Administrative Divisions:
8 departments
Population: 12.5 million
Ethnic Groups: Hausa (54%),
Djerma (21%), Taureg (9%)
Language: French, Hausa,
other indigenous languages

Religion:
Muslim (90%), Animists
GDP per capita: 900 US$
Currency:
1 CFA franc = 100 centimes

Nigeria
Nigeria

Location: West Africa
Area: 923,768 sq km
Highest Point:
Chappal Waddi (2,419 m)
Important Rivers/Body of Water:
Niger, Benue, Lake Chad
Capital: Abuja
Government:
Presidential republic
Administrative Divisions:
36 states, 1 capital district
Population: 132 million
Ethnic Groups: Hausa-Fulani (21%),
Yoruba (21%), Ibo (18%), Ibibo (6%),
430 other ethnicities
Language: English, Arabic,
indigenous languages
Religion: Christians (49%),
Muslim (45%), Animists
GDP per capita: 1,400 US$
Currency: 1 Naira = 100 Kobo

République Centrafricaine
Central African Republic

Location: Central Africa
Area: 622,984 sq km
Highest Point: Ngaoui (1,420 m)
Important River: Ubangi
Capital: Bangui
Government: Presidential republic
Administrative Divisions:
16 prefectures, 1 district
Population: 4.3 million
Ethnic Groups: Banda (30%),
Baya (24%), Sara (11%)

Language: French, Sangho
Religion: Animists (57%),
Christians (35%), Muslims (8%)
GDP per capita: 1,200 US$
Currency:
1 CFA franc = 100 centimes

Rwanda
Rwanda

Location: East Africa
Area: 26,338 sq km
Highest Point:
Karisimbi (4,519 m)
Important Body of Water:
Lake Kivu
Capital: Kigali
Government: Presidential republic
Administrative Divisions:
11 prefectures
Population: 8.6 million
Ethnic Groups:
Hutu and related ethnicities (85%),
Tutsi (14%), Pygmies (1%)
Language: Kinya-rwanda,
French, Swahili, English,
Indigenous Languages
Religion:
Catholic (45%), Protestants (10%),
Muslims (10%), Animists
GDP per capita: 1,500 US$
Currency: 1 Rwandan franc =
100 centimes

São Tomé e Príncipe
Sao Tome and Principe

Location: West Africa
Area: 1,001 sq km
Highest Point:
Pico de Sao Tome (2,024 m)
Capital: Sao Tome
Government: Republic
Administrative Divisions:
District of Sao Tome and autonomou
island of Principe

Population: 194,000
Ethnic Groups:
Black Africans, Mixed Afro-European
descent, Portuguese
Language: Portuguese, Creole
Religion: Catholic (90%),
Protestant (5%), Animists
GDP per capita: 1,200 US$
Currency: 1 dobra = 100 centimes

Sénégal
Senegal

Location: West Africa
Area: 196,722 sq km
Important River: Senegal
Capitol: Dakar
Government: Presidential republic
Administrative Divisions:
10 regions
Population: 12 million
Ethnic Groups:
Wolof (44%), Serer (15%), other
major ethnic groups (35%)
Language: French, Wolof
Religion: Muslims (94%),
Christians (5%), Animists
GDP per capita: 1,800 US$
Currency:
1 CFA franc = 100 centimes

Seychelles
Seychelles

Location:
Islands off the East African coast
Area: 454 sq km
Capital: Victoria
Government: Republic
Administrative Divisions:
23 districts
Population: 81,000
Ethnic Groups:
Creoles (89%), Indians (5%),
Madagascans (3%), Chinese (2%),
Malays, Whites

Language:
English, French, Creole
Religion: Catholic (89%),
Anglicans (8%), Hindus (1%)
GDP per capita: 7,800 US$
Currency:
1 Seychelles rupee = 100 cents

Sierra Leone
Sierra Leone

Location: West Africa
Area: 71,740 sq km
Highest Point:
Loma Monsa (1,948 m)
Capital: Freetown
Government: Republic
Administrative Divisions:
4 provinces, 1 District
Population: 6 million
Ethnic Groups: Mende (35%),
Temne (32%), Creoles (10%),
small Arab Minority
Language: English, Creole
Religion: Animists (53%),
Muslims (39%), Christians (8%)
GDP per capita: 800 US$
Currency: 1 leone = 100 cents

Soomaaliya
Somalia

Location: Northeastern Africa
Area: 637,657 sq km
Highest Point:
Shimbiris (2,416 m)
Capital: Mogadishu
Government: Republic
Administrative Divisions:
18 provinces
Population: 8.8 million
Ethnic Groups: Somali
ethnicities (95%), Arab and Bantu
speaking minorities
Language:
Somali, Arabic, English, Italian

Religion: Muslims (99%),
Christians (less than 1%)
GDP per capita: 600 US$
Currency:
1 Somali shilling = 100 centesimi

South Africa/ Suid-Afrika
South Africa

Location: Southern Africa
Area: 1,219,912 sq km
Highest Point: Njesuthi (3,408 m)
Important River: Orange, Vaal
Capital: Pretoria
Government: Republic
Administrative Divisions:
9 provinces
Population: 44.1 million
Ethnic Groups:
Black Africans, mostly Zulu and Bantu
ethnicities (76%), European descent
(13%), Mixed Afro-European descent
(9%), Asians (3%)
Language: English, Afrikaans, Zulu,
Bantu languages
Religion:
Christians (78%), Hindus (2%),
Muslims (1%), Animists
GDP per capita: 12,000 US$
Currency: 1 rand = 100 cents

Swaziland (kaNgwane)
Swaziland

Location: Southern Africa
Area: 17,363 sq km
Capital: Mbabane
Government:
Constitutional monarchy
Administrative Divisions:
273 clan districts
Population: 1.1 million
Ethnic Groups:
Swazis (97%), Zulus, Tsonga
Language: English, Swazi

Religion:
Christians (70%), Animists (30%)
GDP per capita: 5,000 US$
Currency:
1 lilangeni = 100 cents

Tanzania
Tanzania

Location: East Africa
Area: 945,087 sq km
Highest Point:
Kilimanjaro (5,895 m)
Important Bodies of Water:
Lake Victoria, Lake Tanganyika
Capital:
Dodoma
Government:
Federal presidential republic
Administrative Divisions:
25 regions
Population: 37.5 million
Ethnic Groups:
Bantu ethnicities (95%), Other Black
Africans (4.5%) Whites, Arabs, Asians
Language: Swahili, English
Religion: Christians (45%),
Muslims (33%), Animists
GDP per capita: 700 US$
Currency:
1 Tanzanian shilling = 100 cents

Tchad
Chad

Location:
Central Africa
Area: 1,284,000 sq km
Important Body of Water:
Lake Chad
Capital: N'Djamena
Government:
Presidential republic
Administrative Divisions:
14 prefectures
Population: 10 million

Ethnic Groups:
Arabs (15%), Sara (30%), Mixed
Arab-African descent (38%)
Language: French, Arabic
Religion: Muslims (45%), Christians
(30%), Animists
GDP per capita: 1,300 US$
Currency:
1 CFA franc = 100 centimes

Togo
Togo

Location: West Africa
Area: 56,785 sq km
Capital: Lomé
Government:
Presidential republic
Administrative Divisions:
5 regions
Population: 5.5 million
Ethnic Groups:
Ewe (46%), Volta ethnicities (43%),
Hausa, Fulbe
Language: French, Ewe, Kabye
Religion:
Animists (50%), Christians (35%)
GDP per capita: 1,700 US$
Currency:
1 CFA franc = 100 centimes

Tūnisiyah/Tunisie
Tunisia

Location: North Africa
Area: 163,610 sq km
Highest Point:
Tellatlas (1,200 m)
Capital: Tunis
Government:
Presidential republic
Administrative Divisions:
23 provinces
Population: 10 million
Ethnic Groups: Arab/Arabic Berbers
(98%), Berbers (1%)

Language: Arabic, French,
Religion: Muslim (99%),
Christian and Jewish minorities
GDP per capita: 8,300 US$
Currency:
1 Tunisian dinar = 1,000 millimes

Uganda
Uganda

Location:
East Africa
Area: 236,040 sq km
Highest Point:
Mt. Stanley (5,109 m)
Important Bodies of Water:
Lake Kyoga, Lake Albert
Capital: Kampala
Government:
Presidential republic
Administrative Divisions:
38 districts
Population: 28.1 million
Ethnic Groups:
Bantu ethnicities (50%), Nilotes
(13%), Sudanese ethnicities (5%)
Language:
Swahili, English, Luganda
Religion:
Catholics (45%), Protestants (25%),
Muslims (5%), Animists
GDP per capita: 1,800 US$
Currency:
1 Ugandan shilling = 100 cents

Zambia
Zambia

Location:
Southern Africa
Area: 752,614 sq km
Highest Point:
Mafinga Hills (2,301 m)
Important River/Body of Water:
Zambezi, Lake Kariba
Capital: Lusaka

Government:
Presidential republic
Administrative Divisions:
9 provinces
Population: 11.5 million
Ethnic Groups:
African ethnic groups, including Luba,
Lunda, Nyanja, Tonga, etc. (98%),
Whites (1%)
Language:
English, Bantu languages
Religion:
Christians (72%), Animists (27%)
GDP per capita: 900 US$
Currency:
1 kwacha = 100 ngwee

Zimbabwe
Zimbabwe

Location:
Southern Africa
Area: 390,580 sq km
Highest Point:
Inyangani (2,592 m)
Important Body of Water:
Lake Kariba
Important River:
Zambezi
Capital: Harare
Government:
Presidential republic
Administrative Divisions:
8 provinces
Population: 12.2 million
Ethnic Groups: Shona (80%),
Ndebele (17%), Whites (2%)
Language:
English, Bantu languages
Religion: Animists (40%),
Protestants (17%), Indigenous
Christian Denominations (14%),
Catholics (12%)
GDP per capita: 2,300 US$
Currency:
1 Zimbabwean dollar = 100 cents

North and Central America

Antigua and Barbuda
Antigua and Barbuda

Location: Caribbean Islands
Area: 442 sq km
Capital: St. John's
Government:
Constitutional monarchy
Administrative Divisions:
6 districts, 2 dependencies
Population: 69,000
Ethnic Groups:
African descent (95%), Mixed Afro-
European descent (4%), European
descent (2%)
Language: English, Creole
Religion: Christians (97%),
Rastafarians (<1%)
GDP per capita: 11,000 US$
Currency: 1 East Caribbean dollar =
100 cents

Bahamas
Bahamas

Location:
Caribbean/Atlantic Ocean Islands
Area: 13,939 sq km
Capital: Nassau
Government:
Parliamentary monarchy
Administrative Divisions:
18 districts
Population: 303,770
Ethnic Groups:
African descent (72%), Mixed Afro-
European descent (14%), European
descent (12%)
Language: English
Religion: Baptists (32%),
Anglicans (20%), Catholics (19%),
other Christians (12%)
GDP per capita: 20,200 US$

Currency:
1 Bahamian dollar = 100 cents

Barbados
Barbados

Location: Caribbean Island
Area: 430 sq km
Highest Point:
Mt. Hillaby (340 m)
Capital: Bridgetown
Government:
Parliamentary monarchy
Administrative Divisions:
11 districts
Population: 279,000
Ethnic Groups: African descent
(92%), Mixed African-European
descent (3%), Whites (3%)
Language:
English, Bajan (local dialect)
Religion: Anglicans (40%), Other
Christian churches (30%)
GDP per capita: 17,000 US$
Currency:
1 Barbados dollar = 100 cents

Belize
Belize

Location: Central America
Area: 22,965 sq km
Highest Point:
Maya Mountains (1,122 m)
Capital: Belmopan
Government:
Constitutional monarchy
Administrative Divisions:
6 districts
Population: 288,000
Ethnic Groups: Mestizos (44%),
Creoles of Afro-European
descent (30%), Amerindians (11%),
Garifuna (7%)
Language:
English, Creole, Spanish

Religion: Catholics (58%), Protestants (28%)
GDP per capita: 6,800 US$
Currency:
1 Belizean dollar = 100 cents

Canada
Canada

Location: North America
Area: 9,984,670 sq km
Highest Point:
Mt. Logan (6,050 m)
Important Rivers:
St. Lawrence, Saskatchewan
Capital: Ottawa
Government:
Parliamentary monarchy
Administrative Divisions:
10 provinces, 3 territories
Population: 33 million
Ethnic Groups:
British/Irish descent (28%), French descent (23%), other European (15%), Mixed descent (26%), Amerindian/Inuit (2%), African/Asian/Arab descent (6%)
Language: English, French
Religion:
Catholic (47%), Protestant (36%), other Christians, Muslims, Jews
GDP per capita: 29,700 US$
Currency:
1 Canadian dollar = 100 cents

Costa Rica
Costa Rica

Location:
Central America
Area: 51,100 sq km
Highest Point:
Cerro Chirripo (3,820 m)
Capital: San Jose
Government:
Presidential republic

Administrative Divisions:
7 provinces
Population: 4 million
Ethnic Groups: European descent; primarily Spanish ancestry (87%), Mestizos (7%), African descent (3%), Asians (2%), Amerindians (1%)
Language: Spanish, English, West Indian Creole
Religion:
Catholics (89%), Protestants (8%)
GDP per capita: 11,100 US$
Currency:
1 colon = 100 centavos

Cuba
Cuba

Location: Carribean Island
Area: 110,860 sq km
Highest Point:
Pico Turquino (1,974 m)
Capital: Havana
Government: Socialist republic
Administrative Divisions:
14 provinces, 1 special administrative zone
Population: 11.3 million
Ethnic Groups:
Mixed Afro-European descent (51%), European descent (37%), African descent (11%), East Asians
Language: Spanish
Religion: Catholics (39%), Protestants (5%), Nondenominational Christians, Atheists
GDP per capita: 3,500 US$
Currency:
1 Cuban peso = 100 centavos

Dominica
Dominica

Location: Caribbean Island
Area: 750 sq km

Highest Point:
Morne Diablotins (1,447 m)
Capital: Roseau
Government: Republic
Administrative Divisions:
10 districts
Population: 69,000
Ethnic Groups:
African descent (91%), Mixed Afro-European descent (6%), East Indians (2%)
Language: English, Patois
Religion:
Catholic (78%), Protestants (16%)
GDP per capita: 5,500 US$
Currency: 1 East Caribbean dollar = 100 cents

El Salvador
El Salvador

Location:
Central America
Area: 21,041 sq km
Highest Point:
Santa Ana (2,381 m)
Important Body of Water:
Ilopango
Capital:
San Salvador
Government:
Presidential republic
Administrative Divisions:
14 departments
Population: 6.8 million
Ethnic Groups:
Mestizos (89%), Amerindians (10%), European descent (1%)
Language:
Spanish, indigenous languages
Religion:
Catholics (83%), Large and fast growing Evangelical minority
GDP per capita: 4,800 US$
Currency: 1 Salvadoran colon = 100 centavos

Grenada
Grenada

Location:
Caribbean Island
Area: 344 sq km
Highest Point:
Mt. Saint Catherine (840 m)
Capital: St. George's
Government:
Constitutional Monarchy
Population: 89,300
Ethnic Groups:
African descent (82%), Mixed Afro-European descent (13%), East Indians
Language: English, Patois
Religion:
Catholic (55%), Protestant (35%)
GDP per capita: 5,000 US$
Currency: 1 East Caribbean dollar = 100 cents

Guatemala
Guatemala

Location:
Central America
Area: 108,889 sq km
Highest Point:
Tajumulco (4,220 m)
Capital: Guatemala City
Government:
Presidential republic
Administrative Divisions:
22 departments
Population: 12.3 million
Ethnic Groups:
Amerindians; including Maya (60%),
Mestizos (30%)
Language:
Spanish, indigenous languages
Religion: Catholics (80%),
Protestants (20%)
GDP per capita: 4,700 US$
Currency:
1 quetzal = 100 centavos

Haïti
Haiti

Location: Caribbean Island
Area: 27,750 sq km
Highest Point:
Morne de la Selle (2,715 m)
Capital: Port au Prince
Government:
Presidential republic
Administrative Divisions:
9 departments
Population: 8.3 million
Ethnic Groups:
Black (95%), Whites and Mixed
Afro-European descent (5%)
Language:
French, Haitian Creole
Religion:
Catholics (80%), Protestants (15%),
Animism including Voodoo
GDP per capita: 1,700 US$
Currency:
1 gourde = 100 centimes

Honduras
Honduras

Location: Central America
Area: 112,088 sq km
Highest Point:
Cerro Las Minas (2,840 m)
Capital: Tegucigalpa
Government:
Presidential republic
Administrative Divisions:
18 districts
Population: 7.3 million
Ethnic Groups:
Mestizos (90%), Indians (6%),
African descent (2%)
Language: Spanish, English,
indigenous languages
Religion: Catholics (85%),
Protestants (10%)
GDP per capita: 2,900 US$

Currency:
1 lempira = 100 centavos

Jamaica
Jamaica

Location: Caribbean Island
Area: 10,990 sq km
Highest Point:
Blue Mountain Peak (2,256 m)
Capital: Kingston
Government:
Parliamentary monarchy
Administrative Divisions:
14 districts
Population: 2.7 million
Ethnic Groups:
African descent (76%), Mixed
Afro-European descent (15%),
East Indians, Chinese
Language: English, Patois
Religion:
Protestants (60%), Catholics (5%),
Rastafarians (5%)
GDP per capita: 4,400 US$
Currency:
1 Jamaican dollar = 100 cents

México
Mexico

Location:
Central America
Area: 1,972,550 sq km
Highest Point:
Citlaltepetl (5,700 m)
Important River: Rio Grande
Capital: Mexico City
Government:
Presidential government
Administrative Divisions:
5 regions, 31 states, 1 federal district
Population: 107.4 million
Ethnic Groups:
Mestizos (75%), Amerindians (14%),
Whites (10%)

Nations of the World
North and Central America

Language:
Spanish, indigenous languages
Religion:
Catholic (90%), Protestants (5%)
GDP per capita: 10,000 US$
Currency: 1 new Mexican peso =
100 centavos

Nicaragua
Nicaragua

Location: Central America
Area: 129,494 sq km
Highest Point:
Cerro Mogoton (2,107 m)
Important Lakes:
Lake Nicaragua, Lake Managua
Capital: Managua
Government:
Presidential republic
Administrative Divisions:
16 departments
Population: 5.6 million
Ethnic Groups:
Mestizos (69%), European descent
(14%), African descent (9%),
Amerindian (4%), Mixed Afro-
European descent
Language: Spanish, Chibcha
Religion: Catholic (90%),
Protestants (5%)
GDP per capita: 2,900 US$
Currency:
1 córdoba = 100 centavos

Panamá
Panama

Location: Central America
Area: 78,200 sq km
Highest Point: Chiriqui (3,475 m)
Capital: Panama City
Government:
Presidential republic
Administrative Divisions:
9 provinces, Canal Zone

Population: 3.1 million
Ethnic Groups: Mestizos (65%),
African descent (13%), Asians (2%),
European descent (10%),
Amerindians (8%),
Language: Spanish, English
Religion: Catholic (95%),
Protestants (5%)
GDP per capita: 7,200 US$
Currency:
1 balboa = 100 centesimo

República Dominicana
Dominican Republic

Location: Caribbean Island
Area: 48,730 sq km
Highest Point:
Pico Duarte (3,175 m)
Capital: Santo Domingo
Government:
Presidential republic
Administrative Divisions:
26 provinces, 1 special district
Population: 9.1 million
Ethnic Groups:
Mixed Afro-European descent (73%),
European descent (14%), African
descent (12%)
Language: Spanish
Religion: Catholic (90%),
Protestants, Jewish, Bahai
GDP per capita: 7,000 US$
Currency: 1 Dominican peso =
100 centavos

Saint Kitts and Nevis
Saint Kitts and Nevis

Location: Caribbean Island
Area: 261.6 sq km
Highest Point:
Mt. Liamuiga (1,156 m)
Capital: Basseterre
Government:
Constitutional monarchy

Administrative Divisions:
14 districts
Population: 39,000
Ethnic Groups:
African descent (86%), Mixed Afro-
European descent (11%), European
descent (2%)
Language: English
Religion:
Anglicans (36%), Methodists (32%),
Catholics (11%)
GDP per capita: 8,800 US$
Currency: 1 East Caribbean dollar =
100 cents

Saint Lucia
Saint Lucia

Location: Caribbean Island
Area: 616.3 km
Highest Point: Mt. Gimie (958 m)
Capital: Castries
Government:
Constitutional monarchy
Administrative Divisions:
11 municipalities
Population: 164,000
Ethnic Groups:
African descent (91%), Mixed Afro-
European descent (6%), Asians (3%),
European descent (1%)
Language: English,
Patois (local French Creole)
Religion: Catholics (77%),
Protestants (15%)
GDP per capita: 5,400 US$
Currency: 1 East Caribbean dollar =
100 cents

Saint Vincent and
the Grenadines
Saint Vincent and the Grenadines

Location: Caribbean Island
Area: 389 sq km
Highest Point: Soufriere (1,234 m)

Capital: Kingstown
Government:
constitutional monarchy
Administrative Divisions:
districts
Population: 117,000
Ethnic Groups: African descent
(66%), Mixed Afro-European descent
(19%), East Indian (6%), Whites
(4%), Zambos of Mixed Afro-
merindian descent (2%)
Language: English
Religion: Protestant (75%),
Catholics (10%)
GDP per capita: 2,900 US$
Currency: 1 East Caribbean dollar =
100 cents

Trinidad and Tobago
Trinidad and Tobago

Location: Caribbean Islands
Area: 5,128 sq km
Capital: Port of Spain
Government: Presidential republic
Administrative Divisions:
8 counties, 3 municipalities, autono-
mous district of Tobago
Population: 1.1 million
Ethnic Groups:
East Indians (40%), African descent
(40%), Mixed descent (19%)
Language: English
Religion:
Catholic (30%), Hindus (24%),
Anglicans (11%), Muslims (6%)
GDP per capita: 16,700 US$
Currency: 1 Trinidad-Tobago dollar =
100 cents

United States
of America
United States of America

Location: North America
Area: 9,631,418 sq km

Highest Point:
Mt. McKinley (6,193 m)
Important Bodies of Water/Rivers:
The Great Lakes, Great Salt Lake,
Mississippi/ Missouri River, Colorado
River, Rio Grande, Arkansas River
Capital: Washington D.C
Government: Federal republic
Administrative Divisions:
50 states, 1 federal district
(Washington D.C)
External Territories:
Northern Marianas, Puerto Rico,
American Virgin Islands,
American Samoa, Guam, Midway
Island
Population: 298 million
Ethnic Groups:
Whites (74%), African-Americans
(13%), Latinos (13%), Asians/Pacific
Islanders (4%), Amerindians (1%)
Language: English, Spanish,
Amerindian Languages
Religion:
Protestant denominations, including
Baptists, Methodists, Presbyterians,
and Lutherans (50%), Catholics
(26%), Jewish (3%), Muslims (2%),
Orthodox Christians (2%)
GDP per capita: 41,800 US$
Currency:
1 US dollar = 100 cents

South America

Argentina
Argentina

Location: Southern S. America
Area: 2,766,889 sq km
Highest Point: Aconcagua (6,959 m)
Important Rivers:
Colorado, Rio Negro/Parana
Capital: Buenos Aires

Government: Federal republic
Administrative Divisions:
22 provinces, 1 federal district,
1 territory
Population: 39.9 million
Ethnic Groups:
European descent (90%), Other
Latin Americans (6%), Mestizos (5%),
Amerindians
Language: Spanish
Religion: Catholic (91%),
Protestant (2%), Jewish (1%)
GDP per capita: 13,100 US$
Currency: 1 Argentinean peso =
100 centavos

Bolivia
Bolivia

Location: Central S. America
Area: 1,098,581 sq km
Highest Point: Illimani (6,882 m)
Important Bodies of Water:
Lake Titicaca, Lake Poopó
Capital: Sucre
Government:
Presidential republic
Administrative Divisions:
9 departments
Population: 9 million
Ethnic Groups:
Amerindians (42%), Mestizos (31%),
European descent (27%)
Language:
Spanish, Quechua, Aymara
Religion:
Catholic (93%), Protestants
GDP per capita: 2,900 US$
Currency:
1 boliviano = 100 centavos

Brasil
Brazil

Location: Eastern S. America
Area: 8,511,996 sq km

Nations of the World
South America

Highest Point:
Pico de Neblina (3,014 m)
Important Rivers:
Amazon, Parana
Capital: Brasilia
Government: Federal republic
Administrative Divisions:
26 states, 1 district
Population: 188 million
Ethnic Groups:
European descent (53%), Mixed
Afro-European descent (34%),
African descent (11%), Mestizos,
Japanese, Arabs, Amerindian
Language: Portuguese,
indigenous languages
Religion: Catholic, (85%),
Protestants (10%), Afro-Brazilian
religious practices
GDP per capita: 8,400 US$
Currency:
1 real = 100 centavos

Chile
Chile

Location:
Southern S. America
Area: 756,950 sq km
Highest Point:
Llullaillaco (6,723 m)
Capital: Santiago de Chile
Government:
Presidential Republic
Administrative Divisions:
12 regions and 1 capital district
Population: 16.1 million
Ethnic Groups: Mestizos and
European descent (92%),
Amerindians (7%), Others (<1%)
Language: Spanish
Religion: Catholics (80%),
Protestants (10%)
GDP per capita: 11,300 US$
Currency: 1 Chilean peso =
100 centavos

Colombia
Colombia

Location:
Northwestern S.America
Area: 1,138,910 sq km
Highest Point:
Nevado del Huila (5,750 m)
Important River: Putumayo
Capital: Bogotá
Government: Republic
Administrative Divisions:
32 departments, 1 capital district
Population: 43.5 million
Ethnic Groups:
Mestizos (58%), European descent
(20%), Mixed Afro-European descent
(14%), African descent and Zambos
of mixed African and Indian descent
(>4%), Amerindians (1%)
Language: Spanish
Religion:
Catholic (95%), Protestant (1%)
GDP per capita: 7,900 US$
Currency: 1 Colombian peso =
100 centavos

Ecuador
Ecuador

Location:
Northwestern S. America
Area: 283,560 sq km
Highest Point:
Chimborazo (6,310 m)
Capital: Quito
Government:
Presidential republic
Administrative Divisions:
22 provinces
Population: 13.5 million
Ethnic Groups: Mestizos (35%),
European descent (25%),
Amerindians (20%), Mixed
Afro-European descent (15%),
African descent (5%)
Language: Spanish,
indigenous languages
Religion: Catholics (93%)
GDP per capita: 4,300 US$
Currency:
1 sucre = 100 centavos

Guyana
Guyana

Location: Northern S. America
Area: 214,969 sq km
Highest Point:
Pico da Neblina (3,014 m)
Important River: Essequibo
Capital: Georgetown
Government:
Presidential republic
Administrative Divisions:
10 regions
Population: 767,200
Ethnic Groups:
East Indians (51%), African descent
(29%),Mixed descent (11%),
Amerindians (5%)
Language: English, Hindi, Urdu
Religion:
Protestants (34%), Hindus (33%),
Catholics (20%), Muslims (8%)
GDP per capita: 4,600 US$
Currency:
1 Guyanese dollar = 100 cents

Paraguay
Paraguay

Location:
Central S. America
Area: 406,752 sq km
Important River: Paraguay
Capital: Asuncion
Government:
Presidential republic
Administrative Divisions:
17 departments
Population: 6.5 million

Ethnic Groups:
Amerindians and Mestizos (95%),
European descent (2%)
Language: Spanish, Guarani
Religion:
Catholic (95%), Protestants (1%)
GDP per capita: 4,900 US$
Currency:
1 guarani = 100 centimos

Perú
Peru

Location: Western S. America
Area: 1,285,216 sq km
Highest Point:
Huascaran (6,768 m)
Important Body of Water:
Lake Titicaca
Capital: Lima
Government:
Presidential republic
Administrative Divisions:
25 regions
Population: 28.3 million
Ethnic Groups:
Amerindians (47%), Mestizos (33%),
European descent (12%),
Afro-Peruvians, East Asians
Language:
Spanish, Quechua, Aymara
Religion: Catholics (90%),
Protestants (3%), Animists
GDP per capita: 5,900 US$
Currency:
1 nuevo sol = 100 centimos

Suriname
Suriname

Location: Northern S. America
Area: 163,265 sq km
Highest Point:
Julianatop (1,280 m)
Important Body of Water:
Lake Van Blommestein

Capital:
Paramaribo
Government:
Presidential republic
Administrative Divisions:
10 districts
Population: 439,000
Ethnic Groups:
East Indians (34%), Creoles of
African and European descent (33%),
Javanese (18%), Maroons (9%),
Amerindians (2%)
Language: Dutch, Hindustani,
Javanese, English
Religion:
Hindus (26%), Catholics (23%),
Muslims (20%), Protestants (19%),
Animists
GDP per capita: 4,100 US$
Currency: 1 Surinamese guilder =
100 cents

Uruguay
Uruguay

Location:
South S. America
Area: 176,215 sq km
Important Rivers:
Rio de la Plata, Uruguay, Rio Negro
Capital:
Montevideo
Government:
Presidential republic
Administrative Divisions:
19 departments
Population: 3.4 million
Ethnic Groups: European
descent (85%), Mestizos (5%),
African descent (3%)
Language: Spanish
Religion: Catholic (75%),
Protestants (2%), Jewish (1%)
GDP per capita: 10,000 US$
Currency: 1 Peso Uruguayo =
100 centesimos

Venezuela
Venezuela

Location: Northern S. America
Area: 912,050 sq km
Highest Point:
Pico Bolivar (5,002 m)
Important River: Orinoco
Capital: Caracas
Government:
Presidential republic
Administrative Divisions:
22 states, 1 district
Population: 25.7 million
Ethnic Groups: Mixed descent
(69%), White (20%), African descent
(9%), Amerindians (2%)
Language: Spanish
Religion:
Catholic (93%), Protestants (5%)
GDP per capita: 6,100 US$
Currency:
1 bolivar = 100 centimos

Index of names

The index explained

All of the places named on the maps in the atlas are listed in the atlas index. The place names are listed alpabetically. Special symbols and letters including accents and umlauts are ignored in the order of the index. For example, the letters Á, Ä, Â are all categorized under A, and Ž, Ż, Z are all treated as the standard Latin letter Z. Written characters consisting of two letters joined together (ligatures) are treated as two separate characters in the index: for example, words beginning with the character Æ would be indexed under A E. Generic geographic terms (sea, bay, etc.) were used in the order of the index: for example, the Gulf of Mexico is listed und **G** and Le Havre, France is listed under **L** . Pictograms make it possible for the user to easily locate and categorize objects in the maps. Each pictogram is followed by the international vehicle number plate code of the country where the object is located. Most of the objects in the atlas can be connected to one country. ISO country codes are used for objects located in regions without a number plate code. Two codes divided by a slash are used if an object is located within two countries. For geographic features that can not be attributed to one nation, such as the Atlantic Ocean, the name is followed by relevant page numbers and map grid references.

The grid references for towns and cities identify the location of the place name on the map. Grid references for countries and territories identify the location of the first letter of the place name.

Symbols used in the index

🏔 Mountains	🌋 Volcano	🏞 Lake	▫ Province
▲ Mountain	❄ Glacier	▱ Sea, Bay	● National Capital
▨ Landscape	🗻 Cape, Coast	▱ Coral reef	◉ Provincial Capital
▣ National Park	🏔 River	▱ Island	◯ Town, village
⊰ Desert	▱ Canal	▪ Undersea landscape	
◉ Oasis	🌊 Waterfall, rapids	▪ Country	

A

Å ◯ N 24 Lf14
Aabenraa ◯ DK 26 Le18
Aabybro ◯ DK 26 Le17
Aalborg ◯ DK 26 Le17
Aalen ◯ D 45 Lf21
Äänekoski ◯ FIN 28 Mc14
Aarau ◯ CH 45 Le22
Aars ◯ DK 26 Le17
Aba ◯ WAN 108 Lb17
Abaco Island ▱ BS 126 Ga13
Abadan ◯ IR 77 Nb12
Abakaliki ◯ WAN 108 Lb17
Abakan ◯ RUS 79 Pc08
Abancay ◉ PE 133 Gb21
Abashiri ◯ J 83 Sa10
Abay Wenz 🏔 ETH 109 Md16
Abbeville ◯ F 35 La20
Abbot Ice Shelf ❄ 140 Fa33
Abéché ◯ TCH 106 Ma16
Abengourou ◯ CI 105 Kd17
Abeokuta ◯ WAN 105 La17
Aberdeen ◯ GB 34 Kj17
Aberdeen ◯ USA 120 Fa09
Abergavenny ◯ GB 35 Kj20
Aberystwyth ◯ GB 35 Kh19
Abganerovo ◯ RUS 61 Nc21
Abha ◯ KSA 77 Na15
Abide ◯ TR 64 Me26
Abidjan ● CI 105 Kd17
Abilene ◯ USA 122 Fa12

Abington ◯ GB 34 Kj18
Abisko ◯ S 22 Lk11
Abisko fjällstation ◯ S 22 Lk11
Abisko n.p. ▣ S 22 Lk11
Åbo = Turku ◉ FIN 22 Mb15
Aboa ◯ 141 Kb33
Aboisso ◯ CI 105 Kd17
Abomey ◯ DY 105 La17
Aborlan ◯ RP 85 Qd17
Abrantes ◯ P 40 Kf26
Abrene = Pytalovo ◯ RUS 30 Md17
Abruzzo ▫ I 49 Lg24
Abruzzo, P.N. d' ▣ I 48 Lg25
Abu Ajram ◯ KSA 76 Md13
Abu Hadiyah ◯ KSA 77 Nb13
Abu Dhabi ● UAE 77 Nc14
Abu Hamad ◯ SUD 107 Mc15
Abuja ● WAN 108 Lb17
Abuná ◯ BOL 133 Gc21
Abuña ◯ BR 133 Gc20
Abune Yosef ▲ ETH 107 Md16
Abu Simbel ▱ ET 107 Mc14
Abuye Meda ▲ ETH 109 Md16
Abyad ◯ SUD 107 Mb16
Acapulco ◯ MEX 124 Fa15
Acaraú ◯ BR 134 Hd19
Acarigua ◯ YV 132 Gc17
Accra ● GH 105 Kd17
Achaguas ◯ YV 132 Gc17
Achill Island ▱ IRL 33 Ke19

Acıgöl ◯ TR 64 Me27
Acînsk ◯ RUS 73 Pc07
Acireale ◯ I 49 Lj27
Acklins Island ▱ BS 127 Gb14
Acquapendente ◯ I 46 Lf24
Acqui Terme ◯ I 46 Le23
Acre ▫ BR 133 Gb20
Acre ◯ BR 133 Gc20
Acri ◯ I 49 Lj26
Acuña ◯ MEX 124 Ed13
Ada ◯ USA 123 Fa12
Adam's Peak ▲ CL 81 Pa17
Adana ◯ TR 76 Md11
Adana ▫ TR 65 Mh27
Adapazarı = Sakarya ◉ TR 64 Mf25
Ad Dahna ⊰ KSA 77 Nb13
Ad-Dakhla ◯ MA 104 Ka14
Ad Dammam ◯ KSA 77 Nb13
Ad Darb ◯ KSA 77 Na15
Ad Dawadami ◯ KSA 77 Rd25 Na14
Addis Ababa ● ETH 109 Md17
Ad Diwaniyah ◯ IRQ 76 Na12
Addoo Atoll ▱ MV 81 Oc19
Adelaide ◉ AUS 97 Rd25
Adelaide Island ▱ 140 Gc32
Adelaide River ◯ AUS 94 Rc21
Ademuz ◯ E 42 Ks25
Aden ◯ YE 77 Nb16
Adi ◯ RI 92 Rc19
Adigrat ◯ ETH 107 Md16

Adilcevaz ◯ TR 66 Nb26
Adirondack Mountains 🏔 USA 121 Gb10
Adi Ugri ◯ ER 107 Md16
Adıyaman ◯ TR 65 Mk27
Adjud ◯ RO 55 Md22
Adler ◯ RUS 66 Mk24
Admiralty Inlet ▱ CDN 118 Fc04
Admiralty Islands ▱ PNG 92 Sb19
Admont ◯ A 52 Lj22
Ado-Ekiti ◯ WAN 108 Lb17
Adra ◯ E 41 Kj27
Adrano ◯ I 49 Lh27
Adrar ▲ DZ 106 Lb13
Adrar des Iforhas 🏔 RMM 105 La15
Adré ◯ TCH 106 Ma16
Adria ◯ I 46 Lg23
Adua ◯ RI 87 Rb19
Adygea ▫ RUS 76 Na10
Aegean Sea ▱ GR/TR 57 Mc26
Afándou ◯ GR 64 Me27
Affollé ▨ RIM 105 Kb15
Afghanistan ▪ AFG 78 Oa12
Aflou ◯ DZ 104 La12
Afognak Island ▱ USA 116 Cb07
Afşin ◯ TR 65 Mj26
Afyon ◯ TR 64 Mf26
Aga Buryat Autonomous District ▫ RUS 82 Qd08

Agadez ⬚ RN 106 Lb15
Agadir ⬚ MA 104 Kc12
Agana ⬚ USA 92 Sa16
Agargar ⬚ MA 104 Kb14
Agartala ⬚ IND 84 Pc14
Agde ⬚ F 38 Lb24
Agen ⬚ F 38 La23
Aggteleki N.P. ⬚ H 53 Ma21
Agiá ⬚ GR 56 Mb26
Agia Galini ⬚ GR 57 Mc28
Agia Pelagia ⬚ GR 56 Mc28
Aginskoe ⬚ RUS 82 Qc08
Agios Charalampos ⬚ GR 57 Mc25
Ágios Efstrátios ⬚ GR 57 Mc26
Ágios Kirikos ⬚ GR 57 Md27
Ágios Nikólaos ⬚ GR 57 Mc28
Aglı ⬚ TR 65 Mg25
Agnew ⬚ AUS 94 Ra24
Agra ⬚ IND 80 Od13
Ágreda ⬚ E 42 Kk25
Ağrı ⬚ TR 76 Na11
Ağrı ⬚ TR 66 Nb26
Agrigento ⬚ I 48 Lg27
Agrinio ⬚ GR 56 Ma26
Agrópoli ⬚ I 49 Ls25
Água Clara ⬚ BR 135 Hb23
Agua Prieta ⬚ MEX 122 Ec12
Aguascalientes ⬚ MEX 124 Ed14
Aguascalientes ⬚ MEX 124 Ed14
Águeda ⬚ P 40 Kf25
Aguilar ⬚ E 41 Kh27
Aguilar de Campóo ⬚ E 40 Kh24
Águilas ⬚ E 43 Kk27
Aguirre Cerda ⬚ 140 Gd31
Ahaus ⬚ D 44 Ld19
Åheim ⬚ N 24 Lc14
Ahlat ⬚ TR 66 Nb26
Ahmadabad ⬚ IND 80 Oc14
Ahmednagar ⬚ IND 81 Oc15
Ahtopol ⬚ BG 55 Md24
Ahtubinsk ⬚ RUS 61 Nd21
Åhus ⬚ S 27 Lh18
Ahvaz ⬚ IR 76 Nb12
Ahvenanmaa = Åland ⬚ FIN 25 Lk15
Ahvenanmeri ⬚ FIN 25 Lk15
Aigues-Mortes ⬚ F 38 Lc24
Aigüestortes i Estany de Sant Maurici, P.N. de ⬚ E 42 La24
Ailinginae Atoll ⬚ MH 93 Tb16
Şimleu Silvaniei ⬚ RO 54 Mb22
Ainaži ⬚ LV 30 Mc17
Ainos N.P. ⬚ GR 56 Ma26
Ainsa ⬚ E 42 La24
Aïn Sefra ⬚ DZ 104 Kd12
Aire-sur-l'Adour ⬚ F 42 Kk24
Airolo ⬚ CH 45 Le22
Aïr ou Azbine ⬚ RN 106 Lb15
Aiteke Bi ⬚ KZ 78 Oa09
Aix-en-Provence ⬚ F 39 Lc24
Aix-les-Bains ⬚ F 39 Lc23
Aizawl ⬚ IND 84 Pc14
Aizenay ⬚ F 38 Kk22
Aizpute ⬚ LV 31 Ma17
Ajaccio ⬚ F 48 Ld24
Ajdabiya ⬚ LAR 106 Ma12
Ajdar ⬚ UA 63 Mk21
Ajka ⬚ H 53 Lj22
Ajmer ⬚ IND 80 Oc13
Aka ⬚ BG 55 Md24
Akçakoca ⬚ TR 64 Mf25

Akçalar ⬚ TR 65 Mj27
Akçalı Dağları ⬚ TR 65 Mg27
Akçay ⬚ TR 66 Nb25
Akcjabrski ⬚ BY 51 Me19
Ak Dağlar ⬚ TR 64 Me27
Akdağmadeni ⬚ TR 65 Mh26
Akhisar ⬚ TR 57 Md26
Akimiski Island ⬚ CDN 120 Fd08
Akıncı Burnu ⬚ TR 65 Mh27
Akita ⬚ J 83 Sa11
Akjoujt ⬚ RIM 104 Kb15
Akkajaure ⬚ S 22 Lj12
Akköy ⬚ TR 65 Mg26
Akkuş ⬚ TR 65 Mj25
Akola ⬚ IND 80 Od14
Ak'ordat ⬚ ER 107 Md15
Akören ⬚ TR 64 Mg27
Akpınar ⬚ TR 65 Mg26
Akrahamn ⬚ N 26 Lc16
Akranes ⬚ IS 32 Jj13
Åkrestrømmen ⬚ N 24 Lf15
Akron ⬚ USA 123 Fd10
Akrotiri Akráthos ⬚ GR 57 Mc25
Akrotiri Kriós ⬚ GR 56 Mb28
Akrotiri Maléas ⬚ GR 57 Mb27
Aksaj ⬚ RUS 63 Mk22
Aksaray ⬚ TR 66 Nb25
Aksaray ⬚ TR 65 Mh26
Akşehir ⬚ TR 64 Mf26
Akşehir Gölü ⬚ TR 64 Mf26
Aksekı ⬚ TR 64 Mf27
Akshatau ⬚ KZ 78 Oc09
Aksu ⬚ CHN 79 Pa10
Aksubaevo ⬚ RUS 60 Nf18
Aksum ⬚ ETH 107 Md16
Aktanys ⬚ RUS 60 Nh18
Aktarsk ⬚ RUS 61 Nc20
Aktau ⬚ TM 76 Nc10
Aktöbe ⬚ KZ 78 Nd08
Aktuzla ⬚ TR 66 Nb26
Akure ⬚ WAN 108 Lb17
Akureyri ⬚ IS 32 Ka13
Akyab ⬚ MYA 84 Pc14
Al ⬚ N 24 Le15
Alabama ⬚ USA 123 Fc12
Alabama ⬚ USA 123 Fc12
Alaca ⬚ TR 65 Mh25
Alacahan ⬚ TR 65 Mj26
Alaçam ⬚ TR 65 Mh25
Alacant ⬚ E 43 Kk26
Alaçatı ⬚ TR 57 Md26
Ala Dağlar ⬚ TR 66 Nb26
Ala DağlarTasarı Milli Parkı ⬚ TR 65 Mh27
Alagoas ⬚ BR 134 Ja20
Alagoas ⬚ BR 134 Ja20
Alagoinhas ⬚ BR 135 Ja21
Al Ain ⬚ OM 77 Nd14
Alajuela ⬚ CR 126 Fd16
Alakanuk ⬚ USA 116 Bd06
Alakol ⬚ KZ 79 Pa09
Alakurtti ⬚ RUS 23 Mf12
Al Amarah ⬚ IRQ 76 Nb12
Alamogordo ⬚ USA 122 Ec12
Alamosa ⬚ USA 122 Ec11
Åland = Ahvenanmaa ⬚ FIN 25 Lk15
Ålandsbro ⬚ S 25 Lj14
Ålands hav ⬚ S 25 Lk15
Alanya ⬚ TR 64 Mf27
Alaotra ⬚ RM 111 Nb22
Alarcón ⬚ E 43 Kj26
Alaşehir ⬚ TR 57 Me26
Alaska ⬚ USA 116 Ca06
Alaska Peninsula ⬚ USA 116 Bd07

Alaska Range ⬚ USA 116 Cb06
Alassio ⬚ I 46 Le24
Alatyr' ⬚ RUS 60 Nc18
Alatyr' ⬚ RUS 60 Nd18
Alavus ⬚ FIN 19 Mb14
Al Awaynat ⬚ LAR 106 Ma14
Al-Ayn ⬚ UAE 77 Nd14
Al-'Ayun ⬚ MA 104 Kb13
Alazejskoe ploskogor'e ⬚ RUS 74 Sb05
Alba ⬚ I 46 Le23
Albac ⬚ RO 54 Mb22
Ålbæk ⬚ DK 26 Lf17
Al Baha ⬚ KSA 77 Na14
Alba Iulia ⬚ RO 54 Mb22
Albalate del Arzobispo ⬚ E 42 Kk25
Albania ⬚ AL 56 Ls25
Albany ⬚ AUS 95 Qd25
Albany ⬚ USA 123 Fd12
Albany ⬚ USA 121 Gb10
Al Basiri ⬚ JOR 76 Md12
Al Basra ⬚ IRQ 77 Nb12
Albatross Bay ⬚ AUS 96 Sa21
Al Bayda ⬚ LAR 106 Ma12
Albenga ⬚ I 46 Le23
Albert ⬚ F 37 Lb20
Alberta ⬚ CDN 117 Ea07
Albert Nile ⬚ EAU 109 Mc18
Albertville ⬚ F 39 Ld23
Albi ⬚ F 38 Lb24
Albina ⬚ SME 134 Hb17
Al Biyad ⬚ KSA 77 Nb14
Albox ⬚ E 41 Kj27
Albufeira ⬚ P 41 Kf27
Albuquerque ⬚ E 40 Kg26
Albuquerque ⬚ USA 122 Ec11
Albury-Wodonga ⬚ AUS 97 Sb26
Alcácer do Sal ⬚ P 41 Kf26
Alcáçovas ⬚ P 41 Kf26
Alcalá de Henares ⬚ E 41 Kh25
Alcalá del Júcar ⬚ E 43 Kk26
Alcalá del Río ⬚ E 41 Kh27
Álcamo ⬚ I 48 Lg27
Alcañiz ⬚ E 42 Kk25
Alcántara ⬚ E 40 Kg26
Alcántara ⬚ BR 134 Hd19
Alcaracejos ⬚ E 41 Kh26
Alcaudete ⬚ E 41 Kh27
Alcázar de San Juan ⬚ E 41 Kj26
Alčevs'k ⬚ UA 63 Mk21
Alcoi ⬚ E 43 Kk26
Alcolea del Pinar ⬚ E 42 Kj25
Alcorisa ⬚ E 42 Kk25
Alcoutim ⬚ P 41 Kg27
Alcoy = Alcoi ⬚ E 43 Kk26
Alcúdia ⬚ E 43 Lb26
Aldabra Group ⬚ SY 101 Na10
Aldan ⬚ RUS 75 Rb07
Aldan ⬚ RUS 75 Rc07
Aldanskoe nagor'e ⬚ RUS 75 Ra07
Aldeyjarfoss ⬚ IS 32 Kb13
Aleg ⬚ RIM 105 Kb15
Alegrete ⬚ BR 136 Ha24
Alëhovščina ⬚ RUS 29 Mg15
Aleksandrov ⬚ RUS 58 Mk17
Aleksandrovsk-Sahalinski ⬚ RUS 75 Sa08
Alekseevka ⬚ RUS 59 Mk20
Alekseevka ⬚ RUS 61 Nb20
Alekseevka ⬚ RUS 60 Nf19

Alekseevskaja ⬚ RUS 61 Nb20
Alekseevskoe ⬚ RUS 60 Nf18
Aleksin ⬚ RUS 59 Mj18
Aleksinac ⬚ SR 54 Ma24
Alençon ⬚ F 36 La21
Alenquer ⬚ BR 134 Hb19
Alentejo ⬚ P 41 Kg26
Alesd ⬚ RO 54 Mb22
Aleppo ⬚ SYR 76 Md11
Alert ⬚ CDN 118 Gd02
Alert Point ⬚ CDN 118 Fb02
Alès ⬚ F 39 Lc23
Alessandria ⬚ I 46 Le23
Ålesund ⬚ N 24 Ld14
Alexander Archipelago ⬚ USA 117 Da07
Alexander Island ⬚ 140 Ga32
Alexandria ⬚ ET 107 Mb12
Alexandria ⬚ RO 55 Mc24
Alexándria ⬚ GR 56 Mb25
Alexandroupoli ⬚ GR 57 Mc25
Al Fashir ⬚ SUD 109 Mb16
Alfatar ⬚ BG 55 Md24
Alföld ⬚ H 53 Ma22
Ålgård ⬚ N 26 Lc16
Algarve ⬚ P 41 Kf27
al-Gazira ⬚ SUD 107 Mc16
Algeciras ⬚ E 41 Kh27
Algeria ⬚ DZ 104 La12
Al Ghaydah ⬚ YE 77 Nc15
Alghero ⬚ I 48 Le25
Algiers ⬚ DZ 104 La11
Al Haditah ⬚ KSA 76 Md12
Al Hajarah ⬚ KSA 76 Na13
Al Hallaniyat Bay ⬚ OM 77 Nd15
Al Hallaniyat Bay ⬚ OM 77 Nd15
Al Harjah ⬚ KSA 77 Na15
Al Harrah ⬚ KSA 76 Md12
Al-Hoceima ⬚ MA 104 Kd11
Al Hudaydah ⬚ YE 77 Na16
Al Huluf ⬚ KSA 77 Nb13
Aliağa ⬚ TR 57 Md26
Aliambata ⬚ TLS 87 Rb20
Alibunar ⬚ SR 54 Ma23
Alicante = Alacant ⬚ E 43 Kk26
Alice Springs ⬚ AUS 94 Rc23
Aligarh ⬚ IND 80 Od13
Alika ⬚ GR 56 Mb27
Aliki ⬚ GR 57 Mc25
Alima ⬚ RCB 108 Ld19
Alingsås ⬚ S 26 Lg17
Aliveri ⬚ GR 57 Mc26
Aliwal-Noord ⬚ ZA 110 Mb25
Aliwal North ⬚ ZA 110 Mb25
Al Jagbub ⬚ LAR 106 Ma13
Aljat ⬚ AZ 76 Nb11
Al Jawf ⬚ KSA 76 Md13
Al Jawf ⬚ LAR 106 Ma14
Aljezur ⬚ P 41 Kf27
Al Jufra Oasis ⬚ LAR 106 Ld13
Al Junaynah ⬚ SUD 106 Ma16
Aljustrel ⬚ P 41 Kf27
Al Kharj ⬚ KSA 77 Nb14
Al Khums ⬚ LAR 106 Lc12
Al-Kidan ⬚ KSA 77 Nb14
Alkmaar ⬚ NL 37 Lc19
a-l Kulandy ⬚ KZ 76 Nc10
Al Kut ⬚ IRQ 76 Na12
Allakaket ⬚ USA 116 Ca05
Allen ⬚ RP 85 Ra16
Allentown ⬚ USA 123 Ga10
Allinge ⬚ DK 27 Lh18

Al Lith ☐ KSA 77 Na14
Almadén ☐ E 41 Kh26
Almagro ☐ E 41 Kj26
Al Majm'ah ☐ KSA 77 Nb13
Al Manama ● BRN 77 Nc13
Almansa ☐ E 43 Kk26
Al Marj ☐ LAR 106 Ma12
Almaty ☐ KZ 79 Od10
Al-Mawsil ☐ IRQ 76 Na11
Almazán ☐ E 42 Kj25
Almeirim ☐ BR 134 Hb19
Almelo ☐ NL 37 Ld19
Almenar de Soria ☐ E 42 Kj25
Almendralejo ☐ E 41 Kg26
Almere ☐ NL 37 Lc19
Almería ☐ E 41 Kj27
Al'met'evsk ☐ RUS 60 Ng18
Älmhult ☐ S 27 Lh17
Almirós ☐ GR 56 Mb26
Almodôvar ☐ P 41 Kf27
Almodóvar del Campo ☐ E 41 Kh26
Almonte ☐ E 41 Kg27
Almudévar ☐ E 42 Kk24
Al Mukalla ☐ YE 77 Nb16
Al Mukha ☐ YE 77 Na16
Almuñécar ☐ E 41 Kj27
Al Muzaylif ☐ KSA 77 Na15
Alnwick ☐ GB 34 Kk18
Alónnisos ☐ GR 56 Mb26
Alor ☐ RI 87 Ra20
Álora ☐ E 41 Kh27
Alotau ☐ PNG 96 Sc21
Alpena ☐ USA 123 Fd09
Alpes Maritimes ☒ F 39 Ld23
Alpi Orobie ☒ I 46 Le22
Alpu ☐ TR 64 Mf26
Al Qa'amiyat ☒ KSA 77 Nb15
al-Qadarif ☐ SUD 107 Mc16
Al Qa'iyah ☐ KSA 77 Na14
Al Qalibah ☐ KSA 76 Md13
Al Qaryah ash Sharqiyah ☐ LAR 106 Lc12
Al Qunfudhan ☐ KSA 77 Na15
Ar Rawdah ☐ YE 77 Nb16
Alsace ☒ F 37 Ld21
Alsfeld ☐ D 44 Le20
Alta ☐ N 23 Mb11
Altamira ☐ BR 134 Hb19
Altamura ☐ I 49 Lj25
Alta Murgia, P.N. dell' ☒ I 49 Lj25
Altay ☐ CHN 79 Pb09
Altay ☐ MNG 79 Pd09
Altay ☒ RUS 79 Pb08
Altay Mountains ☒ MNG 79 Pc09
Altdorf ☐ CH 45 Le22
Altea ☐ E 43 Kk26
Altenburg ☐ D 44 Lg20
Altındere Vadisi Milli Parkı ☒ TR 66 Mk25
Altınkaya Baraj ☐ TR 65 Mh25
Altıntaş ☐ TR 64 Mf26
Altiplano ☒ BOL 133 Gc22
Alto Araguaia ☐ BR 135 Hb22
Alto Garças ☐ BR 135 Hb22
Alto Molócue ☐ MOC 111 Md22
Alton ☐ USA 123 Fb11
Alto Purus ☒ PE 133 Gb21
Altötting ☐ D 45 Lg21
Altun Shan ☒ CHN 79 Pb11
Altura ☐ E 43 Kk26
Alturas ☐ USA 120 Dd10
Altus ☐ USA 122 Fa12
Al 'Ula ☐ KSA 76 Md13

Alunda ☐ S 25 Lk15
Alupka ☐ UA 63 Mh23
Alušta ☐ UA 63 Mh23
Alvdal ☐ N 24 Lf14
Älvdalen ☐ S 25 Lh15
Alvesta ☐ S 27 Lh17
Älvros ☐ S 25 Lh14
Älvsbyn ☐ S 25 Ma13
Al Wajh ☐ KSA 76 Md13
Al Widyan ☒ IRQ/KSA 76 Na12
Alytus ☐ LT 31 Mc18
Alzey ☐ D 45 Le21
Amadjuak Lake ☐ CDN 119 Gb05
Amahai ☐ RI 87 Rb19
Åmål ☐ S 26 Lg16
Amaliáda ☐ GR 56 Ma27
Amamapare ☐ RI 92 Rd19
Amapá ☐ BR 134 Hb18
Amarante ☐ P 40 Kf25
Amarillo ☐ USA 122 Ed11
Amasya ☐ TR 65 Mh25
Amazon ☒ BR 134 Hb19
Amazonas ☐ BR 133 Gc20
Amazon Lowlands ☒ 132 Gb19
Ambala ☐ IND 80 Od12
Ambalantota ☐ CL 81 Pa17
Ambam ☐ CAM 108 Lc18
Ambanja ☐ RM 111 Nb21
Ambato ☐ EC 132 Ga19
Ambatondrazaka ☐ RM 111 Nb21
Amberg ☐ D 45 Lf21
Ambérieu-en-Bugey ☐ F 39 Lc23
Ambert ☐ F 38 Lb23
Ambikapur ☐ IND 80 Pa14
Ambilobe ☐ RM 111 Nb21
Ambjörby ☐ S 24 Lg15
Ambohitra ☒ RM 111 Nb21
Amboise ☐ F 38 La22
Ambon ☐ RI 87 Rb19
Ambon ☒ RI 87 Rb19
Ambondromamy ☐ RM 111 Nb22
Ambovombe ☐ RM 111 Nb24
Ambrim ☒ VU 98 Tb22
Amderma ☐ RUS 72 Oa05
Am Djemena ☐ TCH 108 Ld16
Ameixial ☐ P 41 Kg27
Amersfoort ☐ NL 37 Lc19
Amery ☐ 141 Oc32
Amery Ice Shelf ☒ 141 Oc32
Ames ☐ USA 123 Fb10
Amfilohía ☐ GR 56 Ma26
Amfissa ☐ GR 56 Mb26
Amga ☒ RUS 75 Rc06
Amga ☒ RUS 75 Rc06
Amiens ☐ F 37 Lb21
Amindeo ☐ GR 56 Ma25
Amirante Islands ☒ SY 101 Nb10
Åmli ☐ N 26 Le16
Amman ● JOR 76 Md12
Ammarnäs ☐ S 25 Lj13
Ammassalik ☐ DK 119 Ja05
Amol ☐ IR 76 Nc11
Amorgós ☐ GR 57 Mc27
Amorgós ☒ GR 57 Mc27
Amos ☐ CDN 121 Ga09
Åmot ☐ N 26 Le16
Åmotfors ☐ S 26 Lg16
Amoy ☐ CHN 85 Qd14
Ampana ☐ RI 87 Ra19
Ampère Seamount ☒ 104 Kb11

Amposta ☐ E 42 La25
Amran ☐ YE 77 Na15
Amritsar ☐ IND 80 Od12
Amrum ☒ D 44 Le18
Amsterdam ● NL 37 Lc19
Amstetten ☐ A 52 Lh21
Am Timan ☐ TCH 108 Ma16
Amudarja ☒ TM 78 Oa11
Amund Ringnes Island ☒ CDN 118 Fa03
Amundsen Bay ☒ 141 Nc32
Amundsen Gulf ☒ CDN 118 Dd03
Amundsen Ridge ☒ 140 Eb32
Amundsen Sea ☒ 140 Ec32
Amuntai ☐ RI 87 Qc19
Amur ☒ RUS 75 Ra08
Amur ☒ RUS/CHN 83 Rb08
Anabar ☒ RUS 73 Qc04
Anabarskoe plato ☒ RUS 73 Qb04
Anadyr ☐ RUS 74 Tc06
Anadyr' ☒ RUS 74 Tc06
Anadyrskoye Ploskogor'ye ☒ RUS 74 Tc05
Anáfi ☒ GR 57 Mc27
Anafonítria ☐ GR 56 Ma27
Anagni ☐ I 48 Lg25
Anamur ☐ TR 64 Mg27
Anamur Burnu ☒ TR 65 Mg27
Anapa ☐ RUS 63 Mj23
Anápolis ☐ BR 135 Hc22
Ancenis ☐ F 36 Kk22
Anchorage ☐ USA 116 Cc06
Ancona ☐ I 47 Lg24
Ancud ☐ RCH 137 Gb27
Anda ☐ CHN 83 Rb09
Åndalsnes ☐ N 24 Ld14
Andalucía ☒ E 41 Kh27
Andaman and Nicobar Islands ☒ IND 81 Pc16
Andaman Islands ☒ IND 81 Pc16
Andaman Sea ☒ 86 Pc16
Andenes ☐ N 22 Lj11
Ånderdalen n.p. ☒ N 22 Lj11
Andermatt ☐ CH 45 Le22
Andernos-les-Bains ☐ F 38 Kk23
Andes ☒ 128 Ga10
Andfjorden ☒ N 22 Lj11
Andhra Pradesh ☒ IND 81 Od15
Andijon ☐ UZ 78 Oc10
Andırın ☐ TR 65 Mj27
Andirio ☐ GR 56 Ma26
Andong ☐ ROK 83 Rb11
Andorra la Vella ● AND 38 La24
Andorska grjada ☒ RUS 58 Mj16
Andøya ☒ N 22 Lh11
Andravida ☐ GR 56 Ma27
Andreapol' ☐ RUS 58 Mg17
Ándria ☐ I 49 Lj25
Andrijevica ☐ CG 54 Lk24
Andrijlvka ☐ UA 63 Mj22
Ándros ☐ GR 57 Mc27
Ándros ☒ GR 57 Mc27
Andros Island ☒ BS 126 Ga14
Andros Town ☐ BS 126 Ga14
Andrušivka ☐ UA 62 Me20
Andselv ☐ N 22 Lk11
Andújar ☐ E 41 Kh26
Anéfis ☐ RMM 105 La15
Angara ☒ RUS 73 Pd07
Angara ☒ RUS 73 Qa07
Angarsk ☐ RUS 82 Qa08

Angarskij krjaž ☒ RUS 73 Qa07
Angaur ☒ PAL 92 Rc17
Ånge ☐ S 25 Lh14
Angeles ☐ RP 85 Ra15
Ängelholm ☐ S 26 Lg17
Angermanland ☒ S 25 Lj14
Angermünde ☐ D 44 Lg19
Angers ☐ F 36 Kk22
Ängesön ☒ S 25 Ma14
Angola ☒ ANG 110 Ld21
Angoulême ☐ F 38 La23
Ångsö n.p. ☒ S 27 Lk16
Anguilla ☒ UK 127 Gd15
Anholt ☒ DK 26 Lf17
Anhui ☒ CHN 85 Qd12
Aniak ☐ USA 116 Ca06
Anina ☐ RO 54 Ma23
Anjou ☒ F 38 Kk22
Anjouan ☒ COM 111 Na21
Anjujskij hrebet ☒ RUS 74 Ta05
Ankang ☐ CHN 82 Qb12
Ankara ● TR 65 Mg26
Anklam ☐ D 44 Lg19
Anna ☐ RUS 61 Na20
Annaba ☐ DZ 106 Lb11
An Nafud ☒ KSA 76 Na12
An Najaf ☐ IRQ 76 Na12
Annam Plateau ☒ LAO/VN 84 Qb15
Annan ☐ GB 34 Kj18
Annapolis ☐ USA 123 Ga11
Annapurna I ☒ NEP 80 Pa13
Ann Arbor ☐ USA 123 Fd10
An Nasiriyah ☐ IRQ 76 Nb12
Annecy ☐ F 39 Ld23
Annino ☐ RUS 58 Mj16
Anniston ☐ USA 123 Fc12
Annonay ☐ F 39 Lc23
Annopol ☐ PL 51 Ma20
Anqing ☐ CHN 85 Qd12
Ansbach ☐ D 45 Lf21
Anshan ☐ CHN 83 Ra10
Anshun ☐ CHN 84 Qb13
Antalya ☐ TR 64 Mf27
Antalya Körfezi ☒ TR 64 Mf27
Antananarivo ● RM 111 Nb22
Antar ☐ RI 87 Ra20
Antarctica ☒ 140 Ga35
Antarctic Peninsula ☒ 140 Gd32
Antequera ☐ E 41 Kh27
Anti-Atlas ☒ MA 104 Kc12
Antiatlas ☒ MA 104 Kc13
Antigua ☒ AG 127 Gd15
Antigua and Barbuda ☒ AG 127 Gd15
Antikíthira ☒ GR 56 Mb28
Antímilos ☒ GR 57 Mc27
Antipajuta ☐ RUS 73 Od05
Antíparos ☒ GR 57 Mc27
Anti-Taurus Mountains ☒ TR 76 Md11
Antnäs ☐ S 25 Ma13
Antofagasta ☐ RCH 136 Gb23
Antofagasta de la Sierra ☐ RA 136 Gc24
Antracyt ☐ UA 63 Mk21
Antrim ☐ GB 33 Kg18
Antsalova ☐ RM 111 Na22
Antsirabe ☐ RM 111 Nb22
Antsiranana ☐ RM 111 Nb21
Antsohihy ☐ RM 111 Nb21
Anuradhapura ☐ CL 81 Pa17
Anxi ☐ CHN 79 Pd10
Anxious Bay ☒ AUS 95 Rc25
Anyang ☐ CHN 82 Qc11

Anykščiai ◎ LT 31 Mc18
Ánzio ◎ I 48 Lg25
Aomori ◎ J 83 Sa10
Aosta ◉ I 46 Ld23
Aoukâr ▨ RIM 104 Kb15
Aoukâr ◁ RMM 104 Kc14
Aphrida ◎ RO 54 Ma22
Aparri ◎ RP 85 Ra15
Apastovo ◎ RUS 60 Ne18
Apatity ◎ RUS 72 Mc05
Apatzingán d.l.Constitución ◎ MEX 124 Ed15
Ape ◎ LV 30 Md17
Apeldoorn ◎ NL 37 Ld19
Apennines ▲ I 20 Lc09
Apiai ◎ BR 135 Hc23
Aporé ▨ BR 135 Hb22
Apostolove ◎ UA 62 Mg22
Apoteri ◎ GUY 132 Ha18
Appalachian Mountains ▲ USA 123 Fd11
Äppelbo ◎ S 24 Lg15
Apšeronsk ◎ RUS 63 Mk23
Apucarana ◎ BR 135 Hb23
Apui ◎ BR 133 Ha20
Apuka ◎ RUS 74 Tb06
Apure ▨ YV 132 Gc17
Apurímac ▨ PE 133 Gb21
Aquile ◎ BOL 133 Gc22
Aquiléia ◎ I 47 Lg23
Aquitaine ▨ F 38 Kk23
Araban ◎ TR 65 Mj27
Arabian Sea ▨ 77 Oa15
Araç ◎ TR 65 Mg25
Aracá ▨ BR 132 Gd18
Aracaju ◎ BR 135 Ja21
Aracati ◎ BR 134 Ja19
Aracatuba ◎ BR 135 Hb23
Aracena ◎ E 41 Kg27
Araçuaí ◎ BR 135 Hd22
Arad ◎ RO 54 Ma22
Arafura Sea ▨ RI/AUS 92 Rc20
Araguaia ▨ BR 135 Hb21
Araguaia ▨ BR 134 Hc20
Araguaína ◎ BR 134 Hc20
Araguatins ◎ BR 134 Hc20
Aralkı ◎ TR 66 Na25
Aral Sea ▨ UZ/KZ 78 Nd10
Aralsk ◎ KZ 78 Oa09
Aranda de Duero ◎ E 42 Kj25
Aran Islands ▨ IRL 33 Kf19
Aranjuez ◎ E 42 Kj25
Araouane ◎ RMM 104 Kd15
Arapiraca ◎ BR 134 Ja20
Arapkir ◎ TR 66 Mk26
'Ar'ar ◎ KSA 76 Na12
Araraquara ◎ BR 135 Hc23
Araras ◎ BR 134 Hb20
Arauca ◎ CO 132 Gb17
Arawa ◎ PNG 93 Sd20
Arba Minch ◎ ETH 109 Md17
Arbatax ◎ I 48 Le26
Arbil ◎ IRQ 76 Na11
Arboga ◎ S 24 Lg15
Arbroath ◎ GB 34 Kj17
Arcachon ◎ F 38 Kk23
Arčadinskaja ◎ RUS 61 Nb21
Archena ◎ E 43 Kk26
Archipelago of the Recherche ▨ AUS 95 Ra25
Archipiélago de Colón ▨ EC 133 Fc18
Arcipelago della Maddalena, P.N. dell' ▨ I 48 Le25
Arcipélago Toscano, P.N. dell' ◉ I 46 Le24
Arcos de la Frontera ◎ E 41 Kh27

Arctic Bay ◎ CDN 118 Fd04
Arctic Ocean ▨ 138 Da02
Arctic Plains ▨ 116 Ca05
Arcyz ◎ UA 55 Me23
Ardahan ◎ TR 66 Nb25
Ardatov ◎ RUS 60 Nb18
Ardennes ▨ B 37 Lc21
Ardeşen ◎ TR 66 Na25
Ardino ◎ BG 57 Mc25
Ards Peninsula ▨ GB 34 Kh18
Åre ◎ S 24 Lg14
Arecibo ◎ USA 127 Gc15
Arenas de San Pedro ◎ E 40 Kh25
Arendal ◎ N 26 Le16
Areópoli ◎ GR 56 Mb27
Arequipa ◎ PE 133 Gb22
Arévalo ◎ E 40 Kh25
Arezzo ◎ I 46 Lf24
Argentan ◎ F 36 La21
Argentina ▨ RA 136 Gc26
Argentina Range ▨ 140 Ja35
Argenton-sur-Creuse ◎ F 38 La22
Argolikós Kólpos ▨ GR 56 Mb27
Árgos ◎ GR 56 Mb27
Árgos Orestikó ◎ GR 56 Ma25
Argostóli ◎ GR 56 Ma26
Argosy Glacier ▨ 141 Sd35
Arguedas ◎ E 42 Kk24
Arhangel'sk ◎ RUS 72 Na06
Arhavi ◎ TR 66 Na25
Århus ◎ DK 26 Lf17
Ariano Irpino ◎ I 49 Lh25
Arica ◎ RCH 133 Gb22
Aridéa ◎ GR 56 Mb25
Arie Atoll ▨ MV 81 Oc18
Arinos ▨ BR 135 Ha21
Aripuanã ▨ BR 133 Gd20
Ariquemes ◎ BR 133 Gd20
Arisba ◎ GR 57 Md26
Arizona ▨ RA 136 Gc26
Arizona ▨ USA 122 Eb12
Ärjäng ◎ S 26 Lg16
Arjeplog ◎ S 22 Lj12
Arjona ◎ CO 132 Ga16
Arkadak ◎ RUS 61 Nb20
Arkalyk ◎ KZ 78 Ob08
Arkansas ▨ USA 122 Fb11
Arkansas ▨ USA 123 Fb11
Arkansas ▨ USA 123 Fb12
Arkitsa ◎ GR 56 Mb26
Arklow ◎ IRL 33 Kg19
Arles ◎ F 39 Lc24
Arlington ◎ USA 123 Ga11
Arlon ◎ B 37 Lc21
Armenia ▨ ARM 76 Na10
Armenia ◎ CO 132 Ga18
Armidale ◎ AUS 97 Sc25
Armjans'k ◎ UA 62 Mg22
Arnäsvall ◎ S 25 Lk14
Arnay-le-Duc ◎ F 39 Lc22
Arneá ◎ GR 56 Mb25
Arnedo ◎ E 42 Kj24
Årnes ◎ N 24 Lf15
Arnhem ◎ NL 37 Lc20
Arnhem Land ▨ AUS 94 Rc21
Arnøy ◎ N 22 Ma10
Arnsberg ◎ D 44 Le20
Arnstadt ◎ D 44 Lf20
Arquipélago dos Bijagós ▨ GNB 105 Ka16
Ar-Rachidia ◎ MA 104 Kd12
ar-Rahad ◎ SUD 107 Mc16
ar-Rahad ◁ SUD 107 Mc16

Ar Ramadi ◎ IRQ 76 Na12
Ar-Rank ◎ SUD 109 Mc16
Ar Rass ◎ KSA 77 Na13
Arravalli Range ▲ IND 80 Oc13
Ar Rawdah ◎ KSA 77 Na14
Ar-Rif ▲ MA 104 Kc12
Ar Rub' al Khali ▨ KSA 77 Nb15
Ar Rutbah ◎ IRQ 76 Na12
Ar Ruweis ◎ Q 77 Nc13
Arsk ◎ RUS 60 Ne17
Arslanköy ◎ TR 65 Mh27
Árta ◎ GR 56 Ma26
Artemisa ◎ C 126 Fd14
Artemivs'k ◎ UA 63 Mk21
Artigas ◎ 140 Ha30
Artois ▨ F 35 La20
Artvin ◎ TR 76 Na10
Artvin ◎ TR 66 Na25
Aruba ◎ NL 127 Gb16
Aruba ◎ NL 127 Gb16
Arunachal Pradesh ▨ IND 84 Pc13
Arusha ◎ EAT 109 Md19
Aruwimi ▨ RDC 109 Mb18
Arvaykheer ◎ MNG 82 Qa09
Arviat ◎ CDN 120 Fb06
Arvidsjaur ◎ S 25 Lk13
Arvika ◎ S 26 Lg16
Arzamas ◎ RUS 60 Nb18
Ås ◎ S 25 Lh14
Aš ◎ CZ 52 Lg20
Aşağı Üçdam ◎ TR 66 Na26
Asahi dake ▲ J 83 Sa10
Asahikawa ◎ J 83 Sa10
Ásarna ◎ S 25 Lh14
Åsbyrgi ▨ IS 32 Kb13
Aschaffenburg ◎ D 45 Le21
Aschersleben ◎ D 44 Lf20
Áscoli Piceno ◎ I 47 Lg24
Aseb ◎ ER 107 Na16
Åseda ◎ S 27 Lh17
Asedjrad ◁ DZ 104 La14
Asela ◎ ETH 109 Md17
Åsele ◎ S 25 Lj13
Åsen ◎ S 24 Lg15
Asenovgrad ◎ BG 55 Mc24
Åseral ◎ N 26 Ld16
Ashburton ◉ AUS 94 Qd23
Ashburton ▨ NZ 99 Tc27
Asheville ◎ USA 123 Fd11
Ashford ◎ GB 35 La20
Ashgabad ◉ TM 78 Nd11
Ashland ◎ USA 120 Fb09
Ash Shurayf ◎ KSA 76 Md13
Asinara, P.N. dell' ▨ I 48 Le25
Asipovičy ◎ BY 51 Me19
Asir ▨ KSA 77 Na14
Asir ▲ KSA 77 Na14
Aşit ◁ RUS 60 Ne17
Aşkale ◎ TR 66 Na26
Askersund ◎ S 27 Lh16
Askim ◎ N 26 Lf16
Askja ▲ IS 32 Kb13
Askvoll ◎ N 24 Lc15
Asmara ◉ ER 107 Md15
Åsmjany ◎ BY 31 Mc18
Asmunti ◎ FIN 28 Md13
Aspres-sur-Buëch ◎ F 39 Lc23
As Salmy ◎ KWT 77 Nb13
Assam ▨ IND 84 Pc13
Assamakka ◎ RN 106 Lb15
Assen ◎ NL 37 Ld19

As Shamiyah ◁ IRQ 76 Nb12
As-Sila ◎ UAE 77 Nc14
Assiut ◎ ET 107 Mc13
Assiût ◎ ET 107 Mc13
As Sulaymaniyah ◎ IRQ 76 Nb13
As Sulayyil ◎ KSA 77 Nb14
Åstad ◎ N 22 Lh12
Astana ◉ KZ 78 Oc08
Astara ◎ IR 76 Nb11
Asti ◎ I 46 Le23
Astipálea ◎ GR 57 Md27
Astipálea ▨ GR 57 Md27
Astorga ◎ E 40 Kg24
Astoria ◎ USA 122 Dd09
Astove Island ▨ SY 111 Nb21
Astradamovka ◎ RUS 60 Nd18
Astrahan' ◎ RUS 76 Nb09
Åsträsk ◎ S 25 Lk13
Astryna ◎ BY 51 Mc19
Asturias ▨ E 40 Kg24
Asuka ◎ 141 Ma33
Asunción ◉ PY 136 Ha24
Aswa ▨ EAU 109 Mc18
Aswàn ◎ ET 107 Mc14
Atakpamé ◎ TG 105 La17
Atalaya ◎ PE 133 Gb21
Atär ◎ RIM 104 Kb14
Atasu ◎ KZ 78 Oc09
Atatürk Baraji ▨ TR 65 Mk27
Atbara ◎ SUD 107 Mc15
'Atbara ▨ SUD 107 Md15
Aterau ◎ KZ 76 Nc09
Ath ◎ B 37 Lb20
Athabasca ◎ CDN 120 Eb07
Athens ◉ GR 57 Mb27
Athens ◎ USA 123 Fd12
Athína ◉ GR 57 Mb27
Athlone ◎ IRL 33 Kg19
Áthos ▨ GR 57 Mc25
Áthos ▲ GR 57 Mc25
Ati ◎ TCH 106 Ld16
Atjaševo ◎ RUS 60 Nd18
Atlanta ◉ USA 123 Fd12
Atlantic Ocean ▨ 101 Kb11
Atlas ▲ MA 104 Kc12
Atlas Saharien ▲ DZ 104 La12
Atlas Tellien ▲ DZ 104 La11
Atlin Lake ▨ CDN 117 Db07
Atol das Rocas ▨ BR 128 Ja10
Atri ◎ I 47 Lg24
At Ta'if ◎ KSA 77 Na14
Attawapiskat ◎ CDN 120 Fd08
Åtvidaberg ◎ S 27 Lh16
Aubagne ◎ F 39 Lc24
Aubenas ◎ F 39 Lc23
Aubigny-sur-Nère ◎ F Lb22
Aubusson ◎ F 38 Lb23
Auckland ◎ NZ 99 Tc26
Aude ▨ F 39 Lb24
Audierne ◎ F 36 Kh21
Audo Range ▲ ETH 109 Na17
Augsburg ◎ D 45 Lf21
Augusta ▨ AUS 95 Qd25
Augusta ◎ I 49 Lh27
Augusta ◎ USA 123 Fd12
Augusta ◎ USA 121 Gc10
Augustów ◎ PL 51 Mb19
Auki ◉ SOL 93 Ta20
Aukštadvaris ◎ LT 31 Mc18
Aukštaitijos n.p. ◉ LT 31 Md18
Aullène ◎ F 46 Le25
Aurangabad ◎ IND 80 Od14

Auray ◻ F 36 Kj22
Aurdal ◻ N 24 Le15
Aure ◻ N 24 Le14
Aurich ◻ D 44 Ld19
Aurillac ◻ F 38 Lb23
Aurlandsvangen ◻ N 24 Ld15
Aursjøen ◻ N 26 Le14
Austad ◻ N 26 Le18
Austin ◻ USA 122 Ea11
Austin ◉ USA 123 Fa12
Australia ◻ AUS 94 Rb23
Australian Capital Territory
A.C.T. ◻ AUS 97 Sb26
Austria ◼ A 52 Lh22
Austvågøya ▲ N 22 Lh11
Auterive ◻ F 42 La24
Autun ◻ F 39 Lc22
Auvergne ◻ F 38 Lb23
Auvergne ▲ F 38 Lb23
Auxerre ◻ F 39 Lb22
Auxonne ◻ F 39 Lc22
Auyántepui ▲ YV 132 Gd17
Avdijivka ◻ UA 59 Mg20
Aveiro ◻ P 40 Kf25
Avellino ◻ I 49 Lh25
Avesta ◻ S 25 Lj15
Avezzano ◻ I 47 Lg24
Aviator Glacier ⧩ 141 Ta33
Aviator Glacier Tongue ⧩ 141 Tb33
Aviemore ◻ GB 34 Kj17
Avignon ◻ F 39 Lc24
Ávila ◻ E 40 Kh24
Avilés ◻ E 40 Kh24
Avlóna ◻ GR 57 Mb26
Avranches ◻ F 36 Kh21
Avrillé ◻ F 38 Kk22
Awanui ◻ NZ 99 Tc26
Awasa ◻ ETH 109 Md17
Awash Wenz ⧩ ETH 109 Na17
Awbari ◻ LAR 106 Lc13
Awbari Sahra ◻ LAR 106 Lc13
Awjilah ◻ LAR 106 Ma13
Axel Heiberg Island ◻ CDN 118 Fb02
Ayacucho ◻ PE 133 Gb21
Ayakoz ◻ KZ 79 Pa09
Ayamonte ◻ E 41 Kg27
Ayancık ◻ TR 65 Mh25
Aydın ◻ TR 57 Md27
Aydın Dağları ▲ TR 57 Md27
Ayers Rock ▲ AUS 94 Rc24
Ayllón ◻ E 42 Kj25
Ayod ◻ SUD 109 Mc17
'Ayoûn el'Atroûs ◻ RIM 105 Kc15
Ayr ◻ AUS 96 Sb22
Ayr ◻ GB 34 Kh18
Ayrancı ◻ TR 65 Mg27
Ayritepe ◻ TR 64 Mf26
Ayutthaya ◻ THA 84 Qa16
Ayvacık ◻ TR 57 Md26
Ayvacık ◻ TR 65 Mj25
Ayvalık ◻ TR 57 Md26
Azaough ⧩ RMM 105 La15
Azaryçy ◻ BY 51 Me19
Azeffâl ⧩ RIM 104 Kb14
Azerbaijan ◼ AZ 76 Nb10
Aznakaevo ◻ RUS 60 Ng18
Azogues ◻ EC 132 Ga19
Azores-Cape Saint Vincent
Ridge ≋ 104 Kb11
Azov ◻ RUS 63 Mk22
Azovo-Syvas'kyj N.P. ◻ UA 63 Mj22
Azrou ◻ MA 104 Kc12
Azuaga ◻ E 41 Kh26
Azul ◻ RA 137 Ha26

B

Babadag ◻ RO 55 Me23
Babaevo ◻ RUS 58 Mh16
Bab al-Mandab ◻ YE/DJI 77 Na16
Babanusa ◻ SUD 109 Mb16
Babar ◻ RI 87 Rb20
Babelthuap ▲ PAL 92 Rc17
Babinda ◻ AUS 96 Sb22
Babiogórski P.N. ◻ PL 50 Lk21
Babrujsk ◻ BY 51 Me19
Babúškin ◻ RUS 82 Qb08
Bacabal ◻ BR 134 Hd19
Bacan ◻ RI 87 Rb19
Bacău ◻ RO 55 Md22
Bachčysaraj ◻ UA 62 Mg23
Bach Ice Shelf ⧩ 140 Gb33
Bachmac ◻ UA 59 Mg20
Bachórz ◻ PL 51 Mb21
Bačka Palanka ◻ SR 54 Lk23
Bačka Topola ◻ SR 54 Lk23
Bäckefors ◻ S 26 Lg16
Bacolod ◻ RP 85 Ra16
Badajoz ◻ E 41 Kg26
Badalona ◻ E 42 Lb25
Bad Bentheim ◻ D 44 Ld19
Bad Doberan ◻ D 44 Lf18
Baden ◻ A 52 Lj21
Baden-Baden ◻ D 45 Le21
Baden-Württemberg ◻ D 45 Le21
Bad Freienwalde ◻ D 44 Lh19
Bad Gastein ◻ A 52 Lg22
Badgingarra ◻ AUS 95 Qd25
Bad Hersfeld ◻ D 44 Le20
Bad Homburg ◻ D 45 Le20
Bad Ischl ◻ A 52 Lg22
Bad Kreuznach ◻ D 45 Ld21
Bad Mergentheim ◻ D 45 Le21
Bad Neustadt ◻ D 45 Lf20
Bado ◻ RI 92 Rd20
Bad Oldesloe ◻ D 44 Lf19
Bad Reichenhall ◻ D 45 Lg22
Badr Hunayn ◻ KSA 76 Md14
Bad Salzuflen ◻ D 44 Le19
Bad Saulgau ◻ D 45 Le21
Bad Segeberg ◻ D 44 Lf19
Bad Tölz ◻ D 45 Lf22
Baeza ◻ E 41 Kj27
Bafatá ◻ GNB 105 Kb16
Baffin Basin ≋ 118 Gc04
Baffin Bay ≋ 118 Gc04
Baffin-Insel ◻ CDN 118 Ga04
Baffin Island ◻ CDN 118 Ga04
Bafia ◻ CAM 108 Lc18
Bafing ⧩ RG 105 Kb16
Bafoussam ◻ CAM 108 Lc17
Bafra ◻ TR 65 Mh25
Bafra Burnu ◻ TR 65 Mh25
Bagamoyo ◻ EAT 111 Mc20
Bagan ◻ MYA 84 Pc14
Bagé ◻ BR 136 Hb25
Baghdad ◉ IRQ 76 Na12
Bagheria ◻ I 48 Lg26
Baghlan ◻ AFG 78 Ob11
Bagn ◻ N 24 Le15
Bagnères-de-Luchon ◻ F 42 La24
Bagno di Romagna ◻ I 46 Lf24
Bagoé ⧩ RMM 105 Kc16
Bago Yoma ▲ MYA 84 Pd14

Baguio ◻ RP 85 Ra15
Baguirmi ◻ TCH 108 Ld16
Bahama Islands ◻ BS 126 Ga13
Bahamas ◼ BS 126 Ga14
Baharija Oasis ◻ ET 107 Mb13
Bahawlapur ◻ PAK 80 Oc13
Bahia ◻ BR 135 Hd21
Bahia Anegada ≋ RA 137 Gd27
Bahia Blanca ◻ RA 137 Gd26
Bahía de Buenaventura ≋ CO 132 Ga18
Bahía de Chetumal ≋ MEX 125 Fc15
Bahía de Coronado ≋ CR 126 Fd17
Bahía de la Ascensión ≋ MEX 125 Fc15
Bahía de San Juan del Norte ≋ NIC 126 Fd16
Bahía de Sebastián Vizcaíno ≋ MEX 124 Eb13
Bahía Grande ≋ RA 137 Gc29
Bahia Kino ◻ MEX 124 Eb13
Bahía Samborombón ≋ RA 136 Ha26
Bahía Solano ◻ CO 132 Ga17
Bahir Dar ◻ ETH 109 Md16
Bahrain ◼ BRN 77 Nc13
Bahr al-Arab ⧩ SUD 109 Mb16
Bahr Aouk ⧩ RCA 108 Ld17
Bahr Salamat ⧩ TCH 108 Ma16
Baia ◻ RO 55 Me23
Baia de Marajó ≋ BR 134 Hc19
Baia de Setúbal ≋ P 41 Kf26
Baía do Maputo ≋ MOC 111 Mc24
Baia Mare ◻ RO 54 Mb22
Baião ◻ BR 134 Hc19
Baicheng ◻ CHN 83 Ra10
Baie-Comeau ◻ CDN 121 Gc09
Baie de Corisco ≋ G 108 Lb18
Baie-du-Poste ◻ CDN 121 Gb08
Baikonur ◻ KZ 78 Oa09
Baile Átha Cliath = Dublin ◉ IRL 33 Kg19
Bailén ◻ E 41 Kj26
Băileşti ◻ RO 54 Mb23
Bailey Ice Stream ⧩ 140 Jb35
Bailundo ◻ ANG 110 Ld21
Baiona ◻ E 40 Kf24
Bairnsdale ◻ AUS 97 Sb26
Baja ◻ H 53 Lk22
Baja California ◻ MEX 122 Ea12
Baja California Norte ◻ MEX 122 Ea12
Baja California Sur ◻ MEX 124 Eb13
Bajdarackaja guba ≋ RUS 72 Oa04
Bajina Bašta ◻ SR 54 Lk24
Bajkal'sk ◻ RUS 82 Qa08
Bajmok ◻ SR 54 Lk23
Bakaly ◻ RUS 60 Ng18
Baker ◻ USA 122 Ea10
Baker Lake ◻ CDN 118 Fa06
Bakersfield ◻ USA 122 Ea11
Bakkafjörður ◻ IS 32 Kc12
Bakkaflói ≋ IS 32 Kc12

Bakkageröi ▲ IS 32 Kd13
Bakoy ⧩ RMM 105 Kc16
Baku ◉ AZ 76 Nb10
Balá ◻ TR 65 Mg26
Balabac ◻ RP 85 Qd17
Balabac ◻ RP 85 Qd17
Balabanovo ◻ RUS 58 Mj18
Balaguer ◻ E 42 La25
Balahna ◻ RUS 60 Nb17
Balaklija ◻ UA 63 Mj21
Balakovo ◻ RUS 61 Nd20
Balandino ◻ RUS 60 Ng19
Balašiha ◻ RUS 58 Mj18
Balašov ◻ RUS 61 Nb20
Balaton ◻ H 53 Lj22
Balatonbozsok ◻ H 53 Lk22
Balaton-felvidéki N.P. ◻ H 53 Lj22
Balatonfüred ◻ H 53 Lj22
Balatonlelle ◻ H 53 Lj22
Balazote ◻ E 43 Kj26
Bălceşti ◻ RO 54 Mb23
Balčik ◻ BG 55 Me24
Balclutha ◻ NZ 99 Tb28
Bald Head ◻ AUS 95 Qd26
Baldy Peak ▲ USA 122 Ec12
Baleares ◻ E 43 Lb26
Balearic Islands ◻ E 43 La26
Bálgarene ◻ BG 55 Mc24
Balhaš ◻ KZ 79 Od09
Bali ◻ RI 87 Qd20
Balik ◻ BG 55 Md24
Balıkesir ◻ TR 57 Md26
Balıkpapan ◻ RI 87 Qc19
Bälinge ◻ S 27 Lj16
Balingen ◻ D 45 Le21
Balışeyh ◻ TR 65 Mg26
Balkan Mountains ▲ BG 55 Mc24
Balkanabat ◻ TM 76 Nc11
Balkhash ◻ KZ 78 Od09
Ballangen ◻ N 22 Lj11
Ballarat ◻ AUS 97 Sa26
Ballina ◻ AUS 97 Sc24
Ballina ◻ IRL 33 Kf18
Ball's Pyramid ◻ AUS 97 Sd25
Ballstad ◻ N 22 Lg11
Ballycastle ◻ GB 33 Kg18
Ballycroy N.P. ◻ IRL 33 Kf18
Ballyhaunis ◻ IRL 33 Kf19
Ballymena ◻ GB 33 Kg18
Ballymoney ◻ GB 33 Kg18
Balş ◻ RO 54 Mc23
Balonne ⧩ AUS 96 Sb24
Balranald ◻ AUS 97 Sa25
Balsas ◻ BR 134 Hc20
Bålsta ◻ S 27 Lj16
Balta ◻ UA 55 Me22
Balta şi ◻ TR 66 Mk26
Baltasound ◻ GB 34 Kk15
Bălţi ◻ MD 55 Md22
Baltijsk ◻ RUS 27 Lk18
Baltimore ◻ USA 123 Ga11
Baluchistan ◻ PAK 77 Oa13
Balvi ◻ LV 30 Md17
Balykchy ◻ KS 78 Od10
Bam ◻ IR 77 Nd13
Bamako ◉ RMM 105 Kc16
Bambari ◻ RCA 108 Ma17
Bamberg ◻ D 45 Lf21
Bamda ◻ CHN 84 Pd12
Bamenda ◻ CAM 108 Lc17
Bamian ◻ AFG 78 Ob12
Banalla ◻ RDC 109 Mb18
Banat ◻ RO 56 Ma23
Banaue ◻ RP 85 Ra15
Banaz ◻ TR 64 Me26
Banbridge ◻ GB 33 Kg18

Banco de Serrana □ CO 126 Fd16
Banco de Serranilla □ CO 126 Ga15
Banda Aceh ◉ RI 86 Pd17
Bandar-e-Abbas □ IR 77 Nd13
Bandarjaya □ RI 86 Qb19
Bandar Lampung ◉ RI 86 Qb20
Bandar Seri Begawan ◉ BRU 87 Qc18
Bandar Sri Aman □ MAL 86 Qc18
Banda Sea ⌷ RI 87 Rb19
Bander-e-Busher □ IR 77 Nc13
Bandiagara ⌷ RMM 105 Kd16
Bandırma □ TR 57 Md25
Bandon □ IRL 33 Kf20
Bandundu □ RDC 108 Lg19
Bandung □ RI 86 Qb20
Bâneasa □ RO 55 Md23
Banff □ CDN 117 Ea08
Banff □ GB 34 Kj17
Banfora □ BF 105 Kd16
Bangalore □ IND 81 Od16
Bangassou ⌷ RCA 108 Ma18
Banggi □ MAL 87 Qd17
Bangka □ RI 86 Qb19
Bangko □ RI 86 Qa19
Bangkok ◉ THA 84 Qa16
Bangladesh ■ BD 84 Pc14
Bangor □ GB 34 Kh18
Bangor □ GB 35 Kh19
Bangor □ IRL 33 Kf18
Bangor □ USA 121 Gc10
Bangui ◉ RDC 108 Ld18
Bangui □ RP 85 Ra15
Bangweulu Swamps ⌷ Z 110 Mb21
Bani ⌷ RMM 105 Kc16
Bani Walid □ LAR 106 Lc12
Banja Luka □ BIH 47 Lj23
Banjarmasin □ RI 87 Qb19
Banjul ◉ WAG 105 Ka16
Banks Island □ CDN 118 Dd03
Banks Islands ⌷ VU 98 Tb21
Banks Peninsula ⌷ NZ 99 Tc27
Banks Strait ⌷ AUS 97 Sb27
Banská Bystrica □ SK 53 Lk21
Bantry □ IRL 33 Kf20
Banyoles □ E 42 Lb24
Banyuwangi □ RI 87 Qb20
Banzare Coast ⌷ 141 Rb32
Baoding □ CHN 82 Qd11
Baoji □ CHN 82 Qb12
Baotou □ CHN 82 Qc10
Baoulé ⌷ RMM 105 Kc16
Ba'qubah □ IRQ 76 Na12
Bar □ CG 56 La24
Bar □ UA 51 Mc20
Barabacena ⌷ BR 135 Hd23
Barabinskaja nizmennost ⌷ RUS 72 Oc07
Barahona □ DOM 127 Gb15
Baranavičy □ BY 51 Md19
Baranivka □ UA 51 Md20
Baranof Island ⌷ USA 117 Da07
Barbados ■ BDS 127 Ha16
Barbastro □ E 42 La24
Barbate □ E 41 Kh27
Barbezieux-Saint-Hilaire □ F 38 Kk23
Barbuda ⌷ AG 127 Gd15

Barcaldine □ AUS 96 Sb23
Barcelona □ YV 127 Gd16
Barcelonnette □ F 39 Ld23
Barcs □ H 47 Lj23
Bardejov □ SK 53 Ma21
Bareilly □ IND 80 Od13
Barentsburg ⌷ N 22 Lf06
Barentsøya ⌷ N 22 Lh06
Barents Sea ⌷ 139 Mc03
Barguzinskij hrebet ⌷ RUS 82 Qb08
Bari □ I 46 Lh23
Barinas □ YV 132 Gb17
Barisan Range ⌷ RI 86 Qa19
Barkam □ CHN 84 Qa12
Barkly Homestead Roadhouse □ AUS 96 Rd22
Barkly Tableland ⌷ AUS 96 Rd22
Bârlad □ RO 55 Md22
Bar-le-Duc □ F 37 Lc21
Barletta □ I 49 Lj25
Barmer □ IND 80 Oc13
Barnaul ◉ RUS 79 Pa08
Barneville-Carteret □ F 36 Kk21
Barnstaple □ GB 35 Kh20
Barotseland ⌷ Z 110 Ma22
Barovo □ MK 56 Mb25
Barquisimeto □ YV 127 Gc16
Barra □ BR 134 Hd21
Barra □ GB 34 Kg17
Barra do Corda □ BR 134 Hc20
Barra do Garças □ BR 135 Hb22
Barragem de Serra da Mesa ⌷ BR 135 Hc21
Barragem de Sobradinho ⌷ BR 134 Hd21
Barranca □ PE 132 Ga19
Barranca □ PE 133 Ga21
Barrancabermeja □ CO 132 Gb17
Barranquilla □ CO 127 Gb16
Barreiras □ BR 135 Hd21
Barreirinhas □ BR 134 Hd19
Barrême □ F 39 Ld24
Barren Grounds ⌷ CDN 118 Ed24
Barretos □ BR 135 Hc23
Barrie □ CDN 123 Ga10
Barriyat al-Bayyuda ⌷ SUD 107 Mc15
Barrow □ USA 116 Ca04
Barrow-in-Furness □ GB 35 Kj18
Barrow Island ⌷ AUS 94 Qd23
Barrow Strait ⌷ CDN 118 Fa04
Barstow □ USA 122 Ea12
Bar-sur-Aube □ F 37 Lc21
Barth □ D 44 Lg18
Bartın □ TR 65 Mg25
Bartlesville □ USA 123 Fa11
Bartoszyce □ PL 50 Ma18
Baruunkharaa ⌷ MNG 82 Qb09
Baruun Urt □ MNG 82 Qc09
Barvinkove □ UA 63 Mj21
Baryš □ RUS 60 Nd19
Barysav □ BY 31 Me18
Basankusu □ RDC 108 Ld18
Basarabeasca □ MD 55 Me22
Basarabi □ RO 56 Me23
Basay □ RP 85 Ra17
Basel □ CH 45 Ld22

Bashkortostan □ RUS 72 Nd08
Basilan □ RP 85 Ra17
Basilicata □ I 49 Lj25
Basingstoke □ GB 35 Kk20
Baška □ HR 47 Lf23
Başkomutan Tarihi Milli Parkı ⌷ TR 64 Me26
Basle □ CH 45 Ld22
Basra = Al Basra □ IRQ 77 Nb12
Bassano del Grappa □ I 46 Lf23
Bassas da India ⌷ F 111 Md23
Bassein □ MYA 84 Pc15
Basse-Normandie ⌷ F 36 Kk21
Basse Santa Su ⌷ WAG 105 Kb16
Basse-Terre ◉ F 127 Gd15
Basseterre ◉ KNA 127 Gd15
Bass Strait ⌷ AUS 97 Sb26
Bassum □ D 44 Le19
Båstad □ S 26 Lg17
Baštanka □ UA 62 Mg22
Bastia □ F 46 Le24
Bastogne □ B 37 Lc21
Bata □ GQ 108 Lb18
Bataga ⌷ RUS 74 Rc05
Batajsk □ RUS 63 Mk22
Batak □ BG 57 Mc25
Batangafo □ RCA 108 Ld17
Batangas □ RP 85 Ra16
Batanta ⌷ RI 87 Rb19
Bátaszék □ H 53 Lk22
Batemans Bay □ AUS 97 Sc26
Bath □ GB 35 Kj20
Batha ⌷ TCH 108 Ld16
Bathurst □ AUS 97 Sb25
Bathurst □ CDN 121 Gc09
Bathurst Inlet □ CDN 118 Ec05
Bathurst Island ⌷ AUS 94 Rc21
Bathurst Island ⌷ CDN 118 Fa03
Bati Menteşe Dağları ⌷ TR 57 Md27
Bati Toroslar ⌷ TR 64 Mf27
Batna □ DZ 106 Lb11
Baton Rouge ◉ USA 123 Fb12
Båtsfjord □ N 23 Me10
Batticaloa □ CL 81 Pa17
Battipáglia □ I 49 Lh25
Batu ⌷ ETH 109 Md17
Batumi □ GE 76 Na10
Baturube □ RI 87 Ra19
Batyrevo □ RUS 60 Nd18
Baubau □ RI 87 Ra20
Bauchi □ WAN 108 Lb16
Bauru □ BR 135 Hc23
Bauska □ LV 31 Mc17
Bautzen □ D 44 Lh20
Bawan □ RI 87 Qb20
Bay of Biscay ⌷ E/F 38 Kj23
Bayamo □ C 126 Ga14
Bayan Har Shan ⌷ CHN 84 Pd12
Bayankhongor □ MNG 82 Qa09
Bayat □ TR 65 Mh25
Bayburt □ TR 66 Na25
Baydhabo □ SP 109 Na18
Bayerischer Wald, N.P. ⌷ D 45 Lg21
Bayern □ D 45 Lf21

Bayeux □ F 36 Kk21
Bayındır □ TR 57 Md26
Bayji □ IRQ 76 Na12
Baykan □ TR 66 Na26
Bay of Bengal ⌷ 81 Pb15
Bay of Campeche ⌷ MEX 125 Fb15
Bay of Fundy ⌷ CDN 121 Gc10
Bay of Plenty ⌷ NZ 99 Td26
Bay of Whales ⌷ 140 Bd34
Bayonne □ F 42 Kk24
Bayramiç □ TR 57 Md26
Bayreuth □ D 45 Lf21
Baytik Shan ⌷ CHN 79 Pc09
Bayu □ RI 87 Ra19
Baza □ E 41 Kj27
Bazarnye Mataki ⌷ RUS 60 Nf18
Bazarnyi Karabulak □ RUS 61 Nd19
Beachport □ AUS 97 Sa26
Beagle Gulf ⌷ AUS 94 Rc21
Beardmore Glacier ⌷ 141 Tc35
Beasain □ E 42 Kj24
Beatty □ USA 122 Ea11
Beauce ⌷ F 36 La21
Beaufort □ MAL 87 Qd17
Beaufort Sea ⌷ 116 Cd04
Beaufort-Wes □ ZA 110 Ma25
Beaufort West □ ZA 110 Ma25
Beaugency □ F 36 La22
Beaumont □ USA 123 Fb12
Beaune □ F 39 Lc22
Beauvais □ F 37 Lb21
Beauvoir-sur-Mer □ F 36 Kj22
Bebra □ D 44 Le20
Bečej □ SR 54 Ma23
Bèchar □ DZ 104 Kd12
Bechuanaland □ ZA 110 Ma24
Bédarieux □ F 38 Lb24
Bedford □ GB 35 Kk19
Beeskow □ D 44 Lh19
Beethoven Peninsula ⌷ 140 Gb33
Behrendt Mountains ⌷ 140 Gb34
Bei'an □ CHN 83 Rb09
Beihai □ CHN 85 Qb14
Beijing ◉ CHN 82 Qd11
Beira □ MOC 111 Mc22
Beirut ◉ RL 76 Md12
Beitbridge □ ZW 111 Mc22
Beiuş □ RO 54 Mb22
Beja □ P 41 Kg27
Bejaia □ DZ 104 La11
Béjar □ E 40 Kh25
Bejneu □ KZ 78 Nd09
Békés □ H 53 Ma22
Békéscsaba □ H 53 Ma22
Belaazërsk □ BY 51 Mc19
Belaga □ MAL 87 Qc18
Belaja Kalitva ⌷ RUS 63 Na21
Belarus ■ BY 31 Mc19
Belavežskaja Pušča, N.P. ⌷ BY 51 Mc19
Bełchatów □ PL 50 Lk20
Belcher Islands ⌷ CDN 120 Fd07
Belchite □ E 42 Kk25
Belém ■ BR 134 Hc19
Belen □ TR 65 Mj27
Belev □ RUS 59 Mj19
Beleya Terara ⌷ ETH 109 Md16

Belfast ◉ GB 34 Kh18
Belfort ☐ F 39 Ld22
Belgaum ☐ IND 81 Oc15
Belgium ☐ B 37 Lc20
Belgorod ☐ RUS 59 Mj20
Belgrade ◉ SR 54 Ma23
Belgrano II ☐ 140 Jb34
Belica ☐ MK 56 Ma25
Beli Manastir ☐ HR 47 Lk23
Belitung ☐ RI 86 Qb19
Belize ☐ BH 125 Fc15
Belize City ☐ BH 125 Fc15
Bel'kovo ☐ RUS 59 Mg19
Bellac ☐ F 38 La22
Bella Coola ☐ CDN 116 Dc08
Belladonia Motel ☐ AUS 95 Ra25
Bellême ☐ F 36 La21
Belley ☐ F 39 Lc23
Bellingshausen ☐ 140 Ha30
Bellingshausen Sea ☐ 140 Fd32
Bellinzona ☐ CH 45 Le22
Bello ☐ CO 132 Ga17
Bellona Island ☐ SOL 96 Sd21
Bell Peninsula ☐ CDN 118 Fd06
Belluno ☐ I 46 Lg22
Belmopan ◉ BH 125 Fc15
Belmullet ☐ IRL 33 Kf18
Belogradčik ☐ BG 54 Mb24
Belo Horizonte ◉ BR 135 Hd22
Belojarskij ☐ RUS 72 Ob06
Belomorsk ☐ RUS 29 Mh13
Belorečensk ☐ RUS 63 Mk23
Bel'skaja vozvyšennost' ☐ RUS 59 Mg18
Beltiug ☐ RO 54 Mb22
Belyj ☐ RUS 58 Mg18
Belzig ☐ D 44 Lg19
Bemaraha ☐ RM 111 Na22
Bemidji ☐ USA 120 Fb09
Benabarre ☐ E 42 La24
Benavente ☐ E 40 Kh25
Bend ☐ USA 122 Dc10
Bendigo ☐ AUS 97 Sa26
Benešov ☐ CZ 52 Lh21
Benevento ☐ I 49 Lh25
Bengbu ☐ CHN 83 Qd12
Benghazi ☐ LAR 106 Ma12
Bengkulu ☐ RI 86 Qa19
Bengtsfors ☐ S 26 Lg19
Benguela ☐ ANG 110 Lc21
Beni ☐ RDC 109 Mb18
Beni ☐ BOL 133 Gc21
Beni ☐ BOL 133 Gc21
Benicarló ☐ E 43 La25
Benicasim = Benicàssim ☐ E 43 La25
Benicàssim ☐ E 43 La25
Benidorm ☐ E 43 Kk26
Benifaió ☐ E 43 Kk26
Beni Mazâr ☐ ET 107 Mc13
Benin ☐ DY 105 La16
Benin City ☐ WAN 108 Lb17
Beni Suéf ☐ ET 107 Mc13
Benjamin Constant ☐ BR 132 Gc19
Benkovac ☐ HR 47 Lh23
Ben Nevis ▲ GB 34 Kh17
Bensheim ☐ D 45 Le21
Benue ⌁ WAN 108 Lb17
Beograd ◉ SR 54 Ma23
Beppu Oita ☐ J 83 Rc12
Berane ☐ CG 54 Lk24
Berat ☐ AL 56 La25
Berazino ☐ BY 51 Me19

Berbérati ☐ RCA 108 Ld18
Berchtesgaden ☐ D 45 Lg22
Berck-Plage ☐ F 35 La20
Berdjans'k ☐ UA 63 Mj22
Berdjans'ka kosa ☒ UA 63 Mj22
Berdsk ☐ RUS 79 Pa08
Berdyčiv ☐ UA 53 Mb21
Berehove ☐ UA 53 Mb21
Berendi ☐ TR 65 Mh27
Berenice ☐ ET 107 Md14
Berens River ⌁ CDN 120 Fa08
Berestečko ☐ UA 51 Mc20
Berezanka ☐ UA 62 Mf22
Berezanskaja ☐ RUS 63 Mk23
Berežany ☐ UA 51 Mc21
Berezinsky Biosphere Nature Reserve ✿ BY 31 Me19
Berezna ☐ UA 59 Mf20
Berezne ☐ UA 51 Ma20
Bereznehuvate ☐ UA 62 Mg22
Berezniki ☐ RUS 72 Nd07
Berezovo ☐ RUS 29 Mk15
Berga ☐ E 42 La24
Bergama ☐ TR 57 Md26
Bergamo ☐ I 46 Le23
Bergen ☐ D 44 Le19
Bergen ☐ D 44 Lg18
Bergen ☐ N 24 Lc15
Bergerac ☐ F 38 La23
Bergsjö ☐ S 25 Lj15
Berhampur ☐ IND 81 Pa15
Bering Glacier ☒ USA 116 Cd06
Bering Sea ☐ USA/RUS 116 Ba06
Bering Strait ☒ USA/RUS 74 Uc05
Berja ☐ E 41 Kj27
Berkåk ☐ N 24 Lf14
Berkner Island ☐ 140 Hc34
Berkovica ☐ BG 54 Mb24
Berlevåg ☐ N 23 Me10
Berlin ◉ D 44 Lg19
Berlin, Mount ▲ 140 Da34
Bermejo ☐ BOL 136 Gd23
Bermejo ⌁ RA 136 Gd23
Bermeo ☐ E 42 Kj24
Bermuda Islands ☒ GB 121 Gd12
Bermuda Rise ⌁ 121 Gc12
Bernay ☐ F 36 La21
Bernburg ☐ D 44 Lf20
Berndorf ☐ A 52 Lj22
Berne ◉ CH 45 Ld22
Berner Alpen ▲ CH 45 Ld22
Bernkastel-Kues ☐ D 45 Ld21
Beroun ☐ CZ 52 Lh21
Beršad' ☐ UA 62 Me21
Bertoua ☐ CAM 108 Lc18
Berwick-upon-Tweed ☐ GB 34 Kj18
Beryslav ☐ UA 62 Mg22
Besalampy ☐ RM 111 Na22
Besançon ☐ F 39 Ld22
Bešankovičy ☐ BY 31 Me18
Besedino ☐ RUS 59 Mj20
Beskid Mountains ▲ PL/SK 53 Ma21
Besni ☐ TR 65 Mj27
Bessarabia ☒ MD 55 Me22
Bessaz tau ▲ KZ 78 Ob10
Betanzos ☐ E 40 Kf24
Bethel ☐ USA 116 Bd06
Bethlehem ☐ ZA 110 Mb24
Béthune ☐ F 37 Lb20

Betong ☐ THA 86 Qa17
Betpak Dala ☐ KZ 78 Ob09
Bettna ☐ S 27 Lj16
Beverley ☐ GB 35 Kk19
Beyazçeşme Şelâlesi ☒ TR 66 Nb26
Bey Dağları ▲ TR 64 Mf27
Beykoz ☐ TR 57 Me25
Beypazarı ☐ TR 64 Mf25
Beyşehir ☐ TR 64 Mf27
Beyşehir Gölü ☒ TR 64 Mf27
Bežanickaja vozvyšennost' ⌁ RUS 30 Me17
Bežanicy ☐ RUS 30 Me17
Bezdan ☐ SR 54 Lk23
Bežeck ☐ RUS 58 Mj17
Bežeckij verhnij ⌁ RUS 58 Mj17
Bezenčuk ☐ RUS 60 Ne19
Béziers ☐ F 38 Lb24
Bhamo ☐ MYA 84 Pd14
Bhavnagar ☐ IND 80 Oc14
Bhilwara ☐ IND 80 Oc13
Bhopal ◉ IND 80 Od13
Bhubaneswar ◉ IND 80 Pb14
Bhutan ☐ BHT 84 Pc13
Biak ☐ RI 92 Rd19
Biak ☐ RI 92 Rd19
Biała Podlaska ☐ PL 51 Mb19
Białobrzegi ☐ PL 50 Ma20
Białogard ☐ PL 50 Lh18
Białowieski P.N. ✿ PL 51 Mb19
Biały Bór ☐ PL 50 Lj19
Białystok ☐ PL 51 Mb19
Biaora ☐ IND 80 Od14
Biarritz ☐ F 42 Kk24
Biasca ☐ CH 45 Le22
Biberach ☐ D 45 Le21
Bicaz ☐ RO 55 Md22
Bickerton Island ☒ AUS 96 Rd21
Bicske ☐ H 53 Lk22
Bida ☐ WAN 108 Lb17
Bideford ☐ GB 35 Kh20
Biebrzański Park Narodowy ✿ PL 51 Mb19
Biecz ☐ PL 50 Ma21
Biedenkopf ☐ D 44 Le20
Biel = Bienne ☐ CH 45 Ld22
Bielefeld ☐ D 44 Le19
Bielsko-Biała ☐ PL 50 Lk21
Bielsk Podlaski ☐ PL 51 Mb19
Bienne = Biel ☐ CH 45 Ld22
Biertan ☐ RO 54 Mc22
Bieszczadzki P.N. ✿ PL 51 Mb21
Biga ☐ TR 57 Md25
Bigadiç ☐ TR 64 Me26
Bight of Benin ☒ DY/WAN 105 La17
Bight of Bonny ☒ CAM 108 Lb18
Big Spring ☐ USA 122 Ed12
Bihać ☐ BIH 47 Lh23
Bihar ☐ IND 80 Pb13
Biharia ☐ RO 54 Ma22
Bijapur ☐ IND 81 Od15
Bijeljina ☐ BIH 47 Lk23
Bijelo Polje ☐ CG 54 Lk24
Bijsk ☐ RUS 79 Pb08
Bikaner ☐ IND 80 Oc13
Bikin ☐ RUS 83 Rc09
Bila Cerkva ☐ UA 62 Mf21
Bilaspur ☐ IND 80 Pa14
Bilbao = Bilbo ☐ E 42 Kj24
Bilbo = Bilbao ☐ E 42 Kj24
Bildudalur ☐ IS 32 Jj13

Bileća ☐ BIH 47 Lk24
Bilecik ☐ TR 57 Me25
Biled ☐ RO 54 Ma23
Bilgoraj ☐ PL 51 Mb20
Bilgorod-Dnistrovs'kij ☐ UA 62 Mf22
Biliasuvar ☐ AZ 76 Nb11
Bilibino ☐ RUS 74 Tb05
Bilisht ☐ AL 56 Ma25
Billdal ☐ S 26 Lf17
Billings ☐ USA 120 Ec09
Bilohors'k ☐ UA 63 Mh23
Bilokurakyne ☐ UA 63 Mk21
Bilopillja ☐ UA 59 Mh20
Bilovec ☐ CZ 53 Lj21
Bilovods'k ☐ UA 63 Mk21
Bilto ☐ N 23 Ma11
Bingen ☐ D 45 Ld21
Binghamton ☐ USA 123 Ga10
Bingöl ☐ TR 76 Na11
Bingöl ☐ TR 66 Na26
Bingöl Dağları ▲ TR 66 Na26
Bingsjö ☐ S 25 Lh15
Bintan ☐ RI 86 Qa18
Bintulu ☐ MAL 87 Qc18
Binzhou ☐ CHN 83 Qd11
Biograd na moru ☐ HR 47 Lh24
Biogradska Gora, N.P. ✿ SR 54 Lk24
Bir 'Ali ☐ YE 77 Nb16
Birao ☐ RCA 108 Ma16
Bi'r Ben Ghimah ☐ LAR 106 Ma12
Birdsville ☐ AUS 96 Rd24
Biri ☐ N 24 Lf15
Birjand ☐ IR 77 Nd12
Birlik ☐ KZ 78 Oc10
Birmingham ◉ GB 35 Kj19
Birmingham ☐ USA 123 Fc12
Bir Mogreïn ☐ RIM 104 Kb13
Birnin-Konni ☐ RN 105 Lb16
Birnin Kudu ☐ WAN 108 Lb16
Birobidžan ☐ RUS 83 Rc09
Birr ☐ IRL 33 Kg19
Biržai ☐ LT 31 Mc17
Biscarrosse ☐ F 38 Kk23
Bischofshofen ☐ A 52 Lg22
Biscoe Islands ☒ 140 Gc32
Bishkek ◉ KS 78 Oc10
Biskra ☐ DZ 106 Lb12
Biskupiec ☐ PL 50 Ma19
Bislig ☐ RP 85 Rb17
Bismarck ☐ USA 120 Ed09
Bismarck Archipelago ☒ PNG 92 Sb19
Bismarck Sea ☒ PNG 92 Sb19
Bismo ☐ N 24 Le15
Bispgården ☐ S 25 Lj14
Bissau ◉ GNB 105 Ka16
Bistrica ☐ SR 54 Lk24
Bistriţa ☐ RO 54 Mc22
Bisztynek ☐ PL 50 Ma18
Bitburg ☐ D 45 Ld21
Bitjug ⌁ RUS 61 Na20
Bitlis ☐ TR 66 Nb26
Bitola ☐ MK 56 Ma25
Bitonto ☐ I 49 Lj25
Bitterfeld ☐ D 44 Lg20
Bitterroot Range ▲ USA 122 Eb09
Bitung ☐ RI 87 Rb18
Biu ☐ WAN 108 Lc16
Bizerte ☐ TN 106 Lb11
Bjahoml' ☐ BY 31 Me18
Bjala ☐ BG 55 Mc24
Bjala ☐ BG 55 Md24
Bjalyničy ☐ BY 51 Me19

Bjarčzina 🗺 BY 31 Me18
Bjargtangar ▣ IS 32 Jh13
Bjaroza ▣ BY 51 Mc19
Bjarozavka ▣ BY 51 Mc19
Bjästa ▣ S 25 Lk14
Bjelovar ▣ HR 47 Lj23
Bjerkvik ▣ N 22 Lj11
Björbo ▣ S 25 Lh15
Björksele ▣ S 25 Lk13
Björna ▣ S 25 Lk14
Bjorne Peninsula ▣ CDN 118 Fc03
Björnlandets n.p. ▣ ▣ S 25 Lk14
Bjurholm ▣ S 25 Lk14
Bjursås ▣ S 25 Lh15
Blace ▣ SR 54 Ma24
Black Forest 🗺 D 45 Le21
Blackall ▣ AUS 96 Sb23
Blackburn ▣ GB 35 Kj19
Black Mountain ▲ AUS 96 Rd23
Blackpool ▣ GB 35 Kj19
Black River ▣ VN 84 Qa14
Black Volta ▣ GH 105 Kd16
Blagoevgrad ▣ BG 56 Mb24
Blagoveščenka ▣ RUS 79 Pa08
Blagoveščensk ▣ RUS 75 Rb08
Blairgowrie ▣ GB 34 Kj17
Blaj ▣ RO 54 Mb22
Blå Jungfrun n.p. ▣ ▣ S 27 Lj17
Blakstad ▣ N 26 Le16
Blanes ▣ E 42 Lb25
Blangy-sur-Bresle ▣ F 36 La21
Blankenberge ▣ B 37 Lb20
Blankenheim ▣ D 45 Ld20
Blantyre ▣ MW 111 Md22
Błaszki ▣ PL 50 Lk20
Bled ▣ SLO 47 Lj22
Bleikvassli ▣ N 24 Lg13
Blenheim ▣ NZ 99 Tc27
Blida ▣ DZ 104 La11
Blinisht ▣ AL 56 Lk25
Bloemfontein ▣ ZA 110 Mb24
Blois ▣ F 38 La22
Blombacka ▣ S 27 Lg16
Blommesteinmeer ▣ SME 134 Ha18
Blönduós ▣ IS 32 Jk13
Błonie ▣ PL 50 Ma19
Bloomington ▣ USA 123 Fc10
Bludenz ▣ A 45 Le22
Bluefield ▣ USA 123 Fd11
Bluefields ▣ NIC 126 Fd16
Blue Nile ▣ SUD 109 Mc16
Blumenau ▣ BR 135 Hc24
Blytheville ▣ USA 123 Fb11
Bo ▣ WAL 105 Kb17
Bołšezemeľskaja tundra 🗺 RUS 72 Na05
Boa Vista ▣ ▣ BR 132 Gd18
Bobbio ▣ I 46 Le23
Bobo-Dioulasso ▣ BF 105 Kd16
Bobolice ▣ PL 50 Lj19
Bobr ▣ BY 31 Me18
Bobrov ▣ RUS 61 Na20
Bobrovycja ▣ UA 62 Mf20
Bobrynec' ▣ UA 62 Mg21
Boby ▲ RM 111 Nb23
Boca do Acre ▣ BR 133 Gc20
Bocaiúva ▣ BR 135 Hd22
Boca Raton ▣ USA 123 Fd13
Boca Santa Maria ▣ MEX 124 Fa13
Bocholt ▣ D 44 Ld20

Bochum ▣ D 44 Ld20
Bocşa ▣ RO 54 Ma23
Boda ▣ S 25 Lh15
Bodélé 🗺 TCH 106 Ld15
Boden ▣ S 25 Ma13
Bodensee 🗺 D 45 Le22
Bodø ▣ N 22 Lj12
Bodrum ▣ TR 57 Md27
Boende ▣ RDC 108 Ma19
Boğazkale ▣ TR 65 Mh25
Boğazkale Milli Parkı ▣ ▣ TR 65 Mh25
Boğazlıyan ▣ TR 65 Mh26
Bogen ▣ N 22 Lj11
Bogia ▣ PNG 92 Sa19
Bogor ▣ RI 86 Qb20
Bogorodick ▣ RUS 59 Mk19
Bogorodsk ▣ RUS 60 Nb17
Bogotá ▣ CO 132 Gb18
Bogučar ▣ RUS 61 Na21
Bo Hai ▣ CHN 83 Qd11
Bohemia 🗺 CZ 52 Lg21
Bohoduchiv ▣ UA 63 Mh20
Bohol ▣ RP 85 Ra17
Böhönye ▣ H 53 Lj22
Bohuslav ▣ UA 62 Mf21
Boise ▣ USA 122 Ea10
Boizenburg ▣ D 44 Lf19
Bøjden ▣ DK 26 Lf18
Bojnurd ▣ IR 78 Nd11
Boké ▣ RG 105 Kb16
Bolayır ▣ TR 57 Md25
Boldeşti Scăeni ▣ RO 55 Md23
Bolesławiec ▣ PL 50 Lh20
Bolezersk ▣ RUS 29 Mj15
Bolgatanga ▣ GH 105 Kd16
Bolhov ▣ RUS 59 Mj19
Bolhrad ▣ UA 55 Me23
Boliden ▣ S 25 Ma13
Bolivia ▣ BOL 133 Gc22
Boljevac ▣ SR 54 Ma24
Bolkar Dağları ▲ TR 65 Mh27
Bollène ▣ F 39 Lc23
Bollnäs ▣ S 25 Lj15
Bollon ▣ AUS 96 Sb24
Bologna ▣ I 46 Lf23
Bologoe ▣ RUS 58 Mh17
Bologovo ▣ RUS 58 Mf17
Boľšaja Glušica ▣ RUS 60 Nf19
Boľšaja Muraškino ▣ RUS 60 Nc18
Boľšakovo ▣ RUS 31 Ma18
Boľševik ▣ RUS 61 Nb20
Boľšoj Enisej ▣ RUS 79 Pc08
Boľšoj Ignatovo ▣ RUS 60 Nc18
Boľšoj Kandala ▣ RUS 60 Ne18
Boľšoj Karaman ▣ RUS 61 Nd20
Boľšoj Kinel' ▣ RUS 60 Nf19
Boľšoj Ozerki ▣ RUS 61 Nd19
Boľšoj Poljana ▣ RUS 59 Mk19
Boľšoj Privalovka ▣ RUS 59 Mk20
Boľšoj Ramen' ▣ RUS 60 Nd17
Boľšoj Selo ▣ RUS 58 Mk17
Boľšoj Tavoložka ▣ RUS 61 Ne19
Bolton ▣ GB 35 Kj19
Bolu ▣ TR 64 Mf25
Bolungarvík ▣ IS 32 Jj12
Bolvadin ▣ TR 64 Mf26
Bolzano = Bozen ▣ I 46 Lf22

Boma ▣ RDC 108 Lc20
Bombay ▣ IND 80 Oc15
Bomberai Peninsula 🗺 RI 92 Rc19
Bomu ▣ RDC 109 Mb17
Bonaire ▣ NL 127 Gc16
Bonaparte Archipelago 🗺 AUS 94 Ra22
Bonavista Bay ▣ CDN 121 Hb09
Bondokodi ▣ RI 87 Qd20
Bondoukou ▣ CI 105 Kd17
Bongor ▣ TCH 108 Ld16
Bonifacio ▣ F 46 Le25
Bonn ▣ D 44 Ld20
Bonneval ▣ F 36 La21
Bono ▣ I 48 Le25
Bonorva ▣ I 48 Le25
Bonyhád ▣ H 53 Lj22
Booligal ▣ AUS 97 Sa25
Boothia Peninsula 🗺 CDN 118 Fb04
Boué ▣ G 108 Lc19
Bor ▣ RUS 73 Pb06
Bor ▣ SR 54 Mb23
Bor ▣ SUD 109 Mc17
Bor ▣ TR 65 Mh27
Borås ▣ S 26 Lg17
Borba ▣ BR 133 Ha19
Borçka ▣ TR 66 Na25
Bordeaux ▣ F 38 Kk23
Borden Peninsula 🗺 CDN 118 Fd04
Borðeyri ▣ IS 32 Jk13
Bordj Messouda ▣ DZ 106 Lb12
Bordj Mokhtar ▣ DZ 104 La14
Bordj Omar Driss ▣ DZ 106 Lb13
Borga = Porvoo ▣ FIN 28 Mc15
Borgarnes ▣ IS 32 Jk13
Børgefjell n.p. ▣ N 24 Lg13
Borgholm ▣ S 27 Lj17
Borgmassivet ▲ 141 Kc33
Borgomanero ▣ I 46 Le23
Borgo San Lorenzo ▣ I 46 Lf24
Borhaug ▣ N 26 Ld16
Borinskoe ▣ RUS 59 Mk19
Borisoglebsk ▣ RUS 61 Nb20
Borisovka ▣ RUS 59 Mj20
Borisovo-Sudskoe ▣ RUS 58 Mj16
Borkum ▣ D 44 Ld19
Borlänge ▣ S 25 Lh15
Borlu ▣ TR 64 Me26
Borneo 🗺 MAL/RI 87 Qb18
Bornholm ▣ DK 27 Lh18
Borşa ▣ RO 54 Mc22
Borodjanka ▣ UA 62 Mf20
Borohoro Shan ▲ CHN 79 Pa10
Borova ▣ UA 63 Mj21
Borovan ▣ BG 54 Mb24
Borovenka ▣ RUS 58 Mg16
Boroviči ▣ RUS 58 Mg16
Borovoj ▣ RUS 29 Mg13
Borovsk ▣ RUS 58 Mj18
Borroloola ▣ AUS 96 Rd22
Borščiv ▣ UA 51 Md21
Børselv ▣ N 23 Mc10
Borskoe ▣ RUS 60 Nf19
Borujerd ▣ IR 76 Nb12
Borynja ▣ UA 53 Mb21
Boryspil' ▣ UA 62 Mf20
Bory Tucholskie, P.N. ▣ ▣ PL 50 Lj19

Borzja ▣ RUS 82 Qd08
Borzna ▣ UA 59 Mg20
Bosa ▣ I 48 Le25
Bosanska Dubica ▣ BIH 47 Lj23
Bosanska Gradiška ▣ BIH 47 Lj23
Bosanska Krupa ▣ BIH 47 Lj23
Bosanski Petrovac ▣ BIH 47 Lj23
Bosanski Grahovo ▣ BIH 47 Lj23
Bose ▣ CHN 84 Qb14
Bosnia and Herzegovina ▣ BIH 47 Lj23
Bosporus 🗺 TR 57 Me25
Bossangoa ▣ RCA 108 Ld17
Bossembélé ▣ RCA 108 Ld17
Bosso ▣ RN 105 La16
Boston ▣ GB 35 Kk19
Boston ▣ USA 121 Gb10
Botevgrad ▣ BG 54 Mb24
Botoşani ▣ RO 55 Md22
Botswana ▣ RB 110 Ma23
Bottenviken ▣ S 23 Mb13
Bottrop ▣ D 44 Ld20
Bouaké ▣ CI 105 Kc17
Bouar ▣ RCA 108 Ld17
Bougainville Island 🗺 PNG 93 Sd20
Bougouni ▣ RMM 105 Kc16
Boujdour ▣ MA 104 Kb13
Boukra ▣ MA 104 Kb13
Boulder ▣ USA 122 Ec11
Boulia ▣ AUS 96 Rd23
Boulogne-sur-Mer ▣ F 35 La20
Bourbon-Lancy ▣ F 39 Lb22
Bourbonne-les-Bains ▣ F 39 Lc22
Bourg-en-Bresse ▣ F 39 Lc22
Bourges ▣ F 38 Lb22
Bourgoin-Jallieu ▣ F 39 Lc23
Bourke ▣ AUS 97 Sb25
Bournemouth ▣ GB 35 Kk20
Bou Saada ▣ DZ 104 La11
Bowling Green ▣ USA 123 Fc11
Bowman ▣ USA 120 Ed09
Boxholm ▣ S 27 Lh16
Boxmeer ▣ NL 37 Ld20
Boyabat ▣ TR 65 Mh25
Boyuibe ▣ BOL 136 Gd23
Bozburun ▣ TR 64 Me27
Bozcaada ▣ TR 57 Md26
Boz Dağları ▲ TR 57 Md26
Bozdoğan ▣ TR 64 Me27
Bozeman ▣ USA 122 Eb09
Bozen = Bolzano ▣ I 46 Lf22
Bozkir ▣ TR 64 Mg27
Bozova ▣ TR 65 Mk27
Bozüyük ▣ TR 64 Mf26
Bozyazı ▣ TR 65 Mg27
Bra ▣ I 46 Ld23
Brač ▲ HR 47 Lj24
Bräcke ▣ S 25 Lh14
Brad ▣ RO 54 Mb22
Bradenton ▣ USA 123 Fd13
Bradford ▣ GB 35 Kk19
Brady ▣ USA 122 Fa12
Braga ▣ P 40 Kf25
Bragança ▣ P 40 Kg25
Brahestad ▣ FIN 28 Mc13
Brahmaputra ▣ IND/BD 84 Pc13
Brăila ▣ RO 55 Md23
Brainerd ▣ USA 120 Fb09
Braintree ▣ GB 35 La20

Brake D 44 Le19
Bramsche D 44 Le19
Brandberg ▲ NAM 110 Lc23
Brandbu N 24 Lf15
Brande DK 26 Le18
Brandenburg D 44 Lg19
Brandenburg D 44 Lg19
Brandon CDN 120 Fa09
Braniewo PL 50 Lk18
Bransfield Strait 140 Ha31
Brańsk PL 51 Mb19
Brantôme F 38 La23
Brasiléia BR 133 Gc21
Brasília ● BR 135 Hc22
Braslav BY 31 Md18
Braslav Lakes N.P. ♠ BY 31 Md18
Braşov RO 55 Mc23
Bratca RO 54 Mb22
Bratislava SK 53 Lj21
Bratsk RUS 73 Qa07
Bratskoe vdhr. RUS 73 Qa07
Brattvåg N 24 Ld14
Braţul Sulina RO 55 Me23
Braunau A 52 Lg21
Braunschweig D 44 Lf19
Bray IRL 33 Kg19
Brazil ■ BR 135 Ha21
Brazilian Highlands ▲ BR 135 Hd22
Brazzaville ● RCB 108 Ld19
Brčko BIH 47 Lk23
Brechin GB 34 Kj17
Břeclav CZ 53 Lj21
Brecon GB 35 Kj20
Brecon Beacons N.P. ♠ GB 35 Kj20
Breda NL 37 Lc20
Bredasdorp ZA 110 Ma25
Bredstedt D 44 Le18
Bregenz A 45 Le22
Breiðafjörður IS 32 Jj13
Breiðdalsvik IS 32 Kd13
Breivkbotn N 23 Mb10
Brejtovo RUS 58 Mj16
Brekken N 24 Lf14
Brekstad N 24 Le14
Bremen ■ D 44 Le19
Bremerhaven D 44 Le19
Bremerton USA 122 Dd09
Bremervörde D 44 Le19
Bréscia I 46 Lf23
Bressanone = Brixen I 46 Lf22
Bressuire F 38 Kk22
Brest F 36 Kh21
Brest BY 51 Mb19
Brewarrina AUS 97 Sb24
Brezoi RO 54 Mc23
Bria RCA 108 Ma17
Briançon F 39 Ld23
Briceni MD 51 Md21
Bridgeport USA 121 Gb10
Bridgetown AUS 95 Qd25
Bridgetown ■ BDS 127 Ha16
Bridgwater GB 35 Kj20
Bridlington GB 35 Kk18
Brienne-le-Château F 37 Lc21
Brienz CH 45 Le22
Brig CH 45 Ld22
Brighton GB 35 Kk20
Brignoles F 39 Ld24
Brijuni, N.P. ♠ HR 47 Lg23
Brilon D 44 Le20
Brindisi I 49 Lj25
Brioude F 38 Lb23
Brisbane ● AUS 96 Sc24

Brisighella I 46 Lf23
Bristol GB 35 Kj20
Bristol Bay USA 116 Bd07
Bristol Channel GB 35 Kj20
British Columbia CDN 116 Dc07
Brittany F 36 Kj21
Brive-la-Gaillarde F 38 La23
Brixen = Bressanone I 46 Lf22
Brjanka UA 63 Mk21
Brjansk RUS 59 Mh19
Brka BIH 47 Lk23
Broad Sound AUS 96 Sb23
Broby S 27 Lh17
Brocken ▲ D 44 Lf20
Brodec'ke UA 62 Me21
Brodeur Peninsula CDN 118 Fc04
Brodnica PL 50 Lk19
Brody UA 51 Mc20
Broken Hill AUS 97 Sa25
Brokopondo SME 134 Ha17
Brønderslev DK 26 Le17
Brønnøysund N 24 Lg13
Brooke's Point RP 87 Qd17
Brooks CDN 117 Eb08
Brooks Range ▲ USA 116 Ca05
Broome AUS 94 Ra22
Brovary UA 62 Mf20
Brownsville USA 123 Fa13
Bruck an der Mur A 52 Lh22
Brüel D 44 Lf19
Brugge B 37 Lb20
Bruneck = Brunico I 46 Lf22
Brunei ■ BRU 87 Qc18
Brunflo S 25 Lh14
Brunico = Bruneck I 46 Lf22
Brunsbüttel D 44 Le19
Brunswick USA 123 Fd12
Bruntál CZ 53 Lj21
Bruny Island AUS 97 Sb27
Brussels ● B 37 Lc20
Bruxelles ● B 37 Lc20
Bryan USA 123 Fa12
Bryan Coast 140 Fd33
Bryne N 26 Lc16
Brzeg PL 50 Lj20
Brzesko PL 50 Ma21
Brzeziny PL 50 Lk20
Brzozów PL 51 Mb21
Buala SOL 93 Sd20
Buča UA 62 Mf20
Bučač UA 51 Mc21
Bucak TR 64 Mf27
Bucaramanga CO 132 Gb17
Bucegi, P.N. ♠ RO 55 Mc23
Buchanan LB 105 Kb17
Buchan Gulf CDN 118 Gb04
Bucharest ● RO 55 Md23
Buchholz D 44 Le19
Bucureşti ● RO 55 Md23
Bud N 24 Ld14
Budaörs H 53 Lk22
Buðardalur IS 32 Jk13
Budd Coast 141 Qc32
Bude GB 35 Kh20
Büdingen D 45 Le20
Budogošč' RUS 30 Mg16
Budva CG 56 Lk24
Buenaventura CO 132 Ga18

Buenos Aires ■ RA 137 Gd26
Buenos Aires ● RA 136 Ha25
Buenos Aires Lérida CO 132 Gb18
Buffalo USA 120 Ec10
Buffalo USA 120 Ed09
Buffalo USA 123 Ga10
Buftea RO 55 Mc23
Bugojno BIH 47 Lj23
Bugul'ma RUS 60 Ng18
Bugul'minsko-Belebeevskaja vozvyšennost' ▲ RUS 60 Nf18
Buguruslan RUS 72 Nc08
Buguruslan RUS 60 Nd18
Buhtarminskoe sukojmasy KZ 79 Pa09
Buhuşi RO 55 Md22
Buin PNG 93 Sd20
Buinsk RUS 60 Ne18
Bujumbura ● BU 109 Mb19
Buka Island PNG 93 Sc20
Bukama RDC 109 Mb20
Bukan IR 76 Nb11
Bukanovskaja RUS 61 Nb21
Bukavu RDC 109 Mb19
Bukhoro UZ 78 Oa11
Bukittinggi RI 86 Qa19
Bükki N.P. ♠ H 53 Ma21
Bukoba EAT 109 Mc19
Buky UA 62 Mf21
Bulanık TR 66 Nb26
Bulanlak TR 66 Mk25
Bulawayo ZW 110 Mb23
Bulgan MNG 82 Qa09
Bulgar RUS 60 Ne18
Bulle CH 45 Ld22
Bulukumba RI 87 Ra20
Bumba RDC 108 Ma18
Bunbury AUS 95 Qd25
Bundaberg AUS 96 Sc23
Bundoran IRL 33 Kf18
Bunger Hills 141 Qa32
Bungle Bungle Ranges ▲ AUS 94 Rb22
Bunia RDC 109 Mc18
Bünyan TR 65 Mh26
Buon Ma Thout VN 84 Qb16
Buraydah KSA 77 Na13
Burdur TR 64 Mf27
Burdur Gölü TR 64 Mf27
Burdwood Bank GB 137 Gd29
Bure ETH 109 Md16
Bureinskij hrebet ▲ RUS 75 Rc08
Bureja RUS 75 Rc08
Burg D 44 Lf19
Burgas BG 55 Md24
Burgos E 42 Kj24
Burgsvik S 27 Lk17
Burgundy F 37 Lb23
Burhaniye TR 57 Md26
Burjassot E 43 Kk26
Burke Island 140 Ec33
Burketown AUS 96 Rd22
Burkina Faso ■ BF 105 Kd16
Burlington USA 123 Fb10
Burlington USA 121 Gb10
Burnie-Somerset AUS 97 Sb27
Burns USA 122 Ea10
Burrel AL 56 Ma25
Burren N.P. ♠ IRL 33 Kf19
Bursa TR 57 Me25
Burton-upon-Trent GB 35 Kk19

Burträsk S 25 Ma13
Buru RI 87 Rb19
Burundi ■ BU 109 Mb19
Buruntuma GNB 105 Kb16
Burwan IND 80 Pb14
Buryatia RUS 82 Qc08
Burylbaital KZ 78 Oc09
Bury Saint Edmunds GB 35 La19
Busan ● ROK 83 Rb11
Businga RDC 108 Ma18
Bus'k UA 51 Mc21
Busko-Zdrój PL 50 Ma20
Busselton AUS 95 Qd25
Büsum D 44 Le18
Buta RDC 109 Ma18
Butare RWA 109 Mb19
Butrint AL 56 Ma26
Butte USA 122 Eb09
Button Bay CDN 120 Fb07
Butuan RP 85 Rb17
Butung RI 87 Ra19
Buturlinovka RUS 61 Na20
Buzançais F 38 La22
Buzău RO 55 Md23
Buzuluk RUS 72 Nc08
Buzuluk  RUS 60 Nf19
Buzuluk RUS 60 Ng19
Byam Martin Channel CDN 118 Ec03
Bychav BY 59 Mf19
Bychawa PL 51 Mb20
Byczyna PL 50 Lk20
Bydgoszcz PL 50 Lj19
Bygland N 26 Ld16
Bykovo RUS 61 Nc21
Bylot Island CDN 118 Ga04
Byrd Glacier 141 Sd35
Byrkjelo N 24 Ld15
Byske S 25 Ma13
Bytom PL 50 Lk20
Bytów PL 50 Lj18
Byxelkrok S 27 Lj17

C

Caatinga BR 134 Hd20
Cabanatuan RP 85 Ra15
Cabañeros, P.N. de ♠ E 41 Kh26
Cabeza del Buey E 41 Kg27
Cabezas Rubias E 41 Kg27
Cabimas YV 127 Gb16
Cabinda ANG 108 Lc20
Cabinda ANG 108 Lc20
Cabo Blanco CR 126 Fc17
Cabo Catoche MEX 125 Fc14
Cabo Corrientes MEX 124 Ec14
Cabo de Gata E 41 Kj27
Cabo de Gracias a Dios HN 126 Fd15
Cabo Delgado MOC 111 Na21
Cabo de Palos E 43 Kk27
Cabo de San Antonio C 125 Fc14
Cabo de Santa María BR 135 Hc24
Cabo de Santa María P 41 Kg27
Cabo de São Roque BR 134 Ja20
Cabo de São Tomé BR 135 Hd23

Cabo de São Vicente ⌕ P 41 Kf27
Cabo Deseado ⌕ RCH 137 Gb29
Cabo do Norte ⌕ BR 134 Hc18
Cabo dos Bahias ⌕ RA 137 Gc27
Cabo Finisterre ⌕ E 40 Kf24
Caborca ⌕ MEX 122 Eb12
Cabo San Diego ⌕ RA 137 Gc29
Cabo San Juan ⌕ GQ 108 Lb18
Cabo San Lucas ⌕ MEX 124 Ec14
Cabo Tres Montes ⌕ RCH 137 Ga28
Cabo Tres Puntas ⌕ RA 137 Gc28
Cabot Strait ⌕ CDN 121 Gd09
Cabo Virgenes ⌕ RA 137 Gc29
Cabrera, P.N.Terrestre-Marítimo de ⌕ E 43 Lb26
Čačak ⌕ SR 54 Ma24
Caçapava ⌕ BR 136 Hb25
Cáceres ⌕ BR 135 Ha22
Cáceres ⌕ E 40 Kg26
Čačérsk ⌕ BY 59 Mf19
Čačévičy ⌕ BY 51 Me19
Cachoeiro de Itapemirim ⌕ BR 135 Hd23
Cacolo ⌕ ANG 110 Ld21
Čadca ⌕ SK 53 Lk21
Cadiz ⌕ RP 85 Ra16
Cádiz ⌕ E 41 Kg27
Caen ⌕ F 36 Kk21
Caernarfon ⌕ GB 35 Kh19
Caetité ⌕ BR 135 Hd21
Čaevo ⌕ RUS 58 Mj16
Cagayan de Oro ⌕ RP 85 Ra17
Čagda ⌕ RUS 75 Rc07
Cagli ⌕ I 46 Lj24
Cagliari ⌕ I 48 Le26
Čagoda ⌕ RUS 58 Mh16
Caguas ⌕ USA 127 Gc15
Cahersiveen ⌕ IRL 33 Ke20
Cahors ⌕ F 38 La23
Cahul ⌕ MD 55 Me23
Caia ⌕ MOC 111 Md22
Caicara del Orinoco ⌕ YV 132 Gc17
Caicos Island ⌕ UK 127 Gb14
Cairns ⌕ AUS 96 Sb22
Cairo ● ET 107 Mc13
Cajamarca ⌕ PE 133 Ga20
Čakino ⌕ RUS 61 Na19
Çakmak Dağı ▲ TR 66 Nb26
Čakovec ⌕ HR 52 Lj22
Calabar ⌕ WAN 108 Lb17
Calabozo ⌕ YV 132 Gc17
Calabria ⌕ I 49 Lj26
Calábria, P.N. della ⌕ I 49 Lj26
Calafat ⌕ RO 54 Mb24
Calahorra ⌕ E 42 Kk24
Calais ⌕ F 35 La20
Calama ⌕ RCH 136 Gc23
Calamian Group ⌕ RP 85 Qd16
Calamocha ⌕ E 42 Kk25
Cala Rajada ⌕ E 43 Lb26
Călărași ⌕ MD 55 Me22
Călărași ⌕ RO 55 Md23
Calatayud ⌕ E 42 Kk25
Calbayog ⌕ RP 85 Ra16

Calçoene ⌕ BR 134 Hb18
Calcutta ⌕ IND 80 Pb14
Caldas da Reinha ⌕ P 40 Kf26
Caldas de Reis ⌕ E 40 Kf24
Caldera ⌕ RCH 136 Gb24
Caldwell ⌕ USA 122 Ea10
Caleta Olivia ⌕ RA 137 Gc28
Calgary ⌕ CDN 117 Eb08
Cali ⌕ CO 132 Ga18
Calicut ⌕ IND 81 Od16
Caliente ⌕ USA 122 Ec11
California ⌕ USA 122 Dd11
Čáliman, P.N. ⌕ RO 55 Mc22
Calingasta ⌕ RA 136 Gc25
Callao ⌕ PE 133 Ga21
Caloundra ⌕ AUS 96 Sc24
Caltagirone ⌕ I 49 Lh27
Caltanissetta ⌕ I 49 Lh27
Calvert ⌕ AUS 96 Rd22
Calvi ⌕ F 46 Le24
Calvinia ⌕ ZA 110 Ld25
Calw ⌕ D 45 Le21
Calzada de Calatrava ⌕ E 41 Kj26
Camabatela ⌕ ANG 108 Ld20
Camaçari ⌕ BR 135 Ja21
Camagüey ⌕ C 126 Ga14
Camana ⌕ PE 133 Gb22
Camardi ⌕ TR 65 Mh27
Camarones ⌕ RA 137 Gc27
Cambodia ⌕ K 84 Qa16
Cambrai ⌕ F 37 Lb20
Cambrian Mountains ▲ GB 35 Kj19
Cambridge ⌕ GB 35 La19
Cambridge Bay ⌕ CDN 118 Ed05
Camenca ⌕ MD 62 Me21
Cameroon ⌕ CAM 108 Lc17
Cameroon Mountain ▲ CAM 108 Lb18
Cametá ⌕ BR 134 Hc19
Çamlidere ⌕ TR 65 Mg25
Camooweal ⌕ AUS 96 Rd22
Campania ⌕ I 49 Lh25
Campbell River ⌕ CDN 116 Dc09
Campbeltown ⌕ GB 34 Kh18
Campeche ⌕ MEX 125 Fb15
Campeche ⌕ MEX 125 Fb15
Campeche Bank ⌕ 125 Fb14
Câmpeni ⌕ RO 54 Mb22
Cam Pha ⌕ VN 84 Qb14
Campiglia Marittima ⌕ I 46 Lf24
Campina Grande ⌕ BR 134 Ja20
Campinas ⌕ BR 135 Hc23
Campinas ⌕ BR 135 Hc23
Campobasso ⌕ I 49 Lh25
Campo Grande ⌕ BR 135 Hb23
Campos ⌕ BR 135 Hd23
Campos ⌕ BR 135 Hd23
Campos Belos ⌕ BR 135 Hc21
Campos Cerrados ⌕ BR 135 Ha21
Câmpulung ⌕ RO 55 Mc23
Camrose ⌕ CDN 117 Eb08
Çan ⌕ TR 57 Md25
Canada ⌕ CDN 117 Db07
Canada Basin ⌕ 116 Cc03
Canadian ⌕ USA 122 Ed11
Canadian Shield ⌕ CDN 120 Eb06
Canaima ⌕ YV 132 Gd17
Çanakkale ⌕ TR 57 Md25

Canals ⌕ E 43 Kk26
Canary Basin ⌕ 104 Kb12
Canary Islands ⌕ E 104 Ka13
Cañaveras ⌕ E 42 Kj25
Canavieiras ⌕ BR 135 Ja22
Cañazas ⌕ PA 132 Ga17
Canberra ● AUS 97 Sd26
Cancún ⌕ MEX 125 Fc14
Çandarlı Körfezi ⌕ TR 57 Md26
Candeleda ⌕ E 40 Kh25
Cândido Rondon ⌕ BR 135 Hb23
Cañete ⌕ E 43 Kk25
Cangas ⌕ E 40 Kf24
Cangas del Narcea ⌕ E 40 Kg24
Cangas de Onis ⌕ E 40 Kh24
Canguaretama ⌕ BR 134 Ja20
Cangzhou ⌕ CHN 83 Qd11
Canicatti ⌕ I 48 Lg27
Canik Dağları ▲ TR 65 Mj25
Canindé ⌕ BR 134 Ja19
Çankırı ⌕ TR 65 Mg25
Cannes ⌕ F 39 Ld24
Cannobio ⌕ I 46 Le22
Cann River ⌕ AUS 97 Sb26
Canoas ⌕ BR 135 Hb24
Canosa di Púglia ⌕ I 49 Lj25
Cantabria ⌕ E 40 Kj24
Cantabria Mountains ▲ E 40 Kg24
Canterbury ⌕ GB 35 La20
Canterbury Bight ⌕ NZ 99 Tc27
Canto do Buriti ⌕ BR 134 Hd20
Canton ⌕ USA 123 Fd10
Canutama ⌕ BR 133 Gd20
Canyon Glacier ⌕ 141 Td34
Cao Bang ⌕ VN 84 Qb14
Čapaev ⌕ KZ 72 Nc08
Čapaevskj ⌕ RUS 60 Ne19
Capanema ⌕ BR 134 Hc19
Cap Beddouza ⌕ MA 104 Kc12
Cap Bougaroun ⌕ DZ 106 Lb11
Cap Boujdour ⌕ MA 104 Kb13
Cap Comorin ⌕ IND 81 Od17
Cap Corse ⌕ F 46 Le24
Cap de Gaspé ⌕ CDN 121 Gd09
Cap de la Hague ⌕ F 36 Kk21
Cape Adair ⌕ CDN 118 Gb04
Cape Adare ⌕ 141 Tc33
Cape Agulhas ⌕ ZA 110 Ma25
Cape Aldrich ⌕ CDN 118 Gd02
Cape Barren Island ⌕ AUS 97 Sb27
Cape Bathurst ⌕ CDN 118 Dc04
Cape Bauld ⌕ CDN 121 Ha08
Cape Bird ⌕ 141 Tb34
Cape Boothby ⌕ 141 Nd32
Cape Borda ⌕ AUS 97 Rd26
Cape Breton ⌕ CDN 121 Ha09
Cape Breton Island ⌕ CDN 121 Gd09
Cape Canaveral ⌕ USA 123 Fd13
Cape Charles ⌕ USA 123 Ga11
Cape Christian ⌕ CDN 119 Gc04

Cape Coast ⌕ GH 105 Kd17
Cape Coast ⌕ GH 105 Kd17
Cape Cod ⌕ USA 121 Gc10
Cape Constantine ⌕ USA 116 Ca07
Cape Crauford ⌕ CDN 118 Fc04
Cape Croker ⌕ AUS 94 Rc21
Cape Darnley ⌕ 141 Oc32
Cape Dart ⌕ 140 Dc33
Cape Discovery ⌕ CDN 118 Ga02
Cape Dorchester ⌕ CDN 118 Ga05
Cape Dorset ⌕ CDN 119 Ga06
Cape Dyer ⌕ CDN 119 Gd05
Cape Evans Memorial Site ⌕ 141 Tb34
Cape Farewell ⌕ NZ 99 Tc27
Cape Fear ⌕ USA 123 Ga12
Cape Felt ⌕ 140 Eb33
Cape Flattery ⌕ AUS 96 Sb21
Cape Flattery ⌕ USA 122 Dd09
Cape Flying Fish ⌕ 140 Ed33
Cape Foulwind ⌕ NZ 99 Tc27
Cape Freshfield ⌕ 141 Sc32
Cape Girardeau ⌕ USA 123 Fc11
Cape Goodenough ⌕ 141 Rb32
Cape Graham Moore ⌕ CDN 118 Ga04
Cape Harrison ⌕ CDN 121 Ha07
Cape Hatteras ⌕ USA 123 Ga11
Cape Hawke ⌕ AUS 97 Sc25
Cape Horn ⌕ RCH 137 Gc30
Cape Howe ⌕ AUS 97 Sc26
Cape Kellet ⌕ CDN 116 Dc04
Cape Knob ⌕ AUS 95 Qd25
Cape Labrador ⌕ CDN 119 Gd06
Cape Leeuwin ⌕ AUS 95 Qc25
Cape Leveque ⌕ AUS 94 Ra22
Cape Lisburne ⌕ USA 116 Bc05
Capel'ka ⌕ RUS 30 Me16
Cape Lookout ⌕ USA 123 Ga12
Cape Low ⌕ CDN 118 Fc06
Cape Melville ⌕ AUS 96 Sa21
Cape Mendocino ⌕ USA 122 Dd10
Cape Mercy ⌕ CDN 119 Gd06
Cape Meredith ⌕ GB 137 Gd29
Cape Mohican ⌕ USA 116 Bc06
Cape Naturaliste ⌕ AUS 95 Qc25
Cape Nelson ⌕ AUS 97 Sa26
Cape Newenham ⌕ USA 116 Bd07
Cape of Good Hope ⌕ ZA 110 Ld25
Cape Otway ⌕ AUS 97 Sa26
Cape Palmer ⌕ 140 Fa33
Cape Parry ⌕ CDN 118 Dd03
Cape Pasley ⌕ AUS 95 Ra25
Cape Poinsett ⌕ 141 Qc32
Cape Prince Albert ⌕ CDN 118 Dd03
Cape Queen ⌕ CDN 118 Ga06

Cape Race ☒ CDN 121 Hb09
Cape Raper ☒ CDN 119 Gc05
Cape Romanzof ☒ USA 116 Bc06
Cape Sable ☒ CDN 121 Gc10
Cape Sable ☒ USA 123 Fd13
Cape Saint George ☒ CDN 123 Fc13
Cape Saint James ☒ CDN 117 Db08
Cape Scott ☒ CDN 116 Dc08
Cape Sherard ☒ CDN 118 Ga04
Cape Sibbald ☒ 141 Tb33
Cape Smith ☒ CDN 120 Ga06
Cape Spencer ☒ AUS 97 Rd26
Cape Town ☒ ZA 110 Ld25
Cape Verde ☒ CV 105 Jd16
Cape Verde Islands ☒ CV 105 Jd15
Cape Wessel ☒ AUS 96 Rd21
Cape Yakataga ☒ USA 116 Cd06
Cape York ☒ AUS 96 Sa21
Cape York Peninsula ☒ AUS 96 Sa21
Cap-Haïtien ☒ RH 127 Gb15
Capim Grosso ☒ BR 135 Hd21
Čapljina ☒ BIH 47 Lj24
Cap Lopez ☒ G 108 Lb19
Čaplygin ☒ RUS 59 Mk19
Čaplynka ☒ UA 62 Mg22
Capo Ísola delle Correnti ☒ I 49 Lh27
Capo San Vito ☒ I 48 Lg26
Capo Spartivento ☒ I 49 Lj27
Cap Palmas ☒ LB/CI 105 Kc18
Cap Rhir ☒ MA 104 Kc12
Caprivi Strip ☒ NAM 110 Ma22
Capu di Muru ☒ F 46 Le25
Capu Rossu ☒ F 46 Le24
Cap Vert ☒ SN 105 Ka16
Caquetá ☒ CO 132 Gb19
Caracal ☒ RO 55 Mc23
Caracarai ☒ BR 132 Gd18
Caracas ● YV 127 Gc16
Carajás ☒ BR 134 Hb20
Caransebeş ☒ RO 54 Mb23
Carauari ☒ BR 132 Gc19
Caravaca de la Cruz ☒ E 43 Kk26
Caravalas ☒ BR 135 Ja22
Carboneras ☒ E 43 Kk27
Carbonia ☒ I 48 Le24
Carcassonne ☒ F 38 Ld24
Carcot Island ☒ 140 Ga32
Çardak ☒ TR 64 Me27
Cardamom Mountains ☒ K 84 Qa16
Cardeña ☒ E 41 Kh26
Cardiff ☒ GB 35 Kj20
Cardigan Bay ☒ GB 35 Kh19
Carei ☒ RO 54 Mb22
Careiro ☒ BR 134 Ha19
Carentan ☒ F 36 Kk21
Carevo ☒ BG 55 Md24
Carhaix-Plouguer ☒ F 36 Kj21
Caribbean Sea ☒ JA 126 Ga15
Caribou ☒ CDN 120 Fa07
Cariñena ☒ E 42 Kk25
Carinhanha ☒ BR 135 Hd21
Cârlibaba ☒ RO 55 Mc22
Carlisle ☒ GB 34 Kj18
Carlow ☒ IRL 33 Kg19

Carlsbad ☒ USA 122 Ed12
Carlson Inlet ☒ 140 Ga34
Carmacks ☒ CDN 116 Da06
Carmagnola ☒ I 46 Le23
Carmarthen ☒ GB 35 Kh20
Carmen de Patagones ☒ RA 137 Gd27
Carmona ☒ E 41 Kh27
Carnarvon ☒ AUS 94 Qc23
Carnot ☒ RCA 108 Ld17
Carolina ☒ BR 134 Hc20
Caroline Islands ☒ FSM 92 Sa17
Caroline Seamounts ☒ FSM 92 Sa17
Caroni ☒ YV 132 Gd17
Carpathian Mountains ☒ UA/RO 54 Mc21
Carpentras ☒ F 39 Lc23
Carpi ☒ I 46 Lf23
Carrara ☒ I 46 Lf23
Carrauntoohil ☒ IRL 33 Kf19
Carrick-on-Shannon ☒ IRL 33 Kf19
Çarşamba ☒ TR 65 Mj25
Carson City ● USA 122 Ea11
Cartagena ☒ CO 132 Ga16
Cartagena ☒ E 43 Kk27
Cartwright ☒ CDN 121 Ha08
Caruaru ☒ BR 134 Ja21
Carúpano ☒ YV 127 Gd16
Casablanca ☒ MA 104 Kc12
Casa Grande ☒ USA 122 Eb12
Casale Monferrato ☒ I 46 Le23
Casalmaggiore ☒ I 46 Lf23
Casamozza ☒ F 46 Le24
Cascade Range ☒ USA 122 Dd09
Cascais ☒ P 40 Kf26
Cascavel ☒ BR 135 Hb23
Casciana Terme ☒ I 46 Lf24
Cáscina ☒ I 46 Lf24
Casentinesi-Monte Falterona-Campigna, P.N. ☒ I 46 Lf24
Caserta ☒ I 49 Lh25
Casey ☒ 141 Qc32
Casey Bay ☒ 141 Nb32
Cashel ☒ IRL 33 Kg19
Casino ☒ AUS 97 Sc24
Casiquiare ☒ YV 132 Gc16
Casma ☒ PE 133 Ga20
Čašniki ☒ BY 31 Me18
Caspe ☒ E 42 Kk25
Casper ☒ USA 120 Ec10
Caspian Depression ☒ RUS/KZ 76 Nb09
Caspian Sea ☒ 76 Nc10
Cassai ☒ ANG 110 Ma21
Cassino ☒ I 49 Lg25
Castanhal ☒ BR 134 Hc19
Casteljaloux ☒ F 38 La23
Castellammare del Golfo ☒ I 48 Lg26
Castellane ☒ F 39 Ld24
Castelló de la Plana ☒ E 43 Kk26
Castelnaudary ☒ F 42 La24
Castelnovo ne'Monti ☒ I 46 Lf23
Castelo Branco ☒ P 40 Kg26
Castelo de Vide ☒ P 40 Kg26
Castelsarrasin ☒ F 38 La23
Casteltérmini ☒ I 48 Lg27
Castelvetrano ☒ I 48 Lg27
Castets ☒ F 42 Kk24
Castiglione delle Stiviere ☒ I 46 Lf23

Castilla la Vieja ☒ E 40 Kh25
Castilla Nueva ☒ E 41 Kj26
Castilla y León ☒ E 40 Kh25
Castilla - La Mancha ☒ E 41 Kh26
Castillonnès ☒ F 38 La23
Castlebar ☒ IRL 33 Kf19
Castlemaine ☒ AUS 97 Sa26
Castlerea ☒ IRL 33 Kf19
Castletown ☒ GB 34 Kh18
Castres ☒ F 38 Lb24
Castries ● WL 127 Gd16
Castro-Urdiales ☒ E 42 Kj25
Castro Verde ☒ P 41 Kf27
Castrovillari ☒ I 49 Lh26
Castuera ☒ E 41 Kh26
Çat ☒ TR 66 Na26
Çatak ☒ TR 66 Nb26
Çatalca Yarımadası ☒ TR 57 Md25
Catalonia ☒ E 42 La25
Catamarca ☒ RA 136 Gc24
Catanduanes ☒ RP 85 Ra16
Catanduva ☒ BR 135 Hc23
Catanzaro ☒ I 49 Lj26
Cateraggio ☒ F 46 Le24
Cat Island ☒ BS 126 Ga14
Cato ☒ BR 134 Ja20
Caucasia ☒ CO 132 Ga17
Caucasus ☒ RUS/GE 76 Na10
Caudry ☒ F 37 Lb20
Čaunskaja guba ☒ RUS 74 Tb05
Căuşeni ☒ MD 55 Me22
Caupolican ☒ BOL 133 Gc21
Caura ☒ YV 132 Gd17
Caussade ☒ F 38 La23
Cavalla ☒ LB 105 Kc17
Cavan ☒ IRL 33 Kg19
Çavdarhisar ☒ TR 64 Me26
Cavtat ☒ HR 47 Lk24
Çavuşy ☒ BY 59 Mf19
Caxais ☒ BR 134 Hd19
Caxias do Sul ☒ BR 135 Hb24
Çay ☒ TR 64 Mf26
Çaybeyi ☒ TR 65 Mj27
Çayeli ☒ TR 66 Na25
Cayenne ● F 134 Hb17
Çayıralan ☒ TR 65 Mh26
Çaylar ☒ TR 66 Na26
Cayman Islands ☒ UK 126 Fd15
Cayman Ridge ☒ 126 Fd15
Cayman Trench ☒ 126 Fd15
Cazalla de la Sierra ☒ E 41 Kh27
Cazorla ☒ E 41 Kj27
Ceahláu, P.N. ☒ RO 55 Mc22
Ceará ☒ BR 134 Ja19
Čeboksary ☒ RUS 72 Nb07
Čeboksary ☒ RUS 60 Nd17
Cebu ☒ RP 85 Ra16
Cebu ☒ RP 85 Ra16
Cece ☒ H 53 Lk22
Čečel'nyk ☒ UA 62 Me21
Cécina ☒ I 46 Lf24
Cedar City ☒ USA 122 Eb11
Cedar Lake ☒ CDN 120 Ed08
Cedar Rapids ☒ USA 123 Fb10
Cedro ☒ BR 134 Ja20
Ceduna ☒ AUS 95 Rc25
Cefalù ☒ I 49 Lh26
Cegléd ☒ H 53 Lk22
Cehegín ☒ E 43 Kk26
Ceheng ☒ CHN 84 Qb14
Čehov ☒ RUS 58 Mj18
Çekerek ☒ TR 65 Mh25

Çekerek Irmağı ☒ TR 65 Mh26
Čekmaguš ☒ RUS 60 Nh18
Čekurdah ☒ RUS 74 Sb05
Celanova ☒ E 40 Kg24
Celaya ☒ MEX 124 Ed14
Čelbas ☒ RUS 63 Mk22
Celbridge ☒ IRL 33 Kg19
Celebes ☒ RI 87 Ra19
Celebes Sea ☒ RI 87 Ra18
Celina ☒ RUS 63 Na22
Čeljabinsk ☒ RUS 72 Oa07
Celjachany ☒ BY 51 Mc19
Celje ☒ SLO 47 Lh22
Celldömölk ☒ H 53 Lj22
Celle ☒ D 44 Lf19
Celtic Sea ☒ GB 35 Kg20
Çemişgezek ☒ TR 66 Mk26
Central African Republic ☒ RCA 108 Ld17
Central Balkan, N.P. ☒ BG 55 Mc24
Central Brahui Range ☒ PAK 80 Ob13
Central Makran Range ☒ PAK 77 Oa13
Central'nojakutskaja ravnina ☒ RUS 75 Qd06
Central'notungusskoe plato ☒ RUS 73 Pd06
Central Range ☒ PNG 92 Sa20
Central Siberian Plateau ☒ RUS 73 Pc05
Centre ☒ F 36 La22
Cerachovka ☒ BY 59 Mf19
Ceram ☒ RI 87 Rb19
Ceram Sea ☒ RI 87 Rb19
Cerbère ☒ F 38 Lb24
Cercal ☒ P 41 Kf27
Čerdakly ☒ RUS 60 Ne18
Čerencovo ☒ RUS 30 Mg16
Čerepovec ☒ RUS 58 Mj16
Ceres ☒ BR 135 Hc22
Cerignola ☒ I 49 Lh25
Çerikli ☒ TR 65 Mg26
Čerkasy ☒ UA 62 Mg21
Čerkesk ☒ RUS 76 Na10
Čerkessk ☒ RUS 76 Na10
Çerkezköy ☒ TR 57 Me25
Čermik ☒ TR 66 Mk26
Čern' ☒ RUS 59 Mj19
Cerna Domogled, P.N. ☒ RO 54 Mb23
Černava ☒ RUS 59 Mk19
Černava ☒ RUS 59 Mk19
Černavoda ☒ RO 55 Me23
Černay ☒ F 39 Ld22
Černihiv ☒ UA 59 Mf20
Černivci ☒ UA 55 Mc21
Černjachiv ☒ UA 62 Me20
Černjachovsk ☒ RUS 31 Ma18
Černjanka ☒ RUS 59 Mj20
Čërrik ☒ AL 56 Lk25
Cerro Aconcagua ☒ RCH/RA 136 Gb25
Cerro del Toro ☒ RCH/RA 136 Gc24
Cerro de Pasco ☒ PE 133 Ga21
Cerro Guanay ☒ YV 132 Gc17
Cerro Lantaro ☒ RCH 137 Gb28
Cerro Paine ☒ RCH 137 Gb29
Cerro San Valentin ☒ RCH 137 Gb28
Cerro Zapaleri ☒ RCH/RA 136 Gc23

Čerskij ☐ RUS 74 Ta05
Čertkovo ☐ RUS 61 Na21
Čerusti ☐ RUS 58 Na18
Červen' ☐ BY 51 Me19
Cérvia ☐ I 46 Lg23
Červonohrad ☐ UA 51 Mc20
Čerykav ☐ BY 59 Mf19
Cesena ☐ I 46 Lg23
Cesenático ☐ I 46 Lg23
Cēsis ☐ LV 30 Mc17
České Budějovice ☐ CZ
  52 Lh21
České Švýcarsko, N.P. ☀ CZ
  52 Lh21
Český Krumlov ☐ CZ 52 Lh21
Çeşme ☐ TR 57 Md26
Cēsskaja guba ☐ RUS
  72 Nb05
Çetinkaya ☐ TR 65 Mj26
Cetraro ☐ I 49 Lh26
Ceuta ☐ E 104 Kc11
Ceuta ☐ E 41 Kh28
Cévennes ☐ F 38 Ld23
Cévennes, P.N. des ☀ F
  38 Ld23
Cevizli ☐ TR 64 Mf27
Ceyhan ☐ TR 65 Mf27
Ceyhan Nehri ☐ TR 65 Mj27
Ceylon = Sri Lanka ■ CL
  81 Pa17
Chabahar ☐ IR 77 Oa13
Chachapoyas ☐ PE 133 Ga20
Chaco ☐ RA 136 Gd24
Chaco Boreal ☐ PY 136 Gd23
Chaco Boreal ☐ RA 136 Gd24
Chaco Central ☐ RA 136
  Gd23
Chad ☐ TCH 106 Ld16
Chaghcharan ☐ AFG 78 Ob12
Chala ☐ PE 133 Gb22
Chalais ☐ F 38 La23
Châlette-sur-Loing ☐ F
  37 Lb21
Challans ☐ F 38 Kk22
Challapata ☐ BOL 133 Gc22
Challenger Deep ☐ 92 Sa16
Châlons-en-Champagne ☐
  F 37 Lb21
Chalon-sur-Saône ☐ F
  39 Lc22
Chalus ☐ IR 76 Nc11
Cham ☐ D 45 Lg21
Chambal ☐ IND 80 Od13
Chambéry ☐ F 39 Lc23
Chamonix-Mont-Blanc ☐ F
  39 Ld23
Champagne ☐ F 37 Lc21
Champagne-Ardenne ☐ F
  37 Lc21
Champagnole ☐ F 39 Lc22
Champaign ☐ USA 123 Fc10
Champotón ☐ MEX 125 Fb15
Chañara ☐ RCH 136 Gc24
Chandeleur Islands ☐ USA
  123 Fc13
Chandigarh ★ IND 80 Od12
Changane ☐ MOC 111 Mc23
Changara ☐ MOC 111 Mc22
Changchun ☐ CHN 83 Rb10
Changde ☐ CHN 85 Qc13
Changhua ☐ RC 85 Ra14
Chang Jiang ☐ CHN 84 Qc12
Changsha ☐ CHN 85 Qc13
Changshou ☐ CHN 84 Qb12
Channel Islands ■ GB
  36 Kj21
Channel-Port-aux-Basques ☐
  CDN 121 Ha09
Chaoyang ☐ CHN 83 Ra10

Chaozhou ☐ CHN 85 Qd14
Chapada dos Parecis ■ BR
  133 Gd21
Chapeco ☐ BR 135 Hb24
Chapleau ☐ CDN 123 Fd09
Charaña ☐ BOL 133 Gc22
Chari ☐ TCH 108 Ld16
Charikar ☐ AFG 78 Ob11
Charity ☐ GUY 134 Ha17
Charkiv ☐ UA 63 Mj21
Charleroi ☐ B 37 Lc20
Charleston ☐ USA 123 Fd11
Charleston ☐ USA 123 Ga12
Charleville ☐ AUS 96 Sb24
Charleville-Mézières ☐ F
  37 Lc21
Charlotte ☐ USA 123 Fd11
Charlotte Amalie ☐ USA
  127 Gd15
Charlottetown ☐ CDN 121
  Gd09
Charlton ☐ AUS 97 Sa26
Charmes ☐ F 37 Lc21
Charters Towers ☐ AUS
  96 Sb23
Chartres ☐ F 36 La21
Châteaubriant ☐ F 36 Kk22
Château-Chinon ☐ F 39 Lb22
Château-du-Loir ☐ F 36 La22
Châteaudun ☐ F 36 La21
Château-Gontier ☐ F 36 Kk22
Châteaumeillant ☐ F 38 Lb22
Château-Renault ☐ F 38 La22
Châteauroux ☐ F 38 La22
Château-Salins ☐ F 37 Ld21
Château- Thierry ☐ F 37 Lb21
Châtelaillon-Plage ☐ F
  38 Kk22
Châtellerault ☐ F 38 La22
Chatham ☐ GB 35 La20
Chatham Islands ■ NZ
  99 Ua27
Chatham Rise ☐ 99 Td27
Châtillon-sur-Seine ☐ F
  39 Lc22
Chattanooga ☐ USA 123
  Fc11
Chaumont ☐ F 37 Lc21
Chauny ☐ F 37 Lb21
Chauvigny ☐ F 38 La22
Chaves ☐ BR 134 Hc19
Chaves ☐ P 40 Kg25
Chazelles-sur-Lyon ☐ F
  39 Lc23
Cheb ☐ CZ 52 Lg20
Cheboygan ☐ USA 123 Fd09
Chechenia ☐ RUS 76 Nb10
Checiny ☐ PL 50 Ma20
Chegga ☐ RIM 104 Kc13
Chegutu ☐ ZW 110 Mb22
Cheile Bizacului-Hăşmaş, P.N.
  ☀ RO 55 Mc22
Cheile Nerei-Beuşniţa, P.N. ☀
  RO 54 Ma23
Cheleken ☐ TM 76 Nc11
Chelforo ☐ RA 137 Gc26
Chelm ☐ PL 51 Mb20
Chelmża ☐ PL 50 Lk19
Chelmno ☐ PL 50 Lk19
Chemillé ☐ F 38 Kk22
Chemnitz ☐ D 45 Lg20
Chenar Shahijan ☐ IR 77 Nc13
Chengde ☐ CHN 83 Qd10
Chengdu ☐ CHN 84 Qa12
Chennai ☐ IND 81 Pa16
Chenzhou ☐ CHN 85 Qc13
Cheonan ☐ ROK 83 Rb11
Cheongjin ☐ PRK 83 Rb10
Chepes ☐ RA 136 Gc25

Cherbourg-Octeville ☐ F
  36 Kk21
Cherskiy Range ■ RUS
  74 Rd05
Cherson ☐ UA 62 Mg22
Chesapeake Bay ☐ USA
  123 Ga11
Chester ☐ GB 35 Kj19
Chesterfield ☐ GB 35 Kk19
Chesterfield Inlet ☐ CDN
  120 Fb06
Chetumal ☐ MEX 125 Fc15
Cheviot Hills ■ GB 35 Kj18
Che'w Bahir ☐ ETH 109 Md18
Cheyenne ☐ USA 122 Ed10
Chhattisgarh ☐ IND 80 Pa14
Chiang Mai ☐ THA 84 Pd15
Chiang Rai ☐ THA 84 Pd15
Chiapas ☐ MEX 125 Fb15
Chiavenna ☐ I 46 Le22
Chiayi ☐ RC 85 Ra14
Chibougamau ☐ CDN 121
  Gb09
Chicago ☐ USA 123 Fc10
Chichagof Island ■ USA
  117 Da07
Chickasha ☐ USA 123 Fa12
Chiclayo ☐ PE 133 Ga20
Chico ☐ RA 137 Gc28
Chico ☐ USA 122 Dd11
Chicoutimi ☐ CDN 121 Gb09
Chieti ☐ I 47 Lh24
Chifeng ☐ CHN 83 Qd10
Chignik ☐ USA 116 Ca07
Chihuahua ☐ MEX 124 Ec13
Chihuahua ☐ MEX 124 Ec13
Chile ■ RCH 136 Gb24
Chilecito ☐ RA 136 Gc24
Chililabombwe ☐ RDC 110
  Mb21
Chillán ☐ RCH 137 Gb26
Chilpancingo de los Bravos ☐
  MEX 124 Fa15
Chimay ☐ B 37 Lc20
Chimbote ☐ PE 133 Ga20
Chimoio ☐ MOC 111 Mc22
China ■ CHN 79 Pc11
Chincha Alta ☐ PE 133 Ga21
Chinchilla de Monte Aragón
  ☐ E 43 Kk26
Chindwinn ☐ MYA 84 Pc14
Chingola ☐ Z 110 Mb21
Chinhoyi ☐ ZW 110 Mc22
Chinko ☐ RCA 109 Ma17
Chinon ☐ F 38 La22
Chióggia ☐ I 46 Lg23
Chios ☐ GR 57 Mc26
Chipata ☐ Z 111 Mc21
Chipiona ☐ E 41 Kg27
Chippenham ☐ GB 35 Kj20
Chirfa ☐ LAR 106 Lc14
Chisasibi ☐ CDN 121 Ga08
Chisinau ★ MD 55 Me22
Chitré ☐ PA 126 Fd17
Chittagong ☐ BD 84 Pc14
Chittoor ☐ IND 81 Od16
Chitungwiza ☐ ZW 111 Mc22
Chiumbe ☐ ANG 108 Ma20
Chivasso ☐ I 46 Ld23
Chivilcoy ☐ RA 136 Gd26
Chlef ☐ DZ 104 La11
Chmel'nyc'kyj ☐ UA 51 Md21
Chmil'nyk ☐ UA 51 Md21
Chobe ☐ NAM 110 Ma22
Chodoriv ☐ UA 51 Mc21
Chodzież ☐ PL 50 Lj19
Choiseul ☐ SOL 93 Sd20
Chojbalsan ☐ MNG 82 Qc09
Chojna ☐ PL 50 Lh19

Chojnice ☐ PL 50 Lj19
Chojniki ☐ BY 51 Me20
Chojnów ☐ PL 50 Lh20
Cholet ☐ F 38 Kk22
Choluteca ☐ HN 125 Fc15
Choma ☐ ZW 110 Mb22
Chomutov ☐ CZ 52 Lg20
Chon Buri ☐ THA 84 Qa16
Chongqing ☐ CHN 84 Qb13
Chongqing ☐ CHN 84 Qb13
Chonos Archipelago ■ RCH
  137 Ga28
Chorol ☐ UA 62 Mg21
Chorzele ☐ PL 50 Ma19
Chos-Malal ☐ RA 137 Gb26
Chota Nagpur Plateau ■ IND
  80 Pa14
Chott Ech Chergui ☐ DZ
  104 La12
Chott el Hodna ☐ DZ 104
  La11
Chott El Jerid ☐ TN 106 Lb12
Chott Melrhir ☐ DZ 106 Lb12
Chotyn ☐ UA 51 Md21
Choûm ☐ RIM 104 Ka14
Chr'aščevka ☐ RUS 60 Ne19
Christchurch ☐ NZ 99 Tc27
Chrystynivka ☐ UA 62 Me21
Chu ■ KZ 78 Oc10
Chubut ☐ RA 137 Gb27
Chubut ☐ RA 137 Gc27
Chukchi Autonomous District
  ☐ RUS 74 Tb05
Chukchi Sea ☐ USA/RUS
  74 Ua04
Chukotskiy Poluostrov ☐
  RUS 74 Ua05
Chulucanas ☐ PE 132 Fd20
Chumphon ☐ THA 86 Pd16
Chunga ☐ ZW 110 Mb22
Chuquicamata ☐ RCH 136
  Gc23
Chur ☐ CH 45 Le22
Churchill ☐ CDN 120 Fa07
Churchill ☐ CDN 120 Fb07
Churchill Falls ☐ CDN 121
  Gd08
Chust ☐ UA 53 Mb21
Chuvashia ☐ RUS 60 Nd18
Chuy ☐ ROU 136 Hb25
Ciadâr-Lunga ☐ MD 55 Me22
Ciamis ☐ RI 86 Qb20
Cidade Medieval de Évora ☐
  P 41 Kg26
Cide ☐ TR 65 Mg25
Ciechanów ☐ PL 50 Ma19
Ciechanowiec ☐ PL 51 Mb19
Ciechocinek ☐ PL 50 Lk19
Cienfuegos ☐ C 126 Fd14
Cieszanów ☐ PL 51 Mb20
Cieszyn ☐ PL 50 Lk21
Cieza ☐ E 43 Kk26
Çifteler ☐ TR 64 Mf26
Cifuentes ☐ E 42 Kj25
Cihanbeyli ☐ TR 65 Mg26
Cihanbeyli Yaylası ■ TR
  65 Mg26
Cikobia ■ FJI 98 Ua22
Cilacap ☐ RI 86 Qb20
Çıldır ☐ TR 66 Nb25
Çıldır Gölü ☐ TR 66 Nb25
Cil'na ☐ RUS 60 Ne18
Çimenliyeniköy ☐ TR 65
  Mg26
Cincinnati ☐ USA 123 Fd11
Çine ☐ TR 64 Me27
Ciney ☐ B 37 Lc20
Cinque Terre, P.N. delle ☀ I
  46 Le23

Čir ⬚ **RUS** 61 Nb21
Circeo, P.N. del ⬚ ▮ **I** 48 Lg25
Cirebon ◯ **RI** 86 Qb20
Cirencester ◯ **GB** 35 Kk20
Čirpan ⬚ **BG** 55 Mc24
Cislău ◯ **RO** 55 Md23
Cišmišlia ⬚ **MD** 55 Me22
Cistierna ◯ **E** 40 Kh24
Čita ⬚ **RUS** 82 Qc08
Città di Castello ◯ **I** 46 Lg24
Ciucea ◯ **RO** 54 Mb22
Ciucurova ◯ **RO** 55 Me23
Ciudad Bolívar ◆ **YV** 132 Gd17
Ciudad Camargo ◯ **MEX** 124 Ec13
Ciudad Constitución ◯ **MEX** 124 Eb13
Ciudad de Guatemala ● **GCA** 125 Fb16
Ciudad del Carmen ◯ **MEX** 125 Fb15
Ciudad del Este ◯ **PY** 135 Hb24
Ciudad de México ● **MEX** 124 Fa15
Ciudad Guayana ◯ **YV** 132 Gd17
Ciudad Guzmán ◯ **MEX** 124 Ed15
Ciudad Juárez ◯ **MEX** 122 Ec12
Ciudad Madero ◯ **MEX** 125 Fa14
Ciudad Mante ◯ **MEX** 124 Fa14
Ciudad Obregón ◯ **MEX** 124 Ec13
Ciudad Ojeda ◯ **YV** 127 Gb16
Ciudad Real ◯ **E** 41 Kj26
Ciudad Rodrigo ◯ **E** 40 Kg25
Ciudad Valles ◯ **MEX** 124 Fa14
Ciudad Victoria ◯ **MEX** 124 Fa14
Ciutadella ◯ **E** 42 Lb25
Civil'sk ⬚ **RUS** 60 Nd18
Cività Castellana ◯ **I** 46 Lg24
Civitanova Marche ◯ **I** 47 Lg24
Civitavécchia ◯ **I** 46 Lf24
Çivril ◯ **TR** 64 Me26
Cizre ◯ **TR** 76 Na11
Cjurupyns'k ◯ **UA** 62 Mg22
Čkalovsk ⬚ **RUS** 58 Nb17
Clamecy ◯ **F** 39 Ld22
Claremorris ◯ **IRL** 33 Kf19
Clarence Island 🞜 **GB** 140 Hb31
Clarksdale ◯ **USA** 123 Fb12
Clarksville ◯ **USA** 123 Fb11
Clay Belt 🞜 **CDN** 120 Fd08
Clelles ◯ **F** 39 Lc23
Clermont ◯ **AUS** 96 Sb23
Clermont ◯ **F** 37 Lb21
Clermont-Ferrand ◯ **F** 38 Lb23
Cleveland ◯ **USA** 123 Fd10
Clifden ◯ **IRL** 33 Kf19
Cliffs of Moher 🞜 **IRL** 33 Kf19
Clinton-Colden Lake 🞜 **CDN** 120 Eb06
Cloncurry ◯ **AUS** 96 Sa23
Clones ◯ **IRL** 33 Kg19
Clonmel ◯ **IRL** 33 Kg19
Cloppenburg ◯ **D** 44 Le19
Clovis ◯ **USA** 122 Ed12
Čl'ton ⬚ **RUS** 61 Nd21
Cluj-Napoca ◯ **RO** 54 Mb22

Cluses ◯ **F** 39 Ld22
Clyde ◯ **CDN** 119 Gc04
Cna ⬚ **RUS** 61 Na19
Coahuila 🞜 **MEX** 124 Ed13
Coari ◯ **BR** 132 Gd19
Coast Mountains 🞜 **CDN** 117 Db07
Coast of Labrador 🞜 **CDN** 121 Gd07
Coast Ranges 🞜 **USA** 122 Dd11
Coats Island 🞜 **CDN** 118 Fd06
Coatsland 🞜 140 Jb34
Coatzacoalcos ◯ **MEX** 125 Fb15
Cobadin ◯ **RO** 55 Me23
Cobán ◯ **GCA** 125 Fb15
Cobar ◯ **AUS** 97 Sb25
Cobija ◯ **BOL** 133 Gc21
Coburg ◯ **D** 44 Lf20
Cochabamba ◯ **BOL** 133 Gc22
Cochin ◯ **IND** 81 Od17
Cockburn Town ◯ **UK** 127 Gb14
Cocos Island 🞜 **CR** 128 Fb09
Cody ◯ **USA** 120 Ec10
Coeroeni ◯ **SME** 134 Ha18
Coeur d'Alene ◯ **USA** 122 Ea09
Coevorden ◯ **NL** 37 Ld19
Coffs Harbour ◯ **AUS** 97 Sc25
Cognac ◯ **F** 38 Kk23
Coihaique ◯ **RCH** 137 Gb28
Coimbatore ◯ **IND** 81 Od16
Coimbra ◯ **P** 40 Kf25
Coín ◯ **E** 41 Kh27
Çokak ◯ **TR** 65 Mj27
Colchester ◯ **GB** 35 La20
Cold Bay ◯ **USA** 116 Bd07
Coleraine ◯ **GB** 33 Kg18
Colesberg ◯ **ZA** 110 Mb25
Colima 🞜 **MEX** 124 Ed15
Colima ◯ **MEX** 124 Ed15
Colinas ◯ **BR** 134 Hd20
Coll 🞜 **GB** 34 Kg17
Colmar ◯ **F** 37 Ld21
Colmenar Viejo ◯ **E** 40 Kj25
Cologne ◯ **D** 44 Ld20
Colombia ▮ **CO** 132 Gb18
Colombia Basin 🞜 127 Ga16
Colombo ● **CL** 81 Od17
Colón ◯ **PA** 132 Ga17
Colonia ◯ **FSM** 92 Rd17
Colonsay 🞜 **GB** 34 Kg17
Colorado 🞜 **RA** 137 Gc26
Colorado 🞜 **USA** 122 Eb11
Colorado 🞜 **USA** 122 Ec11
Colorado Springs ◯ **USA** 122 Ed11
Columbia 🞜 **USA** 122 Dd09
Columbia ◯ **USA** 123 Fd12
Columbia Plateau 🞜 **USA** 122 Ea10
Columbia Plateau 🞜 **USA** 122 Eb11
Columbus ◯ **USA** 123 Fd11
Columbus ◯ **USA** 123 Fd12
Comácchio ◯ **I** 46 Lg23
Comănești ◯ **RO** 55 Md22
Comitán de Domínguez ◯ **MEX** 125 Fb15
Commentry ◯ **F** 38 Lb22
Commercy ◯ **F** 37 Lc21
Committee Bay 🞜 **CDN** 118 Fc05
Commonwealth Bay 🞜 141 Sa32

Como ◯ **I** 46 Le23
Comodoro Rivadavia ◯ **RA** 137 Gc28
Comoé ◯ **CI** 105 Kd17
Comoros ▮ **COM** 111 Na21
Comoros 🞜 **COM** 111 Na21
Compiègne ◯ **F** 37 Lb21
Comrat ◯ **MD** 55 Me22
Conakry ● **RG** 105 Kb17
Concarneau ◯ **F** 36 Kj22
Conceição do Araguaia ◯ **BR** 134 Hc20
Concepción ◯ **PY** 136 Ha23
Concepción ◯ **RCH** 137 Gb26
Concepción del Oro ◯ **MEX** 124 Ed14
Conches-en-Ouche ◯ **F** 36 La21
Concord ◯ **USA** 121 Gb10
Concordia ◯ **RA** 136 Ha25
Condom ◯ **F** 42 La24
Conegliano ◯ **I** 46 Lg23
Confolens ◯ **F** 38 La22
Congo ▮ **RCB** 108 Ld18
Congo 🞜 **RDC** 108 Ma18
Congo Basin 🞜 **RDC** 108 Ma18
Congonhas ◯ **BR** 135 Hd23
Connacht 🞜 **IRL** 33 Kf19
Connecticut 🞜 **USA** 121 Gb10
Connemara N.P. ▮ **IRL** 33 Kf19
Constanța ◯ **RO** 55 Me23
Constantine ◯ **DZ** 106 Lb11
Constitución ◯ **RCH** 136 Gb26
Contwoyto Lake 🞜 **CDN** 118 Ec05
Conway ◯ **USA** 123 Fb11
Coober Pedy ◯ **AUS** 94 Rc24
Coșești ◯ **RO** 55 Mc23
Cook Ice Shelf 🞜 141 Sc32
Cook Inlet 🞜 **USA** 116 Cb06
Cookstown ◯ **GB** 33 Kg18
Cook Strait 🞜 **NZ** 99 Tc27
Cooktown ◯ **AUS** 96 Sb22
Coolgardie ◯ **AUS** 95 Ra25
Cooma ◯ **AUS** 97 Sb26
Coonabarabran ◯ **AUS** 97 Sb25
Coonamble ◯ **AUS** 97 Sb25
Cooperation Sea 🞜 141 Od32
Coorabie ◯ **AUS** 95 Rc25
Coos Bay ◯ **USA** 122 Dd10
Cootamundra ◯ **AUS** 97 Sb25
Copenhagen ● **DK** 26 Lg18
Copiapó ◯ **RCH** 136 Gc24
Copperbelt 🞜 **Z** 110 Mb21
Coquimbo ◯ **RCH** 136 Gb25
Corabia ◯ **RO** 55 Mc24
Coral Basin 🞜 **AUS** 96 Sb21
Coral Gables ◯ **USA** 123 Fd13
Coral Harbour ◯ **CDN** 118 Fd06
Coral Sea 🞜 96 Sc22
Corby ◯ **GB** 35 Kk19
Corcaigh = Cork ◯ **IRL** 33 Kf20
Cordajás ◯ **BR** 132 Gd19
Cordillera Bética 🞜 **E** 41 Kh27
Cordillera Central 🞜 **E** 40 Kh25
Cordillera Central 🞜 **PE** 133 Ga20

Cordillera Central 🞜 **PE** 133 Gb21
Cordillera de la Costa 🞜 **RCH** 136 Gb25
Cordillera de Mérida 🞜 **YV** 132 Gb17
Cordillera Occidental 🞜 **PE** 133 Ga21
Cordillera Oriental 🞜 **BOL** 133 Gc22
Cordillera Oriental 🞜 **PE** 133 Ga20
Cordillera Patagónica 🞜 **RCH** 137 Gb27
Córdoba ◯ **RA** 136 Gd25
Córdoba ◯ **RA** 136 Gd25
Corfu 🞜 **GR** 56 Lk26
Çorhu Nehri 🞜 **TR** 66 Na25
Coria ◯ **E** 40 Kg26
Corinto ◯ **BR** 135 Hd22
Cork = Corcaigh ◯ **IRL** 33 Kf20
Çorlu ◯ **TR** 57 Md25
Corner Brook ◯ **CDN** 121 Ha09
Corno Grande ▮ **I** 47 Lg24
Çornomors'ke ◯ **UA** 62 Mg23
Čornuchy ◯ **UA** 62 Mg20
Cornwall 🞜 **CDN** 35 Kk26
Cornwallis Island 🞜 **CDN** 118 Fa03
Coro ◯ **YV** 127 Gc16
Coromandel Peninsula 🞜 **NZ** 99 Td26
Coron ◯ **RP** 85 Ra16
Coronation Gulf 🞜 **CDN** 118 Eb05
Coronel Pringles ◯ **RA** 137 Gd26
Çorovodë ◯ **AL** 56 Ma25
Corpus Christi ◯ **USA** 123 Fa13
Correntina ◯ **BR** 135 Hd21
Corrientes ◯ **RA** 136 Ha24
Corrientes 🞜 **RA** 136 Ha24
Corsica 🞜 **F** 48 Le24
Corte ◯ **F** 46 Le24
Cortijos Nuevos ◯ **E** 41 Kj26
Cortina d'Ampezzo ◯ **I** 46 Lg22
Čortkiv ◯ **UA** 51 Mc21
Cortona ◯ **I** 46 Lg24
Çorum ◯ **TR** 65 Mh25
Corumbá ◯ **BR** 135 Ha22
Corvallis ◯ **USA** 122 Dd10
Corwen ◯ **GB** 35 Kj19
Cosenza ◯ **I** 49 Lj26
Cosmo Newbery Mission ◯ **AUS** 94 Ra24
Cosne-Cours-sur-Loire ◯ **F** 38 Lb22
Costa Blanca 🞜 **E** 43 Kk27
Costa Brava 🞜 **E** 42 Lb25
Costa Cálida 🞜 **E** 43 Kk27
Costa Daurada 🞜 **E** 42 La25
Costa de Almería 🞜 **E** 41 Kj27
Costa de la Luz 🞜 **E** 41 Kg27
Costa del Azahar 🞜 **E** 42 La25
Costa del Sol 🞜 **E** 41 Kh27
Costa del Sud 🞜 **I** 48 Le26
Costa de Miskitos 🞜 **NIC** 126 Fd16
Costa de València 🞜 **E** 43 Kk26
Costa Rica ▮ **CR** 125 Fc16
Costa Smeralda 🞜 **I** 48 Le25
Costa Vasca 🞜 **E** 42 Kj24
Costa Verde 🞜 **E** 40 Kg24

Costa Verde P 40 Kf25
Costeşti MD 55 Md22
Costeşti RO 55 Md23
Cotabato RP 85 Ra17
Côte d'Azur F 39 Ld24
Cotonou DY 105 La17
Cottbus D 44 Lh20
Coulman Island 141 Tc33
Coulommiers F 37 Lb21
Council Bluffs USA 123 Fa10
Courland LV 30 Mb17
Courland Lagoon RUS/LT 31 Ma18
Cournon-d'Auvergne F 38 Lb23
Coutances F 36 Kh21
Coutras F 38 Kh23
Covadonga y Picos de Europa, P.N. de E 40 Kh24
Coventry GB 35 Kk19
Covilhã P 40 Kg25
Cowra AUS 97 Sb25
Coxim BR 135 Hb22
Cox's Bazar BD 84 Pc14
Cozia, P.N. RO 55 Mc23
Cozumel MEX 125 Fc14
Cracow PL 50 Lk20
Crailsheim D 45 Lf21
Craiova RO 54 Mb23
Cranbourne AUS 97 Sb26
Cranbrook CDN 122 Ea09
Crary Mountains 140 Ea34
Crater Lake USA 122 Dd10
Cratéus BR 134 Hd20
Crawley GB 35 Kk20
Cree Lake CDN 120 Ec07
Cremona I 46 Lf23
Cres HR 47 Lh23
Cres HR 47 Lh23
Crescent City USA 122 Dd10
Crest F 39 Lc23
Crete GR 56 Mc28
Creuse F 38 La22
Crieff GB 34 Kj17
Crikvenica HR 47 Lh23
Crimea UA 63 Mh23
Cristopol' RUS 60 Nf18
Croatia HR 47 Lj23
Cromer GB 35 La19
Cromwell NZ 99 Tb28
Crooked Island BS 127 Gb14
Crosson Ice Shelf 140 Ec33
Crotone I 49 Lj26
Croyden AUS 96 Sa22
Crozon F 36 Kh21
Crucea RO 55 Me23
Cruz Alta BR 135 Hb24
Cruzeiro do Sul BR 133 Gb20
Csongrád H 53 Ma22
Csorna H 53 Lj22
Cuamba MOC 111 Md21
Cuando ANG 110 Ma22
Cuanza ANG 108 Ld24
Cuauhtémoc MEX 124 Ec13
Cuba C 126 Fd14
Cubango ANG 110 Ld22
Čučkovo RUS 58 Na18
Çubuk TR 65 Mg25
Čudovo RUS 30 Mf16

Čudzin BY 51 Md19
Cuéllar E 40 Kh25
Cuenca E 42 Kj25
Cuenca EC 132 Ga19
Cuernavaca MEX 124 Fa15
Cuers F 39 Ld24
Cugango ANG 108 Ld20
Čuhujiv UA 63 Mj21
Cuiabá BR 135 Ha22
Cuito ANG 110 Ld22
Çukurköprü TR 65 Mh27
Çukurova TR 65 Mh27
Culiacán Rosales MEX 124 Ec14
Cullen GB 34 Kj17
Cullera E 43 Kk26
Čul'man RUS 75 Rb07
Culuene BR 135 Hb21
Čulym RUS 73 Pa07
Cumaná YV 127 Gd16
Cumberland Peninsula CDN 119 Gc05
Cumberland Sound CDN 119 Gc05
Cumbrian Mountains GB 34 Kj18
Čumikan RUS 75 Rd08
Cuminá BR 134 Ha19
Cumnock GB 34 Kh18
Çumra TR 65 Mg27
Čuna RUS 73 Pd07
Cunene ANG 110 Lc22
Cúneo I 46 Ld23
Cunnamulla AUS 96 Sb24
Cuorgnè I 46 Ld23
Curaçao NL 127 Gc16
Curitiba BR 135 Hc24
Currais Novos BR 134 Ja20
Currie AUS 97 Sa26
Curtea de Argeş RO 55 Mc23
Curtici RO 54 Ma22
Curtis Island AUS 96 Sc23
Curtis Island NZ 99 Ua25
Curup RI 86 Qa19
Čuteevo RUS 60 Nd18
Čutove UA 63 Mh21
Cuttack IND 80 Pb14
Cuxhaven D 44 Le19
Cuyuni GUY 132 Gd17
Cuzco PE 133 Gb21
Cybinka PL 50 Lh19
Cyclades GR 57 Mc27
Čyhyryn UA 62 Mg21
Cyprus CY 107 Mc12
Cyrenaica LAR 106 Ma12
Czaplinek PL 50 Lj19
Czarna Białostocka PL 51 Mb19
Czarnków PL 50 Lj19
Czech Republic CZ 52 Lh21
Czersk PL 50 Lj19
Częstochowa PL 50 Lk20
Człopa PL 50 Lj19
Człuchów PL 50 Lj19

D

Dal'nerečensk RUS 83 Rc09
Daba Shan CHN 82 Qb12
Dabeiba CO 132 Ga17
Dabie Shan CHN 85 Qc12
Dąbrowa Białostocka PL 51 Mb19

Dąbrowa Tarnowska PL 50 Ma20
Dabryn' BY 51 Me20
Dachstein A 52 Lg22
Dacia Seamount 104 Kb12
Daegu ROK 83 Rb11
Daejeon ROK 83 Rb11
Dáfni GR 56 Mb26
Dáfni GR 56 Mb26
Dagda LV 31 Md17
Dagestan RUS 76 Nb10
Dagomys RUS 66 Mk24
Dahlak Archipelago ER 107 Md15
Daimiel E 41 Kj26
Dairût ET 107 Mc13
Daito Islands J 83 Rc13
Dajarra AUS 96 Rd23
Dakar SN 105 Ka16
Dakhla Oasis ET 107 Mb13
Đakovica SR 56 Ma24
Đakovo HR 47 Lk23
Dakshin Gangotri 141 Lc32
Dalaman TR 64 Me27
Dalanzadgad MNG 82 Qa10
Dalarna S 24 Lg15
Da Lat VN 85 Qb16
Dalbandīn PAK 77 Oa13
Dalby AUS 96 Sc24
Dale N 24 Lc15
Dale N 24 Lc15
Dalen N 26 Le16
Dalgaranga Hill AUS 95 Qd24
Dâlgopol BG 55 Md24
Dalhart USA 122 Ed11
Dali CHN 84 Qa13
Dalian CHN 83 Ra11
Dalj HR 47 Lk23
Dallas USA 123 Fa12
Dalmatia HR 47 Lh24
Dal'negorsk RUS 75 Rd10
Daloa CI 105 Kc17
Dalsbruk = Taalintehdas FIN 22 Mb15
Dalvík IS 32 Ka13
Daly Waters AUS 94 Rc22
Daman IND 80 Oc14
Damar RI 87 Rb20
Damaraland NAM 110 Ld23
Damascus SYR 76 Md12
Damba ANG 108 Ld20
Damiette ET 107 Mc12
Damlacık TR 65 Mk27
Damme D 44 Le19
Dampier AUS 94 Qd23
Dampier Archipelago AUS 94 Qd23
Dampier Land AUS 94 Ra22
Danakil Depression ETH 107 Na16
Danakil Desert ETH 107 Na16
Da Nang VN 85 Qb15
Dandong CHN 83 Ra10
Dangriga BH 125 Fc15
Danilovgrad CG 54 Lk24
Danilovka RUS 61 Nc20
Dankov RUS 59 Mk19
Dannenberg D 44 Lf19
Danube 52 Lh21
Danville USA 123 Ga11
Darabani RO 55 Md21
Daran IR 76 Nc12
Dardanelles TR 57 Md25
Darende TR 65 Mj26

Dar es Salaam EAT 109 Md20
Darfo-Boário Terme I 46 Lf23
Darfur SUD 106 Ma16
Darıca TR 65 Mj26
Darjeeling IND 80 Pb13
Darling AUS 97 Sa25
Darling Downs AUS 96 Sb24
Darling Range AUS 95 Qd25
Darlington GB 34 Kk18
Darłowo PL 50 Lj18
Darmstadt D 45 Le21
Darnah LAR 106 Ma12
Daroca E 42 Kk25
Darß D 44 Lg18
Dartmoor N.P. GB 35 Kj20
Dartmouth GB 35 Kj20
Daru PNG 92 Sa20
Daruvar HR 47 Lj23
Darvaze TM 78 Nd10
Darwin AUS 94 Rc21
Darwin Glacier 141 Sd34
Dashoguz TM 78 Nd10
Dašt-e Lut IR 77 Nd12
Datça TR 57 Md27
Datong CHN 82 Qc10
Daugavpils LT 31 Md18
Daun D 45 Ld20
Dauphin CDN 120 Ed08
Dauphiné F 39 Lc23
Davangere IND 81 Od16
Davao RP 85 Rb17
Davenport USA 123 Fb10
David PA 126 Fd17
David Glacier 141 Ta34
Davis 141 Od32
Davis Sea 141 Pc31
Davis Strait 119 Ha05
Davos CH 45 Le22
Davyd-Haradok BY 51 Md19
Dawna Range MYA 84 Pd15
Dawson AUS 96 Sb23
Dawson CDN 116 Da06
Dawson Creek CDN 117 Dd07
Dax F 42 Kh24
Daxian CHN 84 Qb12
Dayton USA 123 Fd11
Daytona Beach USA 123 Fd13
De Aar ZA 110 Ma25
Deakin AUS 95 Rb25
Deán Funes RA 136 Gd25
Dease Lake CDN 116 Dc07
Dease Strait CDN 118 Ec05
Death Valley USA 122 Ea11
Debal'ceve UA 63 Mk21
Debar MK 56 Ma25
Dębica PL 50 Ma20
Dęblin PL 51 Ma20
Debre Birhan ETH 109 Md17
Debrecen H 53 Ma22
Debre Markos ETH 109 Md16
Decatur USA 123 Fc12
Decazeville F 38 Lb23
Deccan IND 81 Od15
Decize F 39 Lb22
Deda RO 55 Mc22
Dedegöl Dağları TR 64 Mf27
Dedenevo RUS 58 Mj17
Dédougou BF 105 Kd16

Dedoviči ☐ RUS 30 Me17
Dedza ☐ MW 111 Mc21
Degeberga ☐ S 27 Lh18
Degerfors ☐ S 27 Lh16
Deggendorf ☐ D 45 Lg21
De Grey ↘ AUS 94 Qd23
Dehiba ☐ TN 106 Lc12
Dehradun ☐ IND 80 Od12
Deir Al Zor ☐ SYR 76 Na11
Dej ☐ RO 54 Mb22
Deje ☐ S 26 Lg16
Dek'emhare ☐ ER 107 Md15
Delano ☐ USA 122 Ea11
Delaware ☐ USA 123 Ga11
Delaware Bay ⌐ USA 121 Gb11
Delémont ☐ CH 45 Ld22
Delft ☐ NL 37 Lc20
Delfzijl ☐ NL 37 Ld19
Delhi ☐ IND 80 Od13
Delicias ☐ MEX 124 Ec13
Delitzsch ☐ D 44 Lg20
Delmenhorst ☐ D 44 Le19
Delnice ☐ HR 47 Lh23
Del Rio ☐ USA 124 Ed13
Delsbo ☐ S 25 Lj15
Delta ☐ USA 122 Eb11
Delta of the Danube ↘ RO 55 Me23
Delta del Ebro ⌐ E 42 La25
Delta Dunării, P.N. ⌐ RO 55 Me23
Dembi Dolo ☐ ETH 109 Md17
Demidov ☐ RUS 59 Mf18
Deming ☐ USA 122 Ec12
Demirci ☐ TR 64 Me26
Demjansk ☐ RUS 58 Mg17
Demmin ☐ D 44 Lg19
Democratic Republic Congo ■ RDC 108 Ma18
Demta ☐ RI 92 Sa19
Denham ☐ AUS 94 Qc24
Den Helder ☐ NL 37 Lc19
Denia ☐ E 43 La26
Deniliquin ☐ AUS 97 Sa26
Denison ☐ USA 123 Fa12
Denizli ☐ TR 64 Me27
Denman Glacier ⌐ 141 Qa32
Denmark ■ DK 26 Le18
Denpasar ☐ RI 87 Qd20
Denton ☐ USA 123 Fa12
Denver ☐ USA 122 Ed11
Deputatskij ☐ RUS 74 Sa05
Dera Ghazi Khan ☐ PAK 80 Oc12
Dera Ismail Khan ☐ PAK 80 Oc12
Derbent ☐ RUS 76 Nb10
Derby ☐ AUS 94 Ra22
Derby ☐ GB 35 Kk19
Đerdap, N.P. ☐ SR 54 Ma23
Dereli ☐ TR 66 Mk25
Derhači ☐ UA 63 Mj20
Derry = Londonderry ☐ GB 33 Kg18
Derudeb ☐ SUD 107 Md15
Derventa ☐ BIH 47 Lj23
Dese ☐ ETH 109 Md16
Desenzano del Garda ☐ I 46 Lf23
Desierto de Atacama ☐ RCH 136 Gc23
Desierto de Sechura ☐ PE 133 Fd20
Deskáti ☐ GR 56 Ma26
Des Moines ☐ USA 123 Fb10
Desna ↘ RUS 59 Mh19
Desna ↘ UA 62 Mf20
Desnyanso-Staroguts'kyj N.P. ☐ UA 59 Mg19

Despotovac ☐ SR 54 Ma23
Dessau ☐ D 44 Lg20
Detmold ☐ D 44 Le20
Detroit ☐ USA 123 Fd10
Détroit de Jacques Cartier ⌐ CDN 121 Gd08
Détroit d'Honguedo ⌐ CDN 121 Gc09
Dettifoss ↘ IS 32 Kb13
Detva ☐ SK 53 Lk21
Deva ☐ RO 54 Mb23
Develi ☐ TR 65 Mh26
Devils Lake ☐ USA 120 Fa09
Devnja ☐ BG 55 Md24
Devon ☐ GB 35 Kh20
Devon-Insel ⌐ CDN 118 Fc03
Devon Island ⌐ CDN 118 Fc03
Devonport ☐ AUS 97 Sb27
Devrek ☐ TR 64 Mf25
Dezful ☐ IR 76 Nb12
Dezhou ☐ CHN 83 Qd11
Dhaka ● BD 84 Pc14
Dhanbad ☐ IND 80 Pb14
Dhaulagiri ▲ NEP 80 Pa13
Dhofar ☐ OM 77 Nc15
Dhofar ☐ OM 77 Nc15
Diamantina ☐ AUS 96 Sa23
Diamantina ☐ BR 135 Hd22
Dianópolis ☐ BR 135 Hc21
Dibble Glacier ⌐ 141 Rc32
Dibrugarh ☐ IND 84 Pd13
Dickinson ☐ USA 120 Ed09
Die ☐ F 39 Lc23
Dien Bien Phu ☐ VN 84 Qa14
Dienné ☐ RMM 105 Kd16
Diepholz ☐ D 44 Le19
Dieppe ☐ F 36 La21
Digne-les-Bains ☐ F 39 Ld23
Digoin ☐ F 39 Lb22
Digor ☐ TR 66 Nb25
Digul ↘ RI 92 Sa20
Dijon ☐ F 39 Lc22
Dikili ☐ TR 57 Md26
Dikson ☐ RUS 73 Pa04
Dili ● TLS 87 Rb20
Diljatyn ☐ UA 55 Mc21
Dillenburg ☐ D 44 Le20
Dillingen ☐ D 45 Lf21
Dillingham ☐ USA 116 Ca07
Dilolo ☐ RDC 110 Ma21
Dimitrovgrad ☐ BG 55 Mc24
Dimitrovgrad ☐ RUS 60 Ne18
Dinagat ↗ RP 85 Rb16
Dinan ☐ F 36 Kj21
Dinant ☐ B 37 Lc20
Dinar ☐ TR 64 Mf26
Dinard ☐ F 36 Kj21
Dinaric Alps ▲ HR/BIH 47 Lh23
Dingle ☐ IRL 33 Ke19
Dinkelsbühl ☐ D 45 Lf21
Diourbel ☐ SN 105 Ka16
Dipolog ☐ RP 85 Ra17
Dirk Hartog Island ⌐ AUS 94 Qc24
Dirráhi ☐ GR 56 Mb27
Dirranbandi ☐ AUS 96 Sb24
Disko Bugt ⌐ DK 119 Hb05
Disko Ø ⌐ DK 119 Hb05
Dispur ☐ IND 84 Pc13
Diu ☐ IND 80 Oc14
Divinópolis ☐ BR 135 Hd23
Divo ☐ CI 105 Kc17
Divriği ☐ TR 66 Mk26
Dixon Entrance ⌐ CDN 117 Db08
Diyarbakır ☐ TR 76 Na15
Djambala ☐ RCB 108 Lc19

Djat'kovo ☐ RUS 59 Mh19
Djebel Al Awaynat ▲ SUD 107 Mb14
Djebel Arknu ▲ LAR 106 Ma14
Djebel Hamoyet ▲ SUD 107 Md15
Djebel Mahrat ▲ YE 77 Nc15
Djebel Manar ▲ YE 77 Nb14
Djebel Marra ▲ SUD 106 Ma16
Djebel Musbih ▲ ET 107 Mc14
Djebel Ouarkziz ▲ MA 104 Kc13
Djebel Rafit ▲ SUD 107 Mc14
Djebel Samhan ▲ OM 77 Nc15
Djebel Timétrine ▲ RMM 105 Kd15
Djebel Toubkal ▲ MA 104 Kc12
Djebel Tuwayq ▲ KSA 77 Nb14
Djelfa ☐ DZ 104 La12
Djerem ↘ CAM 108 Lc17
Djibouti ● DJI 109 Na16
Djibouti ■ DJI 109 Na16
Djougou ☐ DY 105 La17
Djúpivogur ☐ IS 32 Kc13
Djurás ☐ S 25 Lh15
Djurö n.p. ⌐ S 26 Lg16
Djurtjuli ☐ RUS 60 Nh18
Dmitrievka ☐ RUS 61 Na19
Dmitriev-L'govskij ☐ RUS 59 Mh19
Dmitrov ☐ RUS 58 Mj17
Dmytrivka ☐ UA 59 Mg20
Dnestrovsc ☐ MD 55 Me22
Dniprodzeržyns'ke vodoschovyšče ⌐ UA 62 Mg21
Dnipro ↘ UA 62 Mg22
Dniprodzeržyns'k ☐ UA 63 Mh21
Dnipropetrovs'k ☐ UA 63 Mh21
Dniprorudne ☐ UA 63 Mh22
Dniprovs'kyj lyman ⌐ UA 62 Mf22
Dnjapro ⌐ BY 59 Mf19
Dno ☐ RUS 30 Me17
Doba ☐ TCH 108 Ld17
Dobbiaco = Toblach ☐ I 46 Lg22
Dobele ☐ LV 31 Mb17
Döbeln ☐ D 44 Lg20
Doberai Peninsula ⌐ RI 92 Rc19
Doboj ☐ BIH 47 Lk23
Dobre Miasto ☐ PL 50 Ma19
Dobrič ☐ BG 55 Md24
Dobrinka ☐ RUS 61 Na19
Dobrjanka ☐ UA 59 Mf19
Dobrjatino ☐ RUS 58 Na18
Dobrodzień ☐ PL 50 Lk20
Dobromyl' ☐ UA 53 Mb21
Dobropillja ☐ UA 63 Mj21
Dobrudžansko Plato ☐ BG 55 Md24
Dobruš ☐ BY 59 Mf19
Docksta ☐ S 25 Lk14
Doctor Pedro P.Peña ☐ PY 136 Gd23
Dodecanese ☐ GR 57 Md27
Dodge City ☐ USA 122 Fa11
Dodoma ● EAT 109 Md20
Dofa ☐ RI 87 Rb19
Doğankent ☐ TR 66 Mk25

Doğanşehir ☐ TR 65 Mj26
Doğansu ☐ TR 66 Nb26
Doğanyol ☐ TR 66 Mk26
Doğu Karadeniz Dağları ▲ TR 66 Mk25
Doha ● Q 77 Nc13
Dokka ☐ N 24 Lf15
Dokkum ☐ NL 37 Ld19
Dokşycy ☐ BY 31 Md18
Dokučajevs'k ☐ UA 63 Mj22
Dolak ⌐ RI 92 Rd20
Dole ☐ F 39 Lc22
Dolný Kubín ☐ SK 53 Lk21
Dolomiti ▲ I 46 Lf22
Dolomiti Bellunesi, P.N. delle ⌐ I 46 Lg22
Dolores ☐ RA 136 Ha26
Dolores ☐ ROU 136 Ha25
Dolphin and Union Strait ⌐ CDN 118 Ea05
Dolyns'ka ☐ UA 62 Mg21
Dolžanskaja ☐ RUS 63 Mj22
Domažlice ☐ CZ 52 Lg21
Dombås ☐ N 24 Le14
Dombóvár ☐ H 53 Lk22
DomeC Concordia ⌐ 141 Ra34
Dome Circe ⌐ 141 Ra33
Domfront ☐ F 36 Kk21
Dominica ■ WD 127 Gd15
Dominican Republic ■ DOM 127 Gb15
Domžale ☐ SLO 47 Lh22
Doñana, P.N. de ⌐ E 41 Kg27
Donau Auen, N.P. ⌐ A 52 Lj21
Donaudurchbruch ⌐ D 45 Lf21
Donautal ☐ A 52 Lg21
Donauwörth ☐ D 45 Lf21
Doncaster ☐ GB 35 Kk19
Dondo ☐ ANG 108 Lc20
Dondra Head ⌐ CL 81 Pa17
Dønduşeni ☐ MD 51 Md21
Donec'k ☐ UA 63 Mj22
Donegal ☐ IRL 33 Kf18
Donga ↘ WAN 108 Lc17
Dongara ☐ AUS 95 Qc24
Dongfang ☐ CHN 84 Qb15
Donggala ☐ RI 87 Qc19
Dong Ha ☐ VN 84 Qb15
Donghae ☐ 83 Rc11
Dong Hoi ☐ VN 84 Qb15
Donji Miholjac ☐ HR 47 Lk23
Donji Žirovac ☐ HR 47 Lj23
Dønna ☐ N 22 Lg12
Donostia = San Sebastián ☐ E 42 Kj24
Donoúsa ☐ GR 57 Mc27
Donqula ☐ SUD 107 Mc15
Donskaja ravnina ▲ RUS 61 Na19
Dorchester ☐ GB 35 Kj20
Dordrecht ☐ NL 37 Lc20
Dorgali ☐ I 44 Le24
Dori ☐ BF 105 Kd16
Dornoch ☐ GB 34 Kh17
Dorohoi ☐ RO 55 Md22
Dorotea ☐ S 25 Lj13
Dortmund ☐ D 44 Ld20
Dörtyol ☐ TR 65 Mh26
Dörtyol ☐ TR 65 Mj26
Dos Hermanas ☐ E 41 Kh27
Dospat ☐ BG 57 Mc25
Dosso ☐ RN 105 La16
Dothan ☐ USA 123 Fc12

Douai ☐ F 37 Lb20
Douala ☉ CAM 108 Lb18
Douarnenez ☐ F 36 Kh21
Doué-la-Fontaine ☐ F 38 Kk22
Douentza ☐ RMM 105 Kd15
Douglas ☐ GB 34 Kh18
Douglas ☉ USA 122 Ec12
Douglas Range ☐ 140 Gb32
Doullens ☐ F 37 Lb20
Dourados ☐ BR 135 Hb23
Dover ☐ GB 35 La20
Dover ☉ USA 123 Ga11
Dovhe ☐ UA 53 Mb21
Dovre ☐ N 24 Le15
Dovrefjell ☑ N 24 Le14
Dovrefjell-Sunndalsfjella n.p. ☑ N 24 Le14
Dovsk ☐ BY 59 Mf19
Downpatrick ☐ GB 34 Kh18
Drabiv ☐ UA 62 Mg21
Drachten ☐ NL 37 Ld19
Drăgăneşti-Olt ☐ RO 55 Mc23
Drăgăneşti-Vlaşca ☐ RO 55 Mc23
Drăgăsani ☐ RO 54 Mc23
Draguignan ☐ F 39 Ld24
Drahičyn ☐ BY 51 Mc19
Drakensberge ▲ ZA 110 Mb25
Drake Passage ⊟ 137 Gc30
Dráma ☐ GR 57 Mc23
Drammen ☐ N 26 Lf16
Drangajökull ☒ IS 32 Jj12
Drangsnes ☐ IS 32 Jk13
Drawieński P.N. ☑ PL 50 Lh19
Drescher ☐ 140 Ka33
Dresden ☉ D 44 Lg20
Dretun' ☐ BY 31 Me18
Dreux ☐ F 36 La21
Driffield ☐ GB 35 Kk19
Drjanovo ☐ BG 55 Mc24
Drøbak ☐ N 26 Lf16
Drobeta-Turnu Severin ☐ RO 54 Mb23
Drobin ☐ PL 50 Lu19
Drochia ☐ MD 55 Md21
Drogheda ☐ IRL 33 Kg19
Drohobyč ☐ UA 53 Mb21
Droning Ingrid Land ☒ DK 119 Hc06
Droning Louise Land ☒ DK 138 Jc03
Dronning Maud Land ▲ 141 Kc34
Droskovo ☐ RUS 59 Mj19
Drozdyn' ☐ UA 51 Md20
Drumheller ☐ CDN 117 Eb08
Drummondville ☐ CDN 121 Gb09
Druskininkai ☐ LT 31 Mb18
Družba ☐ UA 59 Mg19
Družnaja II ☐ 140 Gc33
Družnaja III ☐ 141 Kb33
Dryden ☐ CDN 120 Fb09
Drygalski Ice Tongue ☒ 141 Tb34
Drygalski Island ☒ 141 Pc32
Drysdale ☐ AUS 94 Rb22
Dry Tortugas ☒ USA 126 Fd14
Duba ☐ KSA 76 Md13
Dubai ☉ UAE 77 Nd13
Dubăsari ☐ MD 55 Me22
Dubawnt Lake ⊟ CDN 120 Ed06
Dubbo ☐ AUS 97 Sb25
Dub'jazy ☐ RUS 60 Ne17

Dublin = Baile Átha Cliath ☉ IRL 33 Kg19
Dubna ☐ RUS 58 Mj17
Dubna ☐ RUS 59 Mj18
Dubno ☐ UA 51 Mc20
Dubove ☐ UA 53 Mb21
Dubovka ☐ RUS 61 Nc21
Dubovyj Ovrag ☐ RUS 61 Nc21
Dubréka ☐ RG 105 Kb17
Dubrivka ☐ UA 51 Md20
Dubrovka ☐ RUS 61 Na20
Dubrovnik ☐ HR 47 Lk24
Dubrovycja ☐ UA 51 Md20
Dubuque ☐ USA 123 Fb10
Dudelange ☐ L 37 Ld21
Dudinka ☒ RUS 73 Pb04
Dugi Otok ▲ HR 47 Lh23
Duhovnickoe ☐ RUS 60 Ne19
Duisburg ☐ D 44 Ld20
Dujiangyan ☐ CHN 84 Qa12
Dukhan ☐ Q 77 Nc13
Dukla ☐ PL 50 Ma21
Dülmen ☐ D 44 Ld20
Dulovo ☐ BG 55 Md24
Duluth ☉ USA 120 Fb09
Dumai ☐ RI 86 Qa18
Dumbarton ☐ GB 34 Kh18
Dumfries ☐ GB 34 Kj18
Dumont d'Urville ☐ 141 Rd32
Dumont d'Urville Sea ⊟ 141 Rc31
Duna-Dráva N.P. ☑ H 53 Lk22
Dunaföldvár ☐ H 53 Lk22
Dunaharaszti ☐ H 53 Lk22
Duna-Ipoly N.P. ☑ H 53 Lk22
Dunajivci ☐ UA 51 Md21
Duna-Tisza-Köze ☑ H 53 Lk22
Dunaújváros ☐ H 53 Lk22
Dundalk ☐ IRL 33 Kg19
Dundas ☐ DK 118 Gc03
Dundee ☐ GB 34 Kj17
Dunedin ☐ NZ 99 Tc28
Dune du Pilat ☒ F 38 Kk23
Dungannon ☐ GB 33 Kg18
Dungarvan ☐ IRL 33 Kg19
Dunglow ☐ IRL 33 Kf18
Dungunab ☐ SUD 107 Md14
Dunhua ☐ CHN 83 Rb10
Dunkerque ☐ F 37 Lb20
Dunkwa ☐ GH 105 Kd17
Dun Laoghaire ☐ IRL 33 Kg19
Dupnica ☐ BG 56 Mb24
Durağan ☐ TR 65 Mh25
Durango ☐ MEX 124 Ed14
Durango ☐ USA 122 Ec11
Durant ☐ USA 123 Fa12
Durban ☐ ZA 110 Mc24
Đurđevac ☐ HR 53 Lj22
Durham ☐ GB 34 Kk18
Durmitor ☐ CG 54 Lk24
Durmitor, N.P. ☑ CG 54 Lk24
Durness ☐ GB 34 Kh16
Durrës ☐ AL 56 Lk25
Dushanbe ☉ TJ 78 Ob11
Düsseldorf ☐ D 44 Ld20
Dutlu ☐ TR 65 Mg25
Duyun ☐ CHN 84 Qb13
Düzce ☐ TR 64 Mf25
Düzici ☐ TR 65 Mj27
Dvor ☐ HR 47 Lj23
Dvoriki ☐ RUS 58 Mk17
Dykan'ka ☐ UA 62 Mh21
Dymer ☐ UA 62 Mf20
Džalil' ☐ RUS 60 Ng17
Džankoj ☐ UA 63 Mh23
Dzaoudzi ☐ F 111 Nb21

Dzeržinsk ☐ RUS 60 Nb17
Działdowo ☐ PL 50 Ma19
Dzierzgoń ☐ PL 50 Lk19
Dziaržynsk ☐ BY 51 Md19
Dzjatlava ☐ BY 51 Mc19
Džubga ☐ RUS 63 Mk23
Dzukijos n.p. ☑ LT 31 Mc18
Dzungarian Basin ☒ CHN 79 Pb09

E

Eagle Pass ☐ USA 124 Ed13
East Frisian Islands ☒ D 44 Ld19
Eastbourne ☐ GB 35 La20
East Cape ☒ NZ 99 Td25
East Caroline Basin ⊟ 92 Sb18
East China Sea ⊟ 83 Ra12
Eastern Desert ☒ ET 107 Mc13
Eastern Fields ☒ PNG 92 Sb21
Eastern Ghats ▲ IND 81 Od16
Eastern Sayan Mountains ▲ RUS 79 Pd08
East Falkland ☒ GB 137 Ha29
East London ☐ ZA 110 Mb25
East Saint Louis ☐ USA 123 Fc11
East Siberian Sea ⊟ RUS 74 Tb05
East Timor ■ TLS 87 Rb20
Eau Claire ☐ USA 123 Fb10
Eauripik Atoll ☒ FSM 92 Sa17
Eauripik Rise ⊟ PAL 92 Sa18
Ebeltoft ☐ DK 26 Lf17
Eber Gölü ⊟ TR 64 Mf26
Eberswalde ☐ D 44 Lg19
Ebola ☒ RDC 108 Ma18
Ebolowa ☐ CAM 108 Lc18
Eceabat ☐ TR 57 Md25
Écija ☐ E 41 Kh27
Eckernförde ☐ D 44 Le18
Eckerö ☐ FIN 25 Lk15
Écrins, P.N. des ☑ F 39 Ld23
Ecuador ■ EC 132 Ga19
Ed ☐ S 26 Lf16
Ede ☐ NL 37 Lc19
Edéa ☐ CAM 108 Lc18
Edefors ☐ S 23 Ma12
Eden ☐ AUS 97 Sb26
Edesbyn ☐ S 25 Lh15
Édessa ☐ GR 56 Mb25
Edfu ☐ ET 107 Mc14
Edgeworth David ☐ 141 Qa32
Edinburgh ☉ GB 34 Kj18
Edineţ ☐ MD 55 Md21
Edirne ☐ TR 57 Md25
Edmonton ☉ CDN 117 Eb08
Edmunston ☐ CDN 121 Gc09
Edremit ☐ TR 57 Md26
Edremit Körfezi ⊟ TR 57 Md26
Edward, Mount ☒ 140 Gc34
Edward River ☐ AUS 96 Sa21
Edwards Plateau ▲ USA 122 Ed12
Étaté ☒ VU 98 Tb22
Efimovskij ☐ RUS 58 Mh16
Efkarpia ☐ GR 56 Mb25
Eflâni ☐ TR 65 Mg25
Efremov ☐ RUS 59 Mk19
Eger ☐ H 53 Ma22

Egersund ☐ N 26 Ld16
Eggenfelden ☐ D 45 Lg21
Egilsstaðir ☐ IS 32 Kc13
Égina ☐ GR 56 Mb25
Égina ☒ GR 57 Mb27
Eginio ☐ GR 56 Mb25
Égio ☐ GR 56 Mb25
Eğirdir ☐ TR 64 Mf27
Eğirdir Gölü ⊟ TR 64 Mf26
Egor'e ☐ RUS 58 Mj18
Egor'evsk ☐ RUS 58 Mk18
Egorlykskaja ☐ RUS 63 Na22
Egvekinot ☐ RUS 74 Ua05
Egypt ■ ET 107 Mb13
Ehinos ☐ GR 57 Mc25
Eibar ☐ E 42 Kj24
Eibiswald ☐ A 52 Lh22
Eichstätt ☐ D 45 Lf21
Eide ☐ N 24 Ld14
Eidfjord ☐ N 24 Ld15
Eidsvåg ☐ N 24 Le14
Eidsvoll ☐ N 24 Lf15
Eifel ▲ D 44 Ld20
Eights Coast ☒ 140 Fa33
Eiken ☐ N 26 Ld16
Eilenburg ☐ D 44 Lg20
Einbeck ☐ D 44 Le20
Eindhoven ☐ NL 37 Lc20
Eirunepé ☐ BR 133 Gb20
Eiseb ☒ NAM 110 Ld23
Eisenach ☐ D 44 Lf20
Eisenhüttenstadt ☐ D 44 Lh19
Eisenstadt ☉ A 52 Lj22
Eisfeld ☐ D 44 Lf20
Eivissa ☒ E 43 La26
Eivissa = Ibiza ☉ E 43 La26
Eja ☐ 63 Mk22
Ejea de los Caballeros ☐ E 42 Kk24
Ejsk ☐ RUS 63 Mk22
Ekaterinovka ☐ RUS 59 Mk19
Ekaterinovka ☐ RUS 61 Nc19
Ekenäs = Tammisaari ☐ FIN 30 Mb16
Ekibastuz ☐ KZ 79 Oc08
Ekimoviči ☐ RUS 59 Mg18
Ekinli ☐ TR 66 Nb26
Ekshärad ☐ S 24 Lg15
Eksjö ☐ S 27 Lh17
Elabuga ☐ RUS 60 Ng18
El-Alamein ☐ ET 107 Mb12
Elan' ☐ RUS 61 Nb20
Elan' ☒ RUS 61 Nb20
Elan'-Kolenovskij ☐ RUS 61 Na20
El Aqaba ☐ JOR 76 Md13
El Arahal ☐ E 41 Kh27
El-Araïch ☐ MA 104 Kc11
El Arish ☐ ET 107 Mc12
Elassóna ☐ GR 56 Mb26
Elat ☐ ET 107 Mc13
Elátia ☐ GR 56 Mb26
Elat'ma ☐ RUS 58 Na18
Elâziğ ☐ TR 76 Md11
Elâziğ ☐ TR 66 Mk26
El Banco ☐ CO 132 Gb17
El Barco de Ávila ☐ E 40 Kh25
Elbasan ☐ AL 56 Ma25
El Bawiti ☐ ET 107 Mb13
El Bayadh ☐ DZ 104 La12
Elbistan ☐ TR 65 Mj26
Elblag ☐ PL 50 Lx18
El Bordo ☐ CO 132 Ga18
Elbrus ▲ RUS 76 Na10
El'brus ▲ RUS 76 Na10
El Burgo de Osma ☐ E 42 Kj25

Elburz Mountains – Falun

Elburz Mountains IR 76 Nc11
El Cajon USA 122 Ea12
El Calafate RA 137 Gb29
El Callao YV 132 Gd17
El Centro USA 122 Ea12
Elche = Elx E 43 Kk26
Elche de la Sierra E 43 Kj26
Elda E 43 Kk26
El Djouf RIM 104 Kc14
El Dorado MEX 124 Ec14
Eldorado RA 135 Hb24
El Dorado USA 123 Fb12
Eldoret EAK 109 Md18
Elec RUS 59 Mk19
Êlektostal' RUS 58 Mk18
Elektrénai LT 31 Mc18
Elephant Island GB 140 Ha31
Elephant Island 140 Hb31
Eleşkirt TR 66 Nb26
Eleuthera Island BS 126 Ga13
Elgin GB 34 Kj17
El Hank RIM 104 Kc14
Elhovka RUS 60 Nf19
Elhovo BG 55 Md24
Elionka RUS 59 Mg19
Élista RUS 19 Na09
Elizabeth City USA 123 Ga11
Elizabeth Reef AUS 97 Sd25
El-Jadida MA 104 Kc12
Etk PL 51 Mb19
El Kef TN 106 Lb11
El Kharga ET 107 Mc13
Elko USA 122 Ea10
El Kufrah Oasis LAR 106 Ma14
Ellef Ringnes Island CDN 118 Ed03
Ellesmere Island CDN 118 Fc02
Elliot Lake CDN 123 Fd09
Elliott AUS 94 Rc22
Ellsworth Land 140 Fc33
Ellsworth Mountains 140 Fc34
Elmalı TR 64 Me27
El–Mansûra ET 107 Mc12
El Ménia DZ 104 La12
El Minia ET 107 Mc13
El Nido RP 85 Qd16
El'nja RUS 59 Mg18
El-Obeid SUD 107 Mc16
El Oued DZ 106 Lb12
El Paso USA 122 Ec12
El Qasr ET 107 Mb12
El Salvador ES 125 Fc16
El Sombrero YV 132 Gd17
Elsterwerda D 44 Lg20
El Sueco MEX 124 Ec13
El Tigre YV 132 Gd17
Elva EST 30 Md16
Elvas P 41 Kg26
el Vendrell E 42 La25
Elverum N 24 Lf15
Elx E 43 Kk26
Ely GB 35 La19
Ely USA 122 Eb11
Embalse Yacyretá Apipé RA 136 Ha24
Embi KZ 78 Nd09
Emden F 39 Ld23
Emden D 44 Ld19
Emerald AUS 96 Sb23
Emet TR 64 Me26

Emi Koussi TCH 106 Ld15
Emilia-Romagna I 46 Lf23
Emirdağ TR 64 Mf26
Emir Dağları TR 64 Mf26
Emirgazi TR 65 Mg27
Emmen NL 37 Ld19
Émpoli I 46 Lf24
Emporia USA 123 Fa11
Êna RUS 23 Mg11
Enånger S 25 Lj15
Encarnación PY 136 Ha24
Encs H 53 Ma21
Ende RI 87 Ra20
Enderbyland 141 Na32
Eneabba AUS 95 Qd24
Enerhodar UA 63 Mh22
Enez TR 57 Md25
Engadin CH 45 Le22
Enge N 24 Le14
Enggano RI 86 Qa20
English Channel GB/F 35 Kj20
English Coast 140 Gb33
Enid USA 123 Fa11
Enisej RUS 73 Pb04
Enisejsk RUS 73 Pc07
Enisejskij zaliv RUS 73 Pa04
Eniwetok Atoll MH 93 Ta16
Enkodak FIN 23 Mb11
Enköping S 27 Lj16
Enna I 49 Lh27
En Nahud SUD 109 Mb16
Ennedi TCH 106 Ma15
Ennis IRL 33 Kf19
Enniscorthy IRL 33 Kg19
Enniskillen GB 33 Kg18
Ennistimon IRL 33 Kf19
Enns A 52 Lh21
Enontekiö FIN 23 Mb11
Enschede NL 37 Ld19
Ensenada MEX 122 Ea12
Entrecasteaux Islands PNG 93 Sc20
Entrecasteaux Islands PNG 93 Sc20
Entre Rios RA 136 Ha25
Entre Rios RA 136 Ha25
Entrevaux F 39 Ld24
Enugu WAN 108 Lb17
Enviken S 25 Lh15
Épernay F 37 Lb21
Épi VU 98 Tb22
Épinal F 37 Ld21
Equatorial Guinea GQ 108 Lb18
Erahtur RUS 58 Na18
Erbaa TR 65 Mj25
Erçek TR 66 Nb26
Erçek Gölü TR 66 Nb26
Erciş TR 66 Nb26
Erd H 53 Lk22
Erdek TR 57 Md25
Erdemli TR 65 Mh27
Erdi TCH 106 Ma15
Erebus, Mount 141 Tc34
Erechim BR 135 Hb24
Ereğli TR 64 Mf25
Ereğli TR 65 Mh27
Ereğli Ovası TR 65 Mg27
Erenhot CHN 82 Qc10
Erenler Dağları TR 64 Mg27
Erentepe TR 66 Na26
Erfurt D 44 Lf20
Ergani TR 66 Mk26
Erg Chech DZ 104 Kd13
Erg du Djourab TCH 106 Ld15

Ergene Çay TR 57 Md25
Erg Iguidi RIM/DZ 104 Kc13
Ergun Youqi CHN 82 Ra08
Ergun Zuoqi CHN 82 Ra08
Erie USA 123 Ga10
Erithrés GR 56 Mb26
Eritrea ER 107 Md15
Erkilet TR 65 Mh26
Erlangen D 45 Lf21
Erldunda AUS 94 Rc24
Ermenek TR 65 Mg27
Ermiš RUS 60 Nb18
Ermoúpoli GR 57 Mc27
Ernée F 36 Kk21
Eromanga Island VU 98 Tb22
Errigal IRL 33 Kf18
Ersekë AL 56 Ma25
Erši RUS 59 Mh18
Értil' RUS 61 Na20
Ertis KZ 79 Pa08
Erzgebirge D/CZ 45 Lg20
Êrzin RUS 79 Pd08
Erzincan TR 66 Mk26
Erzurum TR 76 Na11
Erzurum TR 66 Na16
Esbjerg DK 26 Le18
Esbo = Espoo FIN 28 Mc15
Escanaba USA 120 Fc09
Eschede D 44 Lf19
Escudero 140 Ha30
Escuintla GCA 125 Fb16
Esenyurt TR 57 Me25
Eskifjörður IS 32 Kd13
Eskil TR 65 Mg26
Eskilstuna S 27 Lj16
Eskipazar TR 65 Mg25
Eskişehir TR 64 Mf26
Eşme TR 64 Me26
Esmeraldas EC 132 Ga18
Espalion F 38 Lb23
Espeland N 24 Lc15
Esperance AUS 95 Ra25
Esperanza RA 137 Gb29
Esperanza 140 Ha31
Espiel E 41 Kh26
Espinho P 40 Kf24
Espírito Santo BR 135 Hd22
Espíritu Santo VU 98 Tb22
Espíritu Santo VU 98 Tb22
Espoo = Esbo FIN 28 Mc15
Esquel RA 137 Gb27
Essej RUS 73 Qa05
Essen D 44 Ld20
Essequibo GUY 134 Ha17
Estância BR 135 Ja21
Estella E 42 Kj24
Estepa E 41 Kh27
Estepona E 41 Kh27
Estevan CDN 120 Ed09
Estonia EST 30 Mc16
Estoril P 40 Kf26
Estrecho de Le Maire RA 137 Gc30
Estreito BR 134 Hc20
Estremoz P 41 Kg26
Esztergom H 53 Lk22
Étampes F 37 Lb21
Ethiopia ETH 109 Md17
Ethiopian Highlands ETH 109 Md17
Etna I 49 Ln27
Etolikó GR 56 Ma26
Etosha Pan NAM 110 Ld22
Ettelbruck L 37 Ld21
Eu F 35 La20
Eucla Basin AUS 95 Rb25

Eucla Motels AUS 95 Rb25
Eugene USA 122 Dd10
Euphrates IRQ 76 Na12
Eura FIN 22 Mb15
Eureka USA 122 Dd10
Euskirchen D 44 Ld20
Eutin D 44 Lf18
Evans Ice Stream 140 Ga34
Evans Strait CDN 118 Fd06
Evansville USA 123 Fc11
Evenki Autonomous District RUS 73 Pc05
Everett USA 122 Dd09
Evertsberg S 24 Lg15
Evesham GB 35 Kk19
Évia GR 56 Mb26
Evijärvi FIN 19 Mb14
Evje N 26 Ld16
Evlanovo RUS 59 Mj19
Evoikós Kólpos GR 56 Mb26
Évora P 41 Kg26
Évreux F 36 La21
Évros GR 57 Md25
Ewaso Ngiro EAK 109 Md18
Exeter GB 35 Kj20
Exmoor N.P. GB 35 Kj20
Exmouth AUS 94 Qc23
Exmouth Plateau AUS 94 Qd22
Extremadura E 40 Kg26
Exuma Sound BS 126 Ga14
Eymoutiers F 38 La23
Eyre Peninsula AUS 97 Rd25
Ezine TR 57 Md26

F

Faaborg DK 26 Lf18
Fåberg N 24 Lf15
Fåboda FIN 19 Mb14
Fabriano I 47 Lg24
Fachi NG 106 Lc15
Fada TCH 106 Ma15
Fada-N'gourma BF 105 La16
Fadhi OM 77 Nd15
Fǎgǎraş RO 55 Mc23
Fagerås S 26 Lg16
Fagernes N 24 Le15
Fagersta S 25 Lh15
Fairbanks USA 116 Cc06
Fair Isle GB 34 Kk16
Faisalabad PAK 80 Oc12
Fais Island FSM 92 Sa17
Fakfak RI 92 Rc19
Fakse DK 26 Lg18
Falaise F 36 Kk21
Falémé RMM 105 Kb16
Fǎleşti MD 55 Md22
Falkenberg S 26 Lg17
Falkland Escarpment 137 Hb28
Falkland Islands GB 137 Gd29
Falkland Plateau 137 Hb29
Falköping S 26 Lg16
Falls City USA 123 Fa10
Falls of Measach GB 34 Kh17
Falmouth GB 35 Kh20
Fǎlticeni RO 55 Md22
Falun S 25 Lh15

Fangchenggang □ CHN 84 Qb14
Fano I 47 Lg24
Faraday ▲ 140 Gd32
Faradje □ RDC 109 Mb18
Farafangana RM 111 Nb23
Farafra Oasis ET 107 Mb13
Farah AFG 78 Oa12
Faranah RG 105 Kb16
Faraulep Atoll FSM 92 Sa17
Färgelanda S 26 Lf16
Fargo □ USA 120 Fa09
Färila S 25 Lh15
Färjestaden S 27 Lj17
Farkadóna GR 56 Mb26
Farmington USA 122 Ec11
Färnebofjärdens n.p. S 25 Lj15
Faro P 41 Kg27
Faroe Islands DK 18 Kc06
Fårösund S 27 Lk17
Fársala GR 56 Mb26
Fasano I 49 Lj25
Fastiv UA 62 Me20
Fatez RUS 59 Mh19
Fátima P 40 Kf26
Fatsa TR 65 Mj25
Fáurei RO 55 Md23
Fauske N 22 Lh12
Fåvang N 24 Lf15
Faxaflói IS 32 Jj13
Fayetteville □ USA 123 Fb11
Fayetteville □ USA 123 Ga11
Fayu Island FSM 93 Sc17
Fécamp F 36 La21
Fedorovka RUS 63 Mk22
Fehérgyarmat H 53 Mb22
Fehmarnbelt D 44 Lf18
Fehmarnbelt DK 26 Lf18
Feira de Santana □ BR 135 Ja21
Feke TR 65 Mh27
Felanitx E 43 Lb26
Feldbach A 52 Lh22
Feldkirch A 45 Le22
Feldkirchen A 52 Lg22
Felixstowe GB 35 La20
Feltre I 47 Lf23
Femund N 24 Lf14
Femundsmarka n.p. N 24 Lf14
Fener Burnu TR 65 Mh27
Fener Burnu TR 66 Mk25
Fengjie CHN 84 Qb12
Feni Islands PNG 93 Sc19
Feodosija UA 63 Mh23
Ferapontovo RUS 58 Mk16
Fergana Valley UZ 78 Oc10
Fergus Falls □ USA 120 Fa09
Fergusson Island PNG 93 Sc23
Ferkessédougou CI 105 Kc17
Ferlo SN 105 Kb16
Fermo I 46 Lg24
Fermoselle E 40 Kg25
Ferrandina I 49 Lj25
Ferrara I 46 Lf23
Ferraz, Com. ▲ 140 Ha31
Ferreira do Alentejo P 40 Kf26
Ferreira Gomes □ BR 134 Hb18
Ferreñave PE 133 Ga20
Ferrol E 40 Kf24
Fertő-Hanság N.P. H 53 Lg22
Fès □ MA 104 Kc12

Fetești RO 55 Md23
Fethiye TR 64 Me27
Fethiye Körfezi TR 64 Me27
Fezzan LAR 106 Lc13
Fezzan LAR 106 Lc13
Fianarantsoa RM 111 Nb23
Fidenza I 46 Lf23
Fier AL 56 Lk25
Fife Ness ▲ GB 34 Kj17
Fifth Cataract SUD 107 Mc15
Figeac F 38 Lb23
Figueira da Foz P 40 Kf25
Figueres E 42 Lb24
Figuig MA 104 Kd12
Fiji Islands FIJ 98 Td22
Fiji Islands FIJ 98 Td22
Filadelfia PY 136 Gd23
Filchner HD 34
Filchner Ice Shelf 140 Hd35
Filiași RO 54 Mb23
Filiátes GR 56 Ma26
Filinskoe RUS 58 Nb18
Filipiáda GR 56 Ma26
Filipstad S 27 Lh16
Filóti GR 57 Mc27
Fimbulheimen ▲ 141 Lb33
Fimbul Ice Shelf 141 Kd33
Finale Ligure I 46 Le23
Finike TR 64 Mf27
Finke AUS 94 Rc24
Finke AUS 96 Rd24
Finland FIN 19 Mb06
Finnmarksvidda N 23 Mb11
Finnsnes N 22 Lk11
Finschhafen PNG 93 Sb20
Finspång S 27 Lh16
Finsterwalde D 44 Lg20
Fiorenzuola d'Arda I 46 Le23
Firat Nehri TR 66 Mk26
Firenze I 46 Lf24
Firovo RUS 58 Mg17
Firozabad IND 80 Od13
First Cataract ET 107 Mc14
Fisher Strait CDN 118 Fd06
Fishguard GB 35 Kh20
Fitjar N 24 Lc16
Fitzroy AUS 94 Ra22
Fitzroy Crossing AUS 94 Rb22
Fivizzano I 46 Lf23
Fizi RDC 109 Mb19
Fjerritslev DK 26 Le17
Flagstaff □ USA 122 Eb11
Flanders B 37 Lb20
Flatey IS 32 Jj13
Fleetwood GB 35 Kj19
Flekkefjord N 26 Ld16
Flen S 27 Lj16
Flensburg D 44 Le18
Flers F 36 Kk21
Fletcher Promontory ▲ 140 Fd34
Flims CH 45 Le22
Flinders AUS 96 Sa22
Flinders Bay AUS 95 Qd25
Flinders Island AUS 95 Rc25
Flinders Island AUS 97 Rd24
Flinders Ranges AUS 97 Rd25
Flinders Reef AUS 96 Sb22
Flin Flon CDN 120 Ed08
Flisa N 24 Lf15
Florac F 38 Lc24
Florence I 46 Lf24

Florence □ USA 123 Fc12
Florence □ USA 123 Fd12
Florencia CO 132 Ga18
Florești MD 55 Me22
Flores GCA 125 Fc15
Flores RI 87 Ra20
Flores Sea RI 87 Ra20
Floriano BR 134 Hd20
Florianópolis □ BR 135 Hc24
Florida ROU 136 Ha25
Florida USA 123 Fd13
Florida Keys USA 126 Fd14
Flórina GR 56 Ma25
Florø N 24 Lc15
Foča BIH 47 Lk24
Foça TR 57 Md26
Focșani RO 55 Md23
Fóggia I 49 Lh25
Föglö FIN 30 Ma16
Föhr D 44 Le18
Fóia ▲ P 41 Kf27
Foix F 42 La24
Fokino RUS 59 Mh19
Folda N 22 Lh12
Folégandros GR 57 Mc27
Foligno I 46 Lg24
Folkestone GB 35 La20
Folldal N 24 Lf14
Föllinge S 25 Lh14
Follónica I 46 Lf24
Fominki RUS 58 Nb18
Fonsagrada E 40 Kg24
Fontainebleau F 37 Lb21
Fontenay-le-Comte F 38 Kk22
Fontevraud-l'Abbaye F 38 La22
Fonyód H 53 Lg22
Forbes AUS 97 Sb25
Forcalquier F 39 Lc24
Forchheim D 45 Lf21
Førde N 24 Lc15
Førdefjorden N 24 Lc15
Ford Ranges ▲ 140 Cc34
Forfar GB 34 Kj17
Forlì I 46 Lg23
Formentera E 43 La26
Fórmia I 49 Lg25
Formosa RA 136 Ha24
Formosa RA 136 Ha24
Formosa do Rio Preto BR 134 Hc21
Formosa = Taiwan RC 85 Ra14
Fornells E 43 Lc25
Forrestal Range ▲ 140 Hb35
Forsayth AUS 96 Sa22
Formso S 25 Lj14
Forsnes N 24 Le14
Forssa FIN 22 Mb15
Forst D 44 Lh20
Fortaleza □ BR 134 Ja19
Fort-Chimo CDN 121 Gc07
Fort Chipewyan CDN 120 Eb07
Fort Collins USA 120 Ec10
Fort-de-France F 127 Gd16
Fort Frances CDN 120 Fb09
Fort Good Hope CDN 116 Dc05
Fort Hope CDN 120 Fc08
Fort Lauderdale USA 123 Fd13
Fort Liard CDN 117 Dd06
Fort McMurray CDN 120 Eb07
Fort McPherson CDN 116 Db05

Fort Myers □ USA 123 Fd13
Fort Nelson CDN 117 Dd07
Fort Peck Lake USA 120 Ec09
Fort Pierce □ USA 123 Fd13
Fort Portal EAU 109 Mc18
Fort Resolution CDN 120 Eb06
Fort Rupert CDN 121 Ga08
Fort Saint John CDN 117 Dd07
Fort Saskatchewan CDN 117 Eb08
Fort Severn CDN 120 Fc07
Fort Simpson CDN 117 Dd06
Fort Smith CDN 120 Eb06
Fort Smith □ USA 123 Fb11
Fort Stockton □ USA 122 Ed12
Fort Vermillion CDN 117 Ea07
Fort Wayne □ USA 123 Fc10
Fort Worth □ USA 123 Fa12
Fort Yukon USA 116 Cd06
Forvika N 24 Lg13
Foshan CHN 85 Qc14
Fosheim Peninsula CDN 118 Fd03
Fosna N 24 Lf14
Fossano I 46 Ld23
Fossil Bluff ▲ 140 Gc33
Fossombrone I 46 Lg24
Fos-sur-Mer F 39 Lc24
Fougères F 36 Kk21
Fourth Cataract SUD 107 Mc15
Foveaux Strait NZ 99 Tb28
Fowler Ice Rise ▲ 140 Ga34
Foxe Basin CDN 118 Ga05
Foxe Channel CDN 118 Fd05
Foxe Peninsula CDN 118 Ga05
Foz do Iguaçu BR 135 Hb24
Fraga E 42 La25
Frakes, Mount ▲ 140 Ea34
Fram Basin 139 Mc02
Fram Peak ▲ 141 Nd32
Franca BR 135 Hc23
Francavilla al Mare I 47 Lh24
Francavilla Fontana I 49 Lj25
France F 20 La08
Franceville G 108 Lc19
Franche-Comté F 39 Lc22
Francistown RB 110 Mb23
Frankenberg D 44 Le20
Frankfort USA 123 Fd11
Frankfurt (Main) D 45 Le20
Frankfurt (Oder) D 44 Lh19
Franklin Bay CDN 116 Dc04
Franklin Strait CDN 118 Fa04
Franz Josef Land RUS 139 Na02
Fraserburgh GB 34 Kj17
Fraser Island AUS 96 Sc24
Fraser Plateau ▲ CDN 117 Dd08
Fredericia DK 26 Le18
Fredericton CDN 121 Gc09
Frederikshåb DK 119 Hc06
Frederikshavn DK 26 Lf17
Frederiksværk DK 26 Lg18
Frederiksberg S 25 Lh15

Fredrikstad ◻ N 26 Lf16
Freeport ◻ BS 126 Ga13
Freetown ● WAL 105 Kb17
Freiberg ◻ D 44 Lg20
Freiburg ◻ D 45 Lf21
Freising ◻ D 45 Lf21
Freistadt ◻ A 52 Lh21
Fréjus ◻ F 39 Ld24
Fremantle ◻ AUS 95 Qd25
French Guiana ◻ F 134 Hb18
Fresnillo ◻ MEX 124 Ed14
Fresno ◻ USA 122 Ea11
Freyung ◻ D 45 Lg21
Fribourg ◻ CH 45 Ld22
Fridtjof Nansen, Mount ▲ 140 Bd36
Friedrichshafen ◻ D 45 Le22
Friggesund ◻ S 25 Lj15
Frillesås ◻ S 24 Lf17
Fristad ◻ S 26 Lg17
Fritzlar ◻ D 44 Le20
Friuli-Vénezia Giùlia ◻ I 46 Lg22
Frjanovo ◻ RUS 58 Mk17
Frobisher Bay ◻ CDN 119 Gc06
Frolovo ◻ RUS 61 Nb21
Frosinone ◻ I 48 Lg25
Frosta ◻ N 24 Lf14
Frövi ◻ S 27 Lh16
Frøya ◻ N 24 Le14
Frozen Strait ◻ CDN 118 Fd05
Frunzivka ◻ UA 55 Me22
Fruška Gora, N.P. ♦ SR 54 Lk23
Frýdek-Mistek ◻ CZ 53 Lk21
Fuengirola ◻ E 41 Kh27
Fuerteventura ◻ E 104 Kb13
Fujairah ◻ UAE 77 Nd13
Fujian ◻ CHN 85 Qd13
Fuji-san ◻ J 83 Sa11
Fukui ◻ J 83 Rd11
Fukuoka ◻ J 83 Rc12
Fukushima ◻ J 83 Sa11
Fulda ◻ D 45 Le20
Fulufjällets n.p. ♦ S 24 Lg15
Fumay ◻ F 37 Lc21
Fumel ◻ F 38 La24
Funafuti Atoll ◻ TUV 98 Td20
Funäsdalen ◻ S 24 Lg14
Funchal ◻ P 104 Ka12
Fundación ◻ CO 127 Gb16
Fundão ◻ BR 135 Hd22
Funtua ◻ WAN 108 Lb16
Furmanov ◻ RUS 58 Na17
Furneaux Group ◻ AUS 97 Sb26
Fürstenberg ◻ D 44 Lg19
Fürstenfeld ◻ A 52 Lj22
Fürstenfeldbruck ◻ D 45 Lf21
Fürth ◻ D 45 Lf21
Fürth im Wald ◻ D 45 Lg21
Furudal ◻ S 25 Lh15
Fushun ◻ CHN 83 Ra10
Füssen ◻ D 45 Lf22
Fuxin ◻ CHN 83 Ra10
Fuyun ◻ CHN 79 Pb09
Füzesabony ◻ H 53 Ma22
Fuzhou ◻ CHN 85 Qd13
Fyn ◻ DK 26 Lf18
Fyresdal ◻ N 26 Le16

G

Gabès ◻ TN 106 Lb12
Gabon ◻ G 108 Lc19
Gaborone  ● RB 110 Mb23
Gabrovo ◻ BG 55 Mc24

Gacé ◻ F 36 La21
Gäddede ◻ S 25 Lh13
Gadsden ◻ USA 123 Fc12
Gaecheon ◻ PRK 83 Rb11
Gǎeşti ◻ RO 55 Mc23
Gaeta ◻ I 48 Lg25
Gaferut Island ◻ FSM 92 Sb17
Gafsa ◻ TN 106 Lb12
Gagino ◻ RUS 60 Nc18
Gagnoa ◻ CI 105 Kc17
Gaillac ◻ F 42 La24
Gainesville ◻ USA 123 Fd13
Gajutino ◻ RUS 58 Mk16
Gálábovo ◻ BG 55 Mc24
Galápagos Islands ◻ EC 133 Fc18
Galashiels ◻ GB 34 Kj18
Galaţi ◻ RO 55 Me23
Galátista ◻ GR 56 Mb25
Galaxídi ◻ GR 56 Mb26
Galela ◻ RI 87 Rb18
Galena ◻ USA 116 Ca06
Galicia ◻ E 40 Kf23
Galicica, N.P. ♦ MK 56 Ma25
Galle ◻ CL 81 Pa17
Gallipoli ◻ I 49 Lj25
Gällivare ◻ S 23 Ma12
Gallup ◻ USA 122 Ec11
Galveston ◻ USA 123 Fb13
Galveston Bay ◻ USA 123 Fb13
Galway ◻ IRL 33 Kf19
Gama ◻ BR 135 Hc22
Gambia ◻ WAG 105 Ka16
Gambie ◻ SN 105 Kb16
Gamboma ◻ RCB 108 Ld19
Gamleby ◻ S 27 Lj17
Gammelstaden ◻ S 23 Mb13
Gamtog ◻ CHN 84 Pd12
Gandajika ◻ RDC 109 Ma20
Gander ◻ CDN 121 Hb09
Gandesa ◻ E 42 La25
Gandhinagar ◻ IND 80 Oc14
Gandia ◻ E 43 Kk26
Ganges ◻ F 38 Lb24
Ganges ◻ IND 80 Pa13
Gangesebene ◻ IND 80 Pa13
Ganggye ◻ PRK 83 Rb10
Gangneung ◻ ROK 83 Rb11
Gangtok ◻ IND 80 Pb13
Gani ◻ RI 87 Rb19
Gannat ◻ F 38 Lb22
Gansu ◻ CHN 79 Pd11
Gänzä ◻ AZ 76 Nb10
Ganzhou ◻ CHN 85 Qc13
Gao ◻ RMM 105 La15
Gaoual ◻ RG 105 Kb16
Gap ◻ F 39 Ld24
Garabogazköl aglagy ◻ TM 76 Nc10
Garanhuns ◻ BR 134 Ja20
Garapu ◻ BR 135 Hb21
Gardelegen ◻ D 44 Lf19
Garden City ◻ USA 122 Ed11
Gárdony ◻ H 53 Lk22
Gargano, P.N. del ♦ I 49 Lj25
Gargzdai ◻ LT 31 Ma18
Garmisch-Partenkirchen ◻ D 45 Lf22
Garoowe ◻ SP 100 Na08
Garoua ◻ CAM 108 Lc17
Garry Lake ◻ CDN 118 Ed05
Garsen ◻ EAK 109 Na19
Gartog ◻ CHN 84 Pd13
Garwa ◻ IND 80 Pa14
Garwolin ◻ PL 50 Ma20
Gary ◻ USA 123 Fc10
Gascogne ◻ F 38 Kk24

Gascoyne ◻ AUS 94 Qc23
Gastonia ◻ USA 123 Fd11
Gastoúni ◻ GR 56 Ma27
Gâtaia ◻ RO 54 Ma23
Gatčina ◻ RUS 30 Mf16
Gatma Dağı ▲ TR 64 Me26
Gau ◻ FIJ 98 Td22
Gaujas n.p. ♦ LV 30 Mc17
Gaujang ◻ N 24 Ld15
Gaussberg ▲ 141 Pb32
Gávdos ◻ GR 57 Mc28
Gävle ◻ S 25 Lj15
Gavrilov-Jam ◻ RUS 58 Mk17
Gávrio ◻ GR 57 Mc27
Gaya ◻ IND 80 Pa14
Gaza ◻ IL 107 Mc12
Gaziantep ◻ TR 76 Md11
Gazıantep ◻ TR 65 Mj27
Gazipaşa ◻ TR 64 Mg27
Gbadolite ◻ RDC 108 Ma18
Gbarnga ◻ LB 105 Kc17
Gdańsk ◻ PL 50 Lk18
Gdov ◻ RUS 30 Md16
Gdynia ◻ PL 50 Lk18
Gebe ◻ RI 87 Rb18
Gebze ◻ TR 57 Me25
Gediz ◻ TR 64 Me26
Gedser ◻ DK 26 Lf18
Geel ◻ B 37 Lc20
Geelong ◻ AUS 97 Sa26
Geilo ◻ N 24 Le15
Geirangerfjorden ◻ N 24 Ld14
Gela ◻ I 49 Lh27
Gelendžik ◻ RUS 63 Mk23
Gelgaudiškis ◻ LT 31 Mb18
Gelibolu ◻ TR 57 Md25
Gelibolu Yarımadası Milli Parkı ♦ TR 57 Md25
Gembi ◻ ETH 109 Md17
Gemena ◻ RDC 108 Ld18
Gemlik ◻ TR 57 Me25
Genale Wenz ◻ ETH 109 Na17
General Acha ◻ RA 137 Gd26
General E.a Garay ◻ PY 136 Gd24
General Güemes ◻ RA 136 Gc23
General Santos ◻ RP 85 Rb17
General Toševo ◻ BG 55 Me24
Geneva ◻ CH 39 Ld22
Genève ◻ CH 39 Ld22
Genlis ◻ F 39 Lc22
Genoa ◻ I 46 Le23
Genova ◻ I 46 Le23
Gent ◻ B 37 Lb20
Genthin ◻ D 44 Lg19
Geographe Bay ◻ AUS 95 Qd25
Geographe Channel ◻ AUS 94 Qc23
George ◻ ZA 110 Ma25
Georgetown ◻ GUY 134 Ha17
Georgetown ◻ MAL 86 Qa17
Georgetown ◻ USA 123 Ga12
Georgetown ◻ UK 126 Fd15
George VI Ice Shelf ◻ 140 Gc33
George V Land ◻ 141 Sb33
Georgia ◻ GE 76 Na10
Georgia ◻ USA 123 Fd12
Georgian Bay ◻ CDN 123 Fd09
Georgievka ◻ KZ 79 Pa09
Georg von Neumayer ◻ 141 Kc33

Gera ◻ D 44 Lg20
Geráki ◻ GR 56 Mb27
Geraldton ◻ AUS 95 Qc24
Geralzinho ◻ BR 135 Hd22
Gérardmer ◻ F 37 Ld21
Gerede ◻ TR 65 Mg25
Gereshk ◻ AFG 78 Oa12
Gérgal ◻ E 41 Kj27
Germany ◻ D 20 Lb07
Gernika ◻ E 42 Kj24
Geta ◻ FIN 25 Lk15
Getafe ◻ E 40 Kj25
Getz Ice Shelf ◻ 140 Dd33
Gevaş ◻ TR 66 Nb26
Gevgelija ◻ MK 56 Mb25
Gex ◻ F 39 Ld22
Geyik Dağları ▲ TR 64 Mf27
Geyve ◻ TR 64 Mf25
Ghadamis ◻ LAR 106 Lb12
Ghana ◻ GH 105 Kd17
Ghanzi ◻ RB 110 Ma23
Ghard Abu Muharrik ◻ ET 107 Mb13
Ghardaïa ◻ DZ 104 La12
Gharyan ◻ LAR 106 Lc12
Ghat ◻ NG 106 Lc14
Ghazni ◻ AFG 78 Od12
Gheorgheni ◻ RO 55 Mc22
Gherla ◻ RO 54 Mb22
Ghimpaţi ◻ RO 55 Mc23
Giżycko ◻ PL 50 Ma18
Gianitsá ◻ GR 56 Mb25
Giarmata ◻ RO 54 Ma23
Giáros ◻ GR 57 Mc27
Gibraleón ◻ E 41 Kg27
Gibraltar ◻ GB 41 Kh27
Gibson Desert ◻ AUS 94 Ra23
Gien ◻ F 38 Lb22
Gießen ◻ D 45 Le20
Gifhorn ◻ D 44 Lf19
Gighera ◻ RO 54 Mb24
Gijón ◻ E 40 Kh24
Gilbert ◻ AUS 96 Sa22
Gilette ◻ USA 120 Ec10
Gilgit ◻ PAK 78 Oc11
Gilgit Mountains ◻ PAK 78 Oc11
Gillam ◻ CDN 120 Fb07
Gimo ◻ S 25 Lk15
Gióia del Colle ◻ I 49 Lj25
Gióia Táuro ◻ I 49 Lh26
Gioúra ◻ GR 57 Mc26
Giresun ◻ TR 66 Mk25
Giresun Dağları ▲ TR 66 Mk25
Girona ◻ E 42 La25
Gironde ◻ F 38 Kk23
Girvan ◻ GB 34 Kh18
Girvas ◻ RUS 29 Mg14
Gisborne ◻ NZ 99 Td26
Gisenyi ◻ RWA 109 Mb19
Gislaved ◻ S 26 Lg17
Gitega ◻ BU 109 Mc19
Githio ◻ GR 56 Mb27
Giulianova ◻ I 47 Lg24
Giurgeni ◻ RO 55 Md23
Giurgiu ◻ RO 55 Mc24
Givet ◻ F 37 Lc20
Givors ◻ F 39 Lc23
Giza ◻ ET 107 Md13
Gizo ◻ SOL 93 Sd20
Gjirokastër ◻ AL 56 Ma25
Gjoa Haven ◻ CDN 118 Fa05
Gjøvik ◻ N 24 Lf15
Gjumri ◻ ARM 76 Na10
Glace Bay ◻ CDN 121 Ha09
Gladstad ◻ N 24 Lf13
Gladstone ◻ AUS 96 Sc23

Glamoč ◻ BIH 47 Lj23
Glarus ◻ CH 45 Le22
Glasgow ◻ GB 34 Kh18
Glastonbury ◻ GB 35 Kj20
Glazaniha ◻ RUS 29 Mk14
Glen Coe ◼ GB 34 Kh17
Glencolumbkille ◻ IRL 33 Kf18
Glendale ◻ USA 122 Eb12
Glendive ◻ USA 120 Ed09
Glen Innes ◻ AUS 96 Sc24
Glennallen ◻ USA 116 Cc06
Glenrothes ◻ GB 34 Kj17
Gleneagly N.P. ◆ IRL 33 Kg18
Glina ◻ HR 47 Lj23
Glittertind ▲ N 24 Le15
Gliwice ◻ PL 50 Lk20
Głodeni ◻ MD 55 Md22
Głogów ◻ PL 50 Lj21
Glommersträsk ◻ S 25 Lk13
Gloucester ◻ GB 35 Kj20
Głubczyce ◻ PL 50 Lj20
Glubokij ◻ RUS 63 Na21
Głuchołazy ◻ PL 50 Lj20
Gluhove ◻ RUS 60 Nb18
Gmünd ◻ A 52 Lg22
Gmunden ◻ A 52 Lg22
Gnarp ◻ S 25 Lj14
Gnesta ◻ S 27 Lj16
Gniezno ◻ PL 50 Lj19
Gnoien ◻ D 44 Lg19
Gnosjö ◻ S 27 Lg17
Goa ◻ IND 81 Oc16
Gobabis ◻ NAM 110 Ld23
Gobi Desert ◻ CHN/MNG 82 Qa10
Goce Delčev ◻ BG 56 Mb25
Godavari ◼ IND 81 Pa15
Godeč ◻ BG 54 Mb24
Godhavn ◻ DK 119 Hb05
Godoy Cruz ◻ RA 136 Gc25
Gods Lake ◻ CDN 120 Fb08
Gods Lake Narrows ◻ CDN 120 Fb08
Godthåb ◻ DK 119 Hb06
Goes ◻ NL 37 Lb20
Goianésia ◻ BR 135 Hc22
Goiânia ◻ BR 135 Hc22
Goiás ◻ BR 135 Hb22
Goiás ◻ BR 135 Hc21
Gökçeada ◻ TR 57 Mc25
Gökçek ◻ TR 66 Mk26
Gökçekaya Baraji ◻ TR 64 Mf25
Gökırmak ◼ TR 65 Mg25
Gökova ◻ TR 64 Me27
Gökova Körfezi ◻ TR 57 Md27
Göksu ◼ TR 66 Nb26
Göksu Milli Parkı ◆ TR 65 Mg27
Göksun ◻ TR 65 Mj26
Gol ◻ N 24 Le15
Gölbaşı ◻ TR 65 Mg26
Gölbaşı ◻ TR 65 Mj27
Gölcük ◻ TR 57 Me25
Gölcük ◻ TR 65 Mh26
Gölcük ◻ TR 66 Mk26
Gołdap ◻ PL 51 Mb18
Gold Coast ◻ AUS 96 Sc24
Gold Coast ◻ GH 105 Kd18
Golden ◻ CDN 117 Ea08
Göle ◻ TR 66 Nb25
Goleniów ◻ PL 50 Lh19
Golf de Sant Jordi ◻ E 42 La25
Golfe de Gabès ◻ TN 106 Lc12
Golfe de Hammamet ◻ TN 106 Lc11
Golfe de Saint-Malo ◻ F 36 Kj21
Golfe du Lion ◻ F 38 Lb24
Golfküstenebene ◻ USA 123 Fa12
Golfo Corcovado ◻ RCH 137 Gb27
Golfo de Almería ◻ E 41 Kj27
Golfo de Batabanó ◻ C 126 Fd14
Golfo de Fonseca ◻ HN 125 Fc16
Golfo de Guayaquil ◻ EC 132 Fd19
Golfo de Honduras ◻ HN 125 Fc15
Golfo de los Mosquitos ◻ PA 126 Fd17
Golfo de Papagayo ◻ CR 125 Fc16
Golfo de Peñas ◻ RCH 137 Gb28
Golfo di Gaeta ◻ I 48 Lg25
Golfo di Manfredónia ◻ I 49 Lj25
Golfo di Orosei e del Gennargentu, P.N. del ◆ I 48 Le25
Golfo di Salerno ◻ I 49 Lh25
Golfo di Sant'Eufémia ◻ I 49 Lj26
Golfo di Squillace ◻ I 49 Lj26
Golfo San Jorge ◻ RA 137 Gc28
Golfo San Matias ◻ RA 137 Gd27
Golf von Thailand ◻ THA 84 Qa16
Gölgeli Dağları ◻ TR 64 Me27
Gölhisar ◻ TR 64 Me27
Golicyno ◻ RUS 58 Mj18
Goljamo Kruševo ◻ BG 55 Md24
Gölköy ◻ TR 65 Mj25
Golmud ◻ CHN 79 Pd11
Golog Shan ◼ CHN 84 Qa12
Golubac ◻ SR 54 Ma23
Goma ◻ RDC 109 Mb19
Gombe ◼ EAT 109 Mc19
Gombe ◻ WAN 108 Lc16
Gómez Palacio ◻ MEX 124 Ed13
Gonabad ◻ IR 77 Nd12
Gonaïves ◻ RH 127 Gb15
Gonbad-e Kavus ◻ IR 78 Nd11
Gonder ◻ ETH 107 Md16
Gondwana ◻ 141 Tc33
Gönen ◻ TR 57 Md25
Gongola ◼ WAN 108 Lc16
Gongpoquan ◻ CHN 79 Pd10
Gonzales Videla, G. ◻ 140 Gd31
Goodenough Island ◻ PNG 93 Sc20
Goodspeed Nunataks ◻ 141 Oa33
Goomalling ◻ AUS 95 Qd25
Goondiwindi ◻ AUS 96 Sc24
Goose Bay ◻ CDN 121 Gd08
Gooty ◻ IND 81 Od16
Göppingen ◻ D 45 Le21
gora Beluha ▲ RUS 79 Pb09
gora Blednaja ▲ RUS 73 Oa03
gora Cuguš ▲ RUS 66 Na24
Góra Kalwaria ◻ PL 50 Ma20
Gorakhpur ◻ IND 80 Pa13
gora Konžakovskij Kamen' ▲ RUS 72 Nd07
gora Ledjanaja ▲ RUS 74 Tc06
gora Narodnaja ▲ RUS 72 Oa05
gora Pajer ▲ RUS 72 Oa05
gora Skalistyj Golec ▲ RUS 75 Qd07
gora Telposiz ▲ RUS 72 Oa06
Goražde ◻ BIH 47 Lk24
Gorczański Park Narodowy ◆ PL 50 Ma21
Gördes ◻ TR 64 Me26
Gore ◻ NZ 99 Tb28
Gorè ◻ TCH 108 Lc17
Gorelki ◻ RUS 59 Mj18
Göreme ◻ TR 65 Mh26
Göreme Milli Parkı ◆ TR 65 Mh26
Gorgan ◻ IR 76 Nc11
Goricy ◻ RUS 58 Mj17
Gorizia ◻ I 47 Lg23
Gorjačij Ključ ◻ RUS 63 Mk23
Gorlice ◻ PL 50 Ma21
Görlitz ◻ D 44 Lh20
Gorna Orjahovica ◻ BG 55 Mc24
Gornja Radgona ◻ SLO 47 Lh22
Gornji Milanovac ◻ SR 54 Ma23
Gorno-Altajsk ◻ RUS 79 Pb08
Gorno-Altaj ◻ RUS 79 Pb08
Goroch'an ▲ ETH 109 Md17
Gorodec ◻ RUS 58 Nb17
Gorodišče ◻ RUS 60 Nc19
Goroka ◻ PNG 92 Sb20
Gorongosa ◼ MOC 111 Mc22
Gorontalo ◻ RI 87 Ra14
Goršečnoe ◻ RUS 59 Mj20
Gór Stołowych, P.N. ◆ PL 50 Lj20
gory Byrranga ◻ RUS 73 Pc04
Gorzów Wielkopolski ◻ PL 50 Lh19
Goslar ◻ D 44 Lf20
Gospić ◻ HR 47 Lh23
Gostyń ◻ PL 50 Lj20
Gostynin ◻ PL 50 Lk19
Göteborg ◻ S 26 Lf17
Götene ◻ S 26 Lg16
Gotha ◻ D 44 Lf20
Gotland ◻ S 27 Lk17
Gotska Sandön ◻ S 27 Lk16
Gotska Sandön n.p. ◆ S 27 Lk16
Göttingen ◻ D 44 Le20
Goulburn ◻ AUS 97 Sc25
Goulburn Islands ◻ AUS 94 Rc21
Goulimine ◻ MA 104 Kb13
Goumbi ◻ G 108 Lc19
Gournay-en-Bray ◻ F 36 La21
Gov' Altayn Nuruu ◻ MNG 82 Qa10
Gove ◻ AUS 96 Rd21
Govenador Valadares ◻ BR 135 Hd22
Gove Peninsula ◻ AUS 96 Rd21
Governador Gregores ◻ RA 137 Gb28
Governor's Harbour ◻ BS 126 Ga13
Gozne ◻ TR 65 Mh27
Gozo ◻ M 49 Lh27
Graaff-Reinet ◻ ZA 110 Ma25
Gračac ◻ HR 47 Lh23
Gračanica ◻ BIH 47 Lk23
Gradačac ◻ BIH 47 Lk23
Grădiştea de Munte-Cioclovina, P.N. ◆ RO 54 Mb23
Grafton ◻ AUS 97 Sc24
Graham Island ◻ CDN 117 Db08
Graham Land ◻ 140 Gd32
Grain Coast ◻ LB 105 Kb17
Grajaú ◻ BR 134 Hc20
Grajewo ◻ PL 51 Mb19
Grajvoron ◻ RUS 59 Mh20
Grampian Mountains ◼ GB 34 Kh17
Gramsh ◻ AL 56 Ma25
Granada ◻ NIC 125 Fc16
Granby ◻ CDN 121 Gb09
Gran Canaria ◻ E 104 Ka13
Gran Chaco ◻ RA 136 Gd23
Grand Ahama Island ◻ BS 126 Ga13
Grand Banks of Newfoundland ◻ CDN 121 Hb09
Grand Canyon ◼ USA 122 Eb11
Grand Cayman ◻ UK 126 Fd15
Grand Centre ◻ CDN 120 Eb08
Grand Comore ◻ COM 111 Na21
Grande Prairie ◻ CDN 117 Ea07
Grand Erg de Bilma ◻ RN 106 Lc15
Grande Terre ◻ SY 111 Nb20
Grand Falls ◻ CDN 121 Ha09
Grand Forks ◻ USA 120 Fa09
Grand Island ◻ USA 122 Fa10
Grand Junction ◻ USA 122 Ec11
Grândola ◻ P 41 Kf26
Grand Prairie ◻ USA 123 Fa12
Grand Rapids ◻ USA 123 Fc10
Grand Récif de Cook ◻ F 98 Ta22
Grand Récif Sud ◻ F 98 Tb23
Grand Teton ◼ USA 122 Eb10
Grangemouth ◻ GB 34 Kj17
Grängesberg ◻ S 25 Lh15
Granite Peak ◼ USA 122 Ea10
Gränna ◻ S 27 Lh16
Granö ◻ S 25 Lk13
Granollers ◻ E 42 Lb25
Gran Paradiso, P.N. del ◆ I 46 Ld23
Gran Sasso e Monti della Laga, P.N. del ◆ I 47 Lg24
Grantham ◻ GB 35 Kh19
Grants Pass ◻ USA 122 Dd10
Granville ◻ F 36 Kk21
Grasse ◻ F 39 Ld24
Gravina in Púglia ◻ I 49 Lj25
Gray ◻ F 37 Lc22
Graz ◻ A 52 Lh22
Great Belt ◻ DK 26 Lf18
Great Britain ◻ GB 34 Kk17
Great Artesian Basin ◻ AUS 96 Sa24
Great Australian Bight ◻ AUS 95 Rb25

Great Bahama Bank ◫ 126 Ga14
Great Barrier Island ◫ NZ 99 Td26
Great Barrier Reef ◫ AUS 96 Sb22
Great Basin ◫ USA 122 Ea11
Great Bear Lake ◫ CDN 118 Dd03
Great Channel ▭ RI 86 Pc17
Great Dividing Range ▲ AUS 97 Sb26
Great Eastern Erg ◫ DZ 104 La13
Greater Antilles ◫ 126 Ga15
Greater Hinggan Range ▲ CHN 83 Qd10
Greater Sunda Islands ◫ RI 86 Qa18
Great Exhibition Bay ▭ NZ 99 Tc25
Great Falls ◫ USA 122 Eb09
Great Inagua Island ◫ BS 127 Gb14
Great Karoo ◫ ZA 110 Ma25
Great Lake ◫ AUS 97 Sb27
Great Nicobar ◫ IND 81 Pc17
Great Plain of the Koukdjuak ◫ CDN 119 Gb05
Great Plains ◫ CDN 117 Ea07
Great Plains ◫ USA 120 Ed09
Great Rift Valley ◫ 109 Mb19
Great Ruaha ◫ EAT 109 Mc20
Great Salt Lake ◫ USA 122 Eb10
Great Salt Lake Desert ◫ USA 122 Eb10
Great Sand Sea ◫ ET 106 Mb13
Great Sandy Desert ◫ AUS 94 Ra23
Great Slave Lake ◫ CDN 120 Eb06
Great Victoria Desert ◫ AUS 94 Rb24
Great Wall ▭ 140 Ha30
Great Western Erg ◫ DZ 104 La12
Great Yarmouth ◫ GB 35 La19
Greece ◫ GR 56 Ma26
Greeley ◫ USA 122 Ed10
Green ◫ USA 122 Ec11
Green Bay ▭ USA 123 Fc10
Green Islands ◫ PNG 93 Sc19
Greenland ◫ DK 119 Hb02
Greenland=Kalaallit Nunaat ◫ DK 119 Hd03
Greenland Sea ◫ 138 Kb03
Greenock ◫ GB 34 Kh18
Green River ◫ USA 122 Eb11
Greensboro ◫ USA 123 Ga11
Greenville ◫ LB 105 Kc17
Greenville ◫ USA 123 Fa13
Greenville ◫ USA 123 Fd12
Greenville ◫ USA 123 Ga11
Greifswald ◫ D 44 Lg18
Greiz ◫ D 45 Lg20
Gremiha ◫ RUS 72 Md05
Gremjač'e ◫ RUS 59 Mz20
Grenaa ◫ DK 26 Lf17
Grenada ◫ WG 127 Gd16
Grenoble ◫ F 39 Lc23
Gressåmoen n.p. ◫ N 24 Lh13
Greven ◫ D 44 Ld19

Grevená ◫ GR 56 Ma25
Grevenmacher ◫ L 37 Ld21
Greymouth ◫ NZ 99 Tc27
Grey Range ▲ AUS 96 Sa24
Greystones ◫ IRL 33 Kg19
Gribanovskij ◫ RUS 61 Na20
Griffith ◫ AUS 97 Sb25
Grigor'evskoe ◫ RUS 58 Nb17
Grigoriopol ◫ MD 55 Me22
Grimma ◫ D 45 Lg20
Grimsby ◫ GB 35 Kk19
Grimsey ◫ IS 32 Kb12
Grimsstaðir ◫ IS 32 Kb13
Grimstad ◫ N 26 Le16
Grimsvötn ▲ IS 32 Kb13
Grindavík ◫ IS 32 Jj14
Grindsted ◫ DK 26 Le18
Grinnel Pen. ◫ CDN 118 Fa03
Grise Fiord ◫ CDN 118 Fd03
Grivenskaja ◫ RUS 63 Mk23
Grivita ◫ RO 55 Md23
Grjady ◫ RUS 30 Mf16
Grjazi ◫ RUS 59 Mk19
Gröjec ◫ PL 50 Ma20
Grong ◫ N 24 Lg13
Groningen ◫ NL 37 Ld19
Groningen ◫ SME 134 Ha17
Grønligrotta ◫ N 22 Lh12
Groote Eylandt ◫ AUS 96 Rd13
Grootfontein ◫ NAM 110 Ld22
Groot Karasberge ▲ NAM 110 Ld24
Großenhain ◫ D 44 Lg20
Grosseto ◫ I 46 Lf24
Großglockner ▲ A 52 Lg22
Grov ◫ N 22 Lj11
Grove Mountains ▲ 141 Oc32
Groznyj ◫ RUS 76 Nb10
Grudziądz ◫ PL 50 Lk19
Grums ◫ S 26 Lg16
Grünau ◫ NAM 110 Ld24
Grunwald ◫ PL 50 Ma19
Gryfice ◫ PL 50 Lh19
Gryllefjord ◫ N 22 Lj11
Guadalajara ◫ E 41 Kj20
Guadalajara ◫ MEX 124 Ed14
Guadalcanal ◫ SOL 93 Sd20
Guadeloupe ▭ F 127 Gd15
Guadelupe ◫ MEX 124 Fa13
Guadix ◫ E 41 Kj27
Guaíra ◫ BR 135 Hb23
Guajará-Mirim ◫ BR 133 Gc21
Gualdo Tadino ◫ I 46 Lg24
Guam ◫ USA 92 Sa16
Guamúchil ◫ MEX 124 Ec13
Gua Musang ◫ MAL 86 Qa18
Guanare ◫ YV 132 Gc17
Guangdong ◫ CHN 85 Qc14
Guangxi Zhuangzu Zizhiqu ◫ CHN 84 Qb14
Guangyuan ◫ CHN 82 Qb12
Guangzhou ◫ CHN 85 Qc14
Guanajuato ◫ MEX 124 Ed14
Guanajuato ◫ MEX 124 Ed14
Guantánamo ◫ C 126 Ga14
Guaporé ◫ BR 133 Gd21
Guaqui ◫ BOL 133 Gc22
Guarai ◫ BR 134 Hc20
Guarantã do Norte ◫ BR 134 Ha20
Guarapuava ◫ BR 135 Hb24
Guarda ◫ P 40 Kj25
Guardo ◫ E 40 Kh24
Guareña ◫ E 41 Kg26

Guarenas ◫ YV 127 Gc16
Guasave ◫ MEX 124 Ec13
Guasdualito ◫ YV 132 Gb17
Guatemala ◫ GCA 125 Fb16
Guatemala Basin ◫ 125 Fa16
Guaviare ◫ CO 132 Gb18
Guayaquil ◫ EC 132 Fd19
Guayaramerín ◫ BOL 133 Gc21
Guaymas ◫ MEX 124 Eb13
guba Buor-Haja ▭ RUS 74 Rc14
Guben ◫ D 44 Lh20
Gubin ◫ PL 50 Lh20
Gubkin ◫ RUS 59 Mj20
Gudbrandsdalen ◫ N 24 Le15
Guéckedou ◫ RG 105 Kb17
Guelb er Richârt ▲ RIM 104 Kb14
Guer ◫ F 36 Kj22
Guérande ◫ F 36 Kj22
Guéret ◫ F 38 La22
Guerrero ◫ MEX 124 Ed15
Gueugnon ◫ F 39 Lc22
Guge ▲ ETH 109 Md17
Guiana Highlands ◫ YV/GUY 132 Gc17
Guiglo ◫ CI 105 Kc17
Guildford ◫ GB 35 Kk20
Guilin ◫ CHN 85 Qc13
Guillestre ◫ F 39 Ld23
Guimarães ◫ P 40 Kf25
Guinea ◫ RG 105 Kb16
Guinea Basin ◫ 105 Kd18
Guinea-Bissau ◫ GNB 105 Ka16
Güines ◫ C 126 Fd14
Guingamp ◫ F 36 Kj21
Güiria ◫ YV 127 Gd16
Guise ◫ F 37 Lb21
Guiyang ◫ CHN 84 Qb13
Guizhou ◫ CHN 84 Qb13
Gujarat ◫ IND 80 Oc14
Gukovo ◫ RUS 61 Mk21
Gujrat ◫ PAK 80 Oc12
Gulbarga ◫ IND 81 Od15
Gulbene ◫ LV 30 Md17
Guldenløves Fjord ▭ DK 119 Hd06
Gulf of Corinth ▭ GR 56 Mb26
Gulf of Finland ▭ FIN/EST 30 Mc16
Gulf of Aden ▭ 77 Nb16
Gulf of Alaska ▭ USA 117 Cc07
Gulf of Aqaba ▭ 76 Md13
Gulf of Bone ▭ RI 87 Ra19
Gulf of Boothia ▭ CDN 118 Fd04
Gulf of California ▭ MEX 124 Eb13
Gulf of Carpentaria ▭ AUS 96 Rd21
Gulf of Darién ▭ CO 132 Ga17
Gulf of Guinea ▭ 105 La18
Gulf of Kachchh ▭ IND 80 Ob14
Gulf of Khambha ▭ IND 80 Oc14
Gulf of Maine ▭ USA 121 Gc10
Gulf of Mannar ▭ IND/CL 81 Od17
Gulf of Martaban ▭ MYA 84 Pd15
Gulf of Masirah ▭ OM 77 Nd15

Gulf of Mexico ▭ 123 Fb13
Gulf of Oman ▭ OM 77 Nd14
Gulf of Panama ▭ PA 132 Ga17
Gulf of Papua ▭ PNG 92 Sa20
Gulf of Saint Lawrence ▭ CDN 121 Gd09
Gulf of Saint Lawrence ▭ CDN 121 Gd09
Gulf of Sirte ▭ LAR 106 Ld12
Gulf of Suez ▭ ET 107 Mc13
Gulf of Tehuantepec ▭ MEX 125 Fb15
Gulf of Thailand ▭ THA 84 Qa16
Gulf of Tolo ▭ RI 87 Ra19
Gulf of Tomini ▭ RI 87 Ra19
Gulf of Tonkin ▭ VN 84 Qb14
Gulf of Venezuela ▭ YV 127 Gb16
Gulfport ◫ USA 123 Fc12
Gulf Saint Vincent ▭ AUS 97 Rd26
Guljanci ◫ BG 55 Mc24
Gullbrandstorp ◫ S 26 Lg17
Gullfoss ▲ IS 32 Jk13
Gullspång ◫ S 27 Lh16
Güllü Dağları ▲ TR 66 Na25
Güllük Körfezi ▭ TR 57 Md27
Gülpınar ◫ TR 57 Md26
Gulu ◫ EAU 109 Mc18
Gummersbach ◫ D 44 Ld20
Gümüşhane ◫ TR 66 Mk25
Güney Doğu Toroslar ▲ TR 65 Mj26
Gunnerus Ridge ▭ 141 Mc32
Guntur ◫ IND 81 Pa15
Gununa ◫ AUS 96 Rd22
Gunung Binaia ▲ RI 87 Rb19
Gunung Bromo ▲ RI 87 Qb20
Gunung Kerinci ▲ RI 86 Qa19
Gunung Kinabalu ▲ MAL 87 Qd17
Gunung Leuser ▲ RI 86 Pd18
Gunung Liangpran ▲ RI 87 Qc18
Gunung Mekongga ▲ RI 87 Ra19
Gunung Merapi ▲ RI 87 Qb20
Gunung Rantemario ▲ RI 87 Qd19
Gunungsitoli ◫ RI 86 Pd18
Günzburg ◫ D 45 Lf21
Gunzenhausen ◫ D 45 Lf21
Gurahonţ ◫ RO 54 Mb22
Gura Humorului ◫ RO 55 Mc22
Gurguélia ◫ BR 134 Hd20
Gurkovo ◫ BG 55 Mc24
Güroymak ◫ TR 67 Na26
Gürün ◫ TR 65 Mj26
Gurupi ◫ BR 134 Hc19
Gurupi ◫ BR 135 Hc21
Gusev ◫ RUS 31 Mb18
Gus'-Hrustal'nyj ◫ RUS 58 Na18
Guspini ◫ I 48 Le26
Güstrow ◫ D 44 Lg19
Gus'-Železnyj ◫ RUS 58 Na18
Gutenko Mountains ▲ 140 Gd33
Gütersloh ◫ D 44 Le20
Gutulia n.p. ◫ N 24 Lg14
Guwahati ◫ IND 84 Pc13
Guyana ◫ GUY 134 Ha17
Güzelsu ◫ TR 66 Nb26
Gvardejsk ◫ RUS 31 Ma18

Gvarv ☐ N 26 Le16
Gwadar ☐ PAK 77 Oa13
Gwalior ☐ IND 80 Od13
Gwanda ☐ ZW 110 Mb23
Gwangju ☐ ROK 83 Rb11
Gweru ☐ ZW 110 Mb22
Gyangze ☐ CHN 80 Pb13
Gyaring Hu ◆ CHN 84 Pd12
Gydanskaja guba ◆ RUS
  73 Od04
Gydanskij p-ov ☐ RUS 73
  Od04
Gyeongju ☐ ROK 83 Rb11
Gylien ☐ S 23 Mb12
Gympie ☐ AUS 96 Sc24
Gyöngyös ☐ H 53 Lk22
Győr ☐ H 53 Lj22
Gyula ☐ H 53 Ma22
Gyzylarbat ☐ TM 78 Nd11
Gżatsk ☐ RUS 58 Mh18

H

Häädemeeste ☐ EST 30
  Mc16
Haag Nunataks ▲ 140 Ga34
Ha'apai Group ☐ TO 98 Ub22
Haapsalu ☐ EST 30 Mb16
Haarlem ☐ NL 52 Lf19
Haast ☐ NZ 99 Tb27
Habarovsk ☐ RUS 75 Rd09
Habarut ☐ OM 77 Nc15
Hachinohe ☐ J 83 Sa10
Hacıbektaş ☐ TR 65 Mh26
Haciömer ☐ TR 66 Na26
Hackås ☐ S 25 Lh14
Haderslev ☐ DK 26 Le18
Hadım ☐ TR 64 Mg27
Hadjač ☐ UA 62 Mh20
Hadramawt ☐ YE 77 Nb15
Hadseløya ☐ N 22 Lh11
Hadsund ☐ DK 26 Lf17
Hægeland ☐ N 26 Ld16
Haeju ☐ PRK 83 Rb11
Hafar al Batin ☐ KSA 77
  Nb13
Hafik ☐ TR 65 Mj26
Hafnarfjörður ☐ IS 32 Jj13
Hagen ☐ D 44 Lg20
Hagenow ☐ D 44 Lf19
Hagerstown ☐ USA 123 Ga11
Hagfors ☐ S 24 Lg15
Häggenås ☐ S 25 Lh14
Haguenau ☐ F 37 Ld21
Hahót ☐ H 53 Lj22
Hai'an ☐ CHN 85 Qc14
Haifa ☐ IL 76 Md12
Haikou ☐ CHN 85 Qc15
Hailar ☐ CHN 82 Qd09
Hailuoto ☐ FIN 28 Mc13
Hailuoto ☐ FIN 28 Mc13
Hainan ☐ CHN 85 Qb15
Hainan Dao ☐ CHN 85 Qc15
Hainan Strait ◆ CHN 85 Qb14
Hainburg ☐ A 53 Lj21
Haines ☐ USA 117 Da07
Haines Junction ☐ CDN
  117 Da06
Hainfeld ☐ A 52 Lh21
Haiphong ☐ VN 84 Qb14
Haiti ☐ RH 127 Gb15
Hajar ☐ OM 77 Nd14
Hajdúböszörmény ☐ H
  53 Ma22
Hajdúszoboszló ☐ H 53 Ma22
Hajnówka ☐ PL 51 Mb19
Hajsyn ☐ UA 62 Me21

Hajyr ☐ RUS 74 Rc04
Hakodate ☐ J 83 Sa10
Halaban ☐ KSA 77 Na14
Halaib ☐ ET 107 Md14
Halawa ☐ USA 117 Cb35
Halden ☐ N 26 Lf16
Haldwani ☐ IND 80 Od13
Hale ◆ AUS 96 Rd23
Halfmoon Bay ☐ NZ 99 Tb28
Halič ☐ UA 51 Mc21
Halifax ☐ CDN 121 Gd10
Halifax Bay ◆ AUS 96 Sb22
Hálki ☐ GR 57 Md27
Halkida ☐ GR 57 Mb26
Halland ☐ S 26 Lg17
Hall Beach ☐ CDN 118 Fd05
Halle (Saale) ☐ D 44 Lf20
Hällefors ☐ S 27 Lh16
Hallen ☐ S 25 Lh14
Halley ☐ 140 Jc34
Hällingsåfallet ◆ S 25 Lh13
Hall Islands ☐ FSM 93 Sc17
Hällnäs ☐ S 25 Lk13
Hall Peninsula ◆ CDN 119
  Gc06
Halls Creek ☐ AUS 94 Rb22
Hallstavik ☐ S 25 Lk15
Halmahera ☐ RI 87 Rb18
Halmahera Sea ◆ RI 87 Rb19
Halmstad ☐ S 26 Lg17
Halong Bay ◆ VN 84 Qb14
Hal'šany ☐ BY 31 Md18
Hälsingland ☐ S 25 Lh15
Hama ☐ SYR 76 Md11
Hamada de Tinrhert ◆ DZ
  106 Lb13
Hamada du Guir ◆ DZ
  104 Kd12
Hamadan ☐ IR 76 Nb12
Hamar ☐ N 24 Lf15
Hamburg ☐ D 44 Lf19
Hämeenkyrö ☐ FIN 22 Mb15
Hämeenlinna ☐ FIN 28 Mc15
Hameln ☐ D 44 Le19
Hamersley Range ▲ AUS
  94 Qd23
Hamheung ☐ PRK 83 Rb11
Hami ☐ CHN 79 Pc10
Hamilton ☐ AUS 97 Sa26
Hamilton ☐ CDN 123 Fd10
Hamilton ☐ GB 121 Gd12
Hamilton ☐ GB 34 Kh18
Hamilton ☐ NZ 99 Td26
Hamim ☐ UAE 77 Nc14
Hamina ☐ FIN 28 Md15
Hamm ☐ D 44 Ld20
Hammamet ☐ TN 106 Lc11
Hammerdal ☐ S 25 Lh14
Hammerfest ☐ N 23 Mb10
Hamnvik ☐ N 22 Lj11
Hamra n.p. ◆ S 25 Lh15
Hamum-e-Jazmuriyan ◆ IR
  77 Nd13
Hamyśki ☐ RUS 66 Na23
Hanak ☐ KSA 76 Md13
Hanak ☐ TR 66 Nb25
Hanau ☐ D 44 Le20
Hancavičy ☐ BY 51 Md19
Hâncești ☐ MD 55 Me22
Handan ☐ CHN 82 Qc11
Handlová ☐ SK 53 Lk21
Handyga ☐ RUS 75 Rd06
Hangö = Hanko ☐ FIN 30
  Mb16
Hangzhou ☐ CHN 83 Ra12
Hani ☐ TR 66 Na26
Hanko = Hangö ☐ FIN 30
  Mb16
Hannover ☐ D 44 Le19

Hannoversch Münden ☐ D
  44 Le20
Hanoi ☐ VN 84 Qb14
Hanstholm ☐ DK 26 Le17
Hanty-Mansijsk ☐ RUS
  72 Ob16
Hanzhong ☐ CHN 82 Qb12
Haparanda ☐ S 19 Mc13
Haparanda skärgårds n.p. ◆
  S 23 Mb13
Harad ☐ KSA 77 Nb14
Harad ☐ YE 77 Na15
Haradok ☐ BY 31 Me18
Haradzdźśća ☐ BY 51 Md19
Harare ☐ ZW 111 Mc22
Harbin ☐ CHN 83 Rb09
Hardangervidda n.p. ◆ N
  24 Ld15
Harihari ☐ NZ 99 Tb27
Härjedalen ☐ S 24 Lg14
Harkány ☐ H 54 Lk23
Hârlău ☐ RO 55 Md22
Harlingen ☐ NL 37 Lc19
Harlingen ☐ USA 124 Fa13
Harlow ☐ GB 35 La20
Harmancık ☐ TR 64 Me26
Härmänkyla ☐ FIN 28 Me13
Harmanli ☐ BG 57 Mc25
Harney Basin ◆ USA 122
  Dd10
Härnösand ☐ S 25 Lj14
Harper ☐ LB 105 Kc18
Harran ☐ TR 65 Mk27
Harrat al 'Uwayrid ◆ KSA
  76 Md13
Harris ◆ GB 34 Kg17
Harrisburg ☐ USA 123 Ga10
Harrogate ☐ GB 35 Kk19
Harstad ☐ N 22 Lj11
Hartberg ☐ A 52 Lh22
Hartford ☐ USA 121 Gb10
Hartlepool ☐ GB 34 Kk18
Hartola ☐ FIN 28 Md15
Harwich ☐ GB 35 La20
Haryana ☐ IND 80 Od13
Harz ▲ D 44 Lf20
Harz, N.P. ◆ D 44 Lf20
Hasakeh ☐ SYR 76 Na11
Hasançelebi ☐ TR 65 Mj26
Haselünne ☐ D 44 Ld19
Haser Gölü ◆ TR 66 Mk26
Haskovo ☐ BG 57 Mc25
Hasle ☐ DK 27 Lh18
Hassa ☐ TR 65 Mj27
Hassela ☐ S 25 Lj14
Hasselt ☐ B 37 Lc20
Haßfurt ☐ D 45 Lf20
Hassi Messaoud ☐ DZ
  106 Lb12
Hässleholm ☐ S 27 Lg17
Hastings ☐ GB 35 La20
Hastings ☐ NZ 99 Td26
Hastings ☐ USA 123 Fa10
Hatanga ◆ RUS 73 Pd04
Hatanga ☐ RUS 73 Qa04
Hatangskij zaliv ◆ RUS
  73 Qb04
Hatay ☐ TR 76 Md11
Hateg ☐ RO 54 Mb23
Ha Tinh ☐ VN 84 Qb15
Hatteras Island ◆ USA
  123 Ga11
Hattfjelldal ☐ N 25 Lh13
Hattiesburg ☐ USA 123 Fc12
Hatvan ☐ H 53 Lk22
Hat Yai ☐ THA 86 Qa17
Haud ◆ ETH 109 Na17
Hauge ☐ N 26 Lc16
Haugesund ☐ N 26 Lc16

Haukeligrend ☐ N 26 Ld16
Haukivesi ◆ FIN 28 Me14
Haukivuori ☐ FIN 28 Md14
Hauraha ☐ SOL 98 Ta21
Hautajärvi ☐ FIN 23 Me12
Haut Atlas ▲ MA 104 Kc12
Haute-Normandie ☐ F
  36 La21
Hautes Fagnes ◆ B 37 Lc20
Havana ☐ C 126 Fc14
Havøysund ☐ N 23 Mc10
Havre ☐ USA 120 Ec09
Havre-Saint-Pierre ☐ CDN
  121 Gd08
Havrylivka ☐ UA 63 Mj21
Havza ☐ TR 65 Mh25
Hawaii ☐ USA 117 Ca35
Hawaii ☐ USA 117 Cc35
Hawaiian Islands ☐ USA
  117 Ca35
Hawera ☐ NZ 99 Tc26
Hawick ☐ GB 34 Kj18
Hawke Bay ◆ NZ 99 Td26
Hawrah ☐ YE 77 Nb15
Hawthorne ☐ USA 122 Ea11
Hay ☐ AUS 97 Sa25
Haya ☐ SUD 107 Md15
Haydere ☐ TR 64 Me27
Hayes Halvø ◆ DK 118 Gc03
Haymana ☐ TR 65 Mg26
Hayrabolu ☐ TR 57 Md25
Hay River ☐ CDN 117 Ea06
Hays ☐ USA 122 Fa11
Hazebrouck ☐ F 37 Lb20
Hazen Strait ◆ CDN 118 Eb03
Head of Bight ◆ AUS 95
  Rc25
Hearst ☐ CDN 123 Fd09
Hebel ☐ CHN 82 Qc11
Hebron ☐ CDN 121 Gd07
Heby ☐ S 27 Lj16
Hecate Strait ◆ CDN 117
  Db08
Hechi ☐ CHN 84 Qb14
Hede ☐ S 24 Lg14
Hedemora ☐ S 25 Lh15
Heerenveen ☐ NL 37 Lc19
Heerlen ☐ NL 37 Ld20
Heezen Fracture Zone ◆
  140 Ea30
Hefei ☐ CHN 85 Qd12
Hegang ☐ CHN 83 Rc09
Heide ☐ D 44 Le18
Heidelberg ☐ D 45 Le21
Heilbronn ☐ D 45 Le21
Heilongjiang ☐ CHN 83 Rb09
Heima ☐ OM 77 Nd15
Heimaey ☐ IS 32 Jk14
Heimerfrontfjella ▲ 141 Kb33
Heinola ☐ FIN 28 Md15
Hejaz ◆ KSA 76 Md13
Hekimhan ☐ TR 65 Mj26
Hekla ▲ IS 32 Ka14
Hel ☐ PL 50 Lk18
Helena ☐ USA 122 Eb09
Helen Glacier ◆ 141 Pc32
Helen Reef ◆ PAL 92 Rc18
Helgoland ☐ D 44 Ld18
Hella ☐ IS 32 Jk14
Helleland ☐ N 26 Lc16
Hellesvikan ☐ N 24 Le14
Hellesylt ☐ N 24 Ld14
Helligdomsklipperne ◆ DK
  27 Lh18
Hellin ☐ E 43 Kk26
Hellisandur ☐ IS 32 Jj13
Hellnar ☐ IS 32 Jj13
Helmond ☐ NL 37 Lc20
Helmsdale ☐ GB 34 Kj16

Segment
Helodrano Atongila – Hurup

Helodrano Atongila ◌ RM 111 Nb22
Helsingborg ◌ S 26 Lg17
Helsingfors ● FIN 28 Mc15
Helsingør ◌ DK 26 Lg17
Helsinki ● FIN 28 Mc15
Helston ◌ GB 35 Kh20
Helvetinjärven kansallispuisto ◌ FIN 19 Mb14
Hemavan ◌ S 25 Lh13
Hemling ◌ S 25 Lk14
Hemmoor ◌ D 44 Le19
Hemnesberget ◌ N 22 Lg12
Hemse ◌ S 27 Lk17
Hemsedal ◌ N 24 Le15
Henan ◌ CHN 82 Qc12
Hendek ◌ TR 64 Mf25
Henderson ◌ USA 122 Eb11
Hengduan Shan ▲ CHN 84 Pd13
Hengyang ◌ CHN 85 Qc13
Heničes'k ◌ UA 63 Mh22
Hennan ◌ S 25 Lh14
Hennebont ◌ F 36 Kj22
Henningsvær ◌ N 22 Lf11
Henzada ◌ MYA 84 Pd15
Herat ◌ AFG 78 Oa12
Herborn ◌ D 45 Le20
Herceg-Novi ◌ CG 56 Lk24
Herðubreið ▲ IS 32 Kb13
Hereford ◌ GB 35 Kj19
Hereke ◌ TR 57 Me25
Hereroland ◌ NAM 110 Ld23
Herford ◌ D 44 Le19
Hermit Islands ◌ PNG 92 Sb19
Hermosillo ◌ MEX 124 Eb13
Herning ◌ DK 26 Le17
Herrera del Duque ◌ E 41 Kh26
Hersónisos Rodópou ◌ GR 56 Mb28
Hervey Bay ◌ AUS 96 Sc23
Herzberg ◌ D 44 Lg20
Hesdin ◌ F 37 Lb20
Hessel Sound ◌ CDN 118 Fa03
Hessen ◌ D 45 Le20
Hevelândia ◌ BR 132 Gd20
Hexham ◌ GB 34 Kj18
Hidalgo ◌ MEX 124 Fa14
Hidalgo del Parral ◌ MEX 124 Ec13
Hierro ◌ E 104 Ka13
High Level ◌ CDN 117 Ea07
Higüey ◌ DOM 127 Gc15
Hiidenporton kansallispuisto ◌ FIN 28 Me14
Hiiumaa ◌ EST 30 Mb16
Hildburghausen ◌ D 45 Lf20
Hildesheim ◌ D 44 Le19
Hilvan ◌ TR 65 Mk27
Hilversum ◌ NL 37 Lc19
Himachal Pradesh ◌ IND 80 Od12
Himalaya ▲ CHN/NEP 80 Od12
Himki ◌ RUS 58 Mj18
Himmetdede ◌ TR 65 Mh26
Hinchinbrook Island ▲ AUS 96 Sb22
Hindu Kush ▲ AFG 78 Ob12
Hınıs ◌ TR 66 Na26
Hinnøya ▲ N 22 Lh11
Hinojosa del Duque ◌ E 41 Kh26
Hınzır Dağı ▲ TR 65 Mj26
Hirflanlı ◌ TR 65 Mg26
Hirflanlı Baraji ⚡ TR 65 Mg26

Hirflanlı Baraji ◌ TR 65 Mg26
Hiroshima ◌ J 83 Rc12
Hirson ◌ F 37 Lc21
Hirtshals ◌ DK 26 Le17
Hisar ◌ IND 80 Od13
Hislaviči ◌ RUS 59 Mg18
Hispaniola ◌ RH/DOM 127 Gb15
Hitachi ◌ J 83 Sa11
Hitra ◌ N 24 Le14
Hizan ◌ TR 66 Nb26
Hjälmaren ◌ S 27 Lh16
Hjelmeland ◌ N 26 Ld16
Hjelset ◌ N 24 Ld14
Hjerkinn ◌ N 26 Le14
Hjo ◌ S 27 Lh16
Hjørring ◌ DK 26 Le17
Hlevacha ◌ UA 62 Mf20
Hlinsko ◌ CZ 52 Lh21
Hlobyne ◌ UA 62 Mg21
Hlohovec ◌ SK 53 Lj21
Hluchiv ◌ UA 59 Mg20
Hlusk ◌ BY 51 Me19
Hlybokae ◌ BY 31 Md18
Hnivan' ◌ UA 62 Me21
Hnúšťa ◌ SK 53 Lk21
Hobart ◌ AUS 97 Sb27
Hobbs ◌ USA 122 Ed12
Hobro ◌ DK 26 Le17
Hochgölling ▲ A 52 Lg22
Hochharz, N.P. ◌ A 44 Lf20
Ho Chi Minh, Thanh Pho ◌ VN 84 Qb16
Höchstadt ◌ D 45 Lf21
Hodh ▲ RIM 105 Kc15
Hódmezővásárhely ◌ H 53 Ma22
Hodonin ◌ CZ 53 Lj21
Hof ◌ D 45 Lf20
Höfn ◌ IS 32 Kc13
Hofors ◌ S 25 Lj15
Hofsjökull ▲ IS 32 Ka13
Hofsós ◌ IS 32 Ka13
Höga Kusten ▲ S 25 Lk14
Höganäs ◌ S 26 Lg17
Hageset ◌ N 24 Le15
Hoggar ▲ DZ 106 Lb14
Högsby ◌ S 27 Lj17
Högyész ◌ H 53 Lk22
Hohe Tauern ▲ A 52 Lg22
Hohe Tauern, N.P. ◌ A 52 Lg22
Hohot ◌ CHN 82 Qc10
Hoi An ◌ VN 85 Qb15
Hoima ◌ EAU 109 Mc18
Hokkaido ◌ J 83 Sa10
Hola Prystan' ◌ UA 62 Mg22
Holguín ◌ C 126 Ga14
Holíč ◌ SK 53 Lj21
Hollabrunn ◌ A 52 Lj21
Hollick-Kenyon Plateau ▲ 140 Ed34
Hollókö ◌ H 53 Lk22
Hollywood ◌ USA 123 Fd13
Holm ◌ N 24 Lg13
Holm ◌ RUS 30 Mf17
Holman Island ◌ CDN 118 Ea04
Hólmavík ◌ IS 32 Jk13
Holmen ◌ S 25 Ma14
Holmestrand ◌ N 26 Lf16
Holmön ▲ S 25 Ma14
Holmsk ◌ RUS 75 Sa09
Holmskij ◌ RUS 63 Mk23
Holmsund ◌ S 25 Ma14
Holmsveden ◌ S 25 Lj15
Holm-Žirkovskij ◌ RUS 59 Mg18
Holstebro ◌ DK 26 Le17
Holsteinsborg ◌ DK 119 Hb05

Holsworthy ◌ GB 35 Kh20
Holyhead ◌ GB 35 Kh19
Holzminden ◌ D 44 Le20
Hombori ◌ RMM 105 Kd15
Home Bay ◌ CDN 119 Gc05
Homel' ◌ BY 59 Mf19
Homer ◌ USA 116 Cb07
Hommelvik ◌ N 24 Lf14
Homs ◌ SYR 76 Md12
Homutovka ◌ RUS 59 Mh20
Honduras ◌ HN 125 Fc15
Hønefoss ◌ N 24 Lf15
Hong Kong ◌ CHN 85 Qc14
Honiara ★ SOL 93 Sd20
Honiton ◌ GB 35 Kj20
Honningsvåg ◌ N 23 Mc10
Honolulu ◌ USA 117 Cb35
Honshu ◌ J 83 Rd11
Honuu ◌ RUS 74 Sa05
Hoogeveen ◌ NL 37 Ld19
Höör ◌ S 26 Lg18
Hoorn ◌ NL 37 Lc19
Hopa ◌ TR 66 Na25
Hopen ◌ N 22 Lh07
Hoper ◌ RUS 61 Na20
Hopseidet ◌ N 23 Md10
Horasan ◌ TR 76 Na10
Horasan ◌ TR 66 Nb25
Hóra Sfakion ◌ GR 57 Mc28
Horb ◌ D 45 Le21
Hörby ◌ S 27 Lg18
Horgoš ◌ SR 54 Lk22
Horki ◌ BY 31 Mf18
Horlick Mountains ▲ 140 Ec36
Horlivka ◌ UA 63 Mk21
Hornavan ▲ S 22 Lj12
Hornbjarg ◌ IS 32 Jj12
Hornsea ◌ GB 35 Kk19
Horochiv ◌ UA 51 Mc20
Horodenka ◌ UA 51 Mc21
Horodnja ◌ UA 59 Mf20
Horodnycja ◌ UA 51 Md20
Horodok ◌ UA 51 Md21
Horodyšče ◌ UA 62 Mf21
Horsens ◌ DK 26 Le18
Horsham ◌ AUS 97 Sa26
Horsham ◌ GB 35 Kk20
Horten ◌ N 26 Lf16
Hoskins ◌ PNG 93 Sc20
Hospet ◌ IND 81 Od15
Hotan ◌ CHN 79 Pa11
Hotazel ◌ ZA 110 Ma24
Hoting ◌ S 25 Lj13
Hot Springs ◌ USA 122 Ed10
Hot Springs ◌ USA 123 Fd12
Houghton ◌ USA 120 Fc09
Houma ◌ USA 123 Fb13
Houston ◌ USA 123 Fa13
Hova ◌ S 27 Lh16
Høyanger ◌ N 24 Ld15
Hoyerswerda ◌ D 44 Lh20
Høylandet ◌ N 24 Lg13
Hradec Králové ◌ CZ 52 Lh20
Hradzy'k ◌ UA 62 Mg21
Hranice ◌ CZ 53 Lj21
Hraničné ◌ SK 53 Ma21
hrebet Pekulnej ▲ RUS 74 Td05
hrebet Suntar-Hajata ▲ RUS 75 Rd04
hrebet Tukuringra ▲ RUS 75 Rb08
hrebet Turana ▲ RUS 75 Rc08
hrebet Ulahan-Bom ▲ RUS 75 Rd06
Hrebinka ◌ UA 62 Mg20

Hrissoúpoli ◌ GR 57 Mc25
Hrodna ◌ BY 31 Mb19
Hrubieszów ◌ PL 51 Mb20
Hrušuvacha ◌ UA 63 Mj21
Hsinchu ◌ RC 85 Ra14
Huacho ◌ PE 133 Ga21
Hua Hin ◌ THA 86 Pd16
Huai'an ◌ CHN 83 Qd12
Huaihua ◌ CHN 84 Qb13
Huainan ◌ CHN 85 Qd12
Hualien ◌ RC 85 Ra14
Huambo ◌ ANG 110 Ld21
Huancane ◌ PE 133 Gc22
Huancavelica ◌ PE 133 Gb21
Huancayo ◌ PE 133 Ga21
Huang He ⚡ CHN 82 Qb10
Huangshan ◌ CHN 85 Qd13
Huangshi ◌ CHN 85 Qd12
Huangyuan ◌ CHN 82 Qa11
Huánuco ◌ PE 133 Ga20
Huara ◌ RCH 133 Gc22
Huaral ◌ PE 133 Ga21
Huaráz ◌ PE 133 Ga20
Huarmey ◌ PE 133 Ga21
Huasco ◌ RCH 136 Gb24
Hubei ◌ CHN 84 Qb12
Hubli ◌ IND 81 Od15
Hubynycha ◌ UA 63 Mh21
Hudiksvall ◌ S 25 Lj15
Hudson Bay ◌ CDN 120 Ed08
Hudson Bay ◌ CDN 120 Fa08
Hudson Mountains ▲ 140 Fa33
Hudson Strait ≋ CDN 119 Gb06
Hue ◌ VN 84 Qb15
Huedin ◌ RO 54 Mb22
Huelma ◌ E 41 Kj27
Huelva ◌ E 41 Kg27
Huéneja ◌ E 41 Kj27
Huércal-Overa ◌ E 43 Kk27
Huesca ◌ E 42 Kk24
Huéscar ◌ E 41 Kj27
Huete ◌ E 42 Kj25
Hughenden ◌ AUS 96 Sa23
Huib-Hochplato ▲ NAM 110 Ld24
Huittinen ◌ FIN 22 Mb15
Huizou ◌ CHN 85 Qc14
Huljajpole ◌ UA 63 Mj22
Hultsfred ◌ S 27 Lh17
Hulun Nur ▲ CHN 82 Qd09
Humaitá ◌ BR 133 Gd20
Humansdorp ◌ ZA 110 Ma25
Humbe ◌ ANG 110 Lc22
Humboldt Gletscher ≋ DK 118 Gd03
Humpolec ◌ CZ 52 Lh21
Humppila ◌ FIN 22 Mb15
Hun ◌ LAR 106 Ld13
Húnaflói ≋ IS 32 Jk13
Hunan ◌ CHN 85 Qc13
Hundorp ◌ N 24 Lf15
Hunedoara ◌ RO 54 Mb23
Hungary ◌ H 53 Lk22
Hunsrück ▲ D 45 Ld21
Huntington ◌ USA 123 Fd11
Huntly ◌ GB 34 Kj17
Huntsville ◌ CDN 121 Ga09
Huntsville ◌ USA 123 Fc12
Hunyuan ◌ CHN 82 Qc11
Huon Gulf ≋ PNG 93 Sb20
Huon Peninsula ▲ PNG 92 Sb20
Hurezani ◌ RO 54 Mb23
Hurghada ◌ ET 107 Mc13
Huron ◌ USA 122 Fa10
Hurtiguruta ▲ N 24 Lf13
Hurup ◌ DK 26 Le17

Hurzuf ◻ UA 63 Mh23
Húsavík ◻ IS 32 Kb12
Huskvarna ◻ S 27 Lh14
Husum ◻ D 44 Le18
Husum ◻ S 25 Lk14
Hutchinson ◻ USA 123 Fa11
Hvalynsk ◻ RUS 60 Ne19
Hvammstangi ◻ IS 32 Jk13
Hvannadalshnúkur ▲ IS 32 Kb13
Hvar ▲ HR 47 Lj24
Hvastoviči ◻ RUS 59 Mh19
Hverageрði ◻ IS 32 Ja13
Hvittingfoss ◻ N 26 Le16
Hvolsvöllur ◻ IS 32 Jk14
Hvorostjanka ◻ RUS 60 Ne19
Hwange ◻ ZW 110 Mb22
Hyderabad ● IND 81 Od15
Hyderabad ◻ PAK 80 Ob13
Hyères ◻ F 39 Ld24

I

Iaşi ◻ RO 55 Md23
Iasmos ◻ GR 57 Mc25
Ibadan ◻ WAN 105 La17
Ibague ◻ CO 132 Ga18
Ibarra ◻ EC 132 Ga18
Ibb ◻ YE 77 Na16
Ibiza = Eivissa ◻ E 43 La26
Ibotirama ◻ BR 135 Hd21
Ibrjaevo ◻ RUS 60 Ng18
Ica ◻ PE 133 Ga21
İçel ◻ TR 65 Mh27
Iceland ◻ IS 32 La13
Iceland ◻ IS 32 Ka13
İçeriçumra ◻ TR 64 Mg27
Ice Stream A ❄ 140 Cd35
Ice Stream B ❄ 140 Cc35
Ice Stream C ❄ 140 Cb35
Ice Stream D ❄ 140 Cd35
Ice Stream E ❄ 140 Cd35
İçnja ◻ UA 62 Mg20
Idaho ◻ USA 122 Ea10
Idaho Falls ◻ USA 122 Eb10
Idar-Oberstein ◻ D 45 Ld21
Idiofa ◻ RDC 108 Ld19
Idlib ◻ SYR 76 Md11
İdra ◻ GR 57 Mb27
İdra ◻ GR 57 Mb27
İdre ◻ S 24 Lg15
Idrija ◻ SLO 47 Lh23
Keipene ◻ LV 30 Mc17
Ieper ◻ B 37 Lb20
Ierápetra ◻ GR 57 Mc28
Ifalik Atoll ◻ FSM 92 Sa17
Ife ◻ WAN 105 La17
Iferouâne ◻ RN 106 Lb15
Ifjord ◻ N 23 Md10
Igarka ◻ RUS 73 Pb04
Iglesias ◻ I 48 Le26
Ignatovo ◻ RUS 29 Mj15
İğneada ◻ TR 57 Md25
Igoumenitsa ◻ GR 56 Ma26
Iguala ◻ MEX 124 Fa15
Ihiala ◻ WAN 108 La17
Ihosy ◻ RM 111 Nb23
Iisalmi ◻ FIN 28 Md14
Ijebu-Ode ◻ WAN 105 La17
IJsselmeer ≋ NL 37 Lc19
Ikaria ◻ GR 57 Md27
Ikast ◻ DK 26 Le17
Ikela ◻ RDC 108 Ma19
Ikerssuaq ◻ DK 119 Ja05
Ikh Nuuruudyn Khotgor ≋ MNG 79 Pc09
Iłża ◻ PL 50 Ma20

Ilagan ◻ RP 85 Ra15
Iława ◻ PL 50 Lk19
İle ◻ KZ 79 Od10
Île Ambrym ◻ VU 98 Tb22
Île Aoba ◻ VU 98 Tb22
Île Aoba ◻ VU 98 Tb22
Île Aurora ◻ VU 98 Tb22
Ilebo ◻ RDC 108 Ma19
Île Clipperton ◻ F 124 Ec16
Île d'Anticosti ◻ CDN 121 Gd09
Île de France ◻ F 37 Lb21
Île de Jerba ◻ TN 106 Lc12
Île de la Madeleine ◻ CDN 121 Gd09
Île des Pins ◻ F 98 Tb23
Île Epi ◻ VU 98 Tb22
Île Erromango ◻ VU 98 Tb22
Île Europa ◻ F 111 Na23
Île Futuna ◻ F 98 Ua21
Île Gaua ◻ VU 98 Tb22
Île Joinville ≋ 140 Hb31
Île Juán de Nova ◻ F 111 Na22
Ileksinskaja ◻ RUS 29 Mk15
Île Mallicolo ◻ VU 98 Tb22
Île Mallicolo ◻ VU 98 Tb22
Île Pentecôte ◻ VU 98 Tb22
Ilesa ◻ WAN 105 La17
Île Santo ◻ VU 98 Tb22
Île Santo ◻ VU 98 Tb22
Îles Banks ◻ VU 98 Tb21
Île Belep ◻ F 98 Ta22
Îles de Kerkenah ≋ TN 106 Lc12
Îles d'Hyères ≋ F 39 Ld24
Îles Glorieuses ◻ F 111 Nb21
Îles Loyauté ≋ F 98 Tb23
Îles Torres ◻ VU 98 Tb21
Îles Wallis ◻ F 98 Ua21
Île Tanna ◻ VU 98 Tb22
Île Vanoua Lava ◻ VU 98 Tb21
Île Vaté ◻ VU 98 Tb22
Ilfracombe ◻ GB 35 Kh20
Ilgaz ◻ TR 65 Mg25
Ilgaz Dağı Milli Parkı ☘ TR 65 Mg25
Ilgaz Dağları ▲ TR 65 Mg25
Ilgın ◻ TR 64 Mf26
Ilha Caviana de Fora ≋ BR 134 Hc18
Ilha de Maracá ≋ BR 134 Hb18
Ilha de Marajó ≋ BR 134 Hc19
Ilha de Santa Catarina ≋ BR 135 Hc24
Ilha de São João ≋ BR 134 Hd19
Ilha de São Sebastião ≋ BR 135 Hc23
Ilha Desertas ☘ P 104 Ka12
Ilha do Bananal ≋ BR 134 Hb21
Ilha Fernando de Noronha ≋ BR 128 Ja10
Ilha Grande de Gurupá ≋ BR 134 Hb19
Ilhas do Bazaruto ☘ MOC 111 Md23
Ilhas Selvagens ☘ P 104 Ka12
Ilhéus ◻ BR 135 Ja21
Iliç ◻ TR 66 Mk26
Iligan ◻ RP 85 Ra17
Il'ino ◻ RUS 59 Mf18
Il'insko-Zaborskoe ◻ RUS 60 Nc17

Ilirska Bistrica ◻ SLO 47 Lh23
Illiči'vs'k ◻ UA 62 Mf22
Illinois ◻ USA 123 Fc10
Illueca ◻ E 42 Kk25
Ilmenau ◻ D 45 Lf20
Iloilo ◻ RP 85 Ra16
Ilok ◻ HR 47 Lk23
Ilomantsi ◻ FIN 29 Mf14
Ilorin ◻ WAN 105 La17
Ilovlja ◻ RUS 61 Nc20
Ilsbo ◻ S 25 Lj15
Ilulissat ◻ DK 119 Hb05
Ilulissat Icefjord ≋ DK 119 Hc05
İmamoğlu ◻ TR 65 Mh27
Imatra ◻ FIN 28 Me15
Immenstadt ◻ D 45 Lf22
Imola ◻ I 46 Lf23
Imotski ◻ HR 47 Lj24
Imperatriz ◻ BR 134 Hc20
Imperia ◻ I 46 Le24
Imphal ● IND 84 Pc14
İmroz ◻ TR 57 Mc25
In Amenas ◻ DZ 106 Lb13
Inanwatan ◻ RI 92 Rc19
Inari ◻ FIN 23 Md11
Inca ◻ E 43 Lb26
İncebel Dağları ▲ TR 65 Mj26
İnce Burnu ▲ TR 65 Mh24
İncekum Burnu ▲ TR 65 Mg27
Indalsälven ≋ S 25 Lh14
Indaw ◻ MYA 84 Pd14
India ● IND 81 Od15
Indiana ◻ USA 123 Fc10
Indianapolis ● USA 123 Fc11
Indian Ocean ≋ 81 Pa18
Indigirka ≋ RUS 74 Sb05
Indispensable Reefs ≋ SOL 96 Sd21
Indispensable Str. ≋ SOL 93 Ta20
Indonesia ■ RI 86 Qb19
Indore ◻ IND 80 Od14
Indre Arna ◻ N 24 Lc15
Indus ≋ PAK 80 Ob13
Indus ≋ PAK 80 Oc12
Inebolu ◻ TR 65 Mg25
İnegöl ◻ TR 57 Me25
Ineu ◻ RO 54 Ma22
Ingelstad ◻ S 27 Lh17
Ingeniero Jacobacci ◻ RA 137 Gc27
Ingham ◻ AUS 96 Sb22
Ingolstadt ◻ D 45 Lf21
Ingraj Bazar ◻ IND 80 Pb13
Inhambane ◻ MOC 111 Md23
Inhul ≋ UA 62 Mg22
Inja ◻ RUS 79 Pb08
Injune ◻ AUS 96 Sb24
Inle Lake ≋ MYA 84 Pd14
Inn ≋ D/A 45 Lg21
Innbygda ◻ N 24 Lg15
Inndyr ◻ N 22 Lh12
Inner Hebrides ≋ GB 34 Kg17
Inner Mongolia ◻ CHN 82 Qa10
Inneston ◻ AUS 97 Rd26
Innsbruck ◻ A 45 Lf22
Innset ◻ N 22 Lk11
Inowrocław ◻ PL 50 Lk19
In Salah ◻ DZ 104 La13
Insar ◻ RUS 60 Nc19
Institute Ice Stream ❄ 140 Gb35
Insula Mică a Brăilei, P.N. ☘ RO 55 Md23
Însurăţei ◻ RO 55 Md23

Inta ◻ RUS 72 Nd05
Interior Highlands ▲ USA 123 Fb11
Interior Plains ▲ USA 123 Fb11
Interlaken ◻ CH 45 Ld22
International Falls ◻ USA 120 Fb09
Inukjuak ◻ CDN 120 Ga07
Inuvik ◻ CDN 116 Db05
Invercargill ◻ NZ 99 Tb28
Invergordon ◻ GB 34 Kh17
Invermoriston ◻ GB 34 Kh17
Inverness ◻ GB 34 Kh17
Inyangani ▲ ZW 111 Mc22
Inza ◻ RUS 60 Nd19
İnžavino ◻ RUS 61 Nb19
Ioánina ◻ GR 56 Ma26
Ionian Islands ≋ GR 56 Lk26
Ios ◻ GR 57 Mc27
Ios ◻ GR 57 Mc27
Iowa ◻ USA 123 Fb10
Ipameri ◻ BR 135 Hc22
Ipatinga ◻ BR 135 Hd22
Ipatinga ◻ BR 135 Hd22
Ipoh ● MAL 86 Qa18
Ipswich ◻ AUS 96 Sc24
Ipswich ◻ GB 35 La19
Iqaluit ◻ CDN 119 Gc06
Iqe ◻ CHN 79 Pc11
Iquique ◻ RCH 136 Gb23
Iquitos ◻ PE 132 Gb19
Iracoubo ◻ F 134 Hb17
Iráklia ◻ GR 57 Mc27
Iráklio ◻ GR 56 Mc28
Iran ■ IR 77 Nd12
Iran Range ▲ MAL/RI 87 Qc18
Iran Shahr ◻ IR 77 Oa13
Irapuato ◻ MEX 124 Ed14
Iraq ■ IRQ 76 Na12
Irbit ◻ RUS 72 Oa07
Ireland ■ IRL 33 Kf19
Iringa ◻ EAT 109 Md20
Iriri ≋ BR 134 Hb19
Irish Sea ≋ GB 35 Kh19
Irituia ◻ BR 134 Hc19
Irklijiv ◻ UA 62 Mg21
Irkutsk ◻ RUS 82 Qa08
Iron Knob ◻ AUS 97 Rd25
Irrawaddy ≋ MYA 84 Pd14
Iršava ◻ UA 53 Mb21
Irtyš ≋ RUS 72 Oc07
Irtyš ◻ KZ 79 Pa08
Irtysh ≋ RUS 72 Oc07
Irun ◻ E 42 Kk24
Iruñea ◻ E 42 Kk24
Irurzun ◻ E 42 Kk24
Irvine ◻ GB 34 Kh18
Isabel Rubio ◻ C 126 Fd14
Isaccea ◻ RO 55 Me23
İsafjarðardjúp ≋ IS 32 Jj12
İsafjörður ◻ IS 32 Jj12
Isar ≋ D 45 Lg21
Iscar ◻ E 40 Kh25
Ischehisar ◻ TR 64 Mf26
Ischia ◻ I 49 Lg25
Isère ≋ F 39 Ld23
Isérnia ◻ I 49 Lh25
İseyin ◻ WAN 105 La17
Isfahan ◻ IR 76 Nc12
Ishinomaki ◻ J 83 Sa11
İšim ◻ RUS 72 Ob07
Isiolo ◻ EAK 109 Md18
Isiro ◻ RDC 109 Mb18
İskenderun ◻ TR 76 Md11
İskenderun ◻ TR 65 Mj27
İskenderun Körfezi ≋ TR 65 Mh27

İskilip ☐ TR 65 Mh25
Isla Campana ☐ RCH 137 Ga28
Isla Cedros ☐ MEX 124 Ea13
Isla de Almagro ☐ RCH 137 Ga29
Isla de Bioco ☐ GQ 108 Lb18
Isla de Chiloé ☐ RCH 137 Gb27
Isla de Cozumel ☐ MEX 125 Fc14
Isla de Guadelupe ☐ MEX 124 Ea13
Isla de la Juventud ☐ C 126 Fd14
Isla de los Estados ☐ RA 137 Gd29
Isla de Malpelo ☐ CO 132 Fd18
Isla de Margarita ☐ YV 127 Gd16
Isla de Providencia ☐ CO 126 Fd16
Isla de San Andrés ☐ CO 126 Fd16
Isla Desolación ☐ RCH 137 Gb29
Isla Duque de York ☐ RCH 137 Ga29
Isla Hanover ☐ RCH 137 Ga29
İslahiye ☐ TR 65 Mj27
Isla Hoste ☐ RCH 137 Gc30
Isla Isabela ☐ EC 133 Fb19
Isla Londonderry ☐ RCH 137 Gb30
Islamabad ● PAK 80 Oc12
Isla Madre de Dios ☐ RCH 137 Ga29
Isla Mocha ☐ RCH 137 Gb26
Isla Navarino ☐ RCH 137 Gc30
Island Lake ☐ CDN 120 Fb08
Isla P.Lynch ☐ RCH 137 Ga28
Isla Puna ☐ EC 132 Fd19
Isla San Cristóbal ☐ EC 133 Fc19
Isla Santa Cruz ☐ EC 133 Fb19
Isla Santa Inés ☐ RCH 137 Gb29
Islas de la Bahia ☐ HN 125 Fc15
Islas del Cisne ☐ HN 126 Fd15
Islas de los Desventurados ☐ RCH 129 Fb12
Islas de Sotavento ☐ YV 127 Gc16
Islas los Roques ☐ YV 127 Gc16
Islas Malvinas ☐ GB 137 Gd29
Islas Marias ☐ MEX 124 Ec14
Islas Revillagigedo ☐ MEX 124 Eb15
Islas Revillagigedo ☐ MEX 124 Eb15
Islas Wollaston ☐ RCH 137 Gc30
Isla Trinidad ☐ RA 137 Gd26
Isla Wellington ☐ RCH 137 Ga28
Islay ☐ GB 33 Kg18
Isle of Lewis ☐ GB 34 Kg16
Isle of Man ☐ GB 34 Kh18
Isle of Mull ☐ GB 34 Kg17
Isle of Wight ☐ GB 35 Kk20
Isles of Scilly ☐ GB 35 Kg21

Ismâiliya ☐ ET 107 Mc12
Isna ☐ ET 107 Mc13
Isojärven kansallispuisto ✿ FIN 28 Mc15
Isoka ☐ Z 111 Mc21
Ísola d'Elba ☐ I 46 Lf24
Ísola del Giglio ☐ I 46 Lf24
Ísola di Capo Rizzuto ☐ I 49 Lj26
Ísola di Capraia ☐ I 46 Le24
Ísola di Capri ☐ I 49 Lh25
Ísola di Pantelleria ☐ I 48 Lf27
Ísola d'Ischia ☐ I 49 Lg25
Ísola Lipari ☐ I 49 Lh26
Ísola Pianosa ☐ I 46 Lf24
Ísola Vulcano ☐ I 49 Lh26
Isparta ☐ TR 64 Mf27
Íspica ☐ I 49 Lh27
İspir ☐ TR 66 Na25
Israel ◼ IL 107 Mc12
Israelite Bay ☐ AUS 95 Ra25
Issano ☐ GUY 132 Ha17
Issoire ☐ F 38 Lb23
Issoudun ☐ F 38 La22
Isthmus of Kra ▲ THA 86 Pd16
Isthmus of Panama ▲ PA 132 Ga17
Isthmus of Tehuantepec ▲ MEX 125 Fd15
Istiéa ☐ GR 56 Mb26
Istra ☐ RUS 58 Mj18
Istres ☐ F 39 Lc24
Istria ☁ SLO/HR 47 Lg23
Isulan ☐ RP 85 Ra17
Itaberaba ☐ BR 135 Hd21
Itabira ☐ BR 135 Hd22
Itabuna ☐ BR 135 Ja21
Itagüí ☐ CO 132 Ga17
Itäisen Suomenlahden kansallispuisto ✿ FIN 28 Md15
Itaituba ☐ BR 134 Ha19
Itajaí ☐ BR 135 Hc24
Italy ◼ I 48 Lg25
Itanagar ☐ IND 84 Pc13
Itapajé ☐ BR 134 Ja19
Itapebi ☐ BR 135 Ja22
Itéa ☐ GR 56 Mb26
Ithaca ☐ USA 123 Ga16
Itháki ☐ GR 56 Ma26
Itháki ☐ GR 56 Ma26
Iti N.P. ✿ GR 56 Mb26
Ittoqqortoormiit ☐ DK 138 Jd04
Ituiutaba ☐ BR 135 Hc22
Itula ☐ RDC 109 Mb19
Itumbiara ☐ BR 135 Hc22
Itzehoe ☐ D 44 Le19
Ivacévičy ☐ BY 51 Mc19
Ivajlovgrad ☐ BG 57 Md25
Ivalo ☐ FIN 23 Md11
Ivanava ☐ BY 51 Mc19
Ivangorod ☐ RUS 30 Me16
Ivanhoe ☐ AUS 97 Sa25
Ivanić Grad ☐ HR 47 Lj23
Ivanivka ☐ UA 63 Mh22
Ivankiv ☐ UA 62 Me20
Ivano-Frankivs'k ☐ UA 51 Mc21
Ivano-Frankove ☐ UA 53 Mb21
Ivanovo ☐ RUS 58 Na17
Ivarrud ☐ N 25 Lh13
Ívesti ☐ RO 55 Md23
Ivindo ☁ G 108 Lc18
Ivjanec ☐ BY 51 Md19
Ivje ☐ BY 51 Mc19

Ivory Coast ◼ CI 105 Kc17
Ivory Coast ☐ CI 105 Kc18
Ivrea ☐ I 46 Ld23
Ivrindi ☐ TR 57 Md26
Ivujivik ☐ CDN 119 Ga06
Iwaki ☐ J 83 Sa11
Iyidere ☐ TR 66 Na25
Izborsk ☐ RUS 30 Md17
Iževsk ☐ RUS 72 Nc07
Izjum ☐ UA 63 Mj21
Izmajil ☐ UA 55 Me23
İzmir ☐ TR 57 Md26
İzmit ☐ TR 57 Me25
İznik ☐ TR 57 Me25
Izu-Shoto ☐ J 83 Rd12

J

Jaala ☐ FIN 28 Md15
Jabalpur ☐ IND 80 Pa14
Jabiru ☐ AUS 94 Rc21
Jablanica ☐ BG 55 Mc24
Jablanica ☐ BIH 47 Lj24
Jablunkov ☐ CZ 53 Lk21
Jabugo ☐ E 41 Kg27
Jaca ☐ E 42 Kk24
Jáchal ☐ RA 136 Gc24
Jackson ☐ USA 123 Fd12
Jackson ☐ USA 123 Fc11
Jackson, Mount ▲ 140 Gd33
Jacksonville ☐ USA 123 Fd12
Jaen ☐ PE 133 Ga21
Jaén ☐ E 41 Kj27
Jaffna ☐ CL 81 Pa17
Jagdalpur ☐ IND 81 Pa15
Jagdaqi ☐ CHN 83 Ra08
Jagodnoe ☐ RUS 74 Sb06
Jahotyn ☐ UA 62 Mf20
Jaipur ☐ IND 80 Od13
Jaisalmer ☐ IND 80 Oc13
Jajce ☐ BIH 47 Lj23
Jakarta ● RI 86 Qb20
Jäkkvik ☐ S 22 Lj12
Jakobabad ☐ PAK 80 Ob13
Jakobshavn ☐ DK 119 Hb05
Jakobstad ☐ FIN 19 Mb14
Jakovlevo ☐ RUS 59 Mj20
Jakunvara ☐ RUS 29 Mf14
Jakutsk ☐ RUS 75 Rb06
Jalalabad ☐ AFG 80 Oc12
Jalance ☐ E 43 Kk26
Jalgaon ☐ IND 80 Od14
Jalisco ☐ MEX 124 Ed14
Jamaame ☐ SP 109 Na18
Jamaica ◼ JA 126 Ga15
Jamaica Channel ☁ 126 Ga15
Jamalpur ☐ BD 80 Pb14
Jambi ☐ RI 86 Qa19
Jambol ☐ BG 55 Md24
James Bay ☁ CDN 120 Fd08
Jamestown ☐ USA 120 Fa09
Jamestown ☐ USA 123 Ga10
Jämjö ☐ S 27 Lh17
Jammu ☐ IND 80 Od12
Jammu and Kashmir ☐ IND 80 Od12
Jamnagar ☐ IND 80 Oc14
Jampil' ☐ UA 62 Me21
Jämsä ☐ FIN 28 Mc15
Jamshedpur ☐ IND 80 Pb14
Jämtland ☁ S 25 Lh14
Jana ☁ RUS 74 Rd05
Jangkar ☐ RI 87 Qb20
Janjina ☐ HR 47 Lj24
Jano-Indigirskaja nízmennost' ☁ RUS 74 Sa04

Janos ☐ MEX 122 Ec12
Janów Lubelski ☐ PL 51 Mb20
Janskij zaliv ☁ RUS 74 Rd04
Janskoe ploskogor'e ☁ RUS 74 Rc05
Jantra ☁ BG 55 Mc24
Januária ☐ BR 135 Hd22
Japan ◼ J 83 Rd12
Japan Basin ☁ 83 Rc10
Japan Trench ☁ 83 Sa11
Japurá ☁ BR 132 Gc19
Jaransk ☐ RUS 60 Nd17
Jarcevo ☐ RUS 59 Mg18
Jaremča ☐ UA 51 Mc21
Jari ☁ BR 134 Hb18
Jarmolynci ☐ UA 51 Md21
Järna ☐ S 25 Lh15
Jarocin ☐ PL 50 Lj20
Jaromêř ☐ CZ 52 Lh20
Jaroslavl' ☐ RUS 58 Mk17
Jarosław ☐ PL 51 Mb20
Järpen ☐ S 24 Lg14
Järvenpää ☐ FIN 28 Mc15
Järvsö ☐ S 25 Lj15
Jasa Tornič ☐ SR 54 Ma23
Jasenskaja ☐ RUS 63 Mk22
Jašiünai ☐ LT 31 Mc18
Jasło ☐ PL 50 Ma21
Jasmund, N.P. ✿ D 44 Lg18
Jasnogorsk ☐ RUS 59 Mj18
Jasper ☐ CDN 117 Ea08
Jastrowie ☐ PL 50 Lj19
Jasynuvata ☐ UA 63 Mj21
Jászapáti ☐ H 53 Ma22
Jatai ☐ BR 135 Hb22
Jättendal ☐ S 25 Lj15
Jaú ☐ BR 135 Hc23
Java ☁ RI 86 Qb20
Javalambre ☁ E 43 Kk25
Javari ☁ BR 133 Gc20
Java Sea ☁ RI 86 Qb19
Java Trench ☁ 86 Qa20
Jávea = Xàbia ☐ E 43 La26
Javoriv ☐ UA 53 Mb21
Javorivskyj N.P. ✿ UA 53 Mb21
Jawor ☐ PL 50 Lj20
Jayapura ☐ RI 92 Sa19
Jaza'ir Farasan ☁ KSA 77 Na15
Jazirat Al Bahrain ☁ KSA 77 Nb13
Jazireh-ye Kark ☁ IR 77 Nc13
Jazireh-ye Kish ☁ IR 77 Nc13
Jebel ☐ RO 54 Ma23
Jędrzejów ☐ PL 50 Ma20
Jefferson City ☐ USA 123 Fb11
Jeju ☐ ROK 83 Rb12
Jeju Do ☁ ROK 83 Rb12
Jēkabpils ☐ LV 31 Mc17
Jelanec' ☐ UA 62 Mf22
Jelbart Ice Shelf ☐ 141 Kd33
Jelenia Góra ☐ PL 50 Lh20
Jelgava ☐ LV 30 Mb17
Jena ☐ D 44 Lf20
Jenakijeve ☐ UA 63 Mk21
Jendouba ☐ TN 106 Lb11
Jenluise Bank ☁ 141 Qb31
Jeonju ☐ ROK 83 Rb11
Jepara ☐ RI 86 Qc20
Jequié ☐ BR 135 Hd21
Jérémie ☐ RH 127 Gb15
Jeremoabo ☐ BR 135 Ja21
Jerez de la Frontera ☐ E 41 Kg27
Jerez de los Caballeros ☐ E 41 Kg26

Jericho ☐ AUS 96 Sb23
Jericho ☐ IL 76 Md12
Jerramungup ☐ AUS 95 Qd25
Jerusalem ● IL 76 Md12
Jesenik ☐ CZ 53 Lj20
Jesi ☐ I 47 Lg24
Jessheim ☐ N 24 Lf15
Jever ☐ D 44 Ld19
Jevnaker ☐ N 24 Lf15
Jevpatorija ☐ UA 63 Mg23
Jewish Autonomous Region
  ☐ RUS 83 Rc09
Jhang ☐ PAK 80 Oc12
Jhansi ☐ IND 80 Pa14
Jharkhand ☐ IND 80 Pa14
Jiamusi ☐ CHN 83 Rc09
Ji'an ☐ CHN 85 Qd13
Jiangsu ☐ CHN 83 Qd12
Jiangxi ☐ CHN 85 Qd13
Jiaojiang ☐ CHN 85 Ra13
Jiayuguan ☐ CHN 79 Pd11
Jibou ☐ RO 54 Mb22
Jiddah ☐ KSA 76 Md14
Jičín ☐ CZ 52 Lh20
Jieznas ☐ LT 31 Mc18
Jihlava ☐ CZ 52 Lh21
Jilib ☐ SP 109 Na18
Jilin ☐ CHN 83 Rb10
Jilin ☐ CHN 83 Rb10
Jima ☐ ETH 109 Md17
Jimbolia ☐ RO 54 Ma23
Jiménez ☐ MEX 124 Ed13
Jinan ☐ CHN 83 Qd11
Jindřichův Hradec ☐ CZ
  52 Lh21
Jingdezhen ☐ CHN 85 Qd13
Jinghong ☐ CHN 84 Qa14
Jinhua ☐ CHN 85 Qd13
Jining ☐ CHN 82 Qc10
Jining ☐ CHN 83 Qd11
Jinja ☐ EAU 109 Mc18
Jinsha Jiang ☐ CHN 84 Pd12
Jinsha Jiang ☐ CHN 84 Qa13
Jinzhou ☐ CHN 83 Ra10
Ji-Paraná ☐ BR 133 Gd21
Jipijapa ☐ EC 132 Fd19
Jishou ☐ CHN 84 Qb13
Jiujiang ☐ CHN 85 Qd13
Jiulong ☐ CHN 85 Qc14
Jiuzhaigou Valley ☐ CHN
  84 Qa12
Jixi ☐ CHN 83 Rc09
Jizzax ☐ UZ 78 Ob10
João Pessoa ☐ BR 134 Jb20
Jodhpur ☐ IND 80 Oc13
Joensuu ☐ FIN 28 Me14
Jõgeva ☐ EST 30 Md16
Johannesburg ☐ ZA 110
  Mb24
Johnson City ☐ USA 123 Fd11
Johor Bahru ☐ MAL 86 Qa18
Joigny ☐ F 38 Lb22
Joinville ☐ BR 135 Hc24
Joinville ☐ F 37 Lc21
Jokkmokk ☐ S 22 Lk12
Jökulsá á Fjöllum ☐ IS
  32 Kb13
Jökulsárlón ☐ IS 32 Kb14
Jolo ☐ RP 85 Ra17
Jolo ☐ RP 85 Ra17
Jonesboro ☐ USA 123 Fb11
Jones Mountains ▲ 140 Fb33
Jones Sound ☐ CDN 118
  Fc03
Joniškis ☐ LT 31 Mb17
Jönköping ☐ S 27 Lh17
Jonzac ☐ F 38 Kk23
Joplin ☐ USA 123 Fb11
Jordan ☐ JOR 76 Md12

Jorhat ☐ IND 84 Pc13
Jörn ☐ S 25 Ma13
Jørpeland ☐ N 26 Ld16
Jos ☐ WAN 108 Lb16
Joškar-Ola ☐ RUS 72 Nb07
Joškar-Ola ☐ RUS 60 Nd17
Jos Plateau ☐ WAN 108 Lb17
Josselin ☐ F 36 Kj22
Jostedalsbreen ☐ N 24 Ld15
Jostedalsbreen n.p. ☐ N
  24 Ld15
Jotunheimen n.p. ☐ N
  24 Le15
Joyce, Mount ▲ 141 Sd34
Juan de Fuca Strait ☐ USA
  122 Dd09
Juanjui ☐ PE 133 Ga20
Juazeiro ☐ BR 134 Hd20
Juazeiro do Norte ☐ BR
  134 Ja20
Juba ☐ SUD 109 Mc18
Jubany ☐ 140 Ha31
Jubilee Lake ☐ AUS 95 Rb24
Juchavičy ☐ BY 31 Me18
Judenburg ☐ A 52 Lh22
Juelsminde ☐ DK 26 Lf18
Jugorskij p-ov ☐ RUS 72
  Oa05
Juhnov ☐ RUS 59 Mh18
Juiz de Fora ☐ BR 135 Hd23
Jujuy ☐ RA 136 Gc23
Jukagirskoe ploskogor'e ☐
  RUS 74 Sc05
Jukkasjärvi ☐ S 22 Ma12
Juliaca ☐ PE 133 Gb22
Julia Creek ☐ AUS 96 Sa23
Julianehåb ☐ DK 119 Hc06
Juma ☐ RUS 29 Mg13
Jumilla ☐ E 43 Kk26
Juneau ☐ USA 117 Db07
Junín ☐ RA 136 Gc25
Junsele ☐ S 25 Lj14
Juodkrantė ☐ LT 31 Ma18
Jur ☐ SUD 109 Mb17
Jura ☐ F 39 Ld22
Jura ☐ GB 34 Kh18
Jurbarkas ☐ LT 31 Mb18
Jur'evec ☐ RUS 58 No17
Jur'ev-Pol'skij ☐ RUS 58
  Mk17
Jur'jivka ☐ UA 63 Mj21
Jürmala ☐ LV 30 Mb17
Jurovo ☐ RUS 58 Nb17
Juruá ☐ BR 133 Gb20
Juruá ☐ BR 132 Gc19
Juruá ☐ BR 132 Gc19
Juruena ☐ BR 134 Ha20
Juruti ☐ BR 134 Ha19
Jüterbog ☐ D 44 Lg20
Juticalpa ☐ HN 125 Fc16
Jutland ☐ DK 26 Le17
Juva ☐ FIN 28 Md15
Juža ☐ RUS 58 Nb17
Južno-Sahalinsk ☐ RUS
  75 Sa09
Južnoukrajins'k ☐ UA 62 Mf22
Južnyj ☐ RUS 31 Ma18
Južnyj ☐ RUS 60 Nf19
Jyväskylä ☐ FIN 28 Mc14

K

K2 ▲ PAK/CHN 78 Od11
Kaamanen ☐ FIN 23 Md11
Kaaresuvanto ☐ FIN 23 Mb11
Kaarina ☐ FIN 22 Mb15
Kabaena ☐ RI 87 Ra20

Kabale ☐ EAU 109 Mb19
Kabalı ☐ TR 65 Mh25
Kabalo ☐ RDC 109 Mb20
Kabanbai ☐ KZ 79 Od09
Kabardino-Balkaria ☐ RUS
  76 Na10
Kabarei ☐ RI 92 Rc19
Kâbdalis ☐ S 23 Ma12
Kabelvåg ☐ N 22 Lh11
Kabinda ☐ RDC 109 Ma20
Kabompo ☐ Z 110 Ma21
Kabul ● AFG 78 Ob12
Kabwe ☐ Z 110 Mb21
Kachovka ☐ UA 62 Mg22
Kachovs'ke vodoschovyšče ☐
  UA 63 Mh22
Kaçkar Dağı ▲ TR 66 Na25
Kadavu ☐ FIJ 98 Td22
Kadınhanı ☐ TR 64 Mg26
Kadirli ☐ TR 65 Mj27
Kadoma ☐ ZW 110 Mb22
Kaduj ☐ RUS 58 Mj16
Kaduna ☐ WAN 108 Lb16
Kadyj ☐ RUS 58 Nb17
Kaédi ☐ RIM 105 Kb15
Kåfjord ☐ N 23 Mc10
Kafue ☐ Z 110 Mb21
Kafue ☐ ZW 110 Mb22
Kaga Bandoro ☐ RCA
  108 Ld17
Kağızman ☐ TR 66 Na25
Kagoshima ☐ J 83 Rc12
Kaharlyk ☐ UA 62 Mf21
Kahramanmaraş ☐ TR
  65 Mj27
Kahraman-Maraş ☐ TR
  76 Md11
Kai Besar ☐ RI 92 Rc20
Kaikoura ☐ NZ 99 Tc27
Kaili ☐ CHN 84 Qb13
Kailu ☐ CHN 83 Ra10
Kaimana ☐ RI 92 Rc19
Käina ☐ EST 30 Mb16
Kainar ☐ KZ 79 Od09
Kainji Reservoir ☐ WAN
  105 La17
Kairouan ☐ TN 106 Lc11
Kaiserslautern ☐ D 45 Ld21
Kaišiadorys ☐ LT 31 Mc18
Kaiyuan ☐ CHN 84 Qa14
Kajaani ☐ FIN 28 Md13
Kajsackoe ☐ RUS 61 Nd21
Kakali ☐ RI 87 Qc19
Kakinada ☐ IND 81 Pa15
Kakuma ☐ EAK 109 Mc18
Kalaallit Nunaat ☐ DK 119
  Hd03
Kalač ☐ RUS 61 Na20
Kalač-na-Donu ☐ RUS 61
  Nb21
Kalahari Desert ☐ RB 110
  Ma23
Kalamáta ☐ GR 56 Mb27
Kalambáka ☐ GR 56 Ma26
Kálamos ☐ GR 56 Ma26
Kalančak ☐ UA 62 Mg22
Kälarne ☐ S 25 Lj14
Kalávrita ☐ GR 56 Mb26
Kalaymyo ☐ MYA 84 Pc14
Kalbarri ☐ AUS 95 Qc24
Kale ☐ TR 64 Me27
Kaledibi ☐ TR 66 Na25
Kalemie ☐ RDC 109 Mb20
Kalevala ☐ RUS 28 Mf13
Kalgoorlie-Boulder ☐ AUS
  95 Ra25
Kalimantan ☐ RI 87 Qb18
Kálimnos ☐ GR 57 Md27
Kálimnos ☐ GR 57 Md27

Kalinina ☐ RUS 60 Nc17
Kaliningrad ☐ RUS 31 Ma18
Kalininsk ☐ RUS 61 Nc20
Kalinkavičy ☐ BY 51 Me19
Kalispell ☐ USA 122 Eb09
Kalisz ☐ PL 50 Lk20
Kalix ☐ S 23 Mb13
Kalixälven ☐ S 23 Mb12
Kaljazin ☐ RUS 58 Mj17
Kalkalpen, N.P. ☐ A 52 Lh22
Kalkan ☐ TR 64 Me27
Kalkaringi ☐ AUS 94 Rc22
Kallinge ☐ S 27 Lh17
Kallsjön ☐ S 24 Lg14
Kalmar ☐ S 27 Lj17
Kalmarsund ☐ S 27 Lj17
Kal'mius ☐ UA 63 Mj22
Kalmykia ☐ RUS 76 Nb09
Kalmykovskij ☐ RUS 61 Nb21
Kaltanénai ☐ LT 31 Mc18
Kaltenkirchen ☐ D 44 Lf19
Kaluga ☐ RUS 59 Mj18
Kalundborg ☐ DK 26 Lf18
Kaluš ☐ UA 51 Mc21
Kalvåg ☐ N 24 Lc15
Kalvarija ☐ LT 31 Mb18
Kalynivka ☐ UA 62 Me21
Kaman ☐ TR 65 Mg26
Kamčatka ☐ RUS 74 Sd07
Kamchatka Peninsula ☐ RUS
  75 Sc07
Kamčija ☐ BG 55 Md24
Kamenica ☐ SR 54 Lk23
Kamenice nad Lipou ☐ CZ
  52 Lh21
Kamenka ☐ RUS 59 Mk20
Kamenka ☐ RUS 61 Nb19
Kamen'-na-Ob' ☐ RUS
  79 Pa08
Kamennogorsk ☐ RUS
  28 Me15
Kamenskij ☐ RUS 61 Nc20
Kamenskoe ☐ RUS 74 Tb06
Kamensk-Šahtinskij ☐ RUS
  63 Na21
Kamensk-Ural'skij ☐ RUS
  72 Oa07
Kameškovo ☐ RUS 58 Na17
Kamień Pomorski ☐ PL
  50 Lh19
Kamina ☐ RDC 109 Mb20
Kamin'-Kašyrs'kyj ☐ UA
  51 Mc20
Kam'janec-Podil's'kyj ☐ UA
  51 Md21
Kamjaniec ☐ BY 51 Mb19
Kam'janka ☐ UA 62 Mg21
Kamjanka-Buz'ka ☐ UA
  51 Mc20
Kamloops ☐ CDN 117 Dd08
Kampala ● EAU 109 Mc18
Kampar ☐ MAL 86 Qa18
Kampinoski P.N. ☐ PL 50
  Ma19
Kamskoe Ust'e ☐ RUS
  60 Ne18
Kamskoe vdhr. ☐ RUS
  72 Nd07
Kamyšin ☐ RUS 61 Nc20
Kananga ☐ RDC 108 Ma20
Kanaš ☐ RUS 60 Nd18
Kanchanaburi ☐ THA 86
  Pd16
Kandahar ☐ AFG 78 Ob12
Kandalakša ☐ RUS 72 Mc05
Kandalakšskaja guba ☐ RUS
  72 Mc05
Kandangan ☐ RI 87 Qc19
Kandel ☐ D 45 Le21

Kandi DY 105 La16
Kandila GR 56 Mb27
Kandıra TR 64 Mf25
Kandla IND 80 Oc14
Kandrian PNG 93 Sb20
Kandy CL 81 Pa17
Kane Basin DK 118 Gc03
Kanevskaja RUS 63 Mk22
Kangal TR 65 Mj26
Kangaroo Island AUS 97 Rd26
Kangasniemi FIN 28 Md15
Kangerlussuaq DK 119 Hb05
Kangerlussuaq DK 119 Hc05
Kangerlussuaq DK 119 Jb05
Kaniv UA 62 Mf21
Kanivs'ke vodoschovysče UA 62 Mf21
Kankaanpää FIN 22 Mb15
Kankan RG 105 Kc16
Kanker IND 80 Pa14
Kano WAN 108 Lb16
Kanona Z 110 Mc21
Kanpur IND 80 Od13
Kansas USA 122 Ed11
Kansas City USA 123 Fb11
Kansk RUS 73 Pd07
Kantchari BF 105 La16
Kantemirovka RUS 61 Mk21
Kao RI 87 Rb18
Kaohsiung RC 85 Ra14
Kaokoveld NAM 110 Lc22
Kaolack SN 105 Ka16
Kap Agulhas ZA 110 Ld25
Kap Farvel DK 119 Hd07
Kap Gustav Holm DK 119 Jb05
Kapıdağı Yarımadası TR 57 Md25
Kapingamarangi Atoll FSM 93 Sc18
Kapiri Mposhi Z 110 Mb21
Kap Morris Jesup DK 119 Ja02
Kap Møstling Tvillingøen DK 119 Hd06
Kaposvár H 53 Lj22
Kap Parry DK 118 Gb03
Kappeln D 44 Le18
Kapp Norvegia 141 Kb33
Kapshagai KZ 79 Od10
Kapshaghai Bögeni KZ 79 Od10
Kapuas Hulu Range MAL/RI 87 Qc18
Kapuvár H 53 Lj22
Kap York DK 118 Gc03
Kara TG 105 La17
Karaadilli TR 64 Mf26
Karabük TR 65 Mg25
Karaburun TR 57 Md26
Karaburun TR 57 Me25
Karacabey TR 57 Me25
Karacasu TR 64 Me27
Karačev RUS 59 Mh19
Karachay-Cherkessia RUS 76 Na10
Karachi PAK 80 Ob14
Karadeniz Boğazı TR 57 Me25
Karaghandy KZ 78 Oc09
Karaginskij zaliv RUS 74 Ta07
Karagöl Dağları TR 66 Na26

Karagüney Dağı TR 65 Mg25
Karaisalı TR 65 Mh27
Kara Kaya Baraj TR 66 Mk26
Karakelong RI 87 Rb18
Karakoçan TR 66 Na26
Karakol KS 79 Od10
Karakorum Range PAK 78 Od14
Kara Kum TM 78 Nd11
Karakurt TR 66 Nb25
Karalyk RUS 61 Ne19
Karaman TR 65 Mg27
Karamay CHN 79 Od10
Karapelit BG 55 Md24
Karapınar TR 65 Mg27
Kararkút H 53 Lj22
Karasavvon FIN 23 Mb11
Karasburg NAM 110 Ld24
Kara Sea RUS 72 Oa04
Karasjok N 23 Mc11
Karasu TR 64 Mf25
Karataş TR 65 Mh27
Karatepe Aslantaş Milli Parkı TR 65 Mj27
Karaurgan TR 66 Nb25
Karayazı TR 66 Nb26
Karbala IRQ 76 Na12
Karcag H 53 Ma22
Karditsa GR 56 Ma26
Kárdžali BG 57 Mc25
Kareli IND 80 Od14
Karelia RUS 29 Mg14
Karesuando S 23 Mb11
Kargasok RUS 73 Pa07
Kargat RUS 73 Pa07
Kargı TR 65 Mh25
Kargopol' RUS 29 Mk15
Karibib NAM 110 Lc23
Karigasniemi FIN 23 Mc11
Karimata Strait RI 86 Qb19
Karis = Karjaa FIN 22 Mb15
Káristos GR 57 Mc26
Karjaa = Karis FIN 22 Mb15
Karjalanselkä ER 28 Me14
Karkaraly KZ 79 Od09
Karkar Island PNG 92 Sb19
Karkonoski P.N. PL 50 Lh20
Karksi-Nuia EST 30 Mc16
Karleby FIN 19 Mb14
Karlino PL 50 Lh18
Karlıova TR 66 Na26
Karlivka UA 63 Mh21
Karlovac HR 47 Lh23
Karlovo BG 55 Mc24
Karlovy Vary CZ 52 Lg20
Karlsborg S 27 Lh16
Karlshamn S 27 Lh17
Karlskoga S 27 Lh16
Karlskrona S 27 Lh17
Karlsruhe D 45 Le21
Karlstad S 27 Lg16
Karlstadt D 45 Le21
Karnal IND 80 Od13
Karnataka IND 81 Od16
Karnische Alpen A 52 Lg22
Karnobat BG 55 Md24
Karonga MW 109 Mc20
Kärpänkylä FIN 28 Me13
Kárpathos GR 21 Mb10
Karpats'kyj nacionalnyj park UA 53 Mb21
Kars TR 66 Nb25
Kārsava LV 30 Md17
Karsun RUS 60 Nd18
Kartuzy PL 50 Lj18
Karula rahvuspark EST 30 Md17

Karumba AUS 96 Sa22
Karungi S 23 Mb12
Karvia FIN 19 Mb14
Karymskoe RUS 82 Qc08
Kaş TR 64 Me27
Kasabonika CDN 120 Fc08
Kasai RDC 108 Ld19
Kasai RDC 108 Ma20
Kasaji RDC 110 Ma21
Kasama Z 111 Mc21
Kasane RB 110 Ma22
Kaščukoviči BY 59 Mg19
Kaščukovka BY 59 Mf19
Kashechewan CDN 120 Fd08
Kashi CHN 78 Od11
Kashmar IR 78 Nd11
Kasimov RUS 58 Na18
Kasırıta RI 87 Rb19
Kaskinen = Kaskö FIN 25 Ma14
Kaskö = Kaskinen FIN 25 Ma14
Kaspijsk RUS 76 Nb10
Kassala SUD 107 Md15
Kassandra GR 56 Mb26
Kassel D 44 Le20
Kasserine TN 106 Lb11
Kastamonu TR 65 Mg25
Kasteli GR 57 Mc28
Kastl D 45 Lf21
Kastoría GR 56 Ma25
Kasungu MW 111 Mc21
Katanga RDC 108 Ma20
Katerini GR 56 Mb25
Katete Z 111 Mc21
Katherine AUS 94 Rc21
Kathmandu NEP 80 Pb13
Katima Mulilo NAM 110 Ma22
Katiola CI 105 Kc17
Káto Nevrokópi GR 56 Mb25
Katowice PL 50 Lk20
Katrançı Dağı TR 64 Mf27
Katrineholm S 27 Lj16
Katsina WAN 108 Lb16
Katsina-Ala WAN 108 Lb17
Kattegat 26 Lf17
Kauai USA 116 Ca07
Kaufbeuren D 45 Lf22
Kauhajoki FIN 19 Mb14
Kauhanevan-Pohjankankaan kansallispuisto FIN 19 Mb14
Kauhava FIN 19 Mb14
Kaukasus RUS 76 Na10
Kaukauveld NAM 110 Ma22
Kaunas LT 31 Mb18
Kautokeino N 23 Mb11
Kavadarci MK 56 Mb25
Kavajë AL 56 Lk25
Kavak TR 65 Mj25
Kavála GR 57 Mc25
Kavaratti IND 81 Oc16
Kavaratti Island IND 81 Oc16
Kavarna BG 55 Me24
Kavir-e Abarkuh IR 77 Nc12
Kavkazskij zapovednik RUS 66 Na24
Kawaihae USA 117 Cc35
Kawakawa NZ 99 Tc26
Kawasaki J 83 Rd11
Kaya BF 105 Kd16
Kayangel Islands PAL 92 Rc17

Kayes RMM 105 Kb16
Kayseri TR 76 Md11
Kayseri TR 65 Mh26
Kayseri TR 65 Mh26
Kayuagung RI 86 Qb19
Kazačka RUS 61 Nb20
Kazakhstan KZ 78 Nd09
Kazakh Uplands KZ 78 Ob09
Kazan' RUS 72 Nb07
Kazan' RUS 60 Nd18
Kazanka UA 62 Mg22
Kazanlâk BG 55 Mc24
Kazanskaja RUS 61 Na21
Kaz Dağı Milli Parkı TR 57 Md26
Kazımkarabekir TR 65 Mg27
Kazincbarcika H 53 Ma21
Kéa GR 57 Mc27
Kearney USA 122 Fa10
Keban TR 66 Mk26
Keban Baraji TR 66 Mk26
Kebnekaise S 22 Lk12
Kecskemét H 53 Lk22
Kédainiai LT 31 Mb18
Kédougou SN 105 Kb16
Keelung RC 85 Ra13
Keetmannshoop NAM 110 Ld24
Kefalonía GR 56 Ma26
Kéfalos GR 57 Md27
Kehl D 45 Ld21
Keila EST 30 Mc16
Keith AUS 97 Sa26
Kékes H 53 Ma22
Kekova Adasi TR 64 Mf27
Kelheim D 45 Lf21
Kelkit TR 66 Mk25
Kelkit Çayı TR 66 Mk25
Kéllé RCB 108 Lc19
Kelloselkä FIN 23 Me12
Kells IRL 33 Kg19
Kelmé LT 31 Mb18
Kelo TCH 108 Ld17
Kelowna CDN 117 Ea08
Kelso GB 34 Kj18
Kem' RUS 72 Mc05
Kem' RUS 29 Mh13
Kemah TR 66 Mk26
Kemalpaşa TR 66 Na25
Kemer TR 64 Mf27
Kemer TR 65 Mj26
Kemerovo RUS 73 Pb07
Kemi FIN 28 Mc14
Kemijärvi FIN 23 Md12
Kemijärvi FIN 23 Md12
Kemijoki FIN 23 Mc12
Kemlja RUS 60 Nc18
Kempele FIN 28 Mc13
Kemp Land 141 Nd32
Kempten D 45 Lf22
Kenai USA 116 Cb06
Kenai Peninsula USA 116 Cb06
Kendal GB 34 Kj18
Kendari RI 87 Ra19
Kenderes H 53 Ma22
Kenema WAL 105 Kb17
Kenge RDC 108 Ld19
Kénitra MA 104 Kc12
Kennacraig GB 34 Kh18
Kennewick USA 122 Ea09
Kenora CDN 120 Fb09
Kenosha USA 123 Fc10
Kenozersky N.P. RUS 29 Mk15
Kent Group AUS 97 Sb26

Kent Peninsula □ CDN 118 Ec05
Kentucky □ USA 123 Fd11
Kenya ■ EAK 109 Md18
Kępno □ PL 50 Lj20
Kepsut □ TR 64 Me26
KepulauanAnambas □ RI 86 Qb18
Kepulauan Aru □ RI 92 Rc20
Kepulauan Asia □ RI 92 Rc18
Kepulauan Ayu □ RI 92 Rc18
Kepulauan Babar □ RI 87 Rb20
Kepulauan Banda □ RI 87 Rb19
Kepulauan Banggai □ RI 87 Ra19
Kepulauan Daya Barat □ RI 87 Rb20
Kepulauan Gorong □ RI 92 Rc19
Kepulauan Kai □ RI 92 Rc20
Kepulauan Kangean □ RI 87 Qd20
KepulauanKarimata □ RI 86 Qb19
KepulauanKarimunjawa □ RI 86 Qc20
KepulauanLaut Kecil □ RI 87 Qd19
KepulauanLingga □ RI 86 Qa18
Kepulauan Mapia □ RI 92 Rc18
Kepulauan Natuna □ RI 86 Qb18
Kepulauan Sangihe □ RI 87 Rb18
Kepulauan Seribu □ RI 86 Qb20
Kepulauan Sula □ RI 87 Ra19
Kepulauan Talaud □ RI 87 Rb18
Kepulauan Tanimbar □ RI 92 Rc20
Kepulauan Togian □ RI 87 Ra19
Kepulauan Watubela □ RI 92 Rc19
Kerala □ IND 81 Od16
Keramoti □ GR 57 Mc25
Kerč □ UA 63 Mj23
Kerčens'ka protoka □ RUS 63 Mj23
Kerdem □ RUS 75 Rb06
Kerema □ PNG 92 Sb20
Kerempe Burnu ▲ TR 65 Mg24
Keri □ GR 56 Ma27
Kerki □ TM 78 Oa11
Kérkira □ GR 56 Lk26
Kermadec Islands □ NZ 99 Ua25
Kermadec Ridge □ NZ 99 Ua25
Kermadec Trench □ NZ 99 Ua25
Kerman □ IR 77 Nd12
Kermanshah □ IR 76 Nb12
Kéros □ GR 57 Mc27
Kerženec □ RUS 60 Nc17
Keşan □ TR 57 Md25
Kesenuma □ J 83 Sa11
Keşiş Dağı ▲ TR 65 Mj25
Keskin □ TR 65 Mg26
Keswick □ GB 34 Kj18
Keszthely □ H 53 Lj22
Ket' □ RUS 73 Pa07
Ketapang □ RI 86 Qb19

Ketchikan □ USA 117 Db07
Kętrzyn □ PL 50 Ma18
Ketsko-Tymskaja ravnina □ RUS 73 Pa06
Kettering □ GB 35 Kk19
Keuruu □ FIN 28 Mc14
Kevlavik □ IS 32 Jj13
Key West □ USA 126 Fd14
Kežmarok □ SK 53 Ma21
Khakassia □ RUS 79 Pc08
Khalkidhiki □ GR 56 Mb25
Khamis Mushayt □ KSA 77 Na15
Khandwa □ IND 80 Od14
Khangaiyn Nuruu ▲ MNG 79 Pd09
Khania □ GR 56 Mb28
Khanty-Mansi Autonomous District □ RUS 72 Ob06
Kharga Oasis □ ET 107 Mc23
Khartoum ★ SUD 107 Mc15
Khartoum North □ SUD 107 Mc15
Khar Us Nuur □ MNG 79 Pc09
Kherlen Gol □ MNG 82 Qc09
Khon Kaen □ THA 84 Qa15
Khorat = Nakhon Ratchasima □ THA 84 Qa15
Khorat Plateau □ THA 84 Qa15
Khorramabad □ IR 76 Nb12
Khorram Shar □ IR 77 Nb12
Khorugh □ TJ 78 Oc11
Khouribga □ MA 104 Kc12
Khovd □ MNG 79 Pc09
Khövsgöl Nuur □ MNG 82 Qa08
Khrebet Dzhugdzhur □ RUS 75 Rc07
Khujand □ TJ 78 Ob10
Khulna □ BD 80 Pb14
Khuraburi □ THA 86 Pd17
Khyargas Nuur □ MNG 79 Pc09
Kiáto □ GR 56 Mb26
Kibali □ RDC 109 Mb18
Kibangou □ RCB 108 Lc19
Kibondo □ EAT 109 Mc19
Kıbrıscık □ TR 64 Mf25
Kibwezi □ EAK 109 Mc19
Kičevo □ MK 56 Ma25
Kidderminster □ GB 35 Kj19
Kideksa □ RUS 58 Na17
Kidira □ SN 105 Kb16
Kiekinkoski □ FIN 28 Mf13
Kiel □ D 44 Lf18
Kielce □ PL 50 Ma20
Kiev ★ UA 62 Mf20
Kiffa □ RIM 105 Kb15
Kigali ★ BU 100 Mc19
Kiği □ TR 66 Na26
Kigoma □ EAT 109 Mb19
Kihnu □ EST 30 Mb16
Kikinda □ SR 54 Ma23
Kiknur □ RUS 60 Nd17
Kikori □ PNG 92 Sa20
Kikwit □ RDC 108 Ld20
Kilawa Masoko □ EAT 109 Md20
Kildare □ IRL 33 Kg19
Kilifi □ EAK 109 Md19
Kilija □ UA 55 Me23
Kilimanjaro ▲ EAT 109 Md19
Kilinailau Islands □ PNG 93 Sd19
Kilingi-Nõmme □ EST 30 Mc16
Kilini □ GR 56 Ma27

Kilis □ TR 65 Mj27
Kilkeel □ GB 34 Kh18
Kilkenny □ IRL 33 Kg19
Kilkis □ GR 56 Mb25
Killarney □ IRL 33 Kf19
Killarney N.P. ☆ IRL 33 Kf20
Killeen □ USA 123 Fa12
Killybegs □ IRL 33 Kf18
Kilmarnock □ GB 34 Kh18
Kilpisjärvi □ FIN 23 Ma11
Kilrush □ IRL 33 Kf19
Kilwa □ RDC 109 Mb20
Kimba □ AUS 97 Rd25
Kimberley □ ZA 110 Ma24
Kimberley Plateau □ AUS 94 Rb22
Kimi □ GR 57 Mc26
Kimmirut □ CDN 119 Gc06
Kimolos □ GR 57 Mc27
Kimovsk □ RUS 59 Mk19
Kimry □ RUS 58 Mj17
Kindersley □ CDN 120 Ec08
Kindia □ RG 105 Kb16
Kindu □ RDC 109 Mb19
Kinel' □ RUS 60 Nf19
Kineshma □ RUS 58 Nb17
Kingaroy □ AUS 96 Sc24
King Edward VIII Gulf □ 141 Nd32
King George Island □ GB 140 Ha31
King George Island □ 140 Ha31
Kingisepp □ RUS 30 Me16
Kingoonya □ AUS 97 Rd25
King Island □ AUS 97 Sa26
King Leopold Ranges ▲ AUS 94 Ra22
Kingman □ USA 122 Eb11
Kingscote □ AUS 97 Rd26
King Sejong □ 140 Ha31
King's Lynn □ GB 35 La19
Kingston □ CDN 123 Ga10
Kingston □ JA 126 Ga15
Kingston South East □ AUS 97 Rd26
Kingston upon Hull □ GB 35 Kk19
Kingstown ▼ WV 127 Gd16
King William Island □ CDN 118 Fa05
Kinkala □ RCB 108 Lc19
Kinna □ S 26 Lg17
Kinsarvik □ N 24 Ld15
Kinshasa ★ RDC 108 Ld19
Kintampo □ GH 105 Kd17
Kintyre □ GB 34 Kh18
Kinyeti ▲ SUD 109 Mc18
Kiparissia □ GR 56 Ma27
Kipini □ FIN 28 Md13
Kipti □ UA 62 Mf20
Kirá Panagiá □ GR 57 Mc26
Kirava □ UA 62 Mf20
Kirchdorf □ A 52 Lh22
Kirchschlag □ A 52 Lj22
Kırıkhan □ TR 65 Mj27
Kırıkkale □ TR 65 Mg26
Kirillov □ RUS 58 Mk16
Kiriwina Island □ PNG 93 Sc20
Kırka □ TR 64 Mf26
Kırkağaç □ TR 57 Md26
Kirkcaldy □ GB 34 Kj17
Kirkenær □ N 24 Lg15
Kirkenes □ N 23 Mf11
Kirkjubæjarklaustur □ IS 32 Ka14

Kirkland Lake □ CDN 123 Fd09
Kırklareli □ TR 57 Md25
Kirkliai □ LT 31 Mb18
Kirkpatrick, Mount ▲ 141 Ta35
Kirkuk □ IRQ 76 Na11
Kirkwall □ GB 34 Kj16
Kirov □ RUS 72 Nc07
Kirov □ RUS 59 Mh18
Kirovakan □ GE 76 Na10
Kirovo-Čepeck □ RUS 72 Nc07
Kirovohrad □ UA 62 Mg21
Kirovsk □ RUS 30 Mf16
Kirovs'ke □ UA 63 Mh23
Kirsanov □ RUS 61 Nb19
Kırşehir □ TR 65 Mh26
Kiruna □ S 22 Ma12
Kiržač □ RUS 58 Mk17
Kisa □ S 27 Lh17
Kisalföld □ H 53 Lj22
Kisangani □ RDC 109 Mb18
Kis-Balaton □ H 53 Lj22
Kiseljak □ BIH 47 Lk23
Kisi □ WAN 105 La17
Kisii □ EAK 109 Mc19
Kiskörös □ H 53 Lk22
Kiskunfélegyháza □ H 53 Lk22
Kiskunhalas □ H 53 Lk22
Kiskunsági N.P. □ H 53 Lk22
Kismaanyo □ SP 109 Na19
Kissamos □ GR 56 Mb28
Kissidougou □ RG 105 Kb17
Kisumu □ EAK 109 Mc19
Kisvárda □ H 53 Mb21
Kitakyushu □ J 83 Rc12
Kitale □ EAK 109 Md18
Kitchener □ CDN 123 Fd10
Kitee □ FIN 29 Mf14
Kithnos □ GR 57 Mc27
Kithnos □ GR 57 Mc27
Kitimat □ CDN 116 Dc08
Kittelfjäll □ S 25 Lh13
Kittilä □ FIN 23 Mc12
Kitwe □ Z 110 Mb21
Kitzbühel □ A 52 Lg22
Kiunga □ PNG 92 Sa20
Kiuruvesi □ FIN 28 Md14
Kiverci □ UA 51 Mc20
Kiviöli □ EST 30 Md16
Kıyıköy □ TR 57 Me25
Kızılcahamam □ TR 65 Mg25
Kızılırmak □ TR 65 Mg25
Kiziltaşskij liman □ RUS 63 Mj23
Kizner □ RUS 60 Nf17
Kjøllefjord □ N 23 Md10
Kjustendil □ BG 56 Mb24
Kladovo □ SR 54 Mb23
Klagenfurt □ A 52 Lh22
Klaipėda □ LT 31 Ma18
Klamath Falls □ USA 122 Dd10
Klatovy □ CZ 52 Lg21
Kle □ LB 105 Kb17
Klerksdorp □ ZA 110 Mb24
Kletnja □ RUS 59 Mg19
Kletskij □ RUS 61 Nb21
Kličav □ BY 51 Me19
Klimavičy □ BY 59 Mf19
Klimovo □ RUS 59 Mg19
Klimovsk □ RUS 58 Mj18
Klin □ RUS 58 Mj17
Klincy □ RUS 59 Mg19
Klintehamn □ S 27 Lk17
Klippan □ S 26 Lg17
Klisura □ BG 55 Mc24

Klitoria ◻ GR 56 Mb27
Kljavino ◻ RUS 60 Ng18
Ključ ◻ BIH 47 Lj23
Ključevskaja Sopka ▲ RUS 74 Ta07
Kłodzko ◻ PL 50 Lj20
Kløfta ◻ N 24 Lf15
Klokkarvik ◻ N 24 Lc15
Kluang ◻ MAL 86 Qa18
Kluczbork ◻ PL 50 Lk20
Knarvik ◻ N 24 Lc15
Kneža ◻ BG 54 Mc24
Knin ◻ HR 47 Lj23
Knittelfeld ◻ A 52 Lh22
Knivsta ◻ S 27 Lj16
Knjaževac ◻ SR 54 Mb24
Knjažiha ◻ RUS 60 Nd18
Knokke-Heist ◻ B 37 Lb20
Knox Coast ◻ ⬚ 141 Qa32
Knoxville ◻ USA 123 Fd11
Knud Rasmussen Land ◻ DK 118 Ha03
Knyszyn ◻ PL 51 Mb19
Kožuchów ◻ PL 50 Lh20
Kobe ◻ J 83 Rd12
Kobeljaky ◻ UA 62 Mh21
København ● DK 26 Lg18
Koblenz ◻ D 45 Ld20
Kobona ◻ RUS 29 Mf15
Koboža ◻ RUS 58 Mh16
Kobroor ◻ RI 92 Rc20
Kobryn ◻ BY 51 Mc19
Kocaeli ◻ TR 57 Me25
Kocaeli Yarımadası ⬚ TR 57 Me25
Koçarlı ◻ TR 57 Md27
Kočetovka ◻ RUS 59 Na19
Kočevje ◻ SLO 47 Lh23
Kochi ◻ IND 81 Od17
Kochi ◻ J 83 Rc12
Kocjubyns'ke ◻ UA 62 Mf20
Kock ◻ PL 51 Mb20
Koćkarlej ◻ RUS 60 Nd19
Koćubej ◻ RUS 76 Nb10
Kodiak ◻ USA 116 Cb07
Kodiak Island ⬚ USA 116 Cb07
Kodinsk ◻ RUS 73 Pd07
Kodyma ◻ UA 62 Me21
Köflach ◻ A 52 Lh22
Koforidua ◻ GH 105 Kd17
Køge ◻ DK 26 Lg18
Køge Bugt ◻ DK 119 Hd06
Kohima ◻ IND 84 Pc13
Koh Kong ◻ K 84 Qa16
Kohler Glacier ⬚ 140 Eb34
Kohler Range ▲ 140 Eb33
Kohma ◻ RUS 58 Na17
Koh Samui ⬚ THA 86 Qa17
Kohtlajärve ◻ EST 30 Md16
Koidu ◻ WAL 105 Kb17
Koivu ◻ FIN 23 Mc12
Kojonup ◻ AUS 95 Qd25
Kokand ◻ UZ 78 Oc10
Kökar ◻ FIN 30 Ma16
Kokkola ◻ FIN 19 Mb14
Kökpınar ◻ TR 66 Na26
Kokšaga ⬚ RUS 60 Nd17
Kokšajsk ◻ RUS 60 Nd17
Kokstad ◻ ZA 110 Mb25
Koktebel' ◻ UA 63 Mh23
Kola ◻ RUS 23 Mg11
Kolaka ◻ RI 87 Ra19
Kola Peninsula ▲ RUS 72 Md05
Kolari ◻ FIN 23 Mb12
Kolárovo ◻ SK 53 Lj22
Kolåsen ◻ S 24 Lg13
Kolašin ◻ CG 54 Lk24

Kolbuszowa ◻ PL 51 Ma20
Kol'čugino ◻ RUS 58 Mk17
Kolding ◻ DK 26 Le18
Kolhan Upland ▲ IND/BD 80 Pb14
Kolhapur ◻ IND 81 Oc15
Kolin kansallispuisto ☘ FIN 28 Me14
Koljučinskaja guba ◻ RUS 74 Ua05
Kolka ◻ LV 30 Mb17
Kolkasrags ◻ LV 30 Mb17
Kolky ◻ UA 51 Mc20
Kollam ◻ IND 81 Od17
Köln ◻ D 44 Ld20
Kolno ◻ PL 50 Ma19
Koło ◻ PL 50 Lk19
Kołobrzeg ◻ PL 50 Lh18
Kolokani ◻ RMM 105 Kc16
Kolokolčovka ◻ RUS 61 Nc20
Kolomna ◻ RUS 58 Mk18
Kolomyja ◻ UA 51 Mc21
Koloveden kansallispuisto ☘ FIN 28 Me14
Kolpaševo ◻ RUS 73 Pa07
Kolpino ◻ RUS 30 Mf16
Kolpny ◻ RUS 59 Mj19
Kólpos Hanión ◻ GR 56 Mb28
Kólpos Orfanoú ◻ GR 56 Mb25
Kólpos Petalíon ◻ GR 57 Mc27
Kolwezi ◻ RDC 110 Mb21
Kolyčivka ◻ UA 59 Mf20
Kolyma ⬚ RUS 74 Sc05
Kolyma Range ▲ RUS 74 Sc06
Kolymskaja nizmennost' ⬚ RUS 74 Sc05
Kolyšlej ◻ RUS 61 Nc19
Komancza ◻ PL 51 Mb21
Komandorskie o-va ⬚ RUS 74 Tb07
Komárno ◻ SK 54 Lk22
Komi ◻ RUS 72 Nc06
Kominternivs'ke ◻ UA 62 Mf22
Komodo ⬚ RI 87 Qd20
Kôm Ombo ◻ ET 107 Mc14
Komoran ⬚ RI 92 Rd20
Komosomol'sk ◻ RUS 58 Na17
Komotini ◻ GR 57 Mc25
Kompong Som = Sihanoukville ◻ K 84 Qa16
Kompong Thom ◻ K 84 Qa16
Komsomol'skaja ◻ 141 Pd33
Komsomol'skij ◻ RUS 60 Nc18
Komsomol'sk-na-Amure ◻ RUS 75 Rd08
Konakovo ◻ RUS 58 Mj17
Kondoa ◻ EAT 109 Md19
Kondol' ◻ RUS 61 Nc19
Kondopoga ◻ RUS 29 Mh14
Kondrovo ◻ RUS 59 Mh18
Koné ◻ F 98 Ta23
Kong Christian IX Land ⬚ DK 119 Jb05
Kong Christian X Land ⬚ DK 138 Jc04
Kong Frederik IX Land ⬚ DK 119 Hc05
Kong Frederik VIII Land ⬚ DK 138 Jd03
Kong Frederik VI Kyst ⬚ DK 119 Hd06

Kongsøya ⬚ N 22 Lj06
Kongsvinger ◻ N 24 Lf15
Kong Wilhelm Land ⬚ DK 138 Jd03
Königswiesen ◻ A 52 Lh21
Konin ◻ PL 50 Lk19
Konjic ◻ BIH 47 Lj24
Konoša ◻ RUS 72 Na06
Konotop ◻ UA 59 Mg20
Końskie ◻ PL 50 Ma20
Konstantinovsk ◻ RUS 63 Na22
Konstanz ◻ D 45 Le22
Kontagora ◻ WAN 108 Lb16
Kontiolahti ◻ FIN 28 Me14
Konya ◻ TR 64 Mg27
Konya Ovası ▲ TR 65 Mg27
Kościan ◻ PL 50 Lj19
Kościerzyna ◻ PL 50 Lj18
Kopaonik, N.P. ☘ SR 54 Ma24
Kópasker ⬚ IS 32 Kb12
Kopejsk ◻ KZ 72 Nc08
Koper ◻ SLO 47 Lg23
Kopervik ◻ N 26 Lc16
Köping ◻ S 27 Lh16
Koplik i Poshtëm ◻ AL 56 Lk24
Koppang ◻ N 24 Lf15
Kopparberg ◻ S 27 Lh16
Koppe Dag ▲ IR/TM 78 Nd11
Kopperå ◻ N 24 Lf14
Koprivnica ◻ HR 47 Lj23
Köprülü Kanyon Milli Parkı ☘ TR 64 Mf27
Kopyčynci ◻ UA 51 Mc21
Korab ▲ SR/AL 56 Ma25
Korablino ◻ RUS 59 Mk19
K'orahe ◻ ETH 109 Na17
Korbach ◻ D 44 Le20
Korbenići ◻ RUS 29 Mh15
Korçe ◻ AL 56 Ma25
Korčevka ◻ RUS 60 Nd18
Korčula ◻ HR 47 Lj24
Korčula ⬚ HR 47 Lj24
Korea Strait ◻ ROK/J 83 Rb12
Korec' ◻ UA 51 Md20
Korenevo ◻ RUS 59 Mh20
Korenovsk ◻ RUS 63 Mk23
Korf ◻ RUS 74 Tb06
Korff Ice Rise ⬚ 140 Gb34
Korgen ◻ N 22 Lg12
Korhogo ◻ CI 105 Kc17
Korjakskaja Sopka ▲ RUS 75 Sd08
Korjukivka ◻ UA 59 Mg20
Korkuteli ◻ TR 64 Mf27
Korla ◻ CHN 79 Pb10
Körmend ◻ H 52 Lj22
Kornat ▲ HR 47 Lh24
Kornati, N.P. ☘ HR 47 Lh24
Koro ⬚ FIJ 98 Td22
Koroča ◻ RUS 59 Mj20
Köroğlu Dağları ▲ TR 64 Mf25
Köroğlu Tepe ▲ TR 64 Mf25
Koróni ◻ GR 56 Ma27
Koronowo ◻ PL 50 Lj19
Korop ◻ UA 59 Mg20
Koror ● PAL 92 Rc17
Koro Sea ◻ FIJ 98 Td22
Körösladány ◻ H 53 Ma22
Körös-Maros N.P. ☘ H 53 Ma22
Korosten' ◻ UA 62 Me20
Korostyšiv ◻ UA 62 Me20
Koroviha ◻ RUS 60 Nc17
Korpilahti ◻ FIN 28 Mc14
Korsnäs ◻ FIN 25 Ma14

Korsun'-Ševčenkivs'kyj ◻ UA 62 Mf21
Kortrijk ◻ B 37 Lb20
Koryak Autonomous District ◻ RUS 74 Tb06
Koryak Range ▲ RUS 74 Tb06
Kós ⬚ GR 57 Md27
Kós ◻ GR 57 Md27
Kosaja Gora ◻ RUS 58 Mj18
Köse ◻ TR 66 Mk25
Köse Dağları ▲ TR 65 Mj25
Kosha ◻ SUD 107 Mc14
Košice ◻ SK 53 Ma21
Kosovo ◻ SR 54 Ma24
Kosovska Mitrovica ◻ SR 54 Ma24
Kosrae ⬚ FSM 93 Ta17
Kostanaj ◻ KZ 78 Oa08
Kostenec ◻ BG 56 Mb24
Kostjantynivka ◻ UA 63 Mj21
Kostomukša ◻ RUS 28 Mf13
Kostopil' ◻ UA 51 Md20
Kostroma ◻ RUS 58 Na17
Kostrzyn ◻ PL 50 Lh19
Koszalin ◻ PL 50 Lj18
Kőszeg ◻ H 52 Lj22
Kota ◻ IND 80 Od13
Kota Bharu ◻ MAL 86 Qa17
Kota Kinabalu ◻ MAL 87 Qd17
Kotamobagu ◻ RI 87 Ra18
Kotel ◻ BG 55 Md24
Kotel'nič ◻ RUS 72 Nb07
Kotel'va ◻ UA 59 Mh20
Kotka ◻ FIN 28 Md15
Kotlas ◻ RUS 72 Nb06
Kotly ◻ RUS 30 Me16
Kotor ◻ CG 54 Lk24
Kotovo ◻ RUS 61 Nc20
Kotovsk ◻ RUS 61 Na19
Kotovs'k ◻ UA 55 Me22
Kötschach ◻ A 52 Lg22
Kotto ◻ RCA 108 Ma17
Kotuj ⬚ RUS 73 Qa04
Kotzebue ◻ USA 116 Bd05
Kotzebue Sound ◻ USA 116 Bc05
Kotzebue Sound ◻ USA 116 Bd05
Koudougou ◻ BF 105 Kd16
Koulamoutou ◻ G 108 Lc19
Kounávi ◻ GR 57 Mc28
Koundara ◻ RG 105 Kb16
Koupéla ◻ BF 105 Kd16
Kourou ◻ F 134 Hb17
Kouvola ◻ FIN 28 Md15
Kovačica ◻ SR 54 Ma23
Kovada Gölü Milli Parkı ☘ TR 64 Mf27
Kovancılar ◻ TR 66 Mk26
Kovdor ◻ RUS 23 Mf12
Kovd ozero ⬚ RUS 23 Mg11
Kovel' ◻ UA 51 Mc20
Kovernino ◻ RUS 58 Nb17
Kovrov ◻ RUS 58 Na17
Kovylkino ◻ RUS 60 Nb18
Kowal ◻ PL 50 Lk19
Kowloon ◻ CHN 85 Qc14
Köyceğiz ◻ TR 64 Me27
Koyulhisar ◻ TR 65 Mj25
Kozaklı ◻ TR 65 Mh26
Kozan ◻ TR 65 Mh27
Kozáni ◻ GR 56 Ma25
Kozara, N.P. ☘ BIH 47 Lj23
Kozel'sk ◻ RUS 59 Mh19
Kozhikode ◻ IND 81 Od16
Kozienice ◻ PL 50 Ma20
Kozjatyn ◻ UA 62 Me21

Kozloduj ◫ BG 54 Mb24
Kozlovka ◫ RUS 60 Ne18
Kozlu ◫ TR 64 Mf25
Kozluk ◫ TR 66 Na26
Kozlupınar ◫ TR 66 Mk26
Koz'modem'jansk ◫ RUS
  60 Nd17
Kpalime ◫ TG 105 La17
Krabi ◫ THA 86 Pd17
Krafla ▲ IS 32 Kb13
Kragerø ◫ N 26 Le16
Kragujevac ◫ SR 54 Ma23
Krakatau ◫ RI 86 Qb20
Kraków ◫ PL 50 Lk20
Kraljevo ◫ SR 54 Ma24
Kramators'k ◫ UA 63 Mj21
Kramfors ◫ S 25 Lj14
Kranidi ◫ GR 56 Mb27
Kranj ◫ SLO 47 Ln22
Kranjska Gora ◫ SLO 47
  Lg22
Kraśnik ◫ PL 51 Mb20
Krapina ◫ HR 47 Lh22
Kräslava ◫ LV 31 Md18
Krasnaja Gora ◫ RUS
  59 Mf19
Krasnaja Gorbatka ◫ RUS
  58 Na18
Krasnaja Jaruga ◫ RUS
  59 Mh20
Krasnaja Poljana ◫ RUS
  66 Na24
Krasnoarmejsk ◫ RUS
  58 Mk17
Krasnoarmejsk ◫ RUS
  61 Nc20
Krasnoarmijs'k ◫ UA 63 Mj21
Krasnodar ◫ RUS 63 Mk23
Krasnodarskoe Vodohranilišče
  ▭ RUS 63 Mk23
Krasnodon ◫ UA 63 Mk21
Krasnoe ◫ RUS 58 Mk19
Krasnohorivka ◫ UA 63 Mj21
Krasnohrad ◫ UA 63 Mh21
Krasnohvardijs'ke ◫ UA
  63 Mh23
Krasnojarsk ◫ RUS 73 Pc07
Krasnokuts'k ◫ UA 63 Mh20
Krasnomajskij ◫ RUS 58
  Mh17
Krasnopavlivka ◫ UA 63 Mj21
Krasnoperekops'k ◫ UA
  62 Mg23
Krasnopillja ◫ UA 59 Mh20
Krasnoslobodsk ◫ RUS
  60 Nb18
Krasnoslobodsk ◫ RUS
  61 Nc21
Krasnotorovka ◫ RUS
  27 Lk18
Krasnoznamensk ◫ RUS
  31 Mb18
Krasnye Baki ◫ RUS 60 Nc17
Krasnyj Holm ◫ RUS 58 Mj16
Krasnyj Jar ◫ RUS 60 Nf19
Krasnyj Kut ◫ RUS 61 Nd20
Krasnyj Luč ◫ UA 63 Mk21
Krasnyj Manyč ◫ RUS
  63 Na22
Krasnystaw ◫ PL 51 Mb20
Krasyliv ◫ UA 51 Md21
Kratovo ◫ MK 56 Mb24
Kremenčuc'ke vodoschovyšče
  ▭ UA 62 Mg21
Kremenčuk ◫ UA 62 Mg21
Kremenec' ◫ UA 51 Mc20
Kremna ◫ SR 54 Lk24
Krems ◫ A 52 Lh21
Kresna ◫ BG 56 Mb25

Krestcy ◫ RUS 58 Mg16
Kretinga ◫ LT 31 Ma18
Kréva ◫ BY 31 Md18
Kribi ◫ CAM 108 Lb18
Krishna ▲ IND 81 Od15
Kristiansand ◫ N 26 Ld16
Kristianstad ◫ S 27 Lh17
Kristiansund ◫ N 24 Ld14
Kristiinankaupunki =
  Kristinestad ◫ FIN 25
  Ma14
Kristinehamn ◫ S 27 Lh16
Kristinestad =
  Kristiinankaupunki ◫ FIN
  25 Ma14
krjaž Čekanovskogo ▲ RUS
  73 Ra04
krjaž Vetrenyj pojas ▲ RUS
  29 Mh14
Krk ▲ HR 47 Lh23
Krk ◫ HR 47 Lh23
Krka, N.P. ▭ HR 47 Lh24
Krkonošský N.P. ▭ CZ
  52 Lh20
Krokom ◫ S 25 Lh14
Krolevec' ◫ UA 59 Mg20
Kromy ◫ RUS 59 Mh19
Kronach ◫ D 45 Lf20
Kronprins Christian Land ▲
  DK 138 Jd02
Kronprins Olav kyst ▲ 141
  Na32
Kronštadt ◫ RUS 29 Me15
Krośniewice ◫ PL 50 Lk19
Kroonstad ◫ ZA 110 Mb24
Krosno ◫ PL 50 Ma21
Krosnojarskoe vdhr. ▭ RUS
  79 Pc08
Krotoszyn ◫ PL 50 Lj20
Krumbach ◫ D 45 Lf21
Krung Thep = Bangkok ●
  THA 84 Qa16
Kruševac ◫ SR 54 Ma24
Kruševo ◫ MK 56 Ma25
Krutec ◫ RUS 61 Nc19
Kryčav ◫ BY 59 Mf19
Krymsk ◫ RUS 63 Mj23
Kryms'ky hory ▲ UA 63 Mh23
Krynica ◫ PL 50 Ma21
Kryve Ozero ◫ UA 62 Mf22
Kryvsk ◫ BY 59 Mf19
Kryvyj Rih ◫ UA 62 Mg22
Kryžopil' ◫ UA 62 Me21
Kśenskij ◫ RUS 59 Mj20
Kstovo ◫ RUS 60 Nc17
Kuala Belait ◫ BRU 87 Qc18
Kuala Dungan ◫ MAL 86
  Qa18
Kuala Lipis ◫ MAL 86 Qa18
Kuala Lumpur ● MAL 86
  Qa18
Kualapembuang ◫ RI 87
  Qb19
Kuala Terengganu ◫ MAL
  86 Qa17
Kuantan ◫ MAL 86 Qa18
Kuaro ◫ RI 87 Qc19
Kuban' ▲ RUS 63 Mk23
Kubrat ◫ BG 55 Md24
Kuching ◫ MAL 86 Qc18
Kudat ◫ MAL 87 Qd17
Kufstein ◫ A 52 Lg22
Kugej ◫ RUS 63 Mk22
Kugluktuk ◫ CDN 118 Ea05
Kuh-e Damavand ▲ IR
  76 Nc11
Kuhha-ye Qohrud ▲ IR
  77 Nc12
Kuhmo ◫ FIN 28 Me13

Kuito ◫ ANG 110 Ld21
Kuivaniemi ◫ FIN 28 Mc13
Kujbyšev ◫ RUS 73 Od07
Kujbyševskoe Vodohranilišče
  ▭ RUS 60 Nd17
Kukës ◫ AL 56 Ma24
Kukkolaforsen ◫ FIN 28
  Mc13
Kukmor ◫ RUS 60 Nf17
Kula ◫ SR 54 Lk23
Kula ◫ TR 64 Me26
Kuldiga ◫ LV 30 Ma17
Kulebaki ◫ RUS 58 Nb18
Kuleši ◫ RUS 59 Mj19
Kulgera ◫ AUS 94 Rc26
Kulmaç Dağları ▲ TR 65 Mj26
Kulmbach ◫ D 45 Lf20
Kulp ◫ TR 66 Na26
Kulu ◫ TR 65 Mg26
Kulundinskaja ravnina ▲ RUS
  79 Od08
Kumanovo ◫ MK 56 Ma24
Kumasi ◫ GH 105 Kd17
Kumba ◫ CAM 108 Lb18
Kümbet ◫ TR 64 Mf26
Kumertau ◫ RUS 78 Nd08
Kumlinge ◫ FIN 25 Ma15
Kumluca ◫ TR 64 Mf27
Kunda ◫ EST 30 Md16
Kunene ▲ NAM 110 Lc22
Kungälv ◫ S 26 Lf17
Kungsbacka ◫ S 26 Lg17
Kungshamn ◫ S 26 Lf16
Kungsör ◫ S 27 Lj16
Kun'je ◫ UA 63 Mj21
Kunlun Shan ▲ CHN 79 Pa11
Kunming ● CHN 84 Qa13
Kununurra ◫ AUS 94 Rb22
Kuop Atoll ◫ FSM 93 Sc17
Kuopio ◫ FIN 28 Md14
Kupang ◫ RI 87 Ra21
Kupiano ◫ PNG 93 Sb21
Kupiškis ◫ LT 31 Mc18
Kup'jans'k ◫ UA 63 Mj21
Kup'jans'k-Vuzlovyj ◫ UA
  63 Mj21
Kupreanof Island ◫ USA
  117 Db07
Kupres ◫ BIH 47 Lj24
Kuqa ◫ CHN 79 Pa10
Kurdistan ▲ TR/IRQ 76 Na11
Kurdufán ◻ SUD 109 Mb16
Küre Dağları ▲ TR 65 Mg25
Kuressaare ◫ EST 30 Mb16
Kurgan ◫ RUS 72 Ob07
Kuria Muria Islands ◫ OM
  77 Nd15
Kurikka ◫ FIN 19 Mb14
Kuril Islands ◫ RUS 75 Sb09
Kuril Trench ▲ 75 Sb10
Kurjenrahkan kansallispuisto
  ▭ FIN 22 Mb15
Kurlin ◫ RUS 60 Nf20
Kurlovskij ◫ RUS 58 Na18
Kurnool ◫ IND 81 Od15
Kurovskoe ◫ RUS 58 Mk18
Kuršėnai ◫ LT 31 Mb17
Kuršiu n.p. ▭ LT 31 Ma18
Kursk ◫ RUS 59 Mj20
Kuršskaja kosa ▲ RUS/LT
  31 Ma18
Kuršumlija ◫ SR 54 Ma24
Kuršunlu ◫ TR 65 Mg25
Kuruktag ▲ CHN 79 Pb10
Kuruman ◫ ZA 110 Ma24
Kuşadası ◫ TR 57 Md27
Kuşadası Körfezi ◫ TR
  57 Md27
Kusaie ◫ FSM 93 Ta17

Kušalino ◫ RUS 58 Mj17
Kuşcennetil Milli Parkı ▮ TR
  57 Md25
Kuşcenneti Milli Parkı ▮ TR
  65 Mh27
Kuščevskaja ◫ RUS 63 Mk22
Kuş Gölü ▭ TR 57 Me25
Kushiro ◫ J 83 Sa10
Kuskokwim ◫ USA 116 Bd06
Kuskokwim Bay ◫ USA
  116 Bd07
Kuskokwim Mountains ▲
  USA 116 Ca06
Kusmuryn ◫ KZ 78 Oa08
Kusti ◫ SUD 107 Mc16
Kütahya ◫ TR 64 Me26
Kutaisi ◫ GE 76 Na10
Kutina ◫ HR 47 Lj23
Kutlu-Bukaš ◫ RUS 60 Nf18
Kutná Hora ◫ CZ 52 Lh21
Kutno ◫ PL 50 Lk19
Kuujjuaq ◫ CDN 121 Gc07
Kuusamo ◫ FIN 28 Me13
Kuusankoski ◫ FIN 28 Md15
Kuvšinovo ◫ RUS 58 Mh17
Kuwait ◾ KWT 77 Nb13
Kuwait ● KWT 77 Nb13
Kuzneck ◫ RUS 60 Nd19
Kuzneckij Alatau ▲ RUS
  79 Pb08
Kuznecovs'k ◫ UA 51 Mc20
Kvaløya ◫ N 22 Lk11
Kvalsund ◫ N 23 Mb10
Kvam ◫ N 24 Le15
Kverkfjöll ▲ IS 32 Kb13
Kvichak Bay ◫ USA 116 Ca07
Kvikkjokk ◫ S 22 Lj12
Kvikkjokk fjällstation ◫ S
  22 Lj12
Kvislavatn ◫ IS 32 Ka13
Kviteseid ◫ N 26 Le16
Kwajalein Atoll ◫ MH 93 Tb17
Kwangdong ◫ RI 87 Ra18
Kwango ▲ RDC 108 Ld20
Kwekwe ◫ ZW 110 Mb22
Kwidzyn ◫ PL 50 Lk19
Kwilu ▲ RDC 108 Ld20
Kwinana ◫ AUS 95 Qd25
Kyaikkami ◫ MYA 84 Pd15
Kyancutta ◫ AUS 97 Rd25
Kyjiv ● UA 62 Mf20
Kyjivs'ke vodoschovyšče ▭
  UA 62 Mf20
Kyjov ◫ CZ 53 Lj21
Kyle of Lochalsh ◫ GB
  34 Kh17
Kynyčky ◫ UA 55 Me23
Kyoto ◫ J 83 Rd11
Kyrgyzstan ◾ KS 78 Oc10
Kyritz ◫ D 44 Lg19
Kyrksæterøra ◫ N 24 Le14
Kyushu ▲ J 83 Rc12
Kyyjärvi ◫ FIN 28 Mc14
Kyzyl ◫ RUS 79 Pc08
Kyzyl Kum ▲ TM 78 Oa10
Kyzylorda ◫ UZ 78 Ob10
Kyzylzhal ◫ KZ 78 Ob09

L

Laa an der Thaya ◫ A 52 Lj21
La Adela ◫ RA 137 Gd26
Laamu Atoll ◫ MV 81 Oc18
La Banda ◫ RA 136 Gd24
La Bañeza ◫ E 40 Kh24
Labasa ◫ FIJ 98 Td22
Labbezzanga ◫ RN 105 La16

Labé ◻ RG 105 Kb16
Labin ◻ HR 47 Lh23
Labrador Basin ▨ 119 Hb07
Labrador City ◻ CDN 121 Gc08
Labrador Peninsula ◣ CDN 121 Gb07
Labrador Sea ▨ 119 Ha06
Labuhanhaji ◻ RI 86 Pd18
Lac Albanel ◻ CDN 121 Gb08
Lacanau-Océan ◻ F 38 Kk23
Lac Aougoundou ◣ RMM 105 Kd15
Lacaune ◻ F 38 Lb24
Laccadive Islands ◻ IND 81 Oc16
Lac Debo ◣ RMM 105 Kd15
Lac de Kossou ◣ CI 105 Kc17
Lac de Manantali ◣ RMM 105 Kb16
Lac du Buyo ◣ CI 105 Kc17
La Ceiba ◻ HN 125 Fc15
Lac Faguibine ◣ RMM 105 Kd15
La Charité-sur-Loire ◻ F 38 Lb22
La Châtaigneraie ◻ F 38 Kk22
La Châtre ◻ F 38 La22
La Chorrera ◻ PA 132 Ga17
La Ciotat ◻ F 39 Lc24
Lac la Martre ◣ CDN 117 Ea06
Lac la Ronge ◣ CDN 120 Ed07
Lac Mai-Ndombe ◣ RDC 108 Ld19
Lac Ntomba ◣ RDC 108 Ld19
La Crosse ◻ USA 123 Fb10
Lac Seul ◣ CDN 120 Fb08
La Dorada ◻ CO 132 Gb17
Laduškin ◻ RUS 31 Ma18
Ladysmith ◻ ZA 110 Md24
Ladyžyn ◻ UA 62 Me21
Lae ◻ PNG 92 Sb20
Lae Atoll ◻ MH 93 Tb17
Lærdalsøyri ◻ N 24 Ld15
La Esmeralda ◻ YV 132 Gc18
Læsø ◻ DK 26 Lf17
Lævvajokgiedde ◻ N 23 Md11
Lafayette ◻ USA 123 Fb12
La Ferté-Bernard ◻ F 36 La21
La-Ferté-Macé ◻ F 36 Kk21
Lafia ◻ WAN 108 Lb17
La Flèche ◻ F 36 Kk22
La Galite ◻ TN 106 Lb13
Lagan ◻ RUS 76 Nb09
Lagan ◻ S 27 Lh17
Lages ◻ BR 135 Hb24
Lagh Bogal ◣ EAK 109 Md18
Laghouart ◻ DZ 104 La12
Lago Ladoga ◣ RUS 29 Mf15
Lagoa dos Patos ◣ BR 136 Hb25
Lagoa Mangueira ◣ BR 136 Hb25
Lagoa Mirim ◣ BR 136 Hb25
Lago Argentino ◣ RA 137 Gb28
Lago Buenos Aires ◣ RA 137 Gb28
Lago Colhué Huapi ◣ RA 137 Gc28
Lago de Cabora Bassa ◣ MOC 111 Mc22
Lago de Maracaibo ◣ YV 132 Gb17

Lago de Nicaragua ◣ NIC 125 Fc16
Lago de Poopó ◣ BOL 133 Gc22
Lago di Bolsena ◣ I 46 Lf24
Lago di Garda ◣ I 46 Lf23
Lago Maggiore ◣ CH/I 46 Le23
La Gomera ◻ E 104 Ka13
Lago Rogagua ◣ BOL 133 Gc21
Lago Rogaguado ◣ BOL 133 Gc21
Lagos ◻ P 41 Kf27
Lagos ◻ WAN 105 La17
Lago San Martin ◣ RA 137 Gb28
Lagos de Moreno ◻ MEX 124 Ed14
Lago Trasimeno ◣ I 46 Lg24
La Grange ◻ USA 94 Ra22
La Grange ◻ USA 123 Fd12
La Gran Sabana ◣ YV 132 Gd17
Laguna ◻ BR 135 Hc24
Laguna de Caratasca ◣ HN 126 Fd15
Laguna de Tamiahua ◣ MEX 125 Fa14
Laguna Madre ◣ USA 125 Fa13
Laguña Mar Chiquita ◣ RA 136 Gd25
Laguna Merin ◣ ROU 136 Hb25
Lahad Datu ◻ MAL 87 Qd17
Lahdenpoh'ja ◻ RUS 29 Mf15
Lahema rahvuspark ◆ EST 30 Mc16
Lahišyn ◻ BY 51 Mc19
Laholm ◻ S 26 Lg17
Laholmsbukten ▨ S 26 Lg17
Lahore ◻ PAK 80 Oc12
Lahr ◻ D 45 Ld21
Lahta ◻ RUS 29 Mg15
Lahti ◻ FIN 28 Mc15
L'Aigle ◻ F 36 La21
L'Aiguillon-sur-Mer ◻ F 38 Kk22
Lake Geneva ◣ F/CH 39 Ld22
Lake Ohrid ◣ MK 56 Ma25
Lake Onega ◣ RUS 29 Mh15
Lake Peipus ◣ EST/RUS 30 Md16
Lake Scutari ◣ CG/AL 54 La24
Lake Abaya ◣ ETH 109 Md17
Lake Albert ◣ RDC/EAU 109 Mc18
Lake Amadeus ◣ AUS 94 Rc23
Lake Argyle ◣ AUS 94 Rb22
Lake Athabasca ◣ CDN 120 Ec07
Lake Austin ◣ AUS 94 Qd24
Lakeba ◻ FJI 98 Ua22
Lake Baikal ◣ RUS 82 Qb08
Lake Balkhash ◣ KZ 78 Oc09
Lake Barlee ◣ AUS 95 Qd24
Lake Blanche ◣ AUS 96 Rd24
Lake Carey ◣ AUS 95 Ra24
Lake Carnegie ◣ AUS 94 Ra24
Lake Chad ◣ TCH 106 Lc16
Lake Charles ◻ USA 123 Fb12
Lake Chilwa ◣ MW 111 Md22

Lake Cowan ◣ AUS 95 Ra25
Lake Diefenbaker ◣ CDN 120 Ec08
Lake Disappointment ◣ AUS 94 Ra23
Lake District N.P. ◆ GB 34 Kj18
Lake Dora ◣ AUS 94 Ra23
Lake Dundas ◣ AUS 95 Ra25
Lake Edward ◣ RDC/EAU 109 Mb19
Lake Erie ◣ USA/CDN 123 Fd10
Lake Everald ◣ AUS 95 Rc23
Lake Eyasi ◣ EAT 109 Md19
Lake Eyre Basin ◣ AUS 96 Rd24
Lake Eyre North ◣ AUS 96 Rd24
Lake Eyre South ◣ AUS 96 Rd24
Lake Francis Case ◣ USA 122 Fa10
Lake Frome ◣ AUS 97 Sa25
Lake Gairdner ◣ AUS 97 Rd25
Lake Garnpung ◣ AUS 97 Sa25
Lake Gordon ◣ AUS 97 Sb27
Lake Grace ◣ AUS 95 Qd25
Lake Havasu City ◻ USA 122 Eb12
Lake Hopkins ◣ AUS 94 Rb23
Lake Huron ◣ USA/CDN 123 Fd09
Lake Issyk-Kul ◣ KS 79 Od10
Lake Kariba ◣ ZW 110 Mb22
Lake Khanka ◣ CHN/RUS 83 Rc09
Lake Kivu ◣ RDC/RWA 109 Mb19
Lake MacDonald ◣ AUS 94 Rb23
Lake Mackay ◣ AUS 94 Rb23
Lake MacLeod ◣ AUS 94 Qc23
Lake Malawi ◣ MW 111 Mc21
Lake Manitoba ◣ CDN 120 Fa08
Lake Maurice ◣ AUS 95 Rc24
Lake Mead ◣ USA 122 Eb11
Lake Melville ◣ CDN 121 Ha08
Lake Michigan ◣ USA/CDN 123 Fc10
Lake Minigwal ◣ AUS 95 Ra24
Lake Moore ◣ AUS 95 Qd24
Lake Murray ◣ PNG 92 Sa20
Lake Mweru ◣ RDC 109 Mb20
Lake Nasser ◣ ET 107 Mc14
Lake Natron ◣ EAT 109 Md19
Lake Nipigon ◣ CDN 120 Fc09
Lake Okeechobee ◣ USA 123 Fd13
Lake Ontario ◣ USA/CDN 123 Ga10
Lake Pedder ◣ AUS 97 Sb27
Lake Powell ◣ USA 122 Eb11
Lake Rebecca ◣ AUS 95 Ra25
Lake Rukwa ◣ EAT 109 Mc20
Lake Superior ◣ USA/CDN 120 Fc09
Lake Tahoe ◣ USA 122 Dd11
Lake Tana ◣ ETH 109 Md16

Lake Tanganyika ◣ EAT 109 Mb23
Lake Taupo ◣ NZ 99 Td26
Lake Te Anau ◣ NZ 99 Tb28
Lake Titicaca ◣ BOL/PE 133 Gb22
Lake Toba ◣ RI 86 Pd18
Lake Torrens ◣ AUS 97 Rd25
Lake Turkana ◣ EAK 109 Md18
Lake Urmia ◣ IR 76 Nb11
Lake Victoria ◣ 109 Mc19
Lake Volta ◣ GH 105 Kd17
Lake Way ◣ AUS 94 Ra24
Lake Wells ◣ AUS 94 Ra24
Lake White ◣ AUS 94 Rb23
Lake Winnipeg ◣ CDN 120 Fa08
Lake Winnipegosis ◣ CDN 120 Ed08
Lake Xau ◣ RB 110 Ma23
Lake Yamma Yamma ◣ AUS 96 Sa24
Läki ◻ BG 57 Mc25
Lakinsk ◻ RUS 58 Mk17
Lakonikós Kólpos ▨ GR 56 Mb27
Lakselv ◻ N 23 Mc10
Lakshadweep ◻ IND 81 Oc16
Lalapaşa ◻ TR 57 Md25
l'Alcora ◻ E 42 Kk25
l'Alcúdia ◻ E 43 Kk26
Lalín ◻ E 40 Kf22
La Linea de la Concepción ◻ E 41 Kh27
La Loche ◻ CDN 120 Ec07
La Louvière ◻ B 37 Lc20
la Maddalena ◻ I 48 Le25
La Mancha ◣ E 41 Kj26
Lamar ◻ USA 122 Ed11
Lamastre ◻ F 39 Lc23
Lamballe ◻ F 36 Kj21
Lambaréné ◻ G 108 Lc19
Lambert Glacier ◆ 141 Ob33
Lambertsbaai ◻ ZA 110 Ld25
Lamberts Bay ◻ ZA 110 Ld25
Lamego ◻ P 40 Kg25
Lamesa ◻ USA 122 Ed12
Lamézia Terme-Nicastro ◻ I 49 Lj26
Lamia ◻ GR 56 Mb26
Lammhult ◻ S 27 Lh17
La Montaña ◣ PE 133 Gb20
Lamotrek Atoll ◻ FSM 92 Sb17
Lampang ◻ THA 84 Pd15
Lampeland ◻ N 26 Le16
La Mure ◻ F 39 Lc23
Lanai ◻ USA 117 Cb35
Lancaster ◻ USA 122 Dd11
Lancaster ◻ USA 123 Ga10
Lancaster Sound ▨ CDN 118 Fc04
Lanciano ◻ I 47 Lh24
Łańcut ◻ PL 51 Mb20
Landau ◻ D 45 Le21
Landau ◻ D 45 Lg21
Landeck ◻ A 45 Lf22
Lander ◻ USA 94 Rc23
Landerneau ◻ F 36 Kh21
Landes ◣ F 42 Kk24
Landete ◻ E 43 Kk26
Landsberg ◻ D 45 Lf21
Landshut ◻ D 45 Lg21
Landskrona ◻ S 26 Lg18
Langå ◻ DK 26 Le17
Langanes ◣ IS 32 Kc12
Langesund ◻ N 26 Le16
Langevåg ◻ N 26 Lc16

Långfjället ⬕ S 24 Lg14
Langjökull ❄ IS 32 Jk13
Langkawi ▣ MAL 86 Pd17
Langogne ▣ F 38 Lb23
Langon ▣ F 38 Kk23
Langoya ▣ N 22 Lh11
Langres ▣ F 39 Lc22
Langsa ▣ RI 86 Pd18
Långshyttan ▣ S 25 Lj15
Långsjöby ▣ S 25 Lj13
Lang Suan ▣ THA 86 Pd17
Långträsk ▣ S 25 Ma13
Languedoc ▣ F 38 Lb24
Languedoc-Roussillon ▣ F 38 Lb24
Lannemezan ▣ F 42 La24
Lannion ▣ F 36 Kj21
Lansing ▣ USA 123 Fd10
Lanškroun ▣ CZ 52 Lj21
Lanusei ▣ I 48 Lc16
Lanzarote ▣ E 104 Kb13
Lanzhou ▣ CHN 82 Qa11
Laoag ▣ RP 85 Ra15
Laon ▣ F 37 Lb21
La Oroya ▣ PE 133 Ga21
Laos ▣ LAO 84 Qa15
Lapalisse ▣ F 39 Lb22
La Palma ▣ E 104 Ka13
La Palma del Condado ▣ E 41 Kg27
La Pampa ▣ RA 137 Gc26
La Paz ● BOL 133 Gc22
La Paz ▣ MEX 124 Ec17
La Paz ▣ RA 136 Gc25
La Perouse Strait ▣ J/RUS 83 Sa10
Lapland ⬕ S/FIN 22 Lj12
La Plata ▣ RA 136 Ha25
Laponia ⬕ S 22 Lj12
Lapovo ▣ SR 54 Ma23
Lappajärvi ▣ FIN 19 Mb14
Lappeenranta ▣ FIN 28 Me15
Lappoluobbal ▣ N 23 Mb11
Låpseki ▣ TR 57 Md25
Laptev Sea ▣ RUS 73 Ra03
Lapua ▣ FIN 19 Mb14
Łapy ▣ PL 51 Mb19
La Quiaca ▣ RA 136 Gc23
L'Áquila ▣ I 47 Lg24
Laramie ▣ USA 120 Ec10
Lärbro ▣ S 27 Lk17
Laredo ▣ E 42 Kj24
Laredo ▣ USA 122 Fa13
La Réole ▣ F 38 Kk23
Largeau Faya ▣ TCH 106 Ld15
Largs ▣ GB 34 Kh18
La Rioja ▣ E 42 Kj24
La Rioja ▣ RA 136 Gc24
La Rioja ▣ RA 136 Gc24
Lárissa ▣ GR 56 Mb26
Larmor-Plage ▣ F 36 Kj22
Larnaka ▣ CY 107 Mc12
Larne ▣ GB 34 Kh18
La Robla ▣ E 40 Kh24
La-Roche-Bernard ▣ F 36 Kj22
La Rochelle ▣ F 38 Kk22
La Roche-sur-Yon ▣ F 38 Kk22
La Roda ▣ E 41 Kj26
La Romana ▣ DOM 127 Gc15
La Ronge ▣ CDN 120 Ec07
Larrey Pt. ▣ AUS 94 Qd22
Larrimah ▣ AUS 94 Rc22
Lars Christensen Coast ▣ 141 Ob32
Larsen Ice Shelf ▣ 140 Gd32
Larsnes ▣ N 24 Lc14

Larvik ▣ N 26 Le16
Lascelles ▣ AUS 97 Sa26
Las Cruces ▣ USA 122 Ec12
La Serena ▣ E 41 Kh26
La Serena ▣ RCH 136 Gb24
Las Flores ▣ RA 137 Ha26
Las Heras ▣ RA 137 Gc28
Lashio ▣ MYA 84 Pd14
Lashkar Gah ▣ AFG 78 Oa12
Łasin ▣ PL 50 Lk19
Łask ▣ PL 50 Lk20
Las Lomitas ▣ RA 136 Gd23
La Souterraine ▣ F 38 La22
Las Palmas de Gran Canaria ▣ E 104 Ka13
La Spezia ▣ I 46 Le23
Las Plumas ▣ RA 137 Gc27
Lassen Peak ▲ USA 122 Dd10
Las Tunas ▣ C 126 Ga14
Las Vegas ▣ USA 122 Ea11
Las Vegas ▣ USA 122 Ec11
Latady Island ▣ 140 Ga33
Latakia ▣ SYR 76 Md11
Latgale ▣ LV 31 Md17
Latina ▣ I 48 Lg25
Latisana ▣ I 47 Lg23
La Toba ▣ E 43 Kk21
Látrabjarg ▣ IS 32 Jj13
La Tremblade ▣ F 38 Kk22
La Tuque ▣ CDN 121 Gb09
Latvia ▣ LV 30 Mc17
Laudio-Llodio ▣ E 42 Kj24
Lauenburg ▣ D 44 Lf19
Laugarbakki ▣ IS 32 Jk13
Lau Group ▣ FIJI 98 Ua22
Lauhanvuoren kansallispuisto ▣ FIN 19 Mb14
Launceston ▣ AUS 97 Sb27
Launceston ▣ GB 35 Kh20
La Unión ▣ E 43 Kk27
La Unión ▣ RCH 137 Gb27
La Urbana ▣ YV 132 Gc17
Lauría ▣ I 49 Lh25
Lausanne ▣ CH 45 Ld22
Laut ▣ RI 87 Qd19
Lauterbach (Hessen) ▣ D 45 Le20
Lautoka ▣ FIJ 98 Td22
Laval ▣ F 36 Kk21
Laverton ▣ AUS 95 Ra24
Lavia ▣ FIN 22 Mb15
La Vila Joiosa ▣ E 43 Kk26
Lavras ▣ BR 135 Hd23
Lavrentija ▣ RUS 74 Ub05
Lavrio ▣ GR 57 Mc27
Lavrovo ▣ RUS 58 Mj16
Lavumisa ▣ SD 111 Mc24
Lawdar ▣ YE 77 Nb16
Law Dome ▣ 141 Qc32
Lawrence ▣ USA 123 Fa11
Lawton ▣ USA 123 Fa12
Laxå ▣ S 27 Lh16
Layla ▣ KSA 77 Nb14
Łaż ▣ RUS 60 Ne17
Lazarevac ▣ SR 54 Ma23
Lazarevskoe ▣ RUS 66 Mk24
Lázaro Cardenas ▣ MEX 124 Ed15
Lazdijai ▣ LT 31 Mb18
Lázio ▣ I 48 Lg24
Lazo ▣ RUS 74 Pd15
Łeba ▣ PL 50 Lj18
Lebanon ▣ RL 107 Mc12
Lebedjan ▣ RUS 59 Mk19
Lebedyn ▣ UA 59 Mh20
Le Blanc ▣ F 38 La22
Łebork ▣ PL 50 Lj18
Le Bourg-d'Oisans ▣ F 39 Ld23

Lebrija ▣ E 41 Kg27
Lecce ▣ I 49 Lk25
Lecco ▣ I 46 Le23
Le Château-d'Oléron ▣ F 38 Kk23
Leči ▣ LV 30 Ma17
Leck ▣ D 44 Le18
Le Conquet ▣ F 36 Kh21
Le Creusot ▣ F 39 Lc22
Le Croisic ▣ F 36 Kj22
Łęczna ▣ PL 51 Mb20
Ledesma ▣ E 40 Kh25
Leeds ▣ GB 35 Kk19
Leer ▣ D 44 Ld19
Leeuwarden ▣ NL 37 Lc19
Leeward Islands ▣ 127 Gd14
Leeward Islands ▣ 127 Gd14
Lefkáda ▣ GR 56 Ma26
Leganés ▣ E 40 Kj25
Legazpi ▣ RP 85 Ra16
Legionowo ▣ PL 50 Ma19
Legkovo ▣ RUS 58 Mk16
Legnago ▣ I 46 Lf23
Legnica ▣ PL 50 Lj20
Le Havre ▣ F 36 La21
Lehliu-Gară ▣ RO 55 Md23
Leibnitz ▣ A 52 Lh22
Leicester ▣ GB 35 Kk19
Leiden ▣ NL 37 Lc19
Leigh Creek ▣ AUS 97 Rd25
Leikanger ▣ N 24 Lc14
Leinefelde ▣ D 44 Lf20
Leinster ▣ IRL 33 Kg19
Leipalingis ▣ LT 31 Mb18
Leipzig ▣ D 44 Lg20
Leira ▣ N 24 Le14
Leiria ▣ P 40 Kf26
Leirvåg ▣ N 24 Lc15
Leirvik ▣ N 26 Lc16
Leivonmäen kansallispuisto ▣ FIN 28 Mc15
Leiyang ▣ CHN 85 Qc13
Leka ▣ N 24 Lf13
Leknes ▣ N 22 Lg11
Leksand ▣ S 25 Lh15
Lel'čycy ▣ BY 51 Me20
Lelu ▣ FSM 93 Ta17
Lelystad ▣ NL 37 Lc19
Le Mans ▣ F 36 La21
Lemmenjoen kansallispuisto ▣ FIN 23 Mc11
Lempäälä ▣ FIN 22 Mb15
Lemvig ▣ DK 26 Le17
Lena ▣ N 24 Lf15
Lena ▣ RUS 75 Ra05
Lena Delta ▣ RUS 73 Rb04
Lendava ▣ SLO 52 Lj22
Lendery ▣ RUS 29 Mf14
Lenggries ▣ D 45 Lf22
Lenhovda ▣ S 27 Lh17
Lenina ▣ BY 59 Mf19
Lenine ▣ UA 63 Mh23
Leningradskaja ▣ 141 Sd32
Leninogorsk ▣ RUS 60 Ng18
Lenin Peak ▲ TJ 78 Oc11
Leninsk ▣ RUS 61 Nc21
Leninskij ▣ RUS 58 Mj18
Leninsk-Kuzneckij ▣ RUS 79 Pb08
Lenkivci ▣ UA 51 Md21
Lenkoran' ▣ AZ 76 Nb11
Leno-Angarskoe plato ▣ RUS 73 Qa07
Lens ▣ F 37 Lb20
Lensk ▣ RUS 73 Qc06
Lent'evo ▣ RUS 58 Mj16
Lenti ▣ H 52 Lj22
Lentini ▣ I 49 Lh27
Lentvaris ▣ LT 31 Mc18

Leoben ▣ A 52 Lh22
Leominster ▣ GB 35 Kj19
León ▣ E 40 Kh24
León ▣ MEX 124 Ed14
León ▣ NIC 125 Fc16
Leonídio ▣ GR 56 Mb27
Leonora ▣ AUS 95 Ra24
Leopold and Astrid Coast ▣ 141 Pa32
Leova ▣ MD 55 Me22
Lepel' ▣ BY 31 Me18
Leppävirta ▣ FIN 28 Md14
Le Puy-en-Velay ▣ F 38 Lb23
Lercara Friddi ▣ I 48 Lg27
Lerma ▣ E 42 Kj24
Lermontovo ▣ RUS 61 Nb19
Léros ▣ GR 57 Md27
Lerwick ▣ GB 34 Kk15
Les Cayes ▣ RH 127 Gb15
Leshan ▣ CHN 84 Qa12
Les Herbiers ▣ F 38 Kk22
Lesko ▣ PL 51 Mb21
Leskovac ▣ SR 54 Ma24
Leskovik ▣ AL 56 Ma25
Lesneven ▣ F 36 Kh21
Lesnoe ▣ RUS 58 Mh16
Lesosibirsk ▣ RUS 73 Pc07
Lesotho ▣ LS 110 Mb24
Lesparre-Médoc ▣ F 38 Kk23
L'Esperance Rock ▣ NZ 99 Ua25
Les Sables-d'Olonne ▣ F 38 Kk22
Lessebo ▣ S 27 Lh17
Lesser Antilles ▣ 127 Gc16
Lesser Hinggan Range ▣ CHN 75 Rb08
Lesser Slave Lake ▣ CDN 117 Ea07
Lesser Slave Lake ▣ CDN 117 Ea07
Lesser Sunda Islands ▣ RI 87 Qd20
Lésvos ▣ GR 57 Mc26
Leszno ▣ PL 50 Lj20
Letca ▣ RO 54 Mb22
Letenye ▣ H 53 Lj22
Lethbridge ▣ CDN 122 Eb09
Lethem ▣ GUY 132 Ha18
Leticia ▣ CO 132 Gc19
Letnij bereg ▣ RUS 29 Mj13
Le Touquet-Paris-Plage ▣ F 35 La20
Letterkenny ▣ IRL 33 Kg18
Letyčiv ▣ UA 51 Md21
Leutkirch ▣ D 45 Lf22
Leuven ▣ B 37 Lc20
Levanger ▣ N 24 Lf14
Levantine Basin ▣ 107 Mb12
Leverkusen ▣ D 44 Ld20
Levice ▣ SK 53 Lk21
Le Vigan ▣ F 38 Lb24
Levitha ▣ GR 57 Md27
Levski ▣ BG 55 Mc24
Lewiston ▣ USA 122 Ea09
Lewiston ▣ USA 121 Gb10
Lexington ▣ USA 123 Fd11
Leyte ▣ RP 85 Rb16
Lezhë ▣ AL 56 Lk25
Lëzna ▣ BY 31 Mf18
L'gov ▣ RUS 59 Mh20
Lhasa ▣ CHN 84 Pc13
Lhaze ▣ CHN 80 Pb13
Lhokseumawe ▣ RI 86 Pd17
Lian Xian ▣ CHN 85 Qc14
Lianyungang ▣ CHN 83 Qd12
Liaoning ▣ CHN 83 Ra10
Liaoyuan ▣ CHN 83 Rb10
Liatorp ▣ S 27 Lh17

Liberal ☐ USA 122 Ed11
Liberec ☐ CZ 52 Lh20
Liberia ☐ CR 125 Fc16
Liberia ■ LB 105 Kb17
Libohovë ☐ AL 56 Ma25
Libourne ☐ F 38 Kd23
Libreville ● G 108 Lb18
Libya ■ LAR 106 Lc13
Libyan Desert ☐ LAR 106 Ma13
Licata ☐ I 49 Lg27
Lice ☐ TR 66 Na26
Lich ☐ D 44 Le20
Lichinga ☐ MOC 111 Md21
Lichtenfels ☐ D 45 Lf20
Lida ☐ BY 51 Mc19
Liden ☐ S 25 Lj14
Lidköping ☐ S 26 Lg16
Lido di Metaponto ☐ I 49 Lj25
Lidoriki ☐ GR 56 Mb26
Lidzbark ☐ PL 50 Lk19
Lidzbark Warmiński ☐ PL 50 Ma18
Lieksa ☐ FIN 29 Mf14
Lienz ☐ A 52 Lg22
Liești ☐ RO 55 Md23
Liesjärven kansallispuisto ☐ FIN 22 Mb15
Liestal ☐ CH 45 Ld22
Lievestuore ☐ FIN 28 Md14
Liezen ☐ A 52 Lh22
Lifou ☐ F 98 Tb23
Lihir Group ☐ PNG 93 Sc19
Liholslavl' ☐ RUS 58 Mh17
Lihou Reefs and Cays ☐ AUS 96 Sc22
Lihovskoj ☐ RUS 63 Na18
Lihula ☐ EST 30 Mb16
Liinahamari ☐ RUS 23 Mf11
Lijiang ☐ CHN 84 Qa13
Likasi ☐ RDC 110 Mb21
Likenäs ☐ S 24 Lg15
Liknes ☐ N 26 Ld16
Lillärdal ☐ S 25 Lh15
Lille ☐ F 37 Lb20
Lillehammer ☐ N 24 Lf15
Lillesand ☐ N 26 Le16
Lillestrøm ☐ N 26 Lf16
Lillie Marleen ☐ 141 Tc33
Lilongwe ■ MW 111 Mc21
Lima ● PE 133 Ga20
Lima ☐ USA 123 Fd10
Limanowa ☐ PL 50 Ma21
Limassol ☐ CY 107 Mc12
Limay ☐ RA 137 Gc26
Limba Limba ☐ EAT 109 Mc20
Limbaži ☐ LV 30 Mc17
Limbé ☐ CAM 108 Lb18
Limburg ☐ D 44 Le20
Limeira ☐ BR 135 Hc23
Limerick ☐ IRL 33 Kf19
Limes ☐ D 44 Le21
Limfjorden ☐ DK 26 Le17
Limingen ☐ N 24 Lg13
Limmen Bight ☐ AUS 96 Rd21
Limmen Bight River ☐ AUS 94 Rc22
Limnos ☐ GR 57 Mc26
Limoges ☐ F 38 La23
Limousin ☐ F 38 La23
Limousin ☐ F 38 La23
Limoux ☐ F 38 Lb24
Limpopo ☐ MOC 111 Mc23
Limpopo ☐ ZA 110 Mb23
Linares ☐ E 41 Kj26
Linares ☐ MEX 124 Fa14
Lináriá ☐ GR 57 Mc26

Lincoln ☐ GB 35 Kk19
Lincoln ● USA 123 Fa10
Lincoln Sea ☐ 118 Ha02
Lindås ☐ N 24 Lc15
Linde ☐ RUS 75 Ra05
Lindesberg ☐ S 27 Lh16
Lindesnes ☐ N 26 Ld17
Lindi ☐ EAT 109 Md20
Lindi ☐ RDC 109 Mb18
Lindi Bay ☐ EAT 109 Md20
Lindos ☐ GR 64 Me27
Lindsdal ☐ S 27 Lj17
Linevo ☐ RUS 61 Nc20
Linfen ☐ CHN 82 Qc11
Lingen ☐ D 44 Ld19
Lingga ☐ RI 86 Qa19
Linguère ☐ SN 105 Ka15
Linhares ☐ BR 135 Hd22
Linköping ☐ S 27 Lh16
Linnansaaren kansallispuisto ☐ FIN 28 Me14
Linxi ☐ CHN 82 Qd10
Linxi ☐ CHN 83 Qd11
Linyanti ☐ RB 110 Ma22
Linz ☐ A 52 Lh21
Lipany ☐ SK 53 Ma21
Lipari ☐ I 49 Lh26
Lipari Islands ☐ I 49 Lh26
Lipeck ☐ RUS 59 Mh18
Liperi ☐ FIN 28 Me14
Lipicy-Zybino ☐ RUS 59 Mj19
Lipik ☐ HR 47 Lj23
Lipin Bor ☐ RUS 58 Mh15
Lipki ☐ RUS 59 Mj19
Lipno ☐ PL 50 Lk19
Lipova ☐ RO 54 Ma22
Lippstadt ☐ D 44 Le20
Lipsi ☐ GR 57 Md27
Lipsko ☐ PL 50 Ma20
Liptovský Hrádok ☐ SK 53 Lk21
Lisala ☐ RDC 108 Ma18
Lisboa ● P 40 Kf26
Lisbon ● P 40 Kf26
Lisburn ☐ GB 33 Kg18
Lisieux ☐ F 36 La21
Liski ☐ RUS 59 Mk20
L'Isle-Jourdain ☐ F 42 La24
Lismore ☐ AUS 96 Sd24
List ☐ D 44 Le18
Lister, Mount ☐ 141 Ta34
Listowel ☐ IRL 33 Kf19
Lithgow ☐ AUS 97 Sc25
Lithuania ■ LT 31 Mb18
Litoměřice ☐ CZ 52 Lh20
Little Andaman ☐ IND 81 Pc16
Little Karoo ☐ ZA 110 Ma25
Little Nicobar ☐ IND 81 Pc17
Little Rock ● USA 123 Fb12
Liupanshui ☐ CHN 84 Qa14
Liuzhou ☐ CHN 84 Qb14
Livadiá ☐ GR 56 Mb26
Līvāni ☐ LV 31 Md17
Liverpool ☐ GB 35 Kj19
Liverpool Bay ☐ GB 35 Kj19
Livingston ☐ CDN 121 Gc08
Livingston ☐ GB 34 Kj18
Livingstone ☐ ZW 110 Mb22
Livingston Island ☐ GB 140 Gd31
Livland ☐ LV 30 Md17
Livno ☐ BIH 47 Lj24
Livny ☐ RUS 59 Mj19
Livorno ☐ I 46 Lf24
Livron-sur-Drôme ☐ F 39 Lc23
Lixoúri ☐ GR 56 Ma26

Ljachaviči ☐ BY 51 Md19
Ljady ☐ RUS 30 Me16
Ljamca ☐ RUS 23 Mj13
Ljig ☐ SR 54 Ma23
Ljørndalen ☐ N 24 Lg14
Ljuban' ☐ BY 51 Me19
Ljuban' ☐ RUS 30 Mf16
Ljubar ☐ UA 51 Md21
Ljubešiv ☐ UA 51 Mc20
Ljubinje ☐ BIH 47 Lk24
Ljuboml' ☐ UA 51 Mc20
Ljubovija ☐ SR 54 Lk23
Ljubymivka ☐ UA 63 Mj22
Ljubytino ☐ RUS 58 Mg16
Ljudinovo ☐ RUS 59 Mh19
Ljugarn ☐ S 27 Lk17
Ljungan ☐ S 24 Lg14
Ljungby ☐ S 27 Lh17
Ljungsbro ☐ S 27 Lh16
Ljusdal ☐ S 25 Lj15
Llandovery ☐ GB 35 Kj20
Llandudno ☐ GB 35 Kj19
Llanes ☐ E 40 Kj24
Llano Estacado ☐ USA 122 Ed12
Llanos de Chiquitos ☐ BOL 133 Gd22
Llanos del Orinoco ☐ CO/YV 132 Gc17
Llanos de Mojos ☐ BOL 133 Gc21
Llay-Llay ☐ RCH 136 Gb25
Lleida ☐ E 42 La25
Llerena ☐ E 41 Kg26
Llíca ☐ BOL 133 Gc22
Lliria ☐ E 43 Kk26
L'Île-Rousse ☐ F 46 Le24
Lloret de Mar ☐ E 42 Lb25
Lloydminster ☐ CDN 120 Eb08
Llucmajor ☐ E 43 Lb26
Lnáře ☐ CZ 52 Lg21
Lobatse ☐ RB 110 Mb24
Löbau ☐ D 44 Lh20
Lobay ☐ RCA 108 Lj18
Lobcovo ☐ RUS 58 Na17
Łobez ☐ PL 50 Lh19
Lobito ☐ ANG 110 Lc21
Locarno ☐ CH 45 Le22
Lochboisdale ☐ GB 34 Kg17
Loch Lomond and The Trossachs N.P. ☐ GB 34 Kh17
Loch Ness ☐ GB 34 Kh17
Lochvycja ☐ UA 62 Mg20
Lockhart River ☐ AUS 96 Sa21
Locminé ☐ F 36 Kj22
Locri ☐ I 49 Lj26
Lodejenoe Pole ☐ RUS 29 Mg15
Lodève ☐ F 38 Lb24
Lodi ☐ I 46 Le23
Løding ☐ N 22 Lh12
Lødingen ☐ N 22 Lj11
Lodja ☐ RDC 108 Ma19
Łódź ☐ PL 50 Lk20
Lofsdalen ☐ S 24 Lg14
Log ☐ RUS 61 Nb21
Logan ☐ USA 122 Eb10
Logange ☐ RDC 108 Ma19
Logone ☐ TCH 108 Lc17
Logroño ☐ E 42 Kj24
Logrosán ☐ E 41 Kh26
Løgstør ☐ DK 26 Le17
Lohja ☐ FIN 28 Mc15
Loi-Kaw ☐ MYA 84 Pd15
Loimaa ☐ FIN 22 Mb15
Loire ☐ F 38 Kk22

Loja ☐ E 41 Kh27
Loja ☐ EC 132 Ga19
Lojmola ☐ RUS 29 Mf15
Lokan tekojärvi ☐ FIN 23 Md12
Lokichar ☐ EAK 109 Md18
Loknja ☐ RUS 30 Mf17
Lokoja ☐ WAN 108 Lb17
Lokot' ☐ RUS 59 Mh19
Lol ☐ SUD 109 Mb17
Lom ☐ BG 54 Mb24
Lom ☐ N 24 Le15
Łomża ☐ PL 51 Mb19
Lomami ☐ RDC 109 Ma19
Lomami ☐ RDC 108 Ma20
Lombardy ☐ I 46 Le23
Lomblen ☐ RI 87 Ra20
Lombok ☐ RI 87 Qd20
Lomé ● TG 105 La17
Lomela ☐ RDC 108 Ma19
Lomonosov ☐ RUS 30 Me16
Lomonosov Ridge ☐ 138 Hb01
Loncoche ☐ RCH 137 Gb26
London ☐ CDN 123 Fd10
London ● GB 35 Kk20
Londonderry ☐ GB 33 Kg18
Londrina ☐ BR 135 Hb23
Longbawan ☐ RI 87 Qd18
Long Beach ☐ USA 122 Dd11
Longford ☐ IRL 33 Kg19
Longhurst, Mount ☐ 141 Sd34
Long Island ☐ BS 126 Ga14
Long Island ☐ PNG 92 Sb20
Long Island ☐ USA 121 Gb10
Longlac ☐ CDN 120 Fc09
Longmen Shan ☐ CHN 84 Qa12
Longnawang ☐ RI 87 Qd18
Longreach ☐ AUS 96 Sa23
Longuyon ☐ F 37 Lc21
Longview ☐ USA 123 Fb12
Longwy ☐ F 37 Lc21
Long Xuyen ☐ VN 84 Qb16
Longyan ☐ CHN 85 Qd13
Longyearbyen ☐ N 22 Lf06
Löningen ☐ D 44 Ld19
Lönsboda ☐ S 27 Lh17
Lons-le-Saunier ☐ F 39 Lc22
Lopatino ☐ RUS 61 Nc19
Lop Nur ☐ CHN 79 Pc10
Lopori ☐ RDC 108 Ma18
Lorca ☐ E 43 Kk27
Lord Howe Island ☐ AUS 97 Sd25
Lord Howe Rise ☐ 98 Ta24
Lord Howe Seamounts ☐ 97 Sd24
Lorengau ☐ PNG 92 Sb19
Loreto ☐ I 47 Lg24
Loreto ☐ MEX 124 Eb13
Lorica ☐ CO 132 Ga17
Lorient ☐ F 36 Kj22
Lörrach ☐ D 45 Ld22
Lorraine ☐ F 37 Lc21
Los ☐ S 25 Lh15
Los Alamos ☐ USA 122 Ec11
Los Angeles ☐ RCH 137 Gb26
Los Angeles ● USA 122 Dd11
Losap Atoll ☐ FSM 93 Sc17
Los Barrancos ☐ YV 132 Gc18
Los Blancos ☐ RA 136 Gd23
Łosice ☐ PL 51 Mb19
Losinyj ostrov N.P. ☐ RUS 58 Mj18
Los Mochis ☐ MEX 124 Ec13

Los Navalmorales E 40 Kh26
Lossen S 24 Lg14
Lossiemouth GB 34 Kj17
Los Vientos RCH 136 Gc23
Los Vilos RCH 136 Gb25
Los Yébenes E 41 Kj26
Lot F 38 La23
Lotošino RUS 58 Mh17
Loubomo RCB 108 Lc19
Loudéac F 36 Kj21
Loudun F 38 La22
Louga SN 105 Ka15
Loughborough GB 35 Kh19
Lough Neagh GB 33 Kg18
Loughrea IRL 33 Kf19
Louhans F 39 Lc22
Louisiade Archipelago PNG 96 Sc21
Louisiana USA 123 Fb12
Louisville USA 123 Fd11
Loulé P 41 Kg27
Louny CZ 52 Lg20
Lourdes F 42 Kk24
Louth AUS 97 Sb25
Louth GB 35 La19
Louviers F 36 La21
Lövånger S 25 Ma13
Lovćen, N.P. SR 54 Lk24
Loveč BG 55 Mc24
Lower Hutt NZ 99 Td27
Lower Peninsula USA 123 Fc10
Lowestoft GB 35 La19
Łowicz PL 50 Lk19
Loznica SR 54 Lk23
Lozova UA 63 Mj21
Luama RDC 109 Mb19
Lu'an CHN 85 Qd12
Luanco E 40 Kh24
Luanda ANG 108 Lc20
Luanginga ANG 110 Ma21
Luangoe ANG 108 Ld20
Luang Prabang LAO 84 Qa15
Luang Prabang Range LAO 84 Qa15
Luangwa Z 111 Mc21
Luanshya Z 110 Mb21
Luarca E 40 Kg24
Lubaanbajo RI 87 Ra20
Lubango ANG 110 Lc21
Lubao RDC 109 Mb20
Lubartów PL 51 Mb20
Lubawa PL 50 Lk19
Lübben (Spreewald) D 44 Lg20
Lübbenau (Spreewald) D 44 Lg20
Lubbock USA 122 Ed12
Lübeck D 44 Lf19
Lubefu RDC 108 Ma19
Lubero RDC 109 Mb19
Lubin PL 50 Lj20
Lubjaniki RUS 58 Na18
Lublin PL 51 Mb20
Lubliniec PL 50 Lk20
Lubny UA 62 Mg21
Lubumbashi RDC 110 Mb21
Lubutu RDC 109 Mb19
Lucca I 46 Lf24
Luce Bay GB 34 Kh18
Lucena E 41 Kh27
Lucena RP 85 Ra16
Lučenec SK 53 La21
Luc'k UA 51 Mc20
Lucknow IND 80 Pa13

Luçon F 38 Kk22
Ludbreg HR 52 Lj22
Lüderitz NAM 110 Ld24
Ludhiana IND 80 Od12
Ludus RO 54 Mc22
Ludvika S 25 Lh15
Ludwigsburg D 45 Le21
Ludwigsfelde D 44 Lg19
Ludwigshafen D 45 Le21
Ludwigslust D 44 Lf19
Ludza LV 30 Md17
Luena ANG 110 Ld21
Luena Z 110 Ma21
Lufkin USA 123 Fb12
Luga RUS 30 Me16
Luga RUS 30 Me16
Lugano CH 46 Le23
Luganville VU 98 Tb22
Luganville VU 98 Tb22
Lugenda MOC 111 Md21
Lugo E 40 Kg24
Lugo I 46 Lf23
Lugoj RO 54 Ma23
Luh RUS 58 Nb17
Luh RUS 58 Nb17
Luhans'k UA 63 Mk21
Luhovicy RUS 58 Mk18
Luhuo CHN 84 Qa12
Luiana ANG 110 Ma22
Luilaka RDC 108 Ma19
Luilu RDC 108 Ma20
Lukavac BIH 47 Lk23
Lukenie RDC 108 Ld19
Lukojanov RUS 60 Nc18
Lukovit BG 55 Mc24
Lukovnikovo RUS 58 Mh17
Łuków PL 51 Mb20
Luleå S 19 Mb13
Luleälven S 25 Ma13
Lüleburgaz TR 57 Md25
Lulonga RDC 108 Ld18
Lulua RDC 108 Ma20
Lumbala ANG 110 Ma21
Lumbrales E 40 Kg25
Lumi PNG 92 Sa19
Lund S 26 Lg18
Lüneburg D 44 Lf19
Lunéville F 37 Ld21
Lunga Z 110 Mb21
Lunga Lunga EAK 109 Md19
Lungué-Bungo ANG 110 Ma21
Luninec BY 51 Md19
Lunino RUS 60 Nc19
Luodian CHN 84 Qb13
Luoyang CHN 82 Qc12
Lure F 39 Ld22
Lúrio MOC 111 Md21
Lusaka ZW 110 Mb22
Lushnjë AL 56 La25
Lüshun CHN 83 Ra11
Lusk USA 122 Ed10
Lutherstadt Eisleben D 44 Lf20
Lutherstadt Wittenberg D 44 Lg20
Lütjenburg D 44 Lf18
Luton GB 35 Kk20
Lutselk'e CDN 120 Eb06
Lutuhyne UA 63 Mk21
Lützow-Holm bukta 141 Md32
Luumäki FIN 28 Md15
Luuq SP 109 Na18
Luvua RDC 109 Mb20
Luwuk RI 87 Ra19
Luxembourg L 37 Ld21
Luxembourg L 37 Ld21

Luxeuil-les-Bains F 39 Ld22
Luxi CHN 84 Pd14
Luxor ET 107 Mc13
Luzern CH 45 Le22
Lzhou CHN 84 Qb13
Luzon RP 85 Ra15
Luzon Strait RP 85 Ra15
Lycksele S 25 Lk13
Lydney GB 35 Kj20
Lyman UA 63 Mj21
Lynchburg USA 123 Ga11
Lyngdal N 26 Ld16
Lyngen N 22 Ma11
Lyngseidet N 22 Ma11
Lynn Lake CDN 120 Ed07
Lyon F 39 Lc23
Lypci UA 63 Mj20
Lypova Dolyna UA 62 Mg20
Lyra Reef PNG 93 Sc19
Lysekil S 26 Lf16
Lyskovo RUS 60 Nc17
Lysoysundet N 24 Le14
Lysÿcans'k UA 63 Mk21
Lysye Gory RUS 61 Nc20
Lyubimets BG 57 Md25

M

Ma'an JOR 76 Md12
Maanselkä FIN 23 Me12
Maanselkä FIN 28 Me14
Maardu EST 30 Mc16
Maarianhamina = Mariehamn FIN 25 Lk15
Maastricht NL 37 Lc20
Mablethorpe GB 35 La19
Macao CHN 85 Qc14
Macapá BR 134 Hb18
Macauley Island NZ 99 Ua25
Macdonnell Ranges AUS 94 Rc23
Macedonia GR 56 Ma25
Macedonia MK 56 Ma25
Maceió BR 134 Ja20
Macerata I 46 Lg24
Machala EC 132 Ga19
Mâcin RO 55 Me23
Mackay AUS 96 Sb23
Mackenzie CDN 116 Dc05
Mackenzie GUY 134 Ha17
Mackenzie Bay CDN 116 Da05
Mackenzie Bay 141 Oc32
Mackenzie King Island CDN 118 Eb03
Mackenzie Mountains CDN 116 Dc06
Maclean Strait CDN 118 Ed03
Macomér I 48 Le25
Macon USA 123 Fd12
Mâcon F 39 Lc22
Mac Robertson Land 141 Nd33
Macumba AUS 96 Rd24
Madagascar RM 111 Nb23
Madagascar Basin 111 Nc24
Madagascar Ridge 111 Na25
Madagaskar RM 111 Nb23
Madan BG 57 Mc25
Madang PNG 92 Sb20
Madeira BR 132 Ha19

Madeira P 104 Ka12
Madeira Rise 104 Ka12
Maden TR 66 Na25
Madera MEX 124 Ec13
Madesimo I 46 Le22
Madhya Pradesh IND 80 Od14
Madison USA 123 Fc10
Madiun RI 86 Qc20
Madona LV 30 Md17
Madrakah OM 77 Nd15
Madras IND 81 Pa16
Madre de Dios BOL 133 Gc21
Madrid E 40 Kj25
Madrid E 40 Kj25
Madridejos E 41 Kj26
Madura RI 87 Qb20
Madurai IND 81 Od16
Maebashi J 83 Rd11
Maewo VU 98 Tb22
Mafia Island EAT 109 Md20
Mafra BR 135 Hc24
Mafraq JOR 76 Md12
Magadan RUS 75 Sc07
Magangué CO 132 Gb17
Magburaka WAL 105 Kb17
Magdeburg D 44 Lf19
Magén Gangri CHN 84 Qa12
Maghera GB 33 Kg18
Maghera RO 55 Md22
Máglie I 49 Lk25
Magnitogorsk RUS 78 Nd08
Magny-en-Vexin F 36 La21
Mahačkala RUS 76 Nb10
Mahajanga RM 111 Nb22
Mahalapye RB 110 Mb23
Mahanadi IND 80 Pa14
Maharashtra IND 81 Od15
Mahdalynivka UA 63 Mh21
Mahilëv BY 59 Mf19
Mahón = Maó E 43 Lc26
Maicao CO 127 Gb16
Maidstone GB 35 La20
Maiduguri WAN 108 Lc16
Maiella, P.N.della I 47 Lh24
Maiko RDC 109 Mb18
Maikoor RI 92 Rc20
Mainburg D 45 Lf21
Maine USA 123 Gc09
Mainland GB 34 Kj16
Mainland GB 34 Kk15
Mainz D 45 Le20
Maitland AUS 97 Sc25
Maitri 141 Lc33
Maja RUS 75 Rd07
Majak Oktjabrja RUS 61 Nc21
Majdan RUS 60 Ne18
Majdan UA 53 Mb21
Majene RI 87 Qc19
Majkop RUS 76 Na10
Majkop RUS 76 Na10
Makale RI 87 Qc19
Makanshy KZ 79 Pa09
Makar'evskaja RUS 29 Mh15
Makarovo RUS 61 Nb19
Makarska HR 47 Lj24
Makassar RI 87 Qc19
Makassar Strait RI 87 Qd19
Makat KZ 76 Nc09
Makeni WAL 105 Kb17
Makgadikgadi Pans RB 110 Mb23
Makkovik CDN 121 Ha07

Makó ☐ H 53 Ma22
Makokou ☐ G 108 Lc18
Maków Mazowiecki ☐ PL 50 Ma19
Makran Coast Range ▲ PAK 77 Oa13
Maksatiha ☐ RUS 58 Mh17
Maku ☐ IR 76 Na11
Makumbako ☐ EAT 109 Mc20
Makurdi ☐ WAN 108 Lb17
Makwe ☐ MYA 84 Pd14
Malå ☐ S 25 Lk13
Malabo ● GQ 108 Lb18
Malacky ☐ SK 53 Lj21
Maladzečna ☐ BY 31 Md18
Malá Fatra, N.P. ▲ SK 53 Lk21
Málaga ☐ E 41 Kh27
Malagón ☐ E 41 Kj26
Malaita ▲ SOL 93 Ta20
Malaja Višera ☐ RUS 58 Mg16
Malakal ☐ SUD 109 Mc17
Malakula ▲ VU 98 Tb22
Malakula ▲ VU 98 Tb22
Malang ☐ RI 87 Qb20
Malanje ☐ ANG 108 Ld20
Mälaren ☐ S 27 Lj16
Malargüe ☐ RA 136 Gc26
Malaryta ☐ BY 51 Mc20
Mala Serdoba ☐ RUS 61 Nc19
Malaspina Glacier ⁎ USA 116 Cd06
Malatya ☐ TR 76 Md11
Malatya ☐ TR 66 Mk26
Mala Vyska ☐ UA 62 Mf21
Malawi ■ MW 111 Mc21
Malay Peninsula ▲ MAL 86 Qa18
Malaysia ■ MAL 86 Qb17
Malazgirt ☐ TR 76 Nb26
Malbork ☐ PL 50 Lk18
Malbuisson ☐ F 39 Ld22
Malchin ☐ D 44 Lg19
Maldives ■ MV 81 Oc17
Maldives ■ MV 81 Oc18
Male ● MV 81 Oc18
Male Atoll ⁎ MV 81 Oc18
Malegaon ☐ IND 80 Oc14
Malesherbes ☐ F 37 Lb21
Mali ■ RMM 105 Kd15
Mali Lošinj ☐ HR 47 Lh23
Malindi ☐ EAK 109 Na19
Maliq ☐ AL 56 Ma25
Malkara ☐ TR 57 Md25
Malko Tărnovo ☐ BG 57 Md25
Mallacoota Inlet ☐ AUS 97 Sc26
Mallaig ☐ GB 34 Kh17
Mallawi ☐ ET 107 Mc13
Mallorca ▲ E 43 Lb26
Mallow ☐ IRL 33 Kf19
Malmberget ☐ S 23 Ma12
Malmédy ☐ B 37 Ld20
Malmö ☐ S 26 Lg18
Malmyž ☐ RUS 72 Nc07
Malmyž ☐ RUS 60 Nf17
Maloarhangel'sk ☐ RUS 59 Mj19
Małopolska ⁎ PL 50 Ma20
Måløy ☐ N 24 Lc15
Malta ■ M 49 Lh27
Malta ☐ M 49 Lh28
Malta ☐ USA 120 Ec09
Malton ☐ GB 35 Kk18
Malung ☐ S 24 Lg15

Malyj Čuraševo ☐ RUS 60 Nd18
Malyj Enisej ☐ RUS 79 Pd08
Malyn ☐ UA 62 Me20
Malyševo ☐ RUS 58 Na18
Mamadys ☐ RUS 60 Nf18
Mambasa ☐ RDC 109 Mb18
Mamberamo ☐ RI 92 Rd19
Mamburao ☐ RP 85 Ra16
Mamelodi ☐ ZA 110 Mb24
Mamers ☐ F 36 La21
Mamonovo ☐ RUS 27 Lk18
Mamoré ☐ BOL 133 Gc21
Mamou ☐ RG 105 Kb16
Mamuju ☐ RI 87 Qc19
Mamuno ☐ RB 110 Ma23
Mamykovo ☐ RUS 60 Nf18
Manacor ☐ E 43 Lb26
Manado ☐ RI 87 Ra18
Managua ● NIC 125 Fc16
Manakara ☐ RM 111 Nb23
Manamensalo ☐ FIN 22 Md13
Mananjary ☐ RM 111 Nb23
Manaus ☐ BR 132 Ha19
Manavgat ☐ TR 64 Mf27
Manavgat Şelâlesi ⁎ TR 64 Mf27
Manchester ☐ GB 35 Kj19
Manchester ☐ USA 121 Gb10
Manchuria ⁎ CHN 83 Ra10
Mandal ☐ N 26 Ld16
Mandalay ☐ MYA 84 Pd14
Mandimba ☐ MOC 111 Md21
Mandúria ☐ I 49 Lj25
Manevyči ☐ UA 51 Mc20
Manfredónia ☐ I 49 Lh25
Manga ☐ NG 106 Lc16
Mangalia ☐ RO 55 Me24
Mangalore ☐ IND 81 Oc16
Mangnai ☐ CHN 79 Pc11
Mangoky ☐ RM 111 Na23
Mangole ▲ RI 87 Rb19
Mangui ☐ CHN 82 Ra08
Manhattan ☐ USA 123 Fa11
Máni ⁎ GR 56 Mb27
Mania ☐ RM 111 Nb22
Manicouagan ☐ CDN 121 Gc08
Manila ● RP 85 Ra16
Maningrida ☐ AUS 94 Rc21
Manipur ⁎ IND 84 Pc13
Manisa ☐ TR 57 Md26
Manitoba ⁎ CDN 120 Fa07
Manitsoq ☐ DK 119 Hb05
Manizales ☐ CO 132 Ga17
Manja ☐ RM 111 Na23
Manjimup ☐ AUS 95 Qd25
Mankato ☐ USA 123 Fb10
Mankato ☐ USA 123 Fb10
Manlleu ☐ E 42 Lb25
Manna ☐ RI 86 Qa19
Mannheim ☐ D 45 Le21
Manokwari ☐ RI 92 Rc19
Manosque ☐ F 39 Lc24
Manresa ☐ E 42 La25
Mansa Konko ☐ WAG 105 Ka16
Mansel Island ▲ CDN 118 Fd06
Mansfield ☐ USA 123 Fd10
Manta ☐ EC 132 Fd19
Mantes-la-Jolie ☐ F 36 La21
Mántova ☐ I 46 Lf23
Mäntsälä ☐ FIN 28 Mc15
Mänttä ☐ FIN 28 Mc14
Manturovo ☐ RUS 60 Nc16
Mäntyharju ☐ FIN 28 Md15
Manus Island ▲ PNG 92 Sb19

Manzanares ☐ E 41 Kj26
Manzanillo ☐ C 126 Ga14
Manzanillo ☐ MEX 124 Ed15
Manzhouli ☐ CHN 82 Qd09
Mao ☐ E 43 Lc26
Mao ☐ TCH 106 Ld16
Maoming ☐ CHN 85 Qc14
Mapinhane ☐ MOC 111 Md23
Mapuera ☐ BR 134 Ha19
Maputo ● MOC 111 Mc24
Maraã ☐ BR 132 Gc19
Maraba ☐ BR 134 Hc20
Maracaibo ☐ YV 127 Gb16
Maracaju ☐ BR 136 Ha23
Maracay ☐ YV 127 Gc16
Maradi ☐ RN 106 Lb16
Maralinga ☐ AUS 95 Rc25
Maramasike ▲ SOL 93 Ta20
Marambio ⁎ 140 Ha31
Maranhão ⁎ BR 134 Hc20
Marañón ☐ PE 132 Ga19
Marañón ☐ PE 133 Ga20
Mărăşeşti ☐ RO 55 Md23
Marawi ☐ SUD 107 Mc15
Marbella ☐ E 41 Kh27
Marble Bar ☐ AUS 94 Qd23
Marble Point ⁎ 141 Tb34
Marburg ☐ D 44 Le20
Marcali ☐ H 53 Lj22
Marche ⁎ I 47 Lg24
Marchinbar Island ▲ AUS 96 Rd21
Mardan ☐ PAK 80 Oc12
Mar del Plata ☐ RA 137 Ha26
Maré ▲ F 98 Tb23
Marennes ☐ F 38 Kk23
Mar'evka ☐ RUS 60 Ne19
Marevo ☐ RUS 58 Mg17
Marfa ☐ M 49 Lh28
Margariti ☐ GR 56 Ma26
Margaritovo ☐ RUS 63 Mk22
Margate ☐ GB 35 La20
Marghita ☐ RO 54 Mb22
Marguerite Bay ⁎ 140 Gc32
Marhanec' ☐ UA 63 Mh22
Mari ⁎ SYR 76 Na12
Maria Island ▲ AUS 96 Rd21
Mariana Trench ⁎ 92 Sa16
Mariannelund ☐ S 27 Lh17
Mariánské Lázně ☐ CZ 52 Lg21
Mariazell ☐ A 52 Lh22
Maribor ☐ SLO 47 Lh22
Maridi ☐ SUD 109 Mb18
Marie-Byrd-Land ⁎ 140 Ed34
Mariehamn = Maarianhamina ☐ FIN 25 Lk15
Mari-El ⁎ RUS 60 Ne17
Mari-El ⁎ RUS 72 Nb07
Mariental ☐ NAM 110 Ld23
Mariestad ☐ S 27 Lg16
Marietta ☐ USA 123 Fd12
Marijampolė ☐ LT 31 Mb18
Marília ☐ BR 135 Hb23
Marina di Léuca ☐ I 49 Lk26
Marinduque ▲ RP 85 Ra16
Mariner Glacier ⁎ 141 Tb33
Maringa ☐ RDC 108 Ma18
Maringá ☐ BR 135 Hb23
Marion Reef ▲ AUS 96 Sc22
Maripasoula ☐ F 134 Hb18
Mariupol' ☐ UA 63 Mj22
Markabygd ☐ N 24 Lf14
Markaryd ☐ S 26 Lg17
Markham, Mount ▲ 141 Tb35
Markivka ☐ UA 61 Mk21
Markivka ☐ UA 63 Mk21
Marktredwitz ☐ D 45 Lg20
Marla ☐ AUS 94 Rc24

Marlborough ☐ AUS 96 Sb23
Marmande ☐ F 38 La23
Marmara Adası ▲ TR 57 Md25
Marmaris ☐ TR 64 Me27
Mármaro ☐ GR 57 Md26
Mar Menor ⁎ E 43 Kk27
Marmolada ▲ I 46 Lf22
Marne ☐ D 44 Le19
Marne ☐ F 37 Lc21
Maroantsetra ☐ RM 111 Nb22
Maromokotro ▲ RM 111 Nb21
Maroni ☐ F 134 Hb18
Maroua ☐ CAM 108 Lc17
Marquette ☐ USA 120 Fc09
Marrakech ☐ MA 104 Kc12
Marree ☐ AUS 97 Rd24
Marsa Alam ☐ ET 107 Md14
Marsabit ☐ EAK 109 Md18
Marsala ☐ I 48 Lg27
Marsa Maţrūḩ ☐ ET 107 Mb12
Marsa Mubārak ☐ ET 107 Mc13
Marseille ☐ F 39 Lc24
Marsga al Burayqaḩ ☐ LAR 106 Ld12
Marshall Islands ■ MH 93 Ta16
Marsh Harbour ☐ BS 126 Ga13
Martapura ☐ RI 86 Qa19
Mártha ☐ GR 57 Mc28
Martigny ☐ CH 45 Ld22
Martigues ☐ F 39 Lc24
Martinique ⁎ F 127 Gd16
Martti ☐ FIN 23 Me12
Marungu ⁎ RDC 109 Mb20
Marvejols ☐ F 38 Lb23
Mary ☐ TM 78 Oa11
Mary Anne Passage ⁎ AUS 94 Qc23
Maryborough ☐ AUS 96 Sc24
Maryland ⁎ USA 123 Ga11
Maryport ☐ GB 34 Kj18
Masai Steppe ⁎ EAT 109 Md19
Masaka ☐ EAU 109 Mc18
Masamba ☐ RI 87 Ra19
Masasi ☐ EAT 111 Md21
Masbate ☐ RP 85 Ra16
Masbate ☐ RP 85 Ra16
Mascarene Basin ⁎ 101 Nb11
Mascarene Plain ⁎ 111 Nc23
Maseru ● LS 110 Mb24
Mashhad ☐ IR 78 Nd11
Masirah ☐ OM 77 Nd14
Masirah ☐ OM 77 Nd14
Masiri ☐ IR 77 Nc12
Mason City ☐ USA 123 Fb10
Massa ☐ I 46 Lf23
Massachusetts ⁎ USA 121 Gb10
Massa Marittima ☐ I 46 Lf24
Massano ☐ MOC 111 Mc22
Masset ☐ CDN 117 Db08
Massif Central ⁎ F 38 Lb23
Massif de l'Adamaoua ▲ CAM 108 Lc17
Massif de l'Adrar ⁎ RIM 104 Kb14
Massif des Bongo ⁎ RCA 108 Ma17
Massif du Kapka ▲ TCH 106 Ma15
Masty ☐ BY 51 Mc19
Masugnsbyn ☐ S 23 Mb12
Masulipatnam ☐ IND 81 Pa15
Masuria ⁎ PL 50 Ma19

Masvingo ☐ ZW 111 Mc22
Matadi ☐ RDC 108 Lc20
Matagalpa ☐ NIC 125 Fc16
Matagorda Bay ⟿ USA 123 Fa13
Matagorda Island ⟿ USA 123 Fa13
Mátala ☐ GR 57 Mc28
Matamoros ☐ MEX 125 Fa13
Ma'tan as Sarah ☐ LAR 106 Ma14
Matandu ⟿ EAT 109 Md20
Matanzas ☐ C 126 Fd14
Mataranka ☐ AUS 94 Rc21
Mataram ☐ RI 87 Qd20
Mataró ☐ E 42 Lb25
Mata Uta ☐ F 98 Ua21
Matehuala ☐ MEX 124 Ed14
Matera ☐ I 49 Lj25
Mátészalka ☐ H 53 Mb22
Matha ☐ F 38 Kk23
Matienzo ⟿ 140 Ha32
Matnog ☐ RP 85 Ra16
Mato Grosso ☐ BR 135 Ha21
Mato Grosso do Sul ☐ BR 135 Ha22
Matrei ⟿ A 52 Lg22
Matsuyama ☐ J 83 Rc12
Matsuzaka ☐ J 83 Rd12
Matterhorn ⟿ CH/I 39 Ld23
Matthews Ridge ☐ GUY 132 Gd17
Matthew Town ☐ BS 127 Gb14
Mattighofen ☐ A 52 Lg21
Matuku ⟿ FIJI 98 Ua22
Maturín ☐ YV 132 Gd17
Matveev Kurgan ☐ RUS 63 Mk22
Maubeuge ☐ F 37 Lb20
Maudheimvidda ⟿ 141 Kc33
Maués ☐ BR 134 Ha19
Maui ⟿ USA 116 Ca07
Maulamyaing ☐ MYA 84 Pd15
Mauléon ☐ F 38 Kk22
Maumere ☐ RI 87 Ra20
Maun ☐ RB 110 Ma22
Mauna Kea ⟿ USA 116 Ca07
Mauna Loa ⟿ USA 117 Cc36
Mauriac ☐ F 38 Lb23
Mauritania ⟿ RIM 104 Ka15
Mauritius ⬛ MS 103 Nb12
Mauterndorf ⟿ A 52 Lg22
Mavrovi Anovi ☐ MK 56 Ma25
Mavrovo Nacionalni Park ⟿ MK 56 Ma25
Mawson ⟿ 141 Oa32
Mawson Coast ⟿ 141 Oa32
Mawson Glacier ⟿ 141 Sd34
Maya ☐ RI 86 Qb19
Mayaguana I. ⟿ BS 127 Gb14
Mayagüez ☐ USA 127 Gc15
Maych'ew ☐ ETH 107 Md16
Mayen ☐ D 45 Ld20
Mayenne ☐ F 36 Kk21
Maynas ⟿ PE 132 Ga19
Mayombé ☐ G 108 Lc19
Mayon ⟿ RP 85 Ra16
Mayotte ⬛ F 111 Nb21
May Pen ☐ JA 127 Gb15
Mayrhofen ⟿ A 45 Lf22
Mazabuka ☐ Z 110 Mb22
Mazagão ☐ BR 134 Hb20
Mazamet ☐ F 38 Lb24
Mazara del Vallo ☐ I 48 Lg27
Mazar-e Sharif ☐ AFG 78 Ob11
Mazarrón ☐ E 43 Kk27
Mazatenango ☐ GCA 125 Fb16

Mazatlán ☐ MEX 124 Ec14
Mažeikiai ☐ LT 31 Mb17
Mazowsze ⟿ PL 50 Ma19
Mazyr ☐ BY 51 Me19
Mbabane ⬛ SD 110 Mc24
Mbale ☐ EAU 109 Mc19
Mbandaka ☐ RDC 108 Ld18
Mbanza-Ngungu ☐ RDC 108 Lc20
Mbarara ☐ EAU 109 Mc19
Mbeya ☐ EAT 109 Mc20
Mbomu ⟿ RDC 108 Ma18
Mbuji-Mayi ☐ RDC 108 Ma20
McAlester ☐ USA 123 Fa12
McAllen ☐ USA 124 Fa13
McClintock Channel ⟿ CDN 118 Ed04
McClintock, Mount ⟿ 141 Sd34
McClure Strait ⟿ CDN 118 Ea04
Mcensk ☐ RUS 59 Mj19
Mc Murdo ⟿ 141 Tb34
McMurdo Sound ⟿ 141 Ta34
Mdantsane ☐ ZA 110 Mb25
Meadow Lake ☐ CDN 120 Ec08
Mebridege ⟿ ANG 108 Lc20
Mecca ☐ KSA 76 Md14
Mechelen ☐ B 37 Lc20
Mecheria ☐ DZ 104 Kd12
Mecitözü ☐ TR 65 Mh25
Mecklenburgische Seenplatte ⟿ D 44 Lg19
Mecklenburg-Vorpommern ⟿ D 44 Lg19
Medan ☐ RI 86 Pd18
Medeland ⟿ S 25 Lh14
Medellín ☐ CO 132 Ga17
Medenine ☐ TN 106 Lc12
Medford ☐ USA 122 Dd10
Mediaş ☐ RO 54 Mc22
Medicine Hat ☐ CDN 117 Eb08
Medina ☐ KSA 76 Md14
Medinaceli ☐ E 42 Kj25
Medina del Campo ☐ E 40 Kh25
Medina de Pomar ☐ E 42 Kj24
Medina de Rioseco ☐ E 40 Kh25
Medina Sidonia ☐ E 41 Kh27
Medinet el-Faijûm ☐ ET 107 Mc13
Médoc ⟿ F 38 Kk23
Medvedica ☐ RUS 61 Nc20
Medvenka ☐ RUS 59 Mj20
Medvež'egorsk ☐ RUS 29 Mh14
Meekatharra ☐ AUS 94 Qd24
Meerut ☐ IND 80 Od13
Mega ☐ ETH 109 Md18
Mega ☐ RI 92 Rc19
Megalópoli ☐ GR 56 Mb27
Mégara ☐ GR 56 Mb26
Meghalaya ⟿ IND 84 Pc13
Mehamn ☐ N 23 Md10
Meihekou ☐ CHN 83 Rb10
Meiktila ☐ MYA 84 Pd14
Meiningen ☐ D 45 Lf20
Meißen ☐ D 44 Lg20
Meizhou ☐ CHN 85 Qd14
Mékambo ☐ G 108 Ld18
Meke Gölü ⟿ TR 65 Mg27
Mek'ele ☐ ETH 107 Md16
Meknès ☐ MA 104 Kc12
Mekong ⟿ CHN 84 Pd12
Mekong ⟿ K/VN 84 Qb16

Mekong ⟿ THA/LAO 84 Qa15
Melá ☐ GR 57 Mc26
Melaka ⬛ MAL 86 Qa18
Melanesia ⟿ 92 Sa19
Melbourne ⬛ AUS 97 Sb26
Melbourne ☐ USA 123 Fd13
Meldorf ☐ D 44 Le18
Melenki ☐ RUS 58 Na18
Melfi ☐ I 49 Lh25
Melfjorden ☐ N 22 Lg12
Melhus ☐ N 24 Lf14
Melide ☐ E 40 Kf24
Melilla ☐ E 104 Kd11
Melilla ⬛ E 41 Kj28
Mélito de Porto Salvo ☐ I 49 Lh27
Melitopol' ☐ UA 63 Mh22
Mellakoski ☐ FIN 23 Mc12
Melle ☐ F 38 Kk22
Mellerud ☐ S 26 Lg16
Melo ☐ ROU 136 Hb25
Mels ☐ CH 45 Le22
Melsungen ☐ D 44 Le20
Melun ☐ F 37 Lb21
Melville Bugt ⟿ DK 118 Gd03
Melville Island ⟿ AUS 94 Rc21
Melville Island ⟿ CDN 118 Ec03
Melville Peninsula ⟿ CDN 118 Fd05
Memmingen ☐ D 45 Lf22
Mempawah ☐ RI 86 Qb18
Memphis ⟿ USA 123 Fc11
Mena ☐ UA 59 Mg20
Menabe ⟿ RM 111 Na23
Menarandra ⟿ RM 111 Na23
Mende ☐ F 38 Lb23
Mendeleevsk ☐ RUS 60 Ng18
Mendi ☐ PNG 92 Sa20
Mendocino Fracture Zone ⟿ 116 Ca05
Mendoza ☐ RA 136 Gc25
Menemen ☐ TR 57 Md26
Menešjärvi ☐ FIN 23 Md11
Menfi ☐ I 48 Lg27
Mengen ☐ TR 65 Mg25
Menggala ☐ RI 86 Qb19
Mengla ☐ CHN 84 Qa14
Mengzi ☐ CHN 84 Qa14
Menindee ☐ AUS 97 Sa25
Menkerja ☐ RUS 75 Ra05
Menongue ☐ ANG 110 Ld21
Menorca ⟿ E 43 Lc25
Mentawai Archipelago ⟿ RI 86 Pd19
Mentawai Strait ⟿ RI 86 Pd19
Menzelinsk ☐ RUS 60 Ng18
Menzies ☐ AUS 95 Ra24
Menzies, Mount ⟿ 141 Oa33
Meppen ☐ D 44 Ld19
Mequinenza ☐ E 42 La25
Merak ☐ RI 86 Qb20
Meran = Merano ☐ I 46 Lf22
Merano = Meran ☐ I 46 Lf22
Meratus Mountains ⟿ RI 87 Qd19
Merauke ☐ RI 92 Sa20
Mercantour, P.N.du ⟿ F 39 Ld23
Merced ☐ USA 122 Dd11
Mercedes ☐ RA 136 Gc25
Mercedes ☐ RA 136 Ha24
Merefa ☐ UA 63 Mh21
Merenkurkku ⟿ FIN/S 25 Ma14
Mergui ☐ MYA 86 Pd16
Mergui Archipelago ⟿ MYA 86 Pd16

Mérida ☐ E 41 Kg26
Mérida ⬛ MEX 125 Fc14
Mérida ☐ YV 132 Gb17
Meridian ☐ USA 123 Fc12
Merikarvia ☐ FIN 25 Ma15
Merir ⟿ PAL 92 Rc18
Merkinė ☐ LT 31 Mc18
Merredin ☐ AUS 95 Qd25
Merrick ⟿ GB 34 Kh18
Mersin = Içel ☐ TR 65 Mh27
Mêrsrags ☐ LV 30 Mb17
Merthyr Tydfil ☐ GB 35 Kj20
Mértola ☐ P 41 Kg27
Mertz Glacier ⟿ 141 Sb32
Meru ☐ EAK 109 Md18
Méru ☐ F 37 Lb21
Merzifon ☐ TR 65 Mh25
Mesa ☐ USA 122 Eb12
Mesagne ☐ I 49 Lj25
Meschede ☐ D 44 Le20
Mescit Dağları ⟿ TR 66 Na25
Meseleforos ⟿ S 25 Lj13
Mesopotamia ⟿ IRQ 76 Na12
Messalo ⟿ MOC 111 Md21
Messejana ☐ BR 134 Ja19
Messina ☐ ZA 110 Mb23
Messiniakós Kólpos ⟿ GR 56 Mb27
Messolóngi ☐ GR 56 Ma26
Mestre ☐ I 46 Lg23
Meta ☐ YV 132 Gc17
Meta Incognita Peninsula ⟿ CDN 119 Gb06
Metema ☐ ETH 107 Md16
Metéora ⟿ GR 56 Ma26
Méthana ☐ GR 56 Mb27
Metković ☐ HR 47 Lj24
Metlika ☐ SLO 47 Lj23
Metoro ☐ MOC 111 Md21
Metsäkylä ☐ FIN 28 Me13
Métsovo ☐ GR 56 Ma26
Mettlach ☐ D 45 Ld21
Metz ☐ F 37 Ld21
Metzingen ☐ D 45 Le21
Meulaboh ☐ RI 86 Pd18
Meuse ⟿ B 37 Lc21
Mexicali ⬛ MEX 122 Ea12
Mexican Plateau ⟿ MEX 124 Ed13
Mexico ⬛ MEX 124 Ec13
Mexico City ⬛ MEX 124 Fa15
Meydancık ☐ TR 66 Nb25
Meymaneh ☐ AFG 78 Oa11
Mezdra ☐ BG 54 Mb24
Mezen' ☐ RUS 72 Na05
Mezőkövesd ☐ H 53 Ma22
Mezőtúr ☐ H 53 Ma22
Mezraa ☐ TR 65 Mk27
Miajadas ☐ E 41 Kh26
Miami ☐ USA 123 Fd13
Miami Beach ☐ USA 123 Fd13
Miandrivazo ☐ RM 111 Nb22
Mianning ☐ CHN 84 Qa13
Mianyang ☐ CHN 84 Qb12
Miass ☐ RUS 72 Oa07
Miastko ☐ PL 50 Lj18
Micfalău ☐ RO 55 Mc22
Michajlovskoe ☐ RUS 60 Nc17
Michalovce ☐ SK 53 Ma21
Michigan ⟿ USA 123 Fc10
Michoacán ⟿ MEX 124 Ed15
Micronesia ⟿ FSM 93 Sc17
Micronesia ⟿ 93 Sd16
Mičurinsk ☐ RUS 59 Na19
Middelburg ☐ NL 37 Lb20
Middelburg ☐ ZA 110 Mb24
Middelfart ☐ DK 26 Le18

Middle America Trench ◨
124 Ed15
Middle Andaman ◨ **IND**
81 Pc16
Middlesboro ◨ **USA** 123 Fd11
Middlesbrough ◨ **GB** 34
Kk18
Middleton Reef ◨ **AUS**
97 Sd25
Midi-Pyrénées ◨ **F** 38 La24
Midland ◨ **USA** 122 Ed12
Midsund ◨ **N** 24 Ld14
Miechów ◨ **PL** 50 Mb20
Międzychód ◨ **PL** 50 Lh19
Międzyrzec Podlaski ◨ **PL**
51 Mb20
Międzyrzecz ◨ **PL** 50 Lh19
Mielec ◨ **PL** 50 Ma20
Miercurea-Ciuc ◨ **RO** 55 Mc22
Mieres ◨ **E** 40 Kh24
Mihajlov ◨ **RUS** 59 Mk18
Mihajlovka ◨ **RUS** 61 Nb20
Mihnevo ◨ **RUS** 58 Mj18
Mikaševičy ◨ **BY** 51 Md19
Mikkeli ◨ **FIN** 28 Md15
Mikonos ◨ **GR** 57 Mc27
Mikre ◨ **BG** 55 Mc24
Milagro ◨ **EC** 132 Ga19
Milan ◨ **I** 46 Le23
Milano ◨ **I** 46 Le23
Milas ◨ **TR** 57 Md27
Milazzo ◨ **I** 49 Lh26
Mildura ◨ **AUS** 97 Sa25
Miles ◨ **AUS** 96 Sc24
Miles City ◨ **USA** 120 Ec09
Mi'leso ◨ **ETH** 109 Na17
Milford Haven ◨ **GB** 35 Kh20
Milford Sound ◨ **NZ** 99 Tb27
Milford Sound ◨ **NZ** 99 Tb27
Milicz ◨ **PL** 50 Lj20
Millau ◨ **F** 38 Lb23
Miller, Mount ▲ 141 Tb35
Millom ◨ **GB** 34 Kj18
Mělnik ◨ **CZ** 52 Lh20
Milo ◨ **RG** 105 Kc17
Milos ◨ **GR** 57 Mc27
Milos ◨ **GR** 57 Mc27
Milparinka ◨ **AUS** 97 Sa24
Milton Keynes ◨ **GB** 35 Kk19
Milwaukee ◨ **USA** 123 Fc10
Mimizan ◨ **F** 38 Kk23
Mimyj ◨ **RUS** 73 Qc06
Minahasa ◨ **RI** 87 Ra18
Minas ◨ **ROU** 136 Ha25
Minas Gerais ◨ **BR** 135 Hc22
Minatitlán ◨ **MEX** 125 Fb15
Mindanao ◨ **RP** 85 Ra17
Minden ◨ **D** 44 Le19
Mindoro ◨ **RP** 85 Ra16
Minehead ◨ **GB** 35 Kj20
Mingechevir ◨ **AZ** 76 Nb10
Minghoshan ◨ **CHN** 79 Pc10
Mingora ◨ **PAK** 80 Oc12
Mingshui ◨ **CHN** 83 Rb09
Minna ◨ **WAN** 108 Lb17
Minna Bluff ▲ 141 Tc34
Minneapolis ◨ **USA** 123 Fb10
Minnesota ◨ **USA** 120 Fb09
Minot ◨ **USA** 120 Ed09
Min Shan ▲ **CHN** 84 Qa12
Minsk ● **BY** 51 Md19
Minto, Mount ▲ 141 Tc33
Minto Reef ◨ **FSM** 93 Sc17
Miquelon ◨ **CDN** 121 Ga09
Mira ◨ **P** 40 Kf25
Miranda ◨ **BR** 136 Ha23
Miranda de Ebro ◨ **E** 42 Kj24
Miranda do Douro ◨ **P**
40 Kg25

Mirande ◨ **F** 42 La24
Mirandela ◨ **P** 40 Kg25
Mirándola ◨ **I** 46 Lf23
Mirbat ◨ **OM** 77 Nc15
Miri ◨ **MAL** 87 Qc18
Mirina ◨ **GR** 57 Mc26
Mirnyj ◨ 141 Pc32
Mirosławiec ◨ **PL** 50 Lj19
Mirow ◨ **D** 44 Lg19
Mirpur Khas ◨ **PAK** 80 Ob13
Mirzapur ◨ **IND** 80 Pa13
Misima Island ◨ **PNG**
96 Sc21
Misiones ◨ **RA** 135 Hb24
Miskolc ◨ **H** 53 Ma21
Mismar ◨ **SUD** 107 Md15
Misool ◨ **RI** 87 Rb19
Misratah ◨ **LAR** 106 Ld12
Mississippi ◨ **USA** 123 Fb12
Mississippi ◨ **USA** 123 Fc11
Mississippi Delta ◨ **USA**
123 Fc13
Missoula ◨ **USA** 122 Eb09
Missouri ◨ **USA** 120 Ec09
Missouri ◨ **USA** 120 Ed09
Missouri ◨ **USA** 123 Fb11
Mitchell ◨ **AUS** 96 Sa22
Mitchell ◨ **USA** 123 Fa10
Mitchelstown ◨ **IRL** 33 Kf19
Mithimna ◨ **GR** 57 Md26
Mitrofanovka ◨ **RUS** 61 Mk21
Mits'iwa ◨ **ER** 107 Md15
Mittersill ◨ **A** 52 Lg22
Mizan Teferi ◨ **ETH** 109 Md17
Mizil ◨ **RO** 55 Md23
Mizoram ◨ **IND** 84 Pc14
Mizuho ◨ 141 Nb32
Mjadzel ◨ **BY** 31 Md18
Mjaksa ◨ **RUS** 58 Mk16
Mjölby ◨ **S** 27 Lh16
Mjøndalen ◨ **N** 26 Le16
Mjøsa ◨ **N** 24 Lf15
Mladenovac ◨ **SR** 54 Ma23
Mława ◨ **PL** 50 Ma19
Mlebniko ◨ **RUS** 60 Ne17
Mljet ◨ **HR** 47 Lj24
Mljet, N.P. ◨ **HR** 47 Lj24
Mlyniv ◨ **UA** 51 Mc20
Mmabatho ◨ **RSA** 110 Mb24
Moa ◨ **RI** 87 Rb20
Moanda ◨ **G** 108 Lc19
Mobile ◨ **USA** 123 Fc12
Mobile Bay ◨ **USA** 123 Fc12
Mobridge ◨ **USA** 120 Ed09
Mocímboa da Praia ◨ **MOC**
111 Na21
Möckern ◨ **D** 44 Lf19
Moctezuma ◨ **MEX** 124 Ec13
Mocuba ◨ **MOC** 111 Md22
Modane ◨ **F** 39 Ld23
Módena ◨ **I** 46 Lf23
Modesto ◨ **USA** 122 Dd11
Módica ◨ **I** 49 Lh27
Moelv ◨ **N** 24 Lf15
Mogadishu ● **SP** 103 Na09
Mogoča ◨ **RUS** 82 Ra08
Mohe ◨ **CHN** 82 Ra08
Mohéli ◨ **COM** 111 Na21
Mohen ◨ **FSM** 93 Sc17
Mohoro ◨ **EAT** 109 Md20
Mohyliv-Podil's'kyj ◨ **UA**
51 Md21
Moi ◨ **N** 26 Ld16
Mo i Rana ◨ **N** 22 Lh12
Moissac ◨ **F** 38 La23
Mojave Desert ◨ **USA** 122
Dd11
Mojynkum ◄ **KZ** 78 Ob10
Mojynkum ◄ **KZ** 78 Oc10

Mokil Atoll ◨ **FSM** 93 Sd17
Mokpo ◨ **J** 83 Rb12
Mokrous ◨ **RUS** 61 Nb20
Mokša ◄ **RUS** 61 Nb19
Mokšan ◨ **RUS** 61 Nc19
Moldava nad Bodvou ◨ **SK**
53 Ma21
Molde ◨ **N** 24 Ld14
Moldova ◨ **MD** 55 Me22
Molepolole ◨ **RB** 110 Mb23
Molėtai ◨ **LT** 31 Mc18
Molfetta ◨ **I** 49 Lj25
Molina ◨ **E** 42 Kk25
Molise ◨ **I** 49 Lh25
Molodežnaja ◨ 141 Na33
Molokai ◨ **USA** 117 Cb35
Molopo ◄ **RB** 110 Ma24
Mólos ◨ **GR** 56 Mb26
Molucca Islands ◨ **RI** 87
Rb19
Molucca Sea ◨ **RI** 87 Ra19
Mombasa ◨ **EAK** 109 Md19
Momskij hrebet ◄ **RUS**
74 Sa05
Monaco ◨ **MC** 39 Ld24
Monaco Deep ◨ 104 Jd12
Monaghan ◨ **IRL** 33 Kg18
Monastyrščina ◨ **RUS**
59 Mf18
Monastyryšče ◨ **UA** 62 Me21
Monastyrys'ka ◨ **UA** 51 Mc21
Moncalvo ◨ **E** 40 Kg24
Mončegorsk ◨ **RUS** 72 Mc05
Mončegorsk ◨ **RUS** 23 Mg11
Mönchengladbach ◨ **D**
44 Ld20
Monclova ◨ **MEX** 124 Ed13
Moncton ◨ **CDN** 121 Gd09
Mondoñedo ◨ **E** 40 Kg24
Mondovì ◨ **I** 46 Ld23
Monemvassía ◨ **GR** 56 Mb27
Monga ◨ **RDC** 108 Ma18
Mongo ◨ **TCH** 108 Ld16
Mongolia ◨ **MNG** 82 Qa09
Mongu ◨ **Z** 110 Ma22
Monólithos ◨ **GR** 57 Md27
Monópoli ◨ **I** 49 Lj25
Monreal del Campo ◨ **E**
42 Kk25
Monreale ◨ **I** 48 Lg26
Monroe ◨ **USA** 123 Fb12
Monrovia ● **LB** 105 Kb17
Mons ◨ **B** 37 Lb20
Monschau ◨ **D** 45 Ld20
Monsélice ◨ **I** 46 Lf23
Møns Klint ◨ **DK** 26 Lg18
Mönsterås ◨ **S** 27 Lj17
Montalbán ◨ **E** 42 Kk25
Montana ◨ **BG** 54 Mb24
Montana ◨ **USA** 120 Ec09
Montargis ◨ **F** 38 Lb22
Montauban ◨ **F** 42 La24
Montbard ◨ **F** 39 Lc22
Montbéliard ◨ **F** 39 Ld22
Mont Blanc ▲ **F/I** 39 Ld23
Montbrison ◨ **F** 39 Lc23
Mont-de-Marsan ◨ **F** 42 Kk24
Montdidier ◨ **F** 37 Lb21
Mont-Dore ◨ **F** 98 Tb23
Monte Alegre do Piauí ◨ **BR**
134 Hc20
Monte Argentário ◨ **I** 46 Lf24
Montebello Islands ◨ **AUS**
94 Qd23
Monte Cinto ▲ **F** 46 Le24
Monteforte de Lemos ◨ **E**
40 Kg24
Montego Bay ◨ **JA** 126 Ga15
Montélimar ◨ **F** 39 Lc23

Montemor-o-Novo ◨ **P**
41 Kf26
Monte Namuli ▲ **MOC** 111
Md22
Montenegro ◨ **CG** 54 Lk24
Monte Pollino ▲ **I** 49 Lj26
Monte Quemado ◨ **RA**
136 Gd24
Montereau ◨ **F** 37 Lb21
Monterey ◨ **USA** 122 Dd11
Monterey Bay ◨ **USA** 122
Dd11
Montería ◨ **CO** 132 Ga17
Monte Roraima ▲ **BR/GUY**
132 Gd17
Monte Rosa ▲ **I/CH** 46 Ld23
Monterrey ◨ **MEX** 124 Ed13
Monte Sant'Angelo ◨ **I**
49 Lh25
Montes Claros ◨ **BR** 135
Hd22
Montevideo ● **ROU** 136 Ha25
Monte Viso ▲ **I** 46 Ld23
Montgomery ◨ **USA** 123 Fc12
Monthey ◨ **CH** 45 Ld22
Monticello ◨ **USA** 122 Ec11
Montilla ◨ **E** 41 Kh27
Monti Sibillini, P.N.dei ◨ **I**
47 Lg24
Mont Laurier ◨ **CDN** 121
Ga09
Montluçon ◨ **F** 38 Lb22
Montmirail ◨ **F** 37 Lb21
Montmorillon ◨ **F** 38 La22
Monto ◨ **AUS** 96 Sc23
Montoro ◨ **E** 41 Kh26
Montpelier ◨ **USA** 121 Gb10
Montpellier ◨ **F** 38 Lb24
Montpon-Ménestérol ◨ **F**
38 La23
Montréal ◨ **CDN** 121 Gb09
Montreux ◨ **CH** 45 Ld22
Montrose ◨ **GB** 34 Kj17
Monts Bagaane ▲ **RN**
106 Lb15
Montserrat ◨ **UK** 127 Gd15
Monts Mitumba ▲ **RDC**
109 Mb19
Monts Nimba ▲ **CILB** 105
Kc17
Monts Notre-Dame ▲ **CDN**
121 Gb09
Monza ◨ **I** 46 Le23
Monzón ◨ **E** 42 La25
Moonie ◨ **AUS** 96 Sc24
Moora ◨ **AUS** 95 Qd25
Moorhead ◨ **USA** 120 Fa09
Moose Jaw ◨ **CDN** 120 Ec08
Moosonee ◨ **CDN** 121 Fd08
Mopti ◨ **RMM** 105 Kd16
Moquegua ◨ **PE** 133 Gb22
Mór ◨ **H** 53 Lk22
Mora ◨ **E** 41 Kj26
Mora ◨ **S** 25 Lh15
Mora de Rubielos ◨ **E**
42 Kk25
Morag ◨ **PL** 50 Lk19
Móra la Nova ◨ **E** 42 La25
Moramanga ◨ **RM** 111 Nb22
Moratuwa ◨ **CL** 81 Pa17
Moravia ◨ **CZ** 52 Lj21
Morawa ◨ **AUS** 95 Qd24
Mordovo ◨ **RUS** 61 Na19
Mordvinia ◨ **RUS** 60 Nc18
More're ◨ **RUS** 29 Mf15
Morecambe ◨ **GB** 35 Kj18
Moreda ◨ **E** 41 Kj27
Moree ◨ **AUS** 97 Sb24
Morehead ◨ **PNG** 92 Sa20

Morelia ◻ MEX 124 Ed15
Morella ◻ E 42 Kk25
Moresby Island ▣ CDN 117 Db08
Moreton Island ▣ AUS 96 Sc24
Morez ◻ F 39 Ld22
Morioka ◻ J 83 Sa11
Morjärv ◻ S 23 Mb12
Morki ◻ RUS 60 Ne17
Morkoka ◥ RUS 73 Qc06
Morlaix ◻ F 36 Kj21
Mornington Island ▣ AUS 96 Rd22
Morobe ◻ PNG 93 Sb20
Morocco ▦ MA 104 Kc12
Morogoro ◻ EAT 109 Mc18
Morombe ◻ RM 111 Na23
Morón ◻ C 126 Ga14
Morón ◻ RA 136 Ha25
Mörön ◻ MNG 82 Qa09
Morondava ◻ RM 111 Na23
Morón de la Frontera ◻ E 41 Kh27
Moroni ◉ COM 111 Na21
Morotai ◻ RI 87 Rb18
Moroto ◻ EAU 109 Mc18
Morozovsk ◻ RUS 63 Na21
Morpeth ◻ GB 34 Kk18
Moršansk ◻ RUS 61 Na19
Mörsil ◻ S 24 Lg14
Morsovo ◻ RUS 61 Nb19
Mørsvik ◻ N 22 Lh12
Mørsvikfjorden ▤ N 22 Lh12
Morteau ◻ F 39 Ld22
Mortlock Islands ▣ FSM 93 Sc17
Morven ◻ AUS 96 Sb24
Morwell ◻ AUS 97 Sb26
Mosal'sk ◻ RUS 59 Mh18
Mosby ◻ N 26 Ld16
Moscow ● RUS 58 Mj18
Moscow University Ice Shelf ▤ 141 Qd32
Moselle ◻ F 37 Ld21
Moses Lake ◻ USA 122 Ea09
Mosfellsbær ◻ IS 32 Jk13
Moshi ◻ EAT 109 Md19
Mosina ◻ PL 50 Lj19
Mosjøen ◻ N 24 Lg13
Moskenesøya ▣ N 22 Lg12
Moskva ● RUS 58 Mj18
Mosnikovskaja ◻ RUS 29 Mj15
Mosonmagyaróvár ◻ H 53 Lj22
Moss ◻ N 26 Lf16
Mosselbaai ◻ ZA 110 Ma25
Mossel Bay ◻ ZA 110 Ma25
Mossman ◻ AUS 96 Sb22
Mossoró ◻ BR 134 Ja20
Most ◻ CZ 52 Lg20
Mostaganem ◻ DZ 104 La11
Mostar ◻ BIH 47 Lj24
Móstoles ◻ E 40 Kj25
Mostovskoj ◻ RUS 66 Na23
Motala ◻ S 27 Lh16
Motilla del Palancar ◻ E 43 Kk26
Motril ◻ E 41 Kj27
Motygino ◻ RUS 73 Pc07
Moudros ◻ GR 57 Mc26
Mould Bay ◻ CDN 118 Ea03
Moulins ◻ F 38 Lb22
Moundou ◻ TCH 108 Ld17
Mount Adam ▲ GB 137 Ha29
Mountain Nile ◥ SUD 109 Mc17
Mount Apo ▲ RP 85 Rb17

Mount Augustus ▲ AUS 94 Qd23
Mount Balbi ▲ PNG 93 Sb20
Mount Berlin ▲ 140 Da34
Mount Binga ▲ ZW 111 Mc22
Mount Cook ▲ NZ 99 Tc27
Mount Edward ▲ 141 Mc22
Mount Elbert ▲ USA 122 Ec11
Mount Elgon ▲ EAU 109 Mc18
Mount Erebus ▲ 141 Tc34
Mount Essendon ▲ AUS 94 Ra23
Mount Everest ▲ CHN/NEP 80 Pb13
Mount Frakes ▲ 140 Ea34
Mount Fridtjof Nansen ▲ 140 Bd36
Mount Gambier ◻ AUS 97 Sa26
Mount Godwin Austen ▲ PAK/CHN 78 Od11
Mount Hagen ◻ PNG 92 Sa20
Mount Hale ▲ AUS 94 Qd24
Mount Hann ▲ AUS 94 Ra22
Mount Hood ▲ USA 122 Dd09
Mount Hope ◻ AUS 97 Rd25
Mount Isa ◻ AUS 96 Rd23
Mount Jackson ▲ 141 Gd33
Mount Joyce ▲ 141 Sd34
Mount Kenya ▲ EAK 109 Md19
Mount Kirkpatrick ▲ 141 Ta35
Mount Kosciuszko ▲ AUS 97 Sb26
Mount Liebig ▲ AUS 94 Rc23
Mount Lister ▲ 141 Ta34
Mount Logan ▲ CDN 116 Cd06
Mount Longhurst ▲ 141 Sd34
Mount Magnet ◻ AUS 95 Qd24
Mount Markham ▲ 141 Tb35
Mount McClintock ▲ 141 Sd34
Mount McKinley ▲ USA 116 Cb06
Mount Menzies ▲ 141 Oa33
Mount Miller ▲ 141 Tb35
Mount Minto ▲ 141 Tc33
Mount Mitchell ▲ USA 123 Fd11
Mount Mulanje ▲ MW 111 Md22
Mount Northampton ▲ 141 Tb33
Mount Olga ▲ AUS 94 Rb23
Mount Ord ▲ AUS 94 Rb22
Mount Petras ▲ 140 Dc34
Mount Pinatubo ▲ RP 85 Ra15
Mount Rainier ▲ USA 122 Dd09
Mount Robson ▲ CDN 116 Dc08
Mount Ruapehu ▲ NZ 99 Td26
Mount Saunders ▲ 141 Tb36
Mount Seelig ▲ 140 Ed35
Mount Shasta ▲ USA 122 Dd10
Mount Sicapoo ▲ RP 85 Ra15
Mount Sidley ▲ 140 Dc34
Mount Sinai ▲ ET 107 Mc13
Mount Sir Thomas ▲ AUS 94 Rb24

Mount Stinear ▲ 141 Ob33
Mount Takahe ▲ 140 Eb34
Mount Taranaki ▲ NZ 99 Tc26
Mount Usborne ▲ GB 137 Ha29
Mount Vernon ◻ USA 123 Fc11
Mount Victor ▲ 141 Mc33
Mount Waddington ▲ CDN 117 Ea08
Mount Wharton ▲ 141 Ta35
Mount Whitney ▲ USA 122 Ea11
Mount Wilhelm ▲ PNG 92 Sa20
Mount Woodroffe ▲ AUS 94 Rc24
Mount Zeil ▲ AUS 94 Rc23
Moura ◻ BR 132 Gd19
Moura ◻ P 41 Kg26
Mouth of the Shannon ◥ IRL 33 Kf19
Mouths of the Amazon ◥ BR 134 Hc18
Mouths of the Ganges ◥ IND/BD 80 Pb14
Moûtiers ◻ F 39 Ld23
Moyale ◻ EAK 109 Md18
Moynak ◻ UZ 78 Nd16
Moyobamba ◻ PE 133 Ga20
Možajsk ◻ RUS 58 Mj18
Mozambique ▦ MOC 111 Md22
Mozambique Basin ▤ 111 Md24
Mozambique Channel ▤ 111 Na22
Mozambique Plateau ▤ MOC 111 Md22
Mozambique Ridge ▤ 111 Md25
Mpanda ◻ EAT 109 Mc20
Mpika ◻ Z 111 Mc21
Mragowo ◻ PL 50 Ma19
Mrkonjić Grad ◻ BIH 47 Lj23
Mscislav ◻ BY 59 Mf19
Mtwara ◻ EAT 111 Na21
Muang Kham ◻ LAO 84 Qa15
Muang Khong ◻ LAO 84 Qb16
Muang Xai ◻ LAO 84 Qa14
Muarabungo ◻ RI 86 Qa19
Muaraenim ◻ RI 86 Qa19
Muarasiberut ◻ RI 86 Pd19
Muarateweh ◻ RI 87 Qb19
Mubi ◻ WAN 108 Lc16
Mucajaí ◻ BR 132 Gd18
Muchinga Mountains ▲ Z 110 Mc21
Mučkapskij ◻ RUS 61 Nb20
Muconda ◻ ANG 110 Ma21
Mucur ◻ TR 65 Mh26
Mudanjiang ◻ CHN 83 Rb10
Mudanya ◻ TR 57 Me25
Muddus n.p. ◆ S 23 Ma12
Mudgee ◻ AUS 97 Sb25
Mufulira ◻ Z 110 Mb21
Muğla ◻ TR 64 Me27
Mühlig-Hofmann-fjella ▲ 141 Lb33
Mui Ca Mau ◥ VN 86 Qa17
Mukačeve ◻ UA 53 Mb21
Mula ◻ E 43 Kk26
Mulegé ◻ MEX 124 Eb13
Muleta ◻ ETH 109 Na17
Mulhouse ◻ F 39 Ld22
Mullewa ◻ AUS 95 Qd24
Müllheim ◻ D 45 Ld22
Mullingar ◻ IRL 33 Kg19
Mullsjö ◻ S 26 Lg17

Mulock Glacier ▤ 141 Sd34
Multan ◻ PAK 80 Oc12
Mulu ◻ MAL 87 Qc18
Mumbai ◉ IND 80 Oc15
Muna ◻ RI 87 Ra19
Muna ◥ RUS 73 Qd05
München ◉ D 45 Lf21
Muncie ◻ USA 123 Fc10
Munera ◻ E 41 Kj26
Mungindi ◻ AUS 96 Sb24
Munich ◉ D 45 Lf21
Munkedal ◻ S 26 Lf16
Munkfors ◻ S 26 Lg16
Munster ◻ D 44 Lf19
Munster ◻ IRL 33 Kf19
Münster ◻ D 44 Ld20
Munţii Codru-Mona ▲ RO 54 Mb22
Munţii Măcinului, P.N. ◆ RO 55 Me23
Munţii Metaliferi ▲ RO 54 Mb22
Muntok ◻ RI 86 Qb19
Munzur Dağları ▲ TR 66 Mk26
Munzur Vadisi Milli Parkı ◆ TR 66 Mk26
Muodoslompolo ◻ S 23 Mb12
Muonio ◻ FIN 23 Mb12
Murat ◻ F 38 Lb23
Murau ◻ A 52 Lh22
Murchison ◥ AUS 94 Qd24
Murcia ◻ E 43 Kk27
Murcia ◻ E 43 Kk27
Muret ◻ F 42 La24
Murfreesboro ◻ USA 123 Fc11
Murgab ◻ TJ 78 Oc11
Muriaé ◻ BR 135 Hd23
Murighiol ◻ RO 55 Me23
Murilo Atoll ◻ FSM 93 Sc17
Muritiba ◻ BR 135 Ja21
Müritz, N.P. ◆ D 44 Lg19
Murmansk ◻ RUS 72 Mc05
Murmansk ◻ RUS 23 Mg11
Murmaši ◻ RUS 23 Mg11
Murom ◻ RUS 60 Nb18
Murray ◥ AUS 97 Sa25
Murray River Basin ◥ AUS 97 Sa25
Murska Sobota ◻ SLO 52 Lj22
Mürzzuschlag ◻ A 52 Lh22
Muş ◻ TR 66 Na26
Muscat ◉ OM 77 Nd14
Musgrave Ranges ▲ AUS 94 Rc24
Muskogee ◻ USA 123 Fa11
Musoma ◻ EAT 109 Mc19
Musorka ◻ RUS 60 Ne19
Mussau Island ▣ PNG 93 Sb19
Musselburgh ◻ GB 34 Kj18
Mustvee ◻ EST 30 Md16
Mut ◻ TR 65 Mg27
Mutare ◻ ZW 111 Mc22
Muttaburra ◻ AUS 96 Sa23
Muztag ◻ CHN 79 Pb11
Muztagata ◻ CHN 78 Od11
Mvuma ◻ ZW 110 Mc22
Mwali ◻ COM 111 Na21
Mwanza ◻ EAT 109 Mc19
Mwene-Ditu ◻ RDC 108 Ma20
Myanmar ▦ MYA 84 Pd14
Mychajlivka ◻ UA 63 Mh22
Myitkyina ◻ MYA 84 Pd13
Mykolajiv ◻ UA 53 Mb21
Mykolajiv ◻ UA 62 Mf22

Mykolajivka UA 62 Mg23
Mynämäki FIN 22 Mb15
Myślibórz PL 50 Lh19
Myrdalsjökull IS 32 Ka14
Myre N 22 Lh11
Myrhorod UA 62 Mg21
Myronivka UA 62 Mf21
Myrtle Beach USA 123 Ga12
Myrviken S 25 Lh14
mys Alevina RUS 75 Sc07
mys Buor-Haja RUS 74 Rc04
mys Elizavety RUS 75 Sa08
mys Južnyj RUS 74 Sd07
mys Kamčatskij RUS 74 Ta07
mys Kanin Nos RUS 72 Na05
mys Kronockij RUS 74 Ta08
mys Lopatka RUS 75 Sd08
mys Navarin RUS 74 Td06
mys Neupokoeva RUS 73 Pd03
mys Oljutorskij RUS 74 Tc07
Mysore IND 81 Od16
mys Ozernoj RUS 74 Ta07
Mys Šmidta RUS 74 Ua05
mys Tajgonos RUS 74 Sd06
mys Terpenija RUS 75 Sa09
mys Tjulenij AZ 76 Nc10
mys Tolstoj RUS 74 Sd07
mys Želanija RUS 73 Ob03
Myszków PL 50 Lk20
Myszyniec PL 50 Ma19
My Tho VN 84 Qb16
Mytilini GR 57 Md26
Mytišči RUS 58 Mj18
Mývatn IS 32 Kb13
Mzuzu MW 111 Mc21

N

Naantali = Nådendal FIN 22 Mb15
Naas IRL 33 Kg19
Naberežnyj Čelny RUS 60 Ng18
Naberežnyje Čelny RUS 72 Nc07
Nabire RI 92 Rd19
Nabouwalu FIJ 98 Td22
Nacaroa MOC 111 Md21
Nachi-Katsuura J 83 Rc12
Náchod CZ 52 Lj20
Nadelkap ZA 110 Ld25
Nådendal = Naantali FIN 22 Mb15
Nădlac RO 54 Ma22
Nadvirna UA 55 Mc21
Nadym RUS 72 Oc05
Nærøyfjorden N 24 Ld15
Næstved DK 26 Lf18
Náfpaktos GR 56 Ma26
Náfplio GR 56 Mb27
Nafud al Mazhur KSA 77 Na13
Nafud as Sirr KSA 77 Na13
Naga RP 85 Ra16
Nagajbakovo RUS 60 Ng18
Nagaland IND 84 Pc13
Nagano J 83 Rd11
Nagappattinam IND 81 Od16
Nagasaki J 83 Rb12

Nagercoil IND 81 Od17
Nagor'e RUS 58 Mk17
Nagornyj RUS 74 Td06
Nagoya J 83 Rd11
Nagpur IND 80 Od14
Nagyatád H 53 Lj22
Nagykanizsa H 53 Lj22
Naha J 83 Rb13
Nahodka RUS 83 Rc10
Naidi FIJ 98 Td22
Naiman Qi CHN 83 Ra10
Nain CDN 121 Gd07
Na'in IR 76 Nc12
Nairn GB 34 Kj17
Nairobi EAK 109 Md19
Naivasha EAK 109 Md19
Nájera E 42 Kj24
Najran KSA 77 Na15
Nakanai Mountains PNG 93 Sc20
Nakanno RUS 73 Qb06
Nak'fa ER 107 Md15
Nakhon Phanon THA 84 Qa15
Nakhon Ratchasima THA 84 Qa16
Nakhon Sawan THA 84 Qa15
Nakhon Si Thammarat THA 86 Pd17
Nakina CDN 120 Fc08
Nakło nad Notecią PL 50 Lj19
Nakskov DK 26 Lf18
Näkten S 25 Lh14
Nakuru EAK 109 Md19
Nalbant RO 55 Me23
Nalčik RUS 76 Na10
Nallıhan TR 64 Mf25
Nalut LAR 106 Lc12
Namaland NAM 110 Ld24
Namaqualand ZA 110 Ld24
Namatanai PNG 93 Sc19
Nam Co CHN 84 Pc12
Namdalen N 24 Lg13
Namib Desert NAM 110 Lc22
Namib Desert NAM 110 Lc22
Namibe ANG 110 Lc22
Namibia NAM 110 Ld23
Namoluk Island FSM 93 Sc17
Namonuito Atoll FSM 93 Sb17
Nampa USA 122 Ea10
Nampo PRK 83 Rb11
Nampula MOC 111 Md22
Namsos N 24 Lf13
Namsskogan N 24 Lg13
Namur B 37 Lc20
Namwala Z 110 Mb22
Namysłów PL 50 Lj20
Nan THA 84 Qa15
Nana RCA 108 Lf17
Nanaimo CDN 122 Dd09
Nanchang CHN 85 Qd13
Nancy F 37 Ld21
Nanda Devi IND 80 Pa12
Nanded IND 81 Od15
Nandi FIJ 98 Td22
Nanga Parbat PAK 78 Oc11
Nanga Tayap RI 86 Qb19
Nanjing CHN 85 Qd12
Nan Ling CHN 84 Qb13
Nanning CHN 84 Qb14
Nanping CHN 85 Qd13
Nansen Sound CDN 118 Fb02

Nantes F 38 Kk22
Nantong CHN 83 Ra12
Nantucket Island USA 121 Gc10
Nanumanga TUV 98 Td20
Nanumea Atoll TUV 98 Td20
Nanuque BR 135 Hd22
Nanutarra Roadhouse AUS 94 Qd23
Nanyang CHN 82 Qc12
Nanyuki EAK 109 Md18
Napier NZ 99 Td26
Napier Mountains 141 Nc32
Naples I 49 Lh25
Naples USA 123 Fd13
Napo PE 132 Gb19
Napoli I 49 Lh25
Nara RMM 105 Kc15
Narač BY 31 Md18
Naracoorte AUS 97 Sa26
Naratasty RUS 60 Ng18
Narathiwat THA 86 Qa17
Narbonne F 38 Lb24
Nardò I 49 Lk25
Nares Strait CDN 118 Gb03
Nar'jan-Mar RUS 72 Nc05
Narlı TR 65 Mj27
Narmada IND 80 Oc14
Narman TR 66 Na25
Narni I 46 Lg24
Narochanski N.P. BY 31 Md18
Naro-Fominsk RUS 58 Mj18
Narovlja BY 51 Me20
Narrabri AUS 97 Sb25
Narrandera AUS 97 Sb25
Narrogin AUS 95 Qd25
Narsarsuaq DK 119 Hc06
Narva EST 30 Md16
Narva laht EST/RUS 30 Md16
Narvik N 22 Lj11
Narwians P.N. PL 51 Mb19
Naryn KS 78 Od10
Naryn KS 78 Od10
Naryškino RUS 59 Mh19
Năsăud RO 54 Mc22
Nashville USA 123 Fc11
Našice HR 47 Lk23
Nassau BS 126 Ga13
Nässjö S 27 Lh17
Nastola FIN 28 Mc15
Nata RB 110 Mb23
Natal BR 134 Ja20
Natal RI 86 Pd18
Natchez USA 123 Fb12
Nationalpark Eifel D 44 Ld20
Natitingou DY 105 La18
Natuna Besar RI 86 Qb18
Natuna Sea RI 86 Qb18
Naturaliste Plateau AUS 95 Qc25
Nauders A 45 Lf22
Nauen D 44 Lg19
Naujoji Akmenė LT 31 Mb17
Naukluft NAM 110 Ld23
Naumburg D 44 Lf20
Nauru NAU 93 Tb19
Nauru NAU 93 Tb19
Naustdal N 24 Lc15
Nauta PE 132 Gb19
Nautsi RUS 23 Me11
Navahrudak BY 51 Mc19
Navalmoral de la Mata E 40 Kh26

Navalvillar de Pela E 41 Kh26
Navan IRL 33 Kg19
Navapolack BY 31 Me18
Navarra E 42 Kk24
Navasëlki BY 51 Me19
Navašino RUS 58 Nb18
Navia E 40 Kg24
Navlja RUS 59 Mh19
Năvodari RO 55 Me23
Navoiy UZ 78 Ob10
Navojoa MEX 124 Ec13
Navoloki RUS 58 Na17
Nawabshah PAK 80 Ob13
Nawakshut RIM 104 Ka15
Náxos GR 57 Mc27
Náxos GR 57 Mc27
Nayarit MEX 124 Ed14
Nazaré P 40 Kf26
Nazareth IL 76 Md12
Nazca PE 133 Gb21
Nazilli TR 64 Me27
Nazran RUS 76 Na10
Nazran RUS 76 Na10
Nazret ETH 109 Md17
Ncue GQ 108 Lc18
Ndélé RCA 108 Ma17
Ndende G 108 Lc19
N'Djaména TCH 108 Ld16
Ndjolé G 108 Lc19
Ndola Z 110 Mb21
Ndzuani COM 111 Na21
Néa Kalikrátia GR 56 Mb25
Néa Moudania GR 56 Mb25
Neápoli GR 56 Ma25
Neápoli GR 56 Mb27
Neápoli GR 57 Mc28
Néa Zihni GR 56 Mb25
Nebolčí RUS 58 Mg16
Nebraska USA 122 Ed10
Nébrodi I 49 Lh27
Necochea RA 137 Ha26
Nedryhajliv UA 59 Mg20
Nedstrand N 26 Lc16
Needles USA 122 Eb12
Neftejugansk RUS 72 Oc06
Negele ETH 109 Md17
Negele ETH 109 Md17
Negotin SR 54 Mb23
Negotino MK 56 Mb25
Negros RP 85 Ra16
Nehaevskij RUS 61 Na20
Neiva CO 132 Ga18
Nekrasovskoe RUS 58 Na17
Nelidovo RUS 58 Mg17
Nellore IND 81 Pa16
Nelson CDN 120 Fa07
Nelson NZ 99 Tc27
Nelspruit ZA 110 Mc24
Néma RIM 105 Kc15
Neman RUS 31 Mb18
Nemours F 37 Lb21
Nemyriv UA 55 Mb20
Nemyriv UA 62 Me21
Nenagh IRL 33 Kf19
Nendo SOL 98 Tb21
Nenets Autonomous District RUS 72 Nd05
Néo Petritsi GR 56 Mb25
Nepal NEP 80 Pa13
Nérac F 38 La23
Nerehta RUS 58 Na17
Nereta LV 31 Mc17
Neringa-Nida LT 31 Ma18
Nerja E 41 Kj27
Nerjungri RUS 75 Ra07
Nerl' RUS 58 Mj17

Nesbyen ☐ N 24 Le15
Nesebăr ☐ BG 55 Md24
Neskaupstaður ☐ IS 32 Kd13
Nesna ☐ N 22 Lg12
Nesterov ☐ RUS 31 Mb18
Nestiary ☐ RUS 60 Nc17
Netherlands ☐ NL 37 Lc19
Netherlands Antilles ☐ NL 127 Gc16
Nettiling Lake ☐ CDN 119 Gb05
Neubrandenburg ☐ D 44 Lg19
Neuchâtel ☐ CH 45 Ld22
Neue Hebriden ☐ VU 98 Tb24
Neufchâteau ☐ F 37 Lc21
Neufchâtel-en-Bray ☐ F 36 La21
Neumarkt in der Oberpfalz ☐ D 45 Lf21
Neumünster ☐ D 44 Le18
Neuquén ☐ RA 137 Gc26
Neuquén ☐ RA 137 Gc26
Neuruppin ☐ D 44 Lg19
Neuss ☐ D 44 Ld20
Neustadt (Aisch) ☐ D 45 Lf21
Neustadt (Weinstraße) ☐ D 45 Le21
Neustrelitz ☐ D 44 Lg19
Neuwied ☐ D 45 Ld20
Nevada ☐ USA 122 Ea11
Nevada ☐ USA 123 Fb11
Nevado Ampato ▲ PE 133 Gb22
Nevado Ausangate ▲ PE 133 Gb21
Nevado Cololo Keasani ▲ BOL 133 Gc21
Nevado Coropuna ▲ PE 133 Gb22
Nevado de Colima ▲ MEX 124 Ed15
Nevado del Huila ▲ CO 132 Ga18
Nevado del Ruiz ▲ CO 132 Ga17
Nevado Ojos del Salado ▲ RCH/RA 136 Gc24
Nevado Sajama ▲ BOL 133 Gc22
Nevel' ☐ RUS 31 Me17
Nevers ☐ F 38 Lb22
Nevşehir ☐ TR 65 Mh26
New Albany ☐ USA 123 Fc11
New Amsterdam ☐ GUY 134 Ha17
Newark ☐ USA 121 Gb10
New Braunfels ☐ USA 124 Fa13
New Britain ☐ PNG 93 Sb20
New Britain Trench ☐ PNG 93 Sc20
New Brunswick ☐ CDN 121 Gc09
Newbury ☐ GB 35 Kb20
New Bussa ☐ WAN 105 La17
New Caledonia ☐ F 98 Ta23
New Caledonia ☐ F 98 Ta23
New Caledonia Basin ☐ 98 Ta24
Newcastle ☐ AUS 97 Sc25
Newcastle upon Tyne ☐ GB 34 Kk18
Newcastle West ☐ IRL 33 Kf19
New Delhi ● IND 80 Od13
New England Seamounts ☐ 121 Gd21
Newfoundland ☐ CDN 121 Ha09

Newfoundland and Labrador ☐ CDN 121 Ha07
Newfoundland Basin ☐ 119 Hb05
New Georgia ☐ SOL 93 Sd20
New Georgia Group ☐ SOL 93 Sd20
New Glasgow ☐ CDN 121 Gd09
New Guinea ☐ RI/PNG 92 Rd20
New Guinea Trench ☐ RI 92 Rd18
New Hampshire ☐ USA 121 Gb10
New Hanover Island ☐ PNG 93 Sc19
Newhaven ☐ GB 35 La20
New Haven ☐ USA 121 Gb10
New Hebrides ☐ VU 98 Tb22
New Hebrides Basin ☐ VU 98 Ta22
New Hebrides Trench ☐ 98 Tb22
New Ireland ☐ PNG 93 Sc19
New Jersey ☐ USA 121 Gb11
Newman ☐ AUS 94 Qd23
New Mexico ☐ USA 122 Ec12
New Orleans ☐ USA 124 Fc13
New Plymouth ☐ NZ 99 Tc26
Newport ☐ GB 35 Kb21
Newquay ☐ GB 35 Kh20
New Ross ☐ IRL 33 Kg19
Newry ☐ GB 33 Kg18
New Schwabenland ☐ 141 Lb33
New Siberian Islands ☐ RUS 74 Sa03
New South Wales ☐ AUS 97 Sa25
Newtontoppen ▲ N 22 Lf06
Newtown ☐ GB 35 Kj19
New York ☐ USA 121 Gb10
New York ☐ USA 121 Gb10
New Zealand ☐ NZ 99 Tb27
Nexø ☐ DK 27 Lh18
Ngala ☐ WAN 108 Lc16
Ngaoundéré ☐ CAM 108 Lc17
Ngatik Atoll ☐ FSM 92 Rd17
Ngazidja ☐ COM 111 Na21
Ngoko ☐ RCB 108 Ld18
Ngoring Hu ☐ CHN 84 Pd12
Ngorongoro Crater ▲ EAT 109 Md19
Ngulu Atoll ☐ FSM 92 Rd17
Nguru ☐ EAK 109 Md19
Nguru ☐ WAN 106 Lc16
Nha Trang ☐ VN 85 Qb16
Nhulunbuy ☐ AUS 96 Rd21
Niagara Falls ☐ USA 123 Ga10
Niah ☐ MAL 87 Qc18
Niamey ● RN 105 La16
Niangara ☐ RDC 109 Mb18
Nia-Nia ☐ RDC 109 Mb18
Nias ☐ RI 86 Pd18
Nibe ☐ DK 26 Le17
Nicaragua ☐ NIC 125 Fc16
Nice ☐ F 39 Ld24
Nickerson Ice Shelf ☐ 140 Cc34
Nicobar Islands ☐ IND 81 Pc17
Nicosia ☐ CY 76 Mc11
Nicosia ☐ I 49 Lh27
Nicoya ☐ CR 125 Fc16
Nidzica ☐ PL 50 Ma19
Niebüll ☐ D 44 Le18
Niedere Tauern ▲ A 52 Lh23

Niedersachsen ☐ D 44 Le19
Niedersächsisches Wattenmeer, N.P. ▲ D 44 Ld19
Niellé ☐ CI 105 Kc16
Niemisel ☐ S 19 Mb13
Nienburg ☐ D 44 Le19
Niesky ☐ D 44 Lh20
Nieuw Nickerie ☐ SME 134 Ha17
Niğde ☐ TR 65 Mh27
Niger ▲ RMM 105 Kd15
Niger ☐ N 106 Lb15
Niger Delta ☐ WAN 108 Lb18
Niger Fan ☐ 105 La18
Nigeria ☐ WAN 108 Lb17
Nigrita ☐ GR 56 Mb25
Niigata ☐ J 83 Rd11
Nijmegen ☐ NL 37 Lc20
Nikea ☐ GR 56 Mb26
Nikel' ☐ RUS 23 Mf11
Nikiniki ☐ RI 87 Ra19
Nikkaluokta ☐ S 22 Lk12
Nikko ☐ J 83 Rd11
Nikolaevka ☐ RUS 60 Nd19
Nikolaevsk ☐ RUS 61 Nc21
Nikolaevsk-na-Amure ☐ RUS 75 Sa08
Nikol'sk ☐ RUS 60 Nd19
Nikopol ☐ BG 55 Mc24
Nikopol' ☐ UA 63 Mh22
Niksar ☐ TR 65 Mj25
Nikšić ☐ CG 54 Lk24
Nile ▲ ET 107 Mc13
Nile Delta ☐ ET 107 Mc12
Nîmes ☐ F 39 Lc24
Nimmitabel ☐ AUS 97 Sb26
Nimrod Glacier ☐ 141 Sd35
Nimule ☐ SUD 109 Mc18
Ningbo ☐ CHN 85 Ra13
Ningjing Shan ▲ CHN 84 Pd12
Ningxia Huizu Zizhiqu ☐ CHN 82 Qb11
Ninigo Group ☐ PNG 92 Rd19
Niobrara ▲ USA 122 Fa10
Nioro du Sahel ☐ RMM 105 Kc15
Niort ☐ F 38 Kk22
Nipigon ☐ CDN 120 Fc09
Niquelândia ☐ BR 135 Hc21
Niš ☐ SR 54 Ma24
Nísíos Strofádhes ☐ GR 56 Ma27
Nisko ☐ PL 51 Mb20
Nisporeni ☐ MD 55 Me22
Nissiros ☐ GR 57 Md27
Nitchequon ☐ CDN 121 Gb08
Niterói ☐ BR 135 Hd23
Nitra ☐ SK 53 Lk21
Niulakita ☐ TUV 98 Td21
Niutao ☐ TUV 98 Td21
Nivala ☐ FIN 28 Mc14
Nizamabad ☐ IND 81 Od15
Nizina Wielkopolska 쉼 PL 50 Lj19
Nizip ☐ TR 65 Mj27
Nízke Tatry, N.P. ▲ SK 53 Lk21
Nizhaja Lomov ☐ RUS 61 Nb19
Nizhnekamsk ☐ RUS 60 Nf18
Nizhnekamskoe Vodohranilišče ☐ RUS 60 Ng18
Nizhnevartovsk ☐ RUS 73 Od06
Nizhnij Novgorod ☐ RUS 60 Nb17
Nizhnij Tagil ☐ RUS 72 Oa07

Nizhnjaja Tunguska ▲ RUS 73 Pc06
Nizhyn ☐ UA 59 Mf20
Njagan' ☐ RUS 72 Ob06
Njasviž ☐ BY 51 Md19
Njombe ☐ EAT 109 Mc20
Njupeskär 쉼 S 24 Lg15
Njurba ☐ RUS 75 Qd06
Njutånger ☐ S 25 Lj15
Nkhotakota ☐ MW 111 Mc21
Nkongsamba ☐ CAM 108 Lb18
Nockberge, N.P. ▲ A 52 Lg22
Nogales ☐ MEX 122 Eb12
Nogales ☐ USA 122 Eb12
Nogent ☐ F 37 Lc21
Nogent-le-Rotrou ☐ F 36 La21
Noginsk ☐ RUS 58 Mk18
Noia ☐ E 40 Kf24
Nokia ☐ FIN 22 Mb15
Nome ☐ USA 116 Bc06
Nomwin Atoll ☐ FSM 93 Sc17
Nonacho Lake ☐ CDN 120 Ec06
Noormarkku ☐ FIN 25 Ma15
Nora ☐ S 27 Lh16
Norberg ☐ S 25 Lh15
Nordaustlandet ☐ N 22 Lh06
Nordaust-Svalbard naturreservat ☐ N 22 Lh06
Nordborg ☐ DK 26 Le18
Norden ☐ D 44 Ld19
Nordenham ☐ D 44 Le19
Norderney ☐ D 44 Ld19
Norderstedt ☐ D 44 Lf19
Nordfold ☐ N 22 Lh12
Nordhausen ☐ D 44 Lf20
Nordkjosbotn ☐ N 22 Lk11
Nord-Kvaløy ☐ N 22 Lk10
Nördlingen ☐ D 45 Lf21
Nordmaling ☐ S 25 Lk14
Nordmøre ☐ N 24 Ld14
Nordøyane ☐ N 24 Ld14
Nord-Pas-de-Calais ☐ F 37 Lb20
Nordrhein-Westfalen ☐ D 44 Ld20
Noresund ☐ N 24 Le15
Norfolk ☐ GB 35 La19
Norfolk ☐ USA 123 Ga11
Norfolk ☐ USA 123 Ga11
Norfolk Island ☐ AUS 99 Tb24
Norfolk Island ☐ AUS 99 Tb24
Norfolk Ridge ☐ 99 Tb24
Norheimsund ☐ N 24 Ld15
Noril'sk ☐ RUS 73 Pb04
Norman ☐ USA 123 Fa11
Normanby Island ☐ PNG 96 Sc21
Normandia ☐ BR 132 Gd18
Normandie ☐ F 36 Kk21
Normanton ☐ AUS 96 Sa22
Norman Wells ☐ CDN 116 Dc05
Norråker ☐ S 25 Lh13
Norra Kvills n.p. ☐ S 27 Lh17
Norram Kvarken ☐ S/FIN 25 Ma14
Nørre Nebel ☐ DK 26 Le18
Norrköping ☐ S 27 Lj16
Norrtälje ☐ S 27 Lk16
Norseman ☐ AUS 95 Ra25
Norsjö ☐ S 25 Lk13
North Cape ☐ N 23 Mc10
North Frisian Islands ☐ D 44 Ld19

Northallerton ☐ GB 34 Kk18
Northam ☐ AUS 95 Qd25
Northampton ☐ GB 35 Kk19
Northampton, Mount ▲
  141 Tb33
Northamton ☐ AUS 95 Qc24
North Andaman ☐ IND
  81 Pc16
North Battleford ☐ CDN
  120 Ec08
North Bay ☐ CDN 121 Ga09
North Cape ◣ NZ 99 Tc25
North Carolina ☐ USA
  123 Ga11
North China Plain ☐ CHN
  83 Qd11
North Dakota ☐ USA 120 Ed09
North Downs ☐ GB 35 Kk20
Northeast Cape ◣ USA
  116 Bc06
Northeim ☐ D 44 Le20
Northern Ireland ☐ GB
  33 Kg18
Northern Sporades ☐ GR
  56 Mb16
Northern Indian Lake ☐ CDN
  120 Fa07
Northern Territory ☐ AUS
  94 Rc23
North Island ▲ NZ 99 Td26
North Korea ■ PRK 83 Rb11
North Land ☐ RUS 73 Pb03
North Platte ↳ USA 122 Ed10
North Platte ☐ USA 122 Ed10
North Pole   139 La0
North Saskatchewan ↳ CDN
  117 Eb08
North Siberian Lowland ☐
  RUS 73 Pb04
North Taranaki Bight ☐ NZ
  99 Tc26
North Uist ☐ GB 34 Kg17
Northumberland N.P. ◆ GB
  34 Kj18
North Walsham ☐ GB
  35 La19
North West Basin ☐ AUS
  94 Qc23
North West Cape ▲ AUS
  94 Qc23
North West Highlands ☐ GB
  34 Kh17
North West River ☐ CDN
  121 Gd08
Northwest Territories ☐ CDN
  117 Dd06
North York Moors N.P. ◆ GB
  35 Kk18
Norton ☐ USA 122 Fa11
Norton Sound ☐ USA 116
  Bd06
Nortorf ☐ D 44 Le18
Norway ■ N 18 Lb06
Norway House ☐ CDN
  120 Fa08
Norwegian Bay ☐ CDN
  118 Fb03
Norwich ☐ GB 35 La19
Nosivka ☐ UA 62 Mf20
Nosliku ☐ RI 87 Rb18
Nosssob ↳ NAM 110 Ld23
Nosy Be ☐ RM 111 Nb21
Nosy Mitsio ☐ RM 111 Nb21
Nosy Ste-Marie ☐ RM 111
  Nb22
Noto ☐ I 49 Lh27
Notodden ☐ N 26 Le16
Notre Dame Bay ☐ CDN
  121 Ha09

Nottingham ☐ GB 35 Kk19
Nouâdhibou ☐ RIM 104 Ka14
Nouakchott ● RIM 104 Ka15
Nouâmghâr ☐ RIM 104 Ka14
Nouméa ■ F 98 Tb23
Nova Alvorada ☐ BR 135
  Hb23
Nova Borova ☐ UA 62 Me20
Nova Ermakovo ☐ RUS
  60 Nf18
Nova Gorica ☐ SLO 47 Lg23
Nova Gradiška ☐ HR 47 Lj23
Nova Iguaçu ☐ BR 135 Hd23
Novaja Ladoga ☐ RUS
  29 Mj15
Nova Kachovka ☐ UA 62
  Mg22
Novalukoml' ☐ BY 31 Me18
Nova Odesa ☐ UA 62 Mf22
Nova Poltavka ☐ RUS 61 Nd20
Novara ☐ I 46 Le23
Nova Scotia ☐ CDN 121 Gd10
Nova Ušycja ☐ UA 51 Md21
Nova Varoš ☐ SR 54 Lk24
Nova Vodolaha ☐ UA 63
  Mh21
Novaya Zemlya ☐ RUS
  72 Nc04
Nova Zagora ☐ BG 55 Md24
Nové Hrady ☐ CZ 52 Lh21
Nové Zámky ☐ SK 54 Lk22
Novgorod ☐ RUS 30 Mf16
Novhorodka ☐ UA 62 Mg21
Novhorod-Sivers'kyj ☐ UA
  59 Mg20
Novi Bilokorovyči ☐ UA
  62 Me20
Novigrad ☐ HR 47 Lg23
Novi Ligure ☐ I 46 Le23
Novi Pazar ☐ BG 55 Md24
Novi Pazar ☐ SR 54 Ma24
Novi Sad ☐ SR 54 Lk23
Novi Sanžary ☐ UA 62 Mh21
Novi Vinodolski ☐ HR 47
  Lh23
Novoanninskij ☐ RUS 61
  Nb20
Novoarchanhel's'k ☐ UA
  62 Mf21
Novoazovs'k ☐ UA 63 Mk22
Novočeboksarsk ☐ RUS
  60 Nd17
Novočerkassk ☐ RUS 63
  Na22
Novofedorivka ☐ UA 62 Mg22
Novo Hamburgo ☐ BR
  135 Hb24
Novohrad-Volyns'kyj ☐ UA
  51 Md20
Novokašpirskij ☐ RUS
  60 Ne19
Novokujbyševsk ☐ RUS
  60 Nf19
Novokuzneck ☐ RUS 79 Pb08
Novolazarevskaja ☐ 141
  Lc33
Novo Mesto ☐ SLO 47 Lh23
Novomičurinsk ☐ RUS
  59 Mk18
Novomihajlovskij ☐ RUS
  63 Mk23
Novomoskovsk ☐ RUS
  59 Mk18
Novomoskovs'k ☐ UA 63
  Mh21
Novomykolajivka ☐ UA
  62 Mg22
Novomykolajivka ☐ UA
  63 Mh22

Novomyrhorod ☐ UA 62 Mf21
Novonikolaevskij ☐ RUS
  61 Nb20
Novooleksijivka ☐ UA 63
  Mh22
Novopokrovka ☐ UA 63 Mh21
Novopokrovskaja ☐ RUS
  63 Na23
Novopskov ☐ UA 63 Mk21
Novoržev ☐ RUS 30 Me17
Novošahtinsk ☐ RUS 63 Mk22
Novoselivs'ke ☐ UA 62 Mg23
Novosibirsk ☐ RUS 79 Pa08
Novosibirskoe vdhr. ☐ RUS
  79 Pa08
Novosokol'niki ☐ RUS
  30 Mf17
Novotroick ☐ RUS 78 Nd08
Novotroickoe ☐ RUS 60 Nc18
Novotrojic'ke ☐ UA 63 Mh22
Novotulka ☐ RUS 61 Nd20
Novoukrajinka ☐ UA 62 Mf21
Novouljanovsk ☐ RUS
  60 Ne18
Novovolyns'k ☐ UA 51 Mc20
Novska ☐ HR 47 Lj23
Nový Bor ☐ CZ 52 Lh20
Novyi Oskol ☐ RUS 59 Mj20
Novyj Buh ☐ UA 62 Mg22
Novyj Port ☐ RUS 72 Oc05
Novyj Urengoj ☐ RUS 73
  Od05
Nowa Dęba ☐ PL 51 Ma20
Nowa Sól ☐ PL 50 Lj20
Nowogard ☐ PL 50 Lh19
Nowy Sącz ☐ PL 50 Ma21
Nowy Targ ☐ PL 50 Ma21
Nowy Tomyśl ☐ PL 50 Lj19
Noyon ☐ F 37 Lb21
Nubia ■ SUD 107 Mc15
Nubian Desert ☐ SUD 107
  Mc14
Nudol' ☐ RUS 58 Mj17
Nueltin Lake ☐ CDN 120 Fa06
Nueva Gerona ☐ C 126 Fd14
Nueva Rosita ☐ MEX 124
  Ed13
Nuevitas ☐ C 126 Ga14
Nuevo Casas Grandes ☐
  MEX 122 Ec12
Nuevo Laredo ☐ MEX
  124 Fa13
Nuevo León ☐ MEX 124 Ed13
Nuguria Islands ☐ PNG
  93 Sc19
Nui ☐ TUV 98 Td20
Nuku'alofa ● TO 98 Ua23
Nukufetau Atoll ☐ TUV
  98 Td20
Nukulaelae Atoll ☐ TUV
  98 Td20
Nukuoro Atoll ☐ FSM 93
  Sd18
Nukus ☐ UZ 78 Nd10
Nullagine ☐ AUS 94 Ra23
Nullarbor Plain ☐ AUS
  95 Rb25
Numan ☐ WAN 108 Lc17
Numfor ☐ RI 92 Rc19
Nunavut ☐ CDN 118 Ec05
Nuoro ☐ I 48 Le25
Nurdağı ☐ TR 65 Mj17
Nur Dağları ▲ TR 65 Mj27
Nurhak ☐ TR 65 Mj17
Nurlat ☐ RUS 60 Nf18
Nurmes ☐ FIN 28 Me14
Nurmijärvi ☐ FIN 28 Mc15
Nürnberg ☐ D 45 Lf21

Nusaybin ☐ TR 76 Na11
Nuuk ☐ DK 119 Hb06
Nyainqêntanglha Shan ▲
  CHN 84 Pc12
Nyakanzi ☐ EAT 109 Mc19
Nyala ☐ SUD 106 Ma16
Nyanga ↳ G 108 Lc19
Nybergsund ☐ N 24 Lf15
Nyborg ☐ DK 26 Lf18
Nybro ☐ S 27 Lh17
Nyékládháza ☐ H 53 Ma22
Nyhammar ☐ S 25 Lh15
Nykøbing F ☐ DK 26 Lf18
Nykøbing M ☐ DK 26 Le17
Nykøbing S ☐ DK 26 Lf18
Nyköping ☐ S 27 Lj16
Nykvarn ☐ S 27 Lj16
Nynäshamn ☐ S 27 Lj16
Nyngan ☐ AUS 97 Sb25
Nyon ☐ CH 45 Ld22
Nyons ☐ F 39 Lc23
Nyrud ☐ N 23 Me11
Nysa ☐ PL 50 Lj20
Nystadt = Uusikaupunki ☐
  FIN 25 Ma15
Nyžni Sirohozy ☐ UA 63
  Mh22
Nyžni Torhaji ☐ UA 63 Mh22
Nyžn'ohirs'kyj ☐ UA 63
  Mh23
Nzega ■ EAT 109 Mc19

O

Oahu ☐ USA 116 Ca07
Oakland ☐ USA 122 Dd11
Oakley ☐ USA 122 Ed11
Oak Ridge ☐ USA 123 Fd11
Oamaru ☐ NZ 99 Tc28
Oasis II ☐ 141 Qa32
Oates Land ☐ 141 Sd33
Oaxaca ☐ MEX 125 Fa15
Oaxaca de Juárez ☐ MEX
  125 Fa15
Ob' ↳ RUS 72 Ob06
Oban ☐ GB 34 Kh17
Obe ☐ VU 98 Tb22
Obe ☐ VU 98 Tb22
Oberhausen ☐ D 44 Ld20
Oberstdorf ☐ D 45 Lf22
Obi ☐ RI 87 Rb19
Óbidos ☐ P 40 Kf26
Obihiro ☐ J 83 Sa10
Obninsk ☐ RUS 59 Mj18
Obo ☐ RCA 109 Mb17
Obojan' ☐ RUS 59 Mj20
Obolon' ☐ UA 62 Mg21
Oborniki ☐ PL 50 Lj19
Obrenovac ☐ SR 54 Ma23
Obruk Yaylası ▲ TR 65 Mg26
Obskaya Guba ☐ RUS 72
  Oc05
Obytičnoa kosa ☐ UA 63 Mj22
Očakiv ☐ UA 62 Mf22
Ocala ☐ USA 123 Fd13
Ocampo ☐ MEX 124 Ec13
Ocaña ☐ E 41 Kj26
Ocaña ☐ CO 132 Gb17
Oceanside ☐ USA 122 Dd11
Očeretuvate ☐ UA 63 Mh22
Ochsenfurt ☐ D 45 Lf21
Ochtyrka ☐ UA 62 Mh20
Ockelbo ☐ S 25 Lj15
Ocotal ☐ NIC 125 Fc16
Ocotlán ☐ MEX 124 Ed14
Odáðahraun ☐ IS 32 Kb13
Odda ☐ N 24 Ld15

Odden Færgehavn ☐ DK 26 Lf18
Odder ☐ DK 26 Lf18
Odemira ☐ P 41 Kf27
Ödemiş ☐ TR 57 Md26
Odensbacken ☐ S 27 Lh16
Odense ☐ DK 26 Lf18
Odessa ☐ USA 122 Ed12
Odienné ☐ CI 105 Kc17
Odincovo ☐ RUS 58 Mj18
Odiongan ☐ RP 85 Ra16
Odorheiu Secuiesc ☐ RO 55 Mc22
Odra ☐ PL 50 Lj20
Odžaci ☐ SR 54 Lk23
Offenbach ☐ D 45 Le20
Offenburg ☐ D 45 Ld21
Ogaden ☐ ETH 109 Na17
Ogbomoso ☐ WAN 105 La17
Ogden ☐ USA 122 Eb10
Ogorelyši ☐ RUS 29 Mh14
Ogre ☐ LV 30 Mc17
Ogulin ☐ HR 47 Lh23
O'Higgins, Gral.B. ☐ 140 Ha31
Ohio ☐ USA 123 Fd10
Ohio ☐ USA 123 Fd11
Ohrid ☐ MK 56 Ma25
Oiapoque ☐ F 134 Hb18
Ojcowski P.N. ☐ PL 50 Lk20
Öje ☐ S 24 Lg15
O-jima ☐ J 83 Rb13
Ojinaga ☐ MEX 124 Ed13
Ojmjakon ☐ RUS 75 Sa06
Oka ☐ RUS 58 Mj18
Okahandja ☐ NAM 110 Ld23
Okavango ☐ ANG/NAM 110 Ld22
Okavango Delta ☐ RB 110 Ma22
Okavango Swamp ☐ RB 110 Ma22
Okayama ☐ J 83 Rc12
Okehampton ☐ GB 35 Kh20
Okhotsk ☐ RUS 75 Sa07
Okinawa Islands ☐ J 83 Rb13
Okinawa-jima ☐ J 83 Rb13
Oklahoma ☐ USA 122 Fa11
Oklahoma City ☐ USA 123 Fa11
Okovcy ☐ RUS 58 Mg17
Øksfjord ☐ N 23 Mb10
Oksovskij ☐ RUS 29 Mh14
Oktjabr'sk ☐ KZ 78 Nd09
Oktjabr'sk ☐ RUS 60 Ne19
Oktjabr'sk ☐ RUS 72 Nc08
Oktjabr'skij ☐ RUS 60 Ng18
Okulovka ☐ RUS 58 Mg16
Ólafsfjörður ☐ IS 32 Ka12
Olaine ☐ LV 30 Mb17
Öland ☐ S 27 Lj17
Olary ☐ AUS 97 Sa25
Olavarría ☐ RA 137 Gd26
Oława ☐ PL 50 Lj20
Olbia ☐ I 48 Le25
Old Crow ☐ CDN 116 Da05
Oldenburg ☐ D 44 Le19
Oldenburg in Holstein ☐ D 44 Lf18
Olderfjord ☐ N 23 Mc10
Olecko ☐ PL 51 Mb18
Olëkma ☐ RUS 75 Ra07
Olëkminsk ☐ RUS 75 Ra06
Olëkminskij Stanovik ☐ RUS 82 Qd08
Oleksandrivka ☐ UA 62 Mf21
Oleksandrivka ☐ UA 62 Mg21
Oleksandrivka ☐ UA 62 Mg21
Oleksandrivka ☐ UA 62 Mg22

Oleksandrivka ☐ UA 63 Mj21
Ølen ☐ N 26 Lc16
Olenëgorsk ☐ RUS 23 Mg11
Olenëk ☐ RUS 73 Qc05
Olenëk ☐ RUS 73 Ra04
Olenëkskij zaliv ☐ RUS 73 Ra04
Olenino ☐ RUS 58 Mg17
Olenivka ☐ UA 62 Mg23
Oleśnica ☐ PL 50 Lj20
Oles'ko ☐ UA 51 Mc21
Olesno ☐ PL 50 Lk20
Olevs'k ☐ UA 51 Md20
Olgastretet ☐ N 22 Lh06
Ölgiy ☐ MNG 79 Pc09
Ol'hi ☐ RUS 59 Na19
Ol'hovatka ☐ RUS 61 Mk20
Ol'hovka ☐ RUS 61 Nc21
Olifantsriver ☐ ZA 110 Mb23
Olimarao Atoll ☐ FSM 92 Sb17
Olimpos Beydağları Milli Parkı ☐ TR 64 Mf27
Olinda ☐ BR 134 Jb20
Oliveira de Azeméis ☐ P 40 Kf25
Oljutorskij zaliv ☐ RUS 74 Tb07
Olmedo ☐ E 40 Kh25
Olmos ☐ PE 133 Ga20
Oloj ☐ RUS 74 Ta05
Olojskij hrebet ☐ RUS 74 Ta05
Olonec ☐ RUS 29 Mg15
Olongapo ☐ RP 85 Ra16
Olot ☐ E 42 Lb24
Ol'ša ☐ RUS 59 Mf18
Olsztyn ☐ PL 50 Ma19
Olsztynek ☐ PL 50 Ma19
Oltenița ☐ RO 55 Md23
Oltu ☐ TR 66 Na25
Olur ☐ TR 66 Nb25
Olvera ☐ E 41 Kh27
Ólymbos ☐ GR 57 Md28
Olympia ☐ USA 122 Dd09
Olympic Peninsula ☐ USA 122 Dd09
Ólympos ☐ GR 56 Mb25
Omagh ☐ GB 33 Kg18
Omaha ☐ USA 123 Fa10
Oman ☐ OM 77 Nd14
Omapere ☐ NZ 99 Tc26
Omatako ☐ NAM 110 Ld22
Omdurman ☐ SUD 107 Mc15
Ometepec ☐ MEX 124 Fa15
Ommen ☐ NL 37 Ld19
Omolon ☐ RUS 74 Sc05
Omolon ☐ RUS 74 Ta05
Omsk ☐ RUS 79 Oc07
Onbimisan ☐ TR 65 Mk27
Onda ☐ E 43 Kk26
Ondjiva ☐ ANG 110 Ld22
Öndörkhaan ☐ MNG 82 Qc09
Onega ☐ RUS 29 Mk14
Onega ☐ RUS 29 Mk14
Onești ☐ RO 55 Md22
Onežskaja guba ☐ RUS 29 Mh13
Onitsha ☐ WAN 108 Lb17
Ono-i-Lau ☐ FJI 98 Ua23
Onslow ☐ AUS 94 Qd23
Ontario ☐ CDN 120 Fb08
Ontario ☐ CDN 120 Fb08
Ontong Java Atoll ☐ SOL 93 Sd20
Ontong-Java Rise ☐ PNG 93 Sd19
Oodnadatta ☐ AUS 96 Rd24

Oświęcim ☐ PL 50 Lk20
Oos-Londen ☐ ZA 110 Mb25
Oostende ☐ B 37 Lb20
Opaka ☐ BG 55 Md24
Opatija ☐ HR 47 Lh23
Opatów ☐ PL 50 Ma20
Opava ☐ CZ 53 Lj21
Opišnja ☐ UA 62 Mh21
Opočka ☐ RUS 30 Me17
Opoczno ☐ PL 50 Ma20
Opole ☐ PL 50 Lj20
Opotiki ☐ NZ 99 Td26
Oppdal ☐ N 26 Le14
Oradea ☐ RO 54 Ma22
Orahovica ☐ HR 47 Lj23
Oral ☐ KZ 72 Nc08
Oran ☐ DZ 104 Kd11
Orange ☐ AUS 97 Sb25
Orange ☐ F 39 Lc23
Orange ☐ NAM 110 Ld24
Orange Fan ☐ 110 Lc25
Oranienburg ☐ D 44 Lg19
Oranje Gebergte ☐ SME 134 Ha18
Oranjemund ☐ NAM 110 Lc24
Oranjeriver ☐ ZA 110 Ld24
Oranjeriver ☐ ZA 110 Ld24
Oranjestad ☐ NL 127 Gb16
Oravița ☐ RO 54 Ma23
Orbost ☐ AUS 97 Sb26
Ordesa y Monte Perdido, P.N.de ☐ E 42 La24
Ordu ☐ TR 65 Mj25
Ordžonikidze ☐ UA 63 Mh22
Orebić ☐ HR 47 Lj24
Örebro ☐ S 27 Lh16
Oredež ☐ RUS 30 Mf16
Oregon ☐ USA 122 Dd10
Orehovo-Zuevo ☐ RUS 58 Mk18
Orel ☐ RUS 58 Mj19
Orel' ☐ UA 63 Mh21
Orenburg ☐ RUS 78 Nd08
Orense = Ourense ☐ E 40 Kg24
Orestiada ☐ GR 57 Md25
Orhaneli ☐ TR 64 Me26
Orhei ☐ MD 55 Me22
Orhomenós ☐ GR 56 Mb26
Orhon gol ☐ MNG 82 Qa09
Orichiv ☐ UA 63 Mh22
Orihuela ☐ E 43 Kk26
Orijahovo ☐ BG 54 Mb24
Orilia ☐ CDN 123 Ga10
Orimattila ☐ FIN 28 Mc15
Orinoco ☐ YV 132 Gc17
Orinoco Delta ☐ YV 132 Gd17
Orissa ☐ IND 80 Pa14
Orissaare ☐ EST 30 Mb16
Oristano ☐ I 48 Le26
Orivesi ☐ FIN 28 Mc15
Orivesi ☐ FIN 28 Me14
Oriximiná ☐ BR 134 Ha19
Orizaba ☐ MEX 125 Fa15
Orkanger ☐ N 24 Le14
Örkelljunga ☐ S 26 Lg17
Orkney Islands ☐ GB 34 Kj16
Orlando ☐ USA 123 Fd13
Orléanais ☐ F 38 La22
Orléans ☐ F 38 La22
Ormara ☐ PAK 77 Oa13
Ormoc ☐ RP 85 Ra16
Ormož ☐ SLO 52 Lj22
Ormtjernkampen n.p. ☐ N 24 Le15
Ørnes ☐ N 22 Lg12
Orneta ☐ PL 50 Ma18
Örnsköldsvik ☐ S 25 Lk14
Orocue ☐ CO 132 Gb18

Oroluk Atoll ☐ FSM 93 Sd17
Orşova ☐ RO 54 Mb23
Oropesa ☐ E 41 Kh26
Orosháza ☐ H 53 Ma22
Óros İdi ☐ GR 57 Mc28
Orsa ☐ S 25 Lh15
Orša ☐ BY 31 Mf18
Örségi N.P. ☐ H 53 Lj22
Orsk ☐ RUS 78 Nd08
Ørsta ☐ N 24 Ld14
Ortaca ☐ TR 64 Me27
Ortahisar ☐ TR 65 Mh26
Ortakonak ☐ TR 65 Mg26
Ortaköy ☐ TR 65 Mh26
Ortaköy ☐ TR 66 Nb25
Orta Toroslar ☐ TR 65 Mg27
Orthez ☐ F 42 Kh24
Ortona ☐ I 47 Lh24
Oruro ☐ BOL 133 Gc22
Orust ☐ S 26 Lf16
Orvieto ☐ I 46 Lg24
Orživ ☐ UA 51 Md20
Oržycja ☐ UA 62 Mg21
Orzysz ☐ PL 50 Ma19
Oš ☐ KS 78 Oc10
Os ☐ N 24 Lf14
Osaka ☐ J 83 Rd12
Osby ☐ S 26 Lg17
Osen ☐ N 24 Lf13
Oshakati ☐ NAM 110 Ld22
Oshawa ☐ CDN 123 Ga10
Oshkosh ☐ USA 123 Fc10
Osijek ☐ HR 47 Lk23
Oskarström ☐ S 26 Lg17
Öskemen ☐ KZ 79 Pa08
Os'kino ☐ RUS 59 Mk20
Öskjuvatn ☐ IS 32 Kb13
Oskol ☐ RUS 59 Mj20
Oslo ☐ N 26 Lf16
Oslofjorden ☐ N 26 Lf16
Osmancık ☐ TR 65 Mh25
Osmaniye ☐ TR 65 Mj27
Os'mino ☐ RUS 30 Me16
Ösmo ☐ S 27 Lj16
Osnabrück ☐ D 44 Le19
Osogbo ☐ WAN 105 La17
Osorno ☐ RCH 137 Gb27
Osorno la Mayor ☐ E 40 Kh24
Osoyro ☐ N 24 Lc15
Osprey Reef ☐ AUS 96 Sb21
Oss ☐ NL 37 Lc20
Ossora ☐ RUS 74 Ta07
Östansjö ☐ S 27 Lh16
Ostaškov ☐ RUS 58 Mg17
Östavall ☐ S 25 Lh14
Östby ☐ N 24 Lg15
Österbotten = Pohjanmaa ☐ FIN 19 Mb14
Österbybruk ☐ S 25 Lj15
Österforse ☐ S 25 Lj14
Osterode ☐ D 44 Lf20
Östersund ☐ S 25 Lh14
Östhammar ☐ S 25 Lk15
Östmark ☐ S 24 Lg15
ostov Bol. Ljahovskij ☐ RUS 74 Sa04
ostov Kotel'nyj ☐ RUS 74 Sa03
Ostrava ☐ CZ 53 Lk21
Ostróda ☐ PL 50 Lk19
Ostrogožsk ☐ RUS 59 Mk20
Ostroh ☐ UA 51 Md20
Ostrołęka ☐ PL 50 Ma19
Ostrov ☐ RUS 30 Me17
ostrov Ajon ☐ RUS 74 Tb05
ostrov Arga-Muora-Sise ☐ RUS 73 Ra04
ostrova Sergeja Kirova ☐ RUS 73 Pb03

ostrov Belyj RUS 73 Oc04
ostrov Bol. Begičev RUS 73 Qc04
ostrov Bol'ševik RUS 73 Qa03
ostrov Gogland RUS 28 Md15
ostrov Iturup RUS 75 Sb10
ostrov Karaginskij RUS 74 Ta07
ostrov Kolgujev RUS 72 Nb05
ostrov Komsomolec RUS 73 Pc02
ostrov Kunašir RUS 75 Sb10
ostrov Moščnyj RUS 30 Md16
ostrov Novaja Sibir' RUS 74 Sb03
ostrov Oktjabr'skoj Revoljucii RUS 73 Pd02
ostrov Onekotan RUS 75 Sc09
ostrov Paramušir RUS 75 Sd08
ostrov Rasšua RUS 75 Sc09
ostrov Seskar RUS 28 Me15
ostrov Šiaškotan RUS 75 Sc09
ostrov Simušir RUS 75 Sc09
ostrov Soloveckie RUS 29 Mh13
ostrov Urup RUS 75 Sc09
ostrov Vajgač RUS 72 Oa04
ostrov Valaam RUS 29 Mf15
Ostrowiec Świętokrzyski PL 50 Ma20
Ostrów Mazowiecka PL 50 Ma19
Ostrów Wielkopolski PL 50 Lj20
Ostrzeszów PL 50 Lj20
Ostuni I 49 Lj25
Osumi Islands J 83 Rc12
Osuna E 41 Kh27
Oswestry GB 35 Kj19
Osypenko UA 63 Mj22
Otavi NAM 110 Ld22
Otelu Roşu RO 54 Mb23
Othoni GR 56 Lk26
Oti CI 105 La17
Otjiwarongo NAM 110 Ld23
Otlukbeli Dağları TR 66 Mk25
Otnes N 24 Lf15
Otočac HR 47 Lh23
Otradnaja RUS 66 Na23
Otradnyj RUS 60 Nf19
Otranto I 49 Lk25
Otta N 24 Le15
Ottawa ● CDN 121 Ga09
Ottawa Islands CDN 120 Fd07
Ottenby S 27 Lj17
Otuzco PE 133 Ga20
Ouadda RCA 108 Ma17
Ouagadougou ● BF 105 Kd16
Ouahigouya BF 105 Kd16
Ouallam RIM 105 Kc15
Ouarâne RIM 104 Kc14
Ouargla DZ 106 Lb12
Ouarzazate MA 104 Kc12

Oubangui RDC 108 Ld18
Oudtshoorn ZA 110 Ma25
Oued Drâa MA 104 Kc13
Oued Irharhar DZ 106 Lb13
Oued Moulouya MA 104 Kd12
Oued Saoura DZ 104 Kc13
Oued Tadant DZ 106 Lb14
Oued Tafassasset DZ 106 Lb14
Oued Tamanrasset DZ 104 La14
Oued Tekouiat DZ 104 La14
Oued Tichkatine DZ 104 La14
Oughterard IRL 33 Kf19
Ouistreham F 36 Kk21
Oujda MA 104 Kd12
Oujda MA 104 Kd12
Oulainen FIN 28 Mc13
Oulangan kansallispuisto FIN 23 Me12
Oulu FIN 28 Mc13
Oulujärvi FIN 28 Md13
Oum-Chalouba TCH 106 Ma15
Ounianga Kébir TCH 106 Ma15
Ouranoúpoli GR 57 Mc25
Ourense = Orense E 40 Kg24
Ourinhos BR 135 Hc23
Ourique P 41 Kf27
Ouro Preto BR 135 Hd23
Ouro Sogui SN 105 Kb15
Outer Hebrides GB 34 Kg17
Outokumpu FIN 28 Me14
Ouvéa F 98 Tb23
Ovacık TR 65 Mh26
Ovacık TR 66 Na25
Ovakışla TR 66 Nb26
Ovalle RCH 136 Gb25
Ovamboland NAM 110 Lc22
Övergård N 22 Lk11
Överkalix S 23 Mb12
Överlida S 26 Lg17
Overpelt B 37 Lc20
Övertorneå S 23 Mb12
Ovidiopol' UA 62 Mf22
Ovidiu RO 55 Me23
Oviedo E 40 Kh24
Ovinišcenskaja vozvyšennosť RUS 58 Mj15
Øvre Anárjohka n.p. N 23 Mc11
Øvre Årdal N 24 Ld15
Øvre Dividal n.p. N 22 Lk11
Øvre Pasvik n.p. N 23 Me11
Øvre Rendal N 24 Lf15
Øvre Soppero S 23 Ma11
Ovruč UA 62 Me20
Owando RCB 108 Ld19
Owensboro USA 123 Fc11
Owen Sound USA 123 Fd10
Owen Stanley Range PNG 92 Sb20
Owo WAN 108 Lb17
Öxarfjörður IS 32 Kb12
Oxelösund S 27 Lj16
Oxford GB 35 Kk20
Oxnard USA 122 Dd11
Oyem G 108 Lc18
Oyonnax F 39 Lc22
Ozark Plateau USA 123 Fb11

Özd H 53 Ma21
Ožerel'e RUS 59 Mk18
Ozerki RUS 61 Nc20
Ozerki RUS 60 Nd17
Ozerki RUS 60 Nd19
ozero Baskunčak RUS 61 Nd21
ozero Beloe RUS 29 Mj15
ozero Čany RUS 79 Od08
ozero El'ton RUS 61 Nd21
ozero Hanskoe RUS 63 Mk22
ozero Il'men' RUS 30 Mf16
ozero Imandra RUS 23 Mg11
ozero Lača RUS 29 Mk15
ozero Nero RUS 58 Mk17
ozero Tajmyr RUS 73 Qa04
ozero Vože RUS 29 Mk15
Ozery RUS 58 Mk18
Ozieri I 48 Le25

P

Paamiut DK 119 Hc06
Paanajarvi N.P. RUS 23 Mf12
Pabradė LT 31 Mc18
Pačelma RUS 61 Nb19
Pachucade Soto MEX 124 Fa14
Padang RI 86 Qa19
Padang Endau MAL 86 Qa18
Padangpanjang RI 86 Qa19
Padangsidempuan RI 86 Pd18
Paderborn D 44 Le20
Padilla BOL 133 Gd22
Padjelanta n.p. S 22 Lj12
Pádova I 46 Lf23
Padre Island USA 123 Fa13
Padstow GB 35 Kh20
Paducah USA 123 Fc11
Pafos CY 107 Mc12
Pag HR 47 Lh23
Pagadian RP 85 Ra17
Pagai Selatan RI 86 Qa19
Pagai Ulatan RI 86 Pd19
Pagalu STP 108 Lb19
Pagatan RI 87 Qc19
Pagégiai LT 31 Ma18
Pagimana RI 87 Ra19
Pahraničny BY 31 Mb19
Paide EST 30 Mc16
Päijänne FIN 28 Mc15
Päijänteen kansallispuisto FIN 28 Mc15
Paimpol F 36 Kj21
Painted Desert USA 122 Eb11
País Vasco E 42 Kj24
Paisley GB 34 Kh18
Pajala S 23 Mb12
Pajęczno PL 50 Lk20
Pakin Atoll FSM 93 Sd17
Pakistan ■ PAK 80 Ob13
Paklenica, N.P. HR 47 Lh23
Paks H 53 Lk22
Paksan LAO 84 Qa15
Pakse LAO 84 Qb15
Pakwach EAU 109 Mc18
Pala TCH 108 Lc17
Palafrugell E 42 Lb25
Palamós E 42 Lb25
Palanga LT 31 Ma18

Palangkaraya RI 86 Qb19
Palanpur IND 80 Oc14
Palau ■ PAL 92 Rc17
Palau Islands PAL 92 Rc17
Palawan RP 85 Qd16
Paldiski EST 30 Mc16
Paleh RUS 58 Na17
Palembang RI 86 Qa19
Palencia E 40 Kh25
Paleohóra GR 56 Mb28
Palesse BY 51 Mc19
Pali IND 80 Oc13
Palikir ● FSM 93 Sd17
Paljavaam RUS 74 Tc05
Palk Strait IND/CL 81 Od17
Pallas-Ounastunturi kansallispuisto FIN 23 Mb11
Palma Del Río E 41 Kh27
Palma de Mallorca E 43 Lb26
Palmar Sur CR 126 Fd17
Palmas BR 134 Hc21
Palmer USA 116 Cc06
Palmer Land 140 Gc33
Palmer Station 140 Gd31
Palmerston North NZ 99 Td27
Palmi I 49 Li26
Palmira CO 132 Ga18
Palm Islands AUS 96 Sb22
Palm Springs USA 122 Dd11
Palojoensuu FIN 23 Mb11
Palpa PE 133 Ga21
Palu RI 87 Qc19
Palu TR 66 Mk26
Pama BF 105 La16
Pamiers F 42 La24
Pamir TJ 78 Oc11
Pampa del Tamarugal RCH 136 Gb23
Pampa Húmeda RA 136 Gd26
Pampas RA 137 Gd26
Pampa Seca RA 136 Gc26
Pamplona CO 132 Gb17
Pamplona E 42 Kk24
Pamukkale TR 64 Me27
Panaji IND 81 Oc15
Panama PA 126 Fd17
Panamá ● PA 132 Ga17
Panama Canal PA 132 Ga17
Panama City USA 123 Fc12
Panay RP 85 Ra16
Pandan RP 85 Ra16
Pandany RUS 29 Mg14
Panetólio GR 56 Ma26
Panevėžys LT 31 Mc18
Panga pank EST 30 Mb16
Pangkalanbun RI 87 Qb19
Pangnirtung CDN 119 Gc05
Panjgur PAK 77 Oa13
Pankalpinang RI 86 Qb19
Pantanal BR 135 Ha22
Pantanal Matogrossense BR 135 Ha22
Pantelleria I 48 Lf27
Pantoja PE 132 Ga19
Panzhihua CHN 84 Qa13
Páola I 49 Lj26
Pápa H 53 Lj22
Papantla MEX 125 Fa14
Papenburg D 44 Ld19
Papey IS 32 Kc13
Papua RI 92 Rd19
Papua New Guinea ■ PNG 92 Sa20

Pará ◎ BR 134 Hb19
Paraburdoo ◎ AUS 94 Qd23
Paracatu ◎ BR 135 Hc22
Paracel Islands ⌐ 85 Qc15
Paraguay ◼ PY 136 Ha23
Paraguay ◪ PY 136 Ha23
Paraíba ◎ BR 134 Ja20
Parainen = Pargas ◎ FIN
  22 Mb15
Paraíso do Tocantins ◎ BR
  134 Hc21
Parakou ◎ DY 105 La17
Paramaribo ◉ SME 134 Ha17
Paramithía ◎ GR 56 Ma26
Paraná ◎ BR 135 Hb23
Paraná ◎ BR 135 Hb23
Paraná ◪ RA 136 Gd25
Paraná ◪ RA 136 Gd25
Paranã ◪ BR 135 Hc21
Paranaguá ◎ BR 135 Hc24
Paranaíba ◎ BR 135 Hb22
Paranaíba ◪ BR 135 Hb22
Paranapanema ◪ BR 135
  Hb23
Paranésti ◎ GR 57 Mc25
Paratinga ◎ BR 135 Hd21
Paray-le-Monial ◎ F 39 Lc22
Parchim ◎ D 44 Lf19
Parc Naturel Régional
  d'Armorique ◆ F 36 Kh21
Parczew ◎ PL 51 Mb20
Pardo ◪ BR 135 Hb23
Pardo ◪ BR 135 Hd22
Pardubice ◎ CZ 52 Lh19
Parent ◎ CDN 121 Gb09
Parepare ◎ RI 87 Qc19
Párga ◎ GR 56 Ma26
Pargas = Parainen ◎ FIN
  22 Mb15
Pargua ◎ RCH 137 Gb27
Parika ◎ GUY 134 Ha17
Paris ◉ F 37 La21
Paris ◎ USA 123 Fa12
Parkano ◎ FIN 19 Mb14
Parkersburg ◎ USA 123 Fd14
Parma ◎ I 46 Lf23
Parnaíba ◪ BR 134 Hc20
Parnaíba ◎ BR 134 Hd19
Parnaíba ◪ BR 134 Hd19
Parnassos N.P. ◆ GR 56
  Mb26
Párnitha N.P. ◆ GR 57 Mb26
Pärnu ◎ EST 30 Mc16
Páros ◎ GR 57 Mc27
Páros ⌐ GR 57 Mc27
Parque Natural de Ria
  Formosa ◆ P 41 Kg27
Parque Natural da Serra da
  Estrela ◆ P 40 Kg25
Parque Natural do Douro
  Internacional ◆ P 40 Kg25
Parque Natural do Sudoeste
  Alentejano e Costa
  Vicentina ◆ P 41 Kf27
Parque Natural do Vale do
  Guadiana ◆ P 41 Kg27
Parry Islands ⌐ CDN 118
  Ea03
Parthenay ◎ F 38 Kk22
Partizánske ◎ SK 53 Lk21
Paru ◪ BR 134 Hb19
Pårvomaj ◎ BG 55 Mc24
Parýčy ◎ BY 51 Me19
Paša ◪ RUS 29 Mg15
Pasadena ◎ USA 122 Dd11
Pasadena ◎ USA 123 Fa13
Pascagoula ◎ USA 123 Fc12
Pasewalk ◎ D 44 Lh19

Pasinler ◎ TR 66 Na25
Paškovskij ◎ RUS 63 Mk23
Pasłęk ◎ PL 50 Lk18
Pasni ◎ PAK 77 Oa13
Passau ◎ D 45 Lg21
Passo Fundo ◎ BR 135 Hb24
Passos ◎ BR 135 Hc23
Pastavy ◎ BY 31 Md19
Pasto ◎ CO 132 Ga18
Pasvalys ◎ LT 31 Mc17
Patagonia ⌐ RA 137 Gb28
Pătârlagele ◎ RO 55 Md23
Pate Island ⌐ EAK 109 Na19
Paterno ◎ I 49 Lh27
Paterson ◎ USA 121 Gb10
Pátmos ◎ GR 57 Md27
Patna ◉ IND 80 Pb13
Patnos ◎ TR 66 Nb26
Patomskoe nagor'e ▲ RUS
  73 Qc07
Patos ◎ BR 134 Ja20
Patos de Minas ◎ BR 135
  Hc22
Patquia ◎ RA 136 Gc23
Patraikos Kólpos ⌐ GR
  56 Ma26
Patreksfjörður ◎ IS 32 Jj13
Pattani ◎ THA 86 Qa17
Pattaya ◎ THA 84 Qa16
Patu ◎ BR 134 Ja20
Patvinsuom kansallispuisto ◆
  FIN 29 Mf14
Pau ◎ F 42 Kk24
Pauillac ◎ F 38 Kk23
Paulatuk ◎ CDN 118 Dd03
Paulistana ◎ BR 134 Hd20
Paulo Afonso ◎ BR 134 Ja20
Pavia ◎ I 46 Le23
Pāvilosta ◎ LV 30 Ma17
Pavlíkeni ◎ BG 55 Mc24
Pavlodar ◎ KZ 79 Od08
Pavlohrad ◎ UA 63 Mh21
Pavlovka ◎ RUS 61 Nd19
Pavlovo ◎ RUS 60 Nb18
Pavlovsk ◎ RUS 61 Na20
Pavlovskaja ◎ RUS 63 Mk22
Pavlovskij Posad ◎ RUS
  58 Mk18
Pavlovskoe ◎ RUS 58 Na17
Pavlyš ◎ UA 62 Mg21
Pavullo nel Frignano ◎ I
  46 Lf23
Paxí ⌐ GR 56 Ma26
Payne's Find ◎ AUS 95 Qd24
Paysandú ◎ ROU 136 Ha25
Pays de la Loire ⌐ F 36 Kk22
Pazar ◎ TR 66 Na25
Pazarcık ◎ TR 65 Mj27
Pazardžik ◎ BG 55 Mc24
Peace River ◪ CDN 117 Ea07
Peace River ◪ CDN 117 Ea07
Peć ◎ SR 54 Ma24
Peak District N.P. ◆ GB
  35 Kk19
Pearl River ◪ CHN 85 Qc14
Peary Channel ⌐ CDN
  118 Ed03
Peary Land ⌐ DK 119 Jb02
Peawanuck ◎ CDN 120 Fc07
Pebas ◎ PE 132 Gb19
Pecica ◎ RO 54 Ma22
Pečora ◪ RUS 72 Nc05
Pečora ◎ RUS 72 Nd05
Pečorskoe more ⌐ RUS
  72 Nc04
Pečory ◎ RUS 30 Md17
Pecos ◪ USA 122 Ed12

Pecos ◎ USA 122 Ed12
Pécs ◎ H 53 Lk22
Pedro Afonso ◎ BR 134 Hc20
Pedro Juan Caballero ◎ PY
  136 Ha23
Peebles ◎ GB 34 Kj18
Peel ◎ GB 34 Kh18
Peel Sound ⌐ CDN 118 Fa04
Peera Peera Poolanna Lake ⌐
  AUS 96 Rd24
Pegasus Bay ⌐ NZ 99 Tc27
Pegnitz ◎ D 45 Lf21
Pego ◎ E 43 Kk26
Pegu ◎ MYA 84 Pd15
Pegunungan Maoke ▲ RI
  92 Rd19
Pehuajó ◎ RA 136 Gd26
Peine ◎ D 44 Lf19
Pekalongan ◎ RI 86 Qd19
Pekanbaru ◎ RI 86 Qa18
Pektubaevo ◎ RUS 60 Ne17
Peleng ⌐ RI 87 Ra19
Pelhřimov ◎ CZ 52 Lh21
Pelješac ⌐ HR 47 Lj24
Pelkosenniemi ◎ FIN 23
  Md17
Pello ◎ FIN 23 Mc12
Pelolas ◎ BR 135 Hb24
Peloponnesus ⌐ GR 56 Ma27
Pelotas ◎ BR 136 Hb25
Pematang Siantar ◎ RI
  86 Pd18
Pemba ◎ MOC 111 Na21
Pemba Channel ⌐ EAT
  109 Md20
Pemba Island ⌐ EAT 109
  Md20
Pembroke ◎ CDN 121 Ga09
Pembroke ◎ GB 35 Kh20
Pembrokeshire Coast N.P. ◆
  GB 35 Kh20
Peñafiel ◎ E 40 Kh25
Penang ◎ MAL 86 Qa17
Peña Prieta ▲ E 40 Kh24
Peñaranda de Bracamonte ◎
  E 40 Kh25
Peñarroya-Pueblonuevo ◎ E
  41 Kh26
Pendleton ◎ USA 122 Ea09
Peneda-Gerês, P.N.da ◆ P
  40 Kf25
Peniche ◎ P 40 Kf26
Península de Teitao ⌐ RCH
  137 Ga28
Península Valdés ⌐ RA
  137 Gd27
Péninsule de Gaspésie ⌐
  CDN 121 Gc09
Péninsule d'Ungava ⌐ CDN
  112 Ga03
Penmar'h ◎ F 36 Kh22
Pennell Coast ⌐ 141 Tb33
Pennines ⌐ GB 35 Kj18
Pennsylvania ⌐ USA 123
  Ga10
Penny Strait ⌐ CDN 118 Fa03
Peno ◎ RUS 58 Mg17
Penong ◎ AUS 95 Rc25
Penrith ◎ GB 34 Kj18
Pensacola ◎ USA 123 Fc12
Pensacola Mountains ▲
  140 Hb35
Pentecost Island ⌐ VU
  98 Tb22
Penticton ◎ CDN 122 Ea09
Penza ◎ RUS 61 Nc19
Penzance ◎ GB 35 Kh20
Penžinskaja guba ⌐ RUS
  74 Ta06

Peoria ◎ USA 123 Fc10
Peqin ◎ AL 56 Lk25
Perämeren kansallispuisto ◆
  FIN 28 Mc13
Perämeri ⌐ FIN 28 Mc13
Peranka ◎ FIN 28 Me13
Percival Lakes ⌐ AUS 94
  Ra23
Perečyn ◎ UA 53 Mb21
Perehins'ke ◎ UA 51 Mc21
Pereira ◎ CO 132 Ga18
Perejaslav-Chmel'nyc'kyj ◎
  UA 62 Mf20
Perekopka ◎ RUS 61 Nb21
Perelešinskij ◎ RUS 61 Na20
Pereljub ◎ RUS 60 Nf20
Pereščepyne ◎ UA 62 Mh21
Pereslavl'-Zalesskij ◎ RUS
  58 Mk17
Pereslavsky N.P. ◆ RUS
  58 Mk17
Perevoz ◎ RUS 60 Nc18
Pergamino ◎ RA 136 Gd25
Periam ◎ RO 54 Ma22
Périgueux ◎ F 38 La23
Peristéra ⌐ GR 56 Mb26
Perito Moreno ◎ RA 137
  Gb28
Perleberg ◎ D 44 Lf19
Perloja ◎ LT 31 Mc18
Perm' ◎ RUS 72 Nd07
Pernambuco ⌐ BR 134 Ja20
Péronne ◎ F 37 Lb21
Perpignan ◎ F 38 Lb24
Perros-Guirec ◎ F 36 Kj21
Persian Gulf ⌐ 77 Nb13
Perth ◉ AUS 95 Qd25
Perth ◎ GB 34 Kj17
Perth Basin ⌐ AUS 95 Qc25
Pertuis ◎ F 39 Lc24
Peru ◼ PE 133 Ga21
Peru Basin ⌐ 128 Fb11
Peru-Chile Trench ⌐ 133
  Fd20
Perúgia ◎ I 46 Lg24
Peruíbe ◎ BR 135 Hc23
Perušić ◎ HR 47 Lj23
Pervomajsk ◎ RUS 60 Nb18
Pervomajs'k ◎ UA 62 Mf21
Pervomajskij ◎ RUS 59 Na19
Pervomajskoe ◎ RUS 28
  Me15
Pervomajskoe ◎ RUS 61
  Nd20
Pervomajs'kyj ◎ UA 63 Mj21
Pervoural'sk ◎ RUS 72 Nd07
Pésaro ◎ I 47 Lg24
Pescanoe ◎ RUS 29 Mh14
Pescara ◎ I 47 Lh24
Pescina ◎ I 47 Lg24
Peshkopi ◎ AL 56 Ma25
Pestovo ◎ RUS 58 Mh16
Pestravka ◎ RUS 60 Ne19
Petchaburi ◎ THA 86 Pd16
Peterborough ◎ GB 35 Kk19
Peterhead ◎ GB 34 Kk17
Peter I Island ⌐ 140 Fb32
Petermann Gletscher ❄ DK
  118 Gd02
Petersburg ◎ USA 117 Db07
Petin ◎ E 40 Kg24
Petkeljärven kansallispuisto
  ◆ FIN 29 Mf14
Petran ◎ AL 56 Ma25
Petras, Mount ▲ 140 Dc34
Petrič ◎ BG 56 Mb25
Petrinja ◎ HR 47 Lj23
Petrivka ◎ UA 62 Mf20
Petrolina ◎ BR 134 Hd20

Petroşani ☐ **RO** 54 Mb23
Petropavl ☐ **KZ** 78 Ob08
Petropavlivka ☐ **UA** 63 Mj21
Petropavlovka ☐ **RUS** 82 Qb08
Petropavlovka ☐ **RUS** 61 Na20
Petropavlovsk-Kamčatskij ☑ **RUS** 75 Sd08
Petrovac ☐ **SR** 54 Ma23
Petrovka ☐ **RUS** 60 Nf19
Petrovo ☐ **RUS** 58 Mh16
Petrovsk ☐ **RUS** 61 Nc19
Petrovskoe ☐ **RUS** 58 Mk17
Petrovskoe ☐ **RUS** 59 Na19
Petrovsk Zabajkal'skij ☐ **RUS** 82 Qb08
Petrozavodsk ☑ **RUS** 29 Mh15
Petrykav ☐ **BY** 51 Me19
Petuški ☐ **RUS** 58 Mk18
Peureulak ☐ **RI** 86 Pd18
Pevek ☐ **RUS** 74 Tc05
Pézenas ☐ **F** 38 Lb24
Pezinok ☐ **SK** 53 Lj21
Pforzheim ☐ **D** 45 Le21
Phalodi ☐ **IND** 80 Oc13
Phang Nga ☐ **THA** 86 Pd17
Phan Thiet ☐ **VN** 85 Qb16
Philadelphia ☐ **USA** 123 Ga15
Philippine Basin ☐ 85 Rb15
Philippines ☐ **RP** 85 Qd16
Philippine Sea ☐ 85 Rb15
Philippine Trench ☐ **RP** 85 Rb16
Philippine Trench ☐ 85 Rb16
Phitsanulok ☐ **THA** 84 Qa15
Phnom Penh ☑ **K** 84 Qa16
Phoenix ☑ **USA** 122 Eb12
Phuket ☐ **THA** 86 Pd17
Piacenza ☐ **I** 46 Le23
Piaski ☐ **PL** 51 Mb20
Piatra ☐ **RO** 55 Mc24
Piatra Craiului, P.N. ☘ **RO** 55 Mc23
Piatra-Neamţ ☐ **RO** 55 Md22
Piauí ☐ **BR** 134 Hd20
Piazza Armerina ☐ **I** 49 Lf27
Pičaevo ☐ **RUS** 61 Nb19
Picardy ☐ **F** 37 Lb21
Pickering ☐ **GB** 34 Kk18
Pico Almanzor ▲ **E** 40 Kh25
Pico Cristóbal Colón ▲ **CO** 127 Gb16
Pico da Bandeira ▲ **BR** 135 Hd23
Pico da Neblina ▲ **BR/YV** 132 Gc18
Pico de Itambé ▲ **BR** 135 Hd22
Picos ☐ **BR** 134 Hd20
Picton ☐ **NZ** 99 Tc27
Pic Touside ▲ **TCH** 106 Ld14
Piedmont ☐ **I** 46 Le23
Piedras Negras ☐ **MEX** 124 Ed13
Piehanal ☐ **RA** 136 Gd23
Pieksämäki ☐ **FIN** 28 Md14
Pielinen ☐ **FIN** 28 Me14
Pieljekaise n.p. ☘ **S** 22 Lj12
Piemonte ☐ **I** 46 Le23
Pieniński P.N. ☘ **PL/SK** 50 Ma21
Pienza ☐ **I** 46 Lf24
Pierre ☑ **USA** 122 Ed10
Pierrelatte ☐ **F** 39 Lc23
Piešťany ☐ **SK** 53 Lj21
Pietarsaari ☐ **FIN** 19 Mb14
Pietermaritzburg ☐ **ZA** 110 Mc24

Pietersburg ☐ **ZA** 110 Mb23
Pieve di Cadore ☐ **I** 46 Lg22
Pikalevo ☐ **RUS** 58 Mh16
Pikelot Island ☐ **FSM** 92 Sb17
PikiutdleqKøge Bugt ☐ **DK** 119 Hd06
pik Sedova ▲ **RUS** 72 Nd04
Piła ☐ **PL** 50 Lj19
Pilar ☐ **PY** 136 Ha24
Pilbara ☐ **AUS** 94 Qd23
Pilcomayo ☘ **PY** 136 Ha23
Pilgrimstad ☐ **S** 25 Lh14
Pilisvörösvár ☐ **H** 53 Lk22
Pilos ☐ **GR** 56 Ma27
Pimba ☐ **AUS** 97 Rd25
Pimenta Bueno ☐ **BR** 133 Gd21
Pınarbaşı ☐ **TR** 65 Mg26
Pınarbaşı ☐ **TR** 65 Mj26
Pinar del Rio ☐ **C** 126 Fd14
Pınarhisar ☐ **TR** 57 Md25
Pınarlar ☐ **TR** 65 Mj26
Pindaré ☘ **BR** 134 Hc19
Pindhos Mountains ▲ **GR** 56 Ma26
Pindos N.P. ☘ **GR** 56 Ma26
Pinduší ☐ **RUS** 29 Mh14
Pine Bluff ☐ **USA** 123 Fb12
Pine Creek ☐ **AUS** 94 Rc21
Pine Island Bay ☐ 140 Ed23
Pine Island Glacier ☒ 140 Ed34
Pinerolo ☐ **I** 46 Ld23
Pingelap Atoll ☐ **FSM** 93 Ta17
Pingyeri ☐ **IS** 32 Jj13
Pingvallavatn ☐ **IS** 32 Jk13
Pingxiang ☐ **CHN** 85 Qc13
Pingyao ☐ **CHN** 82 Qc11
Pinheiro ☐ **BR** 134 Hc19
Pinhel ☐ **P** 40 Kg25
Pini ☐ **RI** 86 Pd18
Pinnaroo ☐ **AUS** 97 Sa26
Pinneberg ☐ **D** 44 Le19
Pinsk ☐ **BY** 51 Md19
Pinto ☐ **RA** 136 Gd24
Piombino ☐ **I** 46 Lf24
Pionki ☐ **PL** 50 Ma20
Piotrków Trybunalski ☐ **PL** 50 Lk20
Pipéri ☐ **GR** 57 Mc26
Piracicaba ☐ **BR** 135 Hc23
Pirai do Sul ☐ **BR** 135 Hc23
Pirámide ▲ **RCH** 137 Gb28
Pirané ☐ **RA** 136 Ha24
Pirapora ☐ **BR** 135 Hd22
Pirgos ☐ **GR** 56 Ma27
Pirin, N.P. ☘ **BG** 56 Mb25
Piripiri ☐ **BR** 134 Hd19
Pirki ☐ **BY** 62 Mf20
Pirmasens ☐ **D** 45 Ld21
Pirna ☐ **D** 44 Lg20
Pirot ☐ **SR** 54 Mb24
Pisa ☐ **I** 46 Lf24
Pisco ☐ **PE** 133 Ga21
Pisek ☐ **CZ** 52 Lh21
Pistilfjörður ☐ **IS** 32 Kc12
Pistoia ☐ **I** 46 Lf24
Pisz ☐ **PL** 50 Ma19
Piteå ☐ **S** 25 Ma13
Pitelino ☐ **RUS** 58 Na18
Piteşti ☐ **RO** 55 Mc23
Pitkjaranta ☐ **RUS** 29 Mf15
Pittsburgh ☐ **USA** 123 Ga10
Piura ☐ **PE** 132 Fd20
Pivdennyj Buh ☘ **UA** 62 Mf22
Piz Bernina ▲ **CH** 45 Le22
Piz Buin ▲ **CH** 45 Lf22
P'jana ☘ **RUS** 60 Nc18
Pjaozero ☐ **RUS** 23 Mf15

Pjasina ☘ **RUS** 73 Pb04
Pjasinskij zaliv ☐ **RUS** 73 Pa04
Pjatigorsk ☐ **RUS** 76 Na10
P'jatychatky ☐ **UA** 62 Mg21
Þjóðgarðurinn í Jökulsárgljúfrum ☘ **IS** 32 Kc13
Þjóðgarðurinn í Skaftafelli ☘ **IS** 32 Kb13
Þjóðgarðurinn Snæfellsjökull ☘ **IS** 32 Jh13
Þjórsá ☘ **IS** 32 Ka13
Placentia Bay ☐ **CDN** 121 Hb09
Plainview ☐ **USA** 122 Ed12
Planalto Central ▲ **BR** 135 Hc21
Planalto do Bié ▲ **ANG** 110 Ld21
Planalto do Mato Grosso ▲ **BR** 135 Ha21
Plasencia ☐ **E** 40 Kg25
Platamónas ☐ **GR** 56 Mb25
Plateau de la Manika ▲ **RDC** 110 Mb21
Plateau du Djado ▲ **RN** 106 Lc14
Plateau du Kasai ▲ **RDC** 108 Ld20
Plateau du Tademaït ▲ **DZ** 104 La13
Plateau Laurentien ▲ **CDN** 121 Gb09
Plateau Laurentien ▲ **CDN** 121 Gb09
Plateau of Tibet ▲ **CHN** 80 Pa12
plato Putorana ▲ **RUS** 73 Pd05
Plattling ☐ **D** 45 Lg21
Plau ☐ **D** 44 Lg19
Plauen ☐ **D** 45 Lg20
Plav ☐ **CG** 54 Lk24
Plavsk ☐ **RUS** 59 Mj19
Pleiku ☐ **VN** 84 Qb16
Pleščanicy ☐ **BY** 31 Md18
Pleszew ☐ **PL** 50 Lj20
Pleven ☐ **BG** 55 Mc24
Plitvička Jezera ☐ **HR** 47 Lh23
Plitvička jezera, N.P. ☘ **HR** 47 Lh23
Pljevlja ☐ **CG** 54 Lk24
Pljussa ☐ **RUS** 30 Me16
Pljussa ☘ **RUS** 30 Me16
Ploče ☐ **HR** 47 Lj24
Płock ☐ **PL** 50 Lk19
Ploërmel ☐ **F** 36 Kj22
Ploieşti ☐ **RO** 55 Md23
Plön ☐ **D** 44 Lf18
Plońsk ☐ **PL** 50 Ma19
Ploskoš' ☐ **RUS** 30 Mf17
Ploudalmézeau ☐ **F** 36 Kh21
Plovdiv ☐ **BG** 56 Mc24
Plumridge Lakes ☐ **AUS** 95 Rb24
Plumtree ☐ **ZW** 110 Mb23
Plungė ☐ **LT** 31 Ma18
Plymouth ☐ **GB** 35 Kh20
Plymouth ☒ **UK** 127 Gd15
Plzeň ☐ **CZ** 52 Lg21
Pniewy ☐ **PL** 50 Lj19
Pô ☐ **BF** 105 Kd16
Pobeda Ice Island ☐ 141 Pd31
Pobedy Peak ▲ **CHN/KS** 79 Pa10
Poča ☐ **RUS** 29 Mk14

Pocatello ☐ **USA** 122 Eb10
Počep ☐ **RUS** 59 Mg19
Počinok ☐ **RUS** 59 Mg18
Pocking ☐ **D** 45 Lg21
Pocklington Reef ☐ **PNG** 96 Sd21
Podberez'e ☐ **RUS** 30 Mf16
Podberez'e ☐ **RUS** 30 Mf17
Podbořany ☐ **CZ** 52 Lg20
Podborov'e ☐ **RUS** 30 Me17
Poddor'e ☐ **RUS** 30 Mf17
Podgorenskij ☐ **RUS** 61 Mk20
Podgorica ☑ **CG** 56 Lk24
Podíš'ka vysočyna ▲ **UA** 51 Md21
Podil ☐ **UA** 62 Mg21
Podkamennaja Tunguska ☘ **RUS** 73 Pd06
Podkova ☐ **BG** 57 Mc25
Podlesnoje ☐ **RUS** 61 Nd20
Podol'sk ☐ **RUS** 58 Mj18
Podoroż'e ☐ **RUS** 29 Mh15
Podravina ☘ **HR** 47 Lj23
Podromanija ☐ **BIH** 47 Lk24
Podsneżnoe ☐ **RUS** 61 Nc19
Podujevo ☐ **SR** 54 Ma24
Podyji, N.P. ☘ **CZ** 53 Lj21
Pogar ☐ **RUS** 59 Mg19
Poggibonsi ☐ **I** 46 Lf24
Pogoanele ☐ **RO** 55 Md23
Pogost ☐ **RUS** 29 Mh15
Pohjanmaa ▲ **FIN** 19 Mb14
Pohrebyšče ☐ **UA** 62 Me21
Pohvistnevo ☐ **RUS** 60 Ng19
Poiana Teiului ☐ **RO** 55 Md22
Point Barrow ☐ **USA** 116 Ca04
Pointe-à-Pitre ☒ **F** 127 Gd15
Pointe-Noire ☐ **RCB** 108 Lc19
Point Hope ☐ **USA** 116 Bc05
Poitiers ☑ **F** 38 La22
Poitou ☘ **F** 38 Kk22
Poitou-Charente ☐ **F** 38 La22
Pojezierze Pomerskie ▲ **PL** 50 Lj19
Pokhara ☒ **NEP** 80 Pa13
Pokka ☐ **FIN** 23 Mc11
Pokrov ☐ **RUS** 58 Mk18
Pokrovsk ☐ **RUS** 61 Nd20
Pokrovs'ke ☐ **UA** 63 Mj22
Pokrovs'ke ☐ **UA** 63 Mk21
Polack ☐ **BY** 31 Me18
Polackaja Nizína ▲ **BY** 31 Md18
Poland ☐ **PL** 50 Lk19
Polanów ☐ **PL** 50 Lj18
Polar Plateau ▲ 140 Eb36
Polatlı ☐ **TR** 64 Mg26
Potczyn-Zdrój ☐ **PL** 50 Lj19
Poleski P.N. ☘ **PL** 51 Mb20
Polessk ☐ **RUS** 31 Ma18
Policoro ☐ **I** 49 Lj25
Poliegos ☐ **GR** 57 Mc27
Polihnítos ☐ **GR** 57 Md26
Polikastro ☐ **GR** 56 Mb25
Polillo Islands ☐ **RP** 85 Ra16
Polis'ke ☐ **UA** 62 Me20
Polkowice ☐ **PL** 50 Lj20
Pollença ☐ **E** 43 Lb26
Pollino, P.N.del ☘ **I** 49 Lj26
Polmak ☐ **N** 23 Me10
Pologoe Zajmišče ☐ **RUS** 61 Nc21
Polohy ☐ **UA** 63 Mj22
Poloniny, Narodný park ☘ **SK** 53 Mb21
Polonnaruwa ☐ **CL** 81 Pa17

Polonne ⬜ UA 51 Md20
Poltava ⬜ UA 62 Mh21
Põltsamaa ⬜ EST 30 Mc16
poluostrov Kanin ▲ RUS 72 Na05
Poluostrov Rybačij ▲ RUS 23 Mf11
Pombal ⬜ P 40 Kf26
Pomio ⬜ PNG 93 Sc20
Pomorie ⬜ BG 55 Md24
Ponape Island ⬜ FSM 93 Sd17
Ponca City ⬜ USA 123 Fa11
Ponce ⬜ USA 127 Gc15
Pondicherry ⬜ IND 81 Oc16
Pond Inlet ⬜ CDN 118 Ga04
Ponferrada ⬜ E 40 Kg24
Poniatowa ⬜ PL 51 Mb20
Ponoj ⬛ RUS 72 Md05
Ponoj ⬜ RUS 72 Na05
Ponta Albina ▲ ANG 110 Lc22
Ponta de Baleia ⬛ BR 135 Ja22
Ponta Delgada ⬜ P 58 Kb08
137 Gc29
Ponta de Pedras ⬜ BR 134 Hc19
Ponta Grossa ⬜ BR 135 Hb24
Pont-à-Mousson ⬜ F 37 Ld21
Ponta Porã ⬜ BR 136 Ha23
Pontarlier ⬜ F 39 Ld22
Ponta São Sebastião ⬛ MOC 111 Md23
Pont-Audemer ⬜ F 36 La21
Pontchâteau ⬜ F 36 Kj22
Ponte da Barca ⬜ P 40 Kf25
Ponte de Sor ⬜ P 40 Kf26
Pontes e Lacerda ⬜ BR 133 Ha22
Pontevedra ⬜ E 40 Kf24
Pontianak ⬜ RI 86 Qb19
Pontivy ⬜ F 36 Kj21
Pont-l'Abbé ⬜ F 36 Kh22
Pontoise ⬜ F 37 Lb21
Pontremoli ⬜ I 46 Le23
Ponts ⬜ E 42 La25
Popayan ⬜ CO 132 Ga18
Poperinge ⬜ B 37 Lb20
Poplar Bluff ⬜ USA 123 Fb11
Popocatépetl ▲ MEX 124 Fa15
Popondetta ⬜ PNG 93 Sb20
Popovo ⬜ BG 55 Md24
Poprad ⬜ SK 53 Ma21
Popsko ⬜ BG 57 Mc25
Porangatu ⬜ BR 135 Hc21
Porazava ⬜ BY 51 Mc19
Porbandar ⬜ IND 80 Ob14
Pordenone ⬜ I 46 Lg23
Poreč ⬜ HR 47 Lg23
Porhov ⬜ RUS 30 Me17
Pori ⬜ FIN 25 Ma15
Pórisvatn ⬛ IS 32 Ka13
Porjus ⬜ S 22 Lk12
Porlákshöfn ⬜ IS 32 Jk14
Porlamar ⬜ YV 127 Gd16
Pornic ⬜ F 36 Kj22
Poronajsk ⬜ RUS 75 Sa09
Póros ⬜ GR 57 Mb27
Porosozero ⬜ RUS 29 Mg14
Porpoise Bay ⬛ 141 Rb32
Porrentruy ⬜ CH 45 Ld22
Porsangerfjorden ⬛ N 23 Mc10
Porsgrunn ⬜ N 26 Le16
Pórshöfn ⬜ IS 32 Kc12
Pórsmörk ⬛ IS 32 Ka14
Portadown ⬜ GB 33 Kg18

Portage la Prairie ⬜ CDN 120 Fa08
Port Alberni ⬜ CDN 122 Dd09
Portalegre ⬜ P 40 Kg26
Port Arthur ⬜ AUS 97 Sb27
Port Arthur ⬜ USA 123 Fb13
Port Askaig ⬜ GB 33 Kg18
Port Augusta ⬜ AUS 97 Rd25
Port-au-Prince ⬛ RH 127 Gb15
Port Blair ⬛ IND 81 Pc16
Port Elizabeth ⬜ ZA 110 Mb25
Port Ellen ⬜ GB 33 Kg18
Port-Gentil ⬜ G 108 Lb19
Port Harcourt ⬜ WAN 108 Lb18
Port Hardy ⬜ CDN 116 Dc08
Port Harrison ⬜ CDN 120 Ga07
Port Hedland ⬜ AUS 94 Qd23
Port Heiden ⬜ USA 116 Ca07
Port Hope Simpson ⬜ CDN 121 Ha08
Portimão ⬜ P 41 Kf27
Portinatx ⬜ E 43 La26
Portland ⬜ AUS 97 Sa26
Portland ⬜ USA 122 Dd09
Portland ⬜ USA 121 Gb10
Port Laoise ⬜ IRL 33 Kf19
Port Lavaca ⬜ USA 125 Fa13
Port Lincoln ⬜ AUS 97 Rd25
Port Macquarie ⬜ AUS 97 Sc25
Port-Menier ⬜ CDN 121 Gd09
Port Moresby ⬛ PNG 92 Sb20
Port Nelson ⬜ CDN 120 Fb07
Porto ⬜ F 46 Le24
Porto ⬜ P 40 Kf25
Porto Alegre ⬛ BR 136 Hb25
Porto de Moz ⬜ BR 134 Hb19
Portoferráio ⬜ I 46 Lf24
Port of Ness ⬜ GB 34 Kg16
Port of Spain ⬛ TT 127 Gd16
Portogruaro ⬜ I 47 Lg23
Porto Nacional ⬜ BR 134 Hc21
Porto-Novo ⬛ DY 105 La17
Portoroz ⬜ SLO 47 Lg23
Porto San Giórgio ⬜ I 47 Lg24
Pórto Santo ⬜ P 104 Ka12
Porto Torres ⬜ I 48 Le25
Porto Vecchio ⬜ F 46 Le25
Porto Velho ⬜ BR 133 Gd20
Portoviejo ⬜ EC 132 Fd19
Port Pirie ⬜ AUS 97 Rd25
Port Radium ⬜ CDN 117 Ea06
Port Said ⬜ ET 107 Mc12
Port Shepstone ⬜ ZA 110 Mc25
Portsmouth ⬜ GB 35 Kk20
Port Sudan ⬜ SUD 107 Md15
Port Talbot ⬜ GB 35 Kj20
Porttipahdan tekojärvi ⬛ FIN 23 Md11
Portugal ■ P 40 Kf26
Port-Vendres ⬜ F 38 Lb24
Port-Vila ⬛ VU 98 Tb22
Port Wakefield ⬜ AUS 97 Rd25
Port Welshpool ⬜ AUS 97 Sb26
Porvoo = Borga ⬜ FIN 28 Mc15
Porzuna ⬜ E 41 Kh26

Posadas ⬜ RA 136 Ha24
Posadas ⬛ RA 136 Ha24
Posehon'e ⬜ RUS 58 Mk16
Posio ⬜ FIN 23 Me12
Poso ⬜ RI 87 Ra19
Posof ⬜ TR 66 Nb25
Posse ⬜ BR 135 Hc21
Pössneck ⬜ D 45 Lf20
Potamós ⬜ GR 56 Mb28
Potcoava ⬜ RO 55 Mc23
Potenza ⬜ I 49 Ln25
Potgietersrus ⬜ ZA 110 Mb23
Potiskum ⬜ WAN 108 Lc16
Potosí ⬜ BOL 133 Gc22
Potsdam ⬜ D 44 Lg19
Pötürge ⬜ TR 66 Mk26
Poum ⬜ F 98 Ta23
Pouso Alegre ⬜ BR 135 Hc23
Považská Bystrica ⬜ SK 53 Lk21
Póvoa de Varzim ⬜ P 40 Kf25
Powell River ⬜ CDN 122 Dd09
Poysdorf ⬜ A 52 Lj21
Požarevac ⬜ SR 54 Ma23
Poza Rica ⬜ MEX 125 Fa14
Požega ⬜ HR 47 Lj23
Požega ⬜ SR 54 Ma23
Poznań ⬜ PL 50 Lj19
Pozo Alcón ⬜ E 41 Kj27
Pozo-Cañada ⬜ E 43 Kh26
Pozo Colorado ⬜ PY 136 Ha23
Prachuap Khirikhan ⬜ THA 86 Pd16
Prades ⬜ F 38 Lb24
Prague ⬛ CZ 52 Lh20
Praha ⬛ CZ 52 Lh20
Praid ⬜ RO 55 Mc22
Prat, C.A. ⬜ 140 Ha31
Prato ⬜ I 46 Lf24
Pravdinsk ⬜ RUS 31 Ma18
Prečistoe ⬜ RUS 59 Mg18
Preikestolen ⬛ N 26 Ld16
Prenzlau ⬜ D 44 Lg19
Přerov ⬜ CZ 53 Lj21
Prescott ⬜ USA 122 Eb12
Presidencia Roque Sáenz Peña ⬜ RA 136 Gd24
Presidente Eduardo Frei ⬜ 140 Ha30
Presidente Epitácio ⬜ BR 135 Hb23
Presidente Prudente ⬜ BR 135 Hb23
Presidio ⬜ USA 124 Ed13
Prešov ⬜ SK 53 Ma21
Préspa N.P. ⬛ GR 56 Ma25
Presque Isle ⬜ USA 121 Gc09
Prestfoss ⬜ N 24 Le15
Preston ⬜ GB 35 Kj19
Preto ⬛ BR 135 Hc22
Pretoria ⬛ ZA 110 Mb24
Préveza ⬜ GR 56 Ma26
Priangarskoe plato ▲ RUS 73 Pd07
Pribilof Islands ⬛ USA 116 Bc07
Příbram ⬜ CZ 52 Lh21
Priego ⬜ E 42 Kj25
Prienai ⬜ LT 31 Mb18
Prievidza ⬜ SK 53 Lk21
Prijedor ⬜ BIH 47 Lj23
Prijepolje ⬜ SR 54 Lk24
Prilenskoe plato ▲ RUS 75 Ra06
Prilep ⬜ BG 55 Md24

Prilep ⬜ MK 56 Ma25
Primorsk ⬜ RUS 27 Lk18
Primorsk ⬜ RUS 28 Me15
Primorsk ⬜ RUS 61 Nc21
Primorsko ⬜ BG 55 Md24
Primorsko-Ahtarsk ⬜ RUS 63 Mk22
Primošten ⬜ HR 47 Lh24
Prince Albert ⬜ CDN 120 Ec08
Prince Albert Mountains ▲ 141 Sd34
Prince Albert Peninsula ▲ CDN 118 Ea04
Prince Albert Sd. ⬛ CDN 118 Ea04
Prince Charles Island ⬛ CDN 118 Ga05
Prince Edward Island ⬛ CDN 121 Gd09
Prince George ⬜ CDN 117 Dd08
Prince of Wales Island ⬛ AUS 96 Sa21
Prince of Wales Island ⬛ CDN 118 Fa04
Prince of Wales Island ⬛ USA 117 Db07
Prince of Wales Strait ⬛ CDN 118 Ea04
Prince Patrick Island ⬛ CDN 118 Dd03
Prince Regent Inlet ⬛ CDN 118 Fb04
Prince Rupert ⬜ CDN 117 Db08
Princess Charlotte Bay ⬛ AUS 96 Sa21
Princess Elizabeth Land ▲ 141 Od33
Prince William Sound ⬛ USA 116 Cc06
Príncipe ⬛ STP 108 Lb18
Príncipe da Beira ⬜ BR 133 Gd21
Prinsesse Ragnhild kyst ⬛ 141 Mb33
Priozersk ⬜ RUS 29 Mf15
Pripjat' ⬛ BY 51 Me19
Pripyatsky N.P. ⬛ BY 51 Md20
Priština ⬜ SR 54 Ma24
Pritzwalk ⬜ D 44 Lg19
Privas ⬜ F 39 Lc23
Privolžsk ⬜ RUS 58 Na17
Prizren ⬜ SR 56 Ma24
Prjamicyno ⬜ RUS 59 Mh20
Prjaža ⬜ RUS 29 Mg15
Prnjavor ⬜ BIH 47 Lj23
Probolinggo ⬜ RI 87 Qb20
Progress ⬜ 141 Od32
Prokop'evsk ⬜ RUS 79 Pb08
Proletarij ⬜ RUS 30 Mf16
proliv Dmitrija Lapteva ⬛ RUS 74 Sa04
proliv Karskie Vorota ⬛ RUS 72 Nd04
proliv Longa ⬛ RUS 74 Td04
proliv Sannikova ⬛ RUS 74 Rd04
proliv Vil'kickogo ⬛ RUS 73 Qa03
Prome ⬛ MYA 84 Pd15
Pronin ⬜ RUS 61 Nb21
Propriano ⬜ F 46 Le25
Proserpine ⬜ AUS 96 Sb23
Prostějov ⬜ CZ 53 Lj21
Provadija ⬜ BG 55 Md24
Provence ⬛ F 39 Ld24

Provence-Alpes-Côte d'Azur ○ F 39 Ld24
Providence ● USA 121 Gb10
Providenija ○ RUS 74 Ub06
Provins ○ F 37 Lb21
Prenja ○ AL 56 Ma25
Provo ○ USA 122 Be10
Prrenjas ○ AL 56 Ma25
Prudentov ○ RUS 61 Nd21
Prudhoe Bay ○ USA 116 Cc04
Prudnik ○ PL 50 Lj20
Prüm ○ D 45 Ld20
Pruszcz Gdański ○ PL 50 Lk18
Pruszków ○ PL 50 Ma19
Prut ○ RO/MD 55 Md22
Prużany ○ BY 51 Mc19
Pryazovs'ka vysočyna ◨ UA 63 Mj22
Pryazovs'ke ○ UA 63 Mh22
Pryčornomors'ka nyzovyna ◨ UA 55 Me23
Pryluky ○ UA 62 Mg20
Prymors'k ○ UA 63 Mj22
Przasnysz ○ PL 50 Ma19
Przedbórz ○ PL 50 Lk20
Przemyśl ○ PL 51 Mb21
Psahná ○ GR 57 Mb26
Psará ▣ GR 57 Mc26
Psebaj ○ RUS 66 Na23
Ps'ol ◨ UA 62 Mg21
Ptolemaída ○ GR 56 Ma25
Ptuj ○ SLO 47 Lh22
Publications Ice Shelf ▨ 141 Od32
Pucallpa ○ PE 133 Gb20
Pucari ● PNG 92 Sa20
Pučež ○ RUS 58 Nb17
Pucheng ○ CHN 85 Qd13
Púchov ○ SK 53 Lk21
Puck ○ PL 50 Lk18
Pudož ○ RUS 29 Mj15
Puebla ○ MEX 124 Fa15
Puebla ○ MEX 125 Fa15
Puebla de Alcocer ○ E 41 Kh26
Pueblo ○ USA 122 Ed11
Puelches ○ RA 137 Gc26
Puente Alto ○ RCH 136 Gb25
Pu'er ○ CHN 84 Qa14
Puerto Acosta ○ BOL 133 Gc22
Puerto Aisén ○ RCH 137 Gb28
Puerto Ángel ○ MEX 125 Fa15
Puerto Ayacucho ○ YV 132 Gc17
Puerto Bahía Negra ○ PY 136 Ha23
Puerto Barrios ○ GCA 125 Fb15
Puerto Cabello ○ YV 127 Gc16
Puerto Cabezas ○ NIC 126 Fd16
Puerto Carreño ○ CO 132 Gc17
Puerto Cortés ○ HN 125 Fc15
Puerto Cumarebo ○ YV 127 Gc16
Puerto Deseado ○ RA 137 Gc28
Puerto Edén ○ RCH 137 Gb28
Puerto Escondido ○ MEX 125 Fa15

Puerto Grether ○ BOL 133 Gd22
Puerto Inírida ○ CO 132 Gc18
Puerto la Cruz ○ YV 127 Gd16
Puerto Limón ○ CR 126 Fd16
Puerto-Ilano ○ E 41 Kh26
Puerto Lumbreras ○ E 43 Kk27
Puerto Maldonado ○ PE 133 Gc21
Puerto Montt ○ RCH 137 Gb27
Puerto Natales ○ RCH 137 Gb29
Puerto Peñasco ○ MEX 122 Eb12
Puerto Plata ○ DOM 127 Gb15
Puerto Princesa ○ RP 87 Qd17
Puerto Rico ▨ USA 127 Gc15
Puerto Rondón ○ CO 132 Gb17
Puerto San Julián ○ RA 137 Gc28
Puerto Suarez ○ BOL 133 Ha22
Puerto Vallarta ○ MEX 124 Ec14
Puerto Williams ○ RCH 137 Gc30
Pugačev ○ RUS 61 Ne19
Puglia ◨ I 49 Lj25
Puhos ○ FIN 28 Me14
Puigcerdà ○ E 42 La24
Puig Major ▲ E 43 Lb26
Puigmal ▲ E 42 La24
Pukë ○ AL 56 Lk24
Pula ○ HR 47 Lg23
Pulap Atoll ▨ FSM 93 Sb17
Pulawy ○ PL 51 Ma20
Pulkkila ○ FIN 28 Mc13
Pulo Anna ▨ PAL 92 Rc18
Pułtusk ○ PL 50 Ma19
Pülümür ○ TR 66 Mk26
Pulusuk Island ▨ FSM 93 Sb17
Puluwat Atoll ▨ FSM 93 Sb17
Puna de Atacama ◨ RA 136 Gc23
Puncak Jaya ▲ RI 92 Rd19
Pune ○ IND 81 Oc15
Punjab ◨ IND 80 Od12
Puno ○ PE 133 Gb22
Punta Abreojos ○ MEX 124 Eb13
Punta Arenas ○ RCH 137 Gb29
Punta Burica ▲ CR 126 Fd17
Punta Carreta ▲ PE 133 Ga21
Punta Carrizal ▲ RCH 136 Gc24
Punta Coconho ▲ BR 134 Ja19
Punta Coles ▲ PE 133 Gb22
Punta del Diablo ▲ ROU 136 Hb25
Punta Eugenia ▲ MEX 124 Ea13
Punta Galera ▲ EC 132 Fd18
Punta Gallinas ▲ CO 127 Gb16
Punta Križa ○ HR 47 Lh23
Punta la Marmora ▲ I 48 Le25
Punta Lengua de Vaca ▲ RCH 136 Gb25
Punta Mala ▲ PA 132 Ga17

Punta Mogotes ▲ RA 137 Ha26
Punta Naranjas ▲ RA 126 Fd17
Punta Negra ▲ PE 133 Fd20
Punta Ninfas ▲ RA 137 Gd27
Punta Norte ▲ RA 137 Gd27
Punta Norte d.C.San Antonio ▲ RA 136 Ha26
Punta Prieta ○ MEX 124 Eb13
Puntarenas ○ CR 126 Fd17
Punta Santo Tomás ▲ MEX 122 Ea12
Punta Stilo ▲ I 49 Lj26
Punto Fijo ○ YV 127 Gb16
Puolanka ○ FIN 28 Md13
Purdoški ○ RUS 60 Nb18
Puri ○ IND 81 Pb15
Purnia ○ IND 80 Pb13
Purus ◨ BR 133 Gb20
Puruvesi ◨ FIN 28 Me15
Purwakarta ○ RI 86 Qb20
Puškino ○ RUS 61 Nd20
Puškinskie Gory ○ RUS 30 Me17
Püspökladány ○ H 53 Ma22
Pustoška ○ RUS 30 Me17
Putao ○ MYA 84 Pd13
Putenhain ○ MYA 84 Pc15
Putnočany ○ RUS 73 Pc06
Puttalam ○ CL 81 Od17
Puttgarden ○ D 44 Lf18
Putumayo ◨ CO/PE 132 Gb19
Putussibau ○ RI 87 Qc18
Putyvl' ○ UA 59 Mg20
Puumala ○ FIN 28 Me15
Puzači ○ RUS 59 Mj20
Pweto ○ RDC 109 Mb20
Pyhä-Hakin kansallispuisto ▨ FIN 28 Mc14
Pyhäntä ○ FIN 28 Md13
Pyhätunturin kansallispuisto ▨ FIN 23 Md12
Pyinmana ○ MYA 84 Pd15
Pyongyang ● PRK 83 Rb11
Pyrénées ◨ F 38 Kk24
Pyrénées, P.N.des ▨ F 42 Kk24
Pyrjatyn ○ UA 62 Mg20
Pyrzyce ○ PL 50 Lh19
Pytalovo ○ RUS 30 Md17

Q

Qaanaaq ○ DK 118 Gc03
Qadimah ○ KSA 76 Md14
Qaidam Pendi ◨ CHN 79 Pc11
Qal'at at Bishah ○ KSA 77 Na14
Qars-e-Shirin ○ IR 76 Nb12
Qarshi ○ UZ 78 Ob11
Qaryat Abu Qurays ○ LAR 106 Ld12
Qasr el Farafra ○ ET 107 Mb13
Qatar ■ Q 77 Nc13
Qattara Depression ◨ ET 107 Mb12
Qazvin ○ IR 76 Nb11
Qena ○ ET 107 Mc13
Qeqertarsuaq ○ DK 119 Hb05
Qiemo ○ CHN 79 Pb11
Qilian Shan ◨ CHN 79 Pd11
Qingdao ○ CHN 83 Ra11
Qinghai ◨ CHN 79 Pd11
Qinghai Hu ◨ CHN 82 Qa11

Qinhuangdao ○ CHN 83 Qd11
Qin Ling ◨ CHN 82 Qb12
Qinzhou ○ CHN 84 Qb14
Qionghai ○ CHN 85 Qc15
Qiqihar ○ CHN 83 Ra09
Qishn ○ YE 77 Nc15
Qom ○ IR 76 Nc12
Quang Ngai ○ VN 85 Qb15
Quanzhou ○ CHN 85 Qd13
Quaqortoq ○ DK 119 Hc06
Quaqtaq ○ CDN 119 Gc06
Quartu Sant' Elena ○ I 48 Le26
Quchan ○ IR 78 Nd11
Québec ◨ CDN 121 Ga08
Québec ● CDN 121 Gb09
Quedlinburg ○ D 44 Lf20
Queen Alexandra Range ▨ 141 Tb35
Queen Charlotte Islands ▨ USA 117 Db08
Queen Charlotte Sound ◨ CDN 116 Dc08
Queen Charlotte Strait ◨ CDN 116 Dc08
Queen Elizabeth Islands ▨ CDN 118 Ea02
Queen Mary Land ▨ 141 Pc33
Queen Maud Gulf ◨ CDN 118 Ed05
Queensland ◨ AUS 96 Sa23
Queenstown ○ AUS 97 Sb27
Queenstown ○ NZ 99 Tb27
Queenstown ○ ZA 110 Mb25
Quelimane ○ MOC 111 Md23
Quellón ○ RCH 137 Gb27
Querétaro ○ MEX 124 Ed14
Querétaro ◨ MEX 124 Fa14
Quesnel ○ CDN 117 Dd08
Quesso ○ RCB 108 Ld18
Quetta ○ PAK 78 Ob13
Quezaltenango ○ GCA 125 Fb16
Quezon ○ RP 87 Qd17
Quibala ○ ANG 110 Lc21
Quibdó ○ CO 132 Ga17
Quiberon ○ F 36 Kj22
Quillan ○ F 38 Lb24
Quilmes ○ RA 136 Ha25
Quilon ○ IND 81 Od17
Quilpie ○ AUS 96 Sa24
Quimper ○ F 36 Kh22
Quimperlé ○ F 36 Kj22
Quincy ○ USA 123 Fb10
Qui Nhon ○ VN 85 Qb16
Quintanar de la Orden ○ E 41 Kj26
Quintana Roo ◨ MEX 125 Fc15
Quito ● EC 132 Ga19
Qujing ○ CHN 84 Qa13
Qullai Kommunizm ▲ TJ 78 Oc11
Qurghonteppa ○ TJ 78 Ob11
Quxu ○ CHN 84 Pc13
Quyen ○ AUS 97 Sa26
Quzhou ○ CHN 85 Qd13

R

Raa Atoll ▨ MV 81 Oc17
Raahe ○ FIN 28 Mc13
Raanujärvi ○ FIN 23 Mc12
Raas Guardafui ▲ SP 100 Nb08

Raas Xaafuun ⬚ SP 100 Nb08
Rab ⬚ HR 47 Lh23
Raba ⬚ RI 87 Qd20
Rabat ⬚ M 49 Lh28
Rabat ⬚ MA 104 Kc12
Rabaul ⬚ PNG 93 Sc19
Rabka-Zdroj ⬚ PL 50 Lk21
Rabočeostrovsk ⬚ RUS 29 Mh13
Rachiv ⬚ UA 55 Mc21
Radaškoviçy ⬚ BY 31 Md18
Rădăuţi ⬚ RO 55 Mc22
Radechiv ⬚ UA 51 Mc20
Radenci ⬚ SLO 52 Lj22
Radom ⬚ PL 50 Ma20
Radomsko ⬚ PL 50 Lk20
Radomyšl' ⬚ UA 62 Me20
Radovan ⬚ RO 54 Mb23
Radoviš ⬚ MK 56 Mb25
Radymno ⬚ PL 51 Mb21
Radziejów ⬚ PL 50 Lk19
Rafaela ⬚ RA 136 Gd25
Rafha ⬚ KSA 76 Na13
Ragaing Yoma ⬛ MYA 84 Pc14
Rago n.p. ✷ N 22 Lk12
Ragusa ⬚ I 49 Lh27
Rahačov ⬚ BY 59 Mf19
Raipur ⬚ IND 80 Pa14
Raisio ⬚ FIN 22 Mb15
Raja-Jooseppi ⬚ FIN 23 Me11
Rajasthan ⬚ IND 80 Oc13
Rajgród ⬚ PL 51 Mb19
Rajkot ⬚ IND 80 Oc14
Raj Nandgaon ⬚ IND 80 Pa14
Rajshahi ⬚ BD 80 Pb14
Rakiraki ⬚ FIJ 98 Td22
Rakops ⬚ RB 110 Ma23
Rakovnik ⬚ CZ 52 Lg20
Rakvere ⬚ EST 30 Md16
Raleigh ✷ USA 123 Ga11
Ralik Chain ⬛ MH 93 Ta16
Rama ⬚ NIC 126 Fd16
Rambouillet ⬚ F 36 La21
Rameški ⬚ RUS 58 Mj17
Ramlat al Sab'atayn ⬛ YE 77 Nb16
Ramlat ar-Rabkha ⬛ OM 77 Nd14
Ramlat Ghafah ⬛ OM 77 Nd14
Ramlat Rabyanah ⬛ LAR 106 Ld14
Ramlat Umm al-Hait ⬛ OM 77 Nc15
Râmnicu Sărat ⬚ RO 55 Md23
Râmnicu Vâlcea ⬚ RO 54 Mc23
Rampar ⬚ IND 80 Od13
Ramsele ⬚ S 25 Lj14
Ramsey ⬚ GB 34 Kh18
Ramsjö ⬚ S 25 Lh14
Ranau ⬚ MAL 87 Qd17
Rancagua ⬚ RCH 136 Gb25
Ranchi ⬚ IND 80 Pb14
Randazzo ⬚ I 49 Lh27
Randers ⬚ DK 26 Lf17
Rangoon ⬚ MYA 84 Pd15
Rann of Kachchh ⬛ IND 80 Ob14
Ransiki ⬚ RI 92 Rc19
Rantauprapat ⬚ RI 86 Pb18
Ranua ⬚ FIN 28 Md13
Râşcani ⬚ MD 55 Md22
Rapallo ⬚ I 46 Le23

Rapid City ⬚ USA 122 Ed10
Räpina ⬚ EST 30 Md16
Rapla ⬚ EST 30 Mc16
Raqqa ⬚ SYR 76 Md11
Ras Dashen = Simien ⬛ ETH 107 Md16
Ras al Khafji ⬚ KSA 77 Nb13
Ras Al-Khaimah ⬚ UAE 77 Nd13
Râs Banas ⬚ ET 107 Md14
Raseiniai ⬚ LT 31 Mb18
Ra's Fartak ⬚ YE 77 Nc15
Rasht ⬚ IR 76 Nb11
Raška ⬚ SR 54 Ma24
Ras Madrakah ⬚ OM 77 Nd15
Râs Muhammad ⬚ ET 107 Mc13
Rasskazovo ⬚ RUS 61 Na19
Rätan ⬚ S 25 Lh14
Ratchaburi ⬚ THA 86 Pd16
Rathenow ⬚ D 44 Lg19
Ratne ⬚ UA 51 Mc20
Rättvik ⬚ S 25 Lh15
Raufarhöfn ⬚ IS 32 Kc12
Raufoss ⬚ N 24 Lf15
Rauma ⬚ FIN 25 Ma15
Raurkela ⬚ IND 80 Pa14
Rautavaara ⬚ FIN 28 Me14
Rautjärvi ⬚ FIN 28 Me15
Rava Rus'ka ⬚ UA 51 Mb20
Ravenna ⬚ I 46 Lg23
Ravensburg ⬚ D 45 Le22
Ravensthorpe ⬚ AUS 95 Qd25
Rawalpindi ⬚ PAK 80 Oc12
Rawicz ⬚ PL 50 Lj20
Rawlinna ⬚ AUS 95 Rb25
Rawlins ⬚ USA 120 Ec10
Rawson ⬚ RA 137 Gc27
Rayner Glacier ⬛ 141 Nb32
Razgrad ⬚ BG 55 Md24
Razlog ⬚ BG 56 Mb25
Reading ⬚ GB 35 Kk20
Realico ⬚ RA 136 Gd26
Reboly ⬚ RUS 29 Mf14
Recaş ⬚ RO 54 Ma23
Récif des Français ⬛ F 98 Ta22
Recife ⬚ BR 134 Jb20
Récifs Bellona ⬛ F 96 Sd23
Récifs d'Entrecasteaux ⬛ F 98 Ta22
Récifs et Chesterfields ⬛ F 96 Sd22
Recklinghausen ⬚ D 44 Ld20
Reconquista ⬚ RA 136 Ha24
Recovery Glacier ⬛ 140 Jb35
Rečyca ⬚ BY 59 Mf19
Recz ⬚ PL 50 Lh19
Reda ⬚ PL 50 Lk18
Red Basin ⬚ CHN 84 Qb12
Red Deer ⬚ CDN 117 Eb08
Redding ⬚ USA 122 Dd10
Redkino ⬚ RUS 58 Mj17
Red Lake ⬚ CDN 120 Fb08
Redon ⬚ F 36 Kj22
Red River ⬛ USA 120 Fa09
Red River ⬛ USA 123 Fa12
Red River ⬛ VN 84 Qa15
Red Sea ⬛ 107 Md14
Reef Islands ⬛ SOL 98 Tb21
Refahiye ⬚ TR 66 Mk26
Regensburg ⬚ D 45 Lg21
Regestan ⬛ AFG 78 Oa12
Reggane ⬚ DZ 104 La13
Réggio di Calábria ⬚ I 49 Lh26
Réggio nell'Emília ⬚ I 46 Lf23
Reghin ⬚ RO 54 Mc22

Regina ✷ CDN 120 Ed08
Rehoboth ⬚ NAM 110 Ld23
Reims ⬚ F 37 Lc21
Reinbolt Hills ⬛ 141 Oc32
Reindeer Lake ⬛ CDN 120 Ed07
Reinosa ⬚ E 40 Kh24
Reisa n.p. ✷ N 23 Mb11
Rena ⬚ N 24 Lf15
Rendsburg ⬚ D 44 Le18
Rengat ⬚ RI 86 Qa19
Renmark ⬚ AUS 97 Sa25
Rennell Island ⬛ SOL 98 Ta21
Rennell Rise ⬛ SOL 98 Sd21
Rennes ✷ F 36 Kk21
Rennick Glacier ⬛ 141 Ta33
Reno ⬚ USA 122 Ea11
Reşiţa ⬚ RO 54 Ma23
Rep'evka ⬚ RUS 59 Mk20
Repoveden kansallispuisto ✷ FIN 28 Md15
Represa de Itaipu ⬛ BR 135 Hb23
Represa de Tucuruí ⬛ BR 134 Hc19
Represa Tres Marias ⬛ BR 135 Hc22
Republican ⬛ USA 123 Fa10
Repulse Bay ⬚ CDN 118 Fc05
Requena ⬚ E 43 Kk26
Requena ⬚ PE 132 Gb20
Reşadiye ⬚ TR 65 Mj25
Réservoir de LG Deux ⬛ CDN 121 Gd08
Réservoir Manicouagan ⬛ CDN 121 Gc08
Rešetylivka ⬚ UA 63 Mh21
Resistencia ⬚ RA 136 Ha24
Resolute ⬚ CDN 118 Fb04
Resolution Island ⬛ NZ 99 Tb28
Rethel ⬚ F 37 Lc21
Réthimno ⬚ GR 57 Mc28
Réunion ⬚ F 103 Nb12
Reus ⬚ E 42 La25
Reutlingen ⬚ D 45 Le21
Revel ⬚ F 42 Lb24
Revelstoke ⬚ CDN 117 Ea08
Rewa ⬚ IND 80 Pa14
Reyðarfjörður ⬚ IS 32 Kc13
Reyhanlı ⬚ TR 65 Mj27
Reykholar ⬚ IS 32 Jj13
Reykholt ⬚ IS 32 Jk13
Reykjahlíð ⬚ IS 32 Kb13
Reykjavík ✷ IS 32 Jk13
Reynosa ⬚ MEX 124 Fa13
Rezé ⬚ F 38 Kk22
Rézekne ⬚ LV 30 Md17
Rezina ⬚ MD 55 Me22
Rezovo ⬚ BG 57 Me25
Rheine ⬚ D 44 Ld19
Rheinfall ⬚ CH 45 Le22
Rheinland-Pfalz ⬚ D 45 Ld20
Rhine ⬛ D 45 Ld20
Rhinelander ⬚ USA 120 Fc09
Rhode Island ⬚ USA 121 Gb10
Rhodes ⬚ GR 57 Mf27
Rhodope Mountains ⬛ BG/GR 56 Mb25
Rhône ⬛ F 39 Ld22
Rhône-Alpes ⬚ F 39 Lc23
Riaño ⬚ E 40 Kh24
Rias Altas ⬛ E 40 Kf24
Rias Baixas = Rias Bajas ⬛ E 40 Kf24
Rias Bajas = Rias Baixas ⬛ E 40 Kf24

Rías Gallegas ⬛ E 40 Kf24
Ribadeo ⬚ E 40 Kg24
Ribadesella ⬚ E 40 Kh24
Ribatejo ⬚ P 40 Kf26
Ribe ⬚ DK 26 Le18
Ribeira = Santa Eugenia ⬚ E 40 Kf24
Ribeirão Preto ⬚ BR 135 Hc23
Riberalta ⬚ BOL 133 Gc21
Ribnica ⬚ BIH 47 Lk23
Ribnica ⬚ SLO 47 Lh23
Ribnitz-Damgarten ⬚ D 44 Lg18
Řičany ⬚ CZ 52 Lh21
Richard's Bay ⬚ ZA 111 Mc24
Richfield ⬚ USA 120 Eb11
Richmond ✷ AUS 96 Sa23
Richmond ⬚ GB 34 Kk18
Richmond ✷ USA 123 Ga11
Ried im Innkreis ⬚ A 52 Lg21
Riedlingen ⬚ D 45 Le21
Riesa ⬚ D 44 Lg20
Rietavas ⬚ LT 31 Ma18
Rieti ⬚ I 46 Lg24
Riga ✷ LV 30 Mc17
Riihimäki ⬚ FIN 28 Mc15
Riiser-Larsen Ice Shelf ⬛ 140 Ka33
Riisitunturin kansallispuisto ✷ FIN 23 Me12
Rijeka ⬚ HR 47 Lh23
Rila, N.P. ⬛ BG 54 Mb24
Rímavská Sobota ⬚ SK 53 Ma21
Rimbo ⬚ S 27 Lk16
Rimini ⬚ I 46 Lg23
Rimouski ⬚ CDN 121 Gc09
Rindal ⬚ N 24 Le14
Ringkøbing ⬚ DK 26 Le17
Ringkøbing Fjord ⬛ DK 26 Le18
Ringsted ⬚ DK 26 Lf18
Ringvassøy ⬛ N 22 Lk11
Rinia ⬚ GR 57 Mc27
Rintala ⬚ RUS 28 Me15
Riobamba ⬚ EC 132 Ga19
Rio Branco ✷ BR 133 Gc20
Rio Branco ⬛ BR 132 Gd18
Rio Bravo ⬚ MEX 124 Fa13
Rio Bravo del Norte ⬛ MEX 124 Ed13
Rio Cuarto ⬚ RA 136 Gd25
Rio dos Mortes ⬛ BR 135 Hb21
Rio de Janeiro ⬚ BR 135 Hd23
Rio de Janeiro ⬚ BR 135 Hd23
Rio de la Plata ⬛ RA 136 Ha25
Rio Douro ⬛ P 40 Kg25
Rio Gallegos ⬚ RA 137 Gc29
Rio Grande ⬚ BR 136 Hb25
Rio Grande ⬚ USA 124 Ed13
Rio Grande ⬚ MEX 124 Ed14
Rio Grande ⬚ RA 137 Gc29
Rio Grande do Norte ⬚ BR 134 Ja20
Rio Grande do Sul ⬚ BR 135 Hb24
Rio Guadalquivir ⬛ E 41 Kg27
Rio Guadiana ⬛ P 41 Kg27
Riohacha ⬚ CO 127 Gb16
Rio Júcar ⬛ E 43 Kk26
Riom ⬚ F 38 Lb23
Rio Miño ⬛ P 40 Kf24
Rio Miño ⬛ E 40 Kg24

Rio Negro · BR 132 Gc19
Rio Negro · BR 132 Gd19
Rio Negro · RA 137 Gc27
Rio Negro · RA 137 Gc26
Rio Tecero · RA 136 Gd25
Rio Verde · BR 135 Hb22
Rio Verde de Mato Grosso · BR 135 Hb22
Ripky · UA 59 Mf20
Ripoll · E 42 Lb24
Ripon · GB 35 Kk18
Risbäck · S 25 Lh13
Riska · N 26 Le16
Risnjak, N.P. · HR 47 Lh23
Risør · N 26 Le16
Risti · EST 30 Mc16
Ristiina · FIN 28 Md15
Ristna neem · EST 30 Mb16
Ritsem · S 22 Lj12
Rivadavia · RCH 136 Gc24
Riva del Garda · I 46 Lf23
Rivera · ROU 136 Ha25
Riverina · AUS 97 Sa26
Riversdale · ZA 110 Ma25
Riverton · USA 120 Ec10
Rivesaltes · F 38 Lb24
Riviera di Levante · I 46 Le23
Riviera di Ponente · I 46 Le24
Rivière-du-Loup · CDN 121 Gc19
Rivne · UA 51 Md20
Rivne · UA 62 Mf21
Riyadh · KSA 77 Nb14
Rize · TR 66 Na25
Rjabovskij · RUS 61 Na20
Rjazan' · RUS 58 Mk18
Rjazanka · RUS 61 Nb19
Rjažsk · RUS 59 Na19
Rjukan · N 26 Le16
Różan · PL 50 Ma19
Roa · N 24 Lf15
Road Town · UK 127 Gd15
Roanne · F 39 Lc22
Roanoke · USA 123 Ga11
Robertsfors · S 25 Ma13
Robertson Bay · 141 Tb33
Rocas Alijos · MEX 124 Ea14
Rocha · ROU 136 Hb25
Rochechouart · F 38 La23
Rochefort · F 38 Kk23
Rochester · USA 123 Fb10
Rochester · USA 123 Ga10
Rockefeller Plateau · 140 Da34
Rockford · USA 123 Fc10
Rockhampton · AUS 96 Sc23
Rock Springs · USA 120 Ec10
Rocky Mount · USA 123 Ga11
Rocky Mountains · CDN 117 Db06
Rocky Mountains · USA 122 Eb09
Rocroi · F 37 Lc21
Rødbyhavn · DK 26 Lf18
Rödeby · S 27 Lh17
Rodez · F 38 Lb23
Roding · D 45 Lg21
Rodna, P.N. · RO 55 Mc22
Rodniki · RUS 58 Na17
Ródos · GR 64 Me27
Rødvig · DK 26 Lg18
Roebourne · AUS 94 Qd23
Roermond · NL 37 Ld20
Roes Welcome Sound · CDN 118 Fc06

Rogačevka · RUS 59 Mk20
Rogliano · I 49 Lj26
Rohrbach · A 52 Lg21
Rohuküla · EST 30 Mb16
Rokiškis · LT 31 Mc18
Rokuan kansallispuisto · FIN 28 Md13
Rokycany · CZ 52 Lg21
Rokytne · UA 51 Md20
Røldal · N 26 Ld16
Roma · AUS 96 Sb24
Roma · I 48 Lg25
Romagna · I 46 Lf23
Roman · RO 55 Md22
Romania · RO 54 Mb22
Romans-sur-Isère · F 39 Lc23
Romáškino · RUS 60 Nf19
Rome · I 48 Lg25
Romilly-sur-Seine · F 37 Lb21
Romny · UA 59 Mg20
Romodan · UA 62 Mg21
Romsdalen · N 24 Ld14
Ronda · E 41 Kh27
Rondane n.p. · N 24 Le15
Rondônia · BR 133 Gd21
Rondonópolis · BR 135 Hb22
Rongelap Atoll · MH 93 Tb16
Rongerik Atoll · MH 93 Tb16
Rønne · DK 27 Lh18
Ronne Bay · 140 Gb33
Ronneby · S 27 Lh17
Ronne Ice Shelf · 140 Gd34
Rönnöfors · S 24 Lg14
Ronuro · BR 135 Hb21
Roșiori de Vede · RO 55 Mc23
Roosendaal · NL 37 Lc20
Roosevelt · BR 133 Gd20
Roper · AUS 96 Rd21
Roper Bar · AUS 94 Rc21
Roquefort · F 38 Kk23
Roquetas de Mar · E 41 Kj27
Roraima · BR 132 Gd18
Røros · N 24 Lf14
Rørvik · N 24 Lf13
Ros' · BY 51 Mc19
Ros' · UA 62 Mf21
Rošal' · RUS 58 Mk18
Rosario · MEX 124 Ec14
Rosario · RA 136 Gd25
Rosário · BR 136 Ha25
Rosario de la Frontera · RA 136 Gc24
Rosario Oeste · BR 135 Ha21
Roščino · RUS 29 Me15
Roscoff · F 36 Kj21
Roscommon · IRL 33 Kf19
Roseau · WD 127 Gd15
Rosebery · AUS 97 Sb27
Rosendal · N 26 Ld16
Rosenheim · D 45 Lg22
Roskilde · DK 26 Lg18
Roslavl' · RUS 59 Mg19
Rossano · I 49 Lj26
Ross Ice Shelf · 140 Bd35
Rosslare Harbour · IRL 33 Kg19
Rosso · RIM 105 Ka15
Ross-on-Wye · GB 35 Kj20
Rossoš' · RUS 61 Na20
Ross River · CDN 117 Db06
Ross Sea · 140 Bd33
Røssvatnet · N 25 Lh13
Røst · N 22 Lg12
Rostock · D 44 Lg18

Rostov · RUS 58 Mk17
Røsvik · N 22 Lh12
Roswell · USA 122 Ed12
Rotenburg (Wümme) · D 44 Le19
Roth · D 45 Lf21
Rothenburg (Tauber) · D 45 Lf21
Rothera · 140 Gc32
Rotherham · GB 35 Kk19
Roti · RI 87 Ra21
Roto · AUS 97 Sb25
Rotorua · NZ 99 Td26
Rotterdam · NL 37 Lc20
Rottweil · D 45 Le21
Rotuma · FIJ 98 Td21
Roubaix · F 37 Lb20
Rouen · F 36 La21
Roundup · USA 120 Ec09
Roussillon · F 39 Lc23
Rouyn-Noranda · CDN 121 Ga09
Rovaniemi · FIN 23 Mc12
Rovato · I 46 Le23
Roven'ki · RUS 61 Na21
Rovereto · I 46 Lf23
Rovigo · I 46 Lf23
Rovinj · HR 47 Lg23
Rovno · RUS 61 Nd20
Rovuma · MOC 111 Md21
Rowley Shoals · AUS 94 Qd22
Roxas · RP 85 Ra20
Roxas · RP 85 Ra16
Royan · F 38 Kk23
Røyrvik · N 24 Lg13
Rozdil'na · UA 62 Mf22
Rozdol'ne · UA 62 Mg23
Rožencovo · RUS 60 Nd17
Rozivka · UA 63 Mj22
Rožňava · SK 53 Ma21
Rožok · RUS 60 Nb18
Roztoczański P.N. · PL 51 Mb20
Rožyšče · UA 51 Mc20
Rtiščevo · RUS 61 Nb19
Ruba · BY 31 Mf18
Rubbestadneset · N 26 Lc16
Rubcovsk · RUS 79 Pa08
Rubehu Mountains · EAT 109 Md20
Rud-e-Karkheh · IR 76 Nb12
Rudkøbing · DK 26 Lf18
Rudky · UA 53 Mb21
Rudna Glava · SR 54 Mb23
Rudnaja Pristan' · RUS 75 Rd10
Rudnja · RUS 59 Mf18
Rudnyj · KZ 78 Oa08
Ruffec · F 38 La22
Rufiji · EAT 109 Md20
Rufino · RA 136 Gd25
Rufunsa · Z 110 Mb22
Rugby · GB 35 Kk19
Rügen · D 44 Lg18
Ruguj · RUS 58 Mg16
Ruhan' · RUS 59 Mg19
Rui'an · CHN 85 Ra13
Ruijin · CHN 85 Qd13
Rum · GB 34 Kg17
Rumbek · SUD 109 Mb17
Rumilly · F 39 Lc23
Runde · ZW 111 Mc23
Rundu · NAM 110 Ld22
Rungwa · EAT 109 Mc20
Ruodiang · CHN 79 Pb11
Ruokojärvi · FIN 23 Mc12
Ruokolahti · FIN 28 Me15
Ruppert Coast · 140 Cd34

Rurrenabaque · BOL 133 Gc21
Ruse · BG 55 Mc24
Rushan · CHN 83 Ra11
Russell Islands · SOL 93 Sd20
Russia · RUS 19 Na06
Russkaja · 140 Da33
Russkij Kameškir · RUS 61 Nd19
Russkiy Sever N.P. · RUS 29 Mk15
Rustavi · GE 76 Nb10
Rustenburg · ZA 110 Mb24
Rusterfjelbma · N 23 Me10
Rutford Ice Stream · 140 Fd34
Rutledalen · N 24 Lc15
Ruunaankosket · FIN 29 Mf14
Ruvuma · EAT 111 Md21
Ruwenzori · RDC/EAU 109 Mc18
Ruza · RUS 58 Mj18
Ruzaevka · RUS 60 Nc18
Ružany · BY 51 Mc19
Ružomberok · SK 53 Lk21
Rwanda · RWA 1 09 Mb19
Rybinsk · RUS 58 Mk16
Rybinsk Reservoir · RUS 58 Mk16
Rybnik · PL 50 Lk20
Rybnoe · RUS 58 Mk18
Rybreka · RUS 29 Mh15
Rychwał · PL 50 Lk19
Ryd · S 27 Lh17
Rydberg Peninsula · 140 Ga33
Rydsnäs · S 27 Lh17
Ryki · PL 51 Ma20
Ryl'sk · RUS 59 Mh20
Rypin · PL 50 Lk19
Ryukyu Islands · J 83 Rb13
Ryukyu Trench · J 83 Rb13
Rzeszów · PL 51 Ma20
Ržev · RUS 58 Mh17
Ržyščiv · UA 62 Mf21

S

Šaľa · SK 53 Lj21
Saalfeld · D 44 Lf20
Saarbrücken · D 45 Ld21
Sääre · EST 30 Mb17
Saaremaa · EST 30 Mb16
Saarijärvi · FIN 28 Mc14
Saaristomeren kansallispuisto = Skärgårdshavets n.p. · FIN 30 Ma16
Saarland · D 45 Ld21
Saarlouis · D 45 Ld21
Šabac · SR 54 Lk23
Sabadell · E 42 Lb25
Sabaki · EAK 109 Md19
Sabanalarga · CO 127 Gb16
Şabanözü · TR 65 Mg25
Sãbãoani · RO 55 Md22
Sabha · LAR 106 Lc13
Sabile · LV 30 Mb17
Sabinas Hidalgo · MEX 124 Ed13
Sabine Peninsula · CDN 118 Eb03
Šabla · BG 55 Me24
Sablé-sur-Sarthe · F 36 Kk22
Sabrina Coast · 141 Ra32
Sabtaev · KZ 78 Ob09

Sabzevar ☐ IR 78 Nd11
Săcele ☐ RO 55 Mc23
Sachsen ☐ D 44 Lg20
Sachsen-Anhalt ☐ D 44 Lf19
Sachs Harbour ☐ CDN 118 Dd03
Sächsische Schweiz, N.P. ☐ D 44 Lh20
Saçıkara ☐ TR 64 Mg26
Šack ☐ RUS 58 Na18
Šack ☐ BY 51 Md19
Šac'k ☐ UA 51 Mb20
Šac'kyj pryrodnyj n.p. ☐ UA 51 Mb20
Sacramento ☐ USA 122 Dd11
Săcueni ☐ RO 54 Mb22
Sa'dah ☐ YE 77 Na15
Šadrinsk ☐ RUS 72 Oa07
Sæby ☐ DK 26 Lf17
Säffle ☐ S 26 Lg16
Safi ☐ MA 104 Kc12
Safonovo ☐ RUS 59 Mg18
Safranbolu ☐ TR 65 Mg25
Sagarmatha ▲ CHN/NEP 80 Pb13
Sagastyr ☐ RUS 73 Rb04
Saginaw ☐ USA 123 Fd10
Saglek Bay ☐ CDN 121 Gd07
Sagres ☐ P 41 Kf27
Sag Sag ☐ PNG 93 Sb20
Sagua la Grande ☐ C 126 Ga14
Sagunt = Sagunto ☐ E 43 Kk26
Sagunto = Sagunt ☐ E 43 Kk26
Sahagún ☐ E 40 Kh24
Sahara ☐ 104 Kc14
Sahel ☐ 106 Lb15
Sahel ☐ 106 Lb15
Sahra' Surt ☐ LAR 106 Ld12
Šahty ☐ RUS 63 Na22
Šahun'ja ☐ RUS 60 Nd17
Šahy ☐ SK 53 Lk21
Saidpur ☐ BD 80 Pb13
Saigon = Thanh Pho Ho Chi Minh ☐ VN 84 Qb16
Saihan Toroi ☐ CHN 82 Qa10
Saimaa ☐ FIN 28 Me15
Saint George's Channel ☐ GB 35 Kg20
Saint Petersburg ☐ RUS 30 Mf16
Saint-Affrique ☐ F 38 Lb24
Saint Albans ☐ GB 35 Kk20
Saint-Amand-Montrond ☐ F 38 Lb22
Saint Andrews ☐ GB 34 Kj17
Saint Anthony ☐ CDN 121 Ha08
Saint-Augustin ☐ CDN 121 Ha08
Saint Austell ☐ GB 35 Kh20
Saint-Avold ☐ F 37 Ld21
Saint-Brieuc ☐ F 36 Kj21
Saint-Céré ☐ F 38 La23
Saint-Chély-d'Apcher ☐ F 38 Lb23
Saint-Claude ☐ F 39 Lc22
Saint Cloud ☐ USA 120 Fb09
Saint Croix ☐ USA 127 Gd15
Saint-Dié-des-Vosges ☐ F 37 Ld21
Saint-Dizier ☐ F 37 Lc21
Sainte-Maxime ☐ F 39 Ld24
Sainte-Menehould ☐ F 37 Lc21
Sainte-Mère-Église ☐ F 36 Kk21
Saintes ☐ F 38 Kk23

Saintes-Maries-de-la-Mer ☐ F 39 Lc24
Saint-Étienne ☐ F 39 Lc23
Saint-Florent ☐ F 46 Le24
Saint-Florentin ☐ F 37 Lb21
Saint-Flour ☐ F 38 Lb23
Saint-Gaudens ☐ F 42 La24
Saint George ☐ AUS 96 Sb24
Saint George ☐ USA 122 Eb11
Saint George's ☐ WG 127 Gd16
Saint George's Bay ☐ CDN 121 Ha09
Saint-Gilles-Croix-de-Vie ☐ F 38 Kk22
Saint-Girons ☐ F 42 La24
Saint Helenabaai ☐ ZA 110 Ld25
Saint Helier ☐ GB 36 Kj21
Saint-Hilaire-du-Harcouët ☐ F 36 Kk21
Saint Ives ☐ GB 35 Kh20
Saint-Jean-d'Angely ☐ F 38 Kk23
Saint-Jean-de-Monts ☐ F 36 Kj22
Saint-Jean-Pied-de-Port ☐ F 42 Kk24
Saint John ☐ CDN 121 Gc09
Saint John's ☐ AG 127 Gd15
Saint John's ☐ CDN 121 Hb09
Saint Joseph ☐ USA 123 Fb11
Saint-Junien ☐ F 38 La23
Saint Kilda ☐ GB 34 Kf17
Saint Kitts and Nevis ☐ KNA 127 Gd15
Saint Lawrence ☐ CDN 121 Gc09
Saint Lawrence Island ☐ USA 116 Bb06
Saint Lawrence River ☐ CDN 121 Gc09
Saint-Léonard-de-Noblat ☐ F 38 La23
Saint Louis ☐ SN 105 Ka15
Saint Louis ☐ USA 123 Fb11
Saint Lucia ☐ WL 127 Gd16
Saint Luciameer ☐ ZA 111 Mc24
Saint-Maixent-l'École ☐ F 38 Kk22
Saint-Malo ☐ F 36 Kj21
Saint-Marc ☐ RH 127 Gb15
Saint-Marcellin ☐ F 39 Lc23
Saint-Martin ☐ F 127 Gd15
Saint-Martin-de-Ré ☐ F 38 Kk22
Saint Marys ☐ AUS 97 Sb27
Saint Matthew Island ☐ USA 116 Bb06
Saint Matthias Group ☐ PNG 93 Sb19
Saint-Médard-en-Jalles ☐ F 38 Kk23
Saint-Méen-le-Grand ☐ F 36 Kj21
Saint-Mihiel ☐ F 37 Lc21
Saint-Nazaire ☐ F 36 Kj22
Saint-Omer ☐ F 37 Lb20
Saint Paul ☐ USA 120 Fb09
Saint Peter-Port ☐ GB 36 Kj21
Saint Petersburg ☐ USA 123 Fd13
Saint-Pierre ☐ F 121 Ha09
Saint Pierre and Miquelon ☐ F 121 Ha09

Saint-Quentin ☐ F 37 Lb21
Saint-Raphaël ☐ F 39 Ld24
Saint-Tropez ☐ F 39 Ld24
Saint-Renan ☐ F 36 Kh21
Saint-Valéry-en-Caux ☐ F 36 La21
Saint Vincent ☐ WV 127 Gd16
Saint Vincent and the Grenadines ☐ WV 127 Gd16
Saint-Yrieix-la-Perche ☐ F 38 La23
Sajano-Šušenskoe-vodohranilišče ☐ RUS 79 Pc08
Sakakah ☐ KSA 76 Na13
Sakarya ☐ TR 64 Mf25
Sakarya = Adapazarı ☐ TR 64 Mf25
Sakata ☐ J 83 Rd11
Sakha ☐ RUS 73 Qc05
Sakhalin ☐ RUS 75 Sa08
Saki ☐ WAN 105 La17
Šakiai ☐ LT 31 Mb18
Sakishima Islands ☐ J 85 Ra14
Sakony ☐ RUS 60 Nb18
Sakskøbing ☐ DK 26 Lf18
Saky ☐ UA 62 Mg23
Sala ☐ S 27 Lj16
Sala Consilina ☐ I 49 Lh25
Salado ☐ RA 136 Gc25
Salado ☐ RA 136 Gd24
Salado ☐ RA 136 Gd24
Salaiman Range ☐ PAK 78 Ob12
Salalah ☐ OM 77 Nc15
Salamajärven kansallispuisto ☐ FIN 28 Mc14
Salamanca ☐ E 40 Kh25
Salamo ☐ PNG 93 Sc20
Salar de Atacama ☐ RCH 136 Gc23
Salar de Uyuni ☐ BOL 136 Gc23
Salas ☐ E 40 Kg24
Salas de los Infantes ☐ E 42 Kj24
Salavat ☐ RUS 72 Nd08
Salawati ☐ RI 87 Rb19
Salawati ☐ RI 92 Rc19
Salbris ☐ F 38 Lb22
Saldus ☐ LV 31 Mb17
Sale ☐ AUS 97 Sb26
Salem ☐ IND 81 Od16
Salem ☐ USA 122 Dd10
Salerno ☐ I 49 Lh25
Salgótarján ☐ H 53 Lk21
Salgueiro ☐ BR 134 Ja20
Salida ☐ USA 122 Ec11
Salihli ☐ TR 64 Me26
Salihorsk ☐ BY 51 Md19
Salina ☐ USA 123 Fa11
Salina Cruz ☐ MEX 125 Fa15
Salinas ☐ USA 122 Dd11
Salinópolis ☐ BR 134 Hc19
Salisbury ☐ GB 35 Kk20
Šalkar ☐ KZ 78 Nd09
Salmon ☐ USA 122 Eb09
Salo ☐ FIN 22 Mb15
Salon-de-Provence ☐ F 39 Lc24
Salonta ☐ RO 54 Ma22
Salpausselkä ▲ FIN 28 Mc15
Salsbruket ☐ N 24 Lf13
Salta ☐ RA 136 Gc23
Salt Desert ☐ IR 76 Nc12
Saltfjellet-Svartisen n.p. ☐ N 22 Lh12

Saltillo ☐ MEX 124 Ed13
Salt Lake City ☐ USA 122 Eb10
Salto ☐ ROU 136 Ha25
Salto Angel ☐ YV 132 Gd17
Salto del Guaira ☐ PY 136 Ha23
Salton Sea ☐ USA 122 Dd11
Saltstraumen ☐ N 22 Lh12
Saluzzo ☐ I 46 Lg23
Salvador ☐ BR 135 Ja21
Salween ☐ 84 Pd13
Šalynyne ☐ UA 59 Mh20
Salzburg ☐ A 52 Lg22
Salzgitter ☐ D 44 Lf19
Salzwedel ☐ D 44 Lf19
Samachvalavičy ☐ BY 51 Md19
Samachvalavičy ☐ BY 51 Md19
Samail ☐ OM 77 Nd14
Samandağ ☐ TR 65 Mh27
Samar ☐ RP 85 Rb16
Samara ☐ RUS 72 Nc08
Samara ☐ RUS 60 Nf19
Samaria N.P. ☐ GR 57 Mc28
Samarinda ☐ RI 87 Qc19
Samarqand ☐ UZ 78 Ob11
Samarskaya Luka N.P. ☐ RUS 60 Ne19
Samba ☐ RDC 109 Mb19
Sambalpur ☐ IND 80 Pa14
Sambas ☐ RI 86 Qb18
Sambir ☐ UA 53 Mb21
Sámi ☐ GR 56 Ma26
Samofalovka ☐ RUS 61 Nc21
Samokov ☐ BG 54 Mb24
Sámos ☐ GR 57 Md27
Sámos ☐ GR 57 Md27
Samothraki ☐ GR 57 Mc25
Samothraki ☐ GR 57 Mc25
Samsu ☐ TR 66 Nb26
Samsun ☐ TR 65 Mj25
San ☐ RMM 105 Kd16
Sanaa ☐ YE 77 Na15
SANAE IV ☐ 141 Kd33
Sanaga ☐ CAM 108 Lc18
Sanana ☐ RI 87 Rb19
Sanandaj ☐ IR 76 Nb11
San Andrés Tuxtla ☐ MEX 125 Fa15
San Angelo ☐ USA 122 Ed12
San Antonio ☐ USA 123 Fa13
San Antonio d.l.Cobres ☐ RA 136 Gc23
San Antonio Oeste ☐ RA 137 Gd27
San Benedetto del Tronto ☐ I 47 Lg24
San Bernardino ☐ USA 122 Dd11
San Bernardo ☐ RCH 136 Gb25
San Blas ☐ MEX 124 Ec13
San Blas ☐ MEX 124 Ec14
San Borja ☐ BOL 133 Gc21
Sancak ☐ TR 66 Na26
San Carlos ☐ RP 85 Ra15
San Carlos ☐ YV 132 Gc17
San Carlos de Bariloche ☐ RA 137 Gb27
San Carlos del Zulia ☐ YV 132 Gb17
Sanchahe ☐ CHN 83 Rb10
San Cristóbal ☐ SOL 98 Ta21
San Cristóbal ☐ YV 132 Gb17
San Cristóbal de las Casas ☐ MEX 125 Fb15
Sancti Spíritus ☐ C 126 Ga14

Sančursk ☐ RUS 60 Nd17
Sand ☐ N 26 Ld16
Sand ☐ N 24 Lf15
Sandakan ☐ MAL 87 Qd17
Sandane ☐ N 24 Ld15
Sandanski ☐ BG 56 Mb25
Sandefjord ☐ N 26 Lf16
Sandefjord Ice Bay ☐ 141 Oc32
Sandercock Nunataks ▲ 141 Nc32
Sandfire Flat Roadhouse ☐ AUS 94 Ra22
Sandi ☐ SUD 107 Mc15
San Diego ☐ USA 122 Dd11
Sandıklı ☐ TR 64 Mf26
Sandnes ☐ N 26 Lc16
Sandnessjøen ☐ N 22 Lg12
Sandomierz ☐ PL 51 Ma20
Sandön ☐ FIN 25 Ma14
Sandover ☐ AUS 94 Rc23
Sandovo ☐ RUS 58 Mj16
Sandoway ☐ MYA 84 Pc15
Šandrivka ☐ UA 63 Mh21
Sandspit ☐ CDN 117 Db08
Sandstad ☐ N 24 Le14
Sandstone ☐ AUS 94 Qd24
Sandvika ☐ N 24 Lg13
Sandviken ☐ S 25 Lj15
Sandy Lake ☐ CDN 120 Fb08
Sandy Lake ☐ CDN 120 Fb08
San Felipe ☐ CO 132 Gc18
San Felipe ☐ MEX 124 Eb12
San Felipe ☐ YV 127 Gc16
San Fernando ☐ E 41 Kg27
San Fernando ☐ MEX 124 Fa14
San Fernando ☐ RP 85 Ra15
San Fernando ☐ TT 127 Gd16
San Fernando d.Valle de Catamarca ☐ RA 136 Gc24
San Fernando de Apure ☐ YV 132 Gc17
San Fernando de Atabapo ☐ YV 132 Gc18
Sånfjällets n.p. ▲ S 24 Lg14
San Francisco ☐ RA 136 Gd25
San Francisco ☐ USA 122 Dd11
San Francisco de Macoris ☐ DOM 127 Gb15
Sangar ☐ RUS 75 Rb06
Sangaste ☐ EST 30 Md17
San Gavino Monreale ☐ I 48 Le24
Sangazi ☐ TR 57 Me25
Sângerei ☐ MD 55 Me22
Sangerhausen ☐ D 44 Lf20
Sangihe ☐ RI 87 Rb18
San Giovanni in Fiore ☐ I 49 Lj26
San Giovanni Rotondo ☐ I 49 Lh25
Sangkulirang ☐ RI 87 Qd18
Sangli ☐ IND 81 Oc15
Sangüesa ☐ E 42 Kk24
San Ignacio de Velasco ☐ BOL 133 Gd22
San Isidro ☐ RA 136 Ha25
San Javier ☐ E 43 Kk27
Sanjiang ☐ CHN 84 Qb13
San Joaquin Valley ☐ USA 122 Dd11
San Jose ☐ RP 85 Ra15
San Jose ☐ RP 85 Ra16
San Jose ☐ USA 122 Dd11
San José ● CR 126 Fd17
San José ☐ E 41 Kj27

San José ☐ RA 136 Gc25
San José de Chiquitos ☐ BOL 133 Gd22
San José del Cabo ☐ MEX 124 Ec14
San José del Guaviare ☐ CO 132 Gb18
San Juan ☐ DOM 127 Gb15
San Juan ☐ RA 136 Gc25
San Juan ☐ RA 136 Gc25
San Juan ☐ USA 127 Gc15
San Juan Bautista ☐ PY 136 Ha24
Sankt Gallen ☐ CH 45 Le22
Sankt Johann ☐ A 52 Lg22
Sankt Moritz ☐ CH 45 Le22
Sankt-Peterburg ☐ RUS 29 Mf16
Sankt Peter-Ording ☐ D 44 Le18
Sankt Pölten ☐ A 52 Lh21
Sankt Veit an der Glan ☐ A 52 Lh22
Sankuru ☐ RDC 108 Ma19
Şanlıurfa ☐ TR 76 Md11
Şanlıurfa ☐ TR 65 Mk27
San Lorenzo ☐ PY 136 Ha24
San Lorenzo de Calatrava ☐ E 41 Kj26
Sanlúcar de Barrameda ☐ E 41 Kg27
San Lucas ☐ MEX 124 Eb14
San Luis ☐ RA 136 Gc25
San Luis ☐ RA 136 Gc25
San Luis Obispo ☐ USA 122 Dd11
San Luis Potosí ☐ MEX 124 Ed14
San Luis Potosí ☐ MEX 124 Ed14
San Luis Rio Colorado ☐ MEX 122 Eb12
San Marino ● RSM 46 Lg24
San Martín ☐ BOL 133 Gd21
San Martín ☐ 140 Gc32
San Miguel ☐ BOL 133 Gd22
San Miguel ☐ ES 125 Fc16
San Miguel de Tucumán ☐ RA 136 Gc24
Sanming ☐ CHN 85 Qd13
San Nicolas d.l.Arroyos ☐ RA 136 Ha25
Sànnicolau Mare ☐ RO 54 Ma22
Sanok ☐ PL 51 Mb21
San Pablo ☐ RP 85 Ra16
San Pablo o ☐ BOL 133 Gd23
San Pedro ☐ PY 136 Ha23
San Pedro ☐ RA 136 Gd23
San Pédro ☐ CI 105 Kc17
San Pédro ☐ CI 105 Kc18
San Pedro de las Colonias ☐ MEX 124 Ed13
San Pedro Sula ☐ HN 125 Fc15
San Quintin. ☐ MEX 122 Ea12
San Rafael ☐ RA 136 Gc25
San Remo ☐ I 46 Ld24
San Roque ☐ E 41 Kh27
San Salvador ● ES 125 Fc16
San Salvador de Jujuy ☐ RA 136 Gc23
Sansanne-Mango ☐ TG 105 La16
San Sebastián ☐ RA 137 Gc29
San Sebastián = Donostia ☐ E 42 Kj24
Sansepolcro ☐ I 46 Lg24

San Severo ☐ I 49 Lh25
Sanski Most ☐ BIH 47 Lj23
San Stéfano di Camastra ☐ I 49 Lh26
Santa Ana ☐ ES 125 Fc16
Santa Ana ☐ MEX 122 Eb12
Santa Ana ☐ USA 122 Dd11
Santa Barbara ☐ USA 122 Dd11
Santa Catarina ☐ BR 135 Hb24
Santa Clara ☐ C 126 Fd14
Santa Comba ☐ E 40 Kf24
Santa Cruz ☐ RA 137 Gb28
Santa Cruz de la Sierra ☐ BOL 133 Gd22
Santa Cruz de Tenerife ☐ E 104 Ka13
Santa Cruz Islands ☐ SOL 98 Tb21
Santa Elena de Uairén ☐ YV 132 Gd18
Santa Eugenia ☐ E 40 Kf24
Santa Fe ☐ USA 122 Ec11
Santa Fé ☐ E 41 Kj27
Santa Fé ☐ RA 136 Gd25
Santa Fé ☐ RA 136 Gd25
Sant'Agata di Militello ☐ I 49 Lh26
Santa Ines ☐ BR 134 Hc19
Santa Isabel ☐ SOL 93 Sd20
Santa Maria ☐ BR 135 Hb24
Santa Maria ☐ USA 122 Dd12
Santa Maria del Camí ☐ E 43 La24
Santa Maria Island ☐ VU 98 Tb21
Santa Marta ☐ CO 127 Gb16
Santana ☐ BR 134 Hb19
Santana do Livramento ☐ BR 136 Ha25
Santander ☐ E 42 Kj24
Santander ☐ RP 85 Ra17
Sant'Antioco ☐ I 48 Le26
Sant Antoni de Portmany ☐ E 43 La26
Santanyí ☐ E 43 Lb26
Santa Olalla del Cala ☐ E 41 Kg27
Sant'Arcángelo ☐ I 49 Lj25
Santarém ☐ BR 134 Hb19
Santarém ☐ P 40 Kf26
Santaren Channel ☐ C 126 Ga14
Santa Rita ☐ BR 134 Hd19
Santa Rita ☐ BR 134 Ja20
Santa Rosa ☐ RA 137 Gd26
Santa Rosa ☐ USA 122 Dd11
Santa Rosalia ☐ MEX 124 Eb13
Santa Teresa Gallura ☐ I 48 Le25
Sant Carles de la Ràpita ☐ E 43 La25
Sant Celoni ☐ E 42 Lb25
Santiago ☐ PA 126 Fd17
Santiago ● RCH 136 Gb25
Santiago de Compostela ● E 40 Kf24
Santiago de Cuba ☐ C 126 Ga15
Santiago del Estero ☐ RA 136 Gd24
Santiago del Estero ☐ RA 136 Gd24
Santiago de los Cabelleros ☐ DOM 127 Gb15
Santiago Ixcuintla ☐ MEX 124 Ec14

Sant Mateu ☐ E 42 La25
Santo André ☐ BR 135 Hc23
Santo Ángelo ☐ BR 135 Hb24
Santo Corazón ☐ BOL 133 Ha22
Santo Domingo ● DOM 127 Gc15
Santo Domingo d.l.Colorados ☐ EC 132 Ga19
Santorini ☐ GR 57 Mc27
Santos ☐ BR 135 Hc23
Santo Tirso ☐ P 40 Kf25
Santo Tomé ☐ RA 136 Ha24
San Vicente de la Barquera ☐ E 40 Kh24
Sanya ☐ CHN 85 Qb15
Sanza ☐ I 49 Lh25
São António da Abunari ☐ BR 132 Gd19
São Carlos ☐ BR 135 Hc23
São Felix do Araguaia ☐ BR 134 Hb21
São Felix do Xingu ☐ BR 134 Hb20
São Francisco ☐ BR 135 Hd21
São Francisco ☐ BR 134 Ja20
São João d.Meriti ☐ BR 135 Hd23
São José do Rio Preto ☐ BR 135 Hc23
São Lourenço ☐ BR 135 Ha22
São Luis ☐ BR 134 Hd19
São Mateus ☐ BR 135 Ja22
São Miguel do Tapuio ☐ BR 134 Hd20
São Paulo ☐ BR 135 Hb23
São Paulo ☐ BR 135 Hc23
Sao Tomé ☐ STP 108 Lb18
Sao Tomé ☐ STP 108 Lb18
São Tomé and Príncipe ☐ STP 108 Lb18
São Vicente ☐ BR 135 Hc23
Sápai ☐ GR 57 Mc25
Sapele ☐ WAN 108 La19
Sapernoe ☐ RUS 29 Me15
Sapiénza ☐ GR 56 Ma27
Sapožok ☐ RUS 59 Na19
Sapporo ☐ J 83 Sa10
Sapri ☐ I 49 Lh25
Sapulut ☐ RI 87 Qd18
Sarabikulovo ☐ RUS 60 Nf18
Sarai ☐ RUS 59 Na19
Säräisniemi ☐ FIN 28 Md13
Sarajevo ● BIH 47 Lk24
Sarandë ☐ AL 56 Ma26
Saransk ☐ RUS 60 Nc18
Sarapul ☐ RUS 72 Nc07
Sarasota ☐ USA 123 Fd13
Šarašova ☐ BY 51 Mc19
Saratov ☐ RUS 61 Nc20
Saratovskoe vodohranilišče ☐ RUS 60 Ne19
Saray ☐ TR 57 Md25
Sarayköy ☐ TR 64 Me27
Sárbogard ☐ H 53 Lk22
Sardinia ☐ I 48 Le25
Sareks n.p. ▲ S 22 Lj12
Sarektjåkka ▲ S 22 Lj12
Sargasso Sea ☐ 113 Ga06
Sarh ☐ TCH 108 Ld17
Šarhorod ☐ UA 62 Me21
Sari ☐ IR 76 Nc11
Saria ☐ GR 57 Md28
Sarie Marais Base ☐ 141 Kd33
Sarıgöl ☐ TR 64 Me26

Sarıkamış ☒ TR 66 Mb25
Sarıkaya ☒ TR 65 Mh26
Sarina ☒ AUS 96 Sb23
Sariñena ☒ E 42 Kk25
Sarıpınar ☒ TR 66 Mk26
Sarir Tibesti ◁ LAR 106 Ld14
Sariwon ☒ PRK 83 Rb11
Sarıyar Baraji ☲ TR 64 Mf25
Šar'ja ☒ RUS 72 Nb07
Šar'ja ☒ RUS 58 Mg16
Šar'ja ☒ RUS 60 Nc16
Sarkadkeresztúr ☒ H 53 Ma22
Šarkavščyna ☒ BY 31 Md18
Šarkikaraağaç ☒ TR 64 Mf26
Şarkışla ☒ TR 65 Mj26
Şarköy ☒ TR 57 Md25
Sarlat-la-Canéda ☒ F 38 La23
Sărmaşag ☒ RO 54 Mb22
Sarmette ☒ VU 98 Tb22
Sarmette ☒ VU 98 Tb22
Sarmi ☒ RI 92 Rd19
Sarmiento ☒ RA 137 Gc28
Särna ☒ S 24 Lg15
Sarnen ☒ CH 45 Le22
Sarnia ☒ CDN 123 Fd10
Sarny ☒ UA 51 Md20
Saronida ☒ GR 57 Mb27
Saronikós Kólpos ☲ GR 56 Mb27
Saros Körfezi ☲ TR 57 Md25
Sarpiniskie ozera ☲ RUS 61 Nc21
Šar Planina, N.P. ♠ SR 56 Ma24
Sarpsborg ☒ N 26 Lf16
Sarrebourg ☒ F 37 Ld21
Sarreguemines ☒ F 37 Ld21
Sarria ☒ E 40 Kg24
Sartène ☒ F 46 Le25
Sárti ☒ GR 57 Mb25
Saruhanlı ☒ TR 57 Md26
Sárvár ☒ H 53 Lj22
Saryesik-Atyrau ☲ KZ 79 Od09
Saryozek ☒ KZ 79 Od10
Saryshaghan ☒ KZ 78 Oc09
Sarysu ☲ KZ 78 Ob09
Šary Tas ☒ KS 78 Oc11
Saskatchewan ☒ CDN 120 Ec07
Saskatchewan ☲ CDN 120 Ed08
Saskatoon ☒ CDN 120 Ec08
Saskylah ☒ RUS 73 Qc04
Sason ☒ TR 66 Na26
Sasovo ☒ RUS 58 Na18
Sassandra ☒ CI 105 Kc18
Sassari ☒ I 48 Le25
Sassnitz ☒ D 44 Lg18
Sasykol ☲ KZ 79 Pa09
Satara ☒ IND 81 Oc15
Satawal Island ☲ FSM 92 Sb17
Satawan Atoll ☲ FSM 93 Sc17
Satpura Range ▲ IND 80 Od14
Satsunan Islands ☲ J 83 Rb13
Satu Mare ☒ RO 54 Mb22
Šatura ☒ RUS 58 Mk18
Sauda ☒ N 26 Ld16
Sauðárkrókur ☒ IS 32 Ka13
Saudi Arabia ■ KSA 77 Na13
Sauland ☒ N 26 Le16
Saulieu ☒ F 39 Lc22
Saulkrasti ☒ LV 30 Mc17
Sault-SainteMarie ☒ CDN 123 Fd09

Saumarez Reef ☲ AUS 96 Sc23
Saumur ☒ F 38 Kk22
Saunders, Mount ▲ 141 Tb36
Saurimo ☒ ANG 108 Ma20
Sauveterre-de-Béarn ☒ F 42 Kk24
Savannah ☒ USA 123 Fd12
Savannakhét ☒ LAO 84 Qa15
Savanna-la-Mar ☒ JA 126 Ga15
Savaştepe ☒ TR 57 Md26
Savè ☒ DY 105 La17
Save ☲ MOC 111 Mc23
Saveh ☒ IR 76 Nc11
Săveni ☒ RO 55 Md22
Savitaipale ☒ FIN 28 Md15
Šavnik ☒ CG 54 Lk24
Savoie ☲ F 39 Ld23
Savona ☒ I 46 Le23
Savonlinna ☒ FIN 28 Me15
Sävsjö ☒ S 27 Lh17
Savu Sea ☲ RI 87 Ra20
Sawu ☒ RI 87 Ra21
Saxnäs ☒ S 25 Lh13
Säyneinen ☒ FIN 28 Me14
Saynshand ☒ MNG 82 Qb10
Scaife Mountains ▲ 140 Gc33
Scarborough ☒ GB 35 Kk18
Ščekino ☒ RUS 59 Mj19
Schaffhausen ☒ CH 45 Le22
Scharbeutz ☒ D 44 Lf18
Schefferville ☒ CDN 121 Gc08
Schiermonnikoog, N.P. ♠ NL 37 Ld19
Schio ☒ I 46 Lf23
Schladming ☒ A 52 Lg22
Schleswig ☒ D 44 Le18
Schleswig-Holstein ☐ D 44 Le18
Schleswig-Holsteinisches Wattenmeer, N.P. ♠ D 44 Le18
Schlüchtern ☒ D 45 Le20
Schongau ☒ D 45 Lf22
Schubert Inlet ☲ 140 Gb33
Schwäbisch Hall ☒ D 45 Le21
Schwandorf ☒ D 45 Lg21
Schwaner Range ▲ RI 87 Qb19
Schwarzenbek ☒ D 44 Lf19
Schwaz ☒ A 45 Lf22
Schwedt ☒ D 44 Lh19
Schweinfurt ☒ D 45 Lf20
Schwerin ◉ D 44 Lf19
Schwyz ☒ CH 45 Le22
Sciacca ☒ I 48 Lg27
Ščigry ☒ RUS 59 Mj20
Scoresby Land ☲ DK 138 Jd04
Scoresby Sound ☲ DK 138 Jd04
Scoresbysund ☒ DK 138 Jd04
Ščors ☒ UA 62 Mf20
Scotia Ridge ☲ 137 Hb29
Scotia Sea ☲ 137 Hb20
Scotland ☐ GB 34 Kh17
Scott Canyon ☲ 141 Td33
Scott Coast ▲ 141 Ta34
Scott Mountains ▲ 141 Nc32
Scottsbluff ☒ USA 122 Ed10
Scourie ☒ GB 34 Kh16
Scranton ☒ USA 123 Ga10
Ščučyn ☒ BY 51 Mc19
Scunthorpe ☒ GB 35 Kk19

Sel'co ☒ RUS 30 Me16
Sea of Azov ☲ UA 63 Mj22
Sea of Crete ☲ GR 57 Mc27
Sea of Marmara ☲ TR 57 Me25
Sea Islands ☲ USA 123 Fd12
Sea of Japan ☲ 83 Rb11
Sea of Okhotsk ☲ RUS 75 Sb08
Seattle ☒ USA 122 Dd09
Šebekino ☒ RUS 59 Mj20
Sebeş ☒ RO 54 Mb23
Sebež ☒ RUS 31 Me17
Sebežskij N.P. ♠ RUS 31 Me17
Şebinkarahisar ☒ TR 66 Mk25
Sebiş ☒ RO 54 Mb22
Sebta ☒ E 41 Kh28
Sečenovo ☒ RUS 60 Nc18
Secuieni ☒ RO 55 Md22
Sedan ☒ F 37 Lc21
Seelig, Mount ▲ 140 Ed35
Seelow ☒ D 44 Lh19
Sées ☒ F 36 La21
Şefaatli ☒ TR 65 Mh26
Seferihisar ☒ TR 57 Md26
Segeža ☒ RUS 29 Mh14
Ségou ☒ RMM 105 Kc16
Segovia ☒ E 40 Kh25
Segozero ☲ RUS 29 Mg14
Segré ☒ F 38 Kk22
Seguedine ☒ RN 106 Lc14
Seinäjoki ☒ FIN 19 Mb14
Seine ☲ F 37 Lb21
Seini ☒ RO 54 Mb22
Seitsemisen kansallispuisto ♠ FIN 22 Mb15
Sejm ☲ UA 59 Mg20
Sejmčan ☒ RUS 74 Sc06
Sejny ☒ PL 51 Mb18
Šeki ☒ AZ 76 Nb10
Sekondi ☒ GH 105 Kd17
Šeksna ☒ RUS 58 Mk16
Selawik ☒ USA 116 Bd05
Selayar ☒ RI 87 Ra20
Selb ☒ D 45 Lg20
Selbekken ☒ N 24 Le14
Selbu ☒ N 24 Lf14
Selçuk ☒ TR 57 Md27
Selebi-Phikwe ☒ RB 110 Mb23
Selehovskaja ☲ RUS 29 Mk15
Selemdža ☲ RUS 75 Rc08
Selendi ☒ TR 64 Me26
Selenge ☲ RDC 108 Lh19
Selenge gol ☲ MNG 82 Qa09
Sélestat ☒ F 37 Ld21
Selfoss ☒ IS 32 Jk14
Selizarovo ☒ RUS 58 Mg17
Selles-sur-Cher ☒ F 38 La22
Selma ☒ USA 123 Fc12
Semarang ☒ RI 86 Qc20
Semenic-Cheile Caraşului, P.N. ♠ RO 54 Ma23
Semenivka ☒ UA 59 Mg19
Semenov ☒ RUS 60 Nc17
Seměnovka ☒ RUS 61 Nc21
Semey ☒ KZ 79 Pa08
Semiluki ☒ RUS 59 Mk20
Semnan ☒ IR 76 Nc11
Šemordan ☒ RUS 60 Nf17
Senador Pompeu ☒ BR 134 Ja20
Señal Huascarán ▲ PE 133 Ga20
Senanga ☒ Z 110 Ma22

Sendai ☒ J 83 Sa11
Senec ☒ SK 53 Lj21
Senegal ■ SN 105 Ka16
Sénégal ☲ SN 105 Kb15
Sengata ☒ RI 87 Qd18
Sengau ☒ RI 86 Qc18
Senhor do Bonfim ☒ BR 134 Hd21
Senica ☒ SK 53 Lj21
Senigállia ☒ I 47 Lg24
Senj ☒ HR 47 Lh23
Senja ☲ N 22 Lj11
Senkaya ☒ TR 66 Nb25
Senlis ☒ F 37 Lb21
Sennar ☒ SUD 107 Mc16
Sennen ☒ GB 35 Kh20
Sens ☒ F 37 Lb21
Senta ☒ SR 54 Ma23
Senyavin Islands ☲ FSM 93 Sd17
Seoul ◉ ROK 83 Rb11
Šepetivka ☒ UA 51 Md20
Sepik ☲ PNG 92 Sa19
Sepólno Krajeńskie ☒ PL 50 Lj19
Sept-Îles ☒ CDN 121 Gc08
Sepúlveda ☒ E 42 Kj25
Serafettin Daglari ▲ TR 66 Na26
Serafimovič ☒ RUS 61 Nb21
Seram ☒ RI 87 Rb19
Serang ☒ RI 86 Qb20
Serbia ■ SR 54 Ma23
Serbia ☐ SR 54 Ma24
Serdobsk ☒ RUS 61 Nc19
Şereflikochisar ☒ TR 65 Mg26
Sereď ☒ SK 53 Lj21
Šeremet'evka ☒ RUS 60 Nf18
Serengeti ☲ EAT 109 Mc19
Séres ☒ GR 56 Mb25
Sergač ☒ RUS 60 Nc18
Sergiev Posad ☒ RUS 58 Mk17
Sergipe ☐ BR 135 Ja21
Serian ☒ MAL 86 Qc18
Sérifos ☲ GR 57 Mc27
Serinhisar ☒ TR 64 Me27
Sermata ☒ RI 87 Rb20
Sernur ☒ RUS 60 Ne17
Serock ☒ PL 50 Ma19
Serov ☒ RUS 72 Oa07
Serowe ☒ RB 110 Mb23
Serpa ☒ P 41 Kg27
Serpuhov ☒ RUS 59 Mj18
Serra Acara ou Acari ▲ BR 132 Gd18
Serra da Chela ▲ ANG 110 Lc22
Serra de Divisor ▲ BR 133 Gb20
Serra do Cachimbo ▲ BR 134 Ha20
Serra do Caiapó ▲ BR 135 Hb22
Serra do Espinhaço ▲ BR 135 Hd22
Serra do Mar ▲ BR 135 Hc24
Serra do Maracaju ▲ BR 136 Ha23
Serra do Neve ▲ ANG 110 Lc21
Serra do Penitente ▲ BR 134 Hc20
Serra do Roncador ▲ BR 135 Hb21
Serra do Tombador ▲ BR 135 Ha21
Serra do Tumucumaque ▲ BR 134 Hb18

Serra San Bruno � I 49 Lj26
Serres ▢ F 39 Lc23
Serrinha ▢ BR 135 Ja21
Sertão ▣ BR 135 Hd21
Sertão de Camapuã ▣ BR 135 Hb22
Serule ▢ RB 110 Mb23
Servi ▢ TR 66 Na26
Sérvia ▢ GR 56 Mb25
Šešma ▭ RUS 60 Nf18
Sestriere ▢ I 46 Ld23
Sestri Levante ▢ I 46 Le23
Sestroreck ▢ RUS 29 Me15
Sète ▢ F 38 Lb24
Sete Lagoas ▢ BR 135 Hd22
Setermoen ▢ N 22 Lk11
Setesdal ◿ N 26 Ld16
Sétif ▢ DZ 106 Lb11
Setraki ▢ RUS 61 Na21
Setúbal ▢ P 41 Kf26
Sevastopol' ▢ UA 63 Mg23
Ševčenkove ▢ UA 63 Mj21
Severnoe ▢ RUS 60 Ng18
Severnye uvaly ▲ RUS 72 Na07
Severomorsk ▢ RUS 72 Mc05
Severomorsk ▢ RUS 23 Mg11
Severitijarvi ▢ FIN 23 Me11
Sevilla ▣ E 41 Kg27
Sevlievo ▢ BG 56 Mc24
Sevsk ▢ RUS 59 Mh19
Seward ▢ USA 116 Cc06
Seward Peninsula ◿ USA 116 Bd05
Seychelles ▪ SY 103 Nb10
Seydiler ▢ TR 65 Mg25
Seydişehir ▢ TR 64 Mf27
Seyðisfjörður ▢ IS 32 Ka13
Seyhan Nehri ▭ TR 65 Mh27
Şeytan Sofrası ▢ TR 57 Md26
Sézanne ▢ F 37 Lb21
Sfântu Gheorghe ▢ RO 55 Mc23
Sfântu Gheorghe ▢ RO 55 Me23
Sfax ▢ TN 106 Lc12
Sfinári ▢ GR 56 Mb28
Shaanxi ▢ CHN 82 Qb12
Shache ▢ CHN 78 Od11
Shackleton Ice Shelf ◿ 141 Pd32
Shackleton Inlet ▭ 141 Tc35
Shackleton Range ▲ 140 Jc35
Shahreza ▢ IR 77 Nc12
Shahrud ▢ IR 76 Nc11
Shakhrisyabz ▢ UZ 78 Ob11
Shandong ▢ CHN 83 Qd11
Shanghai ▣ CHN 83 Ra12
Shanghai Deepwater Port ▢ CHN 83 Ra12
Shangzhi ▢ CHN 83 Rb09
Shan Plateau ▲ MYA 84 Pd14
Shantarskiye Ostrova ◿ RUS 75 Rd07
Shantipur ▢ IND 80 Pb14
Shantou ▢ CHN 85 Qd14
Shanxi ▢ CHN 82 Qc11
Shaoguan ▢ CHN 85 Qc13
Shaoyang ▢ CHN 85 Qc13
Shark Bay ◿ AUS 94 Qc24
Sharm-el-Sheikh ▢ ET 107 Mc13
Shashemene ▢ ETH 109 Md17
Shashi ▢ CHN 85 Qc12
Shatt-el-Arab ▭ IRQ 77 Nb12
Shawnee ▢ USA 123 Fa11
Sheffield ▢ GB 35 Kk19

Shelikof Strait ▭ USA 116 Cb07
Shenyang ▣ CHN 83 Ra10
Shenzhen ▢ CHN 85 Qc14
Shepparton-Mooroopna ▢ AUS 97 Sb26
Sherbrooke ▢ CDN 121 Gb09
Sheridan ▢ USA 120 Ec10
's-Hertogenbosch ▢ NL 37 Lc20
Shetland Islands ◿ GB 34 Kk15
Shibin el-Kom ▢ ET 107 Mc12
Shieli ▢ UZ 78 Ob10
Shihezi ▢ CHN 79 Pb10
Shijiazhuang ▣ CHN 82 Qc11
Shikarpur ▢ PAK 80 Ob13
Shikoku ◿ J 83 Rc12
Shillong ▢ IND 84 Pc13
Shimla ▢ IND 80 Od12
Shindand ▢ AFG 78 Oa12
Shinyanga ▢ EAT 109 Mc19
Shiquan ▢ CHN 82 Qb12
Shirame-san ▲ J 83 Rd11
Shiraz ▢ IR 77 Nc13
Shiyan ▢ CHN 82 Qc12
Shiza ◿ GR 56 Ma27
Shizuishan ▢ CHN 82 Qb11
Shkodër = Skutari ▢ AL 56 Lk24
Sholapur ▢ IND 81 Od15
Shreveport ▢ USA 123 Fb12
Shrewsbury ▢ GB 35 Kj19
Shu Chu ▭ KZ 78 Oc10
Shuqra ▢ YE 77 Nb16
Shymkent ▢ UZ 78 Ob10
Sianów ▢ PL 50 Lj18
Siaton ▢ RP 85 Ra17
Siau ◿ RI 87 Rb18
Siauliai ▢ LT 31 Mb18
Sibari ▢ I 49 Lj26
Šibenik ▢ HR 47 Lh24
Siberia ◿ RUS 73 Pa06
Siberut ◿ RI 86 Pd19
Sibirskie uvaly ▲ RUS 72 Oc06
Sibiu ▢ RO 54 Mc23
Sib Kuh ▲ IR 77 Nc13
Sibolga ▢ RI 86 Pd18
Sibu ▢ MAL 86 Qc18
Sibut ▢ RCA 108 Ld17
Sibuyan ◿ RP 85 Ra16
Sichuan ▢ CHN 84 Qa12
Sicily ◿ I 49 Lh27
Sicuani ▢ PE 133 Gb21
Sidensjö ▢ S 25 Lk14
Sidi Bel Abbes ▢ DZ 104 Kd11
Sidirókastro ▢ GR 56 Mb25
Sidley, Mount ▲ 140 Dc34
Siedlce ▢ PL 51 Mb19
Siegburg ▢ D 44 Ld20
Siegen ▢ D 44 Le20
Siemiatycze ▢ PL 51 Mb19
Siem Reap ▢ K 84 Qa16
Siena ▢ I 46 Lf24
Sieniawa ▢ PL 51 Mb20
Sieradz ▢ PL 50 Lk20
Sierpc ▢ PL 50 Lk19
Sierra Colorada ▢ RA 137 Gc27
Sierra de Córdoba ▲ RA 136 Gd25
Sierra de Guampi ▲ YV 132 Gc17
Sierra Grande ▢ RA 137 Gc27
Sierra Leone ▪ WAL 105 Kb17

Sierra Madre ▲ RP 85 Ra15
Sierra Madre del Sur ▲ MEX 124 Ed15
Sierra Madre Occidental ▲ MEX 124 Ec13
Sierra Madre Oriental ▲ MEX 124 Fa14
Sierra Morena ▲ E 41 Kg27
Sierra Nevada ▲ E 41 Kj27
Sierra Nevada ▲ USA 122 Ea11
Sierra Nevada, P.N.de ▲ E 41 Kj27
Sífnos ◿ GR 57 Mc27
Siggerud ▢ N 26 Lf16
Sighetu Marmaţiei ▢ RO 54 Mb22
Sighișoara ▢ RO 55 Mc23
Sigli ▢ RI 86 Pc18
Siglufjörður ▢ IS 32 Ka12
Sigmaringen ▢ D 45 Le22
Şigony ▢ RUS 60 Ne19
Sigsbee Deep ◿ 125 Fb14
Sigüenza ▢ E 42 Kj25
Siguiri ▢ RG 105 Kc16
Sigulda ▢ LV 30 Mc17
Sihanoukville ▢ K 84 Qa16
Sihany ▢ RUS 60 Ne19
Siilinjärvi ▢ FIN 28 Md14
Sikar ▢ IND 80 Od13
Sikasso ▢ RMM 105 Kc16
Sikhote-Alin ▲ RUS 83 Rd09
Síkinos ◿ GR 57 Mc27
Sikkim ▢ IND 80 Pb13
Siktjah ▢ RUS 75 Ra15
Šile ▢ TR 57 Me25
Silifke ▢ TR 65 Mg27
Siliguri ▢ IND 80 Pb13
Siling Co ◿ CHN 80 Pb12
Silistra ▢ BG 56 Md23
Silivri ▢ TR 57 Me25
Siljan ◿ N 26 Le16
Siljan ◿ S 25 Lh15
Siljansnäs ▢ S 25 Lh15
Šilka ▭ RUS 82 Qd08
Silkeborg ▢ DK 26 Le17
Sillamäe ▢ EST 30 Md16
Šilovo ▢ RUS 59 Mk19
Silovo ▢ RUS 59 Na18
Šilute ▢ LT 31 Ma18
Silvan ▢ TR 66 Na26
Silvan Baraj ◿ TR 66 Na26
Silvassa ▣ IND 80 Oc14
Silver Plains ▢ AUS 96 Sa21
Simakivka ▢ UA 62 Me20
Šimanovsk ▢ RUS 75 Rb08
Simav ▢ TR 64 Me25
Simbirsk = Uljanovsk ▢ RUS 60 Ne18
Simen Mountains ▲ ETH 107 Md16
Simeria ▢ RO 54 Mb23
Simeulue ◿ RI 86 Pd18
Simferopol' ▢ UA 63 Mh23
Simi ◿ GR 57 Md27
Simien ▲ ETH 107 Md16
Simnas ▢ LT 31 Mb18
Simo ▢ FIN 28 Mc13
Simpang ▢ RI 86 Qa19
Simpson Desert ◿ AUS 96 Rd24
Simrishamn ▢ S 27 Lh18
Simsk ▢ RUS 30 Mf16
Sinabang ▢ RI 86 Pd18
Sinai ◿ ET 107 Mc13
Sinaia ▢ RO 55 Mc23
Sinaloa ▢ MEX 124 Ec13
Sincan ▢ TR 65 Mg25
Sincan ▢ TR 65 Mj26

Sincelejo ▢ CO 132 Ga17
Sindal ▢ DK 26 Lf17
Sindelfingen ▢ D 45 Le21
Sındırgı ▢ TR 64 Me26
Sines ▢ P 41 Kf27
Singa ▢ SUD 107 Mc16
Singapore ▪ SGP 86 Qa18
Singapore ▣ SGP 86 Qa18
Singen ▢ D 45 Le22
Singida ▢ EAT 109 Mc19
Singilej ▢ RUS 60 Ne19
Singkawang ▢ RI 86 Qb18
Singletown ▢ AUS 97 Sc25
Sinie Lipjagi ▢ RUS 59 Mk20
Siniscóla ▢ I 48 Le25
Sinj ▢ HR 47 Lj24
Sinjavka ▢ BY 51 Md19
Sinkep ◿ RI 86 Qa19
Sinkiang ▢ CHN 79 Pa11
Sinodskoe ▢ RUS 61 Nd20
Sinop ▢ BR 135 Ha21
Sinop ▢ TR 65 Mh25
Sinop Burnu ▲ TR 65 Mh24
Sinsheim ▢ D 45 Le21
Sintang ▢ RI 86 Qc18
Sintea Mare ▢ RO 54 Ma22
Sint Maarten ◿ NL 127 Gd15
Sintra ▢ P 40 Kf26
Siófok ▢ H 53 Lk22
Sion ▢ CH 45 Ld22
Sioux City ▢ USA 123 Fa10
Sioux Falls ▢ USA 123 Fa10
Sioux Lookout ▢ CDN 120 Fb08
Siple Dome ◿ 140 Cc35
Siple, Mount ▲ 140 Dc33
Sipura ◿ RI 86 Pd19
Şiran ▢ TR 66 Na26
Sir Edward Pellew Group ◿ AUS 96 Rd22
Siret ▢ RO 55 Md22
Sirevåg ▢ N 26 Lc16
Sirjan ▢ IR 77 Nd13
Sirna ◿ GR 57 Md27
Síros ◿ GR 57 Mc27
Sirsa ▢ IND 80 Od13
Sirsova Ridge ◿ RUS 74 Tc07
Širvintos ▢ LT 31 Mc18
Sisak ▢ HR 47 Lj23
Sisimut ▢ DK 119 Hb05
Sisteron ▢ F 39 Lc23
Sitakund ▢ BD 84 Pc14
Sitapur ▢ IND 80 Pa13
Sitasjaure ◿ S 22 Lj12
Sitges ▢ E 42 La24
Sithonia ◿ GR 57 Mc26
Sitka ▢ USA 117 Da07
Sittwe ▢ MYA 84 Pc14
Sivas ▢ TR 76 Md11
Sivas ▢ TR 65 Mj26
Siverskij ▢ RUS 30 Mf16
Sivers'kyi Donec' ▭ UA 63 Mj21
Sivrihisar ▢ TR 64 Mf26
Siwa ▢ ET 106 Mb13
Siwa Oasis ◿ ET 106 Mb13
Sixth Cataract ◿ SUD 107 Mc15
Själland ▢ DK 26 Lf18
Sjanno ▢ BY 31 Me18
Sjas'stroj ▢ RUS 29 Mg15
Sjaunja naturreservat ◿ S 22 Lk12
Sjeverni Velebit, N.P. ◿ HR 47 Lh23
Sjeverodonec'k ▢ UA 63 Mk21
Sjoasen ▢ N 24 Lf13
Sjøbo ▢ S 27 Lg18

Sjøholt ◻ N 24 Ld14
Sjötorp ◻ S 26 Lg16
Sjøvegan ◻ N 22 Lj11
Skadarsko jezero, N.P. ◻ CG 56 Lk24
Skadovs'k ◻ UA 62 Mg22
Skærbæk ◻ DK 26 Le18
Skagaströnd ◻ IS 32 Jk13
Skagen ◻ DK 26 Lf17
Skagerak ◻ 26 Le17
Skagway ◻ USA 117 Da07
Skálafellsjökull ◊ IS 32 Kb13
Skala-Podil's'ka ◻ UA 51 Md21
Skaloti ◻ GR 57 Mc25
Skanderborg ◻ DK 26 Le17
Skåne ◻ S 26 Lg18
Skånevik ◻ N 26 Lc16
Skarżysko-Kamienna ◻ PL 50 Ma20
Skarberget ◻ N 22 Lj11
Skärgårdshavets n.p. = Saaristomeren kansallispuisto ◻ FIN 30 Ma16
Skarness ◻ N 24 Lf15
Skattungbyn ◻ S 25 Lh15
Skegness ◻ GB 35 La19
Skei ◻ N 24 Ld15
Skei ◻ N 24 Ld15
Skei ◻ N 24 Le14
Skeiðarársandur ◻ IS 32 Kb14
Skeldon ◻ GUY 134 Ha17
Skeleton Coast ◻ NAM 110 Lc22
Skellefteå ◻ S 25 Ma13
Skellefteälven ◻ S 25 Lk13
Skelleftehamn ◻ S 25 Ma13
Skelton Glacier ◻ 141 Sd34
Skiathos ◻ GR 56 Mb26
Skibotn ◻ N 22 Ma11
Skidal' ◻ BY 51 Mc19
Skien ◻ N 26 Le16
Skierniewice ◻ PL 50 Ma20
Skikda ◻ DZ 106 Lb11
Skillingaryd ◻ S 27 Lh17
Skinnskatteberg ◻ S 27 Lh16
Skiros ◻ GR 57 Mc26
Skive ◻ DK 26 Le17
Skjern ◻ DK 26 Le18
Skjervøy ◻ N 22 Ma10
Skjolden ◻ N 24 Ld15
Skjønhaug ◻ N 26 Lf16
Šklov ◻ BY 31 Mf18
Skógafoss ◻ IS 32 Ka14
Skógar ◻ IS 32 Ka14
Skoki ◻ PL 50 Lj19
Skole ◻ UA 53 Mb21
Skolivs'ki Beskydy N.P. ◻ UA 53 Mb21
Skópelos ◻ GR 57 Mb26
Skopin ◻ RUS 59 Mk19
Skopje ● MK 56 Ma24
Skorodnoe ◻ RUS 59 Mj20
Skorovatn ◻ N 24 Lg13
Skotterud ◻ N 26 Lg16
Skottsund ◻ S 25 Lj14
Skövde ◻ S 27 Lg16
Skovorodino ◻ RUS 75 Ra08
Skradin ◻ HR 47 Lh24
Skudeneshavn ◻ N 26 Lc16
Skuleskogens n.p. ◻ S 25 Lk14
Skulgam ◻ N 22 Lk11
Skuodas ◻ LT 31 Ma17
Skutari = Shkodër ◻ AL 56 Lk24
Skutskär ◻ S 25 Lj15
Skvyra ◻ UA 62 Me21

Skwierzyna ◻ PL 50 Lh19
Sky Blu ◻ 140 Gb33
Skye ◻ GB 34 Kg17
Skytrain Ice Rise ◻ 140 Ga34
Slagelse ◻ DK 26 Lf18
Slancy ◻ RUS 30 Mf16
Slano ◻ HR 47 Lj24
Slaný ◻ CZ 52 Lh20
Śląskie ◻ PL 50 Lj20
Slatina ◻ HR 47 Lj23
Slatina ◻ RO 55 Mc23
Slave Coast ◻ TG/DY 105 La17
Slave Lake ◻ CDN 117 Eb07
Slavharad ◻ BY 59 Mf19
Slavjansk na-Kubani ◻ RUS 63 Mk23
Slavkoviči ◻ RUS 30 Me17
Slavonia ◻ HR 47 Lj23
Slavonski Brod ◻ HR 47 Lk23
Slavsk ◻ RUS 31 Ma18
Slavuta ◻ UA 51 Md20
Sławno ◻ PL 50 Lj18
Slieve League ◻ IRL 33 Kf18
Sligo ◻ IRL 33 Kf18
Šlissel'burg ◻ RUS 30 Mf16
Slite ◻ S 27 Lk17
Sliven ◻ BG 55 Md24
Slobozia ◻ RO 55 Md23
Slonim ◻ BY 51 Mc19
Slovakia ◻ SK 53 Lk21
Slovenia ◻ SLO 47 Lh23
Slovenska Bistrica ◻ SLO 47 Lh22
Slovenské rudohorie ◻ PL/SK 53 Lk21
Slov'jans'k ◻ UA 63 Mj21
Słowiński P.N. ◻ PL 50 Lj18
Słubice ◻ PL 50 Lh19
Sluč ◻ UA 51 Md20
Sluck ◻ BY 51 Md19
Slunj ◻ HR 47 Lh23
Słupsk ◻ PL 50 Lj18
Slussfors ◻ S 25 Lj13
Småland ◻ S 27 Lh17
Smålandsstenar ◻ S 26 Lg17
Smaljavičy ◻ BY 31 Me18
Smallwood Res. ◻ CDN 121 Gd08
Smara ◻ MA 104 Kb13
Smarhon' ◻ BY 31 Md18
Smederevo ◻ SR 54 Ma23
Smedjebacken ◻ S 25 Lh15
Smila ◻ UA 62 Mf21
Smiltene ◻ LV 30 Mc17
Smith Bay ◻ CDN 118 Ga03
Smithton ◻ AUS 97 Sb27
Smjadovo ◻ BG 55 Md24
Smøla ◻ N 24 Ld14
Smolensk ◻ RUS 59 Mg18
Smolensko-Moskovskaja vozvýšennost' ◻ RUS 59 Mg18
Smoljan ◻ BG 57 Mc25
Smyley Island ◻ 140 Ga33
Smyšljaevsk ◻ RUS 60 Nf19
Snæfell ◻ IS 32 Kc13
Snake River ◻ USA 122 Ea09
Snåsa ◻ N 24 Lg13
Snåsavatnet ◻ N 24 Lf13
Sneek ◻ NL 37 Lc19
Sniezka ◻ CZ/PL 52 Lh20
Snihurivka ◻ UA 62 Mg22
Snina ◻ SK 53 Mb21
Snjatyn ◻ UA 55 Mc21
Snøhetta ◻ N 26 Le14
Snowdonia N.P. ◻ GB 35 Kj19
Sobat ◻ SUD 109 Mc17

Sobinka ◻ RUS 58 Na18
Sobolevo ◻ RUS 59 Na18
Sobral ◻ BR 134 Hd19
Sobrance ◻ SK 53 Mb21
Sochinsky nacional'nyj park ◻ RUS 63 Mk23
Sochumi ◻ GE 76 Na10
Soči ◻ RUS 66 Mk24
Socorro ◻ CO 132 Gb17
Socotra ◻ YE 77 Nc15
Sodankylä ◻ FIN 23 Md12
Söderhamn ◻ S 25 Lj15
Söderköping ◻ S 27 Lh16
Södertälje ◻ S 27 Lj16
Sofades ◻ GR 56 Mb26
Sofia ● BG 54 Mb24
Sofia ◻ RM 111 Nb22
Sofija ● BG 54 Mb24
Sofijivka ◻ UA 62 Mg21
Sofporog ◻ RUS 23 Mf13
Sogamoso ◻ CO 132 Gb17
Sogndal ◻ N 24 Ld15
Sognefjorden ◻ N 24 Lc15
Sogod ◻ RP 85 Ra16
Soğuksu Milli Parkı ◻ TR 65 Mg25
Söğüt ◻ TR 64 Me27
Söğütlü ◻ TR 66 Na26
Sohåg ◻ ET 107 Mc13
Sohar ◻ OM 77 Nd14
Soini ◻ FIN 28 Mc14
Soissons ◻ F 37 Lb21
Sojol ◻ RI 87 Ra18
Sojuz ◻ 140 Gc33
Sokal' ◻ UA 51 Mc20
Söke ◻ TR 57 Md27
Sokodé ◻ TG 105 La17
Sokółka ◻ PL 51 Mb19
Sokolov Podlaski ◻ PL 51 Mb19
Sokoto ◻ WAN 105 La17
Sokoto ◻ WAN 105 Lb16
Solberg ◻ S 25 Lj14
Sol'cy ◻ RUS 30 Mf16
Solec Kujawski ◻ PL 50 Lk19
Soledad ◻ CO 127 Gb16
Solhan ◻ TR 66 Na26
Solikamsk ◻ RUS 72 Nd07
Solimões ◻ BR 132 Gc19
Solleftå ◻ S 25 Lj14
Sollentuna ◻ S 27 Lj16
Solncevo ◻ RUS 59 Mj20
Solnečnogorsk ◻ RUS 58 Mj17
Solo ◻ RI 86 Qc20
Šolohovskij ◻ RUS 63 Na21
Solomon Islands ◻ SOL 93 Sd20
Solomon Islands ◻ SOL 93 Sd20
Solomon Sea ◻ PNG 93 Sc20
Solone ◻ UA 63 Mh21
Solothurn ◻ CH 45 Ld22
Soloveckie ◻ RUS 29 Mh13
Solsvik ◻ N 24 Lc15
Soltau ◻ D 44 Le19
Soltvadkert ◻ H 53 Lk22
Sölvesborg ◻ S 27 Lh17
Solway Firth ◻ GB 34 Kj18
Solwezi ◻ Z 110 Mb21
Soma ◻ TR 57 Md26
Somalia ◻ 103 Na09
Somali Basin ◻ 101 Na14
Sombor ◻ SR 54 Lk23
Somero ◻ FIN 22 Mb15
Somerset-East ◻ ZA 110 Mb25
Somerset Island ◻ CDN 118 Fb04

Somerset-Oos ◻ ZA 110 Mb25
Somme ◻ F 35 La20
Sompolno ◻ PL 50 Lj19
Sóndalo ◻ I 46 Lf22
Sønderborg ◻ DK 26 Le18
Søndrestrømfjord ◻ DK 119 Hc05
Sondrio ◻ I 46 Le22
Songea ◻ EAT 111 Md21
Songkhla ◻ THA 86 Qa17
Sonid Youqi ◻ CHN 82 Qc10
Sonkovo ◻ RUS 58 Mj17
Sonneberg ◻ D 44 Lf20
Sonora ◻ MEX 124 Eb13
Sonoyta ◻ MEX 122 Eb12
Sonseca ◻ E 41 Kj26
Sonsorol Island ◻ PAL 92 Rc17
Sonthofen ◻ D 45 Lf22
Soomaa rahvuspark ◻ EST 30 Mc16
Sopot ◻ PL 50 Lk18
Sopron ◻ H 52 Lj22
Sora ◻ I 49 Lg25
Sorbas ◻ E 41 Kj27
Sorel ◻ CDN 121 Gb09
Sør-Flatanger ◻ N 24 Lf13
Sorgun ◻ TR 65 Mh26
Sør-Gutvika ◻ N 24 Lf13
Soria ◻ E 42 Kj25
Sørli ◻ N 24 Lg13
Soroca ◻ MD 62 Me21
Sorocaba ◻ BR 135 Hc23
Soroč'i Gory ◻ RUS 60 Nf18
Sorol Atoll ◻ FSM 92 Sa17
Sorong ◻ RI 92 Rc19
Soroti ◻ EAU 109 Mc18
Sorsele ◻ S 25 Lj13
Sørstraumen ◻ N 23 Ma11
Sortavala ◻ RUS 29 Mf15
Sortland ◻ N 22 Lh11
Sørvågen ◻ N 22 Lg12
Sosedka ◻ RUS 61 Nb19
Sosnenskij ◻ RUS 59 Mj19
Sosnogorsk ◻ RUS 72 Nc06
Sosnove ◻ UA 51 Md20
Sosnovka ◻ RUS 61 Na19
Sosnovka ◻ RUS 60 Nf17
Sosnovyj Bor ◻ RUS 30 Me16
Sosnowiec ◻ PL 50 Lk20
Sospel ◻ F 39 Ld24
Šostka ◻ UA 59 Mg20
Soubré ◻ CI 105 Kc17
Soufli ◻ GR 57 Md25
Souillac ◻ F 38 La23
Souk Ahras ◻ DZ 106 Lb11
Sousa ◻ BR 134 Ja20
Sousse ◻ TN 106 Lc11
South Africa ◻ ZA 110 Ma24
Southampton ◻ GB 35 Kk20
Southampton Island ◻ CDN 118 Fd06
South Andaman ◻ IND 81 Pc16
South Australia ◻ AUS 95 Rc24
South Australian Basin ◻ 95 Ra26
South Bend ◻ USA 123 Fc10
South Carolina ◻ USA 123 Fd12
South China Basin ◻ 85 Qd16
South China Mountains ◻ CHN 84 Qb13
South China Sea ◻ 85 Qc15
South Dakota ◻ USA 122 Ed10

South Downs ◫ GB 35 Kk20
South East Cape ⬱ AUS 97 Sb27
South East Point ⬱ AUS 97 Sb26
Southend ◫ CDN 120 Ed07
Southend-on-Sea ◫ GB 35 La20
Southern Sporades ⬱ GR 57 Mc27
Southern Alps ⬱ NZ 99 Tb27
Southern Cross ◫ AUS 95 Qd25
Southern Indian Lake ◫ CDN 120 Fa07
Southern Uplands ⬱ GB 34 Kh18
South Fiji Ridge ⬱ 99 Ua24
South Island ⬱ NZ 99 Tb27
South Korea ■ ROK 83 Rb11
South Molton ◫ GB 35 Kj20
South Pole ● 140 Ga36
Southport ◫ GB 35 Kj19
South Saskatchewan ⌇ CDN 117 Eb08
South Scotia Ridge ⬱ GB 140 Hb31
South Shetland Islands ⬱ GB 140 Gd31
South Solomon Trench ⬱ SOL 98 Ta21
South Taranaki Bight ⬱ NZ 99 Tc27
South Tasman Rise ⬱ 97 Sb28
South Uist ⬱ GB 34 Kg17
South West Cape ⬱ AUS 97 Sb27
Sovata ◫ RO 55 Mc22
Sovetskaja ◫ RUS 61 Nb21
Sovetskaja ◫ 141 Pb34
Sovetskij ◫ RUS 60 Ne17
Soweto ◫ ZA 110 Mb24
Spa ◫ B 37 Lc20
Spain ■ E 20 Kd09
Spalding ◫ GB 35 Kk19
Spanish Town ◫ JA 126 Ga15
Spartanburg ◫ USA 123 Fd12
Spárti ◫ GR 56 Mb27
Spas-Klepiki ◫ RUS 58 Na18
Spassk-Dal'nij ◫ RUS 83 Rc10
Spassk-Rjazanskij ◫ RUS 58 Na18
Spearfish ◫ USA 122 Ed10
Spencer Gulf ⬱ AUS 97 Rd25
Spétses ◫ GR 56 Mb27
Speyer ◫ D 45 Le21
Spirovo ◫ RUS 58 Mh17
Spittal an der Drau ◫ A 52 Lg22
Spitzkoppe ⬱ NAM 110 Ld23
Split ◫ HR 47 Lj24
Špogi ◫ LV 31 Md17
Spokane ◫ USA 122 Ea09
Špola ◫ UA 62 Mf21
Spratly Islands ⬱ 85 Qc16
Spreewald ⬱ D 44 Lh20
Sprengisandur ⬱ IS 32 Ka13
Springbok ◫ ZA 110 Ld24
Springfield ◫ USA 122 Dd10
Springfield ◫ USA 123 Fb11
Springfield ◫ USA 123 Fc11
Springfield ◫ USA 123 Fd12
Springfield ◫ USA 121 Gb10
Springs ◫ ZA 110 Mb24
Springsure ◫ AUS 96 Sb23
Srbobran ◫ SR 54 Lk23
Sredec ◫ BG 55 Md24

Sredinnyj hrebet ⬱ RUS 74 Ta07
Srednerusskaja vozvyšennost' ⬱ RUS 59 Mj18
Sremska Mitrovica ◫ SR 54 Lk23
Sremski Karlovci ◫ SR 54 Lk23
Sribne ◫ UA 62 Mg20
Sri Lanka ■ CL 81 Pa17
Srinagar ◫ IND 80 Od12
Stabbursdalen n.p. ⬱ N 23 Mc10
Stachanov ◫ UA 63 Mk21
Stad ⬱ N 24 Lc14
Stade ◫ D 44 Le19
Stadskanaal ◫ NL 37 Ld19
Stafford ◫ GB 35 Kj19
Staked Plain = Llano Estacado ⬱ USA 122 Ed12
Staloluokta ⬱ S 22 Lj12
Staloluokta fjällstation ⬱ S 22 Lj12
Stambolijski ◫ BG 55 Mc24
Stamford ◫ GB 35 Kk19
Stamsund ◫ N 22 Lg11
Stanica Bagaevskaja ◫ RUS 63 Na22
Stanley ⬱ GB 137 Ha29
Stanovoe ◫ RUS 59 Mk19
Stanovoye Nagor'ye ⬱ RUS 73 Qc07
Stanovoy Khrebet ⬱ RUS 75 Ra07
Stanyčno-Luhans'ke ◫ UA 63 Mk21
Staraja Russa ◫ RUS 30 Mf17
Stara Sajmyrzino ◫ RUS 60 Nd18
Stargard Szczeciński ◫ PL 50 Lh19
Starica ◫ RUS 58 Mh17
Starica ◫ RUS 59 Mh19
Starigrad ◫ HR 47 Lj24
Starnberg ◫ D 45 Lf21
Starobil's'k ◫ UA 63 Mk21
Starobin ◫ BY 51 Md19
Starodub ◫ RUS 59 Mg19
Starogard Gdański ◫ PL 50 Lk19
Starojur'evo ◫ RUS 59 Na19
Starokostjantyniv ◫ UA 51 Md21
Starominskaja ◫ RUS 63 Mk22
Starotitarovskaja ◫ RUS 63 Mj23
Starožilovo ◫ RUS 59 Mk18
Stary Dvor ◫ RUS 58 Na17
Staryi Oskol ◫ RUS 59 Mj20
Stary Ivanovka ◫ RUS 60 Nf18
Staryja Darohi ◫ BY 51 Me19
Staryj Bajsarovo ◫ RUS 60 Ng18
Staryj Kulatka ◫ RUS 60 Nd19
Staryj Račejka ◫ RUS 60 Ne19
Staszów ◫ PL 50 Ma20
Stăuceni ◫ MD 55 Me22
Staunton ◫ USA 123 Ga11
Stavanger ◫ N 26 Lc16
Stavre ⬱ S 25 Lh14
Stawiski ◫ PL 51 Mb19
Steamboat Springs ◫ USA 120 Ec10
Steenstrup Gletscher ⬱ DK 119 Ha03

Stefansson Island ⬱ CDN 118 Ec04
Stege ◫ DK 26 Lg18
Steinbach ◫ CDN 120 Fa09
Steine ⬱ N 22 Lh11
Steinkjer ◫ N 24 Lf14
Stellenbosch ◫ ZA 110 Ld25
Stélvio, P.N.delle = Stilfser Joch, N.P. ⬱ I 46 Lf22
Stenay ◫ F 37 Lc21
Stendal ◫ D 44 Lf19
Stenó Andikíthira ⬱ GR 56 Mb28
Stenó Kíthira ⬱ GR 56 Mb27
Stenungsund ◫ S 26 Lf16
Štepivka ◫ UA 59 Mh20
Stepnoe Matjunico ◫ RUS 60 Nd19
Sterling ◫ USA 122 Ed10
Sterlitamak ◫ RUS 72 Nd08
Šternberk ◫ CZ 53 Lj21
Stevenage ◫ GB 35 Kk20
Stewart Crossing ◫ CDN 116 Da06
Stewart Island ⬱ NZ 99 Tb28
Stewart Islands ⬱ SOL 93 Ta20
Steyr ◫ A 52 Lh21
Stilfser Joch, N.P. = Stélvio, P.N.delle ⬱ I 46 Lf22
Stilida ◫ GR 56 Mb26
Stinear, Mount ⬱ 141 Od33
Štip ◫ MK 56 Mb25
Stirling ◫ GB 34 Kj17
Stjørdal ◫ N 24 Lf14
Stockerau ◫ A 52 Lj21
Stockholm ● S 27 Lk16
Stockton ◫ USA 122 Dd11
Stoczek Lukowski ◫ PL 50 Ma20
Stöde ◫ S 25 Lj14
Stødi ⬱ N 22 Lh12
Stoke-on-Trent ◫ GB 35 Kj19
Stokkvågen ◫ N 22 Lg12
Stokmarknes ◫ N 22 Lh11
Stolac ◫ BIH 47 Lj24
Stolin ◫ BY 51 Md20
Stöllet ⬱ S 24 Lg15
Stonehaven ◫ GB 34 Kj17
Stonglandet ◫ N 22 Lh11
Stony Rapids ◫ CDN 120 Ec07
Stony River ◫ USA 116 Ca06
Storå ⬱ S 27 Lh16
Stora Sjöfallets n.p. ⬱ S 22 Lj12
Storavan ⬱ S 25 Lk13
Stordalen ⬱ N 24 Ld14
Store mosse n.p. ⬱ S 26 Lg17
Støren ◫ N 24 Lf14
Storfjorden ⬱ N 22 Lg07
Storfors ⬱ S 27 Lh16
Storforsen ⬱ S 25 Ma13
Storjord ⬱ N 22 Lh12
Storjorda ⬱ N 22 Lg12
Storkerson Peninsula ⬱ CDN 118 Ec04
Storm Bay ⬱ AUS 97 Sb27
Stornoway ◫ GB 34 Kg16
Storožynec' ◫ UA 55 Mc21
Storsjön ⬱ S 25 Lh14
Storuman ⬱ S 25 Lj13
Stovbcy ◫ BY 51 Md19
Støvring ◫ DK 26 Le17
Stowmarket ◫ GB 35 La19
Strabane ◫ GB 33 Kg18
Stradella ◫ I 46 Le23
Strait of Dover ⬱ GB/F 35 La20

Strait of Gibraltar ⬱ E/MA 41 Kh28
Strait of Messina ⬱ I 49 Lh27
Strait of Otranto ⬱ I/AL 49 Lk25
Strait of Belle Isle ⬱ CDN 121 Ha08
Strait of Hormuz ⬱ IR/OM 77 Nd13
Strait of Magellan ⬱ RCH 137 Gb29
Strait of Malacca ⬱ RI/MAL 86 Qa18
Straits of Florida ⬱ USA/C 126 Fd14
Strakonice ◫ CZ 52 Lg21
Straldža ◫ BG 55 Md24
Stralsund ◫ D 44 Lg18
Stranda ⬱ N 24 Ld14
Strängnäs ◫ S 27 Lk16
Stranraer ◫ GB 34 Kh18
Stråšeni ◫ MD 55 Me22
Stratford-upon-Avon ◫ GB 35 Kk19
Straubing ◫ D 45 Lg21
Straumnes ⬱ IS 32 Jj12
Streaky Bay ⬱ AUS 95 Rc25
Strehaia ◫ RO 54 Mb23
Strelča ◫ BG 55 Mc24
Strenči ◫ LV 30 Mc17
Strezovce ◫ SR 54 Ma24
Stříbro ◫ CZ 52 Lg21
Stromness ◫ GB 34 Kj16
Strömsnäsbruk ◫ S 27 Lg17
Strömstad ◫ S 26 Lf16
Strömsund ◫ S 25 Lh14
Ströms Vattudal ⬱ S 25 Lh13
Strumica ◫ MK 56 Mb25
Stryj ◫ UA 53 Mb21
Stryn ⬱ N 24 Ld14
Strzelce Krajeńskie ◫ PL 50 Lh19
Strzelno ◫ PL 50 Lk19
Stugun ⬱ S 25 Lh14
Stung Treng ◫ LAO 84 Qb16
Stupino ◫ RUS 59 Mk18
Sturt ⌇ AUS 94 Rb22
Sturt Stony Desert ⬱ AUS 96 Rd24
Stuttgart ◫ D 45 Le21
Stykkishólmur ◫ IS 32 Jj13
Styr ⌇ BY 51 Md19
Suakin ◫ SUD 107 Md15
Subaşı ◫ TR 78 Me25
Subate ◫ LV 30 Mc17
Subi Besar ⬱ RI 86 Qb18
Subotica ◫ SR 54 Lk22
Suceava ◫ RO 55 Md22
Sucre ● BOL 133 Gc22
Sudak ◫ UA 63 Mh23
Sudan ▶ SUD 107 Mb15
Sudan ⬱ 105 La16
Sudbury ◫ CDN 123 Fd09
Sudbury ◫ GB 35 La19
Sudd ⬱ SUD 109 Mc17
Sudetes ⬱ PL 50 Lh20
Sudislavl' ◫ RUS 58 Na17
Sudogda ◫ RUS 58 Na18
Sudova Vyšnja ◫ UA 53 Mb21
Süd-Shetland-Inseln ⬱ 140 Ha31
Sudža ◫ RUS 59 Mh20
Sue ⌇ SUD 109 Mb17
Suez ◫ ET 107 Mc13
Suez Canal ⌇ ET 107 Mc12
Suffolk ◫ GB 35 La19
Suffolk ◫ USA 123 Ga11
Suğla Gölü ⬱ TR 64 Mf27

Sugoj ⚓ RUS 74 Sd06
Suhiniči ◎ RUS 59 Mh18
Suhl ◎ D 45 Lf20
Suhodol ◎ RUS 60 Nf19
Suide ◎ CHN 82 Qc11
Suihua ◎ CHN 83 Rb09
Šuja ◎ RUS 58 Na17
Sükhbaatar ◻ MNG 82 Qb08
Sukhothai ◎ THA 84 Pd15
Sukkertoppen ◎ DK 119 Hb05
Sukkur ◎ PAK 80 Ob13
Sukomo ◎ J 83 Rc12
Sula ⚓ UA 62 Mg21
Sulawesi ◙ RI 86 Qa19
Sulawesi ◙ RI 87 Ra19
Sulechów ◎ PL 50 Lh19
Sulina ◎ RO 55 Me23
Sulingen ◎ D 44 Le19
Sulitjelma ◙ N 22 Lj12
Sulitjelma ◙ N S 22 Lj12
Sullana ◎ PE 132 Fz19
Sullorssuaq Vaigat ◺ DK 119 Ha04
Sully-sur-Loire ◎ F 38 Lb22
Sulmona ◎ I 47 Lj24
Sultanhanı ◎ TR 65 Mg26
Sulu Archipelago ◙ RP 87 Ra17
Sülüklü ◎ TR 64 Mg26
Sulu Sea ◺ RP 85 Qd17
Sulzberger Ice Shelf ⊿ 140 Cc34
Sumatra ◙ RI 86 Pd18
Šumava ◙ CZ 52 Lg21
Šumava, N.P. ⚲ CZ 52 Lg21
Sumba ◙ RI 87 Qd20
Sumbawa ◙ RI 87 Qd20
Sumbawa Besar ◎ RI 87 Qd20
Sumbawanga ◎ EAT 109 Mc20
Sumbe ◎ ANG 110 Lc21
Sumburgh ◎ GB 34 Kk16
Sumburgh Head ◺ GB 34 Kk16
Sümeg ◎ H 53 Lj22
Šumen ◙ BG 55 Md24
Šumerlja ◎ RUS 60 Na18
Summit Lake ◎ CDN 117 Dd07
Šumperk ◎ CZ 53 Lj21
Sumy ◎ UA 59 Mh20
Sunbury ◎ AUS 97 Sb26
Suncheon ◎ ROK 83 Rb17
Sundarbans ⚲ IND/BD 80 Pb14
Sunda Strait ◺ RI 86 Qb20
Sunday Strait ◺ AUS 94 Ra22
Sunderland ◎ GB 34 Kk18
Sündiken Dağları ◣ TR 64 Mf26
Sundsvall ◎ S 25 Lj14
Sungaidareh ◎ RI 86 Qa19
Sungaipenuh ◎ RI 86 Qa19
Sungurlu ◎ TR 65 Mh25
Sunja ◎ HR 47 Lj23
Sunndalsøra ◎ N 24 Le14
Sunne ◎ S 25 Lh14
Sunnmøre ◙ N 24 Ld14
Sunyani ◎ GH 105 Kd17
Suojarvi ◎ RUS 29 Mg14
Suomenselkä ◙ FIN 28 Mc14
Suomussalmi ◎ FIN 28 Me13
Suonenjoki ◎ FIN 28 Md14
Superior ◎ USA 120 Fb09
Supetar ◎ HR 47 Lj24
Süphan Dağı ◣ TR 66 Nb26
Support Force Glacier ⊿ 140 Hd35

Sur ◎ OM 77 Nd14
Sura ⚓ RUS 60 Na18
Surabaya ◎ RI 87 Qb20
Surat ◎ IND 80 Oc14
Surat Thani ◎ THA 86 Pd17
Suraž ◎ RUS 59 Mg19
Surgères ◎ F 38 Kk22
Surgut ◎ RUS 72 Oc06
Surigao ◎ RP 85 Rb17
Suriname ◻ SME 134 Ha18
Surrey ◙ CDN 122 Dd09
Surskoe ◎ RUS 60 Na18
Surt ◎ LAR 106 Ld12
Surtsey ◙ IS 32 Jk14
Suruç ◎ TR 65 Mk27
Susa ◎ I 46 Ld23
Suşat ◎ RUS 61 Mj27
Suşehri ◎ TR 66 Mk25
Sušice ◎ CZ 52 Lg21
Suslonger ◎ RUS 60 Ne17
Susuman ◎ RUS 74 Sb06
Susurluk ◎ TR 64 Me26
Susz ◎ PL 50 Lk19
Sutjeska, N.P. ⚲ BIH 47 Lk24
Sutlej ⚓ PAK 80 Oc13
Suva ● FIJ 98 Td22
Suvorov ◎ RUS 59 Mj18
Suwałki ◎ PL 51 Mb18
Suzdal' ◎ RUS 58 Na17
Suzhou ◎ CHN 83 Qd12
Suzhou ◎ CHN 83 Ra12
Suzzara ◎ I 46 Lf23
Svalbarðseyri ◎ IS 32 Kb13
Svaljava ◎ UA 53 Mb21
Svaneke ◎ DK 27 Lh18
Svappavaara ◎ S 23 Ma12
Svartå ◎ S 27 Lh16
Svartvik ◎ S 25 Lj14
Svatove ◎ UA 63 Mk21
Svea ◿ 141 Kb33
Svedala ◎ S 26 Lg18
Sveg ◎ S 25 Lh14
Svegssjön ⚓ S 25 Lh14
Svelgen ◎ N 24 Lc15
Svelvik ◎ N 26 Lf16
Svendborg ◎ DK 26 Lf18
Svenes ◎ N 26 Le16
Svenljunga ◎ S 26 Lg17
Svensby ◎ N 22 Lk11
Svenstavik ◎ S 25 Lh14
Sverdlove ◎ UA 62 Mf22
Sverdlovs'k ◎ UA 63 Mk21
Sverdrup Ch. ◺ CDN 118 Fa02
Sverdrup Islands ◙ CDN 118 Fa03
Svetlahorsk ◎ BY 51 Me19
Svetlogorsk ◎ RUS 31 Ma18
Svetlyi Jar ◎ RUS 61 Nc21
Svetogorsk ◎ RUS 28 Me15
Svidník ◎ SK 53 Ma21
Svijaga ⚓ RUS 60 Ne18
Svilengrad ◎ BG 57 Md25
Svir' ⚓ RUS 29 Mf15
Svislač ◎ BY 51 Mc19
Svislač ◎ BY 51 Me19
Svištov ◎ BG 55 Mc24
Svitlovods'k ◎ UA 62 Mg21
Svoge ◎ BG 54 Mb24
Svolvær ◎ N 22 Lh11
Svorkmo ◎ N 24 Le14
Svyati Gory N.P. ⚲ UA 63 Mj21
Swain Reefs ◙ AUS 96 Sc23
Swakopmnd ◎ NAM 110 Lc23
Swan Hill ◎ AUS 97 Sa26
Swan River ◎ CDN 120 Ed08
Swansea ◎ GB 35 Kj20

Swaziland ◻ SD 111 Mc24
Sweden ◻ S 18 Ld06
Sweeney Mountains ◣ 140 Gb33
Swift Current ◎ CDN 120 Ec08
Swindon ◎ GB 35 Kk20
Switzerland ◻ CH 45 Ld22
Syčevka ◎ RUS 58 Mh18
Syców ◎ PL 50 Lj20
Sydney ◻ AUS 97 Sc25
Sydney ◎ CDN 121 Gd09
Syke ◎ D 44 Le19
Sykkylven ◎ N 24 Ld14
Syktyvkar ◎ RUS 72 Nc06
Sylhet ◎ BD 84 Pc14
Sylt ◙ D 44 Le18
Synel'nykove ◎ UA 63 Mh21
Synevyr, N.P. ⚲ UA 53 Mb21
Syötekylä ◎ FIN 28 Md13
Syötteen kansallispuisto ⚲ FIN 28 Md13
Syowa ◿ 141 Md32
Syracuse ◎ USA 123 Ga10
Syrdarja ⚓ UZ 78 Ob10
Syria ◻ SYR 76 Md11
Syrian Desert ◺ SYR 76 Md12
Šyrjajeve ◎ UA 62 Mf23
Šyroke ◎ UA 62 Mg22
Šyšcycy ◎ BY 51 Md19
Syssleback ◎ S 24 Lg15
Syzran' ◎ RUS 60 Ne19
Szarvas ◎ H 53 Ma22
Szczebrzeszyn ◎ PL 51 Mb20
Szczecin ◎ PL 50 Lh19
Szczecinek ◎ PL 50 Lj19
Szczekociny ◎ PL 50 Lk20
Szczuczyn ◎ PL 51 Mb19
Szczytno ◎ PL 50 Ma19
Szécsény ◎ H 53 Lk21
Szeged ◎ H 53 Ma22
Székesfehérvár ◎ H 53 Lk22
Szekszárd ◎ H 53 Lk22
Szentes ◎ H 53 Ma22
Szerencs ◎ H 53 Ma21
Szigetvár ◎ H 53 Lj22
Szolnok ◎ H 53 Ma22
Szombathely ◎ H 52 Lj22
Szprotawa ◎ PL 50 Lh20
Szydłowiec ◎ PL 50 Ma20

T

Taalintehdas = Dalsbruk ◎ FIN 30 Mb15
Tabar Islands ◙ PNG 93 Sc19
Tabas ◎ IR 77 Nd12
Tabasco ◙ MEX 125 Fb15
Tabernas ◎ E 41 Kj27
Tablas ◙ RP 85 Ra16
Tablas de Daimiel, P.N.de las ⚲ E 41 Kj26
Tábor ◎ CZ 52 Lh21
Tabora ◎ EAT 109 Mc20
Tabou ◎ CI 105 Kc18
Tabriz ◎ IR 76 Nb11
Tabuk ◎ KSA 76 Md13
Tabwemasana ◣ VU 98 Tb22
Tabwemasana ◣ VU 98 Tb22
Täby ◎ S 27 Lk16
Tacheng ◎ CHN 79 Pa09
Tachov ◎ CZ 52 Lg21
Tacinskij ◙ RUS 63 Na21
Tacloban ◎ RP 85 Ra16
Tacna ◎ PE 133 Gb22

Tacoma ◎ USA 122 Dd09
Tacuarembo ◎ ROU 136 Ha25
Tadmur ◎ SYR 76 Md12
Tafalla ◎ E 42 Kk22
Tagaj ⚓ RUS 60 Nd18
Taganrog ◎ RUS 63 Mk22
Taganrogskij zaliv ◺ UA/RUS 63 Mk22
Taguatinga ◎ BR 135 Hc22
Tagula Island ◙ PNG 96 Sc21
Tagum ◎ RP 85 Rb17
Tahat ◣ DZ 106 Ld14
Tahoua ◎ RN 105 Lb16
Tahtalı Dağları ◣ TR 65 Mj26
Tai'an ◎ CHN 83 Qd11
Taichung ◎ RC 85 Ra14
Tailai ◎ CHN 83 Ra09
Tailem Bend ◎ AUS 97 Rd26
Tainan ◎ RC 85 Ra14
Taipei ● RC 85 Ra14
Taiping ◎ MAL 86 Qa18
Taitung ◎ RC 85 Ra14
Taiwan ◻ RC 85 Ra14
Taiwan Strait ◺ CHN/RC 85 Qd14
Taiyuan ◎ CHN 82 Qc11
Ta'izz ◎ YE 77 Na16
Tajikistan ◻ TJ 78 Ob11
Tajšet ◎ RUS 73 Pd07
Takahe, Mount ◣ 140 Eb34
Takapuna ◎ NZ 99 Tc26
Takla Makan Desert ◺ CHN 79 Pa11
Takua Pa ◎ THA 86 Pd17
Talaçyn ◎ BY 51 Me19
Talara ◎ PE 132 Fd19
Talata Mafara ◎ WAN 108 Lb16
Talavera de la Reina ◎ E 41 Kh26
Talbus Qi ◎ CHN 82 Qd10
Talca ◎ RCH 136 Gb26
Talcahuano ◎ RCH 137 Gb26
Taldom ◎ RUS 58 Mj17
Taldykorgan ◎ KZ 79 Od09
Taliabu ◙ RI 87 Ra19
Tallahassee ◎ USA 123 Fd12
Tallinn ● EST 30 Mc16
Tallsjö ◎ S 25 Lk13
Tålmaciu ◎ RO 54 Mc23
Talnah ◎ RUS 73 Pb04
Tal'ne ◎ UA 62 Mf21
Talos Dome ◿ 141 Sd33
Talovaja ◎ RUS 61 Na20
Taloyoak ◎ CDN 118 Fb04
Talsi ◎ LV 30 Mb17
Tamala ◙ GH 105 Kd17
Tamala ◎ RUS 61 Nb19
Tamanrasset ◎ DZ 106 Lb14
Tamási ◎ H 53 Lk22
Tamaulipas ◙ MEX 124 Fa14
Tambacounda ◎ SN 105 Kb16
Tambo ◎ AUS 96 Sb23
Tambov ◎ RUS 61 Na19
Tamil Nadu ◙ IND 81 Od16
Tammisaaren saariston kansallispuisto = Ekenäs skärgårds n.p. ⚲ FIN 30 Mb16
Tammisaari = Ekenäs ◎ FIN 30 Mb16
Tampa ◎ USA 123 Fd13
Tampere ◎ FIN 22 Mb15
Tampico ◎ MEX 124 Fa14
Tamworth ◎ AUS 97 Sc25
Tana ⚓ EAK 109 Md19

Tana � VU 98 Tb22
Tana bru ◻ N 23 Me10
Tanahbala ◻ RI 86 Pd19
Tanahmasa ◻ RI 86 Pd19
Tanami Desert ◻ AUS 94 Rc22
Tanana ◻ USA 116 Ca05
Tandil ◻ RA 137 Ha26
Tanega-jima ◻ J 83 Rc12
Tanezrouft ◻ DZ/RMM 104 Kd14
Tanga ◻ EAT 109 Md20
Tanga Islands ◻ PNG 93 Sc19
Tangermünde ◻ D 44 Lf19
Tanggula Shan ◻ CHN 84 Pc12
Tangier ◻ MA 104 Kc11
Tangshan ◻ CHN 83 Qd11
Taninthari ◻ MYA 86 Pd16
Tanjona Babaomby ◻ RM 111 Nb21
Tanjona Masoala ◻ RM 111 Nc22
Tanjona Vilanandro ◻ RM 111 Na22
Tanjona Vohimena ◻ RM 111 Nb24
Tanjung Mangkalihat ◻ RI 87 Qd18
Tanjungpandan ◻ RI 86 Qb19
Tanjung Puting ◻ RI 86 Qb19
Tanjungredeb ◻ RI 87 Qd18
Tanjung Sambar ◻ RI 86 Qb19
Tanjung South ◻ RI 87 Qb19
Tanjung Vals ◻ RI 92 Rd20
Tankavaara ◻ FIN 23 Md11
Tännforsen ◻ S 24 Lg19
Tannu-Ola Range ◻ RUS 79 Pc08
Tanout ◻ RN 106 Lb16
Tanta ◻ ET 107 Mc12
Tan Tan ◻ MA 104 Kb13
Tanumshede ◻ S 26 Lf16
Tanzania ◻ EAT 109 Mc20
Tășnad ◻ RO 54 Mb22
Taormina ◻ I 49 Lh27
Taoudenni ◻ RMM 104 Kd14
Tapa ◻ EST 30 Mc16
Tapachula ◻ MEX 125 Fb16
Tapajos ◻ BR 134 Ha19
Tapini ◻ PNG 92 Sb20
Taquari ◻ BR 135 Ha22
Tara ◻ RUS 72 Oc07
Tara, N.P. ◻ SR 54 Lk24
Taraclia ◻ MD 55 Me22
Tarakan ◻ RI 87 Qd18
Tarancón ◻ E 40 Kj25
Tarapoto ◻ PE 133 Ga20
Tarare ◻ F 39 Lc23
Tarašča ◻ UA 62 Mf21
Tarascon ◻ F 39 Lc24
Tarauacá ◻ BR 133 Gb20
Taraz ◻ KZ 78 Oc10
Tarazona ◻ E 42 Kk25
Tarazona de la Mancha ◻ E 43 Kk26
Tarbagatai Žotasy ◻ KZ 79 Pa09
Tarbert ◻ GB 34 Kg17
Tarbes ◻ F 42 La24
Tarcoola ◻ AUS 95 Rc25
Tarento ◻ MA 104 Kb13
Târgoviște ◻ RO 55 Mc23
Târgoviște ◻ BG 55 Md24
Târgu Jiu ◻ RO 54 Mb23
Târgu Mureș ◻ RO 54 Mc22
Târgu-Neamț ◻ RO 55 Md22

Târgu Ocna ◻ RO 55 Md22
Târgu Secuiesc ◻ RO 55 Md23
Tarhunah ◻ LAR 106 Lc12
Tarifa ◻ E 41 Kh27
Tarija ◻ BOL 136 Gd23
Tarim ◻ YE 77 Nb15
Tarim Basin ◻ CHN 79 Pa11
Taritatu ◻ RI 92 Rd19
Tarlac ◻ RP 85 Ra15
Tarma ◻ PE 133 Ga21
Tárnaby ◻ S 25 Lh13
Tarnobrzeg ◻ PL 51 Ma20
Tarnogród ◻ PL 51 Mb20
Tarnów ◻ PL 50 Ma20
Tarnowskie Góry ◻ PL 50 Lk20
Taroom ◻ AUS 96 Sb24
Taroudannt ◻ MA 104 Kc12
Tarquinia ◻ I 46 Lf24
Tarragona ◻ E 42 La25
Tàrrega ◻ E 42 La25
Tarso Emissi ◻ TCH 106 Ld14
Tarsus ◻ TR 65 Mh27
Tartus ◻ SYR 76 Md12
Tarusa ◻ RUS 59 Mj18
Tarvisio ◻ I 47 Lg22
Tașeli Yaylası ◻ TR 64 Mg27
Tashkent ● UZ 78 Ob10
Taskesken ◻ KZ 79 Pa09
Taşköprü ◻ TR 65 Mh25
Tasman Basin ◻ 97 Sc27
Tasman Bay ◻ NZ 99 Tc27
Tasmania ◻ AUS 97 Sb27
Tasmania ◻ AUS 97 Sb27
Tasman Sea ◻ 97 Sd26
Tașova ◻ TR 65 Mj25
Tassili du Hoggar ◻ DZ 106 Lb14
Tassili N'Ajjer ◻ DZ 106 Lb13
Tata ◻ H 53 Lk22
Tatabánya ◻ H 53 Lk22
Tatanovo ◻ RUS 61 Na19
Tatarbunary ◻ UA 55 Me23
Tatarskiy Proliv ◻ RUS 75 Sa08
Tatarstan ◻ RUS 72 Nc08
Tatarstan ◻ RUS 60 Nf18
Tathlith ◻ KSA 77 Na15
Tatišćevo ◻ RUS 61 Nc20
Tatra Mountains ◻ PL/SK 53 Ma21
Tatra Mountains ◻ PL/SK 53 Lk21
Tatranský národný park ◻ SK 53 Lk21
Tatvan ◻ TR 66 Nb26
Tau ◻ N 26 Lc16
Tauá ◻ BR 134 Hd20
Taubaté ◻ BR 135 Hc23
Tauberbischofsheim ◻ D 45 Le21
Taufkirchen ◻ D 45 Lg21
Taunggyi ◻ MYA 84 Pd14
Taunus ◻ D 44 Le20
Taupo ◻ NZ 99 Td26
Tauragė ◻ LT 31 Mb18
Tauranga ◻ NZ 99 Td26
Tauu Islands ◻ PNG 93 Sd19
Tavas ◻ TR 64 Me27
Tavda ◻ RUS 72 Ob07
Tavernes de la Valldigna ◻ E 43 Kk26
Taveuni ◻ FIJ 98 Td22
Tavoy ◻ MYA 86 Pd16
Tavșanlı ◻ TR 64 Me26
Tawau ◻ RI 87 Qd18
Tawi-Tawi ◻ RP 87 Ra17
Taxkorgan ◻ CHN 78 Od11

Taybad ◻ IR 78 Oa12
Tayma ◻ KSA 76 Md13
Taymyr (Dolgan-Nenets) Autonomous District ◻ RUS 73 Pb04
Taymyr Peninsula ◻ RUS 73 Pc03
Taytay ◻ RP 85 Qd16
Taza ◻ MA 104 Kd12
Tazovskaya guba ◻ RUS 73 Od05
Tazovskij ◻ RUS 73 Od05
Tchibanga ◻ G 108 Lc19
Tczew ◻ PL 50 Lk18
Teaca ◻ RO 54 Mc22
Te Anau ◻ NZ 99 Tb28
Teano ◻ I 49 Lh25
Te Araroa ◻ NZ 99 Td26
Tebessa ◻ DZ 106 Lb11
Tebingtinggi ◻ RI 86 Pd18
Tecate ◻ MEX 122 Ea12
Tecer Dağları ◻ TR 65 Mj26
Tecka ◻ RA 137 Gb27
Tecomán ◻ MEX 124 Ed15
Tecuci ◻ RO 55 Md23
Tegcheng ◻ CHN 84 Pd13
Tegernsee ◻ D 45 Lf22
Tegucigalpa ● HN 125 Fc16
Teheran ● IR 76 Nc11
Tehuacán ◻ MEX 125 Fa15
Tehuantepec Ridge ◻ 124 Fa16
Teignmouth ◻ GB 35 Kj20
Teiuș ◻ RO 54 Mb22
Tejkovo ◻ RUS 58 Na17
Tekirdağ ◻ TR 57 Md25
Tekman ◻ TR 66 Na26
Tel Aviv ◻ IL 107 Mc12
Telč ◻ CZ 52 Lh21
Telefomin ◻ PNG 92 Sa20
Telemark ◻ N 26 Lc19
Telese ◻ I 49 Lh25
Teles Pires ◻ BR 133 Ha20
Telfer ◻ AUS 94 Ra23
Telford ◻ GB 35 Kj19
Telfs ◻ A 45 Lf22
Teller ◻ USA 116 Bc05
Tel'manove ◻ UA 63 Mk22
Telsen ◻ RA 137 Gc27
Teluk Berau ◻ RI 92 Rc19
Teluk Cenderawasih ◻ RI 92 Rd19
Tembenči ◻ RUS 73 Pd05
Temerloh ◻ MAL 86 Qa18
Temirtau ◻ KZ 78 Oc09
Tempio Pausania ◻ I 48 Le25
Temple ◻ USA 123 Fa12
Templin ◻ D 44 Lg19
Temrjuk ◻ RUS 63 Mj23
Temuco ◻ RCH 137 Gb26
Tenasserim ◻ MYA 86 Pd16
Tenby ◻ GB 35 Kh20
Ten Degree Channel ◻ IND 81 Pc17
Tendrara ◻ MA 104 Kd12
Ténéré ◻ RN 106 Lc15
Ténéré du Tafassasset ◻ RN 106 Lc14
Tenerife ◻ E 104 Ka13
Ténès ◻ DZ 104 La11
Teniente Luis Carvajal ◻ 140 Gc32
Tennant Creek ◻ AUS 94 Rc22
Tennessee ◻ USA 123 Fc11
Tenom ◻ MAL 87 Qd17
Teófilo Otoni ◻ BR 135 Hd22
Teofipol ◻ UA 51 Md21
Tepehuanes ◻ MEX 124 Ec13

Tepic ◻ MEX 124 Ec14
Teplice ◻ CZ 52 Lg20
Teploe ◻ RUS 59 Mj19
Tera ◻ RN 105 La16
Téramo ◻ I 47 Lg24
Terbuny ◻ RUS 59 Mk19
Tercan ◻ TR 66 Na26
Terebovlja ◻ UA 51 Mc21
Teren'ga ◻ RUS 60 Ne19
Teresina ◻ BR 134 Hd20
Termachivka ◻ UA 62 Me20
Terme ◻ TR 65 Mj25
Termessos Milli Parkı ◻ TR 64 Mf27
Termiz ◻ UZ 78 Ob11
Térmoli ◻ I 49 Lh24
Ternate ◻ RI 87 Rb18
Terni ◻ I 46 Lg24
Ternitz ◻ A 52 Lj22
Ternopil' ◻ UA 51 Mc21
Terrace ◻ CDN 116 Dc08
Terracina ◻ I 48 Lg25
Terråk ◻ N 24 Lg13
Terra Nova B. ◻ 141 Tc33
Terrassa ◻ E 42 Lb25
Terre Adélie ◻ 141 Rd32
Terre Clarie ◻ 141 Rd32
Terre Haute ◻ USA 123 Fc11
Terschelling ◻ NL 37 Lc19
Teruel ◻ E 43 Kk25
Tervel ◻ BG 55 Md24
Tervo ◻ FIN 28 Md14
Tervola ◻ FIN 23 Mc12
Tessalit ◻ RMM 104 La14
Tete ◻ MOC 111 Mc22
Teteriv ◻ UA 62 Me20
Teterow ◻ D 44 Lg19
Tetijiv ◻ UA 62 Me21
Tetlin Junction ◻ USA 116 Cd06
Tétouan ◻ MA 104 Kc11
Tetovo ◻ MK 56 Ma25
Teuva ◻ FIN 25 Ma14
Texarkana ◻ USA 123 Fb12
Texas ◻ USA 122 Fa12
Texel ◻ NL 37 Lc19
Thaa Atoll ◻ MV 81 Oc18
Thailand ◻ THA 84 Qa15
Thai Nguyen ◻ VN 84 Qb14
Thames ◻ GB 35 La20
Thamun ◻ YE 77 Nc15
Thanh Hóa ◻ VN 84 Qb14
Thanh Pho Ho Chi Minh ◻ VN 84 Qb16
Thar Desert ◻ IND 80 Oc13
Thargomindah ◻ AUS 96 Sa24
Thássos ◻ GR 57 Mc25
Thássos ◻ GR 57 Mc25
Thayatal, N.P. ◻ A 52 Lh21
The Sound ◻ DK/S 26 Lg18
The Calvados Chain ◻ PNG 96 Sc21
The Everglades ◻ USA 123 Fd13
The Johnston Lakes ◻ AUS 95 Ra25
The New Forest ◻ GB 35 Kk20
The Pas ◻ CDN 120 Ed08
Theron Mountains ◻ 140 Jc34
Thessalia ◻ GR 56 Ma26
The Steppe ◻ KZ 78 Oa09
Thetford ◻ GB 35 La19
The Valley ◻ UK 127 Gd15
The Wash ◻ GB 35 La19
Thiel Mountains ◻ 140 Fc36
Thiers ◻ F 38 Lb23

Thiès ☑ SN 105 Ka16
Thiesi ☑ I 48 Le25
Thika ☑ EAK 109 Md19
Thimphu ☀ BHT 80 Pb13
Thio ☑ F 98 Tb23
Thionville ☑ F 37 Ld21
Thira ☑ GR 57 Mc27
Thira = Santorini ☑ GR 57 Mc27
Third Cataract ☑ SUD 107 Mc15
Thirsk ☑ GB 34 Kk18
Thiruvananthapuram ☑ IND 81 Od17
Thisted ☑ DK 26 Le17
Thiva ☑ GR 57 Mc26
Thompson ☑ CDN 120 Fa07
Thomson ☑ AUS 94 Sa23
Thorshavnheiane ▲ 141 Mc33
Thouars ☑ F 38 Kk22
Thrace ☑ GR 57 Md25
Three Gorges Dam ⬗ CHN 85 Qc12
Three Kings Islands ☑ NZ 99 Tc25
Thuir ☑ F 38 Lb24
Thule ☑ DK 118 Gc03
Thun ☑ CH 45 Ld22
Thunder Bay ☑ CDN 120 Fc09
Thüringen ☑ D 44 Lf20
Thüringer Wald ▲ D 45 Lf20
Thurles ☑ IRL 33 Kg19
Thurso ☑ GB 34 Kj16
Thusis ☑ CH 45 Le22
Thwaites Glacier ⬦ 140 Ec34
Thyborøn ☑ DK 26 Le17
Tianjin ● CHN 83 Qd11
Tianjun ☑ CHN 79 Pd11
Tian Shan ▲ KS/CHN 79 Pa10
Tiaret ☑ DZ 104 La11
Tibana ☑ RO 55 Ma22
Tibati ☑ CAM 108 Lc17
Tiber ☑ I 46 Lg24
Tibesti ▲ TCH 106 Ld15
Tibet ☑ CHN 80 Pa12
Tibet ☑ CHN 80 Pb12
Tibilisi ☀ GE 76 Na10
Tibro ☑ S 27 Lh16
Tidaholm ☑ S 27 Lg16
Tierp ☑ S 25 Lj15
Tierra del Fuego ☑ RA 137 Gc29
Tierra del Fuego ☑ RA 137 Gc29
Tietê ☑ BR 135 Hb23
Tighina ☑ MD 55 Me22
Tigris ☑ IRQ 76 Na12
Tihama ☑ YE 77 Na15
Tihoreck ☑ RUS 63 Na23
Tihvin ☑ RUS 58 Mg16
Tihvinskaja grjada ⬙ RUS 58 Mh16
Tiilikkajärven kansallispuisto ⬗ FIN 28 Me14
Tijuana ☑ MEX 122 Ea12
Tikanlik ☑ CHN 79 Pb10
Tikša ☑ RUS 29 Mg13
Tilal an-Nuba ☑ SUD 107 Mc16
Tilburg ☑ NL 37 Lc20
Tilemsi ⬙ RMM 104 La15
Tilos ☑ GR 57 Md27
Tim ☑ RUS 59 Mj20
Timanskij krjaž ⬙ RUS 72 Nb06

Timaru ☑ NZ 99 Tc27
Timaševsk ☑ RUS 63 Mk23
Timber Creek ☑ AUS 94 Rb21
Timimoun ☑ DZ 104 La13
Timişoara ☑ RO 54 Ma23
Timmins ☑ CDN 123 Fd09
Timohino ☑ RUS 58 Mj16
Timor ☑ RI/TLS 87 Rb20
Timor Sea ☑ 87 Rb21
Timor Trough ☑ 87 Rb21
Timošino ☑ RUS 60 Nc17
Timoudi ☑ DZ 104 Kd13
Timrå ☑ S 25 Lj14
Tindouf ☑ DZ 104 Kc13
Tingmiarmiut Fjord ☑ DK 119 Hd06
Tingo Maria ☑ PE 133 Ga20
Tingsryd ☑ S 27 Lh17
Tingvoll ☑ N 24 Le14
Tinos ☑ GR 57 Mc27
Tinos ☑ GR 57 Mc27
Tinputz ☑ PNG 93 Sc20
Tintina ☑ RA 136 Gd24
Tioman ☑ MAL 86 Qa18
Tipperary ☑ IRL 33 Kf19
Tirana ☀ AL 56 Lk25
Tiranë ☀ AL 56 Lk25
Tirapata ☑ PE 133 Gb21
Tiraspol ☑ MD 55 Me22
Tire ☑ TR 57 Md26
Tirebolu ☑ TR 66 Mk25
Tirnavos ☑ GR 56 Mb26
Tirth Raj Prayag ☑ IND 80 Pa13
Tirupati ☑ IND 81 Od16
Tiszaföldvár ☑ H 53 Ma22
Tiszavasvári ☑ H 53 Ma22
Titan Dome ▲ 141 Tb36
Titisee-Neustadt ☑ D 45 Le22
Titran ☑ N 24 Le14
Titule ☑ RDC 109 Mb18
Titusville ☑ USA 123 Fd13
Tiverton ☑ GB 35 Kj20
Tivoli ☑ I 48 Lg25
Tizimin ☑ MEX 125 Fc14
Tiznit ☑ MA 104 Kc13
Tjačiv ☑ UA 53 Mb21
Tjörn ☑ S 26 Lf17
Tjøtta ☑ N 24 Lg13
Tjumen' ☑ RUS 72 Ob07
Tlaquepaque ☑ MEX 124 Ed14
Tlaxcala ☑ MEX 124 Fa15
Tlemcen ☑ DZ 104 Kd12
Toamasina ☑ RM 111 Nb22
Tobago ☑ TT 127 Gd16
Toba Kakar Range ▲ PAK 78 Ob12
Tobermory ☑ GB 34 Kg17
Tobi ☑ PAL 92 Rc18
Toblach = Dobbiaco ☑ I 46 Lg22
Toboali ☑ RI 86 Qb19
Tobol ☑ RUS 72 Ob07
Toboli ☑ RI 87 Ra19
Tobol'sk ☑ RUS 72 Ob07
Tocantins ⬙ BR 134 Hc21
Tocantins ⬙ BR 134 Hc21
Tocopilla ☑ RCH 136 Gb23
Todi ☑ I 46 Lg24
Töfsingdalens n.p. ⬗ S 24 Lg14
Toft ☑ GB 34 Kk15
Toftlund ☑ DK 26 Le18
Togo ☑ TG 105 La17
Toholampi ☑ FIN 28 Mc14
Toivakka ☑ FIN 28 Md14
Tokaj ☑ H 53 Ma21

Tokara Islands ☑ J 83 Rb13
Tokarevka ☑ RUS 61 Na19
Tokat ☑ TR 65 Mj25
Tokmak ☑ UA 63 Mh22
Toko ☑ RUS 74 Rb12
Toktogul ☑ KS 78 Oc10
Tokuno-jima ☑ J 83 Rb13
Tokushima ☑ J 83 Rc12
Tokyo ☀ J 83 Rd11
Tôlanaro ☑ RM 111 Nb24
Toledo ☑ E 40 Kh26
Toledo ☑ USA 123 Fd10
Toledo Bend Res. ⬙ USA 123 Fb12
Tolentino ☑ I 47 Lg24
Tolga ☑ N 24 Lf14
Toliara ☑ RM 111 Na23
Tolitoli ☑ RI 87 Ra18
Tol'jatti ☑ RUS 60 Ne19
Tolmezzo ☑ I 47 Lg22
Tolosa ☑ E 41 Kj24
Toluca ☑ MEX 124 Fa15
Tomakivka ☑ UA 63 Mh22
Tomakomai ☑ J 83 Sa10
Tomaniivi ▲ FIJ 98 Td22
Tomar ☑ P 40 Kf26
Tomarovka ☑ RUS 59 Mj20
Tomarza ☑ TR 66 Mh26
Tomašpil' ☑ UA 62 Me21
Tomaszów Lubelski ☑ PL 51 Mb20
Tomaszów Mazowiecki ☑ PL 50 Ma20
Tombouctou ☑ RMM 105 Kd15
Tomelilla ☑ S 26 Lg18
Tomelloso ☑ E 41 Kj26
Tomești ☑ RO 55 Ma22
Tomini ☑ RI 87 Ra18
Tomislavgrad ☑ BIH 47 Lj24
Tomkinson Ranges ▲ AUS 94 Rb24
Tomma ▲ N 22 Lg12
Tom Price ☑ AUS 94 Qd23
Tomsk ☑ RUS 73 Pb07
Tomtor ☑ RUS 75 Sa06
Tønder ☑ DK 26 Le18
Tonga ☑ TO 98 Ua22
Tonga Islands ☑ TO 98 Ua23
Tongatapu ☑ TO 98 Ub23
Tongatapu Group ☑ TO 98 Ua23
Tonghe ☑ CHN 83 Rb09
Tongliao ☑ CHN 83 Ra10
Tongling ☑ CHN 85 Qd12
Tonkino ☑ RUS 60 Nd17
Tonlé Sap ☑ K 84 Qa16
Tonneins ☑ F 38 La23
Tonnerre ☑ F 38 Lb22
Tönning ☑ D 44 Le18
Tonopah ☑ USA 122 Ea11
Tonšaevo ☑ RUS 60 Nd17
Tønsberg ☑ N 26 Lf16
Tonstad ☑ N 26 Ld16
Tonya ☑ TR 66 Mk25
Tooele ☑ USA 122 Eb10
Toowoomba ☑ AUS 96 Sc24
Topeka ⊡ USA 123 Fa11
Topliţa ☑ RO 55 Mc22
Topola ☑ SK 54 Ma23
Topol'čany ☑ SK 53 Lk21
Topozero ☑ RUS 29 Mg13
Top Springs ☑ AUS 94 Rc22
Torbali ☑ TR 57 Md26
Tordesillas ☑ E 40 Kh26
Töre ☑ S 19 Mb13
Töreboda ☑ S 27 Lh16
Torekov ☑ S 26 Lg17
Toreno ☑ E 40 Kg24

Torgun ⬙ RUS 61 Nd20
Torhout ☑ B 37 Lb20
Torino ☑ I 46 Ld23
Torit ☑ SUD 109 Mc18
Tornal'a ☑ SK 53 Ma21
Torneälven ⬙ S 23 Ma12
Torneträsk ☑ S 22 Lk11
Torneträsk ⬙ S 22 Lk11
Tornio ☑ FIN 23 Mb13
Törökszentmiklós ☑ H 53 Ma22
Toronto ● CDN 123 Ga10
Toropec ☑ RUS 58 Mf17
Tororo ☑ EAU 109 Mc18
Torpo ☑ N 24 Le15
Torpshammar ☑ S 25 Lj14
Torquay ☑ GB 35 Kj20
Torre de la Higuera ☑ E 41 Kg27
Torre del Greco ☑ I 49 Lh25
Torredonjimeno ☑ E 41 Kj27
Torrelaguna ☑ E 42 Kj25
Torrelavega ☑ E 40 Kh24
Torremolinos ☑ E 41 Kh27
Torrent ☑ E 43 Kk26
Torréon ☑ MEX 124 Ed13
Torres ☑ BR 135 Hb24
Torres Islands ☑ VU 98 Tb21
Torres Strait ☑ AUS 96 Sa21
Torres Trench ☑ VU 98 Tb21
Torrevieja ☑ E 43 Kk27
Torrijos ☑ E 41 Kh26
Tørring ☑ N 24 Lf13
Toronuson kansallispuisto ⬗ FIN 22 Mb15
Torsby ☑ S 24 Lg15
Tórshavn ⊡ DK 32 Kg14
Tortona ☑ I 46 Le23
Tortosa ☑ E 42 La25
Torul ☑ TR 66 Mk25
Toruń ☑ PL 50 Lk19
Toržkovskaja grjada ⬙ RUS 58 Mf17
Toržok ☑ RUS 58 Mh17
Tosbotn ☑ N 24 Lg13
Tosno ☑ RUS 30 Mf16
Tostado ☑ RA 136 Gd24
Tosya ☑ TR 65 Mh25
Totana ☑ E 43 Kk27
Tottori ☑ J 83 Rc11
Touba ☑ CI 105 Kc17
Touggourt ☑ DZ 106 Lb12
Touho ☑ F 98 Tb23
Toul ☑ F 37 Lc21
Toulépleu ☑ LB 105 Kc17
Toulon ☑ F 39 Lc24
Toulouse ☑ F 42 La24
Toungoo ☑ MYA 84 Pd15
Touraine ⬙ F 38 La22
Tournon-sur-Rhône ☑ F 39 Lc23
Tournus ☑ F 39 Lc22
Touros ☑ BR 134 Ja20
Tours ☑ F 38 La22
Tovarkovskij ☑ RUS 59 Mk19
Townsville ☑ AUS 96 Sb22
Toyama ☑ J 83 Rd11
Trail ☑ CDN 122 Ea09
Traku istorinis n.p. ⬗ LT 31 Mc18
Tralee ☑ IRL 33 Kf19
Trän ☑ BG 54 Mb24
Tranås ☑ S 27 Lh16
Trancas ☑ RA 136 Gc24
Tranemo ☑ S 26 Lg17
Trang ☑ THA 86 Pd17
Trangan ☑ RI 92 Rc20
Transantarctic Mountains ▲ 140 Jc35

Transhimalaya CHN 80 Pa12
Transylvania RO 54 Mc22
Transylvanian Alps RO 54 Mc23
Trápani I 48 Lg26
Trappstegsforsarna S 25 Lh13
Trârza RIM 105 Ka15
Trás os Montes P 40 Kg25
Trat THA 84 Qa16
Traunstein D 45 Lg22
Travemünde D 44 Lf19
Traverse City USA 123 Fc10
Travnik BIH 47 Lj23
Třebíč CZ 52 Lh21
Trebinje BIH 47 Lk24
Treblinka PL 50 Ma19
Treinta y Tres ROU 136 Hb25
Trekljano BG 54 Mb24
Trelew RA 137 Gc27
Trelleborg S 26 Lg18
Tremp E 42 La24
Trenčín SK 53 Lk21
Trento I 46 Lf22
Trenton USA 121 Gb10
Tres Arroyos RA 137 Gd26
Três Lagoas BR 135 Hb23
Tresticklans n.p. S 26 Lf16
Tretten N 24 Lf15
Treviso I 46 Lf22
Trieben A 52 Lh22
Trier D 45 Ld21
Trieste I 47 Lg23
Triglav SLO 47 Lg22
Triglavski narodni park SLO 47 Lg22
Trignac F 36 Kj22
Trikala GR 56 Ma26
Trim IRL 33 Kg19
Trincomalee CL 81 Pa17
Trinidad BOL 133 Gd21
Trinidad C 126 Ga14
Trinidad TT 127 Gd16
Trinidad USA 122 Ed11
Trinidad and Tobago TT 127 Gd16
Trinity USA 123 Fa12
Trinity Peninsula 140 Ha31
Tripoli LAR 106 Lc12
Tripoli RL 76 Md12
Tripoli GR 56 Mb27
Tripolitania LAR 106 Lc12
Tripura IND 84 Pc14
Trnava SK 53 Lj21
Trobriand Islands PNG 93 Sc20
Troekurovo RUS 59 Mk19
Trofors N 24 Lg13
Trogir HR 47 Lj24
Troglav HR/BIH 47 Lj24
Troick RUS 78 Oa08
Troickaja RUS 63 Mk23
Trois-Rivières CDN 121 Gb09
Trojan BG 55 Mc24
Trollhättan S 26 Lg16
Tromsø N 22 Lk11
Trøndelag N 24 Lf14
Trondheim N 24 Lf14
Trondheimsfjorden N 24 Lf14
Trosa S 27 Lj16
Trosna RUS 59 Mh19
Trostan' RUS 59 Mg19
Trostjanskij RUS 61 Nb20

Trouville-sur-Mer F 36 La21
Troyes F 37 Lc21
Trstenik SR 54 Ma24
Trubčevsk RUS 59 Mg19
Trubetčino RUS 59 Mk19
Trujillo E 40 Kh26
Trujillo HN 125 Fc15
Trujillo PE 133 Ga20
Trujillo YV 132 Gb17
Truk Islands FSM 93 Sc17
Truro CDN 121 Gd09
Truro GB 35 Kh20
Trustrup DK 26 Lf17
Trutnov CZ 52 Lj18
Trzciel PL 50 Lh19
Trzebinia PL 50 Lj20
Tsetserleg MNG 82 Qa09
Tshikapa RDC 108 Ma20
Tshuapa RDC 108 Ma19
Tsiafajavona RM 111 Nb22
Tsiroanomandidy RM 111 Nb22
Tsugaru Strait J 83 Sa10
Tsumeb NAM 110 Ld22
Tuam IRL 33 Kf19
Tuangku RI 86 Pd18
Tuapse RUS 63 Mk23
Tubarão BR 135 Hc24
Tubbataha Reef RP 87 Qd17
Tubek Tub-Karagan KZ 76 Nc10
Tübingen D 45 Le21
Tubruq LAR 106 Ma12
Tucano BR 135 Ja21
Tuchola PL 50 Lj19
Tuchów PL 50 Ma21
Tucker Glacier 141 Tb33
Tucson USA 122 Eb12
Tucumán RA 136 Gc24
Tucupita YV 132 Gd17
Tucuruí BR 134 Hc19
Tudela E 42 Kk24
Tufi PNG 93 Sb20
Tuguegarao RP 85 Ra15
Tui E 40 Kf24
Tujmazy RUS 60 Ng18
Tuktoyatuk CDN 116 Db05
Tukums LV 30 Mb17
Tukuyu EAT 109 Mc20
Tula RUS 58 Mj18
Tulancingo MEX 124 Fa14
Tulare RUS 55 Me23
Tul'čyn UA 62 Me21
Tuloma RUS 72 Mc05
Tulsa USA 123 Fa11
Tuluá CO 132 Ga18
Tulun RUS 82 Qa08
Tuma RUS 58 Na18
Tumaco CO 132 Ga19
Tumbes PE 132 Fd19
Tumeremo YV 132 Gd17
Tumkur IND 81 Od16
Tunceli TR 66 Mc26
Tunduma EAT 109 Mc20
Tunduru EAT 111 Md21
Tungting Lake CHN 85 Qc13
Tunis TN 106 Lc11
Tunisia TN 106 Lb12
Tunja CO 132 Gb17
Tupelo USA 123 Fc12
Tura RUS 73 Qa06
Turan Lowland TM/UZ 78 Oa10
Turayf KSA 76 Md12
Turbat PAK 77 Oa13
Turbo CO 132 Ga17

Turda RO 54 Mb22
Turek PL 50 Lk19
Turfan Depression CHN 79 Pb10
Turgajskoje plato KZ 78 Oa08
Turgutlu TR 57 Md26
Türi EST 30 Mc16
Turiaçu BR 134 Hc19
Turijs'k UA 51 Mc20
Turin I 46 Ld23
Turiščevo RUS 59 Mh19
Turka UA 53 Mb21
Turkistan UZ 78 Ob10
Turkmenabat TM 78 Oa11
Türkmenbaşhi KZ 76 Nc10
Turkmenistan TM 78 Nd11
Türkoğlu TR 65 Mj27
Turks and Caicos Islands UK 127 Gb14
Turks Island UK 127 Gb14
Turku = Åbo FIN 22 Mb15
Turkwel EAK 109 Md18
Turnhout B 37 Lc20
Turnov CZ 52 Lh20
Turnu Măgurele RO 55 Mc24
Turpan CHN 79 Pb10
Turuhansk RUS 73 Pb04
Turzovka SK 53 Lk21
Tuscaloosa USA 123 Fc12
Tuscany I 46 Lf24
Tutaev RUS 58 Mk17
Tutak TR 66 Nb26
Tuticorin IND 81 Od17
Tutrakan BG 55 Md24
Tuttlingen D 45 Le22
Tutuala TLS 87 Rb20
Tuusniemi FIN 28 Me14
Tuusula FIN 28 Mc15
Tuva RUS 79 Pd08
Tuvalu TUV 98 Td20
Tuvalu Islands TUV 98 Td20
Tuvana-i-Ra FJI 98 Ua23
Túxpan MEX 125 Fa14
Tuxtepec MEX 125 Fa15
Tuxtla Gutiérrez MEX 125 Fb15
Tuy Hoa VN 85 Qb16
Tuža RUS 60 Nd17
Tuz Gölü TR 65 Mg26
Tuzla BIH 47 Lk23
Tvååker S 26 Lg17
Tvedestrand N 26 Le16
Tver' RUS 58 Mh17
Twilight Cove AUS 95 Rb25
Twin Falls USA 122 Eb10
Tyler USA 123 Fa12
Tynset N 24 Lf14
Tyresta n.p. S 27 Lj16
Tyrrhenian Sea I 48 Lf25
Tyškivka UA 62 Mf21

U

Uapés BR 132 Gc18
Uatuma BR 132 Ha19
Ubangi RCB 108 Ld18
Úbeda E 41 Kj26
Uberaba BR 135 Hc22
Uberlândia BR 134 Ha18
Uberlândia BR 135 Hc22
Ubon Ratchathani THA 84 Qa15
Ucayali PE 133 Gb20

Uckfield GB 35 La20
Udačnyj RUS 73 Qc05
Udaipur IND 80 Oc14
Udbina HR 47 Lh23
Uddevalla S 26 Lf16
Uddheden S 26 Lg16
Uddjaure S 25 Lj13
Údine I 47 Lg22
Udmurtia RUS 72 Nc07
Udomlja RUS 58 Mh17
Udon Thani THA 84 Qa15
Ueckermünde D 44 Lh19
Uele RDC 109 Ma18
Uèlen RUS 74 Ub05
Uelzen D 44 Lf19
Ufa RUS 72 Nd07
Ufa RUS 72 Nd08
Uganda EAU 109 Mc18
Ugep WAN 108 Lb17
Uglegorsk RUS 75 Sa09
Uglič RUS 58 Mk17
Ugol'noye Kopi RUS 74 Td06
Ugra RUS 59 Mh18
Uğurlu TR 64 Mf27
Uğurlu Baraji TR 65 Mj25
Uherské Hradiště CZ 53 Lj21
Uhniv UA 51 Mb20
Uhta RUS 72 Nc06
Uithuizen NL 37 Ld19
Ujae Atoll MH 93 Tb17
Ujar RUS 73 Pc07
Ujelang Atoll MH 93 Ta17
Újfehértó H 53 Ma22
Ujście Warty, P.N. PL 50 Lh19
Ujung Pandang RI 87 Qc19
Ukiah USA 122 Dd11
Ukmergé LT 31 Mc18
Ukraine UA 21 Mb08
Ulaangom MNG 79 Pc09
Ulan Bator MNG 82 Qb09
Ulanhot CHN 83 Ra09
Ulan-Udè RUS 82 Qb08
Ulaş TR 65 Mj26
Ulcinj CG 56 Lk25
Ulefoss N 26 Le16
Uliastay MNG 79 Pd09
Ulindi RDC 109 Ma19
Ulithi Atoll FSM 92 Rd16
Ul'janovka UA 62 Mf21
Uljanovsk RUS 60 Ne18
Ullapool GB 34 Kh17
Ullared S 26 Lg17
Ullatti S 23 Ma12
Ulm D 45 Lf21
Ulricehamn S 26 Lg17
Ulu RUS 75 Rb06
Ulubat Gölü TR 57 Me25
Ulubey TR 64 Me26
Uluçınar TR 65 Mh27
Uludağ Milli Parkı TR 57 Me25
Uludağ Tepe TR 57 Me25
Ulukışla TR 65 Mh27
Ulvik N 24 Ld15
Ulvsvåg N 22 Lh11
Umag HR 47 Lg22
Uman' UA 62 Mf21
Umanak Fjord DK 119 Ha04
Umboi Island PNG 92 Sb20
Umbria I 46 Lg24
Umeå S 25 Ma14
Umeälven S 25 Lj13
Umm al Aranib LAR 106 Lc12
Umm Dafag SUD 108 Ma16
Umm Hisin UAE 77 Nc14

Umm Sa'ad ☐ LAR 106 Ma12
Umtata ☐ ZA 110 Mb25
Umuarama ☐ BR 135 Hb23
Unai ☐ BR 135 Hc22
Unalakleet ☐ USA 116 Bd06
Unari ☐ FIN 23 Mc12
Undersåker ☐ S 24 Lg14
Undva neem ☒ EST 30 Ma16
Uneča ☐ RUS 59 Mg19
Ungava Bay ☐ CDN 121 Gc07
Ungheni ☐ MD 55 Md22
Ungwana Bay ☒ EAK 109 Na19
Uniejów ☐ PL 50 Lk20
Unimak Island ☒ USA 116 Bd08
United Kingdom ■ GB 35 La19
United Arab Emirates ■ UAE 77 Nc14
United States ■ USA 122 Fa11
Unpongkor ☐ VU 98 Tb22
Unst ☒ GB 34 Kk15
Unteres Odertal, N.P. ☒ D 44 Lh19
Ünye ☐ TR 65 Mj25
Upata ☐ YV 132 Gd17
Upernavik ☐ DK 119 Ha04
Upington ☐ ZA 110 Ma24
Upper Karoo ☒ ZA 110 Ma25
Upper Peninsula ☒ USA 120 Fc09
Uppland ☒ S 25 Lj15
Uppsala ☐ S 27 Lj16
Ural ☒ KZ 76 Nc09
Ural ☒ RUS 72 Nd08
Ural Mountains ▲ RUS 19 Nd06
Ural Mountains ▲ RUS 72 Oa07
Urandi ☐ BR 135 Hd21
Uranium City ☐ CDN 120 Ec07
Ura-Vajgurore ☐ AL 56 Lk25
Urbino ☐ I 46 Lg24
Uren ☐ RUS 60 Nc17
Urganch ☐ UZ 78 Oa10
Ürgüp ☐ TR 65 Mh26
Urho Kekkosen kansallispuisto ☒ FIN 23 Me11
Urjupinsk ☐ RUS 61 Na20
Urla ☐ TR 57 Md26
Urmary ☐ RUS 60 Nc18
Urmia ☐ IR 76 Nb11
Uroševac ☐ SR 56 Ma24
Uruapan d.Pr. ☐ MEX 124 Ed15
Urubamba ☐ PE 133 Gb21
Urucará ☐ BR 134 Ha19
Uruçui ☐ BR 134 Hd20
Uruguai ☐ BR 135 Hb24
Uruguaiana ☐ BR 136 Ha24
Uruguay ☐ ROU 136 Ha25
Uruguay ☐ ROU/RA 136 Ha24
Ürümqi ☒ CHN 79 Pb10
Ürünlü ☐ TR 64 Mf27
Urussu ☐ RUS 60 Ng18
Urziceni ☐ RO 55 Md23
Ušačy ☐ BY 31 Me18
Usadišče ☐ RUS 58 Mg16
Uşak ☐ TR 64 Me26
Ušakovskoe ☐ RUS 74 Ua04
Usambara Mountains ▲ EAT 109 Md19
Usarp Mountains ▲ 141 Ta33
Uschodni ☐ BY 51 Md19

Usedom ☒ D 44 Lh18
Ushuaia ☐ RA 137 Gc29
Usf-Kamčatsk ☐ RUS 74 Ta07
Usf-Kujga ☐ RUS 74 Rd04
Usf-Maja ☐ RUS 75 Rc06
Usman' ☐ RUS 59 Mk19
Usol'e-Sibirskoe ☐ RUS 82 Qa08
Usovo ☐ RUS 61 Nb19
Ussel ☐ F 38 Lb23
Ussurijsk ☐ RUS 83 Rc10
Usta ☒ RUS 60 Nd17
Ust'-Cil'ma ☐ RUS 72 Nc05
Ust'-Ilimsk ☐ RUS 73 Qa07
Ústí nad Labem ☐ CZ 52 Lh20
Ustiprača ☐ BIH 47 Lk24
Ustjurt Plateau ☒ KZ 78 Nd10
Ustjužna ☐ RUS 58 Mj16
Ustka ☐ PL 50 Lj18
Ust'-Kut ☐ RUS 73 Qb07
Ust'-Labinsk ☐ RUS 63 Mk23
Ust'-Luga ☐ RUS 30 Me16
Ust'-Nera ☐ RUS 74 Sa06
Ust'-Omčug ☐ RUS 74 Sb06
Ust'-Ordynsk Buryat Autonomous District ☐ RUS 82 Qa08
Ust'-Ordynskij ☐ RUS 82 Qa08
Ustrzyki Dolne ☐ PL 51 Mb21
Ustyluh ☐ RUS 51 Mc20
Usu ☐ CHN 79 Pa10
Ust-Varga ☐ RUS 72 Na06
Usvjaty ☐ RUS 31 Mf18
Utah ☒ USA 122 Eb11
Utajärvi ☐ FIN 28 Md13
Utansjö ☐ S 25 Lj14
Utena ☐ LT 31 Mc18
Utica ☐ USA 123 Ga10
Utiel ☐ E 43 Kk26
Utrecht ☐ NL 37 Lc19
Utrera ☐ E 41 Kh27
Utsjoki ☐ FIN 23 Md11
Uttaranchal ☐ IND 80 Cd12
Uttar Pradesh ☐ IND 80 Pa13
Utupua ☒ SOL 98 Tb21
Uummannaq ☐ DK 118 Gc03
Uummannarsuaq ☒ DK 119 Hd07
Uurainen ☐ FIN 28 Mc14
Uusikaupunki = Nystadt ☐ FIN 25 Ma15
Uvarovo ☐ RUS 61 Nb20
Uvs Nuur ☒ MNG 79 Pc08
Uyuni ☐ BOL 136 Gc23
Uzangwa Range ☒ EAT 109 Md20
Uzbekistan ☒ UZ 78 Oa10
Uzerche ☐ F 38 Lb23
Uzès ☐ F 39 Lc24
Uzgen ☐ KS 78 Oc10
Užhorod ☐ UA 53 Mb21
Užice ☐ SR 54 Lk24
Uzlovaja ☐ RUS 59 Mk19
Užovka ☐ RUS 60 Nc18
Üzümlü ☐ TR 66 Mk26
Uzunköprü ☐ TR 57 Md25
Uzyn ☐ UA 62 Mf21

V

Vaalimaa ☐ FIN 28 Md15
Vaalriver ☒ ZA 110 Mb24
Vaasa ☐ FIN 25 Ma14
Vác ☐ H 53 Lk22
Vacaria ☐ BR 135 Hb24

Vadheim ☐ N 24 Lc15
Vadodara ☐ IND 80 Oc14
Vadsø ☐ N 23 Me11
Vaduz ■ FL 45 Le22
Vadvetjåkka n.p. ☒ S 22 Lk11
Værøy ▲ N 22 Lg12
Vågaholmen ☐ N 22 Lg12
Vågåmo ☐ N 24 Le15
Vaganski vrh ▲ HR 47 Lh23
Vägsele ☐ S 25 Lk13
Vaiaku ● TUV 98 Td20
Vaitupu ☒ TUV 98 Td20
Vakhkebir ☐ TR 66 Ma25
Valandovo ☐ MK 56 Mb25
Valašské Meziříčí ☐ CZ 53 Lj21
Vålberg ☐ S 26 Lg16
Val d'Agri e Lagonegrese, P.N. ☒ I 49 Lj25
Valdaisky N.P. ☒ RUS 58 Mg17
Valdaj ☐ RUS 58 Mg17
Valdayskaya Vozvyshennost' ☒ RUS 58 Mg17
Valdemarsvik ☐ S 27 Lj16
Valdemoro ☐ E 40 Kj25
Valdepeñas ☐ E 41 Kj26
Valdez ☐ USA 116 Cc06
Valdivia ☐ RCH 137 Gb26
Val d'Or ☐ CDN 121 Ga09
Valdosta ☐ USA 123 Fd12
Valea lui Mihai ☐ RO 54 Mb22
Valença ☐ BR 135 Ja21
Valence ☐ F 39 Lc23
València ☐ E 43 Kk26
Valencia ☒ YV 127 Gc16
Valenciennes ☐ F 37 Lb20
Valentine ☐ USA 122 Ed10
Våler ☐ N 24 Lf15
Valera ☐ YV 132 Gb17
Valevåg ☐ N 26 Lc16
Valga ☐ EST 30 Md17
Val Grande, P.N.della ☒ I 46 Le22
Valka ☐ LV 30 Mc17
Valkeakoski ☐ FIN 28 Mc15
Valkmusan kansallispuisto ☒ FIN 28 Md15
Valky ☐ UA 63 Mh21
Valkyrjedomen ▲ 141 Md33
Valladolid ☐ E 40 Kh25
Valladolid ☐ MEX 125 Fc15
Valle ☐ N 26 Ld16
Valle d'Aosta ☒ I 46 Ld23
Valle de la Pascua ☐ YV 132 Gc17
Valledupar ☐ CO 127 Gb16
Vallejo ☐ USA 122 Dd11
Vallenar ☐ RCH 136 Gc24
Vallentuna ☐ S 27 Lk16
Valls ☐ E 42 La25
Vallsta ☐ S 25 Lj15
Valmiera ☐ LV 30 Mc17
Valognes ☐ F 36 Kk21
Valøy ☐ N 24 Lf13
Valožyn ☐ BY 31 Md18
Valparaíso ☐ RCH 136 Gb25
Valréas ☐ F 39 Lc23
Valset ☐ N 24 Le14
Valsjöbyn ☐ S 25 Lh13
Valujki ☐ RUS 59 Mk20
Valverde del Camino ☐ E 41 Kg27
Vâmhus ☐ S 25 Lh15
Vammala ☐ FIN 22 Mb15
Van ☐ TR 76 Na11
Van ☐ TR 66 Nb26

Vanavara ☐ RUS 73 Qa06
Vancouver ☒ CDN 122 Dd09
Vancouver Island ☒ CDN 116 Dc09
Vanda ☐ 141 Tb34
Vanda = Vantaa ☐ FIN 28 Mc15
Vanderhoof ☐ CDN 117 Dd08
Van Diemen Gulf ☒ AUS 94 Rc21
Vänern ☒ S 26 Lg16
Vänersborg ☐ S 26 Lg16
Vangaindrano ☐ RM 111 Nb23
Van Gölü ☒ TR 76 Na11
Vangunu ☒ SOL 93 Sd20
Van Horn ☐ USA 122 Ed12
Vanikolo ☒ SOL 98 Tb21
Vanimo ☐ PNG 92 Sa19
Vanino ☐ RUS 75 Sa09
Vänju Mare ☐ RO 54 Mb23
Vanna ☒ N 22 Lk10
Vannareid ☒ N 22 Lk10
Vännäs ☐ S 25 Lk14
Vannes ☐ F 36 Kj22
Vanoise, P.N.de la ☒ F 39 Ld23
Vanrhynsdorp ☐ ZA 110 Ld25
Vansbro ☐ S 25 Lh15
Vantaa = Vanda ☐ FIN 28 Mc15
Vanttauskoski ☐ FIN 23 Md12
Vanua Balavu ☒ FJI 98 Ua22
Vanua Lava ☒ VU 98 Ta21
Vanua Levu ☒ FIJ 98 Td22
Vanuatu ■ VU 98 Ta21
Vanvikan ☐ N 24 Lf14
Vara ☐ S 26 Lg16
Varanasi ☐ IND 80 Pa13
Varangerbotn ☐ N 23 Me10
Varangerfjorden ☒ N 23 Mf10
Varangerhalvøya ▲ N 23 Me10
Varaždin ☐ HR 52 Lj22
Varazze ☐ I 46 Le23
Varberg ☐ S 26 Lg17
Varde ☐ DK 26 Le18
Vardø ☐ N 23 Mf10
Varel ☐ D 44 Le19
Varennes-sur-Allier ☐ F 38 Lb22
Vareš ☐ I 46 Le23
Vårgårda ☐ S 26 Lg16
Varkaus ☐ FIN 28 Md14
Varmahlíð ☒ IS 32 Ka13
Värmland ☒ S 26 Lg16
Varna ☒ BG 55 Md24
Värnamo ☐ S 27 Lh17
Varto ☐ TR 66 Na26
Varva ☐ UA 62 Mg20
Várzea Grande ☐ BR 135 Ha22
Vásárosnamény ☐ H 53 Mb21
Vasil'evo ☐ RUS 60 Ne18
Vasjuganskaja ravnina ☒ RUS 73 Od07
Vasknarva ☐ EST 30 Md16
Vaslui ☐ RO 55 Md22
Vassilikó ☐ GR 56 Mb26
Västansjö ☐ S 25 Lh13
Västerås ☐ S 27 Lj16
Västerbotten ☒ S 25 Ma13
Västerhaninge ☐ S 27 Lk16
Västervik ☐ S 27 Lj17
Vasto ☐ I 47 Lh24
Västra Ämtervik ☐ S 26 Lg16
Vasylivka ☐ UA 63 Mh22
Vasyl'kiv ☐ UA 62 Mf20
Vasyl'kivka ☐ UA 63 Mj21

Vasyščeve – Vitória da Conquista

Vasyščeve ☐ UA 63 Mj21
Vatican City ◼ V 48 Lg25
Vatnajökull ☒ IS 32 Kb13
Vatoa ◉ FJI 98 Ua22
Vatra Dornei ☐ RO 55 Mc22
Vatulele ◉ FIJ 98 Td22
Vatutine ☐ UA 62 Mf21
Vaucouleurs ☐ F 37 Lc21
Vaughn ☐ USA 122 Ec12
Vavkavysk ☐ BY 51 Mc19
Växjö ☐ S 27 Lh17
Vechta ☐ D 44 Le19
Vedea ☐ RO 55 Mc24
Vedrovo ☐ RUS 58 Nb17
Vega ☐ N 24 Lf13
Vegamót ☐ IS 32 Jj13
Vegaøyan ☐ N 24 Lf13
Vejdelevka ☐ RUS 59 Mk20
Vejen ☐ DK 26 Le18
Vejle ☐ DK 26 Le18
Velenje ☐ SLO 47 Lh22
Veles ☒ MK 56 Ma25
Velestíno ☐ GR 56 Mb26
Vélez Blanco ☐ E 41 Kj27
Vélez-Málaga ☐ E 41 Kh27
Velikaja Guba ☐ RUS 29 Mh14
Velikie Luki ☐ RUS 30 Mf17
Veliki Novosilka ☐ UA 63 Mj22
Veliki Preslav ☐ BG 55 Md24
Veliki Zdenci ☐ HR 47 Lj23
Veliko Tărnovo ☐ BG 55 Mc24
Velimlje ☐ CG 54 Lk24
Veliž ☐ RUS 59 Mf18
Vel'ke Kapušany ☐ SK 53 Mb21
Velké Meziříčí ☐ CZ 52 Lh21
Vella Lavella ☐ SOL 93 Sd20
Velletri ☐ I 48 Lg25
Vel'sk ☐ RUS 72 Na06
Velyka Lepetycha ☐ UA 62 Mg22
Velyka Pysarivka ☐ UA 59 Mh20
Velyki Dederkaly ☐ UA 51 Md21
Velykyj Burluk ☐ UA 63 Mj21
Vemb ☐ DK 26 Le17
Vemdalen ☐ S 24 Lg14
Venable Ice Shelf ☐ 140 Fc33
Venado Tuerto ☐ RA 136 Gd25
Vendée ☐ F 38 Kk22
Vendôme ☐ F 36 La22
Venec ☐ BG 55 Md24
Véneto ☐ I 46 Lg23
Venev ☐ RUS 59 Mk18
Venèzia ◉ I 46 Lg23
Venezuela ◼ YV 132 Gc17
Venice ◉ I 46 Lg23
Venjan ☐ S 24 Lg15
Venlo ☐ NL 37 Ld20
Vennesla ☐ N 26 Ld16
Ventimiglia ☐ I 46 Ld24
Ventspils ☐ LV 30 Ma17
Vera ☐ E 43 Kk27
Vera ☐ RA 136 Gd24
Veracruz ☒ MEX 125 Fa15
Veracruz ☐ MEX 125 Fa15
Veraval ☐ IND 80 Oc14
Verbania ☐ I 46 Le23
Vercelli ☐ I 46 Le23
Verchnjadzvinsk ☐ BY 31 Md18
Verchnie Syn'ovydne ☐ UA 53 Mb21

Verchn'odniprovs'k ☐ UA 62 Mh21
Verdalsøra ☐ N 24 Lf14
Verde ☐ BR 135 Ha21
Verden (Aller) ☐ D 44 Le19
Verdun ☐ F 37 Lc21
Vereeniging ☐ ZA 110 Mb24
Verhneimbatsk ☐ RUS 73 Pb06
Verhnetulomskij ☐ RUS 23 Mg11
Verhnetulomskoe Vodohranilišče ☐ RUS 23 Mf11
Verhnezejskaja ravnina ☐ RUS 75 Rb08
Verhnij Baskunčak ☐ RUS 61 Nd21
Véria ☐ GR 56 Mb25
Verín ☐ E 40 Kg25
Verinsko ☐ BG 54 Mb25
Verkhoyanskiy Mountains ☒ RUS 74 Rb05
Vermont ☐ USA 121 Gb10
Vernadsky ☐ 140 Gc32
Verneuil-sur-Avre ☐ F 36 La21
Vernon ☐ CDN 117 Ea08
Vernon ☐ F 36 La21
Verona ☐ I 46 Lf23
Versailles ☐ F 37 Lb21
Vertelim ☐ RUS 60 Nc18
Vertijivka ☐ UA 59 Mf20
Vervins ☐ F 37 Lb21
Ves'egonsk ☐ RUS 58 Mj16
Vesele ☐ UA 63 Mh22
Veselí nad Lužnicí ☐ CZ 52 Lh21
Veselovskoe vodohranilišče ☐ RUS 63 Na22
Veselynove ☐ UA 62 Mf22
Vešenskaja ☐ RUS 61 Na21
Vesoul ☐ F 39 Ld22
Vesterålen ☒ N 22 Lh11
Vesterli ☐ N 22 Ln12
Vestfjorden ☐ N 22 Lg12
Vestmannaeyjar ☒ IS 32 Jk14
Vestnes ☐ N 24 Ld14
Vestvågøy ☒ N 22 Lg11
Vesuvio ▲ I 49 Lh25
Veszprém ☐ H 53 Lj22
Vetlanda ☐ S 27 Lh17
Vetluga ☒ RUS 60 Nc17
Vetluga ☒ RUS 60 Nc17
Vevelstad = Forvika ☐ N 24 Lg13
Vezirköprü ☐ TR 65 Mh25
Vi ☐ S 25 Lj14
Viana do Castelo ☐ P 40 Kf25
Viangchan ◼ LAO 84 Qa15
Viareggio ☐ I 46 Lf24
Viborg ☐ DK 26 Le17
Vibo Valéntia ☐ I 49 Lj26
Vic ☐ E 42 Lb25
Vicenza ☐ I 46 Lf23
Vichada ☒ CO 132 Gb18
Vichy ☐ F 38 Lb22
Victor Harbor ☐ AUS 97 Rd26
Victoria ☐ AUS 97 Sa26
Victoria ☐ CDN 122 Dd09
Victoria ☐ M 49 Lh27
Victoria ☐ RCH 137 Gb26
Victoria ☐ SY 103 Nb10
Victoria ◼ USA 125 Fa13
Victoria de Durango ☐ MEX 124 Ed14
Victoria Falls ☒ ZW 110 Mb22
Victoria Island ☒ CDN 118 Eb04

Victoria Land ☒ 141 Tb33
Victoria Strait ☒ CDN 118 Ed05
Victoria West ☐ ZA 110 Ma25
Victor, Mount ▲ 141 Mc33
Vičuga ☐ RUS 58 Na17
Videle ☐ RO 55 Mc23
Vidin ☐ BG 54 Mb24
Vidra ☐ RO 55 Md23
Vidsel ☐ S 25 Ma13
Vidzy ☐ BY 31 Md18
Viedma ☒ RA 137 Gd27
Vielha ☐ E 42 La24
Vienna ☒ A 52 Lj21
Vienne ☒ F 38 La22
Vienne ☐ F 39 Lc23
Vientiane ◼ LAO 84 Qa15
Vierzon ☐ F 38 Lb22
Vieste ☐ I 49 Lj25
Vietas ☐ S 22 Lk12
Vietnam ◼ VN 85 Qb15
Viet Tri ☐ VN 84 Qb14
Vigan ☐ RP 85 Ra15
Vigevano ☐ I 46 Le23
Vignola ☐ I 46 Lf23
Vigo ☐ E 40 Kf24
Vihanti ☐ FIN 28 Mc13
Viiala ☐ FIN 22 Mb15
Viitasaari ☐ FIN 28 Mc14
Vijayawada ☐ IND 81 Pa15
Vík ☐ IS 32 Ka14
Vikajärvi ☐ FIN 23 Md12
Vikersund ☐ N 26 Le16
Vikna ☐ N 24 Lf13
Vikos-Aoos N.P. ☐ GR 56 Ma26
Vikran ☐ N 22 Lk11
Viksøyri ☐ N 24 Ld15
Vila Franca de Xira ☐ P 40 Kf26
Vilalba = Villalba ☐ E 40 Kg24
Vila Nova de Foz Côa ☐ P 40 Kg24
Vila-real ☐ E 43 Kk26
Vila Real ☐ P 40 Kg25
Vila Real de Santo António ☐ P 41 Kg27
Vilejka ☐ BY 31 Md18
Vilhelmina ☐ S 25 Lj13
Vilhena ☐ BR 133 Gd21
Viljandi ☐ EST 30 Mc16
Viljuj ☒ RUS 75 Ra06
Viljujsk ☐ RUS 75 Ra06
Viljujskoe plato ☒ RUS 73 Qc05
Viljujskoe vdhr. ☒ RUS 73 Qc06
Vilkaviškis ☐ LT 31 Mb18
Vilkacillo ☐ E 41 Kj26
Villach ☐ A 52 Lg22
Villacidro ☐ I 48 Le26
Villafranca di Verona ☐ I 46 Lf23
Villahermosa ☒ MEX 125 Fb15
Villalba = Vilalba ☐ E 40 Kg24
Villa María ☐ RA 136 Gd25
Villamartín ☐ E 41 Kh27
Villa Montes ☐ BOL 136 Gd23
Villandraut ☐ F 38 Kk23
Villanueva de Córdoba ☐ E 41 Kh26
Villanueva de la Serena ☐ E 41 Kh26
Villanueva de los Infantes ☐ E 41 Kj26
Villapalacios ☐ E 41 Kj26
Villareal de los Infantes = Vila-real ☐ E 43 Kk26

Villarrobledo ☐ E 41 Kj26
Villa Velha ☐ BR 135 Hd23
Villavicencio ☒ CO 132 Gb18
Villaviciosa ☐ E 40 Kh24
Villedieu-les-Poêles ☐ F 36 Kk21
Villefranche-de-Rouergue ☐ F 38 Lb23
Villefranche-sur-Saône ☐ F 39 Lc23
Villena ☐ E 43 Kk26
Villeneuve-sur-Lot ☐ F 38 La23
Villingen-Schwenningen ☐ D 45 Le21
Vilnius ☒ LT 31 Mc18
Vil'njans'k ☐ UA 63 Mh22
Vil'nohirs'k ☐ UA 62 Mg22
Vilppula ☐ FIN 28 Mc14
Vilsandi rahvuspark ☐ EST 30 Ma16
Vil'šany ☐ UA 63 Mh20
Vilsbiburg ☐ D 45 Lg21
Vilshofen ☐ D 45 Lg21
Vimianzo ☐ E 40 Kf24
Vimmerby ☐ S 27 Lh17
Viña del Mar ☐ RCH 136 Gb25
Vincennes Bay ☐ 141 Qb32
Vindeln ☐ S 25 Lk13
Vindhya Range ☒ IND 80 Od14
Vindrej ☐ RUS 60 Nb18
Vinh ☐ VN 84 Qb15
Vinica ☐ MK 56 Mb25
Vinkovci ☐ HR 47 Lk23
Vinnycja ☐ UA 62 Me21
Vinson Massif ▲ 140 Fd34
Vinstra ☐ N 24 Le15
Vişeu de Sus ☐ RO 54 Mc22
Vişina ☐ RO 55 Mc24
Vire ☐ F 36 Kk21
Virginha ☐ BR 135 Hc23
Virginia ☐ USA 120 Fb09
Virginia ☐ USA 123 Ga11
Virginia Beach ☐ USA 123 Ga11
Virgin Islands ☒ UK 127 Gd15
Virgin Islands ☒ USA 127 Gd15
Virihaure ☐ S 22 Lj12
Virovitica ☐ HR 47 Lj23
Virrat ☐ FIN 19 Mb14
Virserum ☐ S 27 Lh17
Virtsu ☐ EST 30 Mb16
Vis ☒ HR 47 Lj23
Visaginas ☐ LT 31 Md18
Visalia ☐ USA 122 Ea11
Visayas ☒ RP 85 Ra16
Visby ☐ S 27 Lk17
Viscount Melville Sound ☐ CDN 118 Ec04
Višegrad ☐ BIH 47 Lk24
Vishakhapatnam ☐ IND 81 Pa15
Vissefjärda ☐ S 27 Lh17
Vistula ☒ PL 50 Ma20
Vištytis ☐ LT 31 Mb18
Vitebsk ☐ BY 31 Mf18
Viterbo ☐ I 46 Lg24
Vitiaz II Deep ☒ TO 98 Ub23
Vitiaz III Deep ☒ NZ 99 Ua25
Vitiaz Strait ☒ PNG 92 Sb20
Vitíchi ☐ BOL 136 Gc23
Viti Levu ☒ FIJ 98 Td22
Vitim ☐ RUS 82 Qc08
Vitória ☒ BR 135 Hd23
Vitória Seamounts ☒ 135 Ja23
Vitória da Conquista ☐ BR 135 Hd21

Vitória de Santo Antão – Western Desert

Vitória de Santo Antão ▢ BR
134 Ja20
Vitoria-Gasteiz ▢ E 42 Kj24
Vitré ▢ F 36 Kk21
Vitry-le-François ▢ F 37 Lc21
Vitteaux ▢ F 39 Lc22
Vittel ▢ F 37 Lc21
Vittória ▢ I 49 Lh27
Vittorio Véneto ▢ I 46 Lg23
Viv ↖ RUS 73 Pd05
Viveiro ▢ E 40 Kg24
Vizianagaram ▲ IND 81 Pa15
Vizille ▢ F 39 Lc23
Vjartsilja ▢ RUS 29 Mf14
Vjatka ▢ RUS 72 Nc07
Vjatka ▢ RUS 60 Nf17
Vjatskoje Poljany ▢ RUS
60 Nf17
Vjatskoe ▢ RUS 58 Na17
Vjaz'ma ▢ RUS 59 Mh18
Vjazniki ▢ RUS 58 Nb17
Vladikavkaz ▢ RUS 76 Na10
Vladikavkaz ▢ RUS 76 Na10
Vladimir ▢ RUS 58 Na17
Vladivostok ▢ RUS 83 Rc10
Vlasenica ▢ BIH 47 Lk23
Vlašim ▢ CZ 52 Lh21
Vlasotince ▢ SR 54 Mb24
Vlieland ▢ NL 37 Lc19
Vlissingen ▢ NL 37 Lb20
Vlorë ▢ AL 56 Lk25
Vodlozersky N.P. ▣ RUS
29 Mj14
Vodňany ▢ CZ 52 Lh21
Voghera ▢ I 46 Le23
Voi ▢ EAK 109 Md19
Voiron ▢ F 39 Lc23
Vojens ▢ DK 26 Le18
Vojinka ▢ UA 62 Mg23
Vojnica ▢ RUS 28 Mf13
Vojnika ▢ BG 55 Md24
Vojvodina ↖ SR 54 Lk23
Volcán Antofalla ▲ RA 136
Gc24
Volcán Cayambe ▲ EC
132 Ga19
Volcán Chimborazo ▲ EC
132 Ga19
Volcán Cotopaxi ▲ EC
132 Ga19
Volcán Cumbal ▲ CO 132
Ga18
Volcán Domuyo ▲ RA 137
Gb26
Volcán Lanin ▲ RCH/RA
137 Gb26
Volcán Llullaillaco ▲ RCH
136 Gc23
Volcán Llullaillaco ▲ RCH/
RA 136 Gc23
Volcán Ollagüe ▲ BOL
136 Gc23
Volcán Puracé ▲ CO 132
Ga18
Volcán Sangay ▲ EC 132
Ga19
Volčki ▢ RUS 61 Na19
Volda ▢ RUS 29 Mj14
Volga ▢ RUS 58 Mk17
Volga ↖ RUS 21 Nb07
Volgogradskoe Vodohranilišče
↖ RUS 61 Nc20
Volgorečensk ▢ RUS 58
Na17
Volhov ▢ RUS 30 Mf16
Volhov ↖ RUS 30 Mg16
Völkermarkt ▢ A 52 Lh22
Volksrust ▢ ZA 110 Mb24
Volnovacha ▢ UA 63 Mj22

Voločanka ▢ RUS 73 Pc04
Voločys'k ▢ UA 51 Md21
Volodarka ▢ UA 62 Me21
Volodarsk ▢ RUS 60 Nb17
Volodymyrec' ▢ UA 51 Md20
Volodymyr-Volyns'kyj ▢ UA
51 Mc20
Vologda ▢ RUS 58 Mk16
Volokolamsk ▢ RUS 58 Mh17
Volokonovka ▢ RUS 59 Mj20
Voloma ▢ RUS 29 Mf14
Vólos ▢ GR 56 Mb26
Volosovo ▢ RUS 30 Me16
Volotovo ▢ RUS 59 Mk20
Volovec' ▢ UA 53 Mb21
Vol'sk ▢ RUS 61 Nd19
Volta Redonda ▢ BR 135
Hd23
Volterra ▢ I 46 Lf24
Volžsk ▢ RUS 60 Ne18
Volžskij ▢ RUS 61 Nc21
Vónitsa ▢ GR 56 Ma26
Vopnafjörður ▢ IS 32 Kc13
Vopnafjörður ▢ IS 32 Kc13
Vordingborg ▢ DK 26 Lf18
Vøringsfossen ▣ N 24 Ld15
Vorkuta ▢ RUS 72 Oa05
Vormsi ▢ EST 30 Mb16
Vorona ▢ RUS 61 Nb19
Voronet ▢ RO 55 Mc22
Voronež ▢ RUS 59 Mk20
Vorotynec ▢ RUS 60 Nc17
Vorožba ▢ UA 59 Mh20
Vorpommersche
Boddenlandschaft, N.P. ▣
D 44 Lg18
Vorskla ↖ UA 63 Mh21
Vorsma ▢ RUS 60 Nb18
Võru ▢ EST 30 Md17
Vosges ↖ F 37 Ld21
Voskresensk ▢ RUS 58 Mk18
Voskresenskoe ▢ RUS
58 Mj17
Voskresenskoe ▢ RUS
60 Nc17
Voss ▢ N 24 Ld15
Vostok ▢ 141 Ob34
Vouliagméni ▢ GR 57 Mb27
Vouzela ▢ P 40 Kf25
Vouziers ▢ F 37 Lc21
Vovčans'k ▢ UA 59 Mj20
Voznesens'k ▢ UA 62 Mf22
Voznesenskoe ▢ RUS 60
Nb18
Vraca ▢ BG 54 Mb24
Vraćanski Balkan, N.P. ▣ BG
54 Mb24
Vrádijivka ▢ UA 62 Mf22
Vranov nad Topl'ou ▢ SK
53 Ma21
Vrigstad ▢ S 27 Lh17
Vrises ▢ GR 57 Mc28
Vrlika ▢ HR 47 Lj24
Vršac ▢ SR 54 Ma23
Vryburg ▢ ZA 110 Ma24
Vsevoložsk ▢ RUS 29 Mf15
Vukovar ▢ HR 47 Lk23
Vulcănești ▢ MD 55 Me23
Vuollerim ▢ S 23 Ma12
Vuottas ▢ S 23 Ma12
Vuranggo ▢ SOL 93 Sd20
Vurnary ▢ RUS 60 Nd18
Vybor ▢ RUS 30 Me17
Vyborg ▢ RUS 28 Me15
Vyčegda ↖ RUS 72 Nb06
Vygoniči ▢ RUS 59 Mh19
Vygozero ▢ RUS 29 Mh14
Vyksa ▢ RUS 58 Nb18
Vylkove ▢ UA 55 Me23

Vynnyky ▢ UA 51 Mc21
Vypolzovo ▢ RUS 58 Mg17
Vyrica ▢ RUS 30 Mf16
Vyša ⊟ RUS 61 Nb19
Vyšhorod ▢ UA 62 Mf20
Vyškov ▢ CZ 53 Lj21
Vyšnij Voloček ▢ RUS 58
Mh17
Vysoké Mýto ▢ CZ 53 Lj21
Vysokovsk ▢ RUS 58 Mj17
Vytegra ▢ RUS 29 Mj15
Vyžnycja ▢ UA 55 Mc21

W

Wabe Gestro ↖ ETH 109
Na17
Wabe Shebele Wenz ↖ ETH
109 Na17
Wąbrzeźno ▢ PL 50 Lk19
Wachau ⊟ S 42 Lh21
Waco ▢ USA 123 Fa12
Wädenswil ▢ CH 45 Le22
Wadi al-Milk ↖ SUD 107 Mb15
Wadi ar Ru'ays ↖ LAR
106 Ld13
Wadi Halfa ▢ SUD 107 Mc14
Wadi Huwar ↖ SUD 107 Mb15
Wadi Zazamt ↖ LAR 106
Lc12
Wad Madani ▢ SUD 107 Mc16
Wagga Wagga ▢ AUS 97
Sb26
Wagin ▢ AUS 95 Qd25
Wagrowiec ▢ PL 50 Lj19
Wahai ▢ RI 87 Rb19
Wahiawa ▢ USA 117 Cb35
Waidhofen an der Thaya ▢
A 52 Lh21
Waidhofen an der Ybbs ▢ A
52 Lh22
Waigeo ▢ RI 92 Rb18
Waimea ▢ USA 117 Cc35
Waingapu ▢ RI 87 Ra20
Waipara ▢ NZ 99 Td27
Wakefield ▢ GB 35 Kk19
Wakkanai ▢ J 75 Sa09
Walachia ⊟ RO 55 Mc23
Wałbrzych ▢ PL 50 Lj20
Wałcz ▢ PL 50 Lj19
Wales ▢ USA 116 Bc05
Walgett ▢ AUS 97 Sb25
Walgreen Coast ⊟ 140 Ed33
Walker Mountains ▲ 140
Fa33
Wallaroo ▢ AUS 97 Rd25
Walla Walla ▢ USA 122 Ea09
Wallis and Futuna ▢ F
98 Ua21
Walpole ▢ AUS 95 Qd25
Walsall ▢ GB 35 Kk19
Walsrode ▢ D 44 Le19
Walvis Bay ⊟ NAM 110 Lc23
Walvis Bay ▢ NAM 110 Lc23
Wamba ▢ RDC 108 Ld20
Wanganui ▢ NZ 99 Td26
Wangaratta ▢ AUS 97 Sb26
Wangen ▢ D 45 Le22
Wanparti ▢ IND 81 Od15
Wan Xian ▢ CHN 84 Qb12
Warburton ▢ AUS 96 Rd24
Ware ↖ CDN 116 Dc07
Waregem ▢ B 37 Lb20
Waren ▢ D 44 Lg19
Waren ▢ RI 92 Rd19
Warka ▢ PL 50 Ma20
Warminster ▢ GB 35 Kj20

Warnemünde ▢ D 44 Lg18
Warrego ↖ AUS 96 Sb24
Warrenton ▢ ZA 110 Ma24
Warri ▢ WAN 108 Lb17
Warri ▢ WAN 108 Lb17
Warrington ▢ GB 35 Kj19
Warrnambool ▢ AUS 97 Sa26
Warsaw ● PL 50 Ma19
Warstein ▢ D 44 Le20
Warszawa ● PL 50 Ma19
Warta ▢ PL 50 Lk20
Waru ▢ RI 92 Rc19
Warwick ▢ AUS 96 Sc24
Wasa ▢ 141 Kb33
Washington ▢ USA 122 Dd09
Washington D.C. ● USA
123 Ga11
Waskaganish ▢ CDN 121
Ga08
Wasserburg ▢ D 45 Lg21
Watampone ▢ RI 87 Ra19
Watarais ▢ PNG 92 Sb20
Waterberg ▲ NAM 110 Ld23
Waterford ▢ IRL 33 Kg19
Waterloo ▢ USA 123 Fb10
Watertown ▢ USA 123 Fa10
Watertown ▢ USA 123 Ga10
Watson Lake ▢ CDN 116
Dc06
Wau ▲ PNG 92 Sb20
Wau ▢ SUD 109 Mb17
Wauchope ▢ AUS 94 Rc23
Wausau ▢ USA 123 Fc10
Wavre ▢ B 37 Lc20
Wawa ▢ CDN 123 Fd09
Waw al Kabir ▢ LAR 106
Ld13
Waycross ▢ USA 123 Fd12
Waza ▢ CAM 108 Lc16
Wearhead ▢ GB 34 Kj18
Weber Basin ⊟ RI 92 Rc20
Webi Jubba ↖ SP 109 Na18
Weddell Sea ⊟ 140 Hb33
Wegorzewo ▢ PL 50 Ma18
Węgrów ▢ PL 51 Mb19
Weida ▢ D 45 Lg20
Weiden ▢ D 45 Lg21
Weifang ▢ CHN 83 Qd11
Weihai ▢ CHN 83 Ra11
Weimar ▢ D 44 Lf20
Weipa ▢ AUS 96 Sa21
Weißwasser ▢ D 44 Lh20
Wejherowo ▢ PL 50 Lk18
Weldiya ▢ ETH 109 Md16
Welkom ▢ ZA 110 Mb24
Wellesley Islands ⌒ AUS
96 Rd22
Wellington ● NZ 99 Tc27
Wellington Channel ⊟ CDN
118 Fb03
Wells ▢ USA 122 Eb10
Wels ▢ A 52 Lh21
Welshpool ▢ GB 35 Kj19
Wendo ▢ ETH 109 Md17
Wentworth ▢ AUS 97 Sa25
Wenzhou ▢ CHN 85 Ra13
Wesel ▢ D 44 Ld20
Wessel Islands ⌒ AUS
96 Rd21
West Bengal ▢ IND 80 Pb14
West Caroline Basin ⊟ PAL
92 Rd18
Westerland ▢ D 44 Le18
Western Australia ▢ AUS
94 Qd24
Western Desert ◁ ET 107
Mb13

Western Ghats IND 81 Oc15
Western Sahara MA 104 Ka14
Western Sayan Mountains RUS 79 Pc08
Westerstede D 44 Ld19
West Falkland GB 137 Gd29
West Fayu Island FSM 92 Sb17
West Ice Shelf 141 Pa32
West Indies 126 Ga14
Weston-super-Mare GB 35 Kj20
West Palm Beach USA 123 Fd13
Westport IRL 33 Kf19
Westport NZ 99 Tc27
West Siberian Plain RUS 72 Ob06
West Virginia USA 123 Fd11
West Wyalong AUS 97 Sb25
West Yellowstone USA 122 Eb10
Wetar RI 87 Rb20
Wete EAT 109 Md20
Wetzlar D 45 Le20
Wevok USA 116 Bc05
Wewak PNG 92 Sa19
Wexford IRL 33 Kg19
Weybridge GB 35 Kk20
Weyburn CDN 120 Ed09
Weyer Markt A 52 Lh22
Weymouth GB 35 Kj20
Whangarei NZ 99 Tc26
Wharton, Mount 141 Ta35
Wha Ti CDN 117 Ea06
Wheeling USA 123 Fd10
Whitby GB 35 Kk18
Whitchurch GB 35 Kj19
White Bay CDN 121 Ha08
White Cliffs AUS 97 Sa25
Whitehaven GB 34 Kj18
Whitehorse CDN 117 Da06
White Nile SUD 109 Mc16
White Sea RUS 72 Md05
White Volta GH 105 Kd17
Whithorn GB 34 Kh19
Whitmore Mountains 140 Ec35
Whyalla AUS 97 Rd25
Wichita USA 123 Fa11
Wichita Falls USA 122 Fa12
Wick GB 34 Kj16
Wicklow IRL 33 Kg19
Wicklow Mountains N.P. IRL 33 Kg19
Wieleń PL 50 Lj19
Wieliczka PL 50 Ma21
Wielkopolski P.N. PL 50 Lj19
Wieluń PL 50 Lk20
Wien A 52 Lj21
Wiener Neustadt A 52 Lj22
Wiesbaden D 45 Le21
Wigan GB 35 Kj19
Wigierski P.N. PL 51 Mb18
Wilcannia AUS 97 Sa25
Wildeshausen D 44 Le19
Wildspitze A 45 Lf22
Wilhelm II Land 141 Pb33
Wilhelmshaven D 44 Le19
Wilkes Land 141 Rc32
Wilkins Ice Shelf 140 Gb33
Wilhelmstad NL 127 Gc16
Williams Lake CDN 117 Dd08

Williamson Glacier 141 Qd32
Williston USA 120 Ed09
Williston Lake CDN 117 Dd07
Wilmington USA 123 Ga12
Wilson Hills 141 Sd32
Wiluna AUS 94 Ra24
Winburg ZA 110 Mb24
Winchester GB 35 Kk20
Windhoek NAM 110 Ld23
Windorah AUS 96 Sa24
Windsor CDN 123 Fd10
Windward Islands 127 Gc16
Winfield USA 123 Fa11
Winnemucca USA 122 Ea10
Winnipeg CDN 120 Fa09
Winona USA 123 Fb10
Winslow USA 122 Eb11
Winston-Salem USA 123 Fd11
Winterberg D 44 Le20
Winterthur CH 45 Le22
Winton AUS 96 Sa23
Wirth Peninsula 140 Fd33
Wisbech GB 35 La19
Wisconsin USA 123 Fb10
Wisconsin Range 140 Dd36
Wiseman USA 116 Ca05
Wisła PL 50 Lk21
Wismar D 44 Lf19
Wittenberge D 44 Lf19
Wittenoom AUS 94 Qd23
Wittingen D 44 Lf19
Wittlich D 45 Ld21
Wittstock D 44 Lg19
Witu Islands PNG 93 Sb19
Witwatersrand ZA 110 Mb24
Władysławowo PL 50 Lk18
Włocławek PL 50 Lk19
Włodawa PL 51 Mb20
Włoszczowa PL 50 Lk20
Wokam RI 92 Rc20
Woldegk D 44 Lg19
Woleai Atoll FSM 92 Sa17
Wolfsberg A 52 Lh22
Wolfsburg D 44 Lf19
Wolgast D 44 Lg18
Woliński P.N. PL 50 Lh19
Wollaston Lake CDN 120 Ed07
Wollaston Lake CDN 120 Ed07
Wollaston Peninsula CDN 118 Ea04
Wollongong AUS 97 Sc25
Wołów PL 50 Lj20
Wolsztyn PL 50 Lj19
Wolvega NL 37 Ld19
Wonju ROK 83 Rb11
Wonsan PRK 83 Rb11
Woodlark Island PNG 93 Sc20
Woomera AUS 97 Rd25
Wooramel Roadhause AUS 94 Qc24
Worcester GB 35 Kj19
Worcester ZA 110 Ld25
Worchester USA 121 Gb10
Wörgl A 52 Lg22
Workington GB 34 Kj18
World Park 141 Tc34
Worms D 45 Le21
Worthington USA 123 Fa10
Wotho Atoll MH 93 Tb16
Wotu RI 87 Ra19

Wrangel Island RUS 74 Ua04
Wrangell USA 117 Db07
Wrexham GB 35 Kj19
Wrigley Gulf 140 Dc33
Wrocław PL 50 Lj20
Wronki PL 50 Lj19
Września PL 50 Lj19
Wschowa PL 50 Lj20
Wubin AUS 95 Qd25
Wuhai CHN 82 Qb11
Wuhan CHN 85 Qc12
Wu Jiang CHN 84 Qb13
Wukari WAN 108 Lb17
Wuliang Shan CHN 84 Qa14
Wuling Shan CHN 84 Qb13
Wunstorf D 44 Le19
Wuppertal D 44 Ld20
Würzburg D 45 Le21
Wuvulu Island PNG 92 Sa19
Wuwei CHN 84 Qa11
Wuxi CHN 83 Ra12
Wuyi Shan CHN 85 Qd14
Wuzhou CHN 85 Qc14
Wyk D 44 Le18
Wyndham AUS 94 Rb22
Wyoming USA 120 Ec10
Wyszków PL 50 Ma19

X

Xàbia E 43 La26
Xai-Xai MOC 111 Mc23
Xalapa MEX 125 Fa15
Xam Neua LAO 84 Qa14
Xánthi GR 57 Mc25
Xiaguan CHN 84 Qa13
Xiamen CHN 85 Qd14
Xi'an CHN 82 Qc12
Xiangfan CHN 82 Qc12
Xichang CHN 84 Qa13
Xigazê CHN 80 Pb13
Xilinhot CHN 82 Qc10
Xinduqiao CHN 84 Qa12
Xingtai CHN 82 Qc11
Xingu  BR 134 Hb21
Xining CHN 82 Qa11
Xinyang CHN 85 Qc12
Xique-Xique BR 134 Hd21
Xuanwei CHN 84 Qa13
Xuchang CHN 82 Qc12
Xuejiadao CHN 83 Ra11
Xuyong CHN 84 Qb13
Xuzhou CHN 83 Qd12

Y

Ya'an CHN 84 Qa13
Yablonovyy Range  RUS 82 Qc08
Yahyalı TR 65 Mh26
Yakeshi CHN 82 Ra09
Yakima USA 122 Dd09
Yakima USA 122 Dd09
Yako BF 105 Kd16
Yaku-jima J 83 Rc12
Yakutat USA 117 Da07
Yakutia RUS 73 Qc05
Yalgoo AUS 95 Qd24
Yalova TR 57 Me25
Yalta UA 63 Mh23
Yalvaç TR 64 Mf26
Yamagata J 83 Sa11

Yamal Poluostrov RUS 73 Ob04
Yamato Rise 83 Rc11
Yamdena RI 92 Rc20
Yamoussoukro CI 105 Kc17
Yamuna IND 80 Cl13
Yan'an CHN 82 Qb11
Yangjiang CHN 85 Qc14
Yangon MYA 84 Pd15
Yangtze CHN 84 Qb12
Yangzhou CHN 83 Qd12
Yanji CHN 83 Rb10
Yanshan CHN 84 Qa14
Yantai CHN 83 Ra11
Yaoundé CAM 108 Lc18
Yapen RI 92 Rd19
Yap Islands FSM 92 Rd17
Yap Trench FSM 92 Rd17
Yaralıgöz Dağı TR 65 Mh25
Yardımcı Burnu TR 64 Mf27
Yaren NAU 93 Tb19
Yari CO 132 Gb18
Yarmouth CDN 121 Gc10
Yarumal CO 132 Ga17
Yasawa Group FIJ 98 Td22
Yasun Burnu TR 65 Mj25
Yatağan TR 64 Me27
Yatsushiro J 83 Rc12
Yavarí PE 132 Gb19
Yavaşlar TR 64 Me26
Yaviza PA 132 Ga17
Yavuzeli TR 65 Mj27
Yazd IR 77 Nc12
Yazıhan TR 66 Mk26
Ybbs A 52 Lh21
Ye MYA 84 Pd15
Yecheng CHN 78 Od11
Yedisu TR 66 Na26
Yei SUD 109 Mc18
Yekaterinburg RUS 72 Oa07
Yela Island PNG 96 Sc21
Yelcho 140 Gd31
Yell GB 34 Kk15
Yellowknife CDN 120 Eb06
Yellow River CHN 82 Qb10
Yellow Sea CHN 83 Ra11
Yellowstone USA 120 Ec09
Yelwa WAN 105 La16
Yemen 77 Nb15
Yendi GH 105 Kd17
Yenibaşak TR 66 Na26
Yeniceoba TR 65 Mg26
Yeniçubuk TR 65 Mj26
Yenihisar TR 57 Md27
Yenişehir TR 57 Me25
Yeo Lake AUS 94 Ra24
Yeovil GB 35 Kj20
Yeppoon AUS 96 Sc23
Yerewan ARM 76 Na10
Yerköprü TR 65 Mg27
Yerköy TR 65 Mh26
Yeşilbağ TR 64 Mf27
Yeşilhisar TR 65 Mh26
Yeşilırmak TR 65 Mh25
Yeşilova TR 64 Me27
Yichun CHN 83 Rb09
Yiğilca TR 64 Mf25
Yıldız Dağları TR 57 Md25
Yıldızeli TR 65 Mj26
Yimuhe CHN 82 Ra08
Yinchuan CHN 82 Qb11
Yingkou CHN 83 Ra10
Yining CHN 79 Pa10
Yiyang CHN 85 Qc13
Ylämaa FIN 28 Me15
Yli-Kitka FIN 23 Me12
Ylitornio FIN 23 Mb12
Ylivieska FIN 28 Mc13

Ylöjärvi ☐ FIN 22 Mb15
Yogyakarta ☐ RI 86 Qc20
Yokohama ☐ J 83 Rd11
Yola ☐ WAN 108 Lc17
Yolcular ☐ TR 66 Nb26
Yölüstü ☐ TR 66 Na26
Yonago ☐ J 83 Rc11
Yongzhou ☐ CHN 85 Qc13
York ☐ GB 35 Kk18
York ☐ GB 35 Kk19
Yorkshire Dales N.P. ☒ GB 35 Kj18
Yorkton ☐ CDN 120 Ed08
Youghal ☐ IRL 33 Kg20
Youngstown ☐ USA 123 Fd10
Yozgat Çamlığı Milli Parkı ☒ TR 65 Mh26
Yssingeaux ☐ F 39 Lc23
Ystad ☐ S 26 Lg18
Ytterhogdal ☐ S 25 Lh14
Yuanjiang ☐ CHN 84 Qa14
Yuba City ☐ USA 122 Dd11
Yucatán ☐ MEX 125 Fc14
Yucatán Basin ☐ 125 Fc14
Yucatan Channel ☐ MEX/C 125 Fc14
Yucatán Peninsula ☒ MEX 125 Fc15
Yücebağ ☐ TR 66 Na26
Yueyang ☐ CHN 85 Qc13
Yuğluk Dağı ▲ TR 65 Mg27
Yukarıçamozü ☐ TR 65 Mj26
Yukarı Sakarya Ovaları ▲ TR 64 Mf26
Yukon ☒ USA 116 Cd05
Yukon Flats ☒ USA 116 Cc05
Yukon Plateau ☒ CDN 116 Da06
Yukon Territory ☐ CDN 116 Da06
Yulara ☐ AUS 94 Rc24
Yulin ☐ CHN 82 Qb11
Yulin ☐ CHN 85 Qc14
Yuma ☐ USA 122 Eb12
Yumen ☐ CHN 79 Pd11
Yunak ☐ TR 64 Mf26
Yungas ☒ BOL 133 Gc22
Yunnan ☐ CHN 84 Qa13
Yunt Dağı ▲ TR 57 Md26
Yunuslar ☐ TR 64 Mf27
Yusufeli ☐ TR 66 Na25
Yutian ☐ CHN 79 Pa11
Yuxi ☐ CHN 84 Qa14
Yverdon ☐ CH 45 Ld22
Yvetot ☐ F 36 La21

Z

Zaangarskoe plato ☒ RUS 73 Pc07
Zaanstad ☐ NL 37 Lc19
Žabalj ☐ SR 54 Ma23
Zabalocce ☐ BY 59 Mf19
Zabid ☐ YE 77 Na16
Žabinka ☐ BY 51 Mb19
Žabno ☐ PL 50 Ma20
Zabol ☐ IR 78 Oa12
Zabrze ☐ PL 50 Lk20
Zacatecas ☐ MEX 124 Ed14
Zacatecas ☐ MEX 124 Ed14
Zadar ☐ HR 47 Lh23
Zadonsk ☐ RUS 59 Mk19
Za'farana ☐ ET 107 Mc13
Zafra ☐ E 41 Kg26
Zagaoua ▲ TCH 106 Ma15
Zagros Mountains ▲ IR 76 Nb12

Zahedan ☐ IR 77 Nd13
Záhony ☐ H 53 Mb21
Zainsk ☐ RUS 60 Ng18
Zaj ☐ RUS 60 Ng18
Zajač'e ☐ RUS 59 Mj20
Zaječar ☐ SR 54 Mb24
Zajsan ☐ KZ 79 Pa09
Zajsan köli ☐ KZ 79 Pa09
Zakarpats'ka nyzovyna ☒ UA 53 Mb21
Zákinthos ☐ GR 56 Ma27
Zákinthos ☐ GR 56 Ma27
Zakopane ☐ PL 50 Lk21
Zalaegerszeg ☐ H 53 Lj22
Zalău ☐ RO 54 Mb22
Zalim ☐ KSA 77 Na14
Zalingei ☐ SUD 106 Ma16
Zalizci ☐ UA 51 Mc21
Zaluč'e ☐ RUS 58 Mf17
Zamárdi ☐ H 53 Lj22
Žambejiti ☐ KZ 72 Nc08
Zambezi ▲ MOC 111 Mc22
Zambezi ▲ Z 110 Ma22
Zambezi ▲ Z 110 Ma22
Zambezi Escarpment ▲ ZW 110 Mb22
Zambia ■ Z 110 Mb21
Zambuanga ☐ RP 85 Ra17
Zamboanga Peninsula ☒ RP 85 Ra17
Zamość ☐ PL 51 Mb20
Zamora ☐ E 40 Kh25
Zanjan ☐ IR 76 Nb11
Zánka ☐ H 53 Lj22
Zanthus ☐ AUS 95 Ra25
Zanzibar ☐ EAT 109 Md20
Zanzibar Channel ☒ EAT 109 Md20
Zanzibar Island ☒ EAT 109 Md20
Zaokskij ☐ RUS 58 Mj18
Zapadnaja Dvina ▲ RUS 58 Mg17
Zapadnoe ☐ KZ 78 Ob08
Zapadno-Karel'skaja vozvyšennost ☒ RUS 29 Mf13
Zapala ☐ RA 137 Gb26
Zapoljarnyj ☐ RUS 23 Mf11
Zaporižžja ☐ UA 63 Mh22
Zaporožskoe ☐ RUS 29 Mf15
Zaprešić ☐ HR 47 Lh23
Zaprudnja ☐ RUS 58 Mj17
Za Qu ▲ CHN 84 Pd12
Zara ☐ TR 65 Mj26
Zarajsk ☐ RUS 59 Mk18
Zaranj ☐ AFG 78 Oa12
Zarasai ☐ LT 31 Md18
Zárate ☐ RA 136 Ha25
Zaria ☐ WAN 108 Lb16
Zärneşti ☐ RO 55 Mc23
Zarskoe Selo ☐ RUS 30 Mf16
Žaškiv ☐ UA 62 Mf21
zatoka Syvaš ☒ UA 63 Mh22
Zavitne ☐ UA 63 Mj23
Zavkhan Gol ▲ MNG 79 Pc09
Zavodoukovsk ☐ RUS 72 Ob07
Zavolž'e ☐ RUS 58 Nb17
Zawiercie ☐ PL 50 Lk20
Zbaraž ☐ UA 51 Mc21
Zboriv ☐ UA 51 Mc21
Žd'ár nad Sázavou ☐ CZ 52 Lh21
Zdolbuniv ☐ UA 51 Md20
Zeja ▲ RUS 75 Rb08

Zejsko-Bureinskaja ravnina ☒ RUS 75 Rb08
Zejskoe vdhr. ☒ RUS 75 Rb08
Zelenivka ☐ UA 63 Mj22
Zelenodol'sk ☐ RUS 60 Ne18
Zelenodol's'k ☐ UA 62 Mg22
Zelenograd ☐ RUS 58 Mj17
Zelenogradsk ☐ RUS 31 Ma18
Železnodorožnyj ☐ RUS 31 Ma18
Železnogorsk ☐ RUS 59 Mh19
Želiezovce ☐ SK 53 Lk21
Zell am See ☐ A 52 Lg22
Žemaičiu Naumiestis ☐ LT 31 Ma18
Žemaitijos n.p. ☒ LT 31 Ma17
Zemio ☐ RCA 109 Mb17
Zenica ☐ BIH 47 Lj23
Žepče ☐ BIH 47 Lk23
Žerdevka ☐ RUS 61 Na20
Zernograd ☐ RUS 63 Na22
Zerqan ☐ AL 56 Ma25
Žeskazgan ☐ KZ 78 Ob09
Žetikara ☐ KZ 78 Oa08
Zeven ☐ D 44 Le19
Zgierz ☐ PL 50 Lk20
Zgorzelec ☐ PL 50 Lh20
Zhalantun ☐ CHN 83 Ra09
Zhanaozen ☐ KZ 76 Nc10
Zhangjiakou ☐ CHN 82 Qc10
Zhangye ☐ CHN 82 Qa11
Zhangzhou ☐ CHN 85 Qd14
Zhanjiang ☐ CHN 85 Qc14
Zhaotong ☐ CHN 84 Qa13
Zharkent ☐ KZ 79 Od10
Zhaxigang ☐ CHN 80 Pa12
Zhejiang ☐ CHN 85 Qd13
Zhengzhou ☐ CHN 82 Qc12
Zhob ☐ PAK 78 Ob12
Zhongdian ☐ CHN 84 Pd13
Zhongshan ☐ CHN 85 Qc14
Zhumadian ☐ CHN 85 Qc14
Zhuzhou ☐ CHN 85 Qc13
Žiar nad Hronom ☐ SK 53 Lk21
Zibo ☐ CHN 83 Qd11
Zicavo ☐ F 46 Le25
Zielona Góra ☐ PL 50 Lh20
Zierikzee ☐ NL 37 Lb20
Žigansk ☐ RUS 75 Ra05
Zighan ☐ LAR 106 Ma13
Zigong ☐ CHN 84 Qa13
Ziguinchor ☐ SN 105 Ka16
Zihuatanejo ☐ MEX 124 Ed15
Zile ☐ TR 65 Mh25
Žilina ☐ SK 53 Lk21
Zima ☐ RUS 82 Qa08
Zimbabwe ■ ZW 110 Mb22
Zimbor ☐ RO 54 Mb22
Zimnicea ☐ RO 55 Mc24
Zinder ☐ RN 106 Lb16
Zingst ☐ D 44 Lg18
Zin'kiv ☐ UA 62 Mh20
Zirnovsk ☐ RUS 61 Nc20
Zittau ☐ D 44 Lh20
Živinice ☐ BIH 47 Lk23
Zlaté Moravce ☐ SK 53 Lk21
Zlatica ☐ BG 55 Mc24
Zlatna ☐ RO 54 Mb22
Zlatoust ☐ RUS 72 Nd07
Zlín ☐ CZ 53 Lj21
Žlobin ☐ BY 59 Mf19
Złocieniec ☐ PL 50 Lj19
Złoczew ☐ PL 50 Lk20
Złotów ☐ PL 50 Lj19
Žmerynka ☐ UA 62 Me21
Zmievka ☐ RUS 59 Mj19
Żmigród ☐ PL 50 Lj20
Zmijiv ☐ UA 63 Mj21

Znamenskoe ☐ RUS 59 Mh19
Znam'janka ☐ UA 62 Mg21
Žnin ☐ PL 50 Lj19
Znojmo ☐ CZ 52 Lj21
Žodzina ☐ BY 31 Me18
Zoločiv ☐ UA 51 Mc21
Zolote ☐ UA 63 Mk21
Zolotonoša ☐ UA 62 Mg21
Zomba ☐ MW 111 Md22
Žongar Alatauï ▲ KZ 79 Od10
Zongshan ☐ 141 Od32
Zonguldak ☐ TR 64 Mf26
Zouar ☐ TCH 106 Ld14
Zouérat ☐ RIM 104 Kb14
Žovkva ☐ UA 51 Mb20
Žovti Vody ☐ UA 62 Mg21
Žovtneve ☐ UA 59 Mh20
Zrenjanin ☐ SR 54 Ma23
Zruč nad Sázavou ☐ CZ 52 Lh21
Zubcov ☐ RUS 58 Mh17
Zubova Poljana ☐ RUS 60 Nb18
Zubovo ☐ RUS 29 Mj15
Zug ☐ CH 45 Le22
Zugspitze ▲ D/A 45 Lf22
Žukovka ☐ RUS 59 Mg19
Zumba ☐ EC 132 Ga19
Zunyi ☐ CHN 84 Qb13
Zürich ☐ CH 45 Le22
Žuromin ☐ PL 50 Lk19
Zuwarah ☐ LAR 106 Lc12
Zuytdorp Cliffs ▲ AUS 94 Qc24
Zvenigorod ☐ RUS 58 Mj18
Zvenigovo ☐ RUS 60 Nd18
Zvenyhorodka ☐ UA 62 Mf21
Zvezdec ☐ BG 55 Md24
Zvolen ☐ SK 53 Lk21
Zvornik ☐ BIH 47 Lk23
Zwedru ☐ LB 105 Kc17
Zwettl ☐ A 52 Lh21
Zwickau ☐ D 45 Lg20
Zwiesel ☐ D 45 Lg21
Zwoleń ☐ PL 50 Ma20
Zwolle ☐ NL 37 Ld19
Žydačiv ☐ UA 51 Mc21
Žyrjanka ☐ RUS 74 Sc05
Žytkavičy ☐ BY 51 Md19
Žytomyr ☐ UA 62 Me20

CREDITS

© 2007 Verlag Wolfgang Kunth GmbH & Co. KG, Munich, Germany
Cartography: © GeoGraphic Publishers GmbH & Co. KG, Munich, Germany

Cover design: Derrick Lim
Cover photograph © NASA

Printed in Slovakia